Praise for Routledge Student Statutes

'The best value and best format books on the market' – Ed Bates, University of Southampton, UK

'Focused content, layout and price – Routledge competes and wins in relation to all of these factors' – Craig Lind, University of Sussex, UK

'comprehensive and reliable' – Andromachi Georgosouli, University of Leicester, UK

'user friendly and sensibly laid out' – John Stanton, Kingston University, UK

'An exciting and valuable selection of the key legislative material' – David Radlett, University of Kent, UK

'I prefer the layout of the Routledge statute book to other statute books that I have seen' – Nicola Haralambous, University of Hertfordshire, UK

'Well-presented and has thorough content [...] clearly a good competitor' – Brian Coggon, University of Lincoln, UK

'... given the addition of the useful web resource and the easy to read section headings, I would be more inclined to recommend this book than other statute texts' – Emma Warner-Reed, Leeds Metropolitan University, UK

'excellent and relevant' – Sarwan Singh, City University London, UK

'I personally prefer the Routledge series as it is better laid out and more accessible' – Jonathan Doak, University of Nottingham, UK

'Routledge Student Statutes are practical and carefully designed for the needs of the students' – Stelios Andreadakis, Oxford Brookes University, UK

'an excellent statute text' – Fang Ma, University of Hertfordshire, UK

'Other statute books are not as attractive in look or feel, not as easy to navigate, more expensive and amendments are less clear' – Jason Lowther, University of Plymouth, UK

'Gives good coverage and certainly includes all elements addressed on our current syllabus. I personally think this statute is more clearly set out than other statute books and is more user friendly for it' – Samantha Pegg, Nottingham Trent University, UK

'This statute book is a student friendly material. Index features as well as the overall content make this book a valuable contribution to student reading lists' – Orkun Akseli, Newcastle University, UK

'A very welcome publication' – Simon Barnett, University of Hertfordshire, UK

'I am sticking with Routledge Student Statutes' – Francis Tansinda, Manchester Metropolitan University, UK

ROUTLEDGE
STUDENT STATUTES

Company Law Statutes
2011–2012

MARC MOORE
Lecturer in the Faculty of Laws, University College London

Routledge
Taylor & Francis Group
LONDON AND NEW YORK

First published 2012
by Routledge
2 Park Square, Milton Park, Abingdon, Oxon OX14 4RN

Simultaneously published in the USA and Canada
by Routledge
711 Third Avenue, New York, NY 10017

Routledge is an imprint of the Taylor & Francis Group, an informa business

British Library Cataloguing in Publication Data
A catalogue record for this book is available from the British Library

Library of Congress Cataloguing in Publication Data
A catalogue record for this book has been requested

ISBN13: 978–0–415–68745–4 (pbk)

Typeset in Sabon
by RefineCatch Limited, Bungay, Suffolk

MIX
Paper from responsible sources
FSC www.fsc.org FSC® C004839

Printed and bound in Great Britain by
TJ International Ltd, Padstow, Cornwall

ROUTLEDGE
STUDENT STATUTES

Company Law Statutes

2011–2012

[illegible]sed content, layout and price – Routledge competes and wins in relation to all of these [illegible]rs' – Craig Lind, University of Sussex, UK

[illegible] value and best format books on the market' – Ed Bates, Southampton University, UK

Routledge Student Statutes present all the legislation students need in one easy-to-use volume. Developed in response to feedback from lecturers and students, this book offers a fully up-to-date, comprehensive, and clearly presented collection of legislation – ideal for LLB and GDL course and exam use.

Routledge Student Statutes are:

- **Exam Friendly:** un-annotated and conforming to exam regulations
- **Tailored to fit your course:** 80% of lecturers we surveyed agree that *Routledge Student Statutes* match their course and cover the relevant legislation
- **Trustworthy:** *Routledge Student Statutes* are compiled by subject experts, updated annually and have been developed to meet student needs through extensive market research
- **Easy to use:** a clear text design, comprehensive table of contents, multiple indexes and highlighted amendments to the law make these books the more student-friendly Statutes on the market
- **Competitively Priced:** *Routledge Student Statutes* offer content and usability rated as good or better than our major competitor, but at a more competitive price
- **Supported by a Companion Website:** presenting scenario questions for interpreting Statutes, annotated web links, and multiple-choice questions, these resources are designed to help students to be confident and prepared.

Dr Marc Moore is a Lecturer in the Faculty of Laws, University College London.

ROUTLEDGE STUDENT STATUTES

Titles in the series:

Company Law Statutes 2011–2012
MARC MOORE

Contract, Tort and Restitution Statutes 2011–2012
JAMES DEVENNEY AND HOWARD JOHNSON

Criminal Law Statutes 2011–2012
JONATHAN HERRING

Employment Law Statutes 2011–2012
JANICE NAIRNS

European Union Legislation 2011–2012
JEFFREY KENNER

Evidence Statutes 2011–2012
CLAIRE MCGOURLAY

Family Law Statutes 2011–2012
PHIL BATES

International Trade Law Statutes and Conventions 2011–2013
INDIRA CARR AND MIRIAM GOLDBY

Property Law Statutes 2011–2012
RUSSELL HEWITSON

Public Law and Human Rights 2011–2012
PHILIP JONES

http://cw.routledge.com/textbooks/statutes

Contents

Preface

This book contains the main pieces of primary and secondary legislation appropriate for undergraduate company law courses in the UK, and also for postgraduate courses in company law and related subjects such as corporate governance and corporate finance.

By far the largest section of the book is devoted to the Companies Act 2006 which, at 1300 section in length, is the largest statute in British legislative history. In recognition of the high level of detail and complexity to much of the companies legislation, and the consequent difficulty faced by students in digesting the material, the book aims to provide only those statutory provisions which are necessary for readers undertaking the academic study (as opposed to professional practice) of company law. It is hoped that this will help to ease the task of identifying and applying those rules that are relevant to any issue or problem with which you are faced over the coming months.

The text of this book incorporates any amendments to the law that are in force on 1st June 2011. At the time of preparation of this book, the Bribery Act 2010 is not yet in force but is due to be fully implemented on 1 July 2011. Since most readers will be beginning their study of the subject after this time, all of these provisions are included in the text of the book. Where relevant, a note is added at the end of each piece of legislation detailing amendments and "coming into force" dates.

An especially notable feature of the book, besides the streamlined nature of much of the text, is its inclusion of highly important non-statutory materials including excerpts from the UK Corporate Governance Code, the UK Stewardship Code, the Takeover Code, and the official UK Listing Rules. Whilst this is not a conventional feature of statute books, the editor is nevertheless of the view that these sources are crucial in order for students to acquire a comprehensive understanding of the various regulatory pressures acting on UK companies, particularly those companies whose shares are traded on public investment markets such as the London Stock Exchange. In using such non-statutory materials, however, students should be acutely aware of the ways in which the enforcement of these provisions differs from conventional legislative enforcement methods.

Very often the main challenge that students encounter when studying company law for the first time is not a lack of information but, rather, a *surplus* of material at their disposal. This can make it difficult to find the proverbial "needle in the haystack". For this reason, the book contains multiple indexes including a thematic index which uses common threads linked to the typical structure of university company law courses.

Finally, the Online Material associated with this book provides some useful guidance on how to use the statute book, together with Multiple Choice Questions, Interpreting the Statutes problems and Think Points. The purpose of these features is not to so much to test your general knowledge of company law, as to sharpen your skills of identifying and applying specific rules of law contained within the pages of this book. Remember that in company law, as in any other area of UK law, statutes will not in themselves provide all the answers to legal problems. An underpinning knowledge of the relevant case law and theoretical concepts is therefore essential in order to make effective use of this resource when studying the subject.

Dr Marc Moore
1st June 2011

Guide to the Companion Website

http://cw.routledge.com/textbooks/statutes/

Visit the Companion Website for Routledge Student Statutes in order to:

- Understand how to use a statute book in tutorials and exams;
- Learn how to interpret statutes and other legislation to maximum effect;
- Gain essential practice in statute interpretation prior to your exams, through unique problem-based scenarios;
- Test your understanding of statutes through a set of Multiple Choice Questions for revision or to check your own progress;
- Understand how the law is developing with updates, additional information and links to useful websites.

Alphabetical Index

Chronological Index

Statutes

Partnership Act 1890

Nature of Partnership

1 DEFINITION OF PARTNERSHIP

(1) Partnership is the relation which subsists between persons carrying on a business in common with a view of profit.

(2) But the relation between members of any company or association which is—

(a) Registered as a company under the Companies Act 2006, or any other Act of Parliament for the time being in force and relating to the registration of joint stock companies; or

(b) Formed or incorporated by or in pursuance of any other Act of Parliament or letters patent, or Royal Charter:

is not a partnership within the meaning of this Act.

2 RULES FOR DETERMINING EXISTENCE OF PARTNERSHIP

In determining whether a partnership does or does not exist, regard shall be had to the following rules:

(1) Joint tenancy, tenancy in common, joint property, common property, or part ownership does not of itself create a partnership as to anything so held or owned, whether the tenants or owners do or do not share any profits made by the use thereof.

(2) The sharing of gross returns does not of itself create a partnership, whether the persons sharing such returns have or have not a joint or common right or interest in any property from which or from the use of which the returns are derived.

(3) The receipt by a person of a share of the profits of a business is prima facie evidence that he is a partner in the business, but the receipt of such a share, or of a payment contingent on or varying with the profits of a business, does not of itself make him a partner in the business; and in particular—

(a) The receipt by a person of a debt or other liquidated amount by instalments, or otherwise out of the accruing profits of a business does not of itself make him a partner in the business or liable as such;
(b) A contract for the remuneration of a servant or agent of a person engaged in a business by a share of the profits of the business does not of itself make the servant or agent a partner in the business or liable as such;
(c) A person being the widow, widower, surviving civil partner or child of a deceased partner, and receiving by way of annuity a portion of the profits made in the business in which the deceased person was a partner, is not by reason only of such receipt a partner in the business or liable as such;
(d) The advance of money by way of loan to a person engaged or about to engage in any business on a contract with that person that the lender shall receive a rate of interest varying with the profits, or shall receive a share of the profits arising from carrying on the business, does not of itself make the lender a partner with the person or persons carrying on the business or liable as such. Provided that the contract is in writing, and signed by or on behalf of all the parties thereto;
(e) A person receiving by way of annuity or otherwise a portion of the profits of a business in consideration of the sale by him of the goodwill of the business is not by reason only of such receipt a partner in the business or liable as such.

3 POSTPONEMENT OF RIGHTS OF PERSON LENDING OR SELLING IN CONSIDERATION OF SHARE OF PROFITS IN CASE OF INSOLVENCY

In the event of any person to whom money has been advanced by way of loan upon such a contract as is mentioned in the last foregoing section, or of any buyer of a goodwill in consideration of a share of the profits of the business, being adjudged a bankrupt, entering into arrangement to pay his creditors less than 100p in the pound, or dying in insolvent circumstances, the lender of the loan shall not be entitled to recover anything in respect of his loan, and the seller of the goodwill shall not be entitled to recover anything in respect of the share of profits contracted for, until the claims of the other creditors of the borrower or buyer for valuable consideration in money or money's worth have been satisfied.

4 MEANING OF FIRM

(1) Persons who have entered into partnership with one another are for the purposes of this Act called collectively a firm, and the name under which their business is carried on is called the firm-name.

(2) In Scotland a firm is a legal person distinct from the partners of whom it is composed, but an individual partner may be charged on a decree or diligence directed against the firm, and on payment of the debts is entitled to relief *pro rata* from the firm and its other members.

Relations of Partners to persons dealing with them

5 POWER OF PARTNER TO BIND THE FIRM

Every partner is an agent of the firm and his other partners for the purpose of the business of the partnership; and the acts of every partner who does any act for carrying on in the usual way business of the kind carried on by the firm of which he is a member bind the firm and his partners, unless the partner so acting has in fact no authority to act for the firm in the particular matter, and the person with whom he is dealing either knows that he has no authority, or does not know or believe him to be a partner.

6 PARTNERS BOUND BY ACTS ON BEHALF OF THE FIRM

An act or instrument relating to the business of the firm and done or executed in the firm-name, or in any other manner showing an intention to bind the firm, by any person thereto authorised, whether a partner or not, is binding on the firm and all the partners.

Provided that this section shall not affect any general rule of law relating to the execution of deeds or negotiable instruments.

7 PARTNER USING CREDIT OF FIRM FOR PRIVATE PURPOSES

Where one partner pledges the credit of the firm for a purpose apparently not connected with the firm's ordinary course of business, the firm is not bound, unless he is in fact specially authorised by the other partners; but this section does not affect any personal liability incurred by an individual partner.

8 EFFECT OF NOTICE THAT FIRM WILL NOT BE BOUND BY ACTS OF PARTNER

If it has been agreed between the partners that any restriction shall be placed on the power of any one or more of them to bind the firm, no act done in contravention of the agreement is binding on the firm with respect to persons having notice of the agreement.

9 LIABILITY OF PARTNERS

Every partner in a firm is liable jointly with the other partners, and in Scotland severally also, for all debts and obligations of the firm incurred while he is a partner; and after his death his estate is also severally liable in a due course of administration for such debts and obligations, so far as they remain unsatisfied, but subject in England or Northern Ireland to the prior payment of his separate debts.

10 LIABILITY OF THE FIRM FOR WRONGS

Where, by any wrongful act or omission of any partner acting in the ordinary course of the business of the firm, or with the authority of his co-partners, loss or injury is caused to any person not being a partner in the firm, or any penalty is incurred, the firm is liable therefor to the same extent as the partner so acting or omitting to act.

11 MISAPPLICATION OF MONEY OR PROPERTY RECEIVED FOR OR IN CUSTODY OF THE FIRM

In the following cases; namely—

(a) Where one partner acting within the scope of his apparent authority receives the money or property of a third person and misapplies it; and

(b) Where a firm in the course of its business received money or property of a third person, and the money or property so received is misapplied by one or more of the partners while it is in the custody of the firm;

the firm is liable to make good the loss.

12 LIABILITY FOR WRONGS JOINT AND SEVERAL

Every partner is liable jointly with his co-partners and also severally for everything for which the firm while he is a partner therein becomes liable under either of the two last preceding sections.

13 IMPROPER EMPLOYMENT OF TRUST PROPERTY FOR PARTNERSHIP PURPOSES

If a partner, being a trustee, improperly employs trust-property in the business or on the account of the partnership, no other partner is liable for the trust-property to the persons beneficially interested therein.

Provided as follows:—

(1) this section shall not affect any liability incurred by any partner by reason of his having notice of a breach of trust; and

(2) nothing in this section shall prevent trust money from being followed and recovered from the firm if still in its possession or under its control.

14 PERSONS LIABLE BY "HOLDING OUT"

(1) Every one who by words spoken or written or by conduct represents himself, or who knowingly suffers himself to be represented, as a partner in a particular firm, is liable as a partner to any one who has on the faith of any such representation given credit to the firm, whether the representation has or has not been made or communicated to the person so giving credit by or with the knowledge of the apparent partner making the representation or suffering it to be made.

(2) Provided that where after a partner's death the partnership business is continued in the old firm-name, the continued use of that name or of the deceased partner's name as part thereof shall not of itself make his executors or administrators estate or effects liable for any partnership debts contracted after his death.

15 ADMISSIONS AND REPRESENTATIONS OF PARTNERS

An admission or representation made by any partner concerning the partnership affairs, and in the ordinary course of its business, is evidence against the firm.

16 NOTICE TO ACTING PARTNER TO BE NOTICE TO THE FIRM

Notice to any partner who habitually acts in the partnership business of any matter relating to partnership affairs operates as notice to the firm, except in the case of a fraud on the firm committed by or with the consent of that partner.

17 LIABILITIES OF INCOMING AND OUTGOING PARTNERS

(1) A person who is admitted as a partner into an existing firm does not thereby become liable to the creditors of the firm for anything done before he became a partner.

(2) A partner who retires from a firm does not cease to be liable for partnership debts or obligations incurred before his retirement.

(3) A retiring partner may be discharged from any existing liabilities, by an agreement to that effect between himself and the members of the firm as newly constituted and the creditors, and this agreement may be either express or inferred as a fact from the course of dealing between the creditors and the firm as newly constituted.

18 REVOCATION CONTINUING GUARANTY BY CHANGE IN FIRM

A continuing guaranty or cautionary obligation given either to a firm or to a third person in respect of the transactions of a firm is, in the absence of agreement to the contrary, revoked as to future transactions by any change in the constitution of the firm to which, or of the firm in respect of the transactions of which, the guaranty or obligation was given.

Relations of Partners to one another

19 VARIATION BY CONSENT OF TERMS OF PARTNERSHIP

The mutual rights and duties of partners, whether ascertained by agreement or defined by this Act, may be varied by the consent of all the partners, and such consent may be either express or inferred from a course of dealing.

20 PARTNERSHIP PROPERTY

(1) All property and rights and interests in property originally brought into the partnership stock or acquired, whether by purchase or otherwise, on account of the firm or for the purposes and in the course of the partnership business, are called in this Act partnership property, and must be held and applied by the partners exclusively for the purposes of the partnership and in accordance with the partnership agreement.

21 PROPERTY BOUGHT WITH PARTNERSHIP MONEY

Unless the contrary intention appears, property bought with money belonging to the firm is deemed to have been bought on account of the firm.

23 PROCEDURE AGAINST PARTNERSHIP PROPERTY FOR A PARTNER'S SEPARATE JUDGMENT DEBT

(1) A writ of execution shall not issue against any partnership property except on a judgment against the firm.

(2) The High Court, or a judge thereof, or a county court, may, on the application by summons of any judgment creditor of a partner, make an order charging that partner's interest in the partnership property and profits with payment of the amount of the judgment debt and interest thereon, and may by the same or a subsequent order appoint a receiver of that partner's share of profits (whether already declared or accruing), and of any other money which may be coming to him in respect of the partnership, and direct all accounts and inquiries, and give all other orders and directions which might have been directed or given if the charge had been made in favour of the judgment creditor by the partner, or which the circumstances of the case may require.

(3) The other partner or partners shall be at liberty at any time to redeem the interest charged, or in case of a sale being directed, to purchase the same.

(5) This section shall not apply to Scotland.

24 RULES AS TO INTERESTS AND DUTIES OF PARTNERS SUBJECT TO SPECIAL AGREEMENT

The interests of partners in the partnership as to property and their rights and duties in relation to the partnership shall be determined, subject to any agreement express or implied between the partners, by the following rules:

(1) All the partners are entitled to share equally in the capital and profits of the business, and must contribute equally towards the losses whether of capital or otherwise sustained by the firm.

(2) The firm must indemnify every partner in respect of payments made and personal liabilities incurred by him—
(a) in the ordinary and proper conduct of the business of the firm; or
(b) in or about anything necessarily done for the preservation of the business or property of the firm.

(3) A partner making, for the purpose of the partnership, any actual payment or advance beyond the amount of capital which he has agreed to subscribe, is entitled to interest at the rate of five per cent per annum from the date of the payment or advance.

(4) A partner is not entitled, before the ascertainment of profits, to interest on the capital subscribed by him.

(5) Every partner may take part in the management of the partnership business.

(6) No partner shall be entitled to remuneration for acting in the partnership business.

(7) No person may be introduced as a partner without the consent of all existing partners.

(8) Any difference arising as to ordinary matters connected with the partnership business may be decided by a majority of the partners, but no change may be made in the nature of the partnership business without the consent of all existing partners.

(9) The partnership books are to be kept at the place of business of the partnership (or the principal place, if there is more than one), and every partner may, when he thinks fit, have access to and inspect and copy any of them.

25 EXPULSION OF PARTNER

No majority of the partners can expel any partner unless a power to do so has been conferred by express agreement between the partners.

26 RETIREMENT FROM PARTNERSHIP AT WILL

(1) Where no fixed term has been agreed upon for the duration of the partnership, any partner may determine the partnership at any time on giving notice of his intention so to do to all the other partners.

(2) Where the partnership has originally been constituted by deed, a notice in writing, signed by the partner giving it, shall be sufficient for this purpose.

27 WHERE PARTNERSHIP FOR TERM IS CONTINUED OVER, CONTINUANCE ON OLD TERMS PRESUMED

(1) Where a partnership entered into for a fixed term is continued after the term has expired, and without any express new agreement, the rights and duties of the partners remain the same as they were at the expiration of the term, so far as is consistent with the incidents of a partnership at will.

(2) A continuance of the business by the partners or such of them as habitually acted therein during the term, without any settlement or liquidation of the partnership affairs, is presumed to be a continuance of the partnership.

28 DUTY OF PARTNERS TO RENDER ACCOUNTS, ETC.

Partners are bound to render true accounts and full information of all things affecting the partnership to any partner or his legal representatives.

29 ACCOUNTABILITY OF PARTNERS FOR PRIVATE PROFITS

(1) Every partner must account to the firm for any benefit derived by him without the consent of the other partners from any transaction concerning the partnership, or from any use by him of the partnership property name or business connection.

(2) This section applies also to transactions undertaken after a partnership has been dissolved by the death of a partner, and before the affairs thereof have been completely wound up, either by any surviving partner or by the representatives of the deceased partner.

30 DUTY OF PARTNER NOT TO COMPETE WITH FIRM

If a partner, without the consent of the other partners, carries on any business of the same nature as and competing with that of the firm, he must account for and pay over to the firm all profits made by him in that business.

31 RIGHTS OF ASSIGNEE OF SHARE IN PARTNERSHIP

(1) An assignment by any partner of his share in the partnership, either absolute or by way of mortgage or redeemable charge, does not, as against the other partners, entitle the assignee, during the continuance of the partnership, to interfere in the management or administration of the partnership business or affairs, or to require any accounts of the partnership transactions, or to inspect the partnership books, but entitles the assignee only to receive the share of profits to which the assigning partner would otherwise be entitled, and the assignee must accept the account of profits agreed to by the partners.

(2) In case of a dissolution of the partnership, whether as respects all the partners or as respects the assigning partner, the assignee is entitled to receive the share of the partnership assets to which the assigning partner is entitled as between himself and the other partners, and, for the purpose of ascertaining that share, to an account as from the date of the dissolution.

Dissolution of Partnership, and its consequences

32 DISSOLUTION BY EXPIRATION OR NOTICE

Subject to any agreement between the partners a partnership is dissolved—

(a) If entered into for a fixed term, by the expiration of that term:

(b) If entered into for a single adventure or undertaking, by the termination of that adventure or undertaking:

(c) If entered into for an undefined time, by any partner giving notice to the other or others of his intention to dissolve the partnership.

In the last-mentioned case the partnership is dissolved as from the date mentioned in the notice as the date of dissolution, or, if no date is so mentioned, as from the date of the communication of the notice.

33 DISSOLUTION BY BANKRUPTCY, DEATH, OR CHARGE

(1) Subject to any agreement between the partners, every partnership is dissolved as regards all the partners by the death or bankruptcy of any partner.

(2) A partnership may, at the option of the other partners, be dissolved if any partner suffers his share of the partnership property to be charged under this Act for his separate debt.

34 DISSOLUTION BY ILLEGALITY OF PARTNERSHIP

A partnership is in every case dissolved by the happening of any event which makes it unlawful for the business of the firm to be carried on or for the members of the firm to carry it on in partnership.

35 DISSOLUTION BY THE COURT

On application by a partner the Court may decree a dissolution of the partnership in any of the following cases:

(a) When a partner is found lunatic by inquisition, or in Scotland by cognition, or is shown to the satisfaction of the Court to be of permanently unsound mind, in either of which cases the application may be made as well on behalf of that partner by his committee or next friend or person having title to intervene as by any other partner.

(b) When a partner, other than the partner suing, becomes in any . . . way permanently incapable of performing his part of the partnership contract.

(c) When a partner, other than the partner suing, has been guilty of such conduct as, in the opinion of the Court, regard being had to the nature of the business, is calculated to prejudicially affect the carrying on of the business.

(d) When a partner, other than the partner suing, wilfully or persistently commits a breach of the partnership agreement, or otherwise so conducts himself in matters relating to the partnership business that it is not reasonably practicable for the other partner or partners to carry on the business in partnership with him.

(e) When the business of the partnership can only be carried on at a loss.

(f) Whenever in any case circumstances have arisen which, in the opinion of the Court, render it just and equitable that the partnership be dissolved.

36 RIGHTS OF PERSONS DEALING WITH FIRM AGAINST APPARENT MEMBERS OF FIRM

(1) When a person deals with a firm after a change in its constitution he is entitled to treat all apparent members of the old firm as still being members of the firm until he has notice of the change.

(2) An advertisement in the London Gazette as to a firm whose principal place of business is in England or Wales, in the Edinburgh Gazette as to a firm whose principal place of business is in Scotland, and in the Belfast Gazette as to a firm whose principal place of business is in Northern Ireland, shall be notice as to persons who had not dealings with the firm before the date of the dissolution or change so advertised.

(3) The estate of a partner who dies, or who becomes bankrupt, or of a partner who, not having been known to the person dealing with the firm to be a partner, retires from the firm, is not liable for partnership debts contracted after the date of the death, bankruptcy, or retirement respectively.

37 RIGHT OF PARTNERS TO NOTIFY DISSOLUTION

On the dissolution of a partnership or retirement of a partner any partner may publicly notify the same, and may require the other partner or partners to concur for that purpose in all necessary or proper acts, if any, which cannot be done without his or their concurrence.

38 CONTINUING AUTHORITY OF PARTNERS FOR PURPOSES OF WINDING UP

After the dissolution of a partnership the authority of each partner to bind the firm, and the other rights and obligations of the partners, continue notwithstanding the dissolution so far as may be necessary to wind up the affairs of the partnership, and to complete transactions begun but unfinished at the time of the dissolution, but not otherwise.

Provided that the firm is in no case bound by the acts of a partner who has become bankrupt; but this proviso does not affect the liability of any person who has after the bankruptcy represented himself or knowingly suffered himself to be represented as a partner of the bankrupt.

39 RIGHTS OF PARTNERS AS TO APPLICATION OF PARTNERSHIP PROPERTY

On the dissolution of a partnership every partner is entitled, as against the other partners in the firm, and all persons claiming through them in respect of their interests as partners, to have the property of the partnership applied in payment of the debts and liabilities of the firm, and to have the surplus assets after such payment applied in payment of what may be due to the partners respectively after deducting what may be due from them as partners to the firm; and for that purpose any partner or his representatives may on the termination of the partnership apply to the Court to wind up the business and affairs of the firm.

44 RULE FOR DISTRIBUTION OF ASSETS ON FINAL SETTLEMENT OF ACCOUNTS

In settling accounts between the partners after a dissolution of partnership, the following rules shall, subject to any agreement, be observed:

(a) Losses, including losses and deficiencies of capital, shall be paid firstly out of profits, next out of capital, and lastly, if necessary, by the partners individually in the proportion in which they were entitled to share profits.

(b) The assets of the firm including the sums, if any, contributed by the partners to make up losses or deficiencies of capital, shall be applied in the following manner and order:
   (1) In paying the debts and liabilities of the firm to persons who are not partners therein:
   (2) In paying to each partner rateably what is due from the firm to him for advances as distinguished from capital:
   (3) In paying to each partner rateably what is due from the firm to him in respect of capital:
   (4) The ultimate residue, if any, shall be divided among the partners in the proportion in which the profits are divisible.

Supplemental

45 DEFINITIONS OF "COURT" AND "BUSINESS"

In this Act, unless the contrary intention appears—

The expression court includes every court and judge having jurisdiction in the case:

The expression "business" includes every trade, occupation, or profession.

46 SAVING FOR RULES OF EQUITY AND COMMON LAW

The rules of equity and of common law applicable to partnership shall continue in force except so far as they are inconsistent with the express provisions of this Act.

47 PROVISION AS TO BANKRUPTCY IN SCOTLAND

(1) In the application of this Act to Scotland the bankruptcy of a firm or of an individual shall mean sequestration under the Bankruptcy (Scotland) Acts, and also in the case of an individual the issue against him of a decree of cessio bonorum.

(2) Nothing in this Act shall alter the rules of the law of Scotland relating to the bankruptcy of a firm or of the individual partners thereof.

As amended by the Statute Law Revision Act 1908; SR & O 1921/1804, art 7; SR & O 1923/405, art 2; Mental Health Act 1959, Schedule 8; Decimal Currency Act 1969, s 10(1); Courts Act 1971, Schedule 11, Part II; Statute Law (Repeals) Act 1998, Schedule 1, Part X, Group 1; Civil Partnership Act 2004, Schedule 27, para 2; Companies Act 2006 (Consequential Amendments, Transitional Provisions and Savings) Order 2009, Schedule 1, para 2.

Limited Partnerships Act 1907

3 INTERPRETATION OF TERMS

In the construction of this Act the following words and expressions shall have the meanings respectively assigned to them in this section, unless there be something in the subject or context repugnant to such construction—

"Firm," "firm name," and "business" have the same meanings as in the Partnership Act 1890;

"General partner" shall mean any partner who is not a limited partner as defined by this Act.

4 DEFINITION AND CONSTITUTION OF LIMITED PARTNERSHIP

(1) ...[L]imited partnerships may be formed in the manner and subject to the conditions by this Act provided.

(2) A limited partnership ... must consist of one or more persons called general partners, who shall be liable for all debts and obligations of the firm, and one or more persons to be called limited partners, who shall at the time of entering into such partnership contribute thereto a sum or sums as capital or property valued at a stated amount, and who shall not be liable for the debts or obligations of the firm beyond the amount so contributed.

(3) A limited partner shall not during the continuance of the partnership, either directly or indirectly, draw out or receive back any part of his contribution, and if he does so draw out or receive back any such part shall be liable for the debts and obligations of the firm up to the amount so drawn out or received back.

(4) A body corporate may be a limited partner.

5 REGISTRATION OF LIMITED PARTNERSHIP REQUIRED

Every limited partnership must be registered as such in accordance with the provisions of this Act, or in default thereof it shall be deemed to be a general partnership, and every limited partner shall be deemed to be a general partner.

6 MODIFICATIONS OF GENERAL LAW IN CASE OF LIMITED PARTNERSHIPS

(1) A limited partner shall not take part in the management of the partnership business, and shall not have power to bind the firm:

Provided that a limited partner may by himself or his agent at any time inspect the books of the firm and examine into the state and prospects of the partnership business, and may advise with the partners thereon.

If a limited partner takes part in the management of the partnership business he shall be liable for all debts and obligations of the firm incurred while he so takes part in the management as though he were a general partner.

(2) A limited partnership shall not be dissolved by the death or bankruptcy of a limited partner, and the lunacy of a limited partner shall not be a ground for dissolution of the partnership by the court unless the lunatic's share cannot be otherwise ascertained and realised.

(3) In the event of the dissolution of a limited partnership its affairs shall be wound up by the general partners unless the court otherwise orders.

(5) Subject to any agreement expressed or implied between the partners—
- (a) any difference arising as to ordinary matters connected with the partnership business may be decided by a majority of the general partners;
- (b) a limited partner may, with the consent of the general partners, assign his share in the partnership, and upon such an assignment the assignee shall become a limited partner with all the rights of the assignor;
- (c) the other partners shall not be entitled to dissolve the partnership by reason of any limited partner suffering his share to be charged for his separate debt;
- (d) a person may be introduced as a partner without the consent of the existing limited partners;
- (e) a limited partner shall not be entitled to dissolve the partnership by notice.

7 LAW AS TO PRIVATE PARTNERSHIPS TO APPLY WHERE NOT EXCLUDED BY THIS ACT

Subject to the provisions of this Act, the Partnership Act 1890, and the rules of equity and of common law applicable to partnerships, except so far as they are inconsistent with the express provisions of the last-mentioned Act, shall apply to limited partnerships.

. . .

14 REGISTER AND INDEX TO BE KEPT

At each of the register offices herein-after referred to the registrar shall keep, in proper books to be provided for the purpose, a register and an index of all the limited partnerships registered as aforesaid, and of all the statements registered in relation to such partnerships.

15 REGISTRAR OF JOINT STOCK COMPANIES TO BE REGISTRAR UNDER ACT

The registrar of joint stock companies shall be the registrar of limited partnerships, and the several offices for the registration of joint stock companies in London, Edinburgh, and [Belfast] shall be the offices for the registration of limited partnerships carrying on business within those parts of the United Kingdom in which they are respectively situated.

As amended by the Companies (Consolidation) Act 1908, Schedule 6; SR & O 1921/1804, art 7(b); Statute Law Revision Act 1927; Banking Act 1979, Schedule 7; Regulatory Reform (Removal of 20 Member Limit in Partnerships etc.) Order 2002, art 3.

Theft Act 1968

17 FALSE ACCOUNTING

(1) Where a person dishonestly, with a view to gain for himself or another or with intent to cause loss to another—
  (a) destroys, defaces, conceals or falsifies any account or any record or document made or required for any accounting purpose; or
  (b) in furnishing information for any purpose produces or makes use of any account, or any such record or document as aforesaid, which to his knowledge is or may be misleading, false or deceptive in a material particular;

he shall, on conviction on indictment, be liable to imprisonment for a term not exceeding seven years.

(2) For purposes of this section a person who makes or concurs in making in an account or other document an entry which is or may be misleading, false or deceptive in a material particular, or who omits or concurs in omitting a material particular from an account or other document, is to be treated as falsifying the account or document.

18 LIABILITY OF COMPANY OFFICERS FOR CERTAIN OFFENCES BY COMPANY

(1) Where an offence committed by a body corporate under section 17 of this Act is proved to have been committed with the consent or connivance of any director, or manager, secretary or other similar officer of the body corporate, or any person who was purporting to act in any such capacity, he as well as the body corporate shall be guilty of that offence, and shall be liable to be proceeded against and punished accordingly.

(2) Where the affairs of a body corporate are managed by its members, this section shall apply in relation to the acts and defaults of a member in connection with his functions of management as if he were a director of the body corporate.

19 FALSE STATEMENTS BY COMPANY DIRECTORS, ETC.

(1) Where an officer of a body corporate or unincorporated association (or person purporting to act as such), with intent to deceive members or creditors of the body corporate or association about its affairs, publishes or concurs in publishing a written statement or account which to his knowledge is or may be misleading, false or deceptive in a material particular, he shall on conviction on indictment be liable to imprisonment for a term not exceeding seven years.

(2) For purposes of this section a person who has entered into a security for the benefit of a body corporate or association is to be treated as a creditor of it.

(3) Where the affairs of a body corporate or association are managed by its members, this section shall apply to any statement which a member publishes or concurs in publishing in connection with his functions of management as if he were an officer of the body corporate or association.

20 SUPPRESSION, ETC. OF DOCUMENTS

(1) A person who dishonestly, with a view to gain for himself or another or with intent to cause loss to another, destroys, defaces or conceals any valuable security, any will or other

testamentary document or any original document of or belonging to, or filed or deposited in, any court of justice or any government department shall on conviction on indictment be liable to imprisonment for a term not exceeding seven years.

(3) For purposes of this section "valuable security" means any document creating, transferring, surrendering or releasing any right to, in or over property, or authorising the payment of money or delivery of any property, or evidencing the creation, transfer, surrender or release of any such right, or the payment of money or delivery of any property, or the satisfaction of any obligation.

As amended by the Fraud Act 2006, Schedule 1, paras 1(a)(iv), 4–5.

Companies Act 1985

Part XIV INVESTIGATION OF COMPANIES AND THEIR AFFAIRS; REQUISITION OF DOCUMENTS

Appointment and functions of inspectors

431 INVESTIGATION OF A COMPANY ON ITS OWN APPLICATION OR THAT OF ITS MEMBERS

(1) The Secretary of State may appoint one or more competent inspectors to investigate the affairs of a company and to report the results of their investigations to him.

(2) The appointment may be made—

(a) in the case of a company having a share capital, on the application either of not less than 200 members or of members holding not less than one-tenth of the shares issued (excluding any shares held as treasury shares),

(b) in the case of a company not having a share capital, on the application of not less than one-fifth in number of the persons on the company's register of members, and

(c) in any case, on application of the company.

(3) The application shall be supported by such evidence as the Secretary of State may require for the purpose of showing that the applicant or applicants have good reason for requiring the investigation.

(4) The Secretary of State may, before appointing inspectors, require the applicant or applicants to give security, to an amount not exceeding £5,000, or such other sum as he may by order specify, for payment of the costs of the investigation.

An order under this subsection shall be made by statutory instrument subject to annulment in pursuance of a resolution of either House of Parliament.

432 OTHER COMPANY INVESTIGATIONS

(1) The Secretary of State shall appoint one or more competent inspectors to investigate the affairs of a company and report the result of their investigations to him, if the court by order declares that its affairs ought to be so investigated.

(2) The Secretary of State may make such an appointment if it appears to him that there are circumstances suggesting—

(a) that the company's affairs are being or have been conducted with intent to defraud its creditors or the creditors of any other person, or otherwise for a fraudulent or unlawful purpose, or in a manner which is unfairly prejudicial to some part of its members, or

(b) that any actual or proposed act or omission of the company (including an act or omission on its behalf) is or would be so prejudicial, or that the company was formed for any fraudulent or unlawful purpose, or

(c) that persons concerned with the company's formation or the management of its affairs have in connection therewith been guilty of fraud, misfeasance or other misconduct towards it or towards its members, or

(d) that the company's members have not been given all the information with respect to its affairs which they might reasonably expect.

(2A) Inspectors may be appointed under subsection (2) on terms that any report they may make is not for publication; and in such a case, the provisions of section 437(3) (availability and publication of inspectors' reports) do not apply.

(3) Subsections (1) and (2) are without prejudice to the powers of the Secretary of State under section 431; and the power conferred by subsection (2) is exercisable with respect to a body corporate notwithstanding that it is in course of being voluntarily wound up.

(4) The reference in subsection (2)(a) to a company's members includes any person who is not a member but to whom shares in the company have been transferred or transmitted by operation of law.

433 INSPECTORS' POWERS DURING INVESTIGATION

(1) If inspectors appointed under section 431 or 432 to investigate the affairs of a company think it necessary for the purposes of their investigation to investigate also the affairs of another body corporate which is or at any relevant time has been the company's subsidiary or holding company, or a subsidiary of its holding company or a holding company of its subsidiary, they have power to do so; and they shall report on the affairs of the other body corporate so far as they think that the results of their investigation of its affairs are relevant to the investigation of the affairs of the company first mentioned above.

434 PRODUCTION OF DOCUMENTS AND EVIDENCE TO INSPECTORS

(1) When inspectors are appointed under section 431 or 432, it is the duty of all officers and agents of the company, and of all officers and agents of any other body corporate whose affairs are investigated under section 433(1)—

(a) to produce to the inspectors all documents of or relating to the company or, as the case may be, the other body corporate which are in their custody or power,

(b) to attend before the inspectors when required to do so, and

(c) otherwise to give the inspectors all assistance in connection with the investigation which they are reasonably able to give.

(2) If the inspectors consider that an officer or agent of the company or other body corporate, or any other person, is or may be in possession of information relating to a matter which they believe to be relevant to the investigation, they may require him—
(a) to produce to them any documents in his custody or power relating to that matter,
(b) to attend before them, and
(c) otherwise to give them all assistance in connection with the investigation which he is reasonably able to give;
and it is that person's duty to comply with the requirement.

(3) An inspector may for the purposes of the investigation examine any person on oath, and may administer an oath accordingly.

(4) In this section a reference to officers or to agents includes past, as well as present, officers or agents (as the case may be); and "agents", in relation to a company or other body corporate, includes its bankers and solicitors and persons employed by it as auditors, whether these persons are or are not officers of the company or other body corporate.

(5) An answer given by a person to a question put to him in exercise of powers conferred by this section (whether as it has effect in relation to an investigation under any of sections 431 to 433, or as applied by any other section in this Part) may be used in evidence against him.

(5A) However, in criminal proceedings in which that person is charged with an offence to which this subsection applies—
(a) no evidence relating to the answer may be adduced, and
(b) no question relating to it may be asked,
by or on behalf of the prosecution, unless evidence relating to it is adduced, or a question relating to it is asked, in the proceedings by or on behalf of that person.

(5B) Subsection (5A) applies to any offence other than—
(a) an offence under section 2 or 5 of the Perjury Act 1911 (false statements made on oath otherwise than in judicial proceedings or made otherwise than on oath),
(b) an offence under section 44(1) or (2) of the Criminal Law (Consolidation) (Scotland) Act 1995 (false statements made on oath or otherwise than on oath), or
(c) an offence under Article 7 or 10 of the Perjury (Northern Ireland) Order 1979 (false statements made on oath otherwise than in judicial proceedings or made otherwise than on oath).

(6) In this section "document" includes information recorded in any form.

(7) The power under this section to require production of a document includes power, in the case of a document not in hard copy form, to require the production of a copy of the document—
(a) in hard copy form, or
(b) in a form from which a hard copy can be readily obtained.

(8) An inspector may take copies of or extracts from a document produced in pursuance of this section.

436 OBSTRUCTION OF INSPECTORS TREATED AS CONTEMPT OF COURT

(1) If any person—
(a) fails to comply with section 434(1)(a) or (c),

(b) refuses to comply with a requirement under section 434(1)(b) or (2), or
(c) refuses to answer any question put to him by the inspectors for the purposes of the investigation,

the inspectors may certify that fact in writing to the court.

(2) If that person—
(a) refuses to produce any book or document which it is his duty under section 434 or 435 to produce, or
(b) refuses to attend before the inspectors when required to do so, or
(c) refuses to answer any question put to him by the inspectors with respect to the affairs of the company or other body corporate (as the case may be),

the inspectors may certify the refusal in writing to the court.

(3) The court may thereupon enquire into the case; and, after hearing any witnesses who may be produced against or on behalf of the alleged offender and after hearing any statement which may be offered in defence, the court may punish the offender in like manner as if he had been guilty of contempt of the court.

437 INSPECTORS' REPORTS

(1) The inspectors may, and if so directed by the Secretary of State shall, make interim reports to the Secretary of State, and on the conclusion of their investigation shall make a final report to him.

(1A) Any persons who have been appointed under section 431 or 432 may at any time and, if the Secretary of State directs them to do so, shall inform him of any matters coming to their knowledge as a result of their investigations.

(2) If the inspectors were appointed under section 432 in pursuance of an order of the court, the Secretary of State shall furnish a copy of any report of theirs to the court.

(2A) If the company is registered under the Companies Act 2006 in Northern Ireland, the Secretary of State must send a copy of any interim or final report by the inspectors to the Department of Enterprise, Trade and Investment in Northern Ireland.

(3) In any case the Secretary of State may, if he thinks fit—
(a) forward a copy of any report made by the inspectors to the company's registered office,
(b) furnish a copy on request and on payment of the prescribed fee to—
(i) any member of the company or other body corporate which is the subject of the report,
(ii) any person whose conduct is referred to in the report,
(iii) the auditors of that company or body corporate,
(iv) the applicants for the investigation,
(v) any other person whose financial interests appear to the Secretary of State to be affected by the matters dealt with in the report, whether as a creditor of the company or body corporate, or otherwise, and
(c) cause any such report to be printed and published.

439 EXPENSES OF INVESTIGATING A COMPANY'S AFFAIRS

(1) The expenses of an investigation under any of the powers conferred by this Part shall be defrayed in the first instance by the Secretary of State, but he may recover those expenses from the persons liable in accordance with this section.

There shall be treated as expenses of the investigation, in particular, such reasonable sums as the Secretary of State may determine in respect of general staff costs and overheads.

(2) A person who is convicted on a prosecution instituted as a result of the investigation may in the same proceedings be ordered to pay those expenses to such extent as may be specified in the order.

(4) A body corporate dealt with by an inspectors' report, where the inspectors were appointed otherwise than of the Secretary of State's own motion, is liable except where it was the applicant for the investigation, and except so far as the Secretary of State otherwise directs.

(5) Where inspectors were appointed—
(a) under section 431, or
(b) on an application under section 442(3),
the applicant or applicants for the investigation is or are liable to such extent (if any) as the Secretary of State may direct.

(6) The report of inspectors appointed otherwise than of the Secretary of State's own motion may, if they think fit, and shall if the Secretary of State so directs, include a recommendation as to the directions (if any) which they think appropriate, in the light of their investigation, to be given under subsection (4) or (5) of this section.

(8) Any liability to repay the Secretary of State imposed by subsection (2) above is (subject to satisfaction of his right to repayment) a liability also to indemnify all persons against liability under subsections (4) and (5).

(9) A person liable under any one of those subsections is entitled to contribution from any other person liable under the same subsection, according to the amount of their respective liabilities under it.

(10) Expenses to be defrayed by the Secretary of State under this section shall, so far as not recovered under it, be paid out of money provided by Parliament.

441 INSPECTORS' REPORT TO BE EVIDENCE

(1) A copy of any report of inspectors appointed under this Part, certified by the Secretary of State to be a true copy, is admissible in any legal proceedings as evidence of the opinion of the inspectors in relation to any matter contained in the report and, in proceedings on an application under section 8 of the Company Directors Disqualification Act 1986 or Article 11 of the Company Directors Disqualification (Northern Ireland) Order 2002, as evidence of any fact stated therein.

(2) A document purporting to be such a certificate as is mentioned above shall be received in evidence and be deemed to be such a certificate, unless the contrary is proved.

Other powers of investigation available to the Secretary of State

442 POWER TO INVESTIGATE COMPANY OWNERSHIP

(1) Where it appears to the Secretary of State that there is good reason to do so, he may appoint one or more competent inspectors to investigate and report on the membership of any company, and otherwise with respect to the company, for the purpose of determining the true persons who are or have been financially interested in the success or failure (real or apparent) of the company or able to control or materially to influence its policy.

(3) If an application for investigation under this section with respect to particular shares or debentures of a company is made to the Secretary of State by members of the company,

and the number of applicants or the amount of shares held by them is not less than that required for an application for the appointment of inspectors under section 431(2)(a) or (b), then, subject to the following provisions, the Secretary of State shall appoint inspectors to conduct the investigation applied for.

(3A) The Secretary of State shall not appoint inspectors if he is satisfied that the application is vexatious; and where inspectors are appointed their terms of appointment shall exclude any matter in so far as the Secretary of State is satisfied that it is unreasonable for it to be investigated.

(3B) The Secretary of State may, before appointing inspectors, require the applicant or applicants to give security, to an amount not exceeding £5,000, or such other sum as he may by order specify, for payment of the costs of the investigation.

An order under this subsection shall be made by statutory instrument which shall be subject to annulment in pursuance of a resolution of either House of Parliament.

(3C) If on an application under subsection (3) it appears to the Secretary of State that the powers conferred by section 444 are sufficient for the purposes of investigating the matters which inspectors would be appointed to investigate, he may instead conduct the investigation under that section.

(4) Subject to the terms of their appointment, the inspectors' powers extend to the investigation of any circumstances suggesting the existence of an arrangement or understanding which, though not legally binding, is or was observed or likely to be observed in practice and which is relevant to the purposes of the investigation.

443 PROVISIONS APPLICABLE ON INVESTIGATION UNDER S. 442

(1) For purposes of an investigation under section 442, sections 433(1), 434, 436 and 437 apply with the necessary modifications of references to the affairs of the company or to those of any other body corporate, subject however to the following subsections.

(2) Those sections apply to—
 (a) all persons who are or have been, or whom the inspector has reasonable cause to believe to be or have been, financially interested in the success or failure or the apparent success or failure of the company or any other body corporate whose membership is investigated with that of the company, or able to control or materially influence its policy (including persons concerned only on behalf of others), and
 (b) any other person whom the inspector has reasonable cause to believe possesses information relevant to the investigation,

as they apply in relation to officers and agents of the company or the other body corporate (as the case may be).

(3) If the Secretary of State is of opinion that there is good reason for not divulging any part of a report made by virtue of section 442 and this section, he may under section 437 disclose the report with the omission of that part; and he may cause to be kept by the registrar of companies a copy of the report with that part omitted or, in the case of any other such report, a copy of the whole report.

444 POWER TO OBTAIN INFORMATION AS TO THOSE INTERESTED IN SHARES, ETC.

(1) If it appears to the Secretary of State that there is good reason to investigate the ownership of any shares in or debentures of a company and that it is unnecessary to appoint

inspectors for the purpose, he may require any person whom he has reasonable cause to believe to have or to be able to obtain any information as to the present and past interests in those shares or debentures and the names and addresses of the persons interested and of any persons who act or have acted on their behalf in relation to the shares or debentures to give any such information to the Secretary of State.

(2) For this purpose a person is deemed to have an interest in shares or debentures if he has any right to acquire or dispose of them or of any interest in them, or to vote in respect of them, or if his consent is necessary for the exercise of any of the rights of other persons interested in them, or if other persons interested in them can be required, or are accustomed, to exercise their rights in accordance with his instructions.

(3) A person who fails to give information required of him under this section, or who in giving such information makes any statement which he knows to be false in a material particular, or recklessly makes any statement which is false in a material particular, commits an offence.

(4) A person guilty of an offence under this section is liable—
- (a) on conviction on indictment, to imprisonment for a term not exceeding two years or a fine (or both);
- (b) on summary conviction—
  - (i) in England and Wales, to imprisonment for a term not exceeding twelve months or to a fine not exceeding the statutory maximum (or both) and, for continued contravention, a daily default fine not exceeding one-fiftieth of the statutory maximum;
  - (ii) in Scotland or Northern Ireland, to imprisonment for a term not exceeding six months, or to a fine not exceeding the statutory maximum (or both) and, for continued contravention, a daily default fine not exceeding one-fiftieth of the statutory maximum.

445 POWER TO IMPOSE RESTRICTIONS ON SHARES AND DEBENTURES

(1) If in connection with an investigation under either section 442 or 444 it appears to the Secretary of State that there is difficulty in finding out the relevant facts about any shares (whether issued or to be issued), he may by order direct that the shares shall until further order be subject to the restrictions of Part XV of this Act.

(1A) If the Secretary of State is satisfied that an order under subsection (1) may unfairly affect the rights of third parties in respect of shares then the Secretary of State, for the purpose of protecting such rights and subject to such terms as he thinks fit, may direct that such acts by such persons or descriptions of persons and for such purposes as may be set out in the order, shall not constitute a breach of the restrictions of Part XV of this Act.

(2) This section, and Part XV in its application to orders under it, apply in relation to debentures as in relation to shares save that subsection (1A) shall not so apply.

Requisition and seizure of books and papers

447 POWER TO REQUIRE DOCUMENTS AND INFORMATION

(1) The Secretary of State may act under subsections (2) and (3) in relation to a company.

(2) The Secretary of State may give directions to the company requiring it—

(a) to produce such documents (or documents of such description) as may be specified in the directions;
(b) to provide such information (or information of such description) as may be so specified.

(3) The Secretary of State may authorise a person (an investigator) to require the company or any other person—
(a) to produce such documents (or documents of such description) as the investigator may specify;
(b) to provide such information (or information of such description) as the investigator may specify.

(4) A person on whom a requirement under subsection (3) is imposed may require the investigator to produce evidence of his authority.

(5) A requirement under subsection (2) or (3) must be complied with at such time and place as may be specified in the directions or by the investigator (as the case may be).

(6) The production of a document in pursuance of this section does not affect any lien which a person has on the document.

(7) The Secretary of State or the investigator (as the case may be) may take copies of or extracts from a document produced in pursuance of this section.

(8) A "document" includes information recorded in any form.

(9) The power under this section to require production of a document includes power, in the case of a document not in hard copy form, to require the production of a copy of the document—
(a) in hard copy form, or
(b) in a form from which a hard copy can be readily obtained.

447A INFORMATION PROVIDED: EVIDENCE

(1) A statement made by a person in compliance with a requirement under section 447 may be used in evidence against him.

448 ENTRY AND SEARCH OF PREMISES

(1) A justice of the peace may issue a warrant under this section if satisfied on information on oath given by or on behalf of the Secretary of State, or by a person appointed or authorised to exercise powers under this Part, that there are reasonable grounds for believing that there are on any premises documents whose production has been required under this Part and which have not been produced in compliance with the requirement.

(3) A warrant under this section shall authorise a constable, together with any other person named in it and any other constables—
(a) to enter the premises specified in the information, using such force as is reasonably necessary for the purpose;
(b) to search the premises and take possession of any documents appearing to be such documents as are mentioned in subsection (1) ..., or to take, in relation to any such documents, any other steps which may appear to be necessary for preserving them or preventing interference with them;
(c) to take copies of any such documents; and
(d) to require any person named in the warrant to provide an explanation of them or to state where they may be found.

(7) Any person who intentionally obstructs the exercise of any rights conferred by a warrant issued under this section or fails without reasonable excuse to comply with any requirement imposed in accordance with subsection (3)(d) is guilty of an offence and liable to a fine.

(9) In the application of this section to Scotland for the references to a justice of the peace substitute references to a justice of the peace or a sheriff, and for the references to information on oath substitute references to evidence on oath.

(10) In this section "document" includes information recorded in any form.

450 PUNISHMENT FOR DESTROYING, MUTILATING, ETC. COMPANY DOCUMENTS

(1) An officer of a company who—
  (a) destroys, mutilates or falsifies, or is privy to the destruction, mutilation or falsification of a document affecting, or relating to the company's property or affairs, or
  (b) makes, or is privy to the making of, a false entry in such a document,
is guilty of an offence, unless he proves that he had no intention to conceal the state of affairs of the company or to defeat the law.

(1A) Subsection (1) applies to an officer of an authorised insurance company which is not a body corporate as it applies to an officer of a company.

(2) Such a person as above mentioned who fraudulently either parts with, alters or makes an omission in any such document or is privy to fraudulent parting with, fraudulent altering or fraudulent making of an omission in, any such document, is guilty of an offence.

(3) A person guilty of an offence under this section is liable—
  (a) on conviction on indictment, to imprisonment for a term not exceeding seven years or a fine (or both);
  (b) on summary conviction—
    (i) in England and Wales, to imprisonment for a term not exceeding twelve months or to a fine not exceeding the statutory maximum (or both);
    (ii) in Scotland or Northern Ireland, to imprisonment for a term not exceeding six months, or to a fine not exceeding the statutory maximum (or both).

(5) In this section "document" includes information recorded in any form.

451 PUNISHMENT FOR FURNISHING FALSE INFORMATION

(1) A person commits an offence if in purported compliance with a requirement under section 447 to provide information—
  (a) he provides information which he knows to be false in a material particular;
  (b) he recklessly provides information which is false in a material particular.

(2) A person guilty of an offence under this section is liable—
  (a) on conviction on indictment, to imprisonment for a term not exceeding two years or a fine (or both);
  (b) on summary conviction—
    (i) in England and Wales, to imprisonment for a term not exceeding twelve months or to a fine not exceeding the statutory maximum (or both);
    (ii) in Scotland or Northern Ireland, to imprisonment for a term not exceeding six months, or to a fine not exceeding the statutory maximum (or both).

453 INVESTIGATION OF OVERSEAS COMPANIES

(1) The provisions of this Part apply to bodies corporate incorporated outside the United Kingdom which are carrying on business in the United Kingdom, or have at any time carried on business there, as they apply to companies under this Act; but subject to the following exceptions, adaptations and modifications.

(1A) The following provisions do not apply to such bodies—
(a) section 431 (investigation on application of company or its members),
(c) sections 442 to 445 (investigation of company ownership and power to obtain information as to those interested in shares, etc.).

(1B) The other provisions of this Part apply to such bodies subject to such adaptations and modifications as may be specified by regulations made by the Secretary of State.

(2) Regulations under this section shall be made by statutory instrument subject to annulment in pursuance of a resolution of either House of Parliament.

453A POWER TO ENTER AND REMAIN ON PREMISES

(1) An inspector or investigator may act under subsection (2) in relation to a company if—
(a) he is authorised to do so by the Secretary of State, and
(b) he thinks that to do so will materially assist him in the exercise of his functions under this Part in relation to the company.

(2) An inspector or investigator may at all reasonable times—
(a) require entry to relevant premises, and
(b) remain there for such period as he thinks necessary for the purpose mentioned in subsection (1)(b).

(3) Relevant premises are premises which the inspector or investigator believes are used (wholly or partly) for the purposes of the company's business.

(4) In exercising his powers under subsection (2), an inspector or investigator may be accompanied by such other persons as he thinks appropriate.

(5) A person who intentionally obstructs a person lawfully acting under subsection (2) or (4) is guilty of an offence.

(5A) A person guilty of an offence under this section is liable—
(a) on conviction on indictment, to a fine;
(b) on summary conviction, to a fine not exceeding the statutory maximum.

(7) An inspector is a person appointed under section 431, 432 or 442.

(8) An investigator is a person authorised for the purposes of section 447.

453C FAILURE TO COMPLY WITH CERTAIN REQUIREMENTS

(1) This section applies if a person fails to comply with a requirement imposed by an inspector, the Secretary of State or an investigator in pursuance of either of the following provisions—
(a) section 447;
(b) section 453A.

(2) The inspector, Secretary of State or investigator (as the case may be) may certify the fact in writing to the court.

(3) If, after hearing—

(a) any witnesses who may be produced against or on behalf of the alleged offender;
(b) any statement which may be offered in defence,
the court is satisfied that the offender failed without reasonable excuse to comply with the requirement, it may deal with him as if he had been guilty of contempt of the court.

Part XV ORDERS IMPOSING RESTRICTIONS ON SHARES (SECTION 445)

454 CONSEQUENCE OF ORDER IMPOSING RESTRICTIONS

(1) So long as any shares are directed to be subject to the restrictions of this Part then, subject to any directions made in relation to an order pursuant to section 445(1A) or 456(1A)—
(a) any transfer of those shares or, in the case of unissued shares, any transfer of the right to be issued with them, and any issue of them, is void;
(b) no voting rights are exercisable in respect of the shares;
(c) no further shares shall be issued in right of them or in pursuance of any offer made to their holder; and
(d) except in a liquidation, no payment shall be made of any sums due from the company on the shares, whether in respect of capital or otherwise.

(2) Where shares are subject to the restrictions of subsection (1)(a), any agreement to transfer the shares or, in the case of unissued shares, the right to be issued with them is void (except such agreement or right as may be made or exercised under the terms of directions made by the Secretary of State or the court under section 445(1A) or 456(1A) or an agreement to transfer the shares on the making of an order under section 456(3)(b) below).

(3) Where shares are subject to the restrictions of subsection (1)(c) or (d), an agreement to transfer any right to be issued with other shares in right of those shares, or to receive any payment on them (otherwise than in a liquidation) is void (except such agreement or right as may be made or exercised under the terms of directions made by the Secretary of State or the court under section 445(1A) or 456(1A) or an agreement to transfer any such right on the transfer of the shares on the making of an order under section 456(3)(b) below).

455 PUNISHMENT FOR ATTEMPTED EVASION OF RESTRICTIONS

(1) Subject to the terms of any directions made under section 445(1A) or 456 a person commits an offence if he—
(a) exercises or purports to exercise any right to dispose of any shares which, to his knowledge, are for the time being subject to the restrictions of this Part or of any right to be issued with any such shares, or
(b) votes in respect of any such shares (whether as holder or proxy), or appoints a proxy to vote in respect of them, or
(c) being the holder of any such shares, fails to notify of their being subject to those restrictions any person whom he does not know to be aware of that fact but does know to be entitled (apart from the restrictions) to vote in respect of those shares whether as holder or as proxy, or
(d) being the holder of any such shares, or being entitled to any right to be issued with other shares in right of them, or to receive any payment on them (otherwise than in a liquidation), enters into any agreement which is void under section 454(2) or (3).

(2) Subject to the terms of any directions made under section 445(1A) or 456 if shares in a company are issued in contravention of the restrictions, an offence is committed by—
(a) the company, and
(c) every officer of the company who is in default.

(2A) A person guilty of an offence under this section is liable—
(a) on conviction on indictment, to a fine;
(b) on summary conviction, to a fine not exceeding the statutory maximum.

456 RELAXATION AND REMOVAL OF RESTRICTIONS

(1) Where shares in a company are by order made subject to the restrictions of this Part, application may be made to the court for an order directing that the shares be no longer so subject.

(1A) Where the court is satisfied that an order subjecting the shares to the restrictions of this Part unfairly affects the rights of third parties in respect of shares then the court, for the purpose of protecting such rights and subject to such terms as it thinks fit and in addition to any order it may make under subsection (1), may direct on an application made under that subsection that such acts by such persons or descriptions of persons and for such purposes, as may be set out in the order, shall not constitute a breach of the restrictions of Part XV of this Act.

Subsection (3) does not apply to an order made under this subsection.

(2) If the order applying the restrictions was made by the Secretary of State, or he has refused to make an order disapplying them, the application may be made by any person aggrieved.

(3) Subject as follows, an order of the court or the Secretary of State directing that shares shall cease to be subject to the restrictions may be made only if—
(a) the court or (as the case may be) the Secretary of State is satisfied that the relevant facts about the shares have been disclosed to the company and no unfair advantage has accrued to any person as a result of the earlier failure to make that disclosure, or
(b) the shares are to be transferred for valuable consideration and the court (in any case) or the Secretary of State (if the order was made under section 445) approves the transfer.

(4) Without prejudice to the power of the court to give directions under subsection (1A), where shares in a company are subject to the restrictions, the court may on application order the shares to be sold, subject to the court's approval as to the sale, and may also direct that the shares shall cease to be subject to the restrictions.

An application to the court under this subsection may be made by the Secretary of State or by the company.

457 FURTHER PROVISIONS ON SALE BY COURT ORDER OF RESTRICTED SHARES

(1) Where shares are sold in pursuance of an order of the court under section 456(4) the proceeds of sale, less the costs of the sale, shall be paid into court for the benefit of the persons who are beneficially interested in the shares; and any such person may apply to the court for the whole or part of those proceeds to be paid to him.

(2) On application under subsection (1) the court shall (subject as provided below) order the payment to the applicant of the whole of the proceeds of sale together with any interest thereon or, if any other person had a beneficial interest in the shares at the time of their sale, such proportion of those proceeds and interest as is equal to the proportion which the value of the applicant's interest in the shares bears to the total value of the shares.

(3) On granting an application for an order under section 456(4) ... the court may order that the applicant's costs be paid out of the proceeds of sale; and if that order is made, the applicant is entitled to payment of his costs out of those proceeds before any person interested in the shares in question receives any part of those proceeds.

As amended by the Insolvency Act 1985, Schedule 6, para 3; Financial Services Act 1986, Schedule 13, para 7; Insolvency Act 1986, Schedule 13, part I; Companies Act 1989, ss 55, 56(2)–(6), 57, 59, 60(1), 61–62, 64(1), 66, 70, Schedule 19, para 10(1)–(2), Schedule 24; The Companies (Disclosure of Interests in Shares) (Orders imposing restrictions on shares) Regulations 1991 (SI 1991/1646), regs 5–8; Youth Justice and Criminal Evidence Act 1999, Schedule 3, para 5; Criminal Justice and Police Act 2001, Schedule 2, para 17; The Financial Services and Markets Act 2000 (Consequential Amendments and Repeals) Order 2001, art 23; The Companies (Acquisition of Own Shares) (Treasury Shares) Regulations 2003 (SI 2003/1116), Schedule, para 28; Companies (Audit, Investigations and Community Enterprise) Act 2004, ss 21, 23–24, Schedule 2, paras 16–17, 19; Companies Act 2006, ss 1035(2)–(5), 1038(1)–(2), 1176(1)–(3), Schedule 3, paras 1–2, 4–7, Schedule 16; The Companies Act 2006 (Commencement No. 3, Consequential Amendments, Transitional Provisions and Savings) Order 2007 (SI 2007/2194), Schedule 4, para 11(3)–(10), Schedule 5; The Companies Act 2006 (Consequential Amendments, Transitional Provisions and Savings) Order 2009 (SI 2009/1941), Schedule 1, para 57.

Company Directors Disqualification Act 1986

Preliminary

1 DISQUALIFICATION ORDERS: GENERAL

(1) In the circumstances specified below in this Act a court may, and under section 6 shall, make against a person a disqualification order, that is to say an order that for a period specified in the order—
- (a) he shall not be a director of a company, act as receiver of a company's property or in any way, whether directly or indirectly, be concerned or take part in the promotion, formation or management of a company unless (in each case) he has the leave of the court, and
- (b) he shall not act as an insolvency practitioner.

(2) In each section of this Act which gives to a court power or, as the case may be, imposes on it the duty to make a disqualification order there is specified the maximum (and, in section 6, the minimum) period of disqualification which may or (as the case may be)

must be imposed by means of the order and, unless the court otherwise orders, the period of disqualification so imposed shall begin at the end of the period of 21 days beginning with the date of the order.

(3) Where a disqualification order is made against a person who is already subject to such an order or to a disqualification undertaking, the periods specified in those orders or, as the case may be, in the order and the undertaking shall run concurrently.

(4) A disqualification order may be made on grounds which are or include matters other than criminal convictions, notwithstanding that the person in respect of whom it is to be made may be criminally liable in respect of those matters.

1A DISQUALIFICATION UNDERTAKINGS: GENERAL

(1) In the circumstances specified in sections 7 and 8 the Secretary of State may accept a disqualification undertaking, that is to say an undertaking by any person that, for a period specified in the undertaking, the person—
   (a) will not be a director of a company, act as receiver of a company's property or in any way, whether directly or indirectly, be concerned or take part in the promotion, formation or management of a company unless (in each case) he has the leave of a court, and
   (b) will not act as an insolvency practitioner.

(2) The maximum period which may be specified in a disqualification undertaking is 15 years; and the minimum period which may be specified in a disqualification undertaking under section 7 is two years.

(3) Where a disqualification undertaking by a person who is already subject to such an undertaking or to a disqualification order is accepted, the periods specified in those undertakings or (as the case may be) the undertaking and the order shall run concurrently.

(4) In determining whether to accept a disqualification undertaking by any person, the Secretary of State may take account of matters other than criminal convictions, notwithstanding that the person may be criminally liable in respect of those matters.

Disqualification for general misconduct in Connection with Companies

2 DISQUALIFICATION ON CONVICTION OF INDICTABLE OFFENCE

(1) The court may make a disqualification order against a person where he is convicted of an indictable offence (whether on indictment or summarily) in connection with the promotion, formation, management, liquidation or striking off of a company, with the receivership of a company's property or with his being an administrative receiver of a company.

(2) "The court" for this purpose means—
   (a) any court having jurisdiction to wind up the company in relation to which the offence was committed, or
   (b) the court by or before which the person is convicted of the offence, or
   (c) in the case of a summary conviction in England and Wales, any other magistrates' court acting in the same local justice area;

   and for the purposes of this section the definition of "indictable offence" in Schedule 1 to the Interpretation Act 1978 applies for Scotland as it does for England and Wales.

(3) The maximum period of disqualification under this section is—
(a) where the disqualification order is made by a court of summary jurisdiction, 5 years, and
(b) in any other case, 15 years.

3 DISQUALIFICATION FOR PERSISTENT BREACHES OF COMPANIES LEGISLATION

(1) The court may made a disqualification order against a person where it appears to it that he has been persistently in default in relation to provisions of the companies legislation requiring any return, account or other document to be filed with, delivered or sent, or notice of any matter to be given, to the registrar of companies.

(2) On an application to the court for an order to be made under this section, the fact that a person has been persistently in default in relation to such provisions as are mentioned above may (without prejudice to its proof in any other manner) be conclusively proved by showing that in the 5 years ending with the date of the application he has been adjudged guilty (whether or not on the same occasion) of three or more defaults in relation to those provisions.

(3) A person is to be treated under subsection (2) as being adjudged guilty of a default in relation to any provision of that legislation if—
(a) he is convicted (whether on indictment or summarily) of an offence consisting in a contravention of or failure to comply with that provision (whether on his own part or on the part of any company), or
(b) a default order is made against him, that is to say an order under any of the following provisions—
(i) section 452 of the Companies Act 2006 (order requiring delivery of company accounts),
(ia) section 456 of that Act (order requiring preparation of revised accounts),
(ii) section 1113 of that Act (enforcement of company's filing obligations),
(iii) section 41 of the Insolvency Act 1986 (enforcement of receiver's or manager's duty to make returns), or
(iv) section 170 of that Act (corresponding provision for liquidator in winding up), in respect of any such contravention of or failure to comply with that provision (whether on his own part or on the part of any company).

(4) In this section "the court" means any court having jurisdiction to wind up any of the companies in relation to which the offence or other default has been or is alleged to have been committed.

(4A) In this section "the companies legislation" means the Companies Acts and Parts 1 to 7 of the Insolvency Act 1986 (company insolvency and winding up).

(5) The maximum period of disqualification under this section is 5 years.

4 DISQUALIFICATION FOR FRAUD, ETC., IN WINDING UP

(1) The court may make a disqualification order against a person if, in the course of the winding up of a company, it appears that he—
(a) has been guilty of an offence for which he is liable (whether he has been convicted or not) under section 993 of the Companies Act 2006 (fraudulent trading), or
(b) has otherwise been guilty, while an officer or liquidator of the company, receiver of the company's property or administrative receiver of the company, of any fraud in relation to the company or of any breach of his duty as such officer, liquidator, receiver or administrative receiver.

(2) In this section "the court" means any court having jurisdiction to wind up any of the companies in relation to which the offence or other default has been or is alleged to have been committed; and "officer" includes a shadow director.

(3) The maximum period of disqualification under this section is 15 years.

5 DISQUALIFICATION ON SUMMARY CONVICTION

(1) An offence counting for the purposes of this section is one of which a person is convicted (either on indictment or summarily) in consequence of a contravention of, or failure to comply with, any provision of the companies legislation requiring a return, account or other document to be filed with, delivered or sent, or notice of any matter to be given, to the registrar of companies (whether the contravention or failure is on the person's own part or on the part of any company).

(2) Where a person is convicted of a summary offence counting for those purposes, the court by which he is convicted (or, in England and Wales, any other magistrates' court acting in the same local justice area) may make a disqualification order against him if the circumstances specified in the next subsection are present.

(3) Those circumstances are that, during the 5 years ending with the date of the conviction, the person has had made against him, or has been convicted of, in total not less than 3 default orders and offences counting for the purposes of this section; and those offences may include that of which he is convicted as mentioned in subsection (2) and any other offence of which he is convicted on the same occasion.

(4) For the purposes of this section—
(a) the definition of "summary offence" in Schedule 1 to the Interpretation Act 1978 applies for Scotland as for England and Wales, and
(b) "default order" means the same as in section 3(3)(b).

(4A) In this section "the companies legislation" means the Companies Acts and Parts 1 to 7 of the Insolvency Act 1986 (company insolvency and winding up).

(5) The maximum period of disqualification under this section is 5 years.

Disqualification for unfitness

6 DUTY OF COURT TO DISQUALIFY UNFIT DIRECTORS OF INSOLVENT COMPANIES

(1) The court shall make a disqualification order against a person in any case where, on an application under this section, it is satisfied—
(a) that he is or has been a director of a company which has at any time become insolvent (whether while he was a director or subsequently), and
(b) that his conduct as a director of that company (either taken alone or taken together with his conduct as a director of any other company or companies) makes him unfit to be concerned in the management of a company.

(2) For the purposes of this section and the next, a company becomes insolvent if—
(a) the company goes into liquidation at a time when its assets are insufficient for the payment of its debts and other liabilities and the expenses of the winding up,
(b) the company enters administration, or
(c) an administrative receiver of the company is appointed; and references to a person's conduct as a director of any company or companies include, where that company or

any of those companies has become insolvent, that person's conduct in relation to any matter connected with or arising out of the insolvency of that company.

(3) In this section and section 7(2), "the court" means—
  (a) where the company in question is being or has been wound up by the court, that court,
  (b) where the company in question is being or has been wound up voluntarily, any court which has or (as the case may be) had jurisdiction to wind it up,
  (c) where neither paragraphs (a) nor (b) applies but an administrator or administrative receiver has at any time been appointed in respect of the company in question, any court which has jurisdiction to wind it up.

(3C) In this section and section 7, "director" includes a shadow director.

(4) Under this section the minimum period of disqualification is 2 years, and the maximum period is 15 years.

7 DISQUALIFICATION ORDER OR UNDERTAKING; AND REPORTING PROVISIONS

(1) If it appears to the Secretary of State that it is expedient in the public interest that a disqualification order under section 6 should be made against any person, an application for the making of such an order against that person may be made—
  (a) by the Secretary of State, or
  (b) if the Secretary of State so directs in the case of a person who is or has been a director of a company which is being or has been wound up by the court in England and Wales, by the official receiver.

(2) Except with the leave of the court, an application for the making under that section of a disqualification order against any person shall not be made after the end of the period of 2 years beginning with the day on which the company of which that person is or has been a director became insolvent.

(2A) If it appears to the Secretary of State that the conditions mentioned in section 6(1) are satisfied as respects any person who has offered to give him a disqualification undertaking, he may accept the undertaking if it appears to him that it is expedient in the public interest that he should do so (instead of applying, or proceeding with an application, for a disqualification order).

(3) If it appears to the office-holder responsible under this section, that is to say—
  (a) in the case of a company which is being wound up by the court in England and Wales, the official receiver,
  (b) in the case of a company which is being wound up otherwise, the liquidator,
  (c) in the case of a company which is in administration, the administrator, or
  (d) in the case of a company of which there is an administrative receiver, that receiver,

that the conditions mentioned in section 6(1) are satisfied as respects a person who is or has been a director of that company, the office-holder shall forthwith report the matter to the Secretary of State.

(4) The Secretary of State or the official receiver may require the liquidator, administrator or administrative receiver of a company, or the former liquidator, administrator or administrative receiver of a company—
  (a) to furnish him with such information with respect to any person's conduct as a director of the company, and

(b) to produce and permit inspection of such books, papers and other records relevant to that person's conduct as such a director,

as the Secretary of State or the official receiver may reasonably require for the purpose of determining whether to exercise, or of exercising, any function of his under this section.

8 DISQUALIFICATION AFTER INVESTIGATION OF COMPANY

(1) If it appears to the Secretary of State from investigative material that it is expedient in the public interest that a disqualification order should be made against a person who is, or has been, a director or shadow director of a company, he may apply to the court for such an order.

(1A) "Investigative material" means—
- (a) a report made by inspectors under—
  - (i) section 437 of the Companies Act 1985, or
  - (ii) section 167, 168, 169 or 284 of the Financial Services and Markets Act 2000; and
- (b) information or documents obtained under—
  - (i) section 437, 446E, 447, 448, 451A or 453A of the Companies Act 1985;
  - (ii) section 2 of the Criminal Justice Act 1987;
  - (iii) section 28 of the Criminal Law (Consolidation)(Scotland) Act 1995;
  - (iv) section 83 of the Companies Act 1989; or
  - (v) section 165, 171, 172, 173 or 175 of the Financial Services and Markets Act 2000.

(2) The court may make a disqualification order against a person where, on an application under this section, it is satisfied that his conduct in relation to the company makes him unfit to be concerned in the management of a company.

(2A) Where it appears to the Secretary of State from such report, information or documents that, in the case of a person who has offered to give him a disqualification undertaking—
- (a) the conduct of the person in relation to a company of which the person is or has been a director or shadow director makes him unfit to be concerned in the management of a company, and
- (b) it is expedient in the public interest that he should accept the undertaking (instead of applying, or proceeding with an application, for a disqualification order),

he may accept the undertaking.

(3) In this section "the court" means the High Court or, in Scotland, the Court of Session.

(4) The maximum period of disqualification under this section is 15 years.

8A VARIATION ETC., OF DISQUALIFICATION UNDERTAKING

(1) The court may, on the application of a person who is subject to a disqualification undertaking—
- (a) reduce the period for which the undertaking is to be in force, or
- (b) provide for it to cease to be in force.

(2) On the hearing of an application under subsection (1), the Secretary of State shall appear and call the attention of the court to any matters which seem to him to be relevant, and may himself give evidence or call witnesses.

(3) In this section "the court" … has the same meaning as in section 7(2) or 8 (as the case may be).

9 MATTERS FOR DETERMINING UNFITNESS OF DIRECTORS

(1) Where it falls to a court to determine whether a person's conduct as a director of any particular company or companies makes him unfit to be concerned in the management of a company, the court shall, as respects his conduct as a director of that company or, as the case may be, each of those companies, have regard in particular—
(a) to the matters mentioned in Part I of Schedule 1 to this Act, and
(b) where the company has become insolvent, to the matters mentioned in Part II of that Schedule;
and references in that Schedule to the director and the company are to be read accordingly.

(1A) In determining whether he may accept a disqualification undertaking from any person the Secretary of State shall, as respects the person's conduct as a director of any company concerned, have regard in particular—
(a) to the matters mentioned in Part I of Schedule 1 to this Act, and
(b) where the company has become insolvent, to the matters mentioned in Part II of that Schedule;
and references in that Schedule to the director and the company are to be read accordingly.

(2) Section 6(2) applies for the purposes of this section and Schedule 1 as it applies for the purposes of sections 6 and 7 and in this section and that Schedule "director" includes a shadow director.

(4) The Secretary of State may by order modify any of the provisions of Schedule 1; and such an order may contain such transitional provisions as may appear to the Secretary of State necessary or expedient.

(5) The power to make orders under this section is exercisable by statutory instrument subject to annulment in pursuance of a resolution of either House of Parliament.

Other cases of disqualification

10 PARTICIPATION IN WRONGFUL TRADING

(1) Where the court makes a declaration under section 213 or 214 of the Insolvency Act 1986 that a person is liable to make a contribution to a company's assets, then, whether or not an application for such an order is made by any person, the court may, if it thinks fit, also make a disqualification order against the person to whom the declaration relates.

(2) The maximum period of disqualification under this section is 15 years.

11 UNDISCHARGED BANKRUPTS

(1) It is an offence for a person to act as director of a company or directly or indirectly take part in or be concerned in the promotion, formation or management of a company, without the leave of the court, at a time when—
(a) he is an undischarged bankrupt, or
(b) a bankruptcy restrictions order is in force in respect of him.

(2) "The court" for this purpose is the court by which the person was adjudged bankrupt or, in Scotland, sequestration of his estates was awarded.

(3) In England and Wales, the leave of the court shall not be given unless notice of intention to apply for it has been served on the official receiver; and it is the latter's duty, if he is of

opinion that it is contrary to the public interest that the application should be granted, to attend on the hearing of the application and oppose it.

(4) In this section "company" includes a company incorporated outside Great Britain that has an established place of business in Great Britain.

...

Consequences of contravention

13 CRIMINAL PENALTIES

If a person acts in contravention of a disqualification order or disqualification undertaking ..., or is guilty of an offence under section 11, he is liable—

(a) on conviction on indictment, to imprisonment for not more than 2 years or a fine, or both; and

(b) on summary conviction, to imprisonment for not more than 6 months or a fine not exceeding the statutory maximum, or both.

14 OFFENCES BY BODY CORPORATE

(1) Where a body corporate is guilty of an offence of acting in contravention of a disqualification order or disqualification undertaking ..., and it is proved that the offence occurred with the consent or connivance of, or was attributable to any neglect on the part of any director, manager, secretary or other similar officer of the body corporate, or any person who was purporting to act in any such capacity he, as well as the body corporate, is guilty of the offence and liable to be proceeded against and punished accordingly.

(2) Where the affairs of a body corporate are managed by its members, subsection (1) applies in relation to the acts and defaults of a member in connection with his functions of management as if he were a director of the body corporate.

15 PERSONAL LIABILITY FOR COMPANY'S DEBTS WHERE PERSON ACTS WHILE DISQUALIFIED

(1) A person is personally responsible for all the relevant debts of a company if at any time—
   (a) in contravention of a disqualification order or disqualification undertaking or in contravention of section 11 ... of this Act he is involved in the management of the company, or
   (b) as a person who is involved in the management of the company, he acts or is willing to act on instructions given without the leave of the court by a person whom he knows at that time—
      (i) to be the subject of a disqualification order made or disqualification undertaking accepted under this Act or under the Company Directors Disqualification (Northern Ireland) Order 2002, or
      (ii) to be an undischarged bankrupt.

(2) Where a person is personally responsible under this section for the relevant debts of a company, he is jointly and severally liable in respect of those debts with the company and any other person who, whether under this section or otherwise, is so liable.

(3) For the purposes of this section the relevant debts of a company are—
(a) in relation to a person who is personally responsible under paragraph (a) of subsection (1), such debts and other liabilities of the company as are incurred at a time when that person was involved in the management of the company, and
(b) in relation to a person who is personally responsible under paragraph (b) of that subsection, such debts and other liabilities of the company as are incurred at a time when that person was acting or was willing to act on instructions given as mentioned in that paragraph.

(4) For the purposes of this section, a person is involved in the management of a company if he is a director of the company or if he is concerned, whether directly or indirectly, or takes part, in the management of the company.

(5) For the purposes of this section a person who, as a person involved in the management of a company, has at any time acted on instructions given without the leave of the court by a person whom he knew at that time—
(a) to be the subject of a disqualification order made or disqualification undertaking accepted under this Act or under the Company Directors Disqualification (Northern Ireland) Order 2002, or
(b) to be an undischarged bankrupt,
is presumed, unless the contrary is shown, to have been willing at any time thereafter to act on any instructions given by that person.

Supplementary provisions

16 APPLICATION FOR DISQUALIFICATION ORDER

(1) A person intending to apply for the making of a disqualification order by the court having jurisdiction to wind up a company shall give not less than 10 days' notice of his intention to the person against whom the order is sought; and on the hearing of the application the last-mentioned person may appear and himself give evidence or call witnesses.

(2) An application to a court with jurisdiction to wind up companies for the making against any person of a disqualification order under any of sections 2 to 4 may be made by the Secretary of State or the official receiver, or by the liquidator or any past or present member or creditor of any company in relation to which that person has committed or is alleged to have committed an offence or other default.

(3) On the hearing of any application under this Act made by a person falling within subsection (4), the applicant shall appear and call the attention of the court to any matters which seem to him to be relevant, and may himself give evidence or call witnesses.

(4) The following fall within this subsection—
(a) the Secretary of State;
(b) the official receiver;. . .
(d) the liquidator. . . .

. . .

21A BANK INSOLVENCY

Section 121 of the Banking Act 2009 provides for this Act to apply in relation to bank insolvency as it applies in relation to liquidation.

21B BANK ADMINISTRATION

Section 155 of the Banking Act 2009 provides for this Act to apply in relation to bank administration as it applies in relation to liquidation.

22 INTERPRETATION

(1) This section has effect with respect to the meaning of expressions used in this Act, and applies unless the context otherwise requires.

(2) "Company" means—
   (a) a company registered under the Companies Act 2006 in Great Britain, or
   (b) a company that may be wound up under Part 5 of the Insolvency Act 1986 (unregistered companies).

(3) Section 247 in Part VII of the Insolvency Act 1986 (interpretation for the first Group of Parts of that Act) applies as regards references to a company's insolvency and to its going into liquidation; and "administrative receiver" has the meaning given by section 251 of that Act and references to acting as an insolvency practitioner are to be read in accordance with section 388 of that Act.

(4) "Director" includes any person occupying the position of director, by whatever name called.

(5) "Shadow director", in relation to a company, means a person in accordance with whose directions or instructions the directors of the company are accustomed to act (but so that a person is not deemed a shadow director by reason only that the directors act on advice given by him in a professional capacity).

(10) Any reference to acting as receiver—
   (a) includes acting as manager or as both receiver and manager, but
   (b) does not include acting as administrative receiver;
   and "receivership" is to be read accordingly.

...

24 EXTENT

(1) This Act extends to England and Wales and to Scotland.

SCHEDULES

SCHEDULE 1 MATTERS FOR DETERMINING UNFITNESS OF DIRECTORS

Part I MATTERS APPLICABLE IN ALL CASES

1. Any misfeasance or breach of any fiduciary or other duty by the director in relation to the company, including in particular any breach by the director of a duty under Chapter 2 of Part 10 of the Companies Act 2006 (general duties of directors) owed to the company.

2. Any misapplication or retention by the director of, or any conduct by the director giving rise to an obligation to account for, any money or other property of the company.

3. The extent of the director's responsibility for the company entering into any transaction liable to be set aside under Part XVI of the Insolvency Act 1986 (provisions against debt avoidance).

4. The extent of the director's responsibility for any failure by the company to comply with any of the following provisions of the Companies Act 2006—
(a) section 113 (register of members);
(b) section 114 (register to be kept available for inspection);
(c) section 162 (register of directors);
(d) section 165 (register of directors' residential addresses);
(e) section 167 (duty to notify registrar of changes: directors);
(f) section 275 (register of secretaries);
(g) section 276 (duty to notify registrar of changes: secretaries);
(h) section 386 (duty to keep accounting records);
(i) section 388 (where and for how long accounting records to be kept);
(j) section 854 (duty to make annual returns);
(k) section 860 (duty to register charges);
(l) section 878 (duty to register charges: companies registered in Scotland).

5. The extent of the director's responsibility for any failure by the directors of the company to comply with the following provisions of the Companies Act 2006—
(a) section 394 or 399 (duty to prepare annual accounts);
(b) section 414 or 450 (approval and signature of abbreviated accounts); or
(c) section 433 (name of signatory to be stated in published copy of accounts).

Part II MATTERS APPLICABLE WHERE COMPANY HAS BECOME INSOLVENT

6. The extent of the director's responsibility for the causes of the company becoming insolvent.

7. The extent of the director's responsibility for any failure by the company to supply any goods or services which have been paid for (in whole or in part).

8. The extent of the director's responsibility for the company entering into any transaction or giving any preference, being a transaction or preference—
(a) liable to be set aside under section 127 or sections 238 to 240 of the Insolvency Act 1986, or
(b) challengeable under section 242 or 243 of that Act or under any rule of law in Scotland.

9. The extent of the director's responsibility for any failure by the directors of the company to comply with section 98 of the Insolvency Act 1986 (duty to call creditors' meeting in creditors' voluntary winding up).

10. Any failure by the director to comply with any obligation imposed on him by or under any of the following provisions of the Insolvency Act 1986—
(a) paragraph 47 of Schedule B1 (company's statement of affairs in administration);
(b) section 47 (statement of affairs to administrative receiver);
(c) section 66 (statement of affairs in Scottish receivership);
(d) section 99 (directors' duty to attend meeting; statement of affairs in creditors' voluntary winding up);
(e) section 131 (statement of affairs in winding up by the court);
(f) section 234 (duty of anyone with company property to deliver it up);
(g) section 235 (duty to co-operate with liquidator, etc.).

As amended by the Financial Services Act 1986, s 198(2); Deregulation and Contracting Out Act 1994, Sch 11, para 6; Companies Act 1989, ss 79, 139(4), Sch 10, para 35; Criminal Justice (Scotland) Act 1987, s 55(b); Criminal Justice Act 1988, s 145(b); Criminal Procedure (Consequential Provision) (Scotland) Act 1995, Schedule 4, para 62; Insolvency Act 2000, ss 5(1)–(3), 6(1)–(6), Schedule 4, paras 1–11, 15, Schedule 5; The Financial Services and Markets Act 2000 (Consequential Amendments and Repeals) Order 2001(SI 2001/3649), art 39; Enterprise Act 2002, s 204(6)–(7); Schedule 17, paras 40–41, Schedule 21, para 5; Courts Act 2003, Schedule 8, para 300; Companies (Audit, Investigations and Community Enterprise) Act 2004, Schedule 2, para 28; The Enterprise Act 2002 (Insolvency) Order 2003 (SI 2003/2096), Schedule, para 12; The Insolvency Act 2000 (Company Directors Disqualification Undertakings) Order 2004 (SI 2004/1941), art 2(5); The Companies Act 2006 (Commencement No. 3, Consequential Amendments, Transitional Provisions and Savings) Order 2007(SI 2007/2194), Schedule 4, para 46; The Companies Act 2006 (Consequential Amendments etc.) Order 2008 (SI 2008/948), Schedule 1, para 106(2), (8); Banking Act 2009, ss 121(4), 155(4); The Companies Act 2006 (Consequential Amendments, Transitional Provisions and Savings) Order 2009 (SI 2009/1941), Schedule 1, para 85.

Insolvency Act 1986

THE FIRST GROUP OF PARTS

COMPANY INSOLVENCY; COMPANIES WINDING UP

Part I COMPANY VOLUNTARY ARRANGEMENTS

The Proposal

1 THOSE WHO MAY PROPOSE AN ARRANGEMENT

(1) The directors of a company (other than one which is in administration or being wound up) may make a proposal under this Part to the company and to its creditors for a composition in satisfaction of its debts or a scheme of arrangement of its affairs (from here on referred to, in either case, as a "voluntary arrangement").

(2) A proposal under this Part is one which provides for some person ("the nominee") to act in relation to the voluntary arrangement either as trustee or otherwise for the purpose of supervising its implementation; and the nominee must be a person who is qualified to act as an insolvency practitioner or authorised to act as nominee, in relation to the voluntary arrangement.

(3) Such a proposal may also be made—
(a) where the company is in administration, by the administrator,
(b) where the company is being wound up, by the liquidator.

(4) In this Part "company" means—
(a) a company registered under the Companies Act 2006 in England and Wales or Scotland,
(b) a company incorporated in an EEA State other than the United Kingdom; or
(c) a company not incorporated in an EEA State but having its centre of main interests in a member State other than Denmark.

(5) In subsection (4), in relation to a company, "centre of main interests" has the same meaning as in the EC Regulation and, in the absence of proof to the contrary, is presumed to be the place of its registered office (within the meaning of that Regulation).

(6) If a company incorporated outside the United Kingdom has a principal place of business in Northern Ireland, no proposal under this Part shall be made in relation to it unless it also has a principal place of business in England and Wales or Scotland (or both in England and Wales or Scotland).

1A MORATORIUM

(1) Where the directors of an eligible company intend to make a proposal for a voluntary arrangement, they may take steps to obtain a moratorium for the company.

(2) The provisions of Schedule A1 to this Act have effect with respect to—
(a) companies eligible for a moratorium under this section,
(b) the procedure for obtaining such a moratorium,
(c) the effects of such a moratorium, and
(d) the procedure applicable (in place of sections 2 to 6 and 7) in relation to the approval and implementation of a voluntary arrangement where such a moratorium is or has been in force.

2 PROCEDURE WHERE NOMINEE IS NOT THE LIQUIDATOR OR ADMINISTRATOR

(1) This section applies where the nominee under section 1 is not the liquidator or administrator of the company and the directors do not propose to take steps to obtain a moratorium under section 1A for the company.

(2) The nominee shall, within 28 days (or such longer period as the court may allow) after he is given notice of the proposal for a voluntary arrangement, submit a report to the court stating—
(a) whether, in his opinion, the proposed voluntary arrangement has a reasonable prospect of being approved and implemented,
(aa) whether, in his opinion, meetings of the company and of its creditors should be summoned to consider the proposal, and
(b) if in his opinion such meetings should be summoned, the date on which, and time and place at which, he proposes the meetings should be held.

(3) For the purposes of enabling the nominee to prepare his report, the person intending to make the proposal shall submit to the nominee—
(a) a document setting out the terms of the proposed voluntary arrangement, and
(b) a statement of the company's affairs containing—
(i) such particulars of its creditors and of its debts and other liabilities and of its assets as may be prescribed, and
(ii) such other information as may be prescribed.

(4) The court may—
(a) on an application made by the person intending to make the proposal, in a case where the nominee has failed to submit the report required by this section or has died, or
(b) on an application made by that person or the nominee, in a case where it is impracticable or inappropriate for the nominee to continue to act as such,
direct that the nominee be replaced as such by another person qualified to act as an insolvency practitioner, or authorised to act as nominee, in relation to the voluntary arrangement.

3 SUMMONING OF MEETINGS

(1) Where the nominee under section 1 is not the liquidator or administrator, and it has been report to the court that such meetings as are mentioned in section 2(2) should be summoned, the person making the report shall (unless the court otherwise directs) summon those meetings for the time, date and place proposed in the report.

(2) Where the nominee is the liquidator or administrator, he shall summon meetings of the company and of its creditors to consider the proposal for such a time, date and place as he thinks fit.

(3) The persons to be summoned to a creditors' meeting under this section are every creditor of the company of whose claim and address the person summoning the meeting is aware.

Consideration and implementation of proposal

4 DECISIONS OF MEETINGS

(1) The meetings summoned under section 3 shall decide whether to approve the proposed voluntary arrangement (with or without modifications).

(2) The modifications may include one conferring the functions proposed to be conferred on the nominee on another person qualified to act as an insolvency practitioner or authorised to act as nominee, in relation to the voluntary arrangement.

But they shall not include any modification by virtue of which the proposal ceases to be a proposal such as is mentioned in section 1.

(3) A meeting so summoned shall not approve any proposal or modification which affects the right of a secured creditor of the company to enforce his security, except with the concurrence of the creditor concerned.

(4) Subject as follows, a meeting so summoned shall not approve any proposal or modification under which—
- (a) any preferential debt of the company is to be paid otherwise than in priority to such of its debts as are not preferential debts, or
- (b) a preferential creditor of the company is to be paid an amount in respect of a preferential debt that bears to that debt a smaller proportion than is borne to another preferential debt by the amount that is to be paid in respect of that other debt.

However, the meeting may approve such a proposal or modification with the concurrence of the preferential creditor concerned.

(5) Subject as above, each of the meetings shall be conducted in accordance with the rules.

(6) After the conclusion of either meeting in accordance with the rules, the chairman of the meeting shall report the result of the meeting to the court, and, immediately after reporting to the court, shall give notice of the result of the meeting to such persons as may be prescribed.

(7) References in this section to preferential debts and preferential creditors are to be read in accordance with section 386 in Part XII of this Act.

4A APPROVAL OF ARRANGEMENT

(1) This section applies to a decision, under section 4, with respect to the approval of a proposed voluntary arrangement.

(2) The decision has effect if, in accordance with the rules—
- (a) it has been taken by both meetings summoned under section 3, or
- (b) (subject to any order made under subsection (4)) it has been taken by the creditors' meeting summoned under that section.

(3) If the decision taken by the creditors' meeting differs from that taken by the company meeting, a member of the company may apply to the court.

(4) An application under subsection (3) shall not be made after the end of the period of 28 days beginning with—
- (a) the day on which the decision was taken by the creditors' meeting, or
- (b) where the decision of the company meeting was taken on a later day, that day.

(5) Where a member of a regulated company, within the meaning given by paragraph 44 of Schedule A1, applies to the court under subsection (3), the Financial Services Authority is entitled to be heard on the application.

(6) On an application under subsection (3), the court may—
- (a) order the decision of the company meeting to have effect instead of the decision of the creditors' meeting, or
- (b) make such other order as it thinks fit.

5 EFFECT OF APPROVAL

(1) This section applies where a decision approving a voluntary arrangement has effect under section 4A.

(2) The voluntary arrangement—
 (a) takes effect as if made by the company at the creditors' meeting, and
 (b) binds every person who in accordance with the rules—
  (i) was entitled to vote at that meeting (whether or not he was present or represented at it), or
  (ii) would have been so entitled if he had had notice of it, as if he were a party to the voluntary arrangement.

(2A) If—
 (a) when the arrangement ceases to have effect any amount payable under the arrangement to a person bound by virtue of subsection (2)(b)(ii) has not been paid, and
 (b) the arrangement did not come to an end prematurely, the company shall at that time become liable to pay to that person the amount payable under the arrangement.

(3) Subject as follows, if the company is being wound up or is in administration, the court may do one or both of the following, namely—
 (a) by order stay or sist all proceedings in the winding up or provide for the appointment of the administrator to cease to have effect;
 (b) give such directions with respect to the conduct of the winding up or the administration as it thinks appropriate for facilitating the implementation of the voluntary arrangement.

(4) The court shall not make an order under subsection (3)(a)—
 (a) at any time before the end of the period of 28 days beginning with the first day on which each of the reports required by section 4(6) has been made to the court, or
 (b) at any time when an application under the next section or an appeal in respect of such an application is pending, or at any time in the period within which such an appeal may be brought.

6 CHALLENGE OF DECISIONS

(1) Subject to this section, an application to the court may be made, by any of the persons specified below, on one or both of the following grounds, namely—
 (a) that a voluntary arrangement which has effect under section 4A unfairly prejudices the interests of a creditor, member or contributory of the company;
 (b) that there has been some material irregularity at or in relation to either of the meetings.

(2) The persons who may apply under subsection (1) are—
 (a) a person entitled, in accordance with the rules, to vote at either of the meetings;
 (aa) a person who would have been entitled, in accordance with the rules, to vote at the creditors' meeting if he had had notice of it;
 (b) the nominee or any person who has replaced him under section 2(4) or 4(2); and
 (c) if the company is being wound up or is in administration, the liquidator or administrator.

(3) An application under this section shall not be made—
 (a) after the end of the period of 28 days beginning with the first day on which each of the reports required by section 4(6) has been made to the court; or

(b) in the case of a person who was not given notice of the creditors' meeting, after the end of the period of 28 days beginning with the day on which he became aware that the meeting had taken place,

but (subject to that) an application made by a person within subsection (2)(aa), on the ground that the voluntary arrangement prejudices his interests may be made after the arrangement has ceased to have effect, unless it came to an end prematurely.

(4) Where on such an application the court is satisfied as to either of the grounds mentioned in subsection (1) ... it may do one or both of the following, namely—

(a) revoke or suspend any decision approving the voluntary arrangement which has effect under section 4A or, in a case falling within subsection (1)(b), any decision taken by the meeting in question which has effect under that section;

(b) give a direction to any person for the summoning of further meetings to consider any revised proposal the person who made the original proposal may make or, in the case falling within subsection (1)(b), a further company or (as the case may be) creditors' meeting to reconsider the original proposal.

(5) Where at any time after giving a direction under subsection (4)(b) for the summoning of meetings to consider a revised proposal the court is satisfied that the person who made the original proposal does not intend to submit a revised proposal, the court shall revoke the direction and revoke or suspend any decision approving the voluntary arrangement which has effect under section 4A.

(6) In a case where the court, on an application under this section with respect to any meeting—

(a) gives a direction under subsection (4)(b), or

(b) revokes or suspends an approval under subsection (4)(a) or (5),

the court may give such supplemental directions as it thinks fit and, in particular, directions with respect to things done under the voluntary arrangement since it took effect.

(7) Except in pursuance of the preceding provisions of this section, a decision taken at a meeting summoned under section 3 is not invalidated by any irregularity at or in relation to the meeting.

6A FALSE REPRESENTATIONS, ETC.

(1) If, for the purpose of obtaining the approval of the members or creditors of a company to a proposal for a voluntary arrangement, a person who is an officer of the company—

(a) makes any false representation, or

(b) fraudulently does, or omits to do, anything,

he commits an offence.

(2) Subsection (1) applies even if the proposal is not approved.

(3) For purposes of this section "officer" includes a shadow director.

(4) A person guilty of an offence under this section is liable to imprisonment or a fine, or both.

7 IMPLEMENTATION OF PROPOSAL

(1) This section applies where a voluntary arrangement has effect under section 4A.

(2) The person who is for the time being carrying out in relation to the voluntary arrangement the functions conferred—

(a) on the nominee by virtue of the approval given at one or both of the meetings summoned under section 3, or

(b) by virtue of section 2(4) or 4(2) on a person other than the nominee,

shall be known as the supervisor of the voluntary arrangement.

(3) If any of the company's creditors or any other person is dissatisfied by any act, omission or decision of the supervisor, he may apply to the court; and on the application the court may—

(a) confirm, reverse or modify any act or decision of the supervisor,

(b) give him directions, or

(c) make such other order as it thinks fit.

(4) The supervisor—

(a) may apply to the court for directions in relation to any particular matter arising under the voluntary arrangement, and

(b) is included among the persons who may apply to the court for the winding up of the company or for an administration order to be made in relation to it.

(5) The court may, whenever—

(a) it is expedient to appoint a person to carry out the functions of the supervisor, and

(b) it is inexpedient, difficult or impracticable for an appointment to be made without the assistance of the court,

make an order appointing a person who is qualified to act as an insolvency practitioner or authorised to act as supervisor, in relation to the voluntary arrangement, either in substitution for the existing supervisor or to fill a vacancy.

(6) The power conferred by subsection (5) is exercisable so as to increase the number of persons exercising the functions of supervisor or, where there is more than one person exercising those functions, so as to replace one or more of those persons.

7A PROSECUTION OF DELINQUENT OFFICERS OF COMPANY

(1) This section applies where a moratorium under section 1A has been obtained for a company or the approval of a voluntary arrangement in relation to a company has taken effect under section 4A or paragraph 36 of Schedule A1.

(2) If it appears to the nominee or supervisor that any past or present officer of the company has been guilty of any offence in connection with the moratorium or, as the case may be, voluntary arrangement for which he is criminally liable, the nominee or supervisor shall forthwith—

(a) report the matter to the appropriate authority, and

(b) provide the appropriate authority with such information and give the authority such access to and facilities for inspecting and taking copies of documents (being information or documents in the possession or under the control of the nominee or supervisor and relating to the matter in question) as the authority requires.

In this subsection, "the appropriate authority" means—

(i) in the case of a company registered in England and Wales, the Secretary of State, and

(ii) in the case of a company registered in Scotland, the Lord Advocate.

(3) Where a report is made to the Secretary of State under subsection (2), he may, for the purpose of investigating the matter reported to him and such other matters relating to the affairs of the company as appear to him to require investigation, exercise any of the powers which are exercisable by inspectors appointed under section 431 or 432 of the Companies Act 1985 to investigate a company's affairs.

(4) For the purpose of such an investigation any obligation imposed on a person by any provision of the Companies Acts to produce documents or give information to, or otherwise to assist, inspectors so appointed is to be regarded as an obligation similarly to assist the Secretary of State in his investigation.

(5) An answer given by a person to a question put to him in exercise of the powers conferred by subsection (3) may be used in evidence against him.

(8) Where a prosecuting authority institutes criminal proceedings following any report under subsection (2), the nominee or supervisor, and every officer and agent of the company past and present (other than the defendant or defender), shall give the authority all assistance in connection with the prosecution which he is reasonably able to give.

For this purpose—

"agent" includes any banker or solicitor of the company and any person employed by the company as auditor, whether that person is or is not an officer of the company,

"prosecuting authority" means the Director of Public Prosecutions, the Lord Advocate or the Secretary of State.

(9) The court may, on the application of the prosecuting authority, direct any person referred to in subsection (8) to comply with that subsection if he has failed to do so.

7B ARRANGEMENTS COMING TO AN END PREMATURELY

For the purposes of this Part, a voluntary arrangement the approval of which has taken effect under section 4A or paragraph 36 of Schedule A1 comes to an end prematurely if, when it ceases to have effect, it has not been fully implemented in respect of all persons bound by the arrangement by virtue of section 5(2)(b)(i) or, as the case may be, paragraph 37(2)(b)(i) of Schedule A1.

Part II ADMINISTRATION

8 ADMINISTRATION

Schedule B1 to this Act (which makes provision about the administration of companies) shall have effect.

Part III RECEIVERSHIP

Chapter I RECEIVERS AND MANAGERS (ENGLAND AND WALES)

Preliminary and general provisions

28 EXTENT OF THIS CHAPTER

(1) In this Chapter "company" means a company registered under the Companies Act 2006 in England and Wales or Scotland.

(2) This Chapter does not apply to receivers appointed under Chapter 2 of this Part (Scotland).

29 DEFINITIONS

(1) It is hereby declared that, except where the context otherwise requires—

(a) any reference in this Act to a receiver or manager of the property of a company, or to a receiver of it, includes a receiver or manager, or (as the case may be) a receiver of part only of that property and a receiver only of the income arising from the property or from part of it; and
(b) any reference in this Act to the appointment of a receiver or manager under powers contained in an instrument includes an appointment made under powers which, by virtue of any enactment, are implied in and have effect as if contained in an instrument.

(2) In this Chapter "administrative receiver" means—
(a) a receiver or manager of the whole (or substantially the whole) of a company's property appointed by or on behalf of the holders of any debentures of the company secured by a charge which, as created, was a floating charge, or by such a charge and one or more other securities; or
(b) a person who would be such a receiver or manager but for the appointment of some other person as the receiver of part of the company's property.

30 DISQUALIFICATION OF BODY CORPORATE FROM ACTING AS RECEIVER

A body corporate is not qualified for appointment as receiver of the property of a company, and any body corporate which acts as such a receiver is liable to a fine.

31 DISQUALIFICATION OF BANKRUPT OR PERSON IN RESPECT OF WHOM A DEBT RELIEF ORDER IS MADE

(1) A person commits an offence if he acts as receiver or manager of the property of a company on behalf of debenture holders while—
(a) he is an undischarged bankrupt,
(aa) a moratorium period under a debt relief order applies in relation to him, or
(b) a bankruptcy restrictions order or a debt relief restrictions order is in force in respect of him.

(2) A person guilty of an offence under subsection (1) shall be liable to imprisonment, a fine or both.

(3) This section does not apply to a receiver or manager acting under an appointment made by the court.

32 POWER FOR COURT TO APPOINT OFFICIAL RECEIVER

Where application is made to the court to appoint a receiver on behalf of the debenture holders or other creditors of a company which is being wound up by the court, the official receiver may be appointed.

Receivers and managers appointed out of court

37 LIABILITY FOR CONTRACTS, ETC.

(1) A receiver or manager appointed under powers contained in an instrument (other than an administrative receiver) is, to the same extent as if he had been appointed by order of the court—

(a) personally liable on any contract entered into by him in the performance of his functions (except in so far as the contract otherwise provides) and on any contract of employment adopted by him in the performance of those functions, and
(b) entitled in respect of that liability to indemnity out of the assets.

(2) For the purposes of subsection (1)(a), the receiver or manager is not to be taken to have adopted a contract of employment by reason of anything done or omitted to be done with 14 days after his appointment.

(3) Subsection (1) does not limit any right to indemnity which the receiver or manager would have apart from it, nor limit his liability on contracts entered into without authority, nor confer any right to indemnity in respect of that liability.

(4) Where at any time the receiver or manager so appointed vacates office—
(a) his remuneration and any expenses properly incurred by him, and
(b) any indemnity to which he is entitled out of the assets of the company,
shall be charged on and paid out of any property of the company which is in his custody or under his control at that time in priority to any charge or other security held by the person by or on whose behalf he was appointed.

Provisions applicable to every receivership

39 NOTIFICATION THAT RECEIVER OR MANAGER APPOINTED

(1) Where a receiver or manager of the property of a company has been appointed—
(a) every invoice, order for goods or services, business letter or order form (whether in hard copy, electronic or any other form) issued by or on behalf of the company or the receiver or manager or the liquidator of the company; and
(b) all the company's websites,
must contain a statement that a receiver or manager has been appointed.

(2) If default is made in complying with this section, the company and any of the following persons, who knowingly and wilfully authorises or permits the default, namely, any officer of the company, any liquidator of the company and any receiver or manager, is liable to a fine.

40 PAYMENT OF DEBTS OUT OF ASSETS SUBJECT TO FLOATING CHARGE

(1) The following applies in the case of a company, where a receiver is appointed on behalf of the holders of any debentures of the company secured by a charge which, as created, was a floating charge.

(2) If the company is not at the time in course of being wound up, its preferential debts (within the meaning given to that expression by section 386 in Part XII) shall be paid out of the assets coming to the hands of the receiver in priority to any claims for principal or interest in respect of the debentures.

(3) Payments made under this section shall be recouped, as far as may be, out of the assets of the company available for payment of general creditors.

Administrative receivers: general

42 GENERAL POWERS

(1) The powers conferred on the administrative receiver of a company by the debentures by virtue of which he was appointed are deemed to include (except in so far as they are

inconsistent with any of the provisions of those debentures) the powers specified in Schedule 1 to this Act.

(2) In the application of Schedule 1 to the administrative receiver of a company—
(a) the words "he" and "him" refer to the administrative receiver, and
(b) references to the property of the company are to the property of which he is or, but for the appointment of some other person as the receiver of part of the company's property, would be the receiver or manager.

(3) A person dealing with the administrative receiver in good faith and for value is not concerned to inquire whether the receiver is acting within his powers.

43 POWER TO DISPOSE OF CHARGED PROPERTY, ETC.

(1) Where, on an application by the administrative receiver, the court is satisfied that the disposal (with or without other assets) of any relevant property which is subject to a security would be likely to promote a more advantageous realisation of the company's assets than would otherwise be effected, the court may by order authorise the administrative receiver to dispose of the property as if it were not subject to the security.

(2) Subsection (1) does not apply in the case of any security held by the person by or on whose behalf the administrative receiver was appointed, or of any security to which a security so held has priority.

(3) It shall be a condition of an order under this section that—
(a) the net proceeds of the disposal, and
(b) where those proceeds are less than such amount as may be determined by the court to be the net amount which would be realised on a sale of the property in the open market by a willing vendor, such sums as may be required to make good the deficiency,

shall be applied towards discharging the sums secured by the security.

(4) Where a condition imposed in pursuance of subsection (3) relates to two or more securities, that condition shall require the net proceeds of the disposal and, where paragraph (b) of that subsection applies, the sums mentioned in that paragraph to be applied towards discharging the sums secured by those securities in the order of their priorities.

(7) In this section "relevant property", in relation to the administrative receiver, means the property of which he is or, but for the appointment of some other person as the receiver of part of the company's property, would be the receiver or manager.

44 AGENCY AND LIABILITY FOR CONTRACTS

(1) The administrative receiver of a company—
(a) is deemed to be the company's agent, unless and until the company goes into liquidation;
(b) is personally liable on any contract entered into by him in the carrying out of his functions (except in so far as the contract otherwise provides) and, to the extent of any qualifying liability, on any contract of employment adopted by him in the carrying out of those functions; and
(c) is entitled in respect of that liability to an indemnity out of the assets of the company.

(2) For the purposes of subsection (1)(b) the administrative receiver is not to be taken to have adopted a contract of employment by reason of anything done or omitted to be done within 14 days after his appointment.

(2A) For the purposes of subsection (1)(b), a liability under a contract of employment is a qualifying liability if—
(a) it is a liability to pay a sum by way of wages or salary or contribution to an occupational pension scheme,
(b) it is incurred while the administrative receiver is in office, and
(c) it is in respect of services rendered wholly or partly after the adoption of the contract.

(2B) Where a sum payable in respect of a liability which is a qualifying liability for the purposes of subsection (1)(b) is payable in respect of services rendered partly before and partly after the adoption of the contract, liability under subsection (1)(b) shall only extend to so much of the sum as is payable in respect of services rendered after the adoption of the contract.

(3) This section does not limit any right to indemnity which the administrative receiver would have apart from it, nor limit his liability on contracts entered into or adopted without authority, nor confer any right to indemnity in respect of that liability.

45 VACATION OF OFFICE

(1) An administrative receiver of a company may at any time be removed from office by order of the court (but not otherwise) and may resign his office by giving notice of his resignation in the prescribed manner to such persons as may be prescribed.

(2) An administrative receiver shall vacate office if he ceases to be qualified to act as an insolvency practitioner in relation to the company.

(3) Where at any time an administrative receiver vacates office—
(a) his remuneration and any expenses properly incurred by him, and
(b) any indemnity to which he is entitled out of the assets of the company,
shall be charged on and paid out of any property of the company which is in his custody or under his control at that time in priority to any security held by the person by or on whose behalf he was appointed.

Administrative receivers: ascertainment and investigation of company's affairs

46 INFORMATION TO BE GIVEN BY ADMINISTRATIVE RECEIVER

(1) Where an administrative receiver is appointed, he shall—
(a) forthwith send to the company and publish in the prescribed manner a notice of his appointment, and
(b) within 28 days after his appointment, unless the court otherwise directs, send such a notice to all the creditors of the company (so far as he is aware of their addresses).

(4) If the administrative receiver without reasonable excuse fails to comply with this section, he is liable to a fine and, for continued contravention, to a daily default fine.

47 STATEMENT OF AFFAIRS TO BE SUBMITTED

(1) Where an administrative receiver is appointed, he shall forthwith require some or all of the persons mentioned below to make out and submit to him a statement in the prescribed form as to the affairs of the company.

(2) A statement submitted under this section shall be verified by a statement of truth by the persons required to submit it and shall show—
(a) particulars of the company's assets, debts and liabilities;
(b) the names and addresses of its creditors;
(c) the securities held by them respectively;
(d) the dates when the securities were respectively given; and
(e) such further or other information as may be prescribed.

(3) The persons referred to in subsection (1) are—
(a) those who are or have been officers of the company;
(b) those who have taken part in the company's formation at any time within one year before the date of the appointment of the administrative receiver;
(c) those who are in the company's employment, or have been in its employment within that year, and are in the administrative receiver's opinion capable of giving the information required;
(d) those who are or have been within that year officers of or in the employment of a company which is, or within that year was, an officer of the company.
In this subsection "employment" includes employment under a contract for services.

(4) Where any persons are required under this section to submit a statement of affairs to the administrative receiver, they shall do so (subject to the next subsection) before the end of the period of 21 days beginning with the day after that on which the prescribed notice of the requirement is given to them by the administrative receiver.

(5) The administrative receiver, if he thinks fit, may—
(a) at any time release a person from an obligation imposed on him under subsection (1) or (2), or
(b) either when giving notice under subsection (4) or subsequently, extend the period so mentioned;
and where the administrative receiver has refused to exercise a power conferred by this subsection, the court, if it thinks fit, may exercise it.

(6) If a person without reasonable excuse fails to comply with any obligation imposed under this section, he is liable to a fine and, for continued contravention, to a daily default fine.

48 REPORT BY ADMINISTRATIVE RECEIVER

(1) Where an administrative receiver is appointed, he shall, within 3 months (or such longer period as the court may allow) after his appointment, send to the registrar of companies, to any trustees for secured creditors of the company and (so far as he is aware of their addresses) to all such creditors a report as to the following matters, namely—
(a) the events leading up to his appointment, so far as he is aware of them;
(b) the disposal or proposed disposal by him of any property of the company and the carrying on or proposed carrying on by him of any business of the company;
(c) the amounts of principal and interest payable to the debenture holders by whom or on whose behalf he was appointed and the amounts payable to preferential creditors; and
(d) the amount (if any) likely to be available for the payment of other creditors.

(2) The administrative receiver shall also, within 3 months (or such longer period as the court may allow) after his appointment, either—
(a) send a copy of the report (so far as he is aware of their addresses) to all unsecured creditors of the company; or

(b) publish in the prescribed manner a notice stating an address to which unsecured creditors of the company should write for copies of the report to be sent to them free of charge,

and (in either case), unless the court otherwise directs, lay a copy of the report before a meeting of the company's unsecured creditors summoned for the purpose on not less than 14 days' notice.

(4) Where the company has gone or goes into liquidation, the administrative receiver—
(a) shall, within 7 days after his compliance with subsection (1) or, if later, the nomination or appointment of the liquidator, send a copy of the report to the liquidator, and
(b) where he does so within the time limited for compliance with subsection (2), is not required to comply with that subsection.

(5) A report under this section shall include a summary of the statement of affairs made out and submitted to the administrative receiver under section 47 and of his comments (if any) upon it.

(6) Nothing in this section is to be taken as requiring any such report to include any information the disclosure of which would seriously prejudice the carrying out by the administrative receiver of his functions.

(8) If the administrative receiver without reasonable excuse fails to comply with this section, he is liable to a fine and, for continued contravention, to a daily default fine.

49 COMMITTEE OF CREDITORS

(1) Where a meeting of creditors is summoned under section 48, the meeting may, if it thinks fit, establish a committee ("the creditors' committee") to exercise the functions conferred on it by or under this Act.

(2) If such a committee is established, the committee may, on giving not less than 7 days' notice, require the administrative receiver to attend before it at any reasonable time and furnish it with such information relating to the carrying out by him of his functions as it may reasonably require.

Chapter II RECEIVERS (SCOTLAND)

50 EXTENT OF THIS CHAPTER

This Chapter extends to Scotland only.

51 POWER TO APPOINT RECEIVER

(1) It is competent under the law of Scotland for the holder of a floating charge over all or any part of the property (including uncalled capital), which may from time to time be comprised in the property and undertaking of an incorporated company (whether a company registered under the Companies Act 2006 or not) —
(a) which the Court of Session has jurisdiction to wind up; or
(b) where paragraph (a) does not apply, in respect of which a court of a member state other than the United Kingdom has under the EU Regulation jurisdiction to open insolvency proceedings,

to appoint a receiver of such part of the property of the company as is subject to the charge.

(2) It is competent under the law of Scotland for the court, on the application of the holder of such a floating charge, to appoint a receiver of such part of the property of the company as is subject to the charge.

(2ZA) But, in relation to a company mentioned in subsection (1)(b), a receiver may be appointed under subsection (1) or (2) only in respect of property situated in Scotland.

(2A) Subsections (1) and (2) are subject to section 72A.

(3) The following are disqualified from being appointed as receiver—
(a) a body corporate;
(b) an undischarged bankrupt;
(ba) a person subject to a bankruptcy restrictions order; and
(c) a firm according to the law of Scotland.

(4) A body corporate or a firm according to the law of Scotland which acts as a receiver is liable to a fine.

(5) An undischarged bankrupt or a person subject to a bankruptcy restrictions order who so acts is liable to imprisonment or a fine, or both.

(6) In this section, "receiver" includes joint receivers; and "bankruptcy restrictions order" means—
(a) a bankruptcy restrictions order made under section 56A of the Bankruptcy (Scotland) Act 1985 (c. 66);
(b) a bankruptcy restrictions undertaking entered into under section 56G of that Act;
(c) a bankruptcy restrictions order made under paragraph 1 of Schedule 4A to this Act; or
(d) a bankruptcy restrictions undertaking entered into under paragraph 7 of that Schedule.

"the EU Regulation" is the Regulation of the Council of the European Union published as Council Regulation (EC) No. 1346/2000 on insolvency proceedings;

"court" is to be construed in accordance with Article 2(d) of the EU Regulation;

"insolvency proceedings" is to be construed in accordance with Article 2(a) of the EU Regulation.

52 CIRCUMSTANCES JUSTIFYING APPOINTMENT

(1) A receiver may be appointed under section 51(1) by the holder of the floating charge on the occurrence of any event which, by the provisions of the instrument creating the charge, entitles the holder of the charge to make that appointment and, in so far as not otherwise provided for by the instrument, on the occurrence of any of the following events, namely—
(a) the expiry of a period of 21 days after the making of a demand for payment of the whole or any part of the principal sum secured by the charge, without payment having been made;
(b) the expiry of a period of 2 months during the whole of which interest due and payable under the charge has been in arrears;
(c) the making of an order or the passing of a resolution to wind up the company;
(d) the appointment of a receiver by virtue of any other floating charge created by the company.

(2) A receiver may be appointed by the court under section 51(2) on the occurrence of any event which, by the provisions of the instrument creating the floating charge, entitles the

holder of the charge to make that appointment and, in so far as not otherwise provided for by the instrument, on the occurrence of any of the following events, namely—

(a) where the court, on the application of the holder of the charge, pronounces itself satisfied that the position of the holder of the charge is likely to be prejudiced if no such appointment is made;

(b) any of the events referred to in paragraphs (a) to (c) of subsection (1).

53 MODE OF APPOINTMENT BY HOLDER OF CHARGE

(1) The appointment of a receiver by the holder of the floating charge under section 51(1) shall be by means of an instrument subscribed in accordance with the Requirements of Writing (Scotland) Act 1995] ("the instrument of appointment")...

(7) On the appointment of a receiver under this section, the floating charge by virtue of which he was appointed attaches to the property then subject to the charge; and such attachment has effect as if the charge was a fixed security over the property to which it has attached.

54 APPOINTMENT BY COURT

(1) Application for the appointment of a receiver by the court under section 51(2) shall be by petition to the court, which shall be served on the company.

(2) On such an application, the court shall, if it thinks fit, issue an interlocutor making the appointment of the receiver.

(6) On the appointment of a receiver under this section, the floating charge by virtue of which he was appointed attaches to the property then subject to the charge; and such attachment has effect as if the charge were a fixed security over the property to which it has attached.

55 POWERS OF RECEIVER

(1) Subject to the next subsection, a receiver has in relation to such part of the property of the company as is attached by the floating charge by virtue of which he was appointed, the powers, if any, given to him by the instrument creating that charge.

(2) In addition, the receiver has under this Chapter the powers as respects that property (in so far as these are not inconsistent with any provision contained in that instrument) which are specified in Schedule 2 to this Act.

(3) Subsections (1) and (2) apply—

(a) subject to the rights of any person who has effectually executed diligence on all or any part of the property of the company prior to the appointment of the receiver, and

(b) subject to the rights of any person who holds over all or any part of the property of the company a fixed security or floating charge having priority, over, or ranking pari passu with, the floating charge by virtue of which the receiver was appointed.

(4) A person dealing with a receiver in good faith and for value is not concerned to enquire whether the receiver is acting within his powers.

56 PRECEDENCE AMONG RECEIVERS

(1) Where there are two or more floating charges subsisting over all or any part of the property of the company, a receiver may be appointed under this Chapter by virtue of each such charge; but a receiver appointed by, or on the application of, the holder of a floating charge having priority of ranking over any other floating charge by virtue of

which a receiver has been appointed has the powers given to a receiver by section 55 and Schedule 2 to the exclusion of any other receiver.

(2) Where two or more floating charges rank with one another equally, and two or more receivers have been appointed by virtue of such charges, the receivers so appointed are deemed to have been appointed as joint receivers.

(3) Receivers appointed, or deemed to have been appointed, as joint receivers shall act jointly unless the instrument of appointment or respective instruments of appointment otherwise provide.

(4) Subject to subsection (5) below, the powers of a receiver appointed by, or on the application of, the holder of a floating charge are suspended by, and as from the date of, the appointment of a receiver by, or on the application of, the holder of a floating charge having priority of ranking over that charge to such extent as may be necessary to enable the receiver second mentioned to exercise his powers under section 55 and Schedule 2; and any powers so suspended take effect again when the floating charge having priority of ranking ceases to attach to the property then subject to the charge...

(5) The suspension of the powers of a receiver under subsection (4) does not have the effect of requiring him to release any part of the property (including any letters or documents) of the company from his control until he receives from the receiver superseding him a valid indemnity (subject to the limit of the value of such part of the property of the company as is subject to the charge by virtue of which he was appointed) in respect of any expenses, charges and liabilities he may have incurred in the performance of his functions as receiver.

(6) The suspension of the powers of a receiver under subsection (4) does not cause the floating charge by virtue of which he was appointed to cease to attach to the property to which it attached by virtue of section 53(7) or 54(6).

(7) Nothing in this section prevents the same receiver being appointed by virtue of two or more floating charges.

57 AGENCY AND LIABILITY OF RECEIVER FOR CONTRACTS

(1) A receiver is deemed to be the agent of the company in relation to such property of the company as is attached by the floating charge by virtue of which he was appointed.

(1A) Without prejudice to subsection (1), a receiver is deemed to be the agent of the company in relation to any contract of employment adopted by him in the carrying out of his functions.

(2) A receiver (including a receiver whose powers are subsequently suspended under section 56) is personally liable on any contract entered into by him in the performance of his functions, except in so far as the contract otherwise provides, and, to the extent of any qualifying liability, on any contract of employment adopted by him in the carrying out of those functions.

(2A) For the purposes of subsection (2), a liability under a contract of employment is a qualifying liability if—

(a) it is a liability to pay a sum by way of wages or salary or contribution to an occupational pension scheme,
(b) it is incurred while the receiver is in office, and
(c) it is in respect of services rendered wholly or partly after the adoption of the contract.

(2B) Where a sum payable in respect of a liability which is a qualifying liability for the purposes of subsection (2) is payable in respect of services rendered partly before and partly after the adoption of the contract, liability under that subsection shall only extend to so much of the sum as is payable in respect of services rendered after the adoption of the contract.

(3) A receiver who is personally liable by virtue of subsection (2) is entitled to be indemnified out of the property in respect of which he was appointed.

(4) Any contract entered into by or on behalf of the company prior to the appointment of a receiver continues in force (subject to its terms) notwithstanding that appointment, but the receiver does not by virtue only of his appointment incur any personal liability on any such contract.

(5) For the purposes of subsection (2), a receiver is not to be taken to have adopted a contract of employment by reason of anything done or omitted to be done within 14 days after his appointment.

(6) This section does not limit any right to indemnity which the receiver would have apart from it, nor limit his liability on contracts entered into or adopted without authority, nor confer any right to indemnity in respect of that liability.

(7) Any contract entered into by a receiver in the performance of his functions continues in force (subject to its terms) although the powers of the receiver are subsequently suspended under section 56.

59 PRIORITY OF DEBTS

(1) Where a receiver is appointed and the company is not at the time of the appointment in course of being wound up, the debts which fall under subsection (2) of this section shall be paid out of any assets coming to the hands of the receiver in priority to any claim for principal or interest by the holder of the floating charge by virtue of which the receiver was appointed.

(2) Debts falling under this subsection are preferential debts (within the meaning given by section 386 in Part XII) which, by the end of a period of 6 months after advertisement by the receiver for claims in the Edinburgh Gazette and in a newspaper circulating in the district where the company carries on business either—
   i. have been intimated to him, or
   ii. have become known to him.

(3) Any payments made under this section shall be recouped as far as may be out of the assets of the company available for payment of ordinary creditors.

60 DISTRIBUTION OF MONEYS

(1) Subject to the next section, and to the rights of any of the following categories of persons (which rights shall, except to the extent otherwise provided in any instrument, have the following order of priority), namely—
   (a) the holder of any fixed security which is over property subject to the floating charge and which ranks prior to, or pari passu with, the floating charge;
   (b) all persons who have effectually executed diligence on any part of the property of the company which is subject to the charge by virtue of which the receiver was appointed;
   (c) creditors in respect of all liabilities, charges and expenses incurred by or on behalf of the receiver;

(d) the receiver in respect of his liabilities, expenses and remuneration, and any indemnity to which he is entitled out of the property of the company; and
(e) the preferential creditors entitled to payment under section 59,

the receiver shall pay moneys received by him to the holder of the floating charge by virtue of which the receiver was appointed in or towards satisfaction of the debt secured by the floating charge.

(2) Any balance of moneys remaining after the provisions of subsection (1) and section 61 below have been satisfied shall be paid in accordance with their respective rights and interests to the following persons, as the case may require—
(a) any other receiver;
(b) the holder of a fixed security which is over property subject to the floating charge;
(c) the company or its liquidator, as the case may be.

61 DISPOSAL OF INTEREST IN PROPERTY

(1) Where the receiver sells or disposes, or is desirous of selling or disposing, of any property or interest in property of the company which is subject to the floating charge by virtue of which the receiver was appointed and which is—
(a) subject to any security or interest of, or burden or encumbrance in favour of, a creditor the ranking of which is prior to, or pari passu with, or postponed to the floating charge, or
(b) property or an interest in property affected or attached by effectual diligence executed by any person,

and the receiver is unable to obtain the consent of such creditor or, as the case may be, such person to such a sale or disposal, the receiver may apply to the court for authority to sell or dispose of the property or interest in property free of such security, interest, burden, encumbrance or diligence.

(1A) For the purposes of subsection (1) above, an inhibition which takes effect after the creation of the floating charge by virtue of which the receiver was appointed is not an effectual diligence.

(1B) For the purposes of subsection (1) above, an arrestment is an effectual diligence only where it is executed before the floating charge, by virtue of which the receiver was appointed, attaches to the property comprised in the company's property and undertaking.

(2) Subject to the next subsection, on such an application the court may, if it thinks fit, authorise the sale or disposal of the property or interest in question free of such security, interest, burden, encumbrance or diligence, and such authorisation may be on such terms or conditions as the court thinks fit.

(3) In the case of an application where a fixed security over the property or interest in question which ranks prior to the floating charge has not been met or provided for in full, the court shall not authorise the sale or disposal of the property or interest in question unless it is satisfied that the sale or disposal would be likely to provide a more advantageous realisation of the company's assets than would otherwise be effected.

(4) It shall be a condition of an authorisation to which subsection (3) applies that—
(a) the net proceeds of the disposal, and
(b) where those proceeds are less than such amount as may be determined by the court to be the net amount which would be realised on a sale of the property or interest in the open market by a willing seller, such sums as may be required to make good the deficiency,

shall be applied towards discharging the sums secured by the fixed security.

(5) Where a condition imposed in pursuance of subsection (4) relates to two or more such fixed securities, that condition shall require the net proceeds of the disposal and, where paragraph (b) of that subsection applies, the sums mentioned in that paragraph to be applied towards discharging the sums secured by those fixed securities in the order of their priorities.

(9) Nothing in this section prejudices the right of any creditor of the company to rank for his debt in the winding up of the company.

62 CESSATION OF APPOINTMENT OF RECEIVER

(1) A receiver may be removed from office by the court under subsection (3) below and may resign his office by giving notice of his resignation in the prescribed manner to such persons as may be prescribed.

(2) A receiver shall vacate office if he ceases to be qualified to act as an insolvency practitioner in relation to the company.

(3) Subject to the next subsection, a receiver may, on application to the court by the holder of the floating charge by virtue of which he was appointed, be removed by the court on cause shown.

(4) Where at any time a receiver vacates office—
  (a) his remuneration and any expenses properly incurred by him, and
  (b) any indemnity to which he is entitled out of the property of the company,
shall be paid out of the property of the company which is subject to the floating charge and shall have priority as provided for in section 60(1).

64 NOTIFICATION THAT RECEIVER APPOINTED

(1) Where a receiver has been appointed—
  (a) every invoice, order for goods or services, business letter or order form (whether in hard copy, electronic or any other form) issued by or on behalf of the company or the receiver or the liquidator of the company; and
  (b) all the company's websites,
must contain a statement that a receiver has been appointed.

(2) If default is made in complying with the requirements of this section, the company and any of the following persons who knowingly and wilfully authorises or permits the default, namely any officer of the company, any liquidator of the company and any receiver, is liable to a fine.

65 INFORMATION TO BE GIVEN BY RECEIVER

(1) Where a receiver is appointed, he shall—
  (a) forthwith send to the company and publish notice of his appointment, and
  (b) within 28 days after his appointment, unless the court otherwise directs, send such notice to all the creditors of the company (so far as he is aware of their addresses).

(4) If a person without reasonable excuse fails to comply with this section, he is liable to a fine and, for continued contravention, to a daily default fine.

66 COMPANY'S STATEMENT OF AFFAIRS

(1) Where a receiver of a company is appointed, the receiver shall forthwith require some or all of the persons mentioned in subsection (3) below to make out and submit to him a statement in the prescribed form as to the affairs of the company.

(2) A statement submitted under this section shall be verified by affidavit by the persons required to submit it and shall show—
(a) particulars of the company's assets, debts and liabilities;
(b) the names and addresses of its creditors;
(c) the securities held by them respectively;
(d) the dates when the securities were respectively given; and
(e) such further or other information as may be prescribed.

(3) The persons referred to in subsection (1) are—
(a) those who are or have been officers of the company;
(b) those who have taken part in the company's formation at any time within one year before the date of the appointment of the receiver;
(c) those who are in the company's employment or have been in its employment within that year, and are in the receiver's opinion capable of giving the information required;
(d) those who are or have been within that year officers of or in the employment of a company which is, or within that year was, an officer of the company.
In this subsection "employment" includes employment under a contract for services.

(4) Where any persons are required under this section to submit a statement of affairs to the receiver they shall do so (subject to the next subsection) before the end of the period of 21 days beginning with the day after that on which the prescribed notice of the requirement is given to them by the receiver.

(5) The receiver, if he thinks fit, may—
(a) at any time release a person from an obligation imposed on him under subsection (1) or (2), or
(b) either when giving the notice mentioned in subsection (4) or subsequently extend the period so mentioned,
and where the receiver has refused to exercise a power conferred by this subsection, the court, if it thinks fit, may exercise it.

(6) If a person without reasonable excuse fails to comply with any obligation imposed under this section, he is liable to a fine and, for continued contravention to a daily default fine.

67 REPORT BY RECEIVER

(1) Where a receiver is appointed under section 51, he shall within 3 months (or such longer period as the court may allow) after his appointment, send to the registrar of companies, to the holder of the floating charge by virtue of which he was appointed and to any trustees for secured creditors of the company and (so far as he is aware of their addresses) to all such creditors a report as to the following matters, namely—
(a) the events leading up to his appointment, so far as he is aware of them;
(b) the disposal or proposed disposal by him of any property of the company and the carrying on or proposed carrying on by him of any business of the company;
(c) the amounts of principal and interest payable to the holder of the floating charge by virtue of which he was appointed and the amounts payable to preferential creditors; and
(d) the amount (if any) likely to be available for the payment of other creditors.

(2) The receiver shall also, within 3 months (or such longer period as the court may allow) after his appointment, either—
(a) send a copy of the report (so far as he is aware of their addresses) to all unsecured creditors of the company, or
(b) publish in the prescribed manner a notice stating an address to which unsecured creditors of the company should write for copies of the report to be sent to them free of charge,

and (in either case), unless the court otherwise directs, lay a copy of the report before a meeting of the company's unsecured creditors summoned for the purpose on not less than 14 days' notice.

(4) Where the company has gone or goes into liquidation, the receiver—
(a) shall, within 7 days after his compliance with subsection (1) or, if later, the nomination or appointment of the liquidator, send a copy of the report to the liquidator, and
(b) where he does so within the time limited for compliance with subsection (2), is not required to comply with that subsection.

(5) A report under this section shall include a summary of the statement of affairs made out and submitted under section 66 and of his comments (if any) on it.

(6) Nothing in this section shall be taken as requiring any such report to include any information the disclosure of which would seriously prejudice the carrying out by the receiver of his functions.

(8) If a person without reasonable excuse fails to comply with this section, he is liable to a fine and, for continued contravention, to a daily default fine.

(9) In this section "secured creditor", in relation to a company, means a creditor of the company who holds in respect of his debt a security over property of the company, and "unsecured creditor" shall be construed accordingly.

68 COMMITTEE OF CREDITORS

(1) Where a meeting of creditors is summoned under section 67, the meeting may, if it thinks fit, establish a committee ("the creditors' committee") to exercise the functions conferred on it by or under this Act.

(2) If such a committee is established, the committee may on giving not less than 7 days' notice require the receiver to attend before it at any reasonable time and furnish it with such information relating to the carrying out by him of his functions as it may reasonably require.

70 INTERPRETATION FOR CHAPTER II

(1) In this Chapter, unless the contrary intention appears, the following expressions have the following meanings respectively assigned to them—

"company" means an incorporated company (whether or not a company registered under the Companies Act 2006) which the Court of Session has jurisdiction to wind up;

"fixed security", in relation to any property of a company, means any security, other than a floating charge or a charge having the nature of a floating charge, which on the winding up of the company in Scotland would be treated as an effective security over that property, and (without prejudice to that generality) includes a security over that property, being a heritable security within the meaning of the M1Conveyancing and Feudal Reform (Scotland) Act 1970;

"instrument of appointment" has the meaning given by section 53(1);

"prescribed" means prescribed by regulations made under this Chapter by the Secretary of State;

"receiver" means a receiver of such part of the property of the company as is subject to the floating charge by virtue of which he has been appointed under section 51;

"register of charges" means the register kept by the registrar of companies for the purposes of Chapter 2 of Part 25 of the Companies Act 2006;

"secured debenture" means a bond, debenture, debenture stock or other security which, either itself or by reference to any other instrument, creates a floating charge over all or any part of the property of the company, but does not include a security which creates no charge other than a fixed security; and

"series of secured debentures" means two or more secured debentures created as a series by the company in such a manner that the holders thereof are entitled pari passu to the benefit of the floating charge.

Chapter III RECEIVERS' POWERS IN GREAT BRITAIN AS A WHOLE

72 CROSS-BORDER OPERATION OF RECEIVERSHIP PROVISIONS

(1) A receiver appointed under the law of either part of Great Britain in respect of the whole or any part of any property or undertaking of a company and in consequence of the company having created a charge which, as created, was a floating charge may exercise his powers in the other part of Great Britain so far as their exercise is not inconsistent with the law applicable there.

(2) In subsection (1) "receiver" includes a manager and a person who is appointed both receiver and manager.

Chapter IV PROHIBITION OF APPOINTMENT OF ADMINISTRATIVE RECEIVER

72A FLOATING CHARGE HOLDER NOT TO APPOINT ADMINISTRATIVE RECEIVER

(1) The holder of a qualifying floating charge in respect of a company's property may not appoint an administrative receiver of the company.

(2) In Scotland, the holder of a qualifying floating charge in respect of a company's property may not appoint or apply to the court for the appointment of a receiver who on appointment would be an administrative receiver of property of the company.

(3) In subsections (1) and (2)—

"holder of a qualifying floating charge in respect of a company's property" has the same meaning as in paragraph 14 of Schedule B1 to this Act, and

"administrative receiver" has the meaning given by section 251.

(4) This section applies—
- (a) to a floating charge created on or after a date appointed by the Secretary of State by order made by statutory instrument, and
- (b) in spite of any provision of an agreement or instrument which purports to empower a person to appoint an administrative receiver (by whatever name).

Part IV WINDING UP OF COMPANIES REGISTERED UNDER THE COMPANIES ACTS

Chapter I PRELIMINARY

Introductory

73 SCHEME OF THIS PART

(1) This Part applies to the winding up of a company registered under the Companies Act 2006 in England and Wales or Scotland.

(2) The winding up may be either—
 (a) voluntary (see Chapters 2 to 5), or
 (b) by the court (see Chapter 6).

(3) This Chapter and Chapters 7 to 10 relate to winding up generally, except where otherwise stated.

Contributories

74 LIABILITY AS CONTRIBUTORIES OF PRESENT AND PAST MEMBERS

(1) When a company is wound up, every present and past member is liable to contribute to its assets to any amount sufficient for payment of its debts and liabilities, and the expenses of the winding up, and for the adjustment of the rights of the contributories among themselves.

(2) This is subject as follows—
 (a) a past member is not liable to contribute if he has ceased to be a member for one year or more before the commencement of the winding up;
 (b) a past member is not liable to contribute in respect of any debt or liability of the company contracted after he ceased to be a member;
 (c) a past member is not liable to contribute, unless it appears to the court that the existing members are unable to satisfy the contributions required to be made by them;
 (d) in the case of a company limited by shares, no contribution is required from any member exceeding the amount (if any) unpaid on the shares in respect of which he is liable as a present or past member;
 (e) nothing in the Companies Acts or this Act invalidates any provision contained in a policy of insurance or other contract whereby the liability of individual members on the policy or contract is restricted, or whereby the funds of the company are alone made liable in respect of the policy or contract;
 (f) a sum due to any member of the company (in his character of a member) by way of dividends, profits or otherwise is not deemed to be a debt of the company, payable to that member in a case of competition between himself and any other creditor not a member of the company, but any such sum may be taken into account for the purpose of the final adjustment of the rights of the contributories among themselves.

(3) In the case of a company limited by guarantee, no contribution is required from any member exceeding the amount undertaken to be contributed by him to the company's assets in the event of its being wound up; but if it is a company with a share capital, every member of it is liable (in addition to the amount so undertaken to be contributed to the assets), to contribute to the extent of any sums unpaid on shares held by him.

79 MEANING OF "CONTRIBUTORY"

(1) In this Act the expression "contributory" means every person liable to contribute to the assets of a company in the event of its being wound up, and for the purposes of all proceedings for determining, and all proceedings prior to the final determination of, the persons who are to be deemed contributories, includes any person alleged to be a contributory.

(2) The reference in subsection (1) to persons liable to contribute to the assets does not include a person so liable by virtue of a declaration by the court under section 213 (imputed responsibility for company's fraudulent trading) or section 214 (wrongful trading) in Chapter X of this Part.

80 NATURE OF CONTRIBUTORY'S LIABILITY

The liability of a contributory creates a debt (in England and Wales in the nature of an ordinary contract debt) accruing due from him at the time when his liability commenced, but payable at the times when calls are made for enforcing the liability.

81 CONTRIBUTORIES IN CASE OF DEATH OF A MEMBER

(1) If a contributory dies either before or after he has been placed on the list of contributories, his personal representatives, and the heirs and legatees of heritage of his heritable estate in Scotland, are liable in a due course of administration to contribute to the assets of the company in discharge of his liability and are contributories accordingly.

82 EFFECT OF CONTRIBUTORY'S BANKRUPTCY

(1) The following applies if a contributory becomes bankrupt, either before or after he has been placed on the list of contributories.

(2) His trustee in bankruptcy represents him for all purposes of the winding up, and is a contributory accordingly.

(3) The trustee may be called on to admit to proof against the bankrupt's estate, or otherwise allow to be paid out of the bankrupt's assets in due course of law, any money due from the bankrupt in respect of his liability to contribute to the company's assets.

(4) There may be proved against the bankrupt's estate the estimated value of his liability to future calls as well as calls already made.

Chapter II VOLUNTARY WINDING UP (INTRODUCTORY AND GENERAL)

Resolutions for, and commencement of, voluntary winding up

84 CIRCUMSTANCES IN WHICH COMPANY MAY BE WOUND UP VOLUNTARILY

(1) A company may be wound up voluntarily—
   (a) when the period (if any) fixed for the duration of the company by the articles expires, or the event (if any) occurs, on the occurrence of which the articles provide that the company is to be dissolved, and the company in general meeting has passed a resolution requiring it be wound up voluntarily;
   (b) if the company resolves by special resolution that it be wound up voluntarily.

(2) In this Act the expression "a resolution for voluntary winding up" means a resolution passed under either of the paragraphs of subsection (1).

(2A) Before a company passes a resolution for voluntary winding up it must give written notice of the resolution to the holder of any qualifying floating charge to which section 72A applies.

(2B) Where notice is given under subsection (2A) a resolution for voluntary winding up may be passed only—

(a) after the end of the period of five business days beginning with the day on which the notice was given, or

(b) if the person to whom the notice was given has consented in writing to the passing of the resolution.

(3) Chapter 3 of Part 3 of the Companies Act 2006 (resolutions affecting a company's constitution) applies to a resolution under paragraph (a) of subsection (1) as well as a special resolution under paragraph (b).

85 NOTICE OF RESOLUTION TO WIND UP

(1) When a company has passed a resolution for voluntary winding up, it shall, within 14 days after the passing of the resolution, give notice of the resolution by advertisement in the Gazette.

(2) If default is made in complying with this section, the company and every officer of it who is in default is liable to a fine and, for continued contravention, to a daily default fine.

For purposes of this subsection the liquidator is deemed an officer of the company.

86 COMMENCEMENT OF WINDING UP

A voluntary winding up is deemed to commence at the time of the passing of the resolution for voluntary winding up.

Consequences of resolution to wind up

87 EFFECT ON BUSINESS AND STATUS OF COMPANY

(1) In case of a voluntary winding up, the company shall from the commencement of the winding up cease to carry on its business, except so far as may be required for its beneficial winding up.

(2) However, the corporate state and corporate powers of the company, notwithstanding anything to the contrary in its articles, continue until the company is dissolved.

88 AVOIDANCE OF SHARE TRANSFERS, ETC., AFTER WINDING-UP RESOLUTION

Any transfer of shares, not being a transfer made to or with the sanction of the liquidator, and any alteration in the status of the company's members, made after the commencement of a voluntary winding up, is void.

Declaration of solvency

89 STATUTORY DECLARATION OF SOLVENCY

(1) Where it is proposed to wind up a company voluntarily, the directors (or, in the case of a company having more than two directors, the majority of them) may at a directors' meeting make a statutory declaration to the effect that they have made a full inquiry into the company's affairs and that, having done so, they have formed the opinion that the company will be able to pay its debts in full, together with interest at the official rate (as defined in section 251), within such period, not exceeding 12 months from the commencement of the winding up, as may be specified in the declaration.

(2) Such a declaration by the directors has no effect for purposes of this Act unless—
 (a) it is made within the 5 weeks immediately preceding the date of the passing of the resolution for winding up, or on that date but before the passing of the resolution, and
 (b) it embodies a statement of the company's assets and liabilities as at the latest practicable date before the making of the declaration.

(3) The declaration shall be delivered to the registrar of companies before the expiration of 15 days immediately following the date on which the resolution for winding up is passed.

(4) A director making a declaration under this section without having reasonable grounds for the opinion that the company will be able to pay its debts in full, together with interest at the official rate, within the period specified is liable to imprisonment or a fine, or both.

(5) If the company is wound up in pursuance of a resolution passed within 5 weeks after the making of the declaration, and its debts (together with interest at the official rate) are not paid or provided for in full within the period specified, it is to be presumed (unless the contrary is shown) that the director did not have reasonable grounds for his opinion.

(6) If a declaration required by subsection (3) to be delivered to the registrar is not so delivered within the time prescribed by that subsection, the company and every officer in default is liable to a fine and, for continued contravention, to a daily default fine.

90 DISTINCTION BETWEEN "MEMBERS'" AND "CREDITORS'" VOLUNTARY WINDING UP

A winding up in the case of which a directors' statutory declaration under section 89 has been made is a "members' voluntary winding up"; and a winding up in the case of which such a declaration has not been made is a "creditors' voluntary winding up".

Chapter III MEMBERS' VOLUNTARY WINDING UP

91 APPOINTMENT OF LIQUIDATOR

(1) In a members' voluntary winding up, the company in general meeting shall appoint one or more liquidators for the purpose of winding up the company's affairs and distributing its assets.

(2) On the appointment of a liquidator all the powers of the directors cease, except so far as the company in general meeting or the liquidator sanctions their continuance.

92 POWER TO FILL VACANCY IN OFFICE OF LIQUIDATOR

(1) If a vacancy occurs by death resignation or otherwise in the office of liquidator appointed by the company, the company in general meeting may, subject to any arrangement with its creditors, fill the vacancy.

(2) For that purpose a general meeting may be convened by any contributory or, if there were more liquidators than one, by the continuing liquidators.

(3) The meeting shall be held in manner provided by this Act or by the articles, or in such manner as may, on application by any contributory or by the continuing liquidators, be determined by the court.

92A PROGRESS REPORT TO COMPANY AT YEAR'S END (ENGLAND AND WALES)

(1) Subject to sections 96 and 102, in the event of the winding up of a company registered in England and Wales continuing for more than one year, the liquidator must—
   (a) for each prescribed period produce a progress report relating to the prescribed matters; and
   (b) within such period commencing with the end of the period referred to in paragraph (a) as may be prescribed send a copy of the progress report to—
      (i) the members of the company; and
      (ii) such other persons as may be prescribed.

(2) A liquidator who fails to comply with this section is liable to a fine.

93 GENERAL COMPANY MEETING AT EACH YEAR'S END

(1) Subject to sections 96 and 102, in the event of the winding up continuing for more than one year, the liquidator shall summon a general meeting of the company at the end of the first year from the commencement of the winding up, and of each succeeding year, or at the first convenient date within 3 months from the end of the year or such longer period as the Secretary of State may allow.

(2) The liquidator shall lay before the meeting an account of his acts and dealings, and of the conduct of the winding up, during the preceding year.

(3) If the liquidator fails to comply with this section, he is liable to a fine.

94 FINAL MEETING PRIOR TO DISSOLUTION

(1) As soon as the company's affairs are fully wound up, the liquidator shall make up an account of the winding up showing how it has been conducted and the company's property has been disposed of, and thereupon shall call a general meeting of the company for the purpose of laying before it the account, and giving an explanation of it.

(6) If the liquidator fails to call a general meeting of the company as required by subsection (1), he is liable to a fine.

95 EFFECT OF COMPANY'S INSOLVENCY

(1) This section applies where the liquidator is of the opinion that the company will be unable to pay its debts in full (together with interest at the official rate) within the period stated in the directors' declaration under section 89.

(2) In the case of the winding up of a company registered in Scotland, the liquidator shall—
   (a) summon a meeting of creditors for a day not later than the 28th day after the day on which he formed that opinion;
   (b) send notices of the creditors' meeting to the creditors by post not less than 7 days before the day on which that meeting is to be held;
   (c) cause notice of the creditors' meeting to be advertised once in the Gazette and once at least in 2 newspapers circulating in the relevant locality (that is to say the locality in which the company's principal place of business in Great Britain was situated during the relevant period); and
   (d) during the period before the day on which the creditors' meeting is to be held, furnish creditors free of charge with such information concerning the affairs of the company as they may reasonably require;

   and the notice of the creditors' meeting shall state the duty imposed by paragraph (d) above.

(2A) In the case of the winding up of a company registered in England and Wales, the liquidator—
   (a) shall summon a meeting of creditors for a day not later than the 28th day after the day on which he formed that opinion;
   (b) shall send notices of the creditors' meeting to the creditors not less than 7 days before the day on which that meeting is to be held;
   (c) shall cause notice of the creditors' meeting to be advertised once in the Gazette;
   (d) may cause notice of the meeting to be advertised in such other manner as he thinks fit; and
   (e) shall during the period before the day on which the creditors' meeting is to be held, furnish creditors free of charge with such information concerning the affairs of the company as they may reasonably require;

   and the notice of the creditors' meeting shall state the duty imposed by paragraph (e) above.

(3) The liquidator shall also—
   (a) make out a statement in the prescribed form as to the affairs of the company;
   (b) lay that statement before the creditors' meeting; and
   (c) attend and preside at that meeting.

(4) The statement as to the affairs of the company shall show—
   (a) particulars of the company's assets, debts and liabilities;
   (b) the names and addresses of the company's creditors;
   (c) the securities held by them respectively;
   (d) the dates when the securities were respectively given; and
   (e) such further or other information as may be prescribed.

(8) If the liquidator without reasonable excuse fails to comply with this section, he is liable to a fine.

96 CONVERSION TO CREDITORS' VOLUNTARY WINDING UP

As from the day on which the creditors' meeting is held under section 95, this Act has effect as if—

(a) the directors' declaration under section 89 had not been made; and

(b) the creditors' meeting and the company meeting at which it was resolved that the company be wound up voluntarily were the meetings mentioned in section 98 in the next Chapter;

and accordingly the winding up becomes a creditors' voluntary winding up.

Chapter IV CREDITORS' VOLUNTARY WINDING UP

97 APPLICATION OF THIS CHAPTER

(1) Subject as follows, this Chapter applies in relation to a creditors' voluntary winding up.

(2) Sections 98 and 99 do not apply where, under section 96 in Chapter III, a members' voluntary winding up has become a creditors' voluntary winding up.

98 MEETING OF CREDITORS

(1) In the case of the winding up of a company registered in Scotland, the company shall—
(a) cause a meeting of its creditors to be summoned for a day not later than the 14th day after the day on which there is to be held the company meeting at which the resolution for voluntary winding up is to be proposed;
(b) cause the notices of the creditors' meeting to be sent by post to the creditors not less than 7 days before the day on which that meeting is to be held; and
cause notice of the creditors' meeting to be advertised once in the Gazette and once at least in two newspapers circulating in the relevant locality (that is to say the locality in which the company's principal place of business in Great Britain was situated during the relevant period).

(1A) In the case of the winding up of a company registered in England and Wales, the company—
(a) shall cause a meeting of its creditors to be summoned for a day not later than the 14th day after the day on which there is to be held the company meeting at which the resolution for voluntary winding up is to be proposed;
(b) shall cause the notices of the creditors' meeting to be sent by post to the creditors not less than 7 days before the day on which that meeting is to be held;
(c) shall cause notice of the creditors' meeting to be advertised once in the Gazette; and
(d) may cause notice of the meeting to be advertised in such other manner as the directors think fit.

(2) The notice of the creditors' meeting shall state either—
(a) the name and address of a person qualified to act as an insolvency practitioner in relation to the company who, during the period before the day on which that meeting is to be held, will furnish creditors free of charge with such information concerning the company's affairs as they may reasonably require; or
(b) a place in the relevant locality where, on the two business days falling next before the day on which that meeting is to be held, a list of the names and addresses of the company's creditors will be available for inspection free of charge.

(6) If the company without reasonable excuse fails to comply with subsection (1), (1A) or (2), it is guilty of an offence and liable to a fine.

99 DIRECTORS TO LAY STATEMENT OF AFFAIRS BEFORE CREDITORS

(1) The directors of the company shall—
(a) make out a statement in the prescribed form as to the affairs of the company;
(b) cause that statement to be laid before the creditors' meeting under section 98; and
(c) appoint one of their number to preside at that meeting;
and it is the duty of the director so appointed to attend the meeting and preside over it.

(2) The statement as to the affairs of the company shall show—
(a) particulars of the company's assets, debts and liabilities;
(b) the names and addresses of the company's creditors;

(c) the securities held by them respectively;
(d) the dates when the securities were respectively given; and
(e) such further or other information as may be prescribed.

(2A) The statement as to the affairs of the company shall be verified by some or all of the directors—
(a) in the case of a winding up of a company registered in England and Wales, by a statement of truth; and
(b) in the case of a winding up of a company registered in Scotland, by affidavit.

(3) If—
(a) the directors without reasonable excuse fail to comply with subsection (1), (2) or (2A); or
(b) any director without reasonable excuse fails to comply with subsection (1), so far as requiring him to attend and preside at the creditors' meeting,

the directors are or (as the case may be) the director is guilty of an offence and liable to a fine.

100 APPOINTMENT OF LIQUIDATOR

(1) The creditors and the company at their respective meetings mentioned in section 98 may nominate a person to be liquidator for the purpose of winding up the company's affairs and distributing its assets.

(2) The liquidator shall be the person nominated by the creditors or, where no person has been so nominated, the person (if any) nominated by the company.

101 APPOINTMENT OF LIQUIDATION COMMITTEE

(1) The creditors at the meeting to be held under section 98 or at any subsequent meeting may, if they think fit, appoint a committee ("the liquidation committee") of not more than 5 persons to exercise the functions conferred on it by or under this Act.

(2) If such a committee is appointed, the company may, either at the meeting at which the resolution for voluntary winding up is passed or at any time subsequently in general meeting, appoint such number of persons as they think fit to act as members of the committee, not exceeding 5.

103 CESSER OF DIRECTORS' POWERS

On the appointment of a liquidator, all the powers of the directors cease, except so far as the liquidation committee (or, if there is no such committee, the creditors) sanction their continuance.

104 VACANCY IN OFFICE OF LIQUIDATOR

If a vacancy occurs, by death, resignation or otherwise, in the office of a liquidator (other than a liquidator appointed by, or by the direction of, the court), the creditors may fill the vacancy.

104A PROGRESS REPORT TO COMPANY AND CREDITORS AT YEAR'S END (ENGLAND AND WALES)

(1) If the winding up of a company registered in England and Wales continues for more than one year, the liquidator must—

(a) for each prescribed period produce a progress report relating to the prescribed matters; and
(b) within such period commencing with the end of the period referred to in paragraph (a) as may be prescribed send a copy of the progress report to—
(i) the members and creditors of the company; and
(ii) such other persons as may be prescribed.

(2) A liquidator who fails to comply with this section is liable to a fine.

105 MEETINGS OF COMPANY AND CREDITORS AT EACH YEAR'S END (SCOTLAND)

(1) If the winding up of a company registered in Scotland continues for more than one year, the liquidator shall summon a general meeting of the company and a meeting of the creditors at the end of the first year from the commencement of the winding up, and of each succeeding year, or at the first convenient date within 3 months from the end of the year or such longer period as the Secretary of State may allow.

(2) The liquidator shall lay before each of the meetings an account of his acts and dealings and of the conduct of the winding up during the preceding year.

(3) If the liquidator fails to comply with this section, he is liable to a fine.

(4) Where under section 96 a members' voluntary winding up has become a creditors' voluntary winding up, and the creditors' meeting under section 95 is held 3 months or less before the end of the first year from the commencement of the winding up, the liquidator is not required by this section to summon a meeting of creditors at the end of that year.

106 FINAL MEETING PRIOR TO DISSOLUTION

(1) As soon as the company's affairs are fully wound up, the liquidator shall make up an account of the winding up, showing how it has been conducted and the company's property has been disposed of, and thereupon shall call a general meeting of the company and a meeting of the creditors for the purpose of laying the account before the meetings and giving an explanation of it.

(6) If the liquidator fails to call a general meeting of the company or a meeting of the creditors as required by this section, he is liable to a fine.

Chapter V PROVISIONS APPLYING TO BOTH KINDS OF VOLUNTARY WINDING UP

107 DISTRIBUTION OF COMPANY'S PROPERTY

Subject to the provisions of this Act as to preferential payments, the company's property in a voluntary winding up shall on the winding up be applied in satisfaction of the company's liabilities pari passu and, subject to that application, shall (unless the articles otherwise provide) be distributed among the members according to their rights and interests in the company.

108 APPOINTMENT OR REMOVAL OF LIQUIDATOR BY THE COURT

(1) If from any cause whatever there is not liquidator acting, the court may appoint a liquidator.

(2) The court may, on cause shown, remove a liquidator and appoint another.

109 NOTICE BY LIQUIDATOR OF HIS APPOINTMENT

(1) The liquidator shall, within 14 days after his appointment, publish in the Gazette and deliver to the registrar of companies for registration a notice of his appointment in the form prescribed by statutory instrument made by the Secretary of State.

(2) If the liquidator fails to comply with this section, he is liable to a fine and, for continued contravention, to a daily default fine.

110 ACCEPTANCE OF SHARES, ETC., AS CONSIDERATION FOR SALE OF COMPANY PROPERTY

(1) This section applies, in the case of a company proposed to be, or being, wound up voluntarily, where the whole or part of the company's business or property is proposed to be transferred or sold—

(a) to another company ("the transferee company"), whether or not the latter is a company registered under the Companies Act 2006, or

(b) to a limited liability partnership (the "transferee limited liability partnership").

(2) With the requisite sanction, the liquidator of the company being, or proposed to be, wound up ("the transferor company") may receive, in compensation or part compensation for the transfer or sale—

(a) in the case of the transferee company, shares, policies or other like interests in the transferee company for distribution among the members of the transferor company, or

(b) in the case of the transferee limited liability partnership, membership in the transferee limited liability partnership for distribution among the members of the transferor company.

(3) The sanction requisite under subsection (2) is—

(a) in the case of a members' voluntary winding up, that of a special resolution of the company, conferring either a general authority on the liquidator or an authority in respect of any particular arrangement, and

(b) in the case of a creditors' voluntary winding up, that of either the court or the liquidation committee.

(4) Alternatively to subsection (2), the liquidator may (with that sanction) enter into any other arrangement whereby the members of the transferor company may—

(a) in the case of the transferee company, in lieu of receiving cash, shares, policies or other like interests (or in addition thereto) participate in the profits of, or receive any other benefit from, the transferee company, or

(b) in the case of the transferee limited liability partnership, in lieu of receiving cash or membership (or in addition thereto), participate in some other way in the profits of, or receive any other benefit from, the transferee limited liability partnership.

(5) A sale or arrangement in pursuance of this section is binding on members of the transferor company.

(6) A special resolution is not invalid for purposes of this section by reason that it is passed before or concurrently with a resolution for voluntary winding up or for appointing liquidators; but, if an order is made within a year for winding up the company by the court, the special resolution is not valid unless sanctioned by the court.

The above version of s 110 extends to England and Wales only; a separate version has been created for Scotland, which is the same as the version applying in England and Wales except that subsection (4) in Scotland is worded as follows:

(4) Alternatively to subsection (2), the liquidator may—
(a) in the case of the transferee company, in lieu of receiving cash, shares, policies or other like interests (or in addition thereto) participate in the profits of, or receive any other benefit from, the company, or
(b) in the case of the transferee limited liability partnership, in lieu of receiving cash, or membership (or in addition thereto) participate in some other way in the profits of, or receive any other benefit from, the limited liability partnership.

111 DISSENT FROM ARRANGEMENT UNDER S. 110

(1) This section applies in the case of a voluntary winding up where, for the purposes of section 110(2) or (4), there has been passed a special resolution of the transferor company providing the sanction requisite for the liquidator under that section.

(2) If a member of the transferor company who did not vote in favour of the special resolution expresses his dissent from it in writing, addressed to the liquidator and left at the company's registered office within 7 days after the passing of the resolution, he may require the liquidator either to abstain from carrying the resolution into effect or to purchase his interest at a price to be determined by agreement or by arbitration under this section.

(3) If the liquidator elects to purchase the member's interest, the purchase money must be paid before the company is dissolved and be raised by the liquidator in such manner as may be determined by special resolution.

112 REFERENCE OF QUESTIONS TO COURT

(1) The liquidator or any contributory or creditor may apply to the court to determine any question arising in the winding up of a company, or to exercise, as respects the enforcing of calls or any other matter, all or any of the powers which the court might exercise if the company were being wound up by the court.

(2) The court, if satisfied that the determination of the question or the required exercise of power will be just and beneficial, may accede wholly or partially to the application on such terms and conditions as it thinks fit, or may make such other order on the application as it thinks just.

(3) A copy of an order made by virtue of this section staying the proceedings in the winding up shall forthwith be forwarded by the company, or otherwise as may be prescribed, to the registrar of companies, who shall enter it in his records relating to the company.

113 COURT'S POWER TO CONTROL PROCEEDINGS (SCOTLAND)

If the court, on the application of the liquidator in the winding up of a company registered in Scotland, so directs, no action or proceeding shall be proceeded with or commenced against the company except by leave of the court and subject to such terms as the court may impose.

115 EXPENSES OF VOLUNTARY WINDING UP

All expenses properly incurred in the winding up, including the remuneration of the liquidator, are payable out of the company's assets in priority to all other claims.

116 SAVING FOR CERTAIN RIGHTS

The voluntary winding up of a company does not bar the right of any creditor or contributory to have it wound up by the court; but in the case of an application by a contributory the court must be satisfied that the rights of the contributories will be prejudiced by a voluntary winding up.

Chapter VI WINDING UP BY THE COURT

Jurisdiction (England and Wales)

117 HIGH COURT AND COUNTY COURT JURISDICTION

(1) The High Court has jurisdiction to wind up any company registered in England and Wales.

(2) Where the amount of a company's share capital paid up or credited as paid up does not exceed £120,000, then (subject to this section) the county court of the district in which the company's registered office is situated has concurrent jurisdiction with the High Court to wind up the company.

(5) Every court in England and Wales having winding-up jurisdiction has for the purposes of that jurisdiction all the powers of the High Court;...

Jurisdiction (Scotland)

120 COURT OF SESSION AND SHERIFF COURT JURISDICTION

(1) The Court of Session has jurisdiction to wind up any company registered in Scotland.

(3) Where the amount of a company's share capital paid up or credited as paid up does not exceed £120,000, the sheriff court of the sheriffdom in which the company's registered office is situated has concurrent jurisdiction with the Court of Session to wind up the company;...

Grounds and effect of winding-up petition

122 CIRCUMSTANCES IN WHICH COMPANY MAY BE WOUND UP BY THE COURT

(1) A company may be wound up by the court if—
- (a) the company has by special resolution resolved that the company be wound up by the court,
- (b) being a public company which was registered as such on its original incorporation, the company has not been issued with a trading certificate under section 761 of the Companies Act (requirement as to minimum share capital) and more than a year has expired since it was so registered,
- (c) it is an old public company, within the meaning of Schedule 3 to the Companies Act 2006 (Consequential Amendments, Transitional Provisions and Savings) Order 2009,

(d) the company does not commence its business within a year from its incorporation or suspends its business for a whole year,

(e) except in the case of a private company limited by shares or by guarantee, the number of members is reduced below 2,

(f) the company is unable to pay its debts,

(fa) at the time at which a moratorium for the company under section 1A comes to an end, no voluntary arrangement approved under Part I has effect in relation to the company,

(g) the court is of the opinion that it is just and equitable that the company should be wound up.

(2) In Scotland, a company which the Court of Session has jurisdiction to wind up may be wound up by the Court if there is subsisting a floating charge over property comprised in the company's property and undertaking, and the court is satisfied that the security of the creditor entitled to the benefit of the floating charge is in jeopardy.

For this purpose a creditor's security is deemed to be in jeopardy if the Court is satisfied that events have occurred or are about to occur which render it unreasonable in the creditor's interests that the company should retain power to dispose of the property which is subject to the floating charge.

123 DEFINITION OF INABILITY TO PAY DEBTS

(1) A company is deemed unable to pay its debts—

(a) if a creditor (by assignment or otherwise) to whom the company is indebted in a sum exceeding £750 then due has served on the company, by leaving it at the company's registered office, a written demand (in the prescribed form) requiring the company to pay the sum so due and the company has for 3 weeks thereafter neglected to pay the sum or to secure or compound for it to the reasonable satisfaction of the creditor, or

(b) if, in England and Wales, execution or other process issued on a judgment, decree or order of any court in favour of a creditor of the company is returned unsatisfied in whole or in part, or

(c) if, in Scotland, the induciae of a charge for payment on an extract decree, or an extract registered bond, or an extract registered protest, have expired without payment being made, or

(d) if, in Northern Ireland, a certificate of unenforceability has been granted in respect of a judgment against the company, or

(e) if it is proved to the satisfaction of the court that the company is unable to pay its debts as they fall due.

(2) A company is also deemed unable to pay its debts if it is proved to the satisfaction of the court that the value of the company's assets is less than the amount of its liabilities, taking into account its contingent and prospective liabilities.

(3) The money sum for the time being specified in subsection (1)(a) is subject to increase or reduction by order under section 416 in Part XV.

124 APPLICATION FOR WINDING UP

(1) Subject to the provisions of this section, an application to the court for the winding up of a company shall be by petition presented either by the company, or the directors, or by any creditor or creditors (including any contingent or prospective creditor or creditors), contributory or contributories, or by a liquidator (within the meaning of Article 2(b) of the EC Regulation) appointed in proceedings by virtue of Article 3(1) of the EC

Regulation or a temporary administrator (within the meaning of Article 38 of the EC Regulation) or by the designated officer for a magistrates' court in the exercise of the power conferred by section 87A of the Magistrates' Courts Act 1980 (enforcement of fines imposed on companies), or by all or any of those parties, together or separately.

(2) Except as mentioned below, a contributory is not entitled to present a winding-up petition unless either—
  (a) the number of members is reduced below 2, or
  (b) the shares in respect of which he is a contributory, or some of them, either were originally allotted to him, or have been held by him, and registered in his name, for at least 6 months during the 18 months before the commencement of the winding up, or have devolved on him through the death of a former holder.

(3) A person who is liable under section 76 to contribute to a company's assets in the event of its being wound up may petition on either of the grounds set out in section 122(1)(f) and (g), and subsection (2) above does not then apply; but unless the person is a contributory otherwise than under section 76, he may not in his character as contributory petition on any other ground....

(3A) A winding-up petition on the ground set out in section 122(1)(fa) may only be presented by one or more creditors.

(4) A winding-up petition may be presented by the Secretary of State—
  (a) if the ground of the petition is that in section 122(1)(b) or (c), or
  (b) in a case falling within section 124A or 124B below.

(5) Where a company is being wound up voluntarily in England and Wales, a winding-up petition may be presented by the official receiver attached to the court as well as by any other person authorised in that behalf under the other provisions of this section; but the court shall not make a winding-up order on the petition unless it is satisfied that the voluntary winding up cannot be continued with due regard to the interests of the creditors or contributories.

124A PETITION FOR WINDING UP ON GROUNDS OF PUBLIC INTEREST

(1) Where it appears to the Secretary of State from—
  (a) any report made or information obtained under Part XIV ... of the Companies Act 1985 (company investigations, etc.),...

that it is expedient in the public interest that a company should be wound up, he may present a petition for it to be wound up if the court thinks it just and equitable for it to be so.

(2) This section does not apply if the company is already being wound up by the court.

124B PETITION FOR WINDING UP OF SE

(1) Where—
  (a) an SE whose registered office is in Great Britain is not in compliance with Article 7 of Council Regulation (EC) No 2157/2001 on the Statute for a European company (the "EC Regulation") (location of head office and registered office), and
  (b) it appears to the Secretary of State that the SE should be wound up, he may present a petition for it to be wound up if the court thinks it is just and equitable for it to be so.

(2) This section does not apply if the SE is already being wound up by the court.

(3) In this section "SE" has the same meaning as in the EC Regulation.

125 POWERS OF COURT ON HEARING OF PETITION

(1) On hearing a winding-up petition the court may dismiss it, or adjourn the hearing conditionally or unconditionally, or make an interim order, or any other order that it thinks fit; but the court shall not refuse to make a winding-up order on the ground only that the company's assets have been mortgaged to an amount equal to or in excess of those assets, or that the company has no assets.

(2) If the petition is presented by members of the company as contributories on the ground that it is just and equitable that the company should be wound up, the court, if it is of opinion—
(a) that the petitioners are entitled to relief either by winding up the company or by some other means, and
(b) that in the absence of any other remedy it would be just and equitable that the company should be wound up,
shall make a winding-up order; but this does not apply if the court is also of the opinion both that some other remedy is available to the petitioners and that they are acting unreasonably in seeking to have the company wound up instead of pursuing that other remedy.

126 POWER TO STAY OR RESTRAIN PROCEEDINGS AGAINST COMPANY

(1) At any time after the presentation of a winding-up petition, and before a winding-up order has been made, the company, or any creditor or contributory, may—
(a) where any action or proceeding against the company is pending in the High Court or Court of Appeal in England and Wales or Northern Ireland, apply to the court in which the action or proceeding is pending for a stay of proceedings therein, and
(b) where any other action or proceeding is pending against the company, apply to the court having jurisdiction to wind up the company to restrain further proceedings in the action or proceeding;
and the court to which the application is so made may (as the case may be) stay, sist or restrain the proceedings accordingly on such terms as it thinks fit.

127 AVOIDANCE OF PROPERTY DISPOSITIONS, ETC.

(1) In a winding up by the court, any disposition of the company's property, and any transfer of shares, or alteration in the status of the company's members, made after the commencement of the winding up is, unless the court otherwise orders, void.

(2) This section has no effect in respect of anything done by an administrator of a company while a winding-up petition is suspended under paragraph 40 of Schedule B1.

128 AVOIDANCE OF ATTACHMENTS, ETC.

(1) Where a company registered in England and Wales is being wound up by the court, any attachment, sequestration, distress or execution put in force against the estate or effects of the company after the commencement of the winding up is void.

(2) This section, so far as relates to any estate or effects of the company situated in England and Wales, applies in the case of a company registered in Scotland as it applies in the case of a company registered in England and Wales.

Annotations:

Commencement of winding up

129 COMMENCEMENT OF WINDING UP BY THE COURT

(1) If, before the presentation of a petition for the winding up of a company by the court, a resolution has been passed by the company for voluntary winding up, the winding up of the company is deemed to have commenced at the time of the passing of the resolution; and unless the court, on proof of fraud or mistake, directs otherwise, all proceedings taken in the voluntary winding up are deemed to have been validly taken.

(1A) Where the court makes a winding-up order by virtue of paragraph 13(1)(e) of Schedule B1, the winding up is deemed to commence on the making of the order.

(2) In any other case, the winding up of a company by the court is deemed to commence at the time of the presentation of the petition for winding up.

130 CONSEQUENCES OF WINDING-UP ORDER

(1) On the making of a winding-up order, a copy of the order must forthwith be forwarded by the company (or otherwise as may be prescribed) to the registrar of companies, who shall enter it in his records relating to the company.

(2) When a winding-up order has been made or a provisional liquidator has been appointed, no action or proceeding shall be proceeded with or commenced against the company or its property, except by leave of the court and subject to such terms as the court may impose.

(4) An order for winding up a company operates in favour of all the creditors and of all contributories of the company as if made on the joint petition of a creditor and of a contributory.

Investigation procedures

131 COMPANY'S STATEMENT OF AFFAIRS

(1) Where the court has made a winding-up order or appointed a provisional liquidator, the official receiver may require some or all of the persons mentioned in subsection (3) below to make out and submit to him a statement in the prescribed form as to the affairs of the company.

(2) The statement shall show—
- (a) particulars of the company's assets, debts and liabilities;
- (b) the names and addresses of the company's creditors;
- (c) the securities held by them respectively;
- (d) the dates when the securities were respectively given; and
- (e) such further or other information as may be prescribed or as the official receiver may require.

(2A) The statement shall be verified by the persons required to submit it—
(a) in the case of an appointment of a provisional liquidator or a winding up by the court in England and Wales, by a statement of truth; and
(b) in the case of an appointment of a provisional liquidator or a winding up by the court in Scotland, by affidavit.

(3) The persons referred to in subsection (1) are—
(a) those who are or have been officers of the company;
(b) those who have taken part in the formation of the company at any time within one year before the relevant date;
(c) those who are in the company's employment, or have been in its employment within that year, and are in the official receiver's opinion capable of giving the information required;
(d) those who are or have been within that year officers of, or in the employment of, a company which is, or within that year was, an officer of the company.

(4) Where any persons are required under this section to submit a statement of affairs to the official receiver, they shall do so (subject to the next subsection) before the end of the period of 21 days beginning with the day after that on which the prescribed notice of the requirement is given to them by the official receiver.

(5) The official receiver, if he thinks fit, may—
(a) at any time release a person from an obligation imposed on him under subsection (1) or (2) above; or
(b) either when giving the notice mentioned in subsection (4) or subsequently, extend the period so mentioned;
and where the official receiver has refused to exercise a power conferred by this subsection, the court, if it thinks fit, may exercise it.

(6) In this section—

"employment" includes employment under a contract for services; and

"the relevant date" means—
(a) in a case where a provisional liquidator is appointed, the date of his appointment; and
(b) in a case where no such appointment is made, the date of the winding-up order.

(7) If a person without reasonable excuse fails to comply with any obligation imposed under this section, he is liable to a fine and, for continued contravention, to a daily default fine.

(8) In the application of this section to Scotland references to the official receiver are to the liquidator or, in a case where a provisional liquidator is appointed, the provisional liquidator.

132 INVESTIGATION BY OFFICIAL RECEIVER

(1) Where a winding-up order is made by the court in England and Wales, it is the duty of the official receiver to investigate—
(a) if the company has failed, the causes of the failure; and
(b) generally, the promotion, formation, business, dealings and affairs of the company,
and to make such report (if any) to the court as he thinks fit.

(2) The report is, in any proceedings, prima facie evidence of the facts stated in it.

133 PUBLIC EXAMINATION OF OFFICERS

(1) Where a company is being wound up by the court, the official receiver or, in Scotland, the liquidator may at any time before the dissolution of the company apply to the court for the public examination of any person who—
(a) is or has been an officer of the company; or
(b) has acted as liquidator or administrator of the company or as receiver or manager or, in Scotland, receiver of its property; or
(c) not being a person falling within paragraph (a) or (b), is or has been concerned, or has taken part, in the promotion, formation or management of the company.

(2) Unless the court otherwise orders, the official receiver or, in Scotland, the liquidator shall make an application under subsection (1) if he is requested in accordance with the rules to do so by—
(a) one-half, in value, of the company's creditors; or
(b) three-quarters, in value, of the company's contributories.

(3) On an application under subsection (1), the court shall direct that a public examination of the person to whom the application relates shall be held on a day appointed by the court; and that person shall attend on that day and be publicly examined as to the promotion, formation or management of the company or as to the conduct of its business and affairs, or his conduct or dealings in relation to the company.

(4) The following may take part in the public examination of a person under this section and may question that person concerning the matters mentioned in subsection (3), namely—
(a) the official receiver;
(b) the liquidator of the company;
(c) any person who has been appointed as special manager of the company's property or business;
(d) any creditor of the company who has tendered a proof or, in Scotland, submitted a claim in the winding up;
(e) any contributory of the company.

134 ENFORCEMENT OF S. 133

(1) If a person without reasonable excuse fails at any time to attend his public examination under section 133, he is guilty of a contempt of court and liable to be punished accordingly.

(2) In a case where a person without reasonable excuse fails at any time to attend his examination under section 133 or there are reasonable grounds for believing that a person has absconded, or is about to abscond, with a view to avoiding or delaying his examination under that section, the court may cause a warrant to be issued to a constable or prescribed officer of the court—
(a) for the arrest of that person; and
(b) for the seizure of any books, papers, records, money or goods in that person's possession.

(3) In such a case the court may authorise the person arrested under the warrant to be kept in custody, and anything seized under such a warrant to be held, in accordance with the rules, until such time as the court may order.

Appointment of liquidator

135 APPOINTMENT AND POWERS OF PROVISIONAL LIQUIDATOR

(1) Subject to the provisions of this section, the court may, at any time after the presentation of a winding-up petition, appoint a liquidator provisionally.

(2) In England and Wales, the appointment of a provisional liquidator may be made at any time before the making of a winding-up order; and either the official receiver or any other fit person may be appointed.

(3) In Scotland, such an appointment may be made at any time before the first appointment of liquidators.

(4) The provisional liquidator shall carry out such functions as the court may confer on him.

(5) When a liquidator is provisionally appointed by the court, his powers may be limited by the order appointing him.

136 FUNCTIONS OF OFFICIAL RECEIVER IN RELATION TO OFFICE OF LIQUIDATOR

(1) The following provisions of this section have effect, subject to section 140 below, on a winding-up order being made by the court in England and Wales.

(2) The official receiver, by virtue of his office, becomes the liquidator of the company and continues in office until another person becomes liquidator under the provisions of this Part.

(3) The official receiver is, by virtue of his office, the liquidator during any vacancy.

(4) At any time when he is the liquidator of the company, the official receiver may summon separate meetings of the company's creditors and contributories for the purpose of choosing a person to be liquidator of the company in place of the official receiver.

137 APPOINTMENT BY SECRETARY OF STATE

(1) In a winding up by the court in England and Wales the official receiver may, at any time when he is the liquidator of the company, apply to the Secretary of State for the appointment of a person as liquidator in his place.

(3) On an application under subsection (1), or a reference made in pursuance of a decision under subsection (2), the Secretary of State shall either make an appointment or decline to make one.

138 APPOINTMENT OF LIQUIDATOR IN SCOTLAND

(1) Where a winding-up order is made by the court in Scotland, a liquidator shall be appointed by the court at the time when the order is made.

(2) The liquidator so appointed (here referred to as "the interim liquidator") continues in office until another person becomes liquidator in his place under this section or the next.

(3) The interim liquidator shall (subject to the next subsection) as soon as practicable in the period of 28 days beginning with the day on which the winding-up order was made or such longer period as the court may allow, summon separate meetings of the company's

creditors and contributories for the purpose of choosing a person (who may be the person who is the interim liquidator) to be liquidator of the company in place of the interim liquidator.

139 CHOICE OF LIQUIDATOR AT MEETINGS OF CREDITORS AND CONTRIBUTORIES

(1) This section applies where a company is being wound up by the court and separate meetings of the company's creditors and contributories are summoned for the purpose of choosing a person to be liquidator of the company.

(2) The creditors and the contributories at their respective meetings may nominate a person to be liquidator.

(3) The liquidator shall be the person nominated by the creditors or, where no person has been so nominated, the person (if any) nominated by the contributories.

140 APPOINTMENT BY THE COURT FOLLOWING ADMINISTRATION OR VOLUNTARY ARRANGEMENT

(1) Where a winding-up order is made immediately upon the appointment of an administrator ceasing to have effect, the court may appoint as liquidator of the company the person whose appointment as administrator has ceased to have effect.

(2) Where a winding-up order is made at a time when there is a supervisor of a voluntary arrangement approved in relation to the company under Part I, the court may appoint as liquidator of the company the person who is the supervisor at the time when the winding-up order is made.

(3) Where the court makes an appointment under this section, the official receiver does not become the liquidator as otherwise provided by section 136(2)...

Liquidation committees

141 LIQUIDATION COMMITTEE (ENGLAND AND WALES)

(1) Where a winding-up order has been made by the court in England and Wales and separate meetings of creditors and contributories have been summoned for the purpose of choosing a person to be liquidator, those meetings may establish a committee ("the liquidation committee") to exercise the functions conferred on it by or under this Act.

142 LIQUIDATION COMMITTEE (SCOTLAND)

(1) Where a winding-up order has been made by the court in Scotland and separate meetings of creditors and contributories have been summoned for the purpose of choosing a person to be liquidator ..., those meetings ... may establish a committee ("the liquidation committee") to exercise the functions conferred on it by or under this Act.

The liquidator's functions

143 GENERAL FUNCTIONS IN WINDING UP BY THE COURT

(1) The functions of the liquidator of a company which is being wound up by the court are to secure that the assets of the company are got in, realised and distributed to the company's creditors and, if there is a surplus, to the persons entitled to it.

(2) It is the duty of the liquidator of a company which is being wound up by the court in England and Wales, if he is not the official receiver—
(a) to furnish the official receiver with such information,
(b) to produce to the official receiver, and permit inspection by the official receiver of, such books, papers and other records, and
(c) to give the official receiver such other assistance,
as the official receiver may reasonably require for the purposes of carrying out his functions in relation to the winding up.

144 CUSTODY OF COMPANY'S PROPERTY

(1) When a winding-up order has been made, or where a provisional liquidator has been appointed, the liquidator or the provisional liquidator (as the case may be) shall take into his custody or under his control all the property and things in action to which the company is or appears to be entitled.

(2) In a winding up by the court in Scotland, if and so long as there is no liquidator, all the property of the company is deemed to be in the custody of the court.

145 VESTING OF COMPANY PROPERTY IN LIQUIDATOR

(1) When a company is being wound up by the court, the court may on the application of the liquidator by order direct that all or any part of the property of whatsoever description belonging to the company or held by trustees on its behalf shall vest in the liquidator by his official name; and thereupon the property to which the order relates vests accordingly.

(2) The liquidator may, after giving such indemnity (if any) as the court may direct, bring or defend in his official name any action or other legal proceeding which relates to that property or which it is necessary to bring or defend for the purpose of effectually winding up the company and recovering its property.

146 DUTY TO SUMMON FINAL MEETING

(1) Subject to the next subsection, if it appears to the liquidator of a company which is being wound up by the court that the winding up of the company is for practical purposes complete and the liquidator is not the official receiver, the liquidator shall summon a final general meeting of the company's creditors which—
(a) shall receive the liquidator's report of the winding up, and
(b) shall determine whether the liquidator should have his release under section 174 in Chapter VII of this Part.

(3) In the carrying out of his functions in the winding up it is the duty of the liquidator to retain sufficient sums from the company's property to cover the expenses of summoning and holding the meeting required by this section.

General powers of court

147 POWER TO STAY OR SIST WINDING UP

(1) The court may at any time after an order for winding up, on the application either of the liquidator or the official receiver or any creditor or contributory, and on proof to the satisfaction of the court that all proceedings in the winding up ought to be stayed or sisted, make an order staying or sisting the proceedings, either altogether or for a limited time, on such terms and conditions as the court thinks fit.

(2) The court may, before making an order, require the official receiver to furnish to it a report with respect to any facts or matters which are in his opinion relevant to the application.

(3) A copy of every order made under this section shall forthwith be forwarded by the company, or otherwise as may be prescribed, to the registrar of companies, who shall enter it in his records relating to the company.

148 SETTLEMENT OF LIST OF CONTRIBUTORIES AND APPLICATION OF ASSETS

(1) As soon as may be after making a winding-up order, the court shall settle a list of contributories ..., and shall cause the company's assets to be collected, and applied in discharge of its liabilities.

149 DEBTS DUE FROM CONTRIBUTORY TO COMPANY

(1) The court may, at any time after making a winding-up order, make an order on any contributory for the time being on the list of contributories to pay, in manner directed by the order, any money due from him (or from the estate of the person who he represents) to the company, exclusive of any money payable by him or the estate by virtue of any call.

150 POWER TO MAKE CALLS

(1) The court may, at any time after making a winding-up order, and either before or after it has ascertained the sufficiency of the company's assets, make calls on all or any of the contributories for the time being settled on the list of the contributories to the extent of their liability, for payment of any money which the court considers necessary to satisfy the company's debts and liabilities, and the expenses of winding up, and for the adjustment of the rights of the contributories among themselves, and make an order for payment of any calls so made.

(2) In making a call the court may take into consideration the probability that some of the contributories may partly or wholly fail to pay it.

153 POWER TO EXCLUDE CREDITORS NOT PROVING IN TIME

The court may fix a time or times within which creditors are to prove their debts or claims or to be excluded from the benefit of any distribution made before those debts are proved.

154 ADJUSTMENT OF RIGHTS OF CONTRIBUTORIES

The court shall adjust the rights of the contributories among themselves and distribute any surplus among the persons entitled to it.

155 INSPECTION OF BOOKS BY CREDITORS, ETC.

(1) The court may, at any time after making a winding-up order, make such order for inspection of the company's books and papers by creditors and contributories as the court thinks just; and any books and papers in the company's possession may be inspected by creditors and contributories accordingly, but not further or otherwise.

156 PAYMENT OF EXPENSES OF WINDING UP

The court may, in the event of the assets being insufficient to satisfy the liabilities, make an order as to the payment out of the assets of the expenses incurred in the winding up in such order of priority as the court thinks just.

157 ATTENDANCE AT COMPANY MEETINGS (SCOTLAND)

In the winding up by the court of a company registered in Scotland, the court has power to require the attendance of any officer of the company at any meeting of creditors or of contributories, or of a liquidation committee, for the purpose of giving information as to the trade, dealings, affairs or property of the company.

158 POWER TO ARREST ABSCONDING CONTRIBUTORY

The court, at any time either before or after making a winding-up order, on proof of probable cause for believing that a contributory is about to quit the United Kingdom or otherwise to abscond or to remove or conceal any of his property for the purpose of evading payment of calls, may cause the contributory to be arrested and his books and papers and moveable personal property to be seized and him and them to be kept safely until such time as the court may order.

159 POWERS OF COURT TO BE CUMULATIVE

Powers conferred on the court by this Act are in addition to, and not in restriction of, any existing powers of instituting proceedings against a contributory or debtor of the company, or the estate of any contributory or debtor, for the recovery of any call or other sums.

Chapter VII LIQUIDATORS

Liquidator's powers and duties

165 VOLUNTARY WINDING UP

(1) This section has effect where a company is being wound up voluntarily, but subject to section 166 below in the case of a creditor's voluntary winding up.

(2) The liquidator may—
  (a) in the case of a members' voluntary winding up, with the sanction of [a] special resolution of the company, and
  (b) in the case of a creditor's voluntary winding up, with the sanction of the court or the liquidation committee (or, if there is no such committee, a meeting of the company's creditors),

exercise any of the powers specified in Part I of Schedule 4 to this Act (payment of debts, compromise of claims, etc.).

(3) The liquidator may, without sanction, exercise either of the powers specified in Part II of that Schedule (institution and defence of proceedings; carrying on the business of the company) and any of the general powers specified in Part III of that Schedule.

(4) The liquidator may—
  (a) exercise the court's power of settling a list of contributories (which list is prima facie evidence of the liability of the persons named in it to be contributories),
  (b) exercise the court's power of making calls,

(c) summon general meetings of the company for the purpose of obtaining its sanction by special resolution or for any other purpose he may think fit.

(5) The liquidator shall pay the company's debts and adjust the rights of the contributories among themselves.

(6) Where the liquidator in exercise of the powers conferred on him by this Act disposes of any property of the company to a person who is connected with the company (within the meaning of section 249 in Part VII), he shall, if there is for the time being a liquidation committee, give notice to the committee of that exercise of his powers.

(Extraordinary resolution references omitted)

166 CREDITORS' VOLUNTARY WINDING UP

(1) This section applies where, in the case of a creditors' voluntary winding up, a liquidator has been nominated by the company.

(2) The powers conferred on the liquidator by section 165 shall not be exercised, except with the sanction of the court, during the period before the holding of the creditors' meeting under section 98 in Chapter IV.

(3) Subsection (2) does not apply in relation to the power of the liquidator—
(a) to take into his custody or under his control all the property to which the company is or appears to be entitled;
(b) to dispose of perishable goods and other goods the value of which is likely to diminish if they are not immediately disposed of; and
(c) to do all such other things as may be necessary for the protection of the company's assets.

(4) The liquidator shall attend the creditors' meeting held under section 98 and shall report to the meeting on any exercise by him of his powers (whether or not under this section or under section 112 or 165).

(5) If default is made—
(a) by the company in complying with subsection (1), (1A) or (2) of section 98, or
(b) by the directors in complying with subsection (1), (2) or (2A) of section 99,
the liquidator shall, within 7 days of the relevant day, apply to the court for directions as to the manner in which that default is to be remedied.

(6) "The relevant day" means the day on which the liquidator was nominated by the company or the day on which he first became aware of the default, whichever is the later.

(7) If the liquidator without reasonable excuse fails to comply with this section, he is liable to a fine.

167 WINDING UP BY THE COURT

(1) Where a company is being wound up by the court, the liquidator may—
(a) with the sanction of the court or the liquidation committee, exercise any of the powers specified in Parts I and II of Schedule 4 to this Act (payment of debts; compromise of claims, etc., institution and defence of proceedings; carrying on of the business of the company), and
(b) with or without that sanction, exercise any of the general powers specified in Part III of that Schedule.

(2) Where the liquidator (not being the official receiver), in exercise of the powers conferred on him by this Act—

(a) disposes of any property of the company to a person who is connected with the company (within the meaning of section 249 in Part VII) or

(b) employs a solicitor to assist him in the carrying out of his functions,

he shall, if there is for the time being a liquidation committee, give notice to the committee of that exercise of his powers.

(3) The exercise by the liquidator in a winding up by the court of the powers conferred by this section is subject to the control of the court, and any creditor or contributory may apply to the court with respect to any exercise or proposed exercise of any of those powers.

168 SUPPLEMENTARY POWERS (ENGLAND AND WALES)

(1) This section applies in the case of a company which is being wound up by the court in England and Wales.

(2) The liquidator may summon general meetings of the creditors or contributories for the purpose of ascertaining their wishes; and it is his duty to summon meetings at such times as the creditors or contributories by resolution (either at the meeting appointing the liquidator or otherwise) may direct, or whenever requested in writing to do so by one-tenth in value of the creditors or contributories (as the case may be).

(3) The liquidator may apply to the court (in the prescribed manner) for directions in relation to any particular matter arising in the winding up.

(4) Subject to the provisions of this Act, the liquidator shall use his own discretion in the management of the assets and their distribution among the creditors.

(5) If any person is aggrieved by an act or decision of the liquidator, that person may apply to the court; and the court may confirm, reverse or modify the act or decision complained of, and make such order in the case as it thinks just.

169 SUPPLEMENTARY POWERS (SCOTLAND)

(1) In the case of a winding up in Scotland, the court may provide by order that the liquidator may, where there is no liquidation committee, exercise any of the following powers, namely—

(a) to bring or defend any action or other legal proceeding in the name and on behalf of the company, or

(b) to carry on the business of the company so far as may be necessary for its beneficial winding up,

without the sanction or intervention of the court.

(2) In a winding up by the court in Scotland, the liquidator has (subject to the rules) the same powers as a trustee on a bankrupt estate.

Removal; vacation of office

171 REMOVAL, ETC. (VOLUNTARY WINDING UP)

(1) This section applies with respect to the removal from office and vacation of office of the liquidator of a company which is being wound up voluntarily.

(2) Subject to the next subsection, the liquidator may be removed from office only by an order of the court or—

(a) in the case of a members' voluntary winding up, by a general meeting of the company summoned specially for that purpose, or
(b) in the case of a creditors' voluntary winding up, by a general meeting of the company's creditors summoned specially for that purpose in accordance with the rules.

(4) A liquidator shall vacate office if he ceases to be a person who is qualified to act as an insolvency practitioner in relation to the company.

(5) A liquidator may, in the prescribed circumstances, resign his office by giving notice of his resignation to the registrar of companies.

(6) Where—
(a) in the case of a members' voluntary winding up, a final meeting of the company has been held under section 94 in Chapter III, or
(b) in the case of a creditors' voluntary winding up, final meetings of the company and of the creditors have been held under section 106 in Chapter IV,
the liquidator whose report was considered at the meeting or meetings shall vacate office as soon as he has complied with subsection (3) of that section and has given notice to the registrar of companies that the meeting or meetings have been held and of the decisions (if any) of the meeting or meetings.

172 REMOVAL, ETC. (WINDING UP BY THE COURT)

(1) This section applies with respect to the removal from office and vacation of office of the liquidator of a company which is being wound up by the court, or of a provisional liquidator.

(2) Subject as follows, the liquidator may be removed from office only by an order of the court or by a general meeting of the company's creditors summoned specially for that purpose in accordance with the rules; and a provisional liquidator may be removed from office only by an order of the court.

(3) Where—
(a) the official receiver is liquidator otherwise than in succession under section 136(3) to a person who held office as a result of a nomination by a meeting of the company's creditors or contributories, or
(b) the liquidator was appointed by the court otherwise than under section ... 140(1), or was appointed by the Secretary of State,
a general meeting of the company's creditors shall be summoned for the purpose of replacing him only if he thinks fit, or the court so directs, or the meeting is requested, in accordance with the rules, by not less than one-quarter, in value, of the creditors.

(4) If appointed by the Secretary of State, the liquidator may be removed from office by a direction of the Secretary of State.

(5) A liquidator or provisional liquidator, not being the official receiver, shall vacate office if he ceases to be a person who is qualified to act as an insolvency practitioner in relation to the company.

(6) A liquidator may, in the prescribed circumstances, resign his office by giving notice of his resignation to the court.

(8) Where a final meeting has been held under section 146 (liquidator's report on completion of winding up), the liquidator whose report was considered at the meeting shall vacate office as soon as he has given notice to the court and the registrar of companies that the meeting has been held and of the decisions (if any) of the meeting.

Chapter VIII PROVISIONS OF GENERAL APPLICATION IN WINDING UP

Preferential debts

175 PREFERENTIAL DEBTS (GENERAL PROVISION)

(1) In a winding up the company's preferential debts (within the meaning given by section 386 in Part XII) shall be paid in priority to all other debts.

(2) Preferential debts—
(a) rank equally among themselves after the expenses of the winding up and shall be paid in full, unless the assets are insufficient to meet them, in which case they abate in equal proportions; and
(b) so far as the assets of the company available for payment of general creditors are insufficient to meet them, have priority over the claims of holders of debentures secured by, or holders of, any floating charge created by the company, and shall be paid accordingly out of any property comprised in or subject to that charge.

Property subject to floating charge

176ZA PAYMENT OF EXPENSES OF WINDING UP (ENGLAND AND WALES)

(1) The expenses of winding up in England and Wales, so far as the assets of the company available for payment of general creditors are insufficient to meet them, have priority over any claims to property comprised in or subject to any floating charge created by the company and shall be paid out of any such property accordingly.

(2) In subsection (1)—
(a) the reference to assets of the company available for payment of general creditors does not include any amount made available under section 176A(2)(a);
(b) the reference to claims to property comprised in or subject to a floating charge is to the claims of—
(i) the holders of debentures secured by, or holders of, the floating charge, and
(ii) any preferential creditors entitled to be paid out of that property in priority to them.

(3) Provision may be made by rules restricting the application of subsection (1), in such circumstances as may be prescribed, to expenses authorised or approved—
(a) by the holders of debentures secured by, or holders of, the floating charge and by any preferential creditors entitled to be paid in priority to them, or
(b) by the court.

(4) References in this section to the expenses of the winding up are to all expenses properly incurred in the winding up, including the remuneration of the liquidator.

176A SHARE OF ASSETS FOR UNSECURED CREDITORS

(1) This section applies where a floating charge relates to property of a company—
(a) which has gone into liquidation,
(b) which is in administration,
(c) of which there is a provisional liquidator, or
(d) of which there is a receiver.

(2) The liquidator, administrator or receiver—
 (a) shall make a prescribed part of the company's net property available for the satisfaction of unsecured debts, and
 (b) shall not distribute that part to the proprietor of a floating charge except in so far as it exceeds the amount required for the satisfaction of unsecured debts.

(3) Subsection (2) shall not apply to a company if—
 (a) the company's net property is less than the prescribed minimum, and
 (b) the liquidator, administrator or receiver thinks that the cost of making a distribution to unsecured creditors would be disproportionate to the benefits.

(4) Subsection (2) shall also not apply to a company if or in so far as it is disapplied by—
 (a) a voluntary arrangement in respect of the company, or
 (b) a compromise or arrangement agreed under Part 26 of the Companies Act 2006 (arrangements and reconstructions).

(5) Subsection (2) shall also not apply to a company if—
 (a) the liquidator, administrator or receiver applies to the court for an order under this subsection on the ground that the cost of making a distribution to unsecured creditors would be disproportionate to the benefits, and
 (b) the court orders that subsection (2) shall not apply.

(6) In subsections (2) and (3) a company's net property is the amount of its property which would, but for this section, be available for satisfaction of claims of holders of debentures secured by, or holders of, any floating charge created by the company.

(7) An order under subsection (2) prescribing part of a company's net property may, in particular, provide for its calculation—
 (a) as a percentage of the company's net property, or
 (b) as an aggregate of different percentages of different parts of the company's net property.

(8) An order under this section—
 (a) must be made by statutory instrument, and
 (b) shall be subject to annulment pursuant to a resolution of either House of Parliament.

(9) In this section—

"floating charge" means a charge which is a floating charge on its creation and which is created after the first order under subsection (2)(a) comes into force, and

"prescribed" means prescribed by order by the Secretary of State.

(10) An order under this section may include transitional or incidental provision.

Miscellaneous matters

187 POWER TO MAKE OVER ASSETS TO EMPLOYEES

(1) On the winding up of a company (whether by the court or voluntarily), the liquidator may, subject to the following provisions of this section, make any payment which the company has, before the commencement of the winding up, decided to make under section 247 of the Companies Act 2006 (power to provide for employees or former employees on cessation or transfer of business).

(2) The liquidator may, after the winding up has commenced, make any such provision as is mentioned in section 247(1) if—

(a) the company's liabilities have been fully satisfied and provision has been made for the expenses of the winding up,
(b) the exercise of the power has been sanctioned by a resolution of the company, and
(c) any requirements of the company's articles as to the exercise of the power conferred by section 247(1) are complied with.

(3) Any payment which may be made by a company under this section (that is, a payment after the commencement of its winding up) may be made out of the company's assets which are available to the members on the winding up.

(4) On a winding up by the court, the exercise by the liquidator of his powers under this section is subject to the court's control, and any creditor or contributory may apply to the court with respect to any exercise or proposed exercise of the power.

(5) Subsections (1) and (2) above have effect notwithstanding anything in any rule of law or in section 107 of this Act (property of company after satisfaction of liabilities to be distributed among members).

188 NOTIFICATION THAT COMPANY IS IN LIQUIDATION

(1) When a company is being wound up, whether by the court or voluntarily—
(a) every invoice, order for goods, business letter or order form (whether in hard copy, electronic or any other form) issued by or on behalf of the company, or a liquidator of the company or a receiver or manager of the company's property, being a document on or in which the name of the company appears, and
(b) all the company's websites,
must contain a statement that the company is being wound up.

(2) If default is made in complying with this section, the company and any of the following persons who knowingly and wilfully authorises or permits the default, namely, any officer of the company, any liquidator of the company and any receiver or manager, is liable to a fine.

189 INTEREST ON DEBTS

(1) In a winding up interest is payable in accordance with this section on any debt proved in the winding up, including so much of any such debt as represents interest on the remainder.

(2) Any surplus remaining after the payment of the debts proved in a winding up shall, before being applied for any other purpose, be applied in paying interest on those debts in respect of the periods during which they have been outstanding since the company went into liquidation.

(3) All interest under this section ranks equally, whether or not the debts on which it is payable rank equally.

(4) The rate of interest payable under this section in respect of any debt ("the official rate" for the purposes of any provision of this Act in which that expression is used) is whichever is the greater of—
(a) the rate specified in section 17 of the Judgments Act 1838 on the day on which the company went into liquidation, and
(b) the rate applicable to that debt apart from the winding up.

(5) In the application of this section to Scotland—
 (a) references to a debt proved in a winding up have effect as references to a claim accepted in a winding up, and
 (b) the reference to section 17 of the Judgments Act 1838 has effect as a reference to the rules.

195 MEETINGS TO ASCERTAIN WISHES OF CREDITORS OR CONTRIBUTORIES

(1) The court may—
 (a) as to all matters relating to the winding up of a company, have regard to the wishes of the creditors or contributories (as proved to it by any sufficient evidence), and
 (b) if it thinks fit, for the purpose of ascertaining those wishes, direct meetings of the creditors or contributories to be called, held and conducted in such manner as the court directs, and appoint a person to act as chairman of any such meeting and report the result of it to the court.

(2) In the case of creditors, regard shall be had to the value of each creditor's debt.

(3) In the case of contributories, regard shall be had to the number of votes conferred on each contributory.

Chapter IX DISSOLUTION OF COMPANIES AFTER WINDING UP

201 DISSOLUTION (VOLUNTARY WINDING UP)

(1) This section applies, in the case of a company wound up voluntarily, where the liquidator has sent to the registrar of companies his final account and return under section 94 (members' voluntary) or section 106 (creditors' voluntary).

(2) The registrar on receiving the account and return shall forthwith register them; and on the expiration of 3 months from the registration of the return the company is deemed to be dissolved.

205 DISSOLUTION OTHERWISE THAN UNDER SS. 202–204

(1) This section applies where the registrar of companies receives—
 (a) a notice served for the purposes of section 172(8) (final meeting of creditors and vacation of office by liquidator), or
 (b) a notice, from the official receiver that the winding up of a company by the court is complete.

(2) The registrar shall, on receipt of the notice, forthwith register it; and, subject, as follows, at the end of the period of 3 months beginning with the day of the registration of the notice, the company shall be dissolved.

Chapter X MALPRACTICE BEFORE AND DURING LIQUIDATION; PENALISATION OF COMPANIES AND COMPANY OFFICERS; INVESTIGATIONS AND PROSECUTIONS

Offences of fraud, deception, etc.

206 FRAUD, ETC., IN ANTICIPATION OF WINDING UP

(1) When a company is ordered to be wound up by the court, or passes a resolution for voluntary winding up, any person, being a past or present officer of the company, is

deemed to have committed an offence if, within the 12 months immediately preceding the commencement of the winding up, he has—

(a) concealed any part of the company's property to the value of £500 or more, or concealed any debt due to or from the company, or
(b) fraudulently removed any part of the company's property to the value of £500 or more, or
(c) concealed, destroyed, mutilated or falsified any book or paper affecting or relating to the company's property or affairs, or
(d) made any false entry in any book or paper affecting or relating to the company's property or affairs, or
(e) fraudulently parted with, altered or made any omission in any document affecting or relating to the company's property or affairs, or
(f) pawned, pledged or disposed of any property of the company which has been obtained on credit and has not been paid for (unless the pawning, pledging or disposal was in the ordinary way of the company's business).

(2) Such a person is deemed to have committed an offence if within the period above mentioned he has been privy to the doing by others of any of the things mentioned in paragraphs (c), (d) and (e) of subsection (1); and he commits an offence if, at any time after the commencement of the winding up, he does any of the things mentioned in paragraphs (a) to (f) of that subsection, or is privy to the doing by others of any of the things mentioned in paragraphs (c) to (e) of it.

(3) For purposes of this section, "officer" includes a shadow director.

(4) It is a defence—

(a) for a person charged under paragraph (a) or (f) of subsection (1) (or under subsection (2) in respect of the things mentioned in either of those two paragraphs) to prove that he had no intent to defraud, and
(b) for a person charged under paragraph (c) or (d) of subsection (1) (or under subsection (2) in respect of the things mentioned in either of those two paragraphs) to prove that he had no intent to conceal the state of affairs of the company or to defeat the law.

(5) Where a person pawns, pledges or disposes of any property in circumstances which amount to an offence under subsection (1)(f), every person who takes in pawn or pledge, or otherwise receives, the property knowing it to be pawned, pledged or disposed of in such circumstances, is guilty of an offence.

(6) A person guilty of an offence under this section is liable to imprisonment or a fine, or both.

(7) The money sums specified in paragraphs (a) and (b) of subsection (1) are subject to increase or reduction by order under section 416 in Part XV.

207 TRANSACTIONS IN FRAUD OF CREDITORS

(1) When a company is ordered to be wound up by the court or passes a resolution for voluntary winding up, a person is deemed to have committed an offence if he, being at the time an officer of the company—

(a) has made or caused to be made any gift or transfer of, or charge on, or has caused or connived at the levying of any execution against, the company's property, or
(b) has concealed or removed any part of the company's property since, or within 2 months before, the date of any unsatisfied judgment or order for the payment of money obtained against the company.

(2) A person is not guilty of an offence under this section—
  (a) by reason of conduct constituting an offence under subsection (1)(a) which occurred more than 5 years before the commencement of the winding up, or
  (b) if he proves that, at the time of the conduct constituting the offence, he had no intent to defraud the company's creditors.

(3) A person guilty of an offence under this section is liable to imprisonment or a fine, or both.

208 MISCONDUCT IN COURSE OF WINDING UP

(1) When a company is being wound up, whether by the court or voluntarily, any person, being a past or present officer of the company, commits an offence if he—
  (a) does not to the best of his knowledge and belief fully and truly discover to the liquidator all the company's property, and how and to whom and for what consideration and when the company disposed of any part of that property (except such part as has been disposed of in the ordinary way of the company's business), or
  (b) does not deliver up to the liquidator (or as he directs) all such part of the company's property as is in his custody or under his control, and which he is required by law to deliver up, or
  (c) does not deliver up to the liquidator (or as he directs) all books and papers in his custody or under his control belonging to the company and which he is required by law to deliver up, or
  (d) knowing or believing that a false debt has been proved by any person in the winding up, fails to inform the liquidator as soon as practicable, or
  (e) after the commencement of the winding up, prevents the production of any book or paper affecting or relating to the company's property or affairs.

(2) Such a person commits an offence if after the commencement of the winding up he attempts to account for any part of the company's property by fictitious losses or expenses; and he is deemed to have committed that offence if he has so attempted at any meeting of the company's creditors within the 12 months immediately preceding the commencement of the winding up.

(3) For purposes of this section, "officer" includes a shadow director.

(4) It is a defence—
  (a) for a person charged under paragraph (a), (b) or (c) of subsection (1) to prove that he had no intent to defraud, and
  (b) for a person charged under paragraph (e) of that subsection to prove that he had no intent to conceal the state of affairs of the company or to defeat the law.

(5) A person guilty of an offence under this section is liable to imprisonment or a fine, or both.

209 FALSIFICATION OF COMPANY'S BOOKS

(1) When a company is being wound up, an officer or contributory of the company commits an offence if he destroys, mutilates, alters or falsifies any books, papers or securities, or makes or is privy to the making of any false or fraudulent entry in any register, book of account or document belonging to the company with intent to defraud or deceive any person.

(2) A person guilty of an offence under this section is liable to imprisonment or a fine, or both.

210 MATERIAL OMISSIONS FROM STATEMENT RELATING TO COMPANY'S AFFAIRS

(1) When a company is being wound up, whether by the court or voluntarily, any person, being a past or present officer of the company, commits an offence if he makes any material omission in any statement relating to the company's affairs.

(2) When a company has been ordered to be wound up by the court, or has passed a resolution for voluntary winding up, any such person is deemed to have committed that offence if, prior to the winding up, he has made any material omission in any such statement.

(3) For purposes of this section, "officer" includes a shadow director.

(4) It is a defence for a person charged under this section to prove that he had no intent to defraud.

(5) A person guilty of an offence under this section is liable to imprisonment or a fine, or both.

211 FALSE REPRESENTATIONS TO CREDITORS

(1) When a company is being wound up, whether by the court or voluntarily, any person, being a past or present officer of the company—
   (a) commits an offence if he makes any false representation or commits any other fraud for the purpose of obtaining the consent of the company's creditors or any of them to an agreement with reference to the company's affairs or to the winding up, and
   (b) is deemed to have committed that offence if, prior to the winding up, he has made any false representation, or committed any other fraud, for that purpose.

(2) For purposes of this section, "officer" includes a shadow director.

(3) A person guilty of an offence under this section is liable to imprisonment or a fine, or both.

Penalisation of directors and officers

212 SUMMARY REMEDY AGAINST DELINQUENT DIRECTORS, LIQUIDATORS, ETC.

(1) This section applies if in the course of the winding up of a company it appears that a person who—
   (a) is or has been an officer of the company,
   (b) has acted as liquidator or administrative receiver of the company, or
   (c) not being a person falling within paragraph (a) or (b), is or has been concerned, or has taken part, in the promotion, formation or management of the company,

has misapplied or retained, or become accountable for, any money or other property of the company, or been guilty of any misfeasance or breach of any fiduciary or other duty in relation to the company.

(2) The reference in subsection (1) to any misfeasance or breach of any fiduciary or other duty in relation to the company includes, in the case of a person who has acted as liquidator of the company, any misfeasance or breach of any fiduciary or other duty in connection with the carrying out of his functions as liquidator of the company.

(3) The court may, on the application of the official receiver or the liquidator, or of any creditor or contributory, examine into the conduct of the person falling within subsection (1) and compel him—
(a) to repay, restore or account for the money or property or any part of it, with interest at such rate as the court thinks just, or
(b) to contribute such sum to the company's assets by way of compensation in respect of the misfeasance or breach of fiduciary or other duty as the court thinks just.

(4) The power to make an application under subsection (3) in relation to a person who has acted as liquidator of the company is not exercisable, except with the leave of the court, after he has had his release.

(5) The power of a contributory to make an application under subsection (3) is not exercisable except with the leave of the court, but is exercisable notwithstanding that he will not benefit from any order the court may make on the application.

213 FRAUDULENT TRADING

(1) If in the course of the winding up of a company it appears that any business of the company has been carried on with intent to defraud creditors of the company or creditors of any other person, or for any fraudulent purpose, the following has effect.

(2) The court, on the application of the liquidator may declare that any persons who were knowingly parties to the carrying on of the business in the manner above-mentioned are to be liable to make such contributions (if any) to the company's assets as the court thinks proper.

214 WRONGFUL TRADING

(1) Subject to subsection (3) below, if in the course of the winding up of a company it appears that subsection (2) of this section applies in relation to a person who is or has been a director of the company, the court, on the application of the liquidator, may declare that that person is to be liable to make such contribution (if any) to the company's assets as the court thinks proper.

(2) This subsection applies in relation to a person if—
(a) the company has gone into insolvent liquidation,
(b) at some time before the commencement of the winding up of the company, that person knew or ought to have concluded that there was no reasonable prospect that the company would avoid going into insolvent liquidation, and
(c) that person was a director of the company at that time;
but the court shall not make a declaration under this section in any case where the time mentioned in paragraph (b) above was before 28th April 1986.

(3) The court shall not make a declaration under this section with respect to any person if it is satisfied that after the condition specified in subsection (2)(b) was first satisfied in relation to him that person took every step with a view to minimising the potential loss to the company's creditors as (assuming him to have known that there was no reasonable prospect that the company would avoid going into solvent liquidation) he ought to have taken.

(4) For the purposes of subsections (2) and (3), the facts which a director of a company ought to know or ascertain, the conclusions which he ought to reach and the steps which he ought to take are those which would be known or ascertained, or reached or taken, by a reasonably diligent person having both—

(a) the general knowledge, skill and experience that may reasonably be expected of a person carrying out the same functions as are carried out by that director in relation to the company, and
(b) the general knowledge, skill and experience that that director has.

(5) The reference in subsection (4) to the functions carried out in relation to a company by a director of the company includes any functions which he does not carry out but which have been entrusted to him.

(6) For the purposes of this section a company goes into insolvent liquidation if it goes into liquidation at a time when its assets are insufficient for the payment of its debts and other liabilities and the expenses of the winding up.

(7) In this section "director" includes a shadow director.

(8) This section is without prejudice to section 213.

215 PROCEEDINGS UNDER SS. 213, 214

(1) On the hearing of an application under section 213 or 214, the liquidator may himself give evidence or call witnesses.

(2) Where under either section the court makes a declaration, it may give such further directions as it thinks proper for giving effect to the declaration; and in particular, the court may—
(a) provide for the liability of any person under the declaration to be a charge on any debt or obligation due from the company to him, or on any mortgage or charge or any interest in a mortgage or charge on assets of the company held by or vested in him, or any person on his behalf, or any person claiming as assignee from or through the person liable or any person acting on his behalf, and
(b) from time to time make such further order as may be necessary for enforcing any charge imposed under this subsection.

(3) For the purposes of subsection (2), "assignee"—
(a) includes a person to whom or in whose favour, by the directions of the person made liable, the debt, obligation, mortgage or charge was created, issued or transferred or the interest created, but
(b) does not include an assignee for valuable consideration (not including consideration by way of marriage or the formation of a civil partnership given in good faith and without notice of any of the matters on the ground of which the declaration is made).

(4) Where the court makes a declaration under either section in relation to a person who is a creditor of the company, it may direct that the whole or any part of any debt owed by the company to that person and any interest thereon shall rank in priority after all other debts owed by the company and after any interest on those debts.

(5) Sections 213 and 214 have effect notwithstanding that the person concerned may be criminally liable in respect of matters on the ground of which the declaration under the section is to be made.

216 RESTRICTION ON RE-USE OF COMPANY NAMES

(1) This section applies to a person where a company ("the liquidating company") has gone into insolvent liquidation on or after the appointed day and he was a director or shadow director of the company at any time in the period of 12 months ending with the day before it went into liquidation.

(2) For the purposes of this section, a name is a prohibited name in relation to such a person if—
(a) it is a name by which the liquidating company was known at any time in that period of 12 months, or
(b) it is a name which is so similar to a name falling within paragraph (a) as to suggest an association with that company.

(3) Except with leave of the court or in such circumstances as may be prescribed, a person to whom this section applies shall not at any time in the period of 5 years beginning with the day on which the liquidating company went into liquidation—
(a) be a director of any other company that is known by a prohibited name, or
(b) in any way, whether directly or indirectly, be concerned or take part in the promotion, formation or management of any such company, or
(c) in any way, whether directly or indirectly, be concerned or take part in the carrying on of a business carried on (otherwise than by a company) under a prohibited name.

(4) If a person acts in contravention of this section, he is liable to imprisonment or a fine, or both.

(5) In subsection (3) "the court" means any court having jurisdiction to wind up companies; and on an application for leave under that subsection, the Secretary of State or the official receiver may appear and call the attention of the court to any matters which seem to him to be relevant.

(6) References in this section, in relation to any time, to a name by which a company is known are to the name of the company at that time or to any name under which the company carries on business at that time.

(7) For the purposes of this section a company goes into insolvent liquidation if it goes into liquidation at a time when its assets are insufficient for the payment of its debts and other liabilities and the expenses of the winding up.

(8) In this section "company" includes a company which may be wound up under Part V of this Act.

217 PERSONAL LIABILITY FOR DEBTS, FOLLOWING CONTRAVENTION OF S. 216

(1) A person is personally responsible for all the relevant debts of a company if at any time—
(a) in contravention of section 216, he is involved in the management of the company, or
(b) as a person who is involved in the management of the company, he acts or is willing to act on instructions given (without the leave of the court) by a person whom he knows at that time to be in contravention in relation to the company of section 216.

(2) Where a person is personally responsible under this section for the relevant debts of a company, he is jointly and severally liable in respect of those debts with the company and any other person who, whether under this section or otherwise, is so liable.

(3) For the purposes of this section the relevant debts of a company are—
(a) in relation to a person who is personally responsible under paragraph (a) of subsection (1), such debts and other liabilities of the company as are incurred at a time when that person was involved in the management of the company, and
(b) in relation to a person who is personally responsible under paragraph (b) of that subsection, such debts and other liabilities of the company as are incurred at a time when that person was acting or was willing to act on instructions given as mentioned in that paragraph.

(4) For the purposes of this section, a person is involved in the management of a company if he is a director of the company or if he is concerned, whether directly or indirectly, or takes part, in the management of the company.

(5) For the purposes of this section a person who, as a person involved in the management of a company, has at any time acted on instructions given (without the leave of the court) by a person whom he knew at that time to be in contravention in relation to the company of section 216 is presumed, unless the contrary is shown, to have been willing at any time thereafter to act on any instructions given by that person.

(6) In this section "company" includes a company which may be wound up under Part V.

Investigation and prosecution of malpractice

218 PROSECUTION OF DELINQUENT OFFICERS AND MEMBERS OF COMPANY

(1) If it appears to the court in the course of a winding up by the court that any past or present officer, or any member, of the company has been guilty of any offence in relation to the company for which he is criminally liable, the court may (either on the application of a person interested in the winding up or of its own motion) direct the liquidator to refer the matter—

(a) in the case of a winding up in England and Wales, to the Secretary of State, and
(b) in the case of a winding up in Scotland, to the Lord Advocate.

(3) If in the case of a winding up by the court in England and Wales it appears to the liquidator, not being the official receiver, that any past or present officer of the company, or any member of it, has been guilty of an offence in relation to the company for which he is criminally liable, the liquidator shall report the matter to the official receiver.

(4) If it appears to the liquidator in the course of a voluntary winding up that any past or present officer of the company, or any member of it, has been guilty of an offence in relation to the company for which he is criminally liable, he shall forthwith report the matter—

(a) in the case of a winding up in England and Wales, to the Secretary of State, and
(b) in the case of a winding up in Scotland, to the Lord Advocate,

and shall furnish to the Secretary of State or (as the case may be) the Lord Advocate such information and give to him such access to and facilities for inspecting and taking copies of documents (being information or documents in the possession or under the control of the liquidator and relating to the matter in question) as the Secretary of State or (as the case may be) the Lord Advocate requires.

(5) Where a report is made to the Secretary of State under subsection (4) he may, for the purpose of investigating the matter reported to him and such other matters relating to the affairs of the company as appear to him to require investigation, exercise any of the powers which are exercisable by inspectors appointed under section 431 or 432 of the Companies Act 1985 to investigate a company's affairs.

(6) If it appears to the court in the course of a voluntary winding up that—

(a) any past or present officer of the company, or any member of it, has been guilty as above-mentioned, and
(b) no report with respect to the matter has been made by the liquidator under subsection (4),

the court may (on the application of any person interested in the winding up or of its own motion) direct the liquidator to make such a report.

On a report being made accordingly, this section has effect as though the report had been made in pursuance of subsection (4).

219 OBLIGATIONS ARISING UNDER S. 218

(1) For the purpose of an investigation by the Secretary of State in consequence of a report made to him under section 218(4), any obligation imposed on a person by any provision of the Companies Act 1985 to produce documents or give information to, or otherwise to assist, inspectors appointed as mentioned in section 218(5) is to be regarded as an obligation similarly to assist the Secretary of State in his investigation.

(2) An answer given by a person to a question put to him in exercise of the powers conferred by section 218(5) may be used in evidence against him.

Part VI MISCELLANEOUS PROVISIONS APPLYING TO COMPANIES WHICH ARE INSOLVENT OR IN LIQUIDATION

Management by administrators, liquidators, etc.

234 GETTING IN THE COMPANY'S PROPERTY

(1) This section applies in the case of a company where—
   (a) the company enters administration, or
   (b) an administrative receiver is appointed, or
   (c) the company goes into liquidation, or
   (d) a provisional liquidator is appointed;

and "the office-holder" means the administrator, the administrative receiver, the liquidator or the provisional liquidator, as the case may be.

(2) Where any person has in his possession or control any property, books, papers or records to which the company appears to be entitled, the court may require that person forthwith (or within such period as the court may direct) to pay, deliver, convey, surrender or transfer the property, books, papers or records to the office-holder.

(3) Where the office-holder—
   (a) seizes or disposes of any property which is not property of the company, and
   (b) at the time of seizure or disposal believes, and has reasonable grounds for believing, that he is entitled (whether in pursuance of an order of the court or otherwise) to seize or dispose of that property,

the next subsection has effect.

(4) In that case the office-holder—
   (a) is not liable to any person in respect of any loss or damage resulting from the seizure or disposal except in so far as that loss or damage is caused by the office-holder's own negligence, and
   (b) has a lien on the property, or the proceeds of its sale, for such expenses as were incurred in connection with the seizure or disposal.

235 DUTY TO CO-OPERATE WITH OFFICE-HOLDER

(1) This section applies as does section 234; and it also applies, in the case of a company in respect of which a winding-up order has been made by the court in England and Wales, as if references to the office-holder included the official receiver, whether or not he is the liquidator.

(2) Each of the persons mentioned in the next subsection shall—
(a) give to the office-holder such information concerning the company and its promotion, formation, business, dealings, affairs or property as the office-holder may at any time after the effective date reasonably require, and
(b) attend on the office-holder at such times as the latter may reasonably require.

(3) The persons referred to above are—
(a) those who are or have at any time been officers of the company,
(b) those who have taken part in the formation of the company at any time within one year before the effective date,
(c) those who are in the employment of the company, or have been in its employment (including employment under a contract for services) within that year, and are in the office-holder's opinion capable of giving information which he requires,
(d) those who are, or have within that year been, officers of, or in the employment (including employment under a contract for services) of, another company which is, or within that year was, an officer of the company in question, and
(e) in the case of a company being wound up by the court, any person who has acted as administrator, administrative receiver or liquidator of the company.

(4) For the purposes of subsections (2) and (3), "the effective date" is whichever is applicable of the following dates—
(a) the date on which the company entered administration,
(b) the date on which the administrative receiver was appointed or, if he was appointed in succession to another administrative receiver, the date on which the first of his predecessors was appointed,
(c) the date on which the provisional liquidator was appointed, and
(d) the date on which the company went into liquidation.

(5) If a person without reasonable excuse fails to comply with any obligation imposed by this section, he is liable to a fine and, for continued contravention, to a daily default fine.

236 INQUIRY INTO COMPANY'S DEALINGS, ETC.

(1) This section applies as does section 234; and it also applies in the case of a company in respect of which a winding-up order has been made by the court in England and Wales as if references to the office-holder included the official receiver, whether or not he is the liquidator.

(2) The court may, on the application of the office-holder, summon to appear before it—
(a) any officer of the company,
(b) any person known or suspected to have in his possession any property of the company or supposed to be indebted to the company, or
(c) any person whom the court thinks capable of giving information concerning the promotion, formation, business, dealings, affairs or property of the company.

(3) The court may require any such person as is mentioned in subsection (2)(a) to (c) to submit to the court an account of his dealings with the company or to produce any books, papers or other records in his possession or under his control relating to the company or the matters mentioned in paragraph (c) of the subsection.

(3A) An account submitted to the court under subsection (3) must be contained in—
(a) a witness statement verified by a statement of truth (in England and Wales), and
(b) an affidavit (in Scotland).

(4) The following applies in a case where—

(a) a person without reasonable excuse fails to appear before the court when he is summoned to do so under this section, or
(b) there are reasonable grounds for believing that a person has absconded, or is about to abscond, with a view to avoiding his appearance before the court under this section.

(5) The court may, for the purpose of bringing that person and anything in his possession before the court, cause a warrant to be issued to a constable or prescribed officer of the court—
(a) for the arrest of that person, and
(b) for the seizure of any books, papers, records, money or goods in that person's possession.

(6) The court may authorise a person arrested under such a warrant to be kept in custody, and anything seized under such a warrant to be held, in accordance with the rules, until that person is brought before the court under the warrant or until such other time as the court may order.

237 COURT'S ENFORCEMENT POWERS UNDER S. 236

(1) If it appears to the court, on consideration of any evidence obtained under section 236 or this section, that any person has in his possession any property of the company, the court may, on the application of the office-holder, order that person to deliver the whole or any part of the property to the office-holder at such time, in such manner and on such terms as the court thinks fit.

(2) If it appears to the court, on consideration of any evidence so obtained, that any person is indebted to the company, the court may, on the application of the office-holder, order that person to pay to the office holder, at such time and in such manner as the court may direct, the whole or any part of the amount due, whether in full discharge of the debt or otherwise, as the court thinks fit.

(3) The court may, if it thinks fit, order that any person who if within the jurisdiction of the court would be liable to be summoned to appear before it under section 236 or this section shall be examined in any part of the United Kingdom where he may for the time being be, or in a place outside the United Kingdom.

(4) Any person who appears or is brought before the court under section 236 or this section may be examined on oath, either orally or (except in Scotland) by interrogatories, concerning the company or the matters mentioned in section 236(2)(c).

Adjustment of prior transactions (administration and liquidation)

238 TRANSACTIONS AT AN UNDERVALUE (ENGLAND AND WALES)

(1) This section applies in the case of a company where—
(a) the company enters administration,
(b) the company goes into liquidation;
and "the office-holder" means the administrator or the liquidator, as the case may be.

(2) Where the company has at a relevant time (defined in section 240) entered into a transaction with any person at an undervalue, the office-holder may apply to the court for an order under this section.

(3) Subject as follows, the court shall, on such an application, make such order as it thinks fit for restoring the position to what it would have been if the company had not entered into that transaction.

(4) For the purposes of this section and section 241, a company enters into a transaction with a person at an undervalue if—
(a) the company makes a gift to that person or otherwise enters into a transaction with that person on terms that provide for the company to receive no consideration, or
(b) the company enters into a transaction with that person for a consideration the value of which, in money or money's worth, is significantly less than the value, in money or money's worth, of the consideration provided by the company.

(5) The court shall not make an order under this section in respect of a transaction at an undervalue if it is satisfied—
(a) that the company which entered into the transaction did so in good faith and for the purpose of carrying on its business, and
(b) that at the time it did so there were reasonable grounds for believing that the transaction would benefit the company.

239 PREFERENCES (ENGLAND AND WALES)

(1) This section applies as does section 238.

(2) Where the company has at a relevant time (defined in the next section) given a preference to any person, the office-holder may apply to the court for an order under this section.

(3) Subject as follows, the court shall, on such an application, make such order as it thinks fit for restoring the position to what it would have been if the company had not given that preference.

(4) For the purposes of this section and section 241, a company gives a preference to a person if—
(a) that person is one of the company's creditors or a surety or guarantor for any of the company's debts or other liabilities, and
(b) the company does anything or suffers anything to be done which (in either case) has the effect of putting that person into a position which, in the event of the company going into insolvent liquidation, will be better than the position he would have been in if that thing had not been done.

(5) The court shall not make an order under this section in respect of a preference given to any person unless the company which gave the preference was influenced in deciding to give it by a desire to produce in relation to that person the effect mentioned in subsection (4)(b).

(6) A company which has given a preference to a person connected with the company (otherwise than by reason only of being its employee) at the time the preference was given is presumed, unless the contrary is shown, to have been influenced in deciding to give it by such a desire as is mentioned in subsection (5).

(7) The fact that something has been done in pursuance of the order of a court does not, without more, prevent the doing or suffering of that thing from constituting the giving of a preference.

240 "RELEVANT TIME" UNDER SS. 238, 239

(1) Subject to the next subsection, the time at which a company enters into a transaction at an undervalue or gives a preference is a relevant time if the transaction is entered into, or the preference given—
(a) in the case of a transaction at an undervalue or of a preference which is given to a person who is connected with the company (otherwise than by reason only of being

its employee), at a time in the period of 2 years ending with the onset of insolvency (which expression is defined below),
(b) in the case of a preference which is not such a transaction and is not so given, at a time in the period of 6 months ending with the onset of insolvency,
(c) in either case, at a time between the making of an administration application in respect of the company and the making of an administration order on that application, and
(d) in either case, at a time between the filing with the court of a copy of notice of intention to appoint an administrator under paragraph 14 or 22 of Schedule B1 and the making of an appointment under that paragraph.

(2) Where a company enters into a transaction at an undervalue or gives a preference at a time mentioned in subsection (1)(a) or (b), that time is not a relevant time for the purposes of section 238 or 239 unless the company—
(a) is at that time unable to pay its debts within the meaning of section 123 in Chapter VI of Part IV, or
(b) becomes unable to pay its debts within the meaning of that section in consequence of the transaction or preference;
but the requirements of this subsection are presumed to be satisfied, unless the contrary is shown, in relation to any transaction at an undervalue which is entered into by a company with a person who is connected with the company.

(3) For the purposes of subsection (1), the onset of insolvency is—
(a) in a case where section 238 or 239 applies by reason of an administrator of a company being appointed by administration order, the date on which the administration application is made,
(aa) in a case where section 238 or 239 applies by reason of a company going into liquidation following conversion of administration into winding up by virtue of Article 37 of the EC Regulation, the date of the presentation of the petition on which the administration order was made,
(b) in a case where section 238 or 239 applies by reason of an administrator of a company being appointed under paragraph 14 or 22 of Schedule B1 following filing with the court of a copy of a notice of intention to appoint under that paragraph, the date on which the copy of the notice is filed,
(c) in a case where section 238 or 239 applies by reason of an administrator of a company being appointed otherwise than as mentioned in paragraph (a) or (b), the date on which the appointment takes effect,
(d) in a case where section 238 or 239 applies by reason of a company going into liquidation either following conversion of administration into winding up by virtue of Article 37 of the EC Regulation or at the time when the appointment of an administrator ceases to have effect, the date on which the company entered administration (or, if relevant, the date on which the application for the administration order was made or a copy of the notice of intention to appoint was filed), and
(e) in a case where section 238 or 239 applies by reason of a company going into liquidation at any other time, the date of the commencement of the winding up.

241 ORDERS UNDER SS. 238, 239

(1) Without prejudice to the generality of sections 238(3) and 239(3), an order under either of those sections with respect to a transaction or preference entered into or given by a company may (subject to the next subsection)—

(a) require any property transferred as part of the transaction, or in connection with the giving of the preference, to be vested in the company,
(b) require any property to be so vested if it represents in any person's hands the application either of the proceeds of sale of property so transferred or of money so transferred,
(c) release or discharge (in whole or in part) any security given by the company,
(d) require any person to pay, in respect of benefits received by him from the company, such sums to the office-holder as the court may direct,
(e) provide for any surety or guarantor whose obligations to any person were released or discharged (in whole or in part) under the transaction, or by the giving of the preference, to be under such new or revived obligations to that person as the court thinks appropriate,
(f) provide for security to be provided for the discharge of any obligation imposed by or arising under the order, for such an obligation to be charged on any property and for the security or charge to have the same priority as a security or charge released or discharged (in whole or in part) under the transaction or by the giving of the preference, and
(g) provide for the extent to which any person whose property is vested by the order in the company, or on whom obligations are imposed by the order, is to be able to prove in the winding up of the company for debts or other liabilities which arose from, or were released or discharged (in whole or in part) under or by, the transaction or the giving of the preference.

(2) An order under section 238 or 239 may affect the property of, or impose any obligation on, any person whether or not he is the person with whom the company in question entered into the transaction or (as the case may be) the person to whom the preference was given; but such an order—
(a) shall not prejudice any interest in property which was acquired from a person other than the company and was acquired in good faith and for value, or prejudice any interest deriving from such an interest, and
(b) shall not require a person who received a benefit from the transaction or preference in good faith and for value to pay a sum to the office-holder, except where that person was a party to the transaction or the payment is to be in respect of a preference given to that person at a time when he was a creditor of the company.

(4) The provisions of sections 238 to 241 apply without prejudice to the availability of any other remedy, even in relation to a transaction or preference which the company had no power to enter into or give.

242 GRATUITOUS ALIENATIONS (SCOTLAND)

(1) Where this subsection applies and—
(a) the winding up of a company has commenced, an alienation by the company is challengeable by—
(i) any creditor who is a creditor by virtue of a debt incurred on or before the date of such commencement, or
(ii) the liquidator;
(b) a company enters administration, an alienation by the company is challengeable by the administrator.

(2) Subsection (1) applies where—
(a) by the alienation, whether before or after 1st April 1986 (the coming into force of section 75 of the Bankruptcy (Scotland) Act 1985), any part of the company's

property is transferred or any claim or right of the company is discharged or renounced, and

(b) the alienation takes place on a relevant day.

(3) For the purposes of subsection (2)(b), the day on which an alienation takes place is the day on which it becomes completely effectual; and in that subsection "relevant day" means, if the alienation has the effect of favouring—

(a) a person who is an associate (within the meaning of the Bankruptcy (Scotland) Act 1985) of the company, a day not earlier than 5 years before the date on which—

(i) the winding up of the company commences, or

(ii) as the case may be, the company enters administration; or

(b) any other person, a day not earlier than 2 years before that date.

(4) On a challenge being brought under subsection (1), the court shall grant decree of reduction or for such restoration of property to the company's assets or other redress as may be appropriate; but the court shall not grant such a decree if the person seeking to uphold the alienation establishes—

(a) that immediately, or at any other time, after the alienation the company's assets were greater than its liabilities, or

(b) that the alienation was made for adequate consideration, or

(c) that the alienation—

(i) was a birthday, Christmas or other conventional gift, or

(ii) was a gift made, for a charitable purpose, to a person who is not an associate of the company,

which, having regard to all the circumstances, it was reasonable for the company to make:

Provided that this subsection is without prejudice to any right or interest acquired in good faith and for value from or through the transferee in the alienation.

(5) In subsection (4) above, "charitable purpose" means any charitable, benevolent or philanthropic purpose, whether or not it is charitable within the meaning of any rule of law.

(6) For the purposes of the foregoing provisions of this section, an alienation in implementation of a prior obligation is deemed to be one for which there was no consideration or no adequate consideration to the extent that the prior obligation was undertaken for no consideration or no adequate consideration.

(7) A liquidator and an administrator have the same right as a creditor has under any rule of law to challenge an alienation of a company made for no consideration or no adequate consideration.

(8) This section applies to Scotland only.

243 UNFAIR PREFERENCES (SCOTLAND)

(1) Subject to subsection (2) below, subsection (4) below applies to a transaction entered into by a company, whether before or after 1st April 1986, which has the effect of creating a preference in favour of a creditor to the prejudice of the general body of creditors, being a preference created not earlier than 6 months before the commencement of the winding up of the company or the company enters administration.

(2) Subsection (4) below does not apply to any of the following transactions—

(a) a transaction in the ordinary course of trade or business;

(b) a payment in cash for a debt which when it was paid had become payable, unless the transaction was collusive with the purpose of prejudicing the general body of creditors;

(c) a transaction whereby the parties to it undertake reciprocal obligations (whether the performance by the parties of their respective obligations occurs at the same time or at different times) unless the transaction was collusive as aforesaid;
(d) the granting of a mandate by a company authorising an arrestee to pay over the arrested funds or part thereof to the arrester where—
(i) there has been a decree for payment or a warrant for summary diligence, and
(ii) the decree or warrant has been preceded by an arrestment on the dependence of the action or followed by an arrestment in execution.

(3) For the purposes of subsection (1) above, the day on which a preference was created is the day on which the preference became completely effectual.

(4) A transaction to which this subsection applies is challengeable by—
(a) in the case of a winding up—
(i) any creditor who is a creditor by virtue of a debt incurred on or before the date of commencement of the winding up, or
(ii) the liquidator; and
(b) where the company has entered administration, the administrator.

(5) On a challenge being brought under subsection (4) above, the court, if satisfied that the transaction challenged is a transaction to which this section applies, shall grant decree of reduction or for such restoration of property to the company's assets or other redress as may be appropriate.

Provided that this subsection is without prejudice to any right or interest acquired in good faith and for value from or through the creditor in whose favour the preference was created.

(6) A liquidator and an administrator have the same right as a creditor has under any rule of law to challenge a preference created by a debtor.

(7) This section applies to Scotland only.

244 EXTORTIONATE CREDIT TRANSACTIONS

(1) This section applies as does section 238, and where the company is, or has been, a party to a transaction for, or involving, the provision of credit to the company.

(2) The court may, on the application of the office-holder, make an order with respect to the transaction if the transaction is or was extortionate and was entered into in the period of 3 years ending with the day on which the company entered administration or went into liquidation.

(3) For the purposes of this section a transaction is extortionate if, having regard to the risk accepted by the person providing the credit—
(a) the terms of it are or were such as to require grossly exorbitant payments to be made (whether unconditionally or in certain contingencies) in respect of the provision of the credit, or
(b) it otherwise grossly contravened ordinary principles of fair dealing;
and it shall be presumed, unless the contrary is proved, that a transaction with respect to which an application is made under this section is or, as the case may be, was extortionate.

(4) An order under this section with respect to any transaction may contain such one or more of the following as the court thinks fit, that is to say—
(a) provision setting aside the whole or part of any obligation created by the transaction,

(b) provision otherwise varying the terms of the transaction or varying the terms on which any security for the purposes of the transaction is held,
(c) provision requiring any person who is or was a party to the transaction to pay to the office-holder any sums paid to that person, by virtue of the transaction, by the company,
(d) provision requiring any person to surrender to the office-holder any property held by him as security for the purposes of the transaction,
(e) provision directing accounts to be taken between any persons.

(5) The powers conferred by this section are exercisable in relation to any transaction concurrently with any powers exercisable in relation to that transaction as a transaction at an undervalue or under section 242 (gratuitious alienations in Scotland).

245 AVOIDANCE OF CERTAIN FLOATING CHARGES

(1) This section applies as does section 238, but applies to Scotland as well as to England and Wales.

(2) Subject as follows, a floating charge on the company's undertaking or property created at a relevant time is invalid except to the extent of the aggregate of—
(a) the value of so much of the consideration for the creation of the charge as consists of money paid, or goods or services supplied, to the company at the same time as, or after, the creation of the charge,
(b) the value of so much of that consideration as consists of the discharge or reduction, at the same time as, or after, the creation of the charge, of any debt of the company, and
(c) the amount of such interest (if any) as is payable on the amount falling within paragraph (a) or (b) in pursuance of any agreement under which the money was so paid, the goods or services were so supplied or the debt was so discharged or reduced.

(3) Subject to the next subsection, the time at which a floating charge is created by a company is a relevant time for the purposes of this section if the charge is created—
(a) in the case of a charge which is created in favour of a person who is connected with the company, at a time in the period of 2 years ending with the onset of insolvency,
(b) in the case of a charge which is created in favour of any other person, at a time in the period of 12 months ending with the onset of insolvency,
(c) in either case, at a time between the making of an administration application in respect of the company and the making of an administration order on that application, or
(d) in either case, at a time between the filing with the court of a copy of notice of intention to appoint an administrator under paragraph 14 or 22 of Schedule B1 and the making of an appointment under that paragraph.

(4) Where a company creates a floating charge at a time mentioned in subsection (3)(b) and the person in favour of whom the charge is created is not connected with the company, that time is not a relevant time for the purposes of this section unless the company—
(a) is at that time unable to pay its debts within the meaning of section 123 in Chapter VI of Part IV, or
(b) becomes unable to pay its debts within the meaning of that section in consequence of the transaction under which the charge is created.

(5) For the purposes of subsection (3), the onset of insolvency is—
(a) in a case where this section applies by reason of an administrator of a company being appointed by administration order, the date on which the administration application is made,

(b) in a case where this section applies by reason of an administrator of a company being appointed under paragraph 14 or 22 of Schedule B1 following filing with the court of a copy of notice of intention to appoint under that paragraph, the date on which the copy of the notice is filed,
(c) in a case where this section applies by reason of an administrator of a company being appointed otherwise than as mentioned in paragraph (a) or (b), the date on which the appointment takes effect, and
(d) in a case where this section applies by reason of a company going into liquidation, the date of the commencement of the winding up.

(6) For the purposes of subsection (2)(a) the value of any goods or services supplied by way of consideration for a floating charge is the amount in money which at the time they were supplied could reasonably have been expected to be obtained for supplying the goods or services in the ordinary course of business and on the same terms (apart from the consideration) as those on which they were supplied to the company.

246 UNENFORCEABILITY OF LIENS ON BOOKS, ETC.

(1) This section applies in the case of a company where—
(a) the company enters administration,
(b) the company goes into liquidation, or
(c) a provisional liquidator is appointed;
and "the office-holder" means the administrator, the liquidator or the provisional liquidator, as the case may be.

(2) Subject as follows, a lien or other right to retain possession of any of the books, papers or other records of the company is unenforceable to the extent that its enforcement would deny possession of any books, papers or other records to the office-holder.

(3) This does not apply to a lien on documents which give a title to property and are held as such.

Remote attendance at meetings

246A REMOTE ATTENDANCE AT MEETINGS

(1) Subject to subsection (2), this section applies to—
(a) any meeting of the creditors of a company summoned under this Act or the rules, or
(b) any meeting of the members or contributories of a company summoned by the office-holder under this Act or the rules, other than a meeting of the members of a company in a members' voluntary winding up.

(2) This section does not apply where—
(a) a company is being wound up in Scotland, or
(b) a receiver is appointed under section 51 in Chapter 2 of Part 3.

(3) Where the person summoning a meeting ("the convener") considers it appropriate, the meeting may be conducted and held in such a way that persons who are not present together at the same place may attend it.

(4) Where a meeting is conducted and held in the manner referred to in subsection (3), a person attends the meeting if that person is able to exercise any rights which that person may have to speak and vote at the meeting.

(5) For the purposes of this section—
  (a) a person is able to exercise the right to speak at a meeting when that person is in a position to communicate to all those attending the meeting, during the meeting, any information or opinions which that person has on the business of the meeting; and
  (b) a person is able to exercise the right to vote at a meeting when—
    (i) that person is able to vote, during the meeting, on resolutions put to the vote at the meeting, and
    (ii) that person's vote can be taken into account in determining whether or not such resolutions are passed at the same time as the votes of all the other persons attending the meeting.

(6) The convener of a meeting which is to be conducted and held in the manner referred to in subsection (3) shall make whatever arrangements the convener considers appropriate to—
  (a) enable those attending the meeting to exercise their rights to speak or vote, and
  (b) ensure the identification of those attending the meeting and the security of any electronic means used to enable attendance.

(7) Where in the reasonable opinion of the convener—
  (a) a meeting will be attended by persons who will not be present together at the same place, and
  (b) it is unnecessary or inexpedient to specify a place for the meeting,

any requirement under this Act or the rules to specify a place for the meeting may be satisfied by specifying the arrangements the convener proposes to enable persons to exercise their rights to speak or vote.

(8) In making the arrangements referred to in subsection (6) and in forming the opinion referred to in subsection (7)(b), the convener must have regard to the legitimate interests of the creditors, members or contributories and others attending the meeting in the efficient despatch of the business of the meeting.

(9) If—
  (a) the notice of a meeting does not specify a place for the meeting,
  (b) the convener is requested in accordance with the rules to specify a place for the meeting, and
  (c) that request is made—
    (i) in the case of a meeting of creditors or contributories, by not less than ten percent in value of the creditors or contributories, or
    (ii) in the case of a meeting of members, by members representing not less than ten percent of the total voting rights of all the members having at the date of the request a right to vote at the meeting,

it shall be the duty of the convener to specify a place for the meeting.

(10) In this section, "the office-holder", in relation to a company, means—
  (a) its liquidator, provisional liquidator, administrator, or administrative receiver, or
  (b) where a voluntary arrangement in relation to the company is proposed or

has taken effect under Part 1, the nominee or the supervisor of the voluntary arrangement.

Use of websites

246B USE OF WEBSITES

(1) Subject to subsection (2), where any provision of this Act or the rules requires the office-holder to give, deliver, furnish or send a notice or other document or information to any person, that requirement is satisfied by making the notice, document or information available on a website—

(a) in accordance with the rules, and
(b) in such circumstances as may be prescribed.

(2) This section does not apply where—
(a) a company is being wound up in Scotland, or
(b) a receiver is appointed under section 51 in Chapter 2 of Part 3.

(3) In this section, "the office-holder" means—
(a) the liquidator, provisional liquidator, administrator, or administrative receiver of a company, or
(b) where a voluntary arrangement in relation to a company is proposed or has taken effect under Part 1, the nominee or the supervisor of the voluntary arrangement.

Part VII INTERPRETATION FOR FIRST GROUP OF PARTS

247 "INSOLVENCY" AND "GO INTO LIQUIDATION"

(1) In this Group of Parts, except in so far as the context otherwise requires, "insolvency", in relation to a company, includes the approval of a voluntary arrangement under Part I, or the appointment of an administrator or administrative receiver.

(2) For the purposes of any provision in this Group of Parts, a company goes into liquidation if it passes a resolution for voluntary winding up or an order for its winding up is made by the court at a time when it has not already gone into liquidation by passing such a resolution.

(3) The reference to a resolution for voluntary winding up in subsection (2) includes a reference to a resolution which is deemed to occur by virtue of—
(a) paragraph 83(6)(b) of Schedule B1, or
(b) an order made following conversion of administration or a voluntary arrangement into winding up by virtue of Article 37 of the EC Regulation.

248 "SECURED CREDITOR", ETC.

In this Group of Parts, except in so far as the context otherwise requires—

(a) "secured creditor", in relation to a company, means a creditor of the company who holds in respect of his debt a security over property of the company, and "unsecured creditor" is to be read accordingly; and

(b) "security" means—
(i) in relation to England and Wales, any mortgage, charge, lien or other security, and
(ii) in relation to Scotland, any security (whether heritable or moveable), any floating charge and any right of lien or preference and any right of retention (other than a right of compensation or set off).

249 "CONNECTED" WITH A COMPANY

For the purposes of any provision in this Group of Parts, a person is connected with a company if—

(a) he is a director or shadow director of the company or an associate of such a director or shadow director, or

(b) he is an associate of the company,

and "associate" has the meaning given by section 435 in Part XVIII of this Act.

250 "MEMBER" OF A COMPANY

For the purposes of any provision in this Group of Parts, a person who is not a member of a company but to whom shares in the company have been transferred, or transmitted by operation of law, is to be regarded as a member of the company, and references to a member or members are to be read accordingly.

251 EXPRESSIONS USED GENERALLY

In this Group of Parts, except in so far as the context otherwise requires—

"administrative receiver" means—
(a) an administrative receiver as defined by section 29(2) in Chapter I of Part III, or
(b) a receiver appointed under section 51 in Chapter II of that Part in a case where the whole (or substantially the whole) of the company's property is attached by the floating charge;

"agent" does not include a person's counsel acting as such;

"books and papers" and "books or papers" includes accounts, deeds, writing and documents;

"business day" means any day other than a Saturday, a Sunday, Christmas Day, Good Friday or a day which is a bank holiday in any part of Great Britain;

...

"contributory" has the meaning given by section 79;

"the court", in relation to a company, means a court having jurisdiction to wind up the company;

"director" includes any person occupying the position of director, by whatever name called;

"document" includes summons, notice, order and other legal process, and registers;

"floating charge" means a charge which, as created, was a floating charge and includes a floating charge within section 462 of the Companies Act (Scottish floating charges);

"the Gazette" means—
(a) as respects companies registered in England and Wales, the London Gazette;
(b) as respects companies registered in Scotland, the Edinburgh Gazette;
...

"officer", in relation to a body corporate, includes a director, manager or secretary;

"the official rate", in relation to interest, means the rate payable under section 189(4);

"prescribed" means prescribed by the rules;

"receiver", in the expression "receiver or manager", does not include a receiver appointed under section 51 in Chapter II of Part III;

...

"the rules" means rules under section 411 in Part XV; and

"shadow director", in relation to a company, means a person in accordance with whose directions or instructions the directors of the company are accustomed to act (but so that a person is not deemed a shadow director by reason only that the directors act on advice given by him in a professional capacity).

THE THIRD GROUP OF PARTS

MISCELLANEOUS MATTERS BEARING ON BOTH COMPANY AND INDIVIDUAL INSOLVENCY; GENERAL INTERPRETATION; FINAL PROVISIONS

Part XII PREFERENTIAL DEBTS IN COMPANY AND INDIVIDUAL INSOLVENCY

386 CATEGORIES OF PREFERENTIAL DEBTS

(1) A reference in this Act to the preferential debts of a company or an individual is to the debts listed in Schedule 6 to this Act (contributions to occupational pension schemes; remuneration, etc. of employees; levies on coal and steel production); and references to preferential creditors are to be read accordingly.

(2) In that Schedule "the debtor" means the company or the individual concerned.

(3) Schedule 6 is to be read with Schedule 4 to the Pension Schemes Act 1993 (occupational pension scheme contributions).

387 "THE RELEVANT DATE"

(1) This section explains references in Schedule 6 to the relevant date (being the date which determines the existence and amount of a preferential debt).

(2) For the purposes of section 4 in Part I (meetings to consider company voluntary arrangement), the relevant date in relation to a company which is not being wound up is—
(a) if the company is in administration, the date on which it entered administration, and
(b) if the company is not in administration, the date on which the voluntary arrangement takes effect.

...

(3) In relation to a company which is being wound up, the following applies—
(a) if the winding up is by the court, and the winding-up order was made immediately upon the discharge of an administration order, the relevant date is the date on which the company entered administration;

...

(b) if the case does not fall within paragraph (a) ... and the company—
(i) is being wound up by the court, and
(ii) had not commenced to be wound up voluntarily before the date of the making of the winding-up order,

the relevant date is the date of the appointment (or first appointment) of a provisional liquidator or, if no such appointment has been made, the date of the winding-up order;

...

(c) if the case does not fall within paragraph (a) ... [or] (b) ..., the relevant date is the date of the passing of the resolution for the winding up of the company.

(3A) In relation to a company which is in administration (and to which no other provision of this section applies) the relevant date is the date on which the company enters administration.

(4) In relation to a company in receivership (where section 40 or, as the case may be, section 59 applies), the relevant date is—
(a) in England and Wales, the date of the appointment of the receiver by debenture-holders, and
(b) in Scotland, the date of the appointment of the receiver under section 53(6) or (as the case may be) 54(5).

Part XVI PROVISIONS AGAINST DEBT AVOIDANCE (ENGLAND AND WALES ONLY)

423 TRANSACTIONS DEFRAUDING CREDITORS

(1) This section relates to transactions entered into at an undervalue; and a person enters into such a transaction with another person if—
(a) he makes a gift to the other person or he otherwise enters into a transaction with the other on terms that provide for him to receive no consideration;
(b) he enters into a transaction with the other in consideration of marriage or the formation of a civil partnership; or
(c) he enters into a transaction with the other for a consideration the value of which, in money or money's worth, is significantly less than the value, in money or money's worth, of the consideration provided by himself.

(2) Where a person has entered into such a transaction, the court may, if satisfied under the next subsection, make such order as it thinks fit for—
(a) restoring the position to what it would have been if the transaction had not been entered into, and
(b) protecting the interests of persons who are victims of the transaction.

(3) In the case of a person entering into such a transaction, an order shall only be made if the court is satisfied that it was entered into by him for the purpose—
(a) of putting assets beyond the reach of a person who is making, or may at some time make, a claim against him, or
(b) of otherwise prejudicing the interests of such a person in relation to the claim which he is making or may make.

(4) In this section "the court" means the High Court or—
(a) if the person entering into the transaction is an individual, any other court which would have jurisdiction in relation to a bankruptcy petition relating to him;
(b) if that person is a body capable of being wound up under Part IV or V of this Act, any other court having jurisdiction to wind it up.

(5) In relation to a transaction at an undervalue, references here and below to a victim of the transaction are to a person who is, or is capable of being, prejudiced by it; and in the following two sections the person entering into the transaction is referred to as "the debtor".

424 THOSE WHO MAY APPLY FOR AN ORDER UNDER S. 423

(1) An application for an order under section 423 shall not be made in relation to a transaction except—
(a) in a case where the debtor has been adjudged bankrupt or is a body corporate which is being wound up or is in administration, by the official receiver, by the trustee of the bankrupt's estate or the liquidator or administrator of the body corporate or (with the leave of the court) by a victim of the transaction;

(b) in a case where a victim of the transaction is bound by a voluntary arrangement approved under Part I or Part VIII of this Act, by the supervisor of the voluntary arrangement or by any person who (whether or not so bound) is such a victim; or

(c) in any other case, by a victim of the transaction.

(2) An application made under any of the paragraphs of subsection (1) is to be treated as made on behalf of every victim of the transaction.

425 PROVISION WHICH MAY BE MADE BY ORDER UNDER S. 423

(1) Without prejudice to the generality of section 423, an order made under that section with respect to a transaction may (subject as follows)—

(a) require any property transferred as part of the transaction to be vested in any person, either absolutely or for the benefit of all the persons on whose behalf the application for the order is treated as made;

(b) require any property to be so vested if it represents, in any person's hands, the application either of the proceeds of sale of property so transferred or of the money so transferred;

(c) release or discharge (in whole or in part) any security given by the debtor;

(d) require any person to pay to any other person in respect of benefits received from the debtor such sums as the court may direct;

(e) provide for any surety or guarantor whose obligations to any person were released or discharged (in whole or in part) under the transaction to be under such new or revived obligations as the court thinks appropriate;

(f) provide for security to be provided for the discharge of any obligation imposed by or arising under the order, for such an obligation to be charged on any property and for such security or charge to have the same priority as a security or charge released or discharged (in whole or in part) under the transaction.

(2) An order under section 423 may affect the property of, or impose any obligation on, any person whether or not he is the person with whom the debtor entered into the transaction; but such an order—

(a) shall not prejudice any interest in property which was acquired from a person other than the debtor and was acquired in good faith, for value and without notice of the relevant circumstances, or prejudice any interest deriving from such an interest, and

(b) shall not require a person who received a benefit from the transaction in good faith, for value and without notice of the relevant circumstances to pay any sum unless he was a party to the transaction.

(3) For the purposes of this section the relevant circumstances in relation to a transaction are the circumstances by virtue of which an order under section 423 may be made in respect of the transaction.

(4) In this section "security" means any mortgage, charge, lien or other security.

Part XVIII INTERPRETATION

435 MEANING OF "ASSOCIATE"

(1) For the purposes of this Act any question whether a person is an associate of another person is to be determined in accordance with the following provisions of this section (any provision that a person is an associate of another person being taken to mean that they are associates of each other).

(2) A person is an associate of an individual if that person is—
(a) the individual's husband or wife or civil partner,
(b) a relative of—
(i) the individual, or
(ii) the individual's husband or wife or civil partner, or
(c) the husband or wife or civil partner of a relative of—
(i) the individual, or
(ii) the individual's husband or wife or civil partner.

(3) A person is an associate of any person with whom he is in partnership, and of the husband or wife or civil partner or a relative of any individual with whom he is in partnership; and a Scottish firm is an associate of any person who is a member of the firm.

(4) A person is an associate of any person whom he employs or by whom he is employed.

(5) A person in his capacity as trustee of a trust other than—
(a) a trust arising under any of the second Group of Parts or the Bankruptcy (Scotland) Act 1985, or
(b) a pension scheme or an employees' share scheme,
is an associate of another person if the beneficiaries of the trust include, or the terms of the trust confer a power that may be exercised for the benefit of, that other person or an associate of that other person.

(6) A company is an associate of another company—
(a) if the same person has control of both, or a person has control of one and persons who are his associates, or he and persons who are his associates, have control of the other, or
(b) if a group of two or more persons has control of each company, and the groups either consist of the same persons or could be regarded as consisting of the same persons by treating (in one or more cases) a member of either group as replaced by a person of whom he is an associate.

(7) A company is an associate of another person if that person has control of it or if that person and persons who are his associates together have control of it.

(8) For the purposes of this section a person is a relative of an individual if he is that individual's brother, sister, uncle, aunt, nephew, niece, lineal ancestor or lineal descendant, treating—
(a) any relationship of the half blood as a relationship of the whole blood and the stepchild or adopted child of any person as his child, and
(b) an illegitimate child as the legitimate child of his mother and reputed father;
and references in this section to a husband or wife include a former husband or wife and a reputed husband or wife, and references to a civil partner include a former civil partner and a reputed civil partner.

(9) For the purposes of this section any director or other officer of a company is to be treated as employed by that company.

(10) For the purposes of this section a person is to be taken as having control of a company if—
(a) the directors of the company or of another company which has control of it (or any of them) are accustomed to act in accordance with his directions or instructions, or
(b) he is entitled to exercise, or control the exercise of, one third or more of the voting power at any general meeting of the company of or another company which has control of it;
and where two or more persons together satisfy either of the above conditions, they are to be taken as having control of the company.

(11) In this section "company" includes any body corporate (whether incorporated in Great Britain or elsewhere); and references to directors and other officers of a company and to voting power at any general meeting of a company have effect with any necessary modifications.

436 EXPRESSIONS USED GENERALLY

(1) In this Act, except in so far as the context otherwise requires (and subject to Parts VII and XI)—

...

"associate" has the meaning given by section 435;

"body corporate" includes a body incorporated outside Great Britain, but does not include—
(a) a corporation sole, or
(b) a partnership that, whether or not a legal person, is not regarded as a body corporate under the law by which it is governed;

...

"the EC Regulation" means Council Regulation (EC) No. 1346/2000;

...

"EEA State" means a state that is a Contracting Party to the Agreement on the European Economic Area signed at Oporto on 2nd May 1992 as adjusted by the Protocol signed at Brussels on 17th March 1993;

...

"transaction" includes a gift, agreement or arrangement, and references to entering into a transaction shall be construed accordingly.

...

(2) The following expressions have the same meaning in this Act as in the Companies Acts—

"articles", in relation to a company (see section 18 of the Companies Act 2006);

"debenture" (see section 738 of that Act);

"holding company" (see sections 1159 and 1160 of, and Schedule 6 to, that Act);

"the Joint Stock Companies Acts" (see section 1171 of that Act);

"overseas company" (see section 1044 of that Act);

"paid up" (see section 583 of that Act);

"private company" and "public company" (see section 4 of that Act);

"registrar of companies" (see section 1060 of that Act);

"share" (see section 540 of that Act);

"subsidiary" (see sections 1159 and 1160 of, and Schedule 6 to, that Act).

...

436B REFERENCES TO THINGS IN WRITING

(1) A reference in this Act to a thing in writing includes that thing in electronic form.

...

SCHEDULES

SCHEDULE A1 MORATORIUM WHERE DIRECTORS PROPOSE VOLUNTARY ARRANGEMENT

Part III EFFECTS OF MORATORIUM

Effect on creditors, etc.

12(1) During the period for which a moratorium is in force for a company—
- (a) no petition may be presented for the winding up of the company,
- (b) no meeting of the company may be called or requisitioned except with the consent of the nominee or the leave of the court and subject (where the court gives leave) to such terms as the court may impose,
- (c) no resolution may be passed or order made for the winding up of the company,
- (d) no administration application may be made in respect of the company,
- (da) no administrator of the company may be appointed under paragraph 14 or 22 of Schedule B1,
- (e) no administrative receiver of the company may be appointed,
- (f) no landlord or other person to whom rent is payable may exercise any right of forfeiture by peaceable re-entry in relation to premises let to the company in respect of a failure by the company to comply with any term or condition of its tenancy of such premises, except with the leave of the court and subject to such terms as the court may impose,
- (g) no other steps may be taken to enforce any security over the company's property, or to repossess goods in the company's possession under any hire-purchase agreement, except with the leave of the court and subject to such terms as the court may impose, and
- (h) no other proceedings and no execution or other legal process may be commenced or continued, and no distress may be levied, against the company or its property except with the leave of the court and subject to such terms as the court may impose.

13(1) This paragraph applies where there is an uncrystallised floating charge on the property of a company for which a moratorium is in force.

(2) If the conditions for the holder of the charge to give a notice having the effect mentioned in sub-paragraph (4) are met at any time, the notice may not be given at that time but may instead be given as soon as practicable after the moratorium has come to an end.

(3) If any other event occurs at any time which (apart from this sub-paragraph) would have the effect mentioned in sub-paragraph (4), then—
- (a) the event shall not have the effect in question at that time, but
- (b) if notice of the event is given to the company by the holder of the charge as soon as is practicable after the moratorium has come to an end, the event is to be treated as if it had occurred when the notice was given.

(4) The effect referred to in sub-paragraphs (2) and (3) is—
- (a) causing the crystallisation of the floating charge, or

(b) causing the imposition, by virtue of provision in the instrument creating the charge, of any restriction on the disposal of any property of the company.

(5) Application may not be made for leave under paragraph 12(1)(g) or (h) with a view to obtaining—
(a) the crystallisation of the floating charge, or
(b) the imposition, by virtue of provision in the instrument creating the charge, of any restriction on the disposal of any property of the company.

14 Security granted by a company at a time when a moratorium is in force in relation to the company may only be enforced if, at that time, there were reasonable grounds for believing that it would benefit the company.

SCHEDULE B1 ADMINISTRATION

NATURE OF ADMINISTRATION

Purpose of administration

3(1) The administrator of a company must perform his functions with the objective of—
(a) rescuing the company as a going concern, or
(b) achieving a better result for the company's creditors as a whole than would be likely if the company were wound up (without first being in administration), or
(c) realising property in order to make a distribution to one or more secured or preferential creditors.

(2) Subject to sub-paragraph (4), the administrator of a company must perform his functions in the interests of the company's creditors as a whole.

(3) The administrator must perform his functions with the objective specified in sub-paragraph (1)(a) unless he thinks either—
(a) that it is not reasonably practicable to achieve that objective, or
(b) that the objective specified in sub-paragraph (1)(b) would achieve a better result for the company's creditors as a whole.

(4) The administrator may perform his functions with the objective specified in sub-paragraph (1)(c) only if—
(a) he thinks that it is not reasonably practicable to achieve either of the objectives specified in sub-paragraph (1)(a) and (b), and
(b) he does not unnecessarily harm the interests of the creditors of the company as a whole.

4. The administrator of a company must perform his functions as quickly and efficiently as is reasonably practicable.

APPOINTMENT OF ADMINISTRATOR BY COURT

Administration order

10. An administration order is an order appointing a person as the administrator of a company.

Conditions for making order

11. The court may make an administration order in relation to a company only if satisfied—
(a) that the company is or is likely to become unable to pay its debts, and

(b) that the administration order is reasonably likely to achieve the purpose of administration.

Administration application

12(1) An application to the court for an administration order in respect of a company (an "administration application") may be made only by—
(a) the company,
(b) the directors of the company,
(c) one or more creditors of the company,
(d) the designated officer for a magistrates' court in the exercise of the power conferred by section 87A of the Magistrates' Courts Act 1980 (c. 43) (fine imposed on company), or
(e) a combination of persons listed in paragraphs (a) to (d).

APPOINTMENT OF ADMINISTRATOR BY HOLDER OF FLOATING CHARGE

Power to appoint

14(1) The holder of a qualifying floating charge in respect of a company's property may appoint an administrator of the company.

APPOINTMENT OF ADMINISTRATOR BY COMPANY OR DIRECTORS

Power to appoint

22(1) A company may appoint an administrator.
(2) The directors of a company may appoint an administrator.

ADMINISTRATION APPLICATION – SPECIAL CASES

Effect of administrative receivership

39(1) Where there is an administrative receiver of a company the court must dismiss an administration application in respect of the company unless—
(a) the person by or on behalf of whom the receiver was appointed consents to the making of the administration order...

(2) Sub-paragraph (1) applies whether the administrative receiver is appointed before or after the making of the administration application.

EFFECT OF ADMINISTRATION

Dismissal of pending winding-up petition

40(1) A petition for the winding up of a company—
(a) shall be dismissed on the making of an administration order in respect of the company, and
(b) shall be suspended while the company is in administration following an appointment under paragraph 14.

Dismissal of administrative or other receiver

41(1) When an administration order takes effect in respect of a company any administrative receiver of the company shall vacate office.

(2) Where a company is in administration, any receiver of part of the company's property shall vacate office if the administrator requires him to.

Moratorium on insolvency proceedings

42(1) This paragraph applies to a company in administration.

(2) No resolution may be passed for the winding up of the company.

(3) No order may be made for the winding up of the company.

(4) Sub-paragraph (3) does not apply to an order made on a petition presented under—
(a) section 124A (public interest), or
(aa) section 124B (SEs)...

(5) If a petition presented under a provision referred to in sub-paragraph (4) comes to the attention of the administrator, he shall apply to the court for directions under paragraph 63.

Moratorium on other legal process

43(1) This paragraph applies to a company in administration.

(2) No step may be taken to enforce security over the company's property except—
(a) with the consent of the administrator, or
(b) with the permission of the court.

(3) No step may be taken to repossess goods in the company's possession under a hire-purchase agreement except—
(a) with the consent of the administrator, or
(b) with the permission of the court.

(4) A landlord may not exercise a right of forfeiture by peaceable re-entry in relation to premises let to the company except—
(a) with the consent of the administrator, or
(b) with the permission of the court.

(5) In Scotland, a landlord may not exercise a right of irritancy in relation to premises let to the company except—
(a) with the consent of the administrator, or
(b) with the permission of the court.

(6) No legal process (including legal proceedings, execution, distress and diligence) may be instituted or continued against the company or property of the company except—
(a) with the consent of the administrator, or
(b) with the permission of the court.

(6A) An administrative receiver of the company may not be appointed.

(7) Where the court gives permission for a transaction under this paragraph it may impose a condition on or a requirement in connection with the transaction.

(8) In this paragraph "landlord" includes a person to whom rent is payable.

PROCESS OF ADMINISTRATION

Business and result of initial creditors' meeting

53(1) An initial creditors' meeting to which an administrator's proposals are presented shall consider them and may—

(a) approve them without modification, or
(b) approve them with modification to which the administrator consents.

(2) After the conclusion of an initial creditors' meeting the administrator shall as soon as is reasonably practicable report any decision taken to—
(a) the court,
(b) the registrar of companies, and
(c) such other persons as may be prescribed.

(3) An administrator commits an offence if he fails without reasonable excuse to comply with sub-paragraph (2).

Revision of administrator's proposals

54(1) This paragraph applies where—
(a) an administrator's proposals have been approved (with or without modification) at an initial creditors' meeting,
(b) the administrator proposes a revision to the proposals, and
(c) the administrator thinks that the proposed revision is substantial.

(2) The administrator shall—
(a) summon a creditors' meeting,
(b) send a statement in the prescribed form of the proposed revision with the notice of the meeting sent to each creditor,
(c) send a copy of the statement, within the prescribed period, to each member of the company of whose address he is aware, and
(d) present a copy of the statement to the meeting.

(5) A creditors' meeting to which a proposed revision is presented shall consider it and may—
(a) approve it without modification, or
(b) approve it with modification to which the administrator consents.

(6) After the conclusion of a creditors' meeting the administrator shall as soon as is reasonably practicable report any decision taken to—
(a) the court,
(b) the registrar of companies, and
(c) such other persons as may be prescribed.

(7) An administrator commits an offence if he fails without reasonable excuse to comply with sub-paragraph (6).

FUNCTIONS OF ADMINISTRATOR

General powers

59(1) The administrator of a company may do anything necessary or expedient for the management of the affairs, business and property of the company.

(2) A provision of this Schedule which expressly permits the administrator to do a specified thing is without prejudice to the generality of sub-paragraph (1).

(3) A person who deals with the administrator of a company in good faith and for value need not inquire whether the administrator is acting within his powers.

60 The administrator of a company has the powers specified in Schedule 1 to this Act.

61 The administrator of a company—

(a) may remove a director of the company, and
(b) may appoint a director of the company (whether or not to fill a vacancy).

62 The administrator of a company may call a meeting of members or creditors of the company.

63 The administrator of a company may apply to the court for directions in connection with his functions.

64(1) A company in administration or an officer of a company in administration may not exercise a management power without the consent of the administrator.

(2) For the purpose of sub-paragraph (1)—
(a) "management power" means a power which could be exercised so as to interfere with the exercise of the administrator's powers,
(b) it is immaterial whether the power is conferred by an enactment or an instrument, and
(c) consent may be general or specific.

Distribution

65(1) The administrator of a company may make a distribution to a creditor of the company.

(2) Section 175 shall apply in relation to a distribution under this paragraph as it applies in relation to a winding up.

(3) A payment may not be made by way of distribution under this paragraph to a creditor of the company who is neither secured nor preferential unless the court gives permission.

66 The administrator of a company may make a payment otherwise than in accordance with paragraph 65 or paragraph 13 of Schedule 1 if he thinks it likely to assist achievement of the purpose of administration.

General duties

67 The administrator of a company shall on his appointment take custody or control of all the property to which he thinks the company is entitled.

68(1) Subject to sub-paragraph (2), the administrator of a company shall manage its affairs, business and property in accordance with—
(a) any proposals approved under paragraph 53,
(b) any revision of those proposals which is made by him and which he does not consider substantial, and
(c) any revision of those proposals approved under paragraph 54.

(2) If the court gives directions to the administrator of a company in connection with any aspect of his management of the company's affairs, business or property, the administrator shall comply with the directions.

(3) The court may give directions under sub-paragraph (2) only if—
(a) no proposals have been approved under paragraph 53,
(b) the directions are consistent with any proposals or revision approved under paragraph 53 or 54,
(c) the court thinks the directions are required in order to reflect a change in circumstances since the approval of proposals or a revision under paragraph 53 or 54, or
(d) the court thinks the directions are desirable because of a misunderstanding about proposals or a revision approved under paragraph 53 or 54.

Administrator as agent of company

69 In exercising his functions under this Schedule the administrator of a company acts as its agent.

Charged property: floating charge

70(1) The administrator of a company may dispose of or take action relating to property which is subject to a floating charge as if it were not subject to the charge.

(2) Where property is disposed of in reliance on sub-paragraph (1) the holder of the floating charge shall have the same priority in respect of acquired property as he had in respect of the property disposed of.

(3) In sub-paragraph (2) "acquired property" means property of the company which directly or indirectly represents the property disposed of.

Charged property: non-floating charge

71(1) The court may by order enable the administrator of a company to dispose of property which is subject to a security (other than a floating charge) as if it were not subject to the security.

(2) An order under sub-paragraph (1) may be made only—
- (a) on the application of the administrator, and
- (b) where the court thinks that disposal of the property would be likely to promote the purpose of administration in respect of the company.

(3) An order under this paragraph is subject to the condition that there be applied towards discharging the sums secured by the security—
- (a) the net proceeds of disposal of the property, and
- (b) any additional money required to be added to the net proceeds so as to produce the amount determined by the court as the net amount which would be realised on a sale of the property at market value.

(4) If an order under this paragraph relates to more than one security, application of money under sub-paragraph (3) shall be in the order of the priorities of the securities.

(5) An administrator who makes a successful application for an order under this paragraph shall send a copy of the order to the registrar of companies before the end of the period of 14 days starting with the date of the order.

(6) An administrator commits an offence if he fails to comply with sub-paragraph (5) without reasonable excuse.

Hire-purchase property

72(1) The court may by order enable the administrator of a company to dispose of goods which are in the possession of the company under a hire-purchase agreement as if all the rights of the owner under the agreement were vested in the company.

(2) An order under sub-paragraph (1) may be made only—
- (a) on the application of the administrator, and
- (b) where the court thinks that disposal of the goods would be likely to promote the purpose of administration in respect of the company.

(3) An order under this paragraph is subject to the condition that there be applied towards discharging the sums payable under the hire-purchase agreement—
- (a) the net proceeds of disposal of the goods, and

(b) any additional money required to be added to the net proceeds so as to produce the amount determined by the court as the net amount which would be realised on a sale of the goods at market value.

(4) An administrator who makes a successful application for an order under this paragraph shall send a copy of the order to the registrar of companies before the end of the period of 14 days starting with the date of the order.

(5) An administrator commits an offence if he fails without reasonable excuse to comply with sub-paragraph (4).

Protection for secured or preferential creditor

73(1) An administrator's statement of proposals under paragraph 49 may not include any action which—

(a) affects the right of a secured creditor of the company to enforce his security,
(b) would result in a preferential debt of the company being paid otherwise than in priority to its non-preferential debts, or
(c) would result in one preferential creditor of the company being paid a smaller proportion of his debt than another.

(2) Sub-paragraph (1) does not apply to—

(a) action to which the relevant creditor consents,
(b) a proposal for a voluntary arrangement under Part I of this Act (although this sub-paragraph is without prejudice to section 4(3)), [or]
(c) a proposal for a compromise or arrangement to be sanctioned under Part 26 of the Companies Act 2006 (arrangements and reconstructions)

…

(3) The reference to a statement of proposals in sub-paragraph (1) includes a reference to a statement as revised or modified.

Challenge to administrator's conduct of company

74(1) A creditor or member of a company in administration may apply to the court claiming that—

(a) the administrator is acting or has acted so as unfairly to harm the interests of the applicant (whether alone or in common with some or all other members or creditors), or
(b) the administrator proposes to act in a way which would unfairly harm the interests of the applicant (whether alone or in common with some or all other members or creditors).

(2) A creditor or member of a company in administration may apply to the court claiming that the administrator is not performing his functions as quickly or as efficiently as is reasonably practicable.

(3) The court may—

(a) grant relief;
(b) dismiss the application;
(c) adjourn the hearing conditionally or unconditionally;
(d) make an interim order;
(e) make any other order it thinks appropriate.

(4) In particular, an order under this paragraph may—

(a) regulate the administrator's exercise of his functions;
(b) require the administrator to do or not do a specified thing;
(c) require a creditors' meeting to be held for a specified purpose;

(d) provide for the appointment of an administrator to cease to have effect;
(e) make consequential provision.

(5) An order may be made on a claim under sub-paragraph (1) whether or not the action complained of—
(a) is within the administrator's powers under this Schedule;
(b) was taken in reliance on an order under paragraph 71 or 72.

(6) An order may not be made under this paragraph if it would impede or prevent the implementation of—
(a) a voluntary arrangement approved under Part I,
(b) a compromise or arrangement sanctioned under Part 26 of the Companies Act 2006 (arrangements and reconstructions), ... or
(c) proposals or a revision approved under paragraph 53 or 54 more than 28 days before the day on which the application for the order under this paragraph is made.

ENDING ADMINISTRATION

Automatic end of administration

76(1) The appointment of an administrator shall cease to have effect at the end of the period of one year beginning with the date on which it takes effect.

(2) But—
(a) on the application of an administrator the court may by order extend his term of office for a specified period, and
(b) an administrator's term of office may be extended for a specified period not exceeding six months by consent.

77(1) An order of the court under paragraph 76—
(a) may be made in respect of an administrator whose term of office has already been extended by order or by consent, but
(b) may not be made after the expiry of the administrator's term of office.

(2) Where an order is made under paragraph 76 the administrator shall as soon as is reasonably practicable notify the registrar of companies.

(3) An administrator who fails without reasonable excuse to comply with sub-paragraph (2) commits an offence.

78(1) In paragraph 76(2)(b) "consent" means consent of—
(a) each secured creditor of the company, and
(b) if the company has unsecured debts, creditors whose debts amount to more than 50% of the company's unsecured debts, disregarding debts of any creditor who does not respond to an invitation to give or withhold consent.

REPLACING ADMINISTRATOR

Vacation of office: discharge from liability

98(1) Where a person ceases to be the administrator of a company (whether because he vacates office by reason of resignation, death or otherwise, because he is removed from office or because his appointment ceases to have effect) he is discharged from liability in respect of any action of his as administrator.

GENERAL

Scotland

115(1) In Scotland, the administrator of a company may make, in or towards the satisfaction of the debt secured by the floating charge, a payment to the holder of a floating charge which has attached to the property subject to the charge.

116 In Scotland, the administrator in making any payment in accordance with paragraph 115 shall make such payment subject to the rights of any of the following categories of persons (which rights shall, except to the extent provided in any instrument, have the following order of priority)—

(a) the holder of any fixed security which is over property subject to the floating charge and which ranks prior to, or pari passu with, the floating charge,

(b) creditors in respect of all liabilities and expenses incurred by or on behalf of the administrator,

(c) the administrator in respect of his liabilities, expenses and remuneration and any indemnity to which he is entitled out of the property of the company,

(d) the preferential creditors entitled to payment in accordance with paragraph 65,

(e) the holder of the floating charge in accordance with the priority of that charge in relation to any other floating charge which has attached, and

(f) the holder of a fixed security, other than one referred to in paragraph (a), which is over property subject to the floating charge.

SCHEDULE 1 POWERS OF ADMINISTRATOR OR ADMINISTRATIVE RECEIVER

1. Power to take possession of, collect and get in the property of the company and, for that purpose, to take such proceedings as may seem to him expedient.

2. Power to sell or otherwise dispose of the property of the company by public auction or private contract or, in Scotland, to sell, hire out or otherwise dispose of the property of the company by public group or private bargain.

3. Power to raise or borrow money and grant security therefore over the property of the company.

4. Power to appoint a solicitor or accountant or other professionally qualified person to assist him in the performance of his functions.

5. Power to bring or defend any action or other legal proceedings in the name and on behalf of the company.

6. Power to refer to arbitration any question affecting the company.

7. Power to effect and maintain insurances in respect of the business and property of the company.

8. Power to use the company's seal.

9. Power to do all acts and to execute in the name and on behalf of the company any deed, receipt or other document.

10. Power to draw, accept, make and endorse any bill of exchange or promissory note in the name and on behalf of the company.

11. Power to appoint any agent to do any business which he is unable to do himself or which can more conveniently be done by an agent and power to employ and dismiss employees.

12. Power to do all such things (including the carrying out of works) as may be necessary for the realisation of the property of the company.

13. Power to make any payment which is necessary or incidental to the performance of his functions.

14. Power to carry on the business of the company.

15. Power to establish subsidiaries of the company.

16. Power to transfer to subsidiaries of the company the whole or any part of the business and property of the company.

17. Power to grant or accept a surrender of a lease or tenancy of any of the property of the company, and to take a lease or tenancy of any property required or convenient for the business of the company.

18. Power to make any arrangement or compromise on behalf of the company.

19. Power to call up any uncalled capital of the company.

20. Power to rank and claim in the bankruptcy, insolvency, sequestration or liquidation of any person indebted to the company and to receive dividends, and to accede to trust deeds for the creditors of any such person.

21. Power to present or defend a petition for the winding up of the company.

22. Power to change the situation of the company's registered office.

23. Power to do all other things incidental to the exercise of the foregoing powers.

SCHEDULE 4 POWERS OF LIQUIDATOR IN A WINDING UP

Part I POWERS EXERCISABLE WITH SANCTION

1. Power to pay any class of creditors in full.

2. Power to make any compromise or arrangement with creditors or persons claiming to be creditors, or having or alleging themselves to have any claim (present or future, certain or contingent, ascertained or sounding only in damages) against the company, or whereby the company may be rendered liable.

3. **In the case of a winding up in Scotland** power to compromise, on such terms as may be agreed—
   (a) all calls and liabilities to calls, all debts and liabilities capable of resulting in debts, and all claims (present or future, certain or contingent, ascertained or sounding only in damages) subsisting or supposed to subsist between the company and a contributory or alleged contributory or other debtor or person apprehending liability to the company, and
   (b) all questions in any way relating to or affecting the assets or the winding up of the company,

   and take any security for the discharge of any such call, debt, liability or claim and give a complete discharge in respect of it.

3A. Power to bring legal proceedings under section 213, 214, 238, 239, 242, 243 or 423.

Part II POWERS EXERCISABLE WITHOUT SANCTION IN VOUNTARY WINDING UP, WITH SANCTION IN WINDING UP BY THE COURT

4. Power to bring or defend any action or other legal proceeding in the name annd on behalf of the company.

5. Power to carry on the business of the company so far as may be necessary for its beneficial winding up.

Part III POWERS EXERCISABLE WITHOUT SANCTION IN ANY WINDING UP

6. Power to sell any of the company's property by public auction or private contract with power to transfer the whole of it to any person or to sell the same in parcels.

6A. In the case of a winding up in England and Wales, power to compromise, on such terms as may be agreed—

(a) all calls and liabilities to calls, all debts and liabilities capable of resulting in debts, and all claims (present or future, certain or contingent, ascertained or sounding only in damages) subsisting or supposed to subsist between the company and a contributory or alleged contributory or other debtor or person apprehending liability to the company, and

(b) subject to paragraph 2 in Part 1 of this Schedule, all questions in any way relating to or affecting the assets or the winding up of the company,

and take any security for the discharge of any such call, debt, liability or claim and give a complete discharge in respect of it.

7. Power to do all acts and execute, in the name and on behalf of the company, all deeds, receipts and other documents and for that purpose to use, when necessary, the company's seal.

8. Power to prove, rank and claim in the bankruptcy, insolvency or sequestration of any contributory for any balance against his estate, and to receive dividends in the bankruptcy, insolvency or sequestration in respect of that balance, as a separate debt due from the bankrupt or insolvent, and rateably with the other separate creditors.

9. Power to draw, accept, make and indorse any bill of exchange or promissory note in the name and on behalf of the company, with the same effect with respect to the company's liability as if the bill or note had been drawn, accepted, made or indorsed by or on behalf of the company in the course of its business.

10. Power to raise on the security of the assets of the company any money requisite.

11. Power to take out in his official name letters of administration to any deceased contributory, and to do in his official name any other act necessary for obtaining payment of any money due from a contributory or his estate which cannot conveniently be done in the name of the company.

In all such cases the money due is deemed, for the purpose of enabling the liquidator to take out the letters of administration or recover the money, to be due to the liquidator himself.

12. Power to appoint an agent to do any business which the liquidator is unable to do himself.

13. Power to do all such other things as may be necessary for winding up the company's affairs and distributing its assets.

SCHEDULE 6 THE CATEGORIES OF PREFERENTIAL DEBTS

Category 4: Contributions to occupational pension schemes, etc.

8. Any sum which is owed by the debtor and is a sum to which Schedule 4 to the Pension Schemes Act 1993 applies (contributions to occupational pension schemes and state scheme premiums).

Category 5: Remuneration, etc. of employees

9. So much of any amount which—
   (a) is owed by the debtor to a person who is or has been an employee of the debtor, and
   (b) is payable by way of remuneration in respect of the whole or any part of the period of 4 months next before the relevant date,

   as does not exceed so much as may be prescribed by order made by the Secretary of State.

10. An amount owed by way of accrued holiday remuneration, in respect of any period of employment before the relevant date, to a person whose employment by the debtor has been terminated, whether before, on or after that date.

11. So much of any sum owed in respect of money advanced for the purpose as has been applied for the payment of a debt which, if it had not been paid, would have been a debt falling within paragraph 9 or 10.

12. So much of any amount which—
   (a) is ordered (whether before or after the relevant date) to be paid by the debtor under the Reserve Forces (Safeguard of Employment) Act 1985, and
   (b) is so ordered in respect of a default made by the debtor before that date in the discharge of his obligations under that Act,

   as does not exceed such amount as may be prescribed by order made by the Secretary of State.

...

Category 6: Levies on coal and steel production

...

As amended by the Court of Session Act 1988, Schedule 2; Criminal Justice Act 1988, s 62(2); Companies Act 1989, s 60(2)–(3); The Companies (Single Member Private Limited Companies) Regulations 1992 (SI 1992/1699), Schedule, para 8; Pension Schemes Act 1993, Schedule 8, para 18; Insolvency Act 1994, ss 2–3; Insolvency (No 2) Act 1994, s 1(1); Requirements of Writing (Scotland) Act 1995, Schedule 4, para 58; Access to Justice Act 1999, Schedule 13, para 133; Abolition of Feudal Tenure etc. (Scotland) Act 2000, Schedule 13, Part 1; Insolvency Act 2000, s 10(1)–(7), Schedule 1, paras 3–4, 6–7; Schedule 2, paras 1–11, Schedule 5; Limited Liability Partnerships Regulations 2001 (SI 2001/1090), Schedule 5, para 15; Limited Liability Partnerships (Scotland) Regulations 2001 (SSI 2001/128), Schedule 4, para 1; Enterprise Act 2002, ss 248(2), 250(1), 251(1),(3), 252–253, Schedule 16, Schedule 17, paras 10–18, 23–26, 28–34, 36–37, Schedule 21, para 1, Schedule 26; The Insolvency Act 1986 (Amendment) Regulations 2002 (SI 2002/1037), reg 4; The Insolvency Act 1986 (Amendment) (No. 2) Regulations 2002 (SI 2002/1240), regs 4, 8, 11, 16; Courts Act 2003, Schedule 8, paras 294, 299; The Enterprise Act 2002 (Insolvency) Order 2003 (SI 2003/2096), arts 2(3), 4, Schedule, Part 1, para 10; Civil Partnership Act 2004, Schedule 27, paras 112, 121–122; Companies (Audit, Investigations and Community Enterprise) Act 2004, Schedule 2, para 27; Energy Act 2004, Schedule 20, para 44(2), (4); The European Public Limited-Liability Company Regulations 2004

(SI 2004/2326), reg 73(3), (4)(a), (c); The Insolvent Partnerships Order 1994 (SI 1994/2421), art 2(1)(2); The Civil Partnership Act 2004 (Overseas Relationships and Consequential, etc. Amendments) Order 2005 (SI 2005/3129), art 4(4), Sch 4, para 8; The Insolvency Act 1986 (Amendment) Regulations 2005 (SI 2005/879), reg 2(2)–(3); Companies Act 2006, s 1282(1); The Companies (Registrar, Languages and Trading Disclosures) Regulations 2006 (SI 2006/3429), reg 7(1); Bankruptcy and Diligence etc. (Scotland) Act 2007, ss 3, 155(2), Schedule 5, para 14(2); Tribunals, Courts and Enforcement Act 2007, Schedule 20, para 2; The Companies Act 2006 (Commencement No. 3, Consequential Amendments, Transitional Provisions and Savings) Order 2007 (SI 2007/2194), Schedule 4, paras 39–43; The Companies Act 2006 (Consequential Amendments etc) Order 2008 (SI 2008/948), Schedule 1, paras 100(a), 102–103; The Companies (Trading Disclosures) (Insolvency) Regulations 2008 (SI 2008/1897), reg 2(1)–(2); The Legislative Reform (Insolvency) (Advertising Requirements) Order 2009 (SI 2009/864), art 3; The Companies Act 2006 (Consequential Amendments, Transitional Provisions and Savings) Order (SI 2009/1941), Schedule 1, paras 71–84; The Legislative Reform (Insolvency) (Miscellaneous Provisions) Order 2010 (SI 2010/18); The Insolvency Act 1986 Amendment (Appointment of Receivers) (Scotland) Regulations 2011 (SI 2011/140), reg 2(1)–(3).

Criminal Justice Act 1993

Part V INSIDER DEALING

The offence of insider dealing

52 THE OFFENCE

(1) An individual who has information as an insider is guilty of insider dealing if, in the circumstances mentioned in subsection (3), he deals in securities that are price-affected securities in relation to the information.

(2) An individual who has information as an insider is also guilty of insider dealing if—
   (a) he encourages another person to deal in securities that are (whether or not that other knows it) price-affected securities in relation to the information, knowing or having reasonable cause to believe that the dealing would take place in the circumstances mentioned in subsection (3); or
   (b) he discloses the information, otherwise than in the proper performance of the functions of his employment, office or profession, to another person.

(3) The circumstances referred to above are that the acquisition or disposal in question occurs on a regulated market, or that the person dealing relies on a professional intermediary or is himself acting as a professional intermediary.

(4) This section has effect subject to section 53.

53 DEFENCES

(1) An individual is not guilty of insider dealing by virtue of dealing in securities if he shows—
(a) that he did not at the time expect the dealing to result in a profit attributable to the fact that the information in question was price-sensitive information in relation to the securities, or
(b) that at the time he believed on reasonable grounds that the information had been disclosed widely enough to ensure that none of those taking part in the dealing would be prejudiced by not having the information, or
(c) that he would have done what he did even if he had not had the information.

(2) An individual is not guilty of insider dealing by virtue of encouraging another person to deal in securities if he shows—
(a) that he did not at the time expect the dealing to result in a profit attributable to the fact that the information in question was price-sensitive information in relation to the securities, or
(b) that at the time he believed on reasonable grounds that the information had been or would be disclosed widely enough to ensure that none of those taking part in the dealing would be prejudiced by not having the information, or
(c) that he would have done what he did even if he had not had the information.

(3) An individual is not guilty of insider dealing by virtue of a disclosure of information if he shows—
(a) that he did not at the time expect any person, because of the disclosure, to deal in securities in the circumstances mentioned in subsection (3) of section 52; or
(b) that, although he had such an expectation at the time, he did not expect the dealing to result in a profit attributable to the fact that the information was price-sensitive information in relation to the securities.

(4) Schedule 1 (special defences) shall have effect.

(5) The Treasury may by order amend Schedule 1.

(6) In this section references to a profit include references to the avoidance of a loss.

Interpretation

54 SECURITIES TO WHICH PART V APPLIES

(1) This Part applies to any security which—
(a) falls within any paragraph of Schedule 2; and
(b) satisfies any conditions applying to it under an order made by the Treasury for the purposes of this subsection;
and in the provisions of this Part (other than that Schedule) any reference to a security is a reference to a security to which this Part applies.

(2) The Treasury may by order amend Schedule 2.

55 "DEALING" IN SECURITIES

(1) For the purposes of this Part, a person deals in securities if—
(a) he acquires or disposes of the securities (whether as principal or agent); or
(b) he procures, directly or indirectly, an acquisition or disposal of the securities by any other person.

(2) For the purposes of this Part, “acquire”, in relation to a security, includes—
(a) agreeing to acquire the security; and
(b) entering into a contract which creates the security.

(3) For the purposes of this Part, “dispose”, in relation to a security, includes—
(a) agreeing to dispose of the security; and
(b) bringing to an end a contract which created the security.

(4) For the purposes of subsection (1), a person procures an acquisition or disposal of a security if the security is acquired or disposed of by a person who is—
(a) his agent,
(b) his nominee, or
(c) a person who is acting at his direction,
in relation to the acquisition or disposal.

(5) Subsection (4) is not exhaustive as to the circumstances in which one person may be regarded as procuring an acquisition or disposal of securities by another.

56 “INSIDE INFORMATION”, ETC.

(1) For the purposes of this section and section 57, “inside information” means information which—
(a) relates to particular securities or to a particular issuer of securities or to particular issuers of securities and not to securities generally or to issuers of securities generally;
(b) is specific or precise;
(c) has not been made public; and
(d) if it were made public would be likely to have a significant effect on the price of any securities.

(2) For the purposes of this Part, securities are “price-affected securities” in relation to inside information, and inside information is “price-sensitive information” in relation to securities, if and only if the information would, if made public, be likely to have a significant effect on the price of the securities.

(3) For the purposes of this section “price” includes value.

57 “INSIDERS”

(1) For the purposes of this Part, a person has information as an insider if and only if—
(a) it is, and he knows that it is, inside information, and
(b) he has it, and knows that he has it, from an inside source.

(2) For the purposes of subsection (1), a person has information from an inside source if and only if—
(a) he has it through—
(i) being a director, employee or shareholder of an issuer of securities; or
(ii) having access to the information by virtue of his employment, office or profession; or
(b) the direct or indirect source of his information is a person within paragraph (a).

58 INFORMATION “MADE PUBLIC”

(1) For the purposes of section 56, “made public”, in relation to information, shall be construed in accordance with the following provisions of this section; but those provisions are not exhaustive as to the meaning of that expression.

(2) Information is made public if—
(a) it is published in accordance with the rules of a regulated market for the purpose of informing investors and their professional advisers;
(b) it is contained in records which by virtue of any enactment are open to inspection by the public;
(c) it can be readily acquired by those likely to deal in any securities—
(i) to which the information relates, or
(ii) of an issuer to which the information relates; or
(d) it is derived from information which has been made public.

(3) Information may be treated as made public even though—
(a) it can be acquired only by persons exercising diligence or expertise;
(b) it is communicated to a section of the public and not to the public at large;
(c) it can be acquired only by observation;
(d) it is communicated only on payment of a fee; or
(e) it is published only outside the United Kingdom.

59 "PROFESSIONAL INTERMEDIARY"

(1) For the purposes of this Part, a "professional intermediary" is a person—
(a) who carries on a business consisting of an activity mentioned in subsection (2) and who holds himself out to the public or any section of the public (including a section of the public constituted by persons such as himself) as willing to engage in any such business; or
(b) who is employed by a person falling within paragraph (a) to carry out any such activity.

(2) The activities referred to in subsection (1) are—
(a) acquiring or disposing of securities (whether as principal or agent); or
(b) acting as an intermediary between persons taking part in any dealing in securities.

(3) A person is not to be treated as carrying on a business consisting of an activity mentioned in subsection (2)—
(a) if the activity in question is merely incidental to some other activity not falling within subsection (2); or
(b) merely because he occasionally conducts one of those activities.

(4) For the purposes of section 52, a person dealing in securities relies on a professional intermediary if and only if a person who is acting as a professional intermediary carries out an activity mentioned in subsection (2) in relation to that dealing.

60 OTHER INTERPRETATION PROVISIONS

(1) For the purposes of this Part, "regulated market" means any market, however operated, which, by an order made by the Treasury, is identified (whether by name or by reference to criteria prescribed by the order) as a regulated market for the purposes of this Part.

(2) For the purposes of this Part an "issuer", in relation to any securities, means any company, public sector body or individual by which or by whom the securities have been or are to be issued.

(3) For the purposes of this Part—
(a) "company" means any body (whether or not incorporated and wherever incorporated or constituted) which is not a public sector body; and
(b) "public sector body" means—

(i) the government of the United Kingdom, of Northern Ireland or of any country or territory outside the United Kingdom;
(ii) a local authority in the United Kingdom or elsewhere;
(iii) any international organisation the members of which include the United Kingdom or another member state;
(iv) the Bank of England; or
(v) the central bank of any sovereign State.

(4) For the purposes of this Part, information shall be treated as relating to an issuer of securities which is a company not only where it is about the company but also where it may affect the company's business prospects.

Miscellaneous

61 PENALTIES AND PROSECUTION

(1) An individual guilty of insider dealing shall be liable—
(a) on summary conviction, to a fine not exceeding the statutory maximum or imprisonment for a term not exceeding six months or to both; or
(b) on conviction on indictment, to a fine or imprisonment for a term not exceeding seven years or to both.

(2) Proceedings for offences under this Part shall not be instituted in England and Wales except by or with the consent of—
(a) the Secretary of State; or
(b) the Director of Public Prosecutions.

(3) In relation to proceedings in Northern Ireland for offences under this Part, subsection (2) shall have effect as if the reference to the Director of Public Prosecutions were a reference to the Director of Public Prosecutions for Northern Ireland.

61A SUMMARY PROCEEDINGS: VENUE AND TIME LIMIT FOR PROCEEDINGS

(1) Summary proceedings for an offence of insider dealing may (without prejudice to any jurisdiction exercisable apart from this subsection) be brought against an individual at any place at which the individual is for the time being.

(2) An information relating to an offence of insider dealing that is triable by a magistrates' court in England and Wales may be so tried if it is laid—
(a) at any time within three years after the commission of the offence, and
(b) within twelve months after the date on which evidence sufficient in the opinion of the Director of Public Prosecutions or the Secretary of State (as the case may be) to justify the proceedings comes to that person's knowledge.

(3) Summary proceedings in Scotland for an offence of insider dealing—
(a) must not be commenced after the expiration of three years from the commission of the offence;
(b) subject to that, may be commenced at any time—
(i) within twelve months after the date on which evidence sufficient in the Lord Advocate's opinion to justify the proceedings came to that person's knowledge, or
(ii) where such evidence was reported to the Lord Advocate by the Secretary of State, within twelve months after the date on which it came to the knowledge of the latter.

Section 136(3) of the Criminal Procedure (Scotland) Act 1995 (date when proceedings deemed to be commenced) applies for the purposes of this subsection as for the purposes of that section.

. . .

(5) For the purposes of this section a certificate of the Director of Public Prosecutions, the Lord Advocate, the Director of Public Prosecutions for Northern Ireland or the Secretary of State (as the case may be) as to the date on which such evidence as is referred to above came to that person's notice is conclusive evidence.

62 TERRITORIAL SCOPE OF OFFENCE OF INSIDER DEALING

(1) An individual is not guilty of an offence falling within subsection (1) of section 52 unless—
   (a) he was within the United Kingdom at the time when he is alleged to have done any act constituting or forming part of the alleged dealing;
   (b) the regulated market on which the dealing is alleged to have occurred is one which, by an order made by the Treasury, is identified (whether by name or by reference to criteria prescribed by the order) as being, for the purposes of this Part, regulated in the United Kingdom; or
   (c) the professional intermediary was within the United Kingdom at the time when he is alleged to have done anything by means of which the offence is alleged to have been committed.

(2) An individual is not guilty of an offence falling within subsection (2) of section 52 unless—
   (a) he was within the United Kingdom at the time when he is alleged to have disclosed the information or encouraged the dealing; or
   (b) the alleged recipient of the information or encouragement was within the United Kingdom at the time when he is alleged to have received the information or encouragement.

63 LIMITS ON SECTION 52

(1) Section 52 does not apply to anything done by an individual acting on behalf of a public sector body in pursuit of monetary policies or policies with respect to exchange rates or the management of public debt or foreign exchange reserves.

(2) No contract shall be void or unenforceable by reason only of section 52.

64 ORDERS

(1) Any power under this Part to make an order shall be exercisable by statutory instrument.

(2) No order shall be made under this Part unless a draft of it has been laid before and approved by a resolution of each House of Parliament.

(3) An order under this Part—
   (a) may make different provision for different cases; and
   (b) may contain such incidental, supplemental and transitional provisions as the Treasury consider expedient.

SCHEDULE 1 SPECIAL DEFENCES

Market makers

1(1) An individual is not guilty of insider dealing by virtue of dealing in securities or encouraging another person to deal if he shows that he acted in good faith in the course of—

(a) his business as a market maker, or
(b) his employment in the business of a market maker.

(2) A market maker is a person who—
(a) holds himself out at all normal times in compliance with the rules of a regulated market or an approved organisation as willing to acquire or dispose of securities; and
(b) is recognised as doing so under those rules.

(3) In this paragraph "approved organisation" means an international securities self-regulating organisation approved by the Treasury under any relevant order under section 22 of the Financial Services and Markets Act 2000].

Market information

2(1) An individual is not guilty of insider dealing by virtue of dealing in securities or encouraging another person to deal if he shows that—
(a) the information which he had as an insider was market information; and
(b) it was reasonable for an individual in his position to have acted as he did despite having that information as an insider at the time.

(2) In determining whether it is reasonable for an individual to do any act despite having market information at the time, there shall, in particular, be taken into account—
(a) the content of the information;
(b) the circumstances in which he first had the information and in what capacity; and
(c) the capacity in which he now acts.

3 An individual is not guilty of insider dealing by virtue of dealing in securities or encouraging another person to deal if he shows—
(a) that he acted—
(i) in connection with an acquisition or disposal which was under consideration or the subject of negotiation, or in the course of a series of such acquisitions or disposals; and
(ii) with a view to facilitating the accomplishment of the acquisition or disposal or the series of acquisitions or disposals; and
(b) that the information which he had as an insider was market information arising directly out of his involvement in the acquisition or disposal or series of acquisitions or disposals.

4 For the purposes of paragraphs 2 and 3 market information is information consisting of one or more of the following facts—
(a) that securities of a particular kind have been or are to be acquired or disposed of, or that their acquisition or disposal is under consideration or the subject of negotiation;
(b) that securities of a particular kind have not been or are not to be acquired or disposed of;
(c) the number of securities acquired or disposed of or to be acquired or disposed of or whose acquisition or disposal is under consideration or the subject of negotiation;
(d) the price (or range of prices) at which securities have been or are to be acquired or disposed of or the price (or range of prices) at which securities whose acquisition or disposal is under consideration or the subject of negotiation may be acquired or disposed of;
(e) the identity of the persons involved or likely to be involved in any capacity in an acquisition or disposal.

Price stabilisation

5(1) An individual is not guilty of insider dealing by virtue of dealing in securities or encouraging another person to deal if he shows that he acted in conformity with the price stabilisation rules or with the relevant provisions of Commission Regulation (EC) No

2273/2003 of 22 December 2003 implementing Directive 2003/6/EC of the European Parliament and of the Council as regards exemptions for buy-back programmes and stabilisation of financial instruments.

(2) "Price stabilisation rules" means rules made under section 144(1) of the Financial Services and Markets Act 2000.

SCHEDULE 2 SECURITIES

Shares

1 Shares and stock in the share capital of a company ("shares").

Debt securities

2 Any instrument creating or acknowledging indebtedness which is issued by a company or public sector body, including, in particular, debentures, debenture stock, loan stock, bonds and certificates of deposit ("debt securities").

Warrants

3 Any right (whether conferred by warrant or otherwise) to subscribe for shares or debt securities ("warrants").

Depositary receipts

4(1) The rights under any depositary receipt.

(2) For the purposes of sub-paragraph (1) a "depositary receipt" means a certificate or other record (whether or not in the form of a document)—
- (a) which is issued by or on behalf of a person who holds any relevant securities of a particular issuer; and
- (b) which acknowledges that another person is entitled to rights in relation to the relevant securities or relevant securities of the same kind.

(3) In sub-paragraph (2) "relevant securities" means shares, debt securities and warrants.

Options

5 Any option to acquire or dispose of any security falling within any other paragraph of this Schedule.

Futures

6(1) Rights under a contract for the acquisition or disposal of relevant securities under which delivery is to be made at a future date and at a price agreed when the contract is made.

(2) In sub-paragraph (1)—
- (a) the references to a future date and to a price agreed when the contract is made include references to a date and a price determined in accordance with terms of the contract; and
- (b) "relevant securities" means any security falling within any other paragraph of this Schedule.

Contracts for differences

7(1) Rights under a contract which does not provide for the delivery of securities but whose purpose or pretended purpose is to secure a profit or avoid a loss by reference to fluctuations in—
- (a) a share index or other similar factor connected with relevant securities;
- (b) the price of particular relevant securities; or
- (c) the interest rate offered on money placed on deposit.

(2) In sub-paragraph (1) "relevant securities" means any security falling within any other paragraph of this Schedule.

As amended by the The Financial Services and Markets Act 2000 (Consequential Amendments and Repeals) Order 2001 (SI 2001/3649), art 341(2)–(3); The Financial Services and Markets Act 2000 (Market Abuse) Regulations 2005 (SI 2005/381), Reg 3; The Companies Act 2006 (Consequential Amendments, Transitional Provisions and Savings) Order 2009 (SI 2009/1941), Schedule 1, para 141.

FINANCIAL SERVICES AND MARKETS ACT 2000

Part VI OFFICIAL LISTING

The competent authority

72 THE COMPETENT AUTHORITY

(1) On the coming into force of this section, the functions conferred on the competent authority by this Part are to be exercised by the Authority.

73 GENERAL DUTY OF THE COMPETENT AUTHORITY

(1) In discharging its general functions the competent authority must have regard to—
  (a) the need to use its resources in the most efficient and economic way;
  (b) the principle that a burden or restriction which is imposed on a person should be proportionate to the benefits, considered in general terms, which are expected to arise from the imposition of that burden or restriction;
  (c) the desirability of facilitating innovation in respect of listed securities and in respect of financial instruments which have otherwise been admitted to trading on a regulated market or for which a request for admission to trading on such a market has been made;
  (d) the international character of capital markets and the desirability of maintaining the competitive position of the United Kingdom;
  (e) the need to minimise the adverse effects on competition of anything done in the discharge of those functions;
  (f) the desirability of facilitating competition in relation to listed securities and in relation to financial instruments which have otherwise been admitted to trading on a regulated market or for which a request for admission to trading on such a market has been made.

(1A) To the extent that those general functions are functions under or relating to transparency rules, subsection (1)(c) and (f) have effect as if the references to a regulated market were references to a market.

(2) The competent authority's general functions are—
  (a) its function of making rules under this Part (considered as a whole);
  (b) its functions in relation to the giving of general guidance in relation to this Part (considered as a whole);
  (c) its function of determining the general policy and principles by reference to which it performs particular functions under this Part.

73A PART 6 RULES

(1) The competent authority may make rules ("Part 6 rules") for the purposes of this Part.

(2) Provisions of Part 6 rules expressed to relate to the official list are referred to in this Part as "listing rules".

(3) Provisions of Part 6 rules expressed to relate to disclosure of information in respect of financial instruments which have been admitted to trading on a regulated market or for which a request for admission to trading on a regulated market has been made, are referred to in this Part as "disclosure rules".

(4) Provisions of Part 6 rules expressed to relate to transferable securities are referred to in this Part as "prospectus rules".

(5) In relation to prospectus rules, the purposes of this Part include the purposes of the prospectus directive.

(6) Tranparency rules and corporate governance rules are not listing rules, disclosure rules or prospectus rules, but are Part 6 rules.

The official list

74 THE OFFICIAL LIST

(1) The competent authority must maintain the official list.

(2) The competent authority may admit to the official list such securities and other things as it considers appropriate.

(3) But—
(a) nothing may be admitted to the official list except in accordance with this Part; and
(b) the Treasury may by order provide that anything which falls within a description or category specified in the order may not be admitted to the official list.

(5) In the following provisions of this Part—

"listing" means being included in the official list in accordance with this Part.

Listing

75 APPLICATIONS FOR LISTING

(1) Admission to the official list may be granted only on an application made to the competent authority in such manner as may be required by listing rules.

(2) No application for listing may be entertained by the competent authority unless it is made by, or with the consent of, the issuer of the securities concerned.

(3) No application for listing may be entertained by the competent authority in respect of securities which are to be issued by a body of a prescribed kind.

(4) The competent authority may not grant an application for listing unless it is satisfied that—
(a) the requirements of listing rules (so far as they apply to the application), and
(b) any other requirements imposed by the authority in relation to the application,
are complied with.

(5) An application for listing may be refused if, for a reason relating to the issuer, the competent authority considers that granting it would be detrimental to the interests of investors.

(6) An application for listing securities which are already officially listed in another EEA State may be refused if the issuer has failed to comply with any obligations to which he is subject as a result of that listing.

76 DECISION ON APPLICATION

(1) The competent authority must notify the applicant of its decision on an application for listing—
(a) before the end of the period of six months beginning with the date on which the application is received; or

(b) if within that period the authority has required the applicant to provide further information in connection with the application, before the end of the period of six months beginning with the date on which that information is provided.

(2) If the competent authority fails to comply with subsection (1), it is to be taken to have decided to refuse the application.

(3) If the competent authority decides to grant an application for listing, it must give the applicant written notice.

(4) If the competent authority proposes to refuse an application for listing, it must give the applicant a warning notice.

(5) If the competent authority decides to refuse an application for listing, it must give the applicant a decision notice.

(6) If the competent authority decides to refuse an application for listing, the applicant may refer the matter to the Tribunal.

(7) If securities are admitted to the official list, their admission may not be called in question on the ground that any requirement or condition for their admission has not been complied with.

77 DISCONTINUANCE AND SUSPENSION OF LISTING

(1) The competent authority may, in accordance with listing rules, discontinue the listing of any securities if satisfied that there are special circumstances which preclude normal regular dealings in them.

(2) The competent authority may, in accordance with listing rules, suspend the listing of any securities.

(2A) The competent authority may discontinue under subsection (1) or suspend under subsection (2) the listing of any securities on its own initiative or on the application of the issuer of those securities.

(3) If securities are suspended under subsection (2) they are to be treated, for the purposes of sections 96 and 99, as still being listed.

(4) This section applies to securities whenever they were admitted to the official list.

(5) If the competent authority discontinues or suspends the listing of any securities, on its own initiative, the issuer may refer the matter to the Tribunal.

78 DISCONTINUANCE OR SUSPENSION: PROCEDURE

(1) A discontinuance or suspension by the competent authority on its own initiative takes effect—

(a) immediately, if the notice under subsection (2) states that that is the case;
(b) in any other case, on such date as may be specified in that notice.

(2) If on its own initiative the competent authority—

(a) proposes to discontinue or suspend the listing of securities, or
(b) discontinues or suspends the listing of securities with immediate effect,

it must give the issuer of the securities written notice.

(3) The notice must—

(a) give details of the discontinuance or suspension;

(b) state the competent authority's reasons for the discontinuance or suspension and for choosing the date on which it took effect or takes effect;
(c) inform the issuer of the securities that he may make representations to the competent authority within such period as may be specified in the notice (whether or not he has referred the matter to the Tribunal);
(d) inform him of the date on which the discontinuance or suspension took effect or will take effect; and
(e) inform him of his right to refer the matter to the Tribunal.

(4) The competent authority may extend the period within which representations may be made to it.

(5) If, having considered any representations made by the issuer of the securities, the competent authority decides—
(a) to discontinue or suspend the listing of the securities, or
(b) if the discontinuance or suspension has taken effect, not to cancel it,
the competent authority must give the issuer of the securities written notice.

(6) A notice given under subsection (5) must inform the issuer of the securities of his right to refer the matter to the Tribunal.

(7) If a notice informs a person of his right to refer a matter to the Tribunal, it must give an indication of the procedure on such a reference.

(8) If the competent authority decides—
(a) not to discontinue or suspend the listing of the securities, or
(b) if the discontinuance or suspension has taken effect, to cancel it, the competent authority must give the issuer of the securities written notice.

(9) The effect of cancelling a discontinuance is that the securities concerned are to be readmitted, without more, to the official list.

(10) If the competent authority has suspended the listing of securities on its own initiative and proposes to refuse an application by the issuer of the securities for the cancellation of the suspension, it must give him a warning notice.

(11) The competent authority must, having considered any representations made in response to the warning notice—
(a) if it decides to refuse the application, give the issuer of the securities a decision notice;
(b) if it grants the application, give him written notice of its decision.

(12) If the competent authority decides to refuse an application for the cancellation of the suspension of listed securities, the applicant may refer the matter to the Tribunal.

(13) "Discontinuance" means a discontinuance of listing under section 77(1).

(14) "Suspension" means a suspension of listing under section 77(2).

78A DISCONTINUANCE OR SUSPENSION AT THE REQUEST OF THE ISSUER: PROCEDURE

(1) A discontinuance or suspension by the competent authority on the application of the issuer of the securities takes effect—
(a) immediately, if the notice under subsection (2) states that this is the case;
(b) in any other case, on such date as may be specified in that notice.

(2) If the competent authority discontinues or suspends the listing of securities on the application of the issuer of the securities it must give him written notice.

(3) The notice must—
(a) give details of the discontinuance or suspension;
(b) inform the issuer of the securities of the date on which the discontinuance or suspension took effect or will take effect; and
(c) inform the issuer of his right to apply for the cancellation of the suspension.

(4) If the competent authority proposes to refuse an application by the issuer of the securities for the discontinuance or suspension of the listing of the securities, it must give him a warning notice.

(5) The competent authority must, having considered any representations made in response to the warning notice, if it decides to refuse the application, give the issuer of the securities a decision notice.

(6) If the competent authority decides to refuse an application by the issuer of the securities for the discontinuance or suspension of the listing of the securities, the issuer may refer the matter to the Tribunal.

(7) If the competent authority has suspended the listing of securities on the application of the issuer of the securities and proposes to refuse an application by the issuer for the cancellation of the suspension, it must give him a warning notice.

(8) The competent authority must, having considered any representations made in response to the warning notice—
(a) if it decides to refuse the application for the cancellation of the suspension, give the issuer of the securities a decision notice;
(b) if it grants the application, give him a written notice of its decision.

(9) If the competent authority decides to refuse an application for the cancellation of the suspension of listed securities, the applicant may refer the matter to the Tribunal.

(10) "Discontinuance" means a discontinuance of listing under section 77(1).

(11) "Suspension" means a suspension of listing under section 77(2).

Listing particulars

79 LISTING PARTICULARS AND OTHER DOCUMENTS

(1) Listing rules may provide that securities of a kind specified in the rules may not be admitted to the official list unless—
(a) listing particulars have been submitted to, and approved by, the competent authority and published; or
(b) in such cases as may be specified by listing rules, such document (other than listing particulars or a prospectus of a kind required by listing rules) as may be so specified has been published.

(2) "Listing particulars" means a document in such form and containing such information as may be specified in listing rules.

(3) For the purposes of this Part, the persons responsible for listing particulars are to be determined in accordance with regulations made by the Treasury.

(3A) Listing rules made under subsection (1) may not specify securities of a kind for which an approved prospectus is required as a result of section 85.

(4) Nothing in this section affects the competent authority's general power to make listing rules.

80 GENERAL DUTY OF DISCLOSURE IN LISTING PARTICULARS

(1) Listing particulars submitted to the competent authority under section 79 must contain all such information as investors and their professional advisers would reasonably require, and reasonably expect to find there, for the purpose of making an informed assessment of—
(a) the assets and liabilities, financial position, profits and losses, and prospects of the issuer of the securities; and
(b) the rights attaching to the securities.

(2) That information is required in addition to any information required by—
(a) listing rules, or
(b) the competent authority,
as a condition of the admission of the securities to the official list.

(3) Subsection (1) applies only to information—
(a) within the knowledge of any person responsible for the listing particulars; or
(b) which it would be reasonable for him to obtain by making enquiries.

(4) In determining what information subsection (1) requires to be included in listing particulars, regard must be had (in particular) to—
(a) the nature of the securities and their issuer;
(b) the nature of the persons likely to consider acquiring them;
(c) the fact that certain matters may reasonably be expected to be within the knowledge of professional advisers of a kind which persons likely to acquire the securities may reasonably be expected to consult; and
(d) any information available to investors or their professional advisers as a result of requirements imposed on the issuer of the securities by a recognised investment exchange, by listing rules or by or under any other enactment.

81 SUPPLEMENTARY LISTING PARTICULARS

(1) If at any time after the preparation of listing particulars which have been submitted to the competent authority under section 79 and before the commencement of dealings in the securities concerned following their admission to the official list—
(a) there is a significant change affecting any matter contained in those particulars the inclusion of which was required by—
(i) section 80,
(ii) listing rules, or
(iii) the competent authority, or
(b) a significant new matter arises, the inclusion of information in respect of which would have been so required if it had arisen when the particulars were prepared,
the issuer must, in accordance with listing rules, submit supplementary listing particulars of the change or new matter to the competent authority, for its approval and, if they are approved, publish them.

(2) "Significant" means significant for the purpose of making an informed assessment of the kind mentioned in section 80(1).

(3) If the issuer of the securities is not aware of the change or new matter in question, he is not under a duty to comply with subsection (1) unless he is notified of the change or new matter by a person responsible for the listing particulars.

(4) But it is the duty of any person responsible for those particulars who is aware of such a change or new matter to give notice of it to the issuer.

(5) Subsection (1) applies also as respects matters contained in any supplementary listing particulars previously published under this section in respect of the securities in question.

82 EXEMPTIONS FROM DISCLOSURE

(1) The competent authority may authorise the omission from listing particulars of any information, the inclusion of which would otherwise be required by section 80 or 81, on the ground—
- (a) that its disclosure would be contrary to the public interest;
- (b) that its disclosure would be seriously detrimental to the issuer; or
- (c) in the case of securities of a kind specified in listing rules, that its disclosure is unnecessary for persons of the kind who may be expected normally to buy or deal in securities of that kind.

(2) But—
- (a) no authority may be granted under subsection (1)(b) in respect of essential information; and
- (b) no authority granted under subsection (1)(b) extends to any such information.

(3) The Secretary of State or the Treasury may issue a certificate to the effect that the disclosure of any information (including information that would otherwise have to be included in listing particulars for which they are themselves responsible) would be contrary to the public interest.

(4) The competent authority is entitled to act on any such certificate in exercising its powers under subsection (1)(a).

(5) This section does not affect any powers of the competent authority under listing rules made as a result of section 101(2).

(6) "Essential information" means information which a person considering acquiring securities of the kind in question would be likely to need in order not to be misled about any facts which it is essential for him to know in order to make an informed assessment.

(7) "Listing particulars" includes supplementary listing particulars.

Transferable securities: public offers and admission to trading

84 MATTERS WHICH MAY BE DEALT WITH BY PROSPECTUS RULES

(1) Prospectus rules may make provision as to—
- (a) the required form and content of a prospectus (including a summary);
- (b) the cases in which a summary need not be included in a prospectus;
- (c) the languages which may be used in a prospectus (including a summary);
- (d) the determination of the persons responsible for a prospectus;
- (e) the manner in which applications to the competent authority for the approval of a prospectus are to be made.

(2) Prospectus rules may also make provision as to—
- (a) the period of validity of a prospectus;
- (b) the disclosure of the maximum price or of the criteria or conditions according to which the final offer price is to be determined, if that information is not contained in a prospectus;
- (c) the disclosure of the amount of the transferable securities which are to be offered to the public or of the criteria or conditions according to which that amount is to be determined, if that information is not contained in a prospectus;

(c) the required form and content of other summary documents (including the languages which may be used in such a document);
(d) the ways in which a prospectus that has been approved by the competent authority may be made available to the public;
(f) the disclosure, publication or other communication of such information as the competent authority may reasonably stipulate;
(g) the principles to be observed in relation to advertisements in connection with an offer of transferable securities to the public or admission of transferable securities to trading on a regulated market and the enforcement of those principles;
(h) the suspension of trading in transferable securities where continued trading would be detrimental to the interests of investors;
  (i) elections under section 87 or under Article 2.1(m)(iii) of the prospectus directive as applied for the purposes of this Part by section 102C.

(3) Prospectus rules may also make provision as to—
(a) access to the register of investors maintained under section 87R; and
(b) the supply of information from that register.

(4) Prospectus rules may make provision for the purpose of dealing with matters arising out of or related to any provision of the prospectus directive.

(5) In relation to cases where the home State in relation to an issuer of transferable securities is an EEA State other than the United Kingdom, prospectus rules may make provision for the recognition of elections made in relation to such securities under the law of that State in accordance with Article 1.3 or 2.1(m)(iii) of the prospectus directive.

(6) In relation to a document relating to transferable securities issued by an issuer incorporated in a non-EEA State and drawn up in accordance with the law of that State, prospectus rules may make provision as to the approval of that document as a prospectus.

(7) Nothing in this section affects the competent authority's general power to make prospectus rules.

85 PROHIBITION OF DEALING ETC. IN TRANSFERABLE SECURITIES WITHOUT APPROVED PROSPECTUS

(1) It is unlawful for transferable securities to which this subsection applies to be offered to the public in the United Kingdom unless an approved prospectus has been made available to the public before the offer is made.

(2) It is unlawful to request the admission of transferable securities to which this subsection applies to trading on a regulated market situated or operating in the United Kingdom unless an approved prospectus has been made available to the public before the request is made.

(3) A person who contravenes subsection (1) or (2) is guilty of an offence and liable—
(a) on summary conviction, to imprisonment for a term not exceeding 3 months or a fine not exceeding the statutory maximum or both;
(b) on conviction on indictment, to imprisonment for a term not exceeding 2 years or a fine or both.

(4) A contravention of subsection (1) or (2) is actionable, at the suit of a person who suffers loss as a result of the contravention, subject to the defences and other incidents applying to actions for breach of statutory duty.

(5) Subsection (1) applies to all transferable securities other than—
(a) those listed in Schedule 11A;
(b) such other transferable securities as may be specified in prospectus rules.

(6) Subsection (2) applies to all transferable securities other than—
(a) those listed in Part 1 of Schedule 11A;
(b) such other transferable securities as may be specified in prospectus rules.

(7) "Approved prospectus" means, in relation to transferable securities to which this section applies, a prospectus approved by the competent authority of the home State in relation to the issuer of the securities.

86 EXEMPT OFFERS TO THE PUBLIC

(1) A person does not contravene section 85(1) if—
(a) the offer is made to or directed at qualified investors only;
(b) the offer is made to or directed at fewer than 100 persons, other than qualified investors, per EEA State;
(c) the minimum consideration which may be paid by any person for transferable securities acquired by him pursuant to the offer is at least 50,000 euros (or an equivalent amount);
(d) the transferable securities being offered are denominated in amounts of at least 50,000 euros (or equivalent amounts); or
(e) the total consideration for the transferable securities being offered cannot exceed 100,000 euros (or an equivalent amount).

(2) Where—
(a) a person who is not a qualified investor ("the client") has engaged a qualified investor falling within Article 2.1(e)(i) of the prospectus directive to act as his agent, and
(b) the terms on which the qualified investor is engaged enable him to make decisions concerning the acceptance of offers of transferable securities on the client's behalf without reference to the client, an offer made to or directed at the qualified investor is not to be regarded for the purposes of subsection (1) as also having been made to or directed at the client.

(3) For the purposes of subsection (1)(b), the making of an offer of transferable securities to—
(a) trustees of a trust,
(b) members of a partnership in their capacity as such, or
(c) two or more persons jointly,
is to be treated as the making of an offer to a single person.

(4) In determining whether subsection (1)(e) is satisfied in relation to an offer ("offer A"), offer A is to be taken together with any other offer of transferable securities of the same class made by the same person which—
(a) was open at any time within the period of 12 months ending with the date on which offer A is first made; and
(b) had previously satisfied subsection (1)(e).

(5) For the purposes of this section, an amount (in relation to an amount denominated in euros) is an "equivalent amount" if it is an amount of equal value denominated wholly or partly in another currency or unit of account.

(6) The equivalent is to be calculated at the latest practicable date before (but in any event not more than 3 working days before) the date on which the offer is first made.

(7) "Qualified investor" means—
(a) an entity falling within Article 2.1(e)(i), (ii) or (iii) of the prospectus directive;
(b) an investor registered on the register maintained by the competent authority under section 87R;
(c) an investor authorised by an EEA State other than the United Kingdom to be considered as a qualified investor for the purposes of the prospectus directive.

87 ELECTION TO HAVE PROSPECTUS

(1) A person who proposes—
(a) to issue transferable securities to which this section applies,
(b) to offer to the public transferable securities to which this section applies, or
(c) to request the admission to a regulated market of transferable securities to which this section applies,
may elect, in accordance with prospectus rules, to have a prospectus in relation to the securities.

(2) If a person makes such an election, the provisions of this Part and of prospectus rules apply in relation to those transferable securities as if, in relation to an offer of the securities to the public or the admission of the securities to trading on a regulated market, they were transferable securities for which an approved prospectus would be required as a result of section 85.

(3) Listing rules made under section 79 do not apply to securities which are the subject of an election.

(4) The transferable securities to which this section applies are those which fall within any of the following paragraphs of Schedule 11A—
(a) paragraph 2,
(b) paragraph 4,
(c) paragraph 8, or
(d) paragraph 9,
where the United Kingdom is the home State in relation to the issuer of the securities.

Approval of prospectus

87A CRITERIA FOR APPROVAL OF PROSPECTUS BY COMPETENT AUTHORITY

(1) The competent authority may not approve a prospectus unless it is satisfied that—
(a) the United Kingdom is the home State in relation to the issuer of the transferable securities to which it relates,
(b) the prospectus contains the necessary information, and
(c) all of the other requirements imposed by or in accordance with this Part or the prospectus directive have been complied with (so far as those requirements apply to a prospectus for the transferable securities in question).

(2) The necessary information is the information necessary to enable investors to make an informed assessment of—
(a) the assets and liabilities, financial position, profits and losses, and prospects of the issuer of the transferable securities and of any guarantor; and
(b) the rights attaching to the transferable securities.

(3) The necessary information must be presented in a form which is comprehensible and easy to analyse.

(4) The necessary information must be prepared having regard to the particular nature of the transferable securities and their issuer.

(5) The prospectus must include a summary (unless the transferable securities in question are ones in relation to which prospectus rules provide that a summary is not required).

(6) The summary must, briefly and in non-technical language, convey the essential characteristics of, and risks associated with, the issuer, any guarantor and the transferable securities to which the prospectus relates.

(7) Where the prospectus for which approval is sought does not include the final offer price or the amount of transferable securities to be offered to the public, the applicant must inform the competent authority in writing of that information as soon as that element is finalised.

(8) "Prospectus" (except in subsection (5)) includes a supplementary prospectus.

87B EXEMPTIONS FROM DISCLOSURE

(1) The competent authority may authorise the omission from a prospectus of any information, the inclusion of which would otherwise be required, on the ground—
  (a) that its disclosure would be contrary to the public interest;
  (b) that its disclosure would be seriously detrimental to the issuer, provided that the omission would be unlikely to mislead the public with regard to any facts or circumstances which are essential for an informed assessment of the kind mentioned in section 87A(2); or
  (c) that the information is only of minor importance for a specific offer to the public or admission to trading on a regulated market and unlikely to influence an informed assessment of the kind mentioned in section 87A(2).

(2) The Secretary of State or the Treasury may issue a certificate to the effect that the disclosure of any information would be contrary to the public interest.

(3) The competent authority is entitled to act on any such certificate in exercising its powers under subsection (1)(a).

(4) This section does not affect any powers of the competent authority under prospectus rules.

(5) "Prospectus" includes a supplementary prospectus.

87C CONSIDERATION OF APPLICATION FOR APPROVAL

(1) The competent authority must notify the applicant of its decision on an application for approval of a prospectus before the end of the period for consideration.

(2) The period for consideration—
  (a) begins with the first working day after the date on which the application is received; but
  (b) if the competent authority gives a notice under subsection (4), is to be treated as beginning with the first working day after the date on which the notice is complied with.

(3) The period for consideration is—
  (a) except in the case of a new issuer, 10 working days; or
  (b) in that case, 20 working days.

(4) The competent authority may by notice in writing require a person who has applied for approval of a prospectus to provide—
(a) specified documents or documents of a specified description, or
(b) specified information or information of a specified description.

(5) No notice under subsection (4) may be given after the end of the period, beginning with the first working day after the date on which the application is received, of—
(a) except in the case of a new issuer, 10 working days; or
(b) in that case, 20 working days.

(6) Subsection (4) applies only to information and documents reasonably required in connection with the exercise by the competent authority of its functions in relation to the application.

(7) The competent authority may require any information provided under this section to be provided in such form as it may reasonably require.

(8) The competent authority may require—
(a) any information provided, whether in a document or otherwise, to be verified in such manner, or
(b) any document produced to be authenticated in such manner,
as it may reasonably require.

(9) The competent authority must notify the applicant of its decision on an application for approval of a supplementary prospectus before the end of the period of 7 working days beginning with the date on which the application is received; and subsections (4) and (6) to (8) apply to such an application as they apply to an application for approval of a prospectus.

(10) The competent authority's failure to comply with subsection (1) or (9) does not constitute approval of the application in question.

(11) "New issuer" means an issuer of transferable securities which—
(a) does not have transferable securities admitted to trading on any regulated market; and
(b) has not previously offered transferable securities to the public.

87D PROCEDURE FOR DECISION ON APPLICATION FOR APPROVAL

(1) If the competent authority approves a prospectus, it must give the applicant written notice.

(2) If the competent authority proposes to refuse to approve a prospectus, it must give the applicant written notice.

(3) The notice must state the competent authority's reasons for the proposed refusal.

(4) If the competent authority decides to refuse to approve a prospectus, it must give the applicant written notice.

(5) The notice must—
(a) give the competent authority's reasons for refusing the application; and
(b) inform the applicant of his right to refer the matter to the Tribunal.

(6) If the competent authority refuses to approve a prospectus, the applicant may refer the matter to the Tribunal.

(7) In this section "prospectus" includes a supplementary prospectus.

Transfer of application for approval of a prospectus

87E TRANSFER BY COMPETENT AUTHORITY OF APPLICATION FOR APPROVAL

(1) The competent authority may transfer an application for the approval of a prospectus or a supplementary prospectus to the competent authority of another EEA State ("the transferee authority").

(2) Before doing so, the competent authority must obtain the agreement of the transferee authority.

(3) The competent authority must inform the applicant of the transfer within 3 working days beginning with the first working day after the date of the transfer.

(4) On making a transfer under subsection (1), the competent authority ceases to have functions under this Part in relation to the application transferred.

87F TRANSFER TO COMPETENT AUTHORITY OF APPLICATION FOR APPROVAL

(1) Where the competent authority agrees to the transfer to it of an application for the approval of a prospectus made to the competent authority of another EEA State—
- (a) the United Kingdom is to be treated for the purposes of this Part as the home State in relation to the issuer of the transferable securities to which the prospectus relates, and
- (b) this Part applies to the application as if it had been made to the competent authority but with the modification in subsection (2).

(2) Section 87C applies as if the date of the transfer were the date on which the application was received by the competent authority.

Supplementary prospectus

87G SUPPLEMENTARY PROSPECTUS

(1) Subsection (2) applies if, during the relevant period, there arises or is noted a significant new factor, material mistake or inaccuracy relating to the information included in a prospectus approved by the competent authority.

(2) The person on whose application the prospectus was approved must, in accordance with prospectus rules, submit a supplementary prospectus containing details of the new factor, mistake or inaccuracy to the competent authority for its approval.

(3) The relevant period begins when the prospectus is approved and ends—
- (a) with the closure of the offer of the transferable securities to which the prospectus relates; or
- (b) when trading in those securities on a regulated market begins.

(4) "Significant" means significant for the purposes of making an informed assessment of the kind mentioned in section 87A(2).

(5) Any person responsible for the prospectus who is aware of any new factor, mistake or inaccuracy which may require the submission of a supplementary prospectus in accordance with subsection (2) must give notice of it to—
- (a) the issuer of the transferable securities to which the prospectus relates, and
- (b) the person on whose application the prospectus was approved.

(6) A supplementary prospectus must provide sufficient information to correct any mistake or inaccuracy which gave rise to the need for it.

(7) Subsection (1) applies also to information contained in any supplementary prospectus published under this section.

Passporting

87H PROSPECTUS APPROVED IN ANOTHER EEA STATE

(1) A prospectus approved by the competent authority of an EEA State other than the United Kingdom is not an approved prospectus for the purposes of section 85 unless that authority has provided the competent authority with—
  (a) a certificate of approval;
  (b) a copy of the prospectus as approved; and
  (c) if requested by the competent authority, a translation of the summary of the prospectus.

(2) A document is not a certificate of approval unless it states that the prospectus—
  (a) has been drawn up in accordance with the prospectus directive; and
  (b) has been approved, in accordance with that directive, by the competent authority providing the certificate.

(3) A document is not a certificate of approval unless it states whether (and, if so, why) the competent authority providing it authorised, in accordance with the prospectus directive, the omission from the prospectus of information which would otherwise have been required to be included.

(4) "Prospectus" includes a supplementary prospectus.

87I PROVISION OF INFORMATION TO HOST MEMBER STATE

(1) The competent authority must, if requested to do so, supply the competent authority of a specified EEA State with—
  (a) a certificate of approval;
  (b) a copy of the specified prospectus (as approved by the competent authority); and
  (c) a translation of the summary of the specified prospectus (if the request states that one has been requested by the other competent authority).

(2) Only the following may make a request under this section—
  (a) the issuer of the transferable securities to which the specified prospectus relates;
  (b) a person who wishes to offer the transferable securities to which the specified prospectus relates to the public in an EEA State other than (or as well as) the United Kingdom;
  (e) a person requesting the admission of the transferable securities to which the specified prospectus relates to a regulated market situated or operating in an EEA State other than (or as well as) the United Kingdom.

(3) A certificate of approval must state that the prospectus—
  (a) has been drawn up in accordance with this Part and the prospectus directive; and
  (b) has been approved, in accordance with those provisions, by the competent authority.

(4) A certificate of approval must state whether (and, if so, why) the competent authority authorised, in accordance with section 87B, the omission from the prospectus of information which would otherwise have been required to be included.

(5) The competent authority must comply with a request under this section—
(a) if the prospectus has been approved before the request is made, within 3 working days beginning with the date of the request; or
(b) if the request is submitted with an application for the approval of the prospectus, on the first working day after the date on which it approves the prospectus.

(6) "Prospectus" includes a supplementary prospectus.

(7) "Specified" means specified in a request made for the purposes of this section.

Transferable securities: powers of competent authority

87J REQUIREMENTS IMPOSED AS CONDITION OF APPROVAL

(1) As a condition of approving a prospectus, the competent authority may by notice in writing—
(a) require the inclusion in the prospectus of such supplementary information necessary for investor protection as the competent authority may specify;
(b) require a person controlling, or controlled by, the applicant to provide specified information or documents;
(c) require an auditor or manager of the applicant to provide specified information or documents;
(d) require a financial intermediary commissioned to assist either in carrying out the offer to the public of the transferable securities to which the prospectus relates or in requesting their admission to trading on a regulated market, to provide specified information or documents.

(2) "Specified" means specified in the notice.

(3) "Prospectus" includes a supplementary prospectus.

87K POWER TO SUSPEND OR PROHIBIT OFFER TO THE PUBLIC

(1) This section applies where a person ("the offeror") has made an offer of transferable securities to the public in the United Kingdom ("the offer").

(2) If the competent authority has reasonable grounds for suspecting that an applicable provision has been infringed, it may—
(a) require the offeror to suspend the offer for a period not exceeding 10 working days;
(b) require a person not to advertise the offer, or to take such steps as the authority may specify to suspend any existing advertisement of the offer, for a period not exceeding 10 working days.

(3) If the competent authority has reasonable grounds for suspecting that it is likely that an applicable provision will be infringed, it may require the offeror to withdraw the offer.

(4) If the competent authority finds that an applicable provision has been infringed, it may require the offeror to withdraw the offer.

(5) "An applicable provision" means—
(a) a provision of this Part,
(b) a provision contained in prospectus rules,
(c) any other provision made in accordance with the prospectus directive,
applicable in relation to the offer.

87L POWER TO SUSPEND OR PROHIBIT ADMISSION TO TRADING ON A REGULATED MARKET

(1) This section applies where a person has requested the admission of transferable securities to trading on a regulated market situated or operating in the United Kingdom.

(2) If the competent authority has reasonable grounds for suspecting that an applicable provision has been infringed and the securities have not yet been admitted to trading on the regulated market in question, it may—
(a) require the person requesting admission to suspend the request for a period not exceeding 10 working days;
(b) require a person not to advertise the securities to which it relates, or to take such steps as the authority may specify to suspend any existing advertisement in connection with those securities, for a period not exceeding 10 working days.

(3) If the competent authority has reasonable grounds for suspecting that an applicable provision has been infringed and the securities have been admitted to trading on the regulated market in question, it may—
(a) require the market operator to suspend trading in the securities for a period not exceeding 10 working days;
(b) require a person not to advertise the securities, or to take such steps as the authority may specify to suspend any existing advertisement in connection with those securities, for a period not exceeding 10 working days.

(4) If the competent authority finds that an applicable provision has been infringed, it may require the market operator to prohibit trading in the securities on the regulated market in question.

(5) "An applicable provision" means—
(a) a provision of this Part,
(b) a provision contained in prospectus rules,
(c) any other provision made in accordance with the prospectus directive,
applicable in relation to the admission of the transferable securities to trading on the regulated market in question.

87M PUBLIC CENSURE OF ISSUER

(1) If the competent authority finds that—
(a) an issuer of transferable securities,
(b) a person offering transferable securities to the public, or
(c) a person requesting the admission of transferable securities to trading on a regulated market,
is failing or has failed to comply with his obligations under an applicable provision, it may publish a statement to that effect.

(2) If the competent authority proposes to publish a statement, it must give the person a warning notice setting out the terms of the proposed statement.

(3) If, after considering any representations made in response to the warning notice, the competent authority decides to make the proposed statement, it must give the person a decision notice setting out the terms of the statement.

(4) "An applicable provision" means—
(a) a provision of this Part,
(b) a provision contained in prospectus rules,

(c) any other provision made in accordance with the prospectus directive, applicable to a prospectus in relation to the transferable securities in question.

(5) "Prospectus" includes a supplementary prospectus.

87N RIGHT TO REFER MATTERS TO THE TRIBUNAL

(1) A person to whom a decision notice is given under section 87M may refer the matter to the Tribunal.

(2) A person to whom a notice is given under section 87O may refer the matter to the Tribunal.

87O PROCEDURE UNDER SECTIONS 87K AND 87L

(1) A requirement under section 87K or 87L takes effect—
(a) immediately, if the notice under subsection (2) states that that is the case;
(b) in any other case, on such date as may be specified in that notice.

(2) If the competent authority—
(a) proposes to exercise the powers in section 87K or 87L in relation to a person, or
(b) exercises any of those powers in relation to a person with immediate effect,
it must give that person written notice.

(3) The notice must—
(a) give details of the competent authority's action or proposed action;
(b) state the competent authority's reasons for taking the action in question and choosing the date on which it took effect or takes effect;
(c) inform the recipient that he may make representations to the competent authority within such period as may be specified by the notice (whether or not he has referred the matter to the Tribunal);
(d) inform him of the date on which the action took effect or takes effect; and
(e) inform him of his right to refer the matter to the Tribunal.

(4) The competent authority may extend the period within which representations may be made to it.

(5) If, having considered any representations made to it, the competent authority decides to maintain, vary or revoke its earlier decision, it must give written notice to that effect to the person mentioned in subsection (2).

(6) A notice given under subsection (5) must inform that person, where relevant, of his right to refer the matter to the Tribunal.

(7) If a notice informs a person of his right to refer a matter to the Tribunal, it must give an indication of the procedure on such a reference.

(8) If a notice under this section relates to the exercise of the power conferred by section 87L(3), the notice must also be given to the person at whose request the transferable securities were admitted to trading on the regulated market.

87P EXERCISE OF POWERS AT REQUEST OF COMPETENT AUTHORITY OF ANOTHER EEA STATE

(1) This section applies if—
(a) the competent authority of an EEA State other than the United Kingdom has approved a prospectus,

(b) the transferable securities to which the prospectus relates have been offered to the public in the United Kingdom or their admission to trading on a regulated market has been requested, and
(c) that competent authority makes a request that the competent authority assist it in the performance of its functions under the law of that State in connection with the prospectus directive.

(2) For the purpose of complying with the request mentioned in subsection (1)(c), the powers conferred by sections 87K and 87L may be exercised as if the prospectus were one which had been approved by the competent authority.

(3) Section 87N does not apply to an exercise of those powers as a result of this section.

(4) Section 87O does apply to such an exercise of those powers but with the omission of subsections (3)(e), (6) and (7).

Rights of investors

87Q RIGHT OF INVESTOR TO WITHDRAW

(1) Where a person agrees to buy or subscribe for transferable securities in circumstances where the final offer price or the amount of transferable securities to be offered to the public is not included in the prospectus, he may withdraw his acceptance before the end of the withdrawal period.

(2) The withdrawal period—
(a) begins with the investor's acceptance; and
(b) ends at the end of the second working day after the date on which the competent authority is informed of the information in accordance with section 87A(7).

(3) Subsection (1) does not apply if the prospectus contains—
(a) in the case of the amount of transferable securities to be offered to the public, the criteria or conditions (or both) according to which that element will be determined, or
(b) in the case of price, the criteria or conditions (or both) according to which that element will be determined or the maximum price.

(4) Where a supplementary prospectus has been published and, prior to the publication, a person agreed to buy or subscribe for transferable securities to which it relates, he may withdraw his acceptance before the end of the period of 2 working days beginning with the first working day after the date on which the supplementary prospectus was published.

Registered investors

87R REGISTER OF INVESTORS

(1) The competent authority must establish and maintain, in accordance with this section and prospectus rules, a register of investors for the purposes of section 86.

(2) An individual may not be entered in the register unless—
(a) he is resident in the United Kingdom; and
(b) he meets at least two of the criteria mentioned in Article 2.2 of the prospectus directive.

(3) A company may not be entered in the register unless—

(a) it falls within the meaning of "small and medium-sized enterprises" in Article 2.1 of the prospectus directive; and
(b) its registered office is in the United Kingdom.

(4) A person who does not fall within subsection (2) or (3) may not be entered in the register.

Sponsors

88 SPONSORS

(1) Listing rules may require a person to make arrangements with a sponsor for the performance by the sponsor of such services in relation to him as may be specified in the rules.

(2) "Sponsor" means a person approved by the competent authority for the purposes of the rules.

(3) Listing rules made by virtue of subsection (1) may—
(a) provide for the competent authority to maintain a list of sponsors;
(b) specify services which must be performed by a sponsor;
(c) impose requirements on a sponsor in relation to the provision of services or specified services;
(d) specify the circumstances in which a person is qualified for being approved as a sponsor.

(4) If the competent authority proposes—
(a) to refuse a person's application for approval as a sponsor, or
(b) to cancel a person's approval as a sponsor otherwise than at his request,
it must give him a warning notice.

(5) If, after considering any representations made in response to the warning notice, the competent authority decides—
(a) to grant the application for approval, or
(b) not to cancel the approval,
it must give the person concerned, and any person to whom a copy of the warning notice was given, written notice of its decision.

(6) If, after considering any representations made in response to the warning notice, the competent authority decides—
(a) to refuse to grant the application for approval, or
(b) to cancel the approval,
it must give the person concerned a decision notice.

(7) A person to whom a decision notice is given under this section may refer the matter to the Tribunal.

89 PUBLIC CENSURE OF SPONSOR

(1) Listing rules may make provision for the competent authority, if it considers that a sponsor has contravened a requirement imposed on him by rules made as a result of section 88(3)(c), to publish a statement to that effect.

(2) If the competent authority proposes to publish a statement it must give the sponsor a warning notice setting out the terms of the proposed statement.

(3) If, after considering any representations made in response to the warning notice, the competent authority decides to make the proposed statement, it must give the sponsor a decision notice setting out the terms of the statement.

(4) A sponsor to whom a decision notice is given under this section may refer the matter to the Tribunal.

Power of competent authority to call for information

89H COMPETENT AUTHORITY'S POWER TO CALL FOR INFORMATION

(1) The competent authority may by notice in writing given to a person to whom this section applies require him—
- (a) to provide specified information or information of a specified description, or
- (b) to produce specified documents or documents of a specified description.

(2) This section applies to—
- (a) an issuer in respect of whom transparency rules have effect;
- (b) a voteholder;
- (c) an auditor of—
  - (i) an issuer to whom this section applies, or
  - (ii) a voteholder;
- (d) a person who controls a voteholder;
- (e) a person controlled by a voteholder;
- (f) a director or other similar officer of an issuer to whom this section applies;
- (g) a director or other similar officer of a voteholder or, where the affairs of a voteholder are managed by its members, a member of the voteholder.

(3) This section applies only to information and documents reasonably required in connection with the exercise by the competent authority of functions conferred on it by or under sections 89A to 89G (transparency rules).

(4) Information or documents required under this section must be provided or produced—
- (a) before the end of such reasonable period as may be specified, and
- (b) at such place as may be specified.

(5) If a person claims a lien on a document, its production under this section does not affect the lien.

89I REQUIREMENTS IN CONNECTION WITH CALL FOR INFORMATION

(1) The competent authority may require any information provided under section 89H to be provided in such form as it may reasonably require.

(2) The competent authority may require—
- (a) any information provided, whether in a document or otherwise, to be verified in such manner as it may reasonably require;
- (b) any document produced to be authenticated in such manner as it may reasonably require.

(3) If a document is produced in response to a requirement imposed under section 89H, the competent authority may—
- (a) take copies of or extracts from the document; or
- (b) require the person producing the document, or any relevant person, to provide an explanation of the document.

(4) In subsection (3)(b) "relevant person", in relation to a person who is required to produce a document, means a person who—
(a) has been or is a director or controller of that person;
(b) has been or is an auditor of that person;
(c) has been or is an actuary, accountant or lawyer appointed or instructed by that person; or
(d) has been or is an employee of that person.

(5) If a person who is required under section 89H to produce a document fails to do so, the competent authority may require him to state, to the best of his knowledge and belief, where the document is.

89J POWER TO CALL FOR INFORMATION: SUPPLEMENTARY PROVISIONS

(1) The competent authority may require an issuer to make public any information provided to the authority under section 89H.

(2) If the issuer fails to comply with a requirement under subsection (1), the competent authority may, after seeking representations from the issuer, make the information public.

(3) In sections 89H and 89I (power of competent authority to call for information)—

"control" and "controlled" have the meaning given by subsection (4) below;

"specified" means specified in the notice;

"voteholder" means a person who—
(a) holds voting rights in respect of any voting shares for the purposes of sections 89A to 89G (transparency rules), or
(b) is treated as holding such rights by virtue of rules under section 89A(3)(b).

(4) For the purposes of those sections a person ("A") controls another person ("B") if—
(a) A holds a majority of the voting rights in B,
(b) A is a member of B and has the right to appoint or remove a majority of the members of the board of directors (or, if there is no such board, the equivalent management body) of B,
(c) A is a member of B and controls alone, pursuant to an agreement with other shareholders or members, a majority of the voting rights in B, or
(d) A has the right to exercise, or actually exercises, dominant influence or control over B.

(5) For the purposes of subsection (4)(b)—
(a) any rights of a person controlled by A, and
(b) any rights of a person acting on behalf of A or a person controlled by A,
are treated as held by A.

Powers exercisable in case of infringement of transparency obligation

89K PUBLIC CENSURE OF ISSUER

(1) If the competent authority finds that an issuer of securities admitted to trading on a regulated market is failing or has failed to comply with an applicable transparency obligation, it may publish a statement to that effect.

(2) If the competent authority proposes to publish a statement, it must give the issuer a warning notice setting out the terms of the proposed statement.

(3) If, after considering any representations made in response to the warning notice, the competent authority decides to make the proposed statement, it must give the issuer a decision notice setting out the terms of the statement.

(4) A notice under this section must inform the issuer of his right to refer the matter to the Tribunal (see section 89N) and give an indication of the procedure on such a reference.

(5) In this section "transparency obligation" means an obligation under—
(a) a provision of transparency rules, or
(b) any other provision made in accordance with the transparency obligations directive.

(6) In relation to an issuer whose home State is a member State other than the United Kingdom, any reference to an applicable transparency obligation must be read subject to section 100A(2).

89L POWER TO SUSPEND OR PROHIBIT TRADING OF SECURITIES

(1) This section applies to securities admitted to trading on a regulated market.

(2) If the competent authority has reasonable grounds for suspecting that an applicable transparency obligation has been infringed by an issuer, it may—
(a) suspend trading in the securities for a period not exceeding 10 days,
(b) prohibit trading in the securities, or
(c) make a request to the operator of the market on which the issuer's securities are traded—
(i) to suspend trading in the securities for a period not exceeding 10 days, or
(ii) to prohibit trading in the securities.

(3) If the competent authority has reasonable grounds for suspecting that a provision required by the transparency obligations directive has been infringed by a voteholder of an issuer, it may—
(a) prohibit trading in the securities, or
(b) make a request to the operator of the market on which the issuer's securities are traded to prohibit trading in the securities.

(4) If the competent authority finds that an applicable transparency obligation has been infringed, it may require the market operator to prohibit trading in the securities.

(5) In this section "transparency obligation" means an obligation under—
(a) a provision contained in transparency rules, or
(b) any other provision made in accordance with the transparency obligations directive.

(6) In relation to an issuer whose home State is a member State other than the United Kingdom, any reference to an applicable transparency obligation must be read subject to section 100A(2).

89M PROCEDURE UNDER SECTION 89L

(1) A requirement under section 89L takes effect—
(a) immediately, if the notice under subsection (2) states that that is the case;
(b) in any other case, on such date as may be specified in the notice.

(2) If the competent authority—

(a) proposes to exercise the powers in section 89L in relation to a person, or
(b) exercises any of those powers in relation to a person with immediate effect,
it must give that person written notice.

(3) The notice must—
(a) give details of the competent authority's action or proposed action;
(b) state the competent authority's reasons for taking the action in question and choosing the date on which it took effect or takes effect;
(c) inform the recipient that he may make representations to the competent authority within such period as may be specified by the notice (whether or not he had referred the matter to the Tribunal);
(d) inform him of the date on which the action took effect or takes effect;
(e) inform him of his right to refer the matter to the Tribunal (see section 89N) and give an indication of the procedure on such a reference.

(4) The competent authority may extend the period within which representations may be made to it.

(5) If, having considered any representations made to it, the competent authority decides to maintain, vary or revoke its earlier decision, it must give written notice to that effect to the person mentioned in subsection (2).

89N RIGHT TO REFER MATTERS TO THE TRIBUNAL

A person—

(a) to whom a decision notice is given under section 89K (public censure), or

(b) to whom a notice is given under section 89M (procedure in connection with suspension or prohibition of trading),

may refer the matter to the Tribunal.

Corporate governance

89O CORPORATE GOVERNANCE RULES

(1) The competent authority may make rules ("corporate governance rules")—
(a) for the purpose of implementing, enabling the implementation of or dealing with matters arising out of or related to, any Community obligation relating to the corporate governance of issuers who have requested or approved admission of their securities to trading on a regulated market;
(b) about corporate governance in relation to such issuers for the purpose of implementing, or dealing with matters arising out of or related to, any Community obligation.

(2) "Corporate governance", in relation to an issuer, includes—
(a) the nature, constitution or functions of the organs of the issuer;
(b) the manner in which organs of the issuer conduct themselves;
(c) the requirements imposed on organs of the issuer;
(d) the relationship between the different organs of the issuer;
(e) the relationship between the organs of the issuer and the members of the issuer or holders of the issuer's securities.

(3) The burdens and restrictions imposed by rules under this section on foreign-traded issuers must not be greater than the burdens and restrictions imposed on UK-traded issuers by—

(a) rules under this section, and
(b) listing rules.

(4) For this purpose—

"foreign-traded issuer" means an issuer who has requested or approved admission of the issuer's securities to trading on a regulated market situated or operating outside the United Kingdom;

"UK-traded issuer" means an issuer who has requested or approved admission of the issuer's securities to trading on a regulated market situated or operating in the United Kingdom.

(5) This section is without prejudice to any other power conferred by this Part to make Part 6 rules.

Compensation for false or misleading statements etc.

90 COMPENSATION FOR STATEMENTS IN LISTING PARTICULARS OR PROSPECTUS

(1) Any person responsible for listing particulars is liable to pay compensation to a person who has—
(a) acquired securities to which the particulars apply; and
(b) suffered loss in respect of them as a result of—
(i) any untrue or misleading statement in the particulars; or
(ii) the omission from the particulars of any matter required to be included by section 80 or 81.

(2) Subsection (1) is subject to exemptions provided by Schedule 10.

(3) If listing particulars are required to include information about the absence of a particular matter, the omission from the particulars of that information is to be treated as a statement in the listing particulars that there is no such matter.

(4) Any person who fails to comply with section 81 is liable to pay compensation to any person who has—
(a) acquired securities of the kind in question; and
(b) suffered loss in respect of them as a result of the failure.

(5) Subsection (4) is subject to exemptions provided by Schedule 10.

(6) This section does not affect any liability which may be incurred apart from this section.

(7) References in this section to the acquisition by a person of securities include references to his contracting to acquire them or any interest in them.

(8) No person shall, by reason of being a promoter of a company or otherwise, incur any liability for failing to disclose information which he would not be required to disclose in listing particulars in respect of a company's securities—
(a) if he were responsible for those particulars; or
(b) if he is responsible for them, which he is entitled to omit by virtue of section 82.

(9) The reference in subsection (8) to a person incurring liability includes a reference to any other person being entitled as against that person to be granted any civil remedy or to rescind or repudiate an agreement.

(10) "Listing particulars", in subsection (1) and Schedule 10, includes supplementary listing particulars.

(11) This section applies in relation to a prospectus as it applies to listing particulars, with the following modifications—
(a) references in this section or in Schedule 10 to listing particulars, supplementary listing particulars or sections 80, 81 or 82 are to be read, respectively, as references to a prospectus, supplementary prospectus and sections 87A, 87G and 87B;
(b) references in Schedule 10 to admission to the official list are to be read as references to admission to trading on a regulated market;
(c) in relation to a prospectus, "securities" means "transferable securities".

(12) A person is not to be subject to civil liability solely on the basis of a summary in a prospectus unless the summary is misleading, inaccurate or inconsistent when read with the rest of the prospectus; and, in this subsection, a summary includes any translation of it.

90A LIABILITY OF ISSUERS IN CONNECTION WITH PUBLISHED INFORMATION

Schedule 10A makes provision about the liability of issuers of securities to pay compensation to persons who have suffered loss as a result of—
(a) a misleading statement or dishonest omission in certain published information relating to the securities, or
(b) a dishonest delay in publishing such information.

90B POWER TO MAKE FURTHER PROVISION ABOUT LIABILITY FOR PUBLISHED INFORMATION

(1) The Treasury may by regulations make provision about the liability of issuers of securities traded on a regulated market, and other persons, in respect of information published to holders of securities, to the market or to the public generally.

(2) Regulations under this section may amend any primary or subordinate legislation, including any provisions of, or made under, this Act.

Penalties

91 PENALTIES FOR BREACH OF PART 6 RULES

(1) If the competent authority considers that—
(a) an issuer of listed securities, or
(b) an applicant for listing,
has contravened any provision of listing rules, it may impose on him a penalty of such amount as it considers appropriate.

(1ZA) If the competent authority considers that—
(a) an issuer who has requested or approved the admission of a financial instrument to trading on a regulated market,
(b) a person discharging managerial responsibilities within such an issuer, or
(c) a person connected with such a person discharging managerial responsibilities,
has contravened any provision of disclosure rules, it may impose on him a penalty of such amount as it considers appropriate.

(1A) If the competent authority considers that—

(a) an issuer of transferable securities,
(b) a person offering transferable securities to the public or requesting their admission to trading on a regulated market,
(c) an applicant for the approval of a prospectus in relation to transferable securities,
(d) a person on whom a requirement has been imposed under section 87K or 87L, or
(e) any other person to whom a provision of the prospectus directive applies,

has contravened a provision of this Part or of prospectus rules, or a provision otherwise made in accordance with the prospectus directive or a requirement imposed on him under such a provision, it may impose on him a penalty of such amount as it considers appropriate.

(1B) If the competent authority considers—
(a) that a person has contravened—
(i) a provision of transparency rules or a provision otherwise made in accordance with the transparency obligations directive, or
(ii) a provision of corporate governance rules, or
(b) that a person on whom a requirement has been imposed under section 89L (power to suspend or prohibit trading of securities in case of infringement of applicable transparency obligation), has contravened that requirement,

it may impose on the person a penalty of such amount as it considers appropriate.

(2) If, in the case of a contravention by a person referred to in subsection (1), (1ZA)(a), (1A) or (1B) ("P"), the competent authority considers that another person who was at the material time a director of P was knowingly concerned in the contravention, it may impose upon him a penalty of such amount as it considers appropriate.

(3) If the competent authority is entitled to impose a penalty on a person under this section in respect of a particular matter it may, instead of imposing a penalty on him in respect of that matter, publish a statement censuring him.

(4) Nothing in this section prevents the competent authority from taking any other steps which it has power to take under this Part.

(5) A penalty under this section is payable to the competent authority.

(6) The competent authority may not take action against a person under this section after the end of the period of two years beginning with the first day on which it knew of the contravention unless proceedings against that person, in respect of the contravention, were begun before the end of that period.

(7) For the purposes of subsection (6)—
(a) the competent authority is to be treated as knowing of a contravention if it has information from which the contravention can reasonably be inferred; and
(b) proceedings against a person in respect of a contravention are to be treated as begun when a warning notice is given to him under section 92.

92 WARNING NOTICES

(1) If the competent authority proposes to take action against a person under section 91, it must give him a warning notice.

(2) A warning notice about a proposal to impose a penalty must state the amount of the proposed penalty.

(3) A warning notice about a proposal to publish a statement must set out the terms of the proposed statement.

(4) If the competent authority decides to take action against a person under section 91, it must give him a decision notice.

(5) A decision notice about the imposition of a penalty must state the amount of the penalty.

(6) A decision notice about the publication of a statement must set out the terms of the statement.

(7) If the competent authority decides to take action against a person under section 91, he may refer the matter to the Tribunal.

93 STATEMENT OF POLICY

(1) The competent authority must prepare and issue a statement ("its policy statement") of its policy with respect to—
  (a) the imposition of penalties under section 91; and
  (b) the amount of penalties under that section.

(2) The competent authority's policy in determining what the amount of a penalty should be must include having regard to—
  (a) the seriousness of the contravention in question in relation to the nature of the requirement contravened;
  (b) the extent to which that contravention was deliberate or reckless; and
  (c) whether the person on whom the penalty is to be imposed is an individual.

(3) The competent authority may at any time alter or replace its policy statement.

(4) If its policy statement is altered or replaced, the competent authority must issue the altered or replacement statement.

(5) In exercising, or deciding whether to exercise, its power under section 91 in the case of any particular contravention, the competent authority must have regard to any policy statement published under this section and in force at the time when the contravention in question occurred.

(6) The competent authority must publish a statement issued under this section in the way appearing to the competent authority to be best calculated to bring it to the attention of the public.

(7) The competent authority may charge a reasonable fee for providing a person with a copy of the statement.

(8) The competent authority must, without delay, give the Treasury a copy of any policy statement which it publishes under this section.

94 STATEMENTS OF POLICY: PROCEDURE

(1) Before issuing a statement under section 93, the competent authority must publish a draft of the proposed statement in the way appearing to the competent authority to be best calculated to bring it to the attention of the public.

(2) The draft must be accompanied by notice that representations about the proposal may be made to the competent authority within a specified time.

(3) Before issuing the proposed statement, the competent authority must have regard to any representations made to it in accordance with subsection (2).

(4) If the competent authority issues the proposed statement it must publish an account, in general terms, of—

(a) the representations made to it in accordance with subsection (2); and
(b) its response to them.

(5) If the statement differs from the draft published under subsection (1) in a way which is, in the opinion of the competent authority, significant, the competent authority must (in addition to complying with subsection (4)) publish details of the difference.

(6) The competent authority may charge a reasonable fee for providing a person with a copy of a draft published under subsection (1).

(7) This section also applies to a proposal to alter or replace a statement.

Miscellaneous

97 APPOINTMENT BY COMPETENT AUTHORITY OF PERSONS TO CARRY OUT INVESTIGATIONS

(1) Subsection (2) applies if it appears to the competent authority that there are circumstances suggesting that—
(a) there may have been a contravention of—
(i) a provision of this Part or of Part 6 rules, or
(ii) a provision otherwise made in accordance with the prospectus directive or the transparency obligations directive;
(b) a person who was at the material time a director of a person mentioned in section 91(1), (1ZA)(a), (1A) or (1B) has been knowingly concerned in a contravention by that person of—
(i) a provision of this Part or of Part 6 rules, or
(ii) a provision otherwise made in accordance with the prospectus directive or the transparency obligations directive;
(d) there may have been a contravention of section 83, 85, 87G or 98.

(2) The competent authority may appoint one or more competent persons to conduct an investigation on its behalf.

100 PENALTIES

(1) In determining its policy with respect to the amount of penalties to be imposed by it under this Part, the competent authority must take no account of the expenses which it incurs, or expects to incur, in discharging its functions under this Part.

(2) The competent authority must prepare and operate a scheme for ensuring that the amounts paid to it by way of penalties imposed under this Part are applied for the benefit of issuers of securities admitted to the official list, and issuers who have requested or approved the admission of financial instruments to trading on a regulated market.

(3) The scheme may, in particular, make different provision with respect to different classes of issuer.

100A EXERCISE OF POWERS WHERE UK IS HOST MEMBER STATE

(1) This section applies to the exercise by the competent authority of any power under this Part exercisable in case of infringement of—
(a) a provision of prospectus rules or any other provision made in accordance with the prospectus directive, or

(b) a provision of transparency rules or any other provision made in accordance with the transparency obligations directive,

in relation to an issuer whose home State is a member State other than the United Kingdom.

(2) The competent authority may act in such a case only in respect of the infringement of a provision required by the relevant directive.
Any reference to an applicable provision or applicable transparency obligation shall be read accordingly.

(3) If the authority finds that there has been such an infringement, it must give a notice to that effect to the competent authority of the person's home State requesting it—

(a) to take all appropriate measures for the purpose of ensuring that the person remedies the situation that has given rise to the notice, and

(b) to inform the authority of the measures it proposes to take or has taken or the reasons for not taking such measures.

(4) The authority may not act further unless satisfied—

(a) that the competent authority of the person's home State has failed or refused to take measures for the purpose mentioned in subsection (3)(a), or

(b) that the measures taken by that authority have proved inadequate for that purpose.

This does not affect exercise of the powers under section 87K(2), 87L(2) or (3) or 89L(2) or (3) (powers to protect market).

(5) If the authority is so satisfied, it must, after informing the competent authority of the person's home State, take all appropriate measures to protect investors.

(6) In such a case the authority must inform the Commission of the measures at the earliest opportunity.

Interpretative provisions

102A MEANING OF "SECURITIES" ETC.

(1) This section applies for the purposes of this Part.

(2) "Securities" means (except in section 74(2) and the expression "transferable securities") anything which has been, or may be, admitted to the official list.

(3) "Transferable securities" means anything which is a transferable security for the purposes of Directive 2004/39/EC of the European Parliament and of the Council on markets in financial instruments, other than money-market instruments for the purposes of that directive which have a maturity of less than 12 months.

(3A) "Debt securities" has the meaning given in Article 2.1(b) of the transparency obligations directive.

(4) "Financial instrument" has (except in section 89F) the meaning given in Article 1.3 of Directive 2003/6/EC of the European Parliament and of the Council of 28 January 2003 on insider dealing and market manipulation (as modified by Article 69 of Directive 2004/39/EC on markets in financial instruments).

(5) "Non-equity transferable securities" means all transferable securities that are not equity securities; and for this purpose "equity securities" has the meaning given in Article 2.1(b) of the prospectus directive.

(6) "Issuer"—

(a) in relation to an offer of transferable securities to the public or admission of transferable securities to trading on a regulated market for which an approved prospectus is required as a result of section 85, means a legal person who issues or proposes to issue the transferable securities in question,

(aa) in relation to transparency rules, means a legal person whose securities are admitted to trading on a regulated market or whose voting shares are admitted to trading on a UK market other than a regulated market, and in the case of depository receipts representing securities, the issuer is the issuer of the securities represented;

(b) in relation to anything else which is or may be admitted to the official list, has such meaning as may be prescribed by the Treasury, and

(c) in any other case, means a person who issues financial instruments.

102B MEANING OF "OFFER OF TRANSFERABLE SECURITIES TO THE PUBLIC" ETC.

(1) For the purposes of this Part there is an offer of transferable securities to the public if there is a communication to any person which presents sufficient information on—

(a) the transferable securities to be offered, and

(b) the terms on which they are offered,

to enable an investor to decide to buy or subscribe for the securities in question.

(2) For the purposes of this Part, to the extent that an offer of transferable securities is made to a person in the United Kingdom it is an offer of transferable securities to the public in the United Kingdom.

(3) The communication may be made—

(a) in any form;

(b) by any means.

(4) Subsection (1) includes the placing of securities through a financial intermediary.

(5) Subsection (1) does not include a communication in connection with trading on—

(a) a regulated market;

(b) a multilateral trading facility; or

(c) a market prescribed by an order under section 130A(3).

(6) "Multilateral trading facility" means a multilateral system, operated by an investment firm or a market operator, which brings together multiple third-party buying and selling interests in financial instruments in accordance with non-discretionary rules so as to result in a contract.

102C MEANING OF "HOME STATE" IN RELATION TO TRANSFERABLE SECURITIES

In this Part, in relation to an issuer of transferable securities, the "home-State" is the EEA State which is the "home Member State" for the purposes of the prospectus directive (which is to be determined in accordance with Article 2.1(m) of that directive).

103 INTERPRETATION OF THIS PART

(1) In this Part, save where the context otherwise requires—

"disclosure rules" has the meaning given in section 73A;

"financial instrument" has the meaning given in Article 1(3) of Directive 2003/6/EC of the European Parliament and the Council of 28 January 2003 on insider dealing and market manipulation (market abuse);

...

"listed securities" means anything which has been admitted to the official list;

"listing" has the meaning given in section 74(5);

"listing particulars" has the meaning given in section 79(2);

"listing rules" has the meaning given in section 73A;

"market operator" means a person who manages or operates the business of a regulated market;

"offer of transferable securities to the public" has the meaning given in section 102B;

"the official list" means the list maintained by the competent authority as that list has effect for the time being;

"Part 6 rules" has the meaning given in section 73A;

"the prospectus directive" means Directive 2003/71/EC of the European Parliament and of the Council of 4 November 2003 on the prospectus to be published when securities are offered to the public or admitted to trading;

"prospectus rules" has the meaning given in section 73A;

"regulated market" has the meaning given in Article 4.1(14) of Directive 2004/39/EC of the European Parliament and of the Council on markets in financial instruments;

"supplementary prospectus" has the meaning given in section 87G;

"the transparency obligations directive" means Directive 2004/109/EC of the European Parliament and of the Council relating to the harmonisation of transparency requirements in relation to information about issuers whose securities are admitted to trading on a regulated market

"transparency rules" has the meaning given by section 89A(5);

. . .

"working day" means any day other tha[n] a Saturday, a Sunday, Christmas Day, Good Friday or a day which is a bank holiday under the Banking and Financial Dealings Act 1971 (c. 80) in any part of the United Kingdom.

(2) In relation to any function conferred on the competent authority by this Part, any reference in this Part to the competent authority is to be read as a reference to the person by whom that function is for the time being exercisable.

. . .

Part VIII PENALTIES FOR MARKET ABUSE

Market abuse

118 MARKET ABUSE

(1) For the purposes of this Act, market abuse is behaviour (whether by one person alone or by two or more persons jointly or in concert) which—

(a) occurs in relation to—
(i) qualifying investments admitted to trading on a prescribed market,
(ii) qualifying investments in respect of which a request for admission to trading on such a market has been made, or
(iii) in the case of subsection (2) or (3) behaviour, investments which are related investments in relation to such qualifying investments, and
(b) falls within any one or more of the types of behaviour set out in subsections (2) to (8).

(2) The first type of behaviour is where an insider deals, or attempts to deal, in a qualifying investment or related investment on the basis of inside information relating to the investment in question.

(3) The second is where an insider discloses inside information to another person otherwise than in the proper course of the exercise of his employment, profession or duties.

(4) The third is where the behaviour (not falling within subsection (2) or (3))—
(a) is based on information which is not generally available to those using the market but which, if available to a regular user of the market, would be, or would be likely to be, regarded by him as relevant when deciding the terms on which transactions in qualifying investments should be effected, and
(b) is likely to be regarded by a regular user of the market as a failure on the part of the person concerned to observe the standard of behaviour reasonably expected of a person in his position in relation to the market.

(5) The fourth is where the behaviour consists of effecting transactions or orders to trade (otherwise than for legitimate reasons and in conformity with accepted market practices on the relevant market) which—
(a) give, or are likely to give, a false or misleading impression as to the supply of, or demand for, or as to the price of, one or more qualifying investments, or
(b) secure the price of one or more such investments at an abnormal or artificial level.

(6) The fifth is where the behaviour consists of effecting transactions or orders to trade which employ fictitious devices or any other form of deception or contrivance.

(7) The sixth is where the behaviour consists of the dissemination of information by any means which gives, or is likely to give, a false or misleading impression as to a qualifying investment by a person who knew or could reasonably be expected to have known that the information was false or misleading.

(8) The seventh is where the behaviour (not falling within subsection (5), (6) or (7))—
(a) is likely to give a regular user of the market a false or misleading impression as to the supply of, demand for or price or value of, qualifying investments, or
(b) would be, or would be likely to be, regarded by a regular user of the market as behaviour that would distort, or would be likely to distort, the market in such an investment,

and the behaviour is likely to be regarded by a regular user of the market as a failure on the part of the person concerned to observe the standard of behaviour reasonably expected of a person in his position in relation to the market.

(9) Subsections (4) and (8) and the definition of "regular user" in section 130A(3) cease to have effect on 31 December 2011 and subsection (1)(b) is then to be read as no longer referring to those subsections.

118A SUPPLEMENTARY PROVISION ABOUT CERTAIN BEHAVIOUR

(1) Behaviour is to be taken into account for the purposes of this Part only if it occurs—

(a) in the United Kingdom, or
(b) in relation to—
(i) qualifying investments which are admitted to trading on a prescribed market situated in, or operating in, the United Kingdom,
(ii) qualifying investments for which a request for admission to trading on such a prescribed market has been made, or
(iii) in the case of section 118(2) and (3), investments which are related investments in relation to such qualifying investments.

(2) For the purposes of subsection (1), as it applies in relation to section 118(4) and (8), a prescribed market accessible electronically in the United Kingdom is to be treated as operating in the United Kingdom.

(3) For the purposes of section 118(4) and (8), the behaviour that is to be regarded as occurring in relation to qualifying investments includes behaviour which—
(a) occurs in relation to anything that is the subject matter, or whose price or value is expressed by reference to the price or value of the qualifying investments, or
(b) occurs in relation to investments (whether or not they are qualifying investments) whose subject matter is the qualifying investments.

(4) For the purposes of section 118(7), the dissemination of information by a person acting in the capacity of a journalist is to be assessed taking into account the codes governing his profession unless he derives, directly or indirectly, any advantage or profits from the dissemination of the information.

(5) Behaviour does not amount to market abuse for the purposes of this Act if—
(a) it conforms with a rule which includes a provision to the effect that behaviour conforming with the rule does not amount to market abuse,
(b) it conforms with the relevant provisions of Commission Regulation (EC) No 2273/2003 of 22 December 2003 implementing Directive 2003/6/EC of the European Parliament and of the Council as regards exemptions for buy-back programmes and stabilisation of financial instruments, or
(c) it is done by a person acting on behalf of a public authority in pursuit of monetary policies or policies with respect to exchange rates or the management of public debt or foreign exchange reserves.

(6) Subsections (2) and (3) cease to have effect on 31 December 2011.

118B INSIDERS

For the purposes of this Part an insider is any person who has inside information—
(a) as a result of his membership of an administrative, management or supervisory body of an issuer of qualifying investments,

(b) as a result of his holding in the capital of an issuer of qualifying investments,

(c) as a result of having access to the information through the exercise of his employment, profession or duties,

(d) as a result of his criminal activities, or

(e) which he has obtained by other means and which he knows, or could reasonably be expected to know, is inside information.

118C INSIDE INFORMATION

(1) This section defines "inside information" for the purposes of this Part.

(2) In relation to qualifying investments, or related investments, which are not commodity derivatives, inside information is information of a precise nature which—
(a) is not generally available,
(b) relates, directly or indirectly, to one or more issuers of the qualifying investments or to one or more of the qualifying investments, and
(c) would, if generally available, be likely to have a significant effect on the price of the qualifying investments or on the price of related investments.

(3) In relation to qualifying investments or related investments which are commodity derivatives, inside information is information of a precise nature which—
(a) is not generally available,
(b) relates, directly or indirectly, to one or more such derivatives, and
(c) users of markets on which the derivatives are traded would expect to receive in accordance with any accepted market practices on those markets.

(4) In relation to a person charged with the execution of orders concerning any qualifying investments or related investments, inside information includes information conveyed by a client and related to the client's pending orders which—
(a) is of a precise nature,
(b) is not generally available,
(c) relates, directly or indirectly, to one or more issuers of qualifying investments or to one or more qualifying investments, and
(d) would, if generally available, be likely to have a significant effect on the price of those qualifying investments or the price of related investments.

(5) Information is precise if it—
(a) indicates circumstances that exist or may reasonably be expected to come into existence or an event that has occurred or may reasonably be expected to occur, and
(b) is specific enough to enable a conclusion to be drawn as to the possible effect of those circumstances or that event on the price of qualifying investments or related investments.

(6) Information would be likely to have a significant effect on price if and only if it is information of a kind which a reasonable investor would be likely to use as part of the basis of his investment decisions.

(7) For the purposes of subsection (3)(c), users of markets on which investments in commodity derivatives are traded are to be treated as expecting to receive information relating directly or indirectly to one or more such derivatives in accordance with any accepted market practices, which is—
(a) routinely made available to the users of those markets, or
(b) required to be disclosed in accordance with any statutory provision, market rules, or contracts or customs on the relevant underlying commodity market or commodity derivatives market.

(8) Information which can be obtained by research or analysis conducted by, or on behalf of, users of a market is to be regarded, for the purposes of this Part, as being generally available to them.

The code

119 THE CODE

(1) The Authority must prepare and issue a code containing such provisions as the Authority considers will give appropriate guidance to those determining whether or not behaviour amounts to market abuse.

(2) The code may among other things specify—
(a) descriptions of behaviour that, in the opinion of the Authority, amount to market abuse;
(b) descriptions of behaviour that, in the opinion of the Authority, do not amount to market abuse;
(c) factors that, in the opinion of the Authority, are to be taken into account in determining whether or not behaviour amounts to market abuse;
(d) descriptions of behaviour that are accepted market practices in relation to one or more specified markets;
(e) descriptions of behaviour that are not accepted market practices in relation to one or more specified markets.

(2A) In determining, for the purposes of subsections (2)(d) and (2)(e) or otherwise, what are and what are not accepted market practices, the Authority must have regard to the factors and procedures laid down in Articles 2 and 3 respectively of Commission Directive 2004/72/EC of 29 April 2004 implementing Directive 2003/6/EC of the European Parliament and of the Council.

(3) The code may make different provision in relation to persons, cases or circumstances of different descriptions.

(4) The Authority may at any time alter or replace the code.

(5) If the code is altered or replaced, the altered or replacement code must be issued by the Authority.

(6) A code issued under this section must be published by the Authority in the way appearing to the Authority to be best calculated to bring it to the attention of the public.

(7) The Authority must, without delay, give the Treasury a copy of any code published under this section.

(8) The Authority may charge a reasonable fee for providing a person with a copy of the code.

120 PROVISIONS INCLUDED IN THE AUTHORITY'S CODE BY REFERENCE TO THE CITY CODE

(1) The Authority may include in a code issued by it under section 119 ("the Authority's code") provision to the effect that in its opinion behaviour conforming with the City Code—
(a) does not amount to market abuse;
(b) does not amount to market abuse in specified circumstances; or
(c) does not amount to market abuse if engaged in by a specified description of person.

(2) But the Treasury's approval is required before any such provision may be included in the Authority's code.

(3) If the Authority's code includes provision of a kind authorised by subsection (1), the Authority must keep itself informed of the way in which the Panel on Takeovers and Mergers interprets and administers the relevant provisions of the City Code.

(4) "City Code" means the City Code on Takeovers and Mergers issued by the Panel as it has effect at the time when the behaviour occurs.

(5) "Specified" means specified in the Authority's code.

121 CODES: PROCEDURE

(1) Before issuing a code under section 119, the Authority must publish a draft of the proposed code in the way appearing to the Authority to be best calculated to bring it to the attention of the public.

(2) The draft must be accompanied by—
(a) a cost benefit analysis; and
(b) notice that representations about the proposal may be made to the Authority within a specified time.

(3) Before issuing the proposed code, the Authority must have regard to any representations made to it in accordance with subsection (2)(b).

(4) If the Authority issues the proposed code it must publish an account, in general terms, of—
(a) the representations made to it in accordance with subsection (2)(b); and
(b) its response to them.

(5) If the code differs from the draft published under subsection (1) in a way which is, in the opinion of the Authority, significant—
(a) the Authority must (in addition to complying with subsection (4)) publish details of the difference; and
(b) those details must be accompanied by a cost benefit analysis.

(6) Subsections (1) to (5) do not apply if the Authority considers that there is an urgent need to publish the code.

(7) Neither subsection (2)(a) nor subsection (5)(b) applies if the Authority considers—
(a) that, making the appropriate comparison, there will be no increase in costs; or
(b) that, making that comparison, there will be an increase in costs but the increase will be of minimal significance.

(8) The Authority may charge a reasonable fee for providing a person with a copy of a draft published under subsection (1).

(9) This section also applies to a proposal to alter or replace a code.

(10) "Cost benefit analysis" means an estimate of the costs together with an analysis of the benefits that will arise—
(a) if the proposed code is issued; or
(b) if subsection (5)(b) applies, from the code that has been issued.

(11) "The appropriate comparison" means—
(a) in relation to subsection (2)(a), a comparison between the overall position if the code is issued and the overall position if it is not issued;
(b) in relation to subsection (5)(b), a comparison between the overall position after the issuing of the code and the overall position before it was issued.

122 EFFECT OF THE CODE

(1) If a person behaves in a way which is described (in the code in force under section 119 at the time of the behaviour) as behaviour that, in the Authority's opinion, does not amount

to market abuse that behaviour of his is to be taken, for the purposes of this Act, as not amounting to market abuse.

(2) Otherwise, the code in force under section 119 at the time when particular behaviour occurs may be relied on so far as it indicates whether or not that behaviour should be taken to amount to market abuse.

Power to impose penalties

123 POWER TO IMPOSE PENALTIES IN CASES OF MARKET ABUSE

(1) If the Authority is satisfied that a person ("A")—
(a) is or has engaged in market abuse, or
(b) by taking or refraining from taking any action has required or encouraged another person or persons to engage in behaviour which, if engaged in by A, would amount to market abuse,
it may impose on him a penalty of such amount as it considers appropriate.

(2) But the Authority may not impose a penalty on a person if, having considered any representations made to it in response to a warning notice, there are reasonable grounds for it to be satisfied that—
(a) he believed, on reasonable grounds, that his behaviour did not fall within paragraph (a) or (b) of subsection (1), or
(b) he took all reasonable precautions and exercised all due diligence to avoid behaving in a way which fell within paragraph (a) or (b) of that subsection.

(3) If the Authority is entitled to impose a penalty on a person under this section it may, instead of imposing a penalty on him, publish a statement to the effect that he has engaged in market abuse.

Statement of policy

124 STATEMENT OF POLICY

(1) The Authority must prepare and issue a statement of its policy with respect to—
(a) the imposition of penalties under section 123; and
(b) the amount of penalties under that section.

(2) The Authority's policy in determining what the amount of a penalty should be must include having regard to—
(a) whether the behaviour in respect of which the penalty is to be imposed had an adverse effect on the market in question and, if it did, how serious that effect was;
(b) the extent to which that behaviour was deliberate or reckless; and
(c) whether the person on whom the penalty is to be imposed is an individual.

(3) A statement issued under this section must include an indication of the circumstances in which the Authority is to be expected to regard a person as—
(a) having a reasonable belief that his behaviour did not amount to market abuse; or
(b) having taken reasonable precautions and exercised due diligence to avoid engaging in market abuse.

(4) The Authority may at any time alter or replace a statement issued under this section.

(5) If a statement issued under this section is altered or replaced, the Authority must issue the altered or replacement statement.

(6) In exercising, or deciding whether to exercise, its power under section 123 in the case of any particular behaviour, the Authority must have regard to any statement published under this section and in force at the time when the behaviour concerned occurred.

(7) A statement issued under this section must be published by the Authority in the way appearing to the Authority to be best calculated to bring it to the attention of the public.

(8) The Authority may charge a reasonable fee for providing a person with a copy of a statement published under this section.

(9) The Authority must, without delay, give the Treasury a copy of any statement which it publishes under this section.

125 STATEMENT OF POLICY: PROCEDURE

(1) Before issuing a statement of policy under section 124, the Authority must publish a draft of the proposed statement in the way appearing to the Authority to be best calculated to bring it to the attention of the public.

(2) The draft must be accompanied by notice that representations about the proposal may be made to the Authority within a specified time.

(3) Before issuing the proposed statement, the Authority must have regard to any representations made to it in accordance with subsection (2).

(4) If the Authority issues the proposed statement it must publish an account, in general terms, of—
- (a) the representations made to it in accordance with subsection (2); and
- (b) its response to them.

(5) If the statement differs from the draft published under subsection (1) in a way which is, in the opinion of the Authority, significant, the Authority must (in addition to complying with subsection (4)) publish details of the difference.

(6) The Authority may charge a reasonable fee for providing a person with a copy of a draft published under subsection (1).

(7) This section also applies to a proposal to alter or replace a statement.

Procedure

126 WARNING NOTICES

(1) If the Authority proposes to take action against a person under section 123, it must give him a warning notice.

(2) A warning notice about a proposal to impose a penalty must state the amount of the proposed penalty.

(3) A warning notice about a proposal to publish a statement must set out the terms of the proposed statement.

127 DECISION NOTICES AND RIGHT TO REFER TO TRIBUNAL

(1) If the Authority decides to take action against a person under section 123, it must give him a decision notice.

(2) A decision notice about the imposition of a penalty must state the amount of the penalty.

(3) A decision notice about the publication of a statement must set out the terms of the statement.

(4) If the Authority decides to take action against a person under section 123, that person may refer the matter to the Tribunal.

Miscellaneous

128 SUSPENSION OF INVESTIGATIONS

(1) If the Authority considers it desirable or expedient because of the exercise or possible exercise of a power relating to market abuse, it may direct a recognised investment exchange or recognised clearing house—
(a) to terminate, suspend or limit the scope of any inquiry which the exchange or clearing house is conducting under its rules; or
(b) not to conduct an inquiry which the exchange or clearing house proposes to conduct under its rules.

(2) A direction under this section—
(a) must be given to the exchange or clearing house concerned by notice in writing; and
(b) is enforceable, on the application of the Authority, by injunction or, in Scotland, by an order under section 45 of the Court of Session Act 1988.

(3) The Authority's powers relating to market abuse are its powers—
(a) to impose penalties under section 123; or
(b) to appoint a person to conduct an investigation under section 168 in a case falling within subsection (2)(d) of that section.

129 POWER OF COURT TO IMPOSE PENALTY IN CASES OF MARKET ABUSE

(1) The Authority may on an application to the court under section 381 or 383 request the court to consider whether the circumstances are such that a penalty should be imposed on the person to whom the application relates.

(2) The court may, if it considers it appropriate, make an order requiring the person concerned to pay to the Authority a penalty of such amount as it considers appropriate.

130 GUIDANCE

(1) The Treasury may from time to time issue written guidance for the purpose of helping relevant authorities to determine the action to be taken in cases where behaviour occurs which is behaviour—
(a) with respect to which the power in section 123 appears to be exercisable; and
(b) which appears to involve the commission of an offence under section 397 of this Act or Part V of the Criminal Justice Act 1993 (insider dealing).

(2) The Treasury must obtain the consent of the Attorney General and the Secretary of State before issuing any guidance under this section.

(3) In this section "relevant authorities"—
(a) in relation to England and Wales, means the Secretary of State, the Authority, the Director of the Serious Fraud Office and the Director of Public Prosecutions;

(b) in relation to Northern Ireland, means the Secretary of State, the Authority, the Director of the Serious Fraud Office and the Director of Public Prosecutions for Northern Ireland.

(4) Subsections (1) to (3) do not apply to Scotland.

(5) In relation to Scotland, the Lord Advocate may from time to time, after consultation with the Treasury, issue written guidance for the purpose of helping the Authority to determine the action to be taken in cases where behaviour mentioned in subsection (1) occurs.

130A INTERPRETATION AND SUPPLEMENTARY PROVISION

(1) The Treasury may by order specify (whether by name or description)—
(a) the markets which are prescribed markets for the purposes of specified provisions of this Part, and
(b) the investments that are qualifying investments in relation to the prescribed markets.

(2) An order may prescribe different investments or descriptions of investment in relation to different markets or descriptions of market.

(3) In this Part—

"accepted market practices" means practices that are reasonably expected in the financial market or markets in question and are accepted by the Authority or, in the case of a market situated in another EEA State, the competent authority of that EEA State within the meaning of Directive 2003/6/EC of the European Parliament and of the Council of 28 January 2003 on insider dealing and market manipulation (market abuse),

"behaviour" includes action or inaction,

"dealing", in relation to an investment, means acquiring or disposing of the investment whether as principal or agent or directly or indirectly, and includes agreeing to acquire or dispose of the investment, and entering into and bringing to an end a contract creating it,

"investment" is to be read with section 22 and Schedule 2,

"regular user", in relation to a particular market, means a reasonable person who regularly deals on that market in investments of the kind in question,

"related investment", in relation to a qualifying investment, means an investment whose price or value depends on the price or value of the qualifying investment.

(4) Any reference in this Act to a person engaged in market abuse is to a person engaged in market abuse either alone or with one or more other persons.

131 EFFECT ON TRANSACTIONS

The imposition of a penalty under this Part does not make any transaction void or unenforceable.

131A PROTECTED DISCLOSURES

(1) A disclosure which satisfies the following three conditions is not to be taken to breach any restriction on the disclosure of information (however imposed).

(2) The first condition is that the information or other matter—
(a) causes the person making the disclosure (the discloser) to know or suspect, or

(b) gives him reasonable grounds for knowing or suspecting, that another person has engaged in market abuse.

(3) The second condition is that the information or other matter disclosed came to the discloser in the course of his trade, profession, business or employment.

(4) The third condition is that the disclosure is made to the Authority or to a nominated officer as soon as is practicable after the information or other matter comes to the discloser.

(5) A disclosure to a nominated officer is a disclosure which is made to a person nominated by the discloser's employer to receive disclosures under this section, and is made in the course of the discloser's employment and in accordance with the procedure established by the employer for the purpose.

(6) For the purposes of this section, references to a person's employer include any body, association or organisation (including a voluntary organisation) in connection with whose activities the person exercises a function (whether or not for gain or reward) and references to employment must be construed accordingly.

Part 8A SHORT SELLING

Short selling rules

131B SHORT SELLING RULES

(1) The Authority may make rules prohibiting in specified cases persons from engaging in short selling in relation to relevant financial instruments (or relevant financial instruments of a specified description).

(2) The Authority may make rules requiring—
(a) a person who has engaged in short selling in relation to relevant financial instruments (or relevant financial instruments of a specified description), or
(b) an authorised person of a specified description who has acted on behalf of such a person, to disclose in specified cases specified information, or information of a specified description, about the short selling.

(3) Rules under subsection (2) may specify the time by which, and the way in which, the disclosure must be made (and may in particular provide for the information to be disclosed to the Authority or published in a specified way).

(4) Rules under subsection (2) may apply in relation to short selling engaged in before the rules are made where the resulting short position is still open when the rules are made.

(5) The reference to a short position being open is to be read in accordance with provision made by the rules.

(6) Rules under this section may apply to short selling wholly outside the United Kingdom by persons outside the United Kingdom, but only in so far as the rules relate to UK financial instruments.

(7) The description of relevant financial instruments that may be specified by the rules includes relevant financial instruments issued by a specified person.

(8) Rules under this section are referred to in this Part as "short selling rules".

(9) The Authority must, when making short selling rules, have regard to any international agreement as to measures to be taken in respect of short selling.

131C SHORT SELLING RULES: DEFINITIONS ETC.

(1) This section supplements section 131B.

(2) The cases in which a person ("S") engages in short selling in relation to a financial instrument (a "shorted instrument") include any case where—
(a) S enters into a transaction which creates, or relates to, another financial instrument; and
(b) the effect (or one of the effects) of the transaction is to confer a financial advantage on S in the event of a decrease in the price or value of the shorted instrument.

(3) "Financial instrument" has the meaning given by Article 4.1(17) of the markets in financial instruments directive.

(4) "Relevant financial instrument" means a financial instrument that—
(a) is admitted to trading on a regulated market or on any other prescribed market in an EEA State; or
(b) has such other connection with a market in an EEA State as may be specified.

(5) "Specified" means specified by short selling rules.

(6) "UK financial instrument" means a financial instrument that is admitted to trading on a market in the United Kingdom.

(7) In the case of a financial instrument that is admitted to trading on—
(a) a market in the United Kingdom or another EEA State, and
(b) one or more markets in a country or territory, or countries or territories, anywhere else in the world,
short selling rules may apply in relation to trading on both or all markets.

(8) In any case where—
(a) a financial instrument ("instrument A") is admitted to trading on a market in the United Kingdom or another EEA State,
(b) another financial instrument ("instrument B") is admitted to trading on one or more markets in a country or territory, or countries or territories, anywhere else in the world, and
(c) the price or value of instrument A depends on the price or value of instrument B (or vice versa),
short selling rules may apply in relation to trading on both or all markets.

(9) In subsection (4)(a) "regulated market" has the meaning given by Article 4.1(14) of the markets in financial instruments directive.

(10) References in this section to a market in a country or territory are to a market situated or operating in the country or territory.

131D SHORT SELLING RULES: PROCEDURE IN URGENT CASES

(1) The Authority may make short selling rules (and may subsequently amend those rules) without complying with section 155 (consultation in relation to proposed rules) if it considers that it is necessary to do so, in order to—
(a) maintain confidence in the UK financial system; or
(b) protect the stability of the UK financial system.

(2) Any rules made by virtue of subsection (1) ("emergency rules") cease to have effect at the end of the period of three months beginning with the day on which the rules are made ("the relevant day"); but this is subject as follows.

(3) The Authority may direct that emergency rules are to cease to have effect at the end of a period (not exceeding six months beginning with the relevant day) specified in the direction.

(4) A direction under subsection (3) may be made only if, immediately before the end of the period mentioned in subsection (2), the Authority considers that it is necessary to do so, in order to—
(a) maintain confidence in the UK financial system; or
(b) protect the stability of the UK financial system.

(5) Such a direction must be published by the Authority in the way appearing to the Authority to be best calculated to bring it to the attention of the public.

(6) Nothing in subsection (2) or (3) prevents the Authority from revoking emergency rules before the end of the periods referred to there.

Power to require information

131E POWER TO REQUIRE INFORMATION

(1) The Authority may, by notice in writing, require a person ("P")—
(a) to provide specified information or information of a specified description; or
(b) to produce specified documents or documents of a specified description.

(2) This section applies only to information and documents that the Authority reasonably requires for the purpose of determining whether P, or a person connected with P, has contravened any provision of short selling rules.

(3) Information or documents required under this section must be provided or produced—
(a) before the end of such reasonable period as may be specified; and
(b) at such place as may be specified.

(4) The Authority may require any information provided under this section to be provided in such form as it may reasonably require.

(5) The Authority may require—
(a) any information provided, whether in a document or otherwise, to be verified in such manner as it may reasonably require; or
(b) any document produced to be authenticated in such manner as it may reasonably require.

(6) In this section "specified" means specified in the notice.

(7) For the purposes of this section a person is connected with another person ("P") if the person is or has at any relevant time been—
(a) a member of P's group;
(b) a controller of P;
(c) any other member of a partnership of which P is a member; or
(d) in relation to P, a person mentioned in Part 1 of Schedule 15 (reading references in that Part to the authorised person as references to P).

131F POWER TO REQUIRE INFORMATION: SUPPLEMENTARY

(1) If the Authority has power under section 131E to require a person to produce a document but it appears that the document is in the possession of a third person, that power may be exercised in relation to the third person.

(2) If a document is produced in response to a requirement imposed under section 131E, the Authority may—
  (a) take copies of or extracts from the document; or
  (b) require the person producing the document, or any relevant person, to provide an explanation of the document.

(3) In subsection (2)(b) "relevant person", in relation to a person who is required to produce a document, means a person who—
  (a) has been or is or is proposed to be a director or controller of that person;
  (b) has been or is an auditor of that person;
  (c) has been or is an actuary, accountant or lawyer appointed or instructed by that person; or
  (d) has been or is an employee of that person.

(4) If a person who is required under section 131E to produce a document fails to do so, the Authority may require the person to state, to the best of the person's knowledge and belief, where the document is.

(5) A lawyer may be required under section 131E to provide the name and address of the lawyer's client.

(6) A person ("P") may not be required under section 131E to disclose information or produce a document in respect of which P owes an obligation of confidence by virtue of carrying on the business of banking unless—
  (a) P is the person under investigation or a member of that person's group;
  (b) the person to whom the obligation of confidence is owed is the person under investigation or a member of that person's group; or
  (c) the person to whom the obligation of confidence is owed consents to the disclosure or production.

(7) If a person claims a lien on a document, its production under section 131E does not affect the lien.

Breach of short selling rules etc.

131G POWER TO IMPOSE PENALTY OR ISSUE CENSURE

(1) This section applies if the Authority is satisfied that a person has contravened—
  (a) any provision of short selling rules; or
  (b) any requirement imposed on the person under section 131E or 131F.

(2) The Authority may impose a penalty of such amount as it considers appropriate on—
  (a) the person who contravened the provision or requirement; or
  (b) any person who was knowingly concerned in the contravention.

(3) It may, instead of imposing a penalty on a person, publish a statement censuring the person.

(4) The Authority may not take action against a person under this section after the end of the limitation period unless, before the end of that period, it has given a warning notice to the person under section 131H.

(5) "The limitation period" means the period of three years beginning with the first day on which the Authority knew of the contravention.

(6) For this purpose the Authority is to be treated as knowing of a contravention if it has information from which the contravention can reasonably be inferred.

131H PROCEDURE AND RIGHT TO REFER TO TRIBUNAL

(1) If the Authority proposes to take action against a person under section 131G, it must give the person a warning notice.

(2) A warning notice about a proposal to impose a penalty must state the amount of the penalty.

(3) A warning notice about a proposal to publish a statement must set out the terms of the statement.

(4) If the Authority decides to take action against a person under section 131G, it must give the person a decision notice.

(5) A decision notice about the imposition of a penalty must state the amount of the penalty.

(6) A decision notice about the publication of a statement must set out the terms of the statement.

(7) If the Authority decides to take action against a person under section 131G, the person may refer the matter to the Tribunal.

131I DUTY ON PUBLICATION OF STATEMENT

After a statement under section 131G(3) is published, the Authority must send a copy of the statement to—

(a) the person in respect of whom it is made; and

(b) any person to whom a copy of the decision notice was given under section 393(4).

131J IMPOSITION OF PENALTIES UNDER SECTION 131G: STATEMENT OF POLICY

(1) The Authority must prepare and issue a statement of its policy with respect to—
(a) the imposition of penalties under section 131G; and
(b) the amount of penalties under that section.

(2) The Authority's policy in determining what the amount of a penalty should be must include having regard to—
(a) the seriousness of the contravention;
(b) the extent to which the contravention was deliberate or reckless; and
(c) whether the person on whom the penalty is to be imposed is an individual.

(3) The Authority may at any time alter or replace a statement issued under this section.

(4) If a statement issued under this section is altered or replaced, the Authority must issue the altered or replaced statement.

(5) The Authority must, without delay, give the Treasury a copy of any statement which it publishes under this section.

(6) A statement issued under this section must be published by the Authority in the way appearing to the Authority to be best calculated to bring it to the attention of the public.

(7) The Authority may charge a reasonable fee for providing a person with a copy of the statement.

(8) In exercising, or deciding whether to exercise, a power under section 131G in the case of any particular contravention, the Authority must have regard to any statement of

policy published under this section and in force at a time when the contravention occurred.

131K STATEMENT OF POLICY: PROCEDURE

(1) Before issuing a statement under section 131J, the Authority must publish a draft of the proposed statement in the way appearing to the Authority to be best calculated to bring it to the attention of the public.

(2) The draft must be accompanied by notice that representations about the proposal may be made to the Authority within a specified time.

(3) Before issuing the proposed statement, the Authority must have regard to any representations made to it in accordance with subsection (2).

(4) If the Authority issues the proposed statement it must publish an account, in general terms, of—
(a) the representations made to it in accordance with subsection (2); and
(b) its response to them.

(5) If the statement differs from the draft published under subsection (1) in a way which is, in the opinion of the Authority, significant, the Authority must (in addition to complying with subsection (4)) publish details of the difference.

(6) The Authority may charge a reasonable fee for providing a person with a copy of a draft published under subsection (1).

(7) This section also applies to a proposal to alter or replace a statement.

Part XI INFORMATION GATHERING AND INVESTIGATIONS

Powers to gather information

165 AUTHORITY'S POWER TO REQUIRE INFORMATION: AUTHORISED PERSONS ETC.

(1) The Authority may, by notice in writing given to an authorised person, require him—
(a) to provide specified information or information of a specified description; or
(b) to produce specified documents or documents of a specified description.

(2) The information or documents must be provided or produced—
(a) before the end of such reasonable period as may be specified; and
(b) at such place as may be specified.

(3) An officer who has written authorisation from the Authority to do so may require an authorised person without delay—
(a) to provide the officer with specified information or information of a specified description; or
(b) to produce to him specified documents or documents of a specified description.

(4) This section applies only to information and documents reasonably required in connection with the exercise by the Authority of functions conferred on it by or under this Act.

(5) The Authority may require any information provided under this section to be provided in such form as it may reasonably require.

(6) The Authority may require—
(a) any information provided, whether in a document or otherwise, to be verified in such manner, or
(b) any document produced to be authenticated in such manner,
as it may reasonably require.

(7) The powers conferred by subsections (1) and (3) may also be exercised to impose requirements on—
(a) a person who is connected with an authorised person;
(b) an operator, trustee or depositary of a scheme recognised under section 270 or 272 who is not an authorised person;
(c) a recognised investment exchange or recognised clearing house.

(8) "Authorised person" includes a person who was at any time an authorised person but who has ceased to be an authorised person.

(9) "Officer" means an officer of the Authority and includes a member of the Authority's staff or an agent of the Authority.

(10) "Specified" means—
(a) in subsections (1) and (2), specified in the notice; and
(b) in subsection (3), specified in the authorisation.

(11) For the purposes of this section, a person is connected with an authorised person ("A") if he is or has at any relevant time been—
(a) a member of A's group;
(b) a controller of A;
(c) any other member of a partnership of which A is a member; or
(d) in relation to A, a person mentioned in Part I of Schedule 15.

165A AUTHORITY'S POWER TO REQUIRE INFORMATION: FINANCIAL STABILITY

(1) The Authority may, by notice in writing given to a person to whom this section applies, require the person—
(a) to provide specified information or information of a specified description; or
(b) to produce specified documents or documents of a specified description.

(2) This section applies to—
(a) a person who has a legal or beneficial interest in any of the assets of a relevant investment fund;
(b) a person who is responsible for the management of a relevant investment fund;
(c) a person (a "service provider") who provides any service to an authorised person;
(d) a person prescribed by an order made by the Treasury or any person of a description prescribed by such an order (and see also section 165C);
(e) a person who is connected with a person to whom this section applies as a result of any of the above paragraphs.

(3) This section applies only to information and documents that the Authority considers are, or might be, relevant to the stability of one or more aspects of the UK financial system.

(4) A notice may be given to a service provider, or to a person who is connected with a service provider, only if the Authority considers that—
(a) the service or the way in which it (or any part of it) is provided, or
(b) any failure to provide the service (or any part of it),

poses, or would be likely to pose, a serious threat to the stability of the UK financial system.

(5) Information or documents required under this section must be provided or produced—
(a) before the end of such reasonable period as may be specified; and
(b) at such place as may be specified.

(6) The Authority may require any information provided under this section to be provided in such form as it may reasonably require.

(7) The Authority may require—
(a) any information provided, whether in a document or otherwise, to be verified in such manner as it may reasonably require; or
(b) any document produced to be authenticated in such manner as it may reasonably require.

(8) In this section—
- "management" includes any of the activities listed in Annex II to the UCITS directive;
- "relevant investment fund" means an investment fund whose assets consist of or include financial instruments which—
  (a) are traded in the United Kingdom; or
  (b) were issued by a body incorporated in the United Kingdom;
- "service" includes facility;
- "specified" means specified in the notice.

(9) For the purposes of the definition of "relevant investment fund"—
(a) arrangements may constitute an investment fund even if there is only one person participating in the arrangements; and
(b) the reference to financial instruments has the meaning given by Article 4.1(17) of the markets in financial instruments directive.

(10) For the purposes of this section a person is connected with another person ("A") if the person is or has at any relevant time been—
(a) a member of A's group;
(b) a controller of A;
(c) any other member of a partnership of which A is a member; or
(d) in relation to A, a person mentioned in Part 1 of Schedule 15 (reading references in that Part to the authorised person as references to A).

165B SAFEGUARDS ETC. IN RELATION TO EXERCISE OF POWER UNDER SECTION 165A

(1) If the Authority proposes to impose a requirement on a person under section 165A, it must give the person a notice in writing warning the person that the Authority is proposing to impose the requirement.

(2) The notice under subsection (1) must—
(a) give the Authority's reasons for proposing to impose the requirement; and
(b) specify a reasonable period within which the person may make representations to the Authority.

(3) The Authority must then decide, within a reasonable period, whether to impose the requirement.

(4) Subsections (1) to (3) do not apply in any case where the Authority is satisfied that it is necessary for the information or documents to be provided or produced without delay.

(5) If the Authority imposes a requirement on a person under section 165A, the notice under that section must give the Authority's reasons for imposing the requirement.

(6) The Authority must prepare a statement of its policy with respect to the exercise of the power conferred by section 165A.

(7) The statement requires the approval of the Treasury.

(8) If the Treasury approve the statement, the Authority must publish it.

(9) The power conferred by section 165A may not be exercised before the statement has been published.

165C ORDERS UNDER SECTION 165A(2)(D)

(1) The Treasury may make an order under section 165A(2)(d) only if they consider that—
(a) the activities carried on by the prescribed person or persons of the prescribed description, or the way in which those activities (or any part of them) are carried on, or
(b) any failure to carry on those activities (or any part of them),
pose, or would be likely to pose, a serious threat to the stability of the UK financial system.

(2) Subject as follows, an order under section 165A(2)(d) may not be made unless a draft of the order has been laid before, and approved by a resolution of, each House of Parliament.

(3) Subsection (2) does not apply in any case where the Treasury are satisfied that it is necessary to make an order under section 165A(2)(d) without laying a draft for approval.

(4) In that case, the order—
(a) must be laid before Parliament after being made; and
(b) ceases to have effect at the end of the relevant period unless before the end of that period it is approved by a resolution of each House of Parliament.

(5) If an order ceases to have effect as a result of subsection (4)(b) that does not affect—
(a) anything done under it; or
(b) the power to make a new one.

(6) "Relevant period" means a period of 28 days beginning with the day on which the order is made.

(7) In calculating the relevant period no account is to be taken of any time during which Parliament is dissolved or prorogued or during which both Houses are adjourned for more than four days.

(8) If a statutory instrument containing an order under section 165A(2)(d) would, apart from this subsection, be treated as a hybrid instrument for the purposes of the Standing Orders of either House of Parliament, it is to proceed in that House as if it were not a hybrid instrument.

166 REPORTS BY SKILLED PERSONS

(1) The Authority may, by notice in writing given to a person to whom subsection (2) applies, require him to provide the Authority with a report on any matter about which the Authority has required or could require the provision of information or production of documents under section 165.

(2) This subsection applies to—
(a) an authorised person ("A"),
(b) any other member of A's group,
(c) a partnership of which A is a member, or
(d) a person who has at any relevant time been a person falling within paragraph (a), (b) or (c),

who is, or was at the relevant time, carrying on a business.

(3) The Authority may require the report to be in such form as may be specified in the notice.

(4) The person appointed to make a report required by subsection (1) must be a person—
(a) nominated or approved by the Authority; and
(b) appearing to the Authority to have the skills necessary to make a report on the matter concerned.

(5) It is the duty of any person who is providing (or who at any time has provided) services to a person to whom subsection (2) applies in relation to a matter on which a report is required under subsection (1) to give a person appointed to provide such a report all such assistance as the appointed person may reasonably require.

(6) The obligation imposed by subsection (5) is enforceable, on the application of the Authority, by an injunction or, in Scotland, by an order for specific performance under section 45 of the Court of Session Act 1988.

Appointment of investigators

167 APPOINTMENT OF PERSONS TO CARRY OUT GENERAL INVESTIGATIONS

(1) If it appears to the Authority or the Secretary of State ("the investigating authority") that there is good reason for doing so, the investigating authority may appoint one or more competent persons to conduct an investigation on its behalf into—
(a) the nature, conduct or state of the business of a recognised investment exchange or an authorised person or of an appointed representative;
(b) a particular aspect of that business; or
(c) the ownership or control of a recognised investment exchange or an authorised person.

(2) If a person appointed under subsection (1) thinks it necessary for the purposes of his investigation, he may also investigate the business of a person who is or has at any relevant time been—
(a) a member of the group of which the person under investigation ("A") is part; or
(b) a partnership of which A is a member.

(3) If a person appointed under subsection (1) decides to investigate the business of any person under subsection (2) he must give that person written notice of his decision.

(4) The power conferred by this section may be exercised in relation to a former authorised person (or appointed representative) but only in relation to—
(a) business carried on at any time when he was an authorised person (or appointed representative); or
(b) the ownership or control of a former authorised person at any time when he was an authorised person.

(5) "Business" includes any part of a business even if it does not consist of carrying on regulated activities.

(6) References in subsection (1) to a recognised investment exchange do not include references to an overseas investment exchange (as defined by section 313(1)).

168 APPOINTMENT OF PERSONS TO CARRY OUT INVESTIGATIONS IN PARTICULAR CASES

(1) Subsection (3) applies if it appears to an investigating authority that there are circumstances suggesting that—
  (a) a person may have contravened any regulation made under section 142; or
  (b) a person may be guilty of an offence under section 177, 191, 346 or 398(1) or under Schedule 4.

(2) Subsection (3) also applies if it appears to an investigating authority that there are circumstances suggesting that—
  (a) an offence under section 24(1) or 397 or under Part V of the Criminal Justice Act 1993 may have been committed;
  (b) there may have been a breach of the general prohibition;
  (c) there may have been a contravention of section 21 or 238; or
  (d) market abuse may have taken place.

(3) The investigating authority may appoint one or more competent persons to conduct an investigation on its behalf.

(4) Subsection (5) applies if it appears to the Authority that there are circumstances suggesting that—
  (a) a person may have contravened section 20;
  (b) a person may be guilty of an offence under prescribed regulations relating to money laundering;
  (c) a person may have contravened a rule made by the Authority;
  (d) an individual may not be a fit and proper person to perform functions in relation to a regulated activity carried on by an authorised or exempt person;
  (e) an individual may have performed or agreed to perform a function in breach of a prohibition order;
  (f) an authorised or exempt person may have failed to comply with section 56(6);
  (g) an authorised person may have failed to comply with section 59(1) or (2);
  (h) a person in relation to whom the Authority has given its approval under section 59 may not be a fit and proper person to perform the function to which that approval relates;
  (ha) a person may have performed a controlled function without approval for the purposes of section 63A;
  (i) a person may be guilty of misconduct for the purposes of section 66; or
  (j) a person may have contravened any provision made by or under this Act for the purpose of implementing the markets in financial instruments directive or by any directly applicable Community regulation made under that directive.

(5) The Authority may appoint one or more competent persons to conduct an investigation on its behalf.

(6) "Investigating authority" means the Authority or the Secretary of State.

Assistance to overseas regulators

169 INVESTIGATIONS ETC. IN SUPPORT OF OVERSEAS REGULATOR

(1) At the request of an overseas regulator, the Authority may—

(a) exercise the power conferred by section 165; or
(b) appoint one or more competent persons to investigate any matter.

(2) An investigator has the same powers as an investigator appointed under section 168(3) (as a result of subsection (1) of that section).

(3) If the request has been made by a competent authority in pursuance of any EU obligation the Authority must, in deciding whether or not to exercise its investigative power, consider whether its exercise is necessary to comply with any such obligation.

(4) In deciding whether or not to exercise its investigative power, the Authority may take into account in particular—
(a) whether in the country or territory of the overseas regulator concerned, corresponding assistance would be given to a United Kingdom regulatory authority;
(b) whether the case concerns the breach of a law, or other requirement, which has no close parallel in the United Kingdom or involves the assertion of a jurisdiction not recognised by the United Kingdom;
(c) the seriousness of the case and its importance to persons in the United Kingdom;
(d) whether it is otherwise appropriate in the public interest to give the assistance sought.

(5) The Authority may decide that it will not exercise its investigative power unless the overseas regulator undertakes to make such contribution towards the cost of its exercise as the Authority considers appropriate.

(6) Subsections (4) and (5) do not apply if the Authority considers that the exercise of its investigative power is necessary to comply with an EU obligation.

(7) If the Authority has appointed an investigator in response to a request from an overseas regulator, it may direct the investigator to permit a representative of that regulator to attend, and take part in, any interview conducted for the purposes of the investigation.

(8) A direction under subsection (7) is not to be given unless the Authority is satisfied that any information obtained by an overseas regulator as a result of the interview will be subject to safeguards equivalent to those contained in Part XXIII.

(9) The Authority must prepare a statement of its policy with respect to the conduct of interviews in relation to which a direction under subsection (7) has been given.

(10) The statement requires the approval of the Treasury.

(11) If the Treasury approve the statement, the Authority must publish it.

(12) No direction may be given under subsection (7) before the statement has been published.

(13) "Overseas regulator" has the same meaning as in section 195.

(14) "Investigative power" means one of the powers mentioned in subsection (1).

(15) "Investigator" means a person appointed under subsection (1)(b).

169A SUPPORT OF OVERSEAS REGULATOR WITH RESPECT TO FINANCIAL STABILITY

(1) At the request of an overseas regulator, the Authority may exercise a corresponding section 165A power.

(2) An "overseas regulator" means an authority in a country or territory outside the United Kingdom which exercises functions with respect to the stability of the financial system operating in that country or territory.

(3) A "corresponding section 165A power" means a power corresponding to the one conferred by section 165A, but reading references in that section to the stability of the UK financial system as references to the stability of the financial system operating in the country or territory of the overseas regulator.

(4) The following provisions apply in relation to the exercise of the corresponding section 165A power—
(a) section 165B(1) to (5); and
(b) section 169(3), (4)(a) and (d), (5) and (6).

(5) In this section "the financial system" includes—
(a) financial markets and exchanges;
(b) activities that would be regulated activities if carried on in the United Kingdom; and
(c) other activities connected with financial markets and exchanges.

Conduct of investigations

170 INVESTIGATIONS: GENERAL

(1) This section applies if an investigating authority appoints one or more competent persons ("investigators") under section 167 or 168(3) or (5) to conduct an investigation on its behalf.

(2) The investigating authority must give written notice of the appointment of an investigator to the person who is the subject of the investigation ("the person under investigation").

(3) Subsections (2) and (9) do not apply if—
(a) the investigator is appointed as a result of section 168(1) or (4) and the investigating authority believes that the notice required by subsection (2) or (9) would be likely to result in the investigation being frustrated; or
(b) the investigator is appointed as a result of subsection (2) of section 168.

(4) A notice under subsection (2) must—
(a) specify the provisions under which, and as a result of which, the investigator was appointed; and
(b) state the reason for his appointment.

(5) Nothing prevents the investigating authority from appointing a person who is a member of its staff as an investigator.

(6) An investigator must make a report of his investigation to the investigating authority.

(7) The investigating authority may, by a direction to an investigator, control—
(a) the scope of the investigation;
(b) the period during which the investigation is to be conducted;
(c) the conduct of the investigation; and
(d) the reporting of the investigation.

(8) A direction may, in particular—
(a) confine the investigation to particular matters;
(b) extend the investigation to additional matters;
(c) require the investigator to discontinue the investigation or to take only such steps as are specified in the direction;
(d) require the investigator to make such interim reports as are so specified.

(9) If there is a change in the scope or conduct of the investigation and, in the opinion of the investigating authority, the person subject to investigation is likely to be significantly

prejudiced by not being made aware of it, that person must be given written notice of the change.

(10) "Investigating authority", in relation to an investigator, means—
(a) the Authority, if the Authority appointed him;
(b) the Secretary of State, if the Secretary of State appointed him.

171 POWERS OF PERSONS APPOINTED UNDER SECTION 167

(1) An investigator may require the person who is the subject of the investigation ("the person under investigation") or any person connected with the person under investigation—
(a) to attend before the investigator at a specified time and place and answer questions; or
(b) otherwise to provide such information as the investigator may require.

(2) An investigator may also require any person to produce at a specified time and place any specified documents or documents of a specified description.

(3) A requirement under subsection (1) or (2) may be imposed only so far as the investigator concerned reasonably considers the question, provision of information or production of the document to be relevant to the purposes of the investigation.

(3A) Where the investigation relates to a recognised investment exchange, an investigator has the additional powers conferred by sections 172 and 173 (and for this purpose references in those sections to an investigator are to be read accordingly).

(4) For the purposes of this section and section 172, a person is connected with the person under investigation ("A") if he is or has at any relevant time been—
(a) a member of A's group;
(b) a controller of A;
(c) a partnership of which A is a member; or
(d) in relation to A, a person mentioned in Part I or II of Schedule 15.

(5) "Investigator" means a person conducting an investigation under section 167.

(6) "Specified" means specified in a notice in writing.

(7) The reference in subsection (3A) to a recognised investment exchange does not include a reference to an overseas investment exchange (as defined by section 313(1)).

172 ADDITIONAL POWER OF PERSONS APPOINTED AS A RESULT OF SECTION 168(1) OR (4)

(1) An investigator has the powers conferred by section 171.

(2) An investigator may also require a person who is neither the subject of the investigation ("the person under investigation") nor a person connected with the person under investigation—
(a) to attend before the investigator at a specified time and place and answer questions; or
(b) otherwise to provide such information as the investigator may require for the purposes of the investigation.

(3) A requirement may only be imposed under subsection (2) if the investigator is satisfied that the requirement is necessary or expedient for the purposes of the investigation.

(4) "Investigator" means a person appointed as a result of subsection (1) or (4) of section 168.

(5) "Specified" means specified in a notice in writing.

173 POWERS OF PERSONS APPOINTED AS A RESULT OF SECTION 168(2)

(1) Subsections (2) to (4) apply if an investigator considers that any person ("A") is or may be able to give information which is or may be relevant to the investigation.

(2) The investigator may require A—
(a) to attend before him at a specified time and place and answer questions; or
(b) otherwise to provide such information as he may require for the purposes of the investigation.

(3) The investigator may also require A to produce at a specified time and place any specified documents or documents of a specified description which appear to the investigator to relate to any matter relevant to the investigation.

(4) The investigator may also otherwise require A to give him all assistance in connection with the investigation which A is reasonably able to give.

(5) "Investigator" means a person appointed under subsection (3) of section 168 (as a result of subsection (2) of that section).

174 ADMISSIBILITY OF STATEMENTS MADE TO INVESTIGATORS

(1) A statement made to an investigator by a person in compliance with an information requirement is admissible in evidence in any proceedings, so long as it also complies with any requirements governing the admissibility of evidence in the circumstances in question.

(2) But in criminal proceedings in which that person is charged with an offence to which this subsection applies or in proceedings in relation to action to be taken against that person under section 123—
(a) no evidence relating to the statement may be adduced, and
(b) no question relating to it may be asked,
by or on behalf of the prosecution or (as the case may be) the Authority, unless evidence relating to it is adduced, or a question relating to it is asked, in the proceedings by or on behalf of that person.

(3) Subsection (2) applies to any offence other than one—
(a) under section 177(4) or 398;
(b) under section 5 of the Perjury Act 1911 (false statements made otherwise than on oath);
(c) under section 44(2) of the Criminal Law (Consolidation)(Scotland) Act 1995 (false statements made otherwise than on oath); or
(d) under Article 10 of the Perjury (Northern Ireland) Order 1979.

(4) "Investigator" means a person appointed under section 167 or 168(3) or (5).

(5) "Information requirement" means a requirement imposed by an investigator under section 171, 172, 173 or 175.

175 INFORMATION AND DOCUMENTS: SUPPLEMENTAL PROVISIONS

(1) If the Authority or an investigator has power under this Part to require a person to produce a document but it appears that the document is in the possession of a third person, that power may be exercised in relation to the third person.

(2) If a document is produced in response to a requirement imposed under this Part, the person to whom it is produced may—

(a) take copies or extracts from the document; or
(b) require the person producing the document, or any relevant person, to provide an explanation of the document.

(3) If a person who is required under this Part to produce a document fails to do so, the Authority or an investigator may require him to state, to the best of his knowledge and belief, where the document is.

(4) A lawyer may be required under this Part to furnish the name and address of his client.

(5) No person may be required under this Part to disclose information or produce a document in respect of which he owes an obligation of confidence by virtue of carrying on the business of banking unless—
(a) he is the person under investigation or a member of that person's group;
(b) the person to whom the obligation of confidence is owed is the person under investigation or a member of that person's group;
(c) the person to whom the obligation of confidence is owed consents to the disclosure or production; or
(d) the imposing on him of a requirement with respect to such information or document has been specifically authorised by the investigating authority.

(6) If a person claims a lien on a document, its production under this Part does not affect the lien.

(7) "Relevant person", in relation to a person who is required to produce a document, means a person who—
(a) has been or is or is proposed to be a director or controller of that person;
(b) has been or is an auditor of that person;
(c) has been or is an actuary, accountant or lawyer appointed or instructed by that person; or
(d) has been or is an employee of that person.

(8) "Investigator" means a person appointed under section 167 or 168(3) or (5).

176 ENTRY OF PREMISES UNDER WARRANT

(1) A justice of the peace may issue a warrant under this section if satisfied on information on oath given by or on behalf of the Secretary of State, the Authority or an investigator that there are reasonable grounds for believing that the first, second or third set of conditions is satisfied.

(2) The first set of conditions is—
(a) that a person on whom an information requirement has been imposed has failed (wholly or in part) to comply with it; and
(b) that on the premises specified in the warrant—
  (i) there are documents which have been required; or
  (ii) there is information which has been required.

(3) The second set of conditions is—
(a) that the premises specified in the warrant are premises of an authorised person or an appointed representative;
(b) that there are on the premises documents or information in relation to which an information requirement could be imposed; and
(c) that if such a requirement were to be imposed—
  (i) it would not be complied with; or
  (ii) the documents or information to which it related would be removed, tampered with or destroyed.

(4) The third set of conditions is—
(a) that an offence mentioned in section 168 for which the maximum sentence on conviction on indictment is two years or more has been (or is being) committed by any person;
(b) that there are on the premises specified in the warrant documents or information relevant to whether that offence has been (or is being) committed;
(c) that an information requirement could be imposed in relation to those documents or information; and
(d) that if such a requirement were to be imposed—
(i) it would not be complied with; or
(ii) the documents or information to which it related would be removed, tampered with or destroyed.

(5) A warrant under this section shall authorise a constable—
(a) to enter the premises specified in the warrant;
(b) to search the premises and take possession of any documents or information appearing to be documents or information of a kind in respect of which a warrant under this section was issued ("the relevant kind") or to take, in relation to any such documents or information, any other steps which may appear to be necessary for preserving them or preventing interference with them;
(c) to take copies of, or extracts from, any documents or information appearing to be of the relevant kind;
(d) to require any person on the premises to provide an explanation of any document or information appearing to be of the relevant kind or to state where it may be found; and
(e) to use such force as may be reasonably necessary.

(6) In England and Wales, sections 15(5) to (8) and section 16 of the Police and Criminal Evidence Act 1984 (execution of search warrants and safeguards) apply to warrants issued under this section.

...

(8) Any document of which possession is taken under this section may be retained—
(a) for a period of three months; or
(b) if within that period proceedings to which the document is relevant are commenced against any person for any criminal offence, until the conclusion of those proceedings.

(9) In the application of this section to Scotland—
(a) for the references to a justice of the peace substitute references to a justice of the peace or a sheriff; and
(b) for the references to information on oath substitute references to evidence on oath.

(10) "Investigator" means a person appointed under section 167 or 168(3) or (5).

(11) "Information requirement" means a requirement imposed—
(a) by the Authority under section 87C, 87J, 165, 165A, 169A or 175; or
(b) by an investigator under section 171, 172, 173 or 175.

Offences

177 OFFENCES

(1) If a person other than the investigator ("the defaulter") fails to comply with a requirement imposed on him under this Part the person imposing the requirement may certify that fact in writing to the court.

(2) If the court is satisfied that the defaulter failed without reasonable excuse to comply with the requirement, it may deal with the defaulter (and in the case of a body corporate, any director or officer) as if he were in contempt; and "officer", in relation to a limited liability partnership, means a member of the limited liability partnership.

(3) A person who knows or suspects that an investigation is being or is likely to be conducted under this Part is guilty of an offence if—
(a) he falsifies, conceals, destroys or otherwise disposes of a document which he knows or suspects is or would be relevant to such an investigation, or
(b) he causes or permits the falsification, concealment, destruction or disposal of such a document,
unless he shows that he had no intention of concealing facts disclosed by the documents from the investigator.

(4) A person who, in purported compliance with a requirement imposed on him under this Part—
(a) provides information which he knows to be false or misleading in a material particular, or
(b) recklessly provides information which is false or misleading in a material particular,
is guilty of an offence.

(5) A person guilty of an offence under subsection (3) or (4) is liable—
(a) on summary conviction, to imprisonment for a term not exceeding six months or a fine not exceeding the statutory maximum, or both;
(b) on conviction on indictment, to imprisonment for a term not exceeding two years or a fine, or both.

(6) Any person who intentionally obstructs the exercise of any rights conferred by a warrant under section 176 is guilty of an offence and liable on summary conviction to imprisonment for a term not exceeding 51 weeks or a fine not exceeding level 5 on the standard scale, or both.

(7) "Court" means—
(a) the High Court;
(b) in Scotland, the Court of Session.

Part XIV DISCIPLINARY MEASURES

205 PUBLIC CENSURE

If the Authority considers that an authorised person has contravened a requirement imposed on him by or under this Act or by any directly applicable Community regulation made under the markets in financial instruments directive, the Authority may publish a statement to that effect.

206 FINANCIAL PENALTIES

(1) If the Authority considers that an authorised person has contravened a requirement imposed on him by or under this Act, or by any directly applicable Community regulation made under the markets in financial instruments directive, it may impose on him a penalty, in respect of the contravention, of such amount as it considers appropriate.

(3) A penalty under this section is payable to the Authority.

206A SUSPENDING PERMISSION TO CARRY ON REGULATED ACTIVITIES ETC.

(1) If the Authority considers that an authorised person has contravened a relevant requirement imposed on the person, it may—
- (a) suspend, for such period as it considers appropriate, any permission which the person has to carry on a regulated activity; or
- (b) impose, for such period as it considers appropriate, such limitations or other restrictions in relation to the carrying on of a regulated activity by the person as it considers appropriate.

(2) In subsection (1)—
- "permission" means any permission that the authorised person has, whether given (or treated as given) by the Authority or conferred by any provision of this Act;
- "relevant requirement" means a requirement imposed—
  - (a) by or under this Act; or
  - (b) by any directly applicable Community regulation made under the markets in financial instruments directive.

(3) The period for which a suspension or restriction is to have effect may not exceed 12 months.

(4) A suspension may relate only to the carrying on of an activity in specified circumstances.

(5) A restriction may, in particular, be imposed so as to require the person concerned to take, or refrain from taking, specified action.

(6) The Authority may—
- (a) withdraw a suspension or restriction; or
- (b) vary a suspension or restriction so as to reduce the period for which it has effect or otherwise to limit its effect.

(7) The power under this section may (but need not) be exercised so as to have effect in relation to all the regulated activities that the person concerned carries on.

(8) Any one or more of the powers under—
- (a) subsection (1)(a) and (b) of this section, and
- (b) sections 205 and 206,

may be exercised in relation to the same contravention.

207 PROPOSAL TO TAKE DISCIPLINARY MEASURES

(1) If the Authority proposes—
- (a) to publish a statement in respect of an authorised person (under section 205),
- (b) to impose a penalty on an authorised person (under section 206), or
- (c) to suspend a permission of an authorised person or impose a restriction in relation to the carrying on of a regulated activity by an authorised person (under section 206A),

it must give the authorised person a warning notice.

(2) A warning notice about a proposal to publish a statement must set out the terms of the statement.

(3) A warning notice about a proposal to impose a penalty, must state the amount of the penalty.

(4) A warning notice about a proposal to suspend a permission or impose a restriction must state the period for which the suspension or restriction is to have effect.

208 DECISION NOTICE

(1) If the Authority decides—
(a) to publish a statement under section 205 (whether or not in the terms proposed),
(b) to impose a penalty under section 206 (whether or not of the amount proposed), or
(c) to suspend a permission or impose a restriction under section 206A (whether or not in the manner proposed),
it must without delay give the authorised person concerned a decision notice.

(2) In the case of a statement, the decision notice must set out the terms of the statement.

(3) In the case of a penalty, the decision notice must state the amount of the penalty.

(3A) In the case of a suspension or restriction, the decision notice must state the period for which the suspension or restriction is to have effect.

(4) If the Authority decides to—
(a) publish a statement in respect of an authorised person under section 205,
(b) impose a penalty on an authorised person under section 206, or
(c) suspend a permission of an authorised person, or impose a restriction in relation to the carrying on of a regulated activity by an authorised person, under section 206A,
the authorised person may refer the matter to the Tribunal.

209 PUBLICATION

After a statement under section 205 is published, the Authority must send a copy of it to the authorised person and to any person on whom a copy of the decision notice was given under section 393(4).

210 STATEMENTS OF POLICY

(1) The Authority must prepare and issue a statement of its policy with respect to—
(a) the imposition of penalties, suspensions or restrictions under this Part;
(b) the amount of penalties under this Part; and
(c) the period for which suspensions or restrictions under this Part are to have effect.

(2) The Authority's policy in determining what the amount of a penalty should be, or what the period for which a suspension or restriction is to have effect should be, must include having regard to—
(a) the seriousness of the contravention in question in relation to the nature of the requirement contravened;
(b) the extent to which that contravention was deliberate or reckless; and
(c) whether the person against whom action is to be taken is an individual.

(3) The Authority may at any time alter or replace a statement issued under this section.

(4) If a statement issued under this section is altered or replaced, the Authority must issue the altered or replacement statement.

(5) The Authority must, without delay, give the Treasury a copy of any statement which it publishes under this section.

(6) A statement issued under this section must be published by the Authority in the way appearing to the Authority to be best calculated to bring it to the attention of the public.

(7) In exercising, or deciding whether to exercise, its power under section 206 or 206A in the case of any particular contravention, the Authority must have regard to any statement

published under this section and in force at the time when the contravention in question occurred.

(8) The Authority may charge a reasonable fee for providing a person with a copy of the statement.

211 STATEMENTS OF POLICY: PROCEDURE

(1) Before issuing a statement under section 210, the Authority must publish a draft of the proposed statement in the way appearing to the Authority to be best calculated to bring it to the attention of the public.

(2) The draft must be accompanied by notice that representations about the proposal may be made to the Authority within a specified time.

(3) Before issuing the proposed statement, the Authority must have regard to any representations made to it in accordance with subsection (2).

(4) If the Authority issues the proposed statement it must publish an account, in general terms, of—
(a) the representations made to it in accordance with subsection (2); and
(b) its response to them.

(5) If the statement differs from the draft published under subsection (1) in a way which is, in the opinion of the Authority, significant, the Authority must (in addition to complying with subsection (4)) publish details of the difference.

(6) The Authority may charge a reasonable fee for providing a person with a copy of a draft published under subsection (1).

(7) This section also applies to a proposal to alter or replace a statement.

Part XXV INJUNCTIONS AND RESTITUTION

Injunctions

380 INJUNCTIONS

(1) If, on the application of the Authority or the Secretary of State, the court is satisfied—
(a) that there is a reasonable likelihood that any person will contravene a relevant requirement, or
(b) that any person has contravened a relevant requirement and that there is a reasonable likelihood that the contravention will continue or be repeated,
the court may make an order restraining (or in Scotland an interdict prohibiting) the contravention.

(2) If on the application of the Authority or the Secretary of State the court is satisfied—
(a) that any person has contravened a relevant requirement, and
(b) that there are steps which could be taken for remedying the contravention,
the court may make an order requiring that person, and any other person who appears to have been knowingly concerned in the contravention, to take such steps as the court may direct to remedy it.

(3) If, on the application of the Authority or the Secretary of State, the court is satisfied that any person may have—
(a) contravened a relevant requirement, or
(b) been knowingly concerned in the contravention of such a requirement,

it may make an order restraining (or in Scotland an interdict prohibiting) him from disposing of, or otherwise dealing with, any assets of his which it is satisfied he is reasonably likely to dispose of or otherwise deal with.

(4) The jurisdiction conferred by this section is exercisable by the High Court and the Court of Session.

(5) In subsection (2), references to remedying a contravention include references to mitigating its effect.

(6) "Relevant requirement"—
(a) in relation to an application by the Authority, means a requirement—
(i) which is imposed by or under this Act or by any directly applicable Community regulation made under the markets in financial instruments directive; or
(ii) which is imposed by or under any other Act and whose contravention constitutes an offence which the Authority has power to prosecute under this Act;
(b) in relation to an application by the Secretary of State, means a requirement which is imposed by or under this Act and whose contravention constitutes an offence which the Secretary of State has power to prosecute under this Act.

(7) In the application of subsection (6) to Scotland—
(a) in paragraph (a)(ii) for "which the Authority has power to prosecute under this Act" substitute "mentioned in paragraph (a) or (b) of section 402(1)"; and
(b) in paragraph (b) omit "which the Secretary of State has power to prosecute under this Act".

381 INJUNCTIONS IN CASES OF MARKET ABUSE

(1) If, on the application of the Authority, the court is satisfied—
(a) that there is a reasonable likelihood that any person will engage in market abuse, or
(b) that any person is or has engaged in market abuse and that there is a reasonable likelihood that the market abuse will continue or be repeated,
the court may make an order restraining (or in Scotland an interdict prohibiting) the market abuse.

(2) If on the application of the Authority the court is satisfied—
(a) that any person is or has engaged in market abuse, and
(b) that there are steps which could be taken for remedying the market abuse,
the court may make an order requiring him to take such steps as the court may direct to remedy it.

(3) Subsection (4) applies if, on the application of the Authority, the court is satisfied that any person—
(a) may be engaged in market abuse; or
(b) may have been engaged in market abuse.

(4) The court make an order restraining (or in Scotland an interdict prohibiting) the person concerned from disposing of, or otherwise dealing with, any assets of his which it is satisfied that he is reasonably likely to dispose of, or otherwise deal with.

(5) The jurisdiction conferred by this section is exercisable by the High Court and the Court of Session.

(6) In subsection (2), references to remedying any market abuse include references to mitigating its effect.

Restitution orders

382 RESTITUTION ORDERS

(1) The court may, on the application of the Authority or the Secretary of State, make an order under subsection (2) if it is satisfied that a person has contravened a relevant requirement, or been knowingly concerned in the contravention of such a requirement, and—
(a) that profits have accrued to him as a result of the contravention; or
(b) that one or more persons have suffered loss or been otherwise adversely affected as a result of the contravention.

(2) The court may order the person concerned to pay to the Authority such sum as appears to the court to be just having regard—
(a) in a case within paragraph (a) of subsection (1), to the profits appearing to the court to have accrued;
(b) in a case within paragraph (b) of that subsection, to the extent of the loss or other adverse effect;
(c) in a case within both of those paragraphs, to the profits appearing to the court to have accrued and to the extent of the loss or other adverse effect.

(3) Any amount paid to the Authority in pursuance of an order under subsection (2) must be paid by it to such qualifying person or distributed by it among such qualifying persons as the court may direct.

(4) On an application under subsection (1) the court may require the person concerned to supply it with such accounts or other information as it may require for any one or more of the following purposes—
(a) establishing whether any and, if so, what profits have accrued to him as mentioned in paragraph (a) of that subsection;
(b) establishing whether any person or persons have suffered any loss or adverse effect as mentioned in paragraph (b) of that subsection and, if so, the extent of that loss or adverse effect; and
(c) determining how any amounts are to be paid or distributed under subsection (3).

(5) The court may require any accounts or other information supplied under subsection (4) to be verified in such manner as it may direct.

(6) The jurisdiction conferred by this section is exercisable by the High Court and the Court of Session.

(7) Nothing in this section affects the right of any person other than the Authority or the Secretary of State to bring proceedings in respect of the matters to which this section applies.

(8) "Qualifying person" means a person appearing to the court to be someone—
(a) to whom the profits mentioned in subsection (1)(a) are attributable; or
(b) who has suffered the loss or adverse effect mentioned in subsection (1)(b).

(9) "Relevant requirement"—
(a) in relation to an application by the Authority, means a requirement—
(i) which is imposed by or under this Act or by any directly applicable Community regulation made under the markets in financial instruments directive; or
(ii) which is imposed by or under any other Act and whose contravention constitutes an offence which the Authority has power to prosecute under this Act;
(b) in relation to an application by the Secretary of State, means a requirement which is imposed by or under this Act and whose contravention constitutes an offence which the Secretary of State has power to prosecute under this Act.

(10) In the application of subsection (9) to Scotland—
(a) in paragraph (a)(ii) for "which the Authority has power to prosecute under this Act" substitute "mentioned in paragraph (a) or (b) of section 402(1); and
(b) in paragraph (b) omit "which the Secretary of State has power to prosecute under this Act"".

383 RESTITUTION ORDERS IN CASES OF MARKET ABUSE

(1) The court may, on the application of the Authority, make an order under subsection (4) if it is satisfied that a person ("the person concerned")—
(a) has engaged in market abuse, or
(b) by taking or refraining from taking any action has required or encouraged another person or persons to engage in behaviour which, if engaged in by the person concerned, would amount to market abuse,
and the condition mentioned in subsection (2) is fulfilled.

(2) The condition is—
(a) that profits have accrued to the person concerned as a result; or
(b) that one or more persons have suffered loss or been otherwise adversely affected as a result.

(3) But the court may not make an order under subsection (4) if it is satisfied that—
(a) the person concerned believed, on reasonable grounds, that his behaviour did not fall within paragraph (a) or (b) of subsection (1); or
(b) he took all reasonable precautions and exercised all due diligence to avoid behaving in a way which fell within paragraph (a) or (b) of subsection (1).

(4) The court may order the person concerned to pay to the Authority such sum as appears to the court to be just having regard—
(a) in a case within paragraph (a) of subsection (2), to the profits appearing to the court to have accrued;
(b) in a case within paragraph (b) of that subsection, to the extent of the loss or other adverse effect;
(c) in a case within both of those paragraphs, to the profits appearing to the court to have accrued and to the extent of the loss or other adverse effect.

(5) Any amount paid to the Authority in pursuance of an order under subsection (4) must be paid by it to such qualifying person or distributed by it among such qualifying persons as the court may direct.

(6) On an application under subsection (1) the court may require the person concerned to supply it with such accounts or other information as it may require for any one or more of the following purposes—
(a) establishing whether any and, if so, what profits have accrued to him as mentioned in subsection (2)(a);
(b) establishing whether any person or persons have suffered any loss or adverse effect as mentioned in subsection (2)(b) and, if so, the extent of that loss or adverse effect; and
(c) determining how any amounts are to be paid or distributed under subsection (5).

(7) The court may require any accounts or other information supplied under subsection (6) to be verified in such manner as it may direct.

(8) The jurisdiction conferred by this section is exercisable by the High Court and the Court of Session.

(9) Nothing in this section affects the right of any person other than the Authority to bring proceedings in respect of the matters to which this section applies.

(10) "Qualifying person" means a person appearing to the court to be someone—
(a) to whom the profits mentioned in paragraph (a) of subsection (2) are attributable; or
(b) who has suffered the loss or adverse effect mentioned in paragraph (b) of that subsection.

Restitution required by Authority

384 POWER OF AUTHORITY TO REQUIRE RESTITUTION

(1) The Authority may exercise the power in subsection (5) if it is satisfied that an authorised person ("the person concerned") has contravened a relevant requirement, or been knowingly concerned in the contravention of such a requirement, and—
(a) that profits have accrued to him as a result of the contravention; or
(b) that one or more persons have suffered loss or been otherwise adversely affected as a result of the contravention.

(2) The Authority may exercise the power in subsection (5) if it is satisfied that a person ("the person concerned")—
(a) has engaged in market abuse, or
(b) by taking or refraining from taking any action has required or encouraged another person or persons to engage in behaviour which, if engaged in by the person concerned, would amount to market abuse,
and the condition mentioned in subsection (3) is fulfilled,

(3) The condition is—
(a) that profits have accrued to the person concerned as a result of the market abuse; or
(b) that one or more persons have suffered loss or been otherwise adversely affected as a result of the market abuse.

(4) But the Authority may not exercise that power as a result of subsection (2) if, having considered any representations made to it in response to a warning notice, there are reasonable grounds for it to be satisfied that—
(a) the person concerned believed, on reasonable grounds, that his behaviour did not fall within paragraph (a) or (b) of that subsection; or
(b) he took all reasonable precautions and exercised all due diligence to avoid behaving in a way which fell within paragraph (a) or (b) of that subsection.

(5) The power referred to in subsections (1) and (2) is a power to require the person concerned, in accordance with such arrangements as the Authority considers appropriate, to pay to the appropriate person or distribute among the appropriate persons such amount as appears to the Authority to be just having regard—
(a) in a case within paragraph (a) of subsection (1) or (3), to the profits appearing to the Authority to have accrued;
(b) in a case within paragraph (b) of subsection (1) or (3), to the extent of the loss or other adverse effect;
(c) in a case within paragraphs (a) and (b) of subsection (1) or (3), to the profits appearing to the Authority to have accrued and to the extent of the loss or other adverse effect.

(6) "Appropriate person" means a person appearing to the Authority to be someone—
(a) to whom the profits mentioned in paragraph (a) of subsection (1) or (3) are attributable; or

(b) who has suffered the loss or adverse effect mentioned in paragraph (b) of subsection (1) or (3).

(7) "Relevant requirement" means—
(a) a requirement imposed by or under this Act or by any directly applicable Community regulation made under the markets in financial instruments directive; and
(b) a requirement which is imposed by or under any other Act and whose contravention constitutes an offence in relation to which this Act confers power to prosecute on the Authority.

(8) In the application of subsection (7) to Scotland, in paragraph (b) for "in relation to which this Act confers power to prosecute on the Authority" substitute "mentioned in paragraph (a) or (b) of section 402(1)".

385 WARNING NOTICES

(1) If the Authority proposes to exercise the power under section 384(5) in relation to a person, it must give him a warning notice.

(2) A warning notice under this section must specify the amount which the Authority proposes to require the person concerned to pay or distribute as mentioned in section 384(5).

386 DECISION NOTICES

(1) If the Authority decides to exercise the power under section 384(5), it must give a decision notice to the person in relation to whom the power is exercised.

(2) The decision notice must—
(a) state the amount that he is to pay or distribute as mentioned in section 384(5);
(b) identify the person or persons to whom that amount is to be paid or among whom that amount is to be distributed; and
(c) state the arrangements in accordance with which the payment or distribution is to be made.

(3) If the Authority decides to exercise the power under section 384(5), the person in relation to whom it is exercised may refer the matter to the Tribunal.

Part XXVI NOTICES

Warning notices

387 WARNING NOTICES

(1) A warning notice must—
(a) state the action which the Authority proposes to take;
(b) be in writing;
(c) give reasons for the proposed action;
(d) state whether section 394 applies; and
(e) if that section applies, describe its effect and state whether any secondary material exists to which the person concerned must be allowed access under it.

(2) The warning notice must specify a reasonable period (which may not be less than 28 days) within which the person to whom it is given may make representations to the Authority.

(3) The Authority may extend the period specified in the notice.

(4) The Authority must then decide, within a reasonable period, whether to give the person concerned a decision notice.

Decision notices

388 DECISION NOTICES

(1) A decision notice must—
  (a) be in writing;
  (b) give the Authority's reasons for the decision to take the action to which the notice relates;
  (c) state whether section 394 applies;
  (d) if that section applies, describe its effect and state whether any secondary material exists to which the person concerned must be allowed access under it; and
  (e) give an indication of—
    (i) any right to have the matter referred to the Tribunal which is given by this Act; and
    (ii) the procedure on such a reference.

(2) If the decision notice was preceded by a warning notice, the action to which the decision notice relates must be action under the same Part as the action proposed in the warning notice.

(3) The Authority may, before it takes the action to which a decision notice ("the original notice") relates, give the person concerned a further decision notice which relates to different action in respect of the same matter.

(4) The Authority may give a further decision notice as a result of subsection (3) only if the person to whom the original notice was given consents.

(5) If the person to whom a decision notice is given under subsection (3) had the right to refer the matter to which the original decision notice related to the Tribunal, he has that right as respects the decision notice under subsection (3).

Conclusion of proceedings

389 NOTICES OF DISCONTINUANCE

(1) If the Authority decides not to take—
  (a) the action proposed in a warning notice, or
  (b) the action to which a decision notice relates,
  it must give a notice of discontinuance to the person to whom the warning notice or decision notice was given.

(2) But subsection (1) does not apply if the discontinuance of the proceedings concerned results in the granting of an application made by the person to whom the warning or decision notice was given.

(3) A notice of discontinuance must identify the proceedings which are being discontinued.

390 FINAL NOTICES

(1) If the Authority has given a person a decision notice and the matter was not referred to the Tribunal within the time required by Tribunal Procedure Rules, the Authority must,

on taking the action to which the decision notice relates, give the person concerned and any person to whom the decision notice was copied a final notice.

(2) If the Authority has given a person a decision notice and the matter was referred to the Tribunal, the Authority must, on taking action in accordance with any directions given by—
(a) the Tribunal, or
(b) a court on an appeal against the decision of the Tribunal,
give that person and any person to whom the decision notice was copied a final notice.

(3) A final notice about a statement must—
(a) set out the terms of the statement;
(b) give details of the manner in which, and the date on which, the statement will be published.

(4) A final notice about an order must—
(a) set out the terms of the order;
(b) state the date from which the order has effect.

(5) A final notice about a penalty must—
(a) state the amount of the penalty;
(b) state the manner in which, and the period within which, the penalty is to be paid;
(c) give details of the way in which the penalty will be recovered if it is not paid by the date stated in the notice.

(6) A final notice about a requirement to make a payment or distribution in accordance with section 384(5) must state—
(a) the persons to whom,
(b) the manner in which, and
(c) the period within which,
it must be made.

(7) In any other case, the final notice must—
(a) give details of the action being taken;
(b) state the date on which the action is to be taken.

(8) The period stated under subsection (5)(b) or (6)(c) may not be less than 14 days beginning with the date on which the final notice is given.

(9) If all or any of the amount of a penalty payable under a final notice is outstanding at the end of the period stated under subsection (5)(b), the Authority may recover the outstanding amount as a debt due to it.

(10) If all or any of a required payment or distribution has not been made at the end of a period stated in a final notice under subsection (6)(c), the obligation to make the payment is enforceable, on the application of the Authority, by injunction or, in Scotland, by an order under section 45 of the Court of Session Act 1988.

Publication

391 PUBLICATION

(1) Neither the Authority nor a person to whom a warning notice is given or copied may publish the notice or any details concerning it.

(1A) A person to whom a decision notice is given or copied may not publish the notice or any details concerning it unless the Authority has published the notice or those details.

(2) A notice of discontinuance must state that, if the person to whom the notice is given consents, the Authority may publish such information as it considers appropriate about the matter to which the discontinued proceedings related.

(3) A copy of a notice of discontinuance must be accompanied by a statement that, if the person to whom the notice is copied consents, the Authority may publish such information as it considers appropriate about the matter to which the discontinued proceedings related, so far as relevant to that person.

(4) The Authority must publish such information about the matter to which a decision notice or final notice relates as it considers appropriate.

(5) When a supervisory notice takes effect, the Authority must publish such information about the matter to which the notice relates as it considers appropriate.

(6) But the Authority may not publish information under this section if publication of it would, in its opinion, be unfair to the person with respect to whom the action was taken or prejudicial to the interests of consumers.

(7) Information is to be published under this section in such manner as the Authority considers appropriate.

(8) For the purposes of determining when a supervisory notice takes effect, a matter to which the notice relates is open to review if—
(a) the period during which any person may refer the matter to the Tribunal is still running;
(b) the matter has been referred to the Tribunal but has not been dealt with;
(c) the matter has been referred to the Tribunal and dealt with but the period during which an appeal may be brought against the Tribunal's decision is still running; or
(d) such an appeal has been brought but has not been determined.

(9) "Notice of discontinuance" means a notice given under section 389.

(10) "Supervisory notice" has the same meaning as in section 395.

(11) Section 425A (meaning of "consumers") applies for the purposes of this section.

Third party rights and access to evidence

392 APPLICATION OF SECTIONS 393 AND 394

Sections 393 and 394 apply to—
(a) a warning notice given in accordance with section 54(1), 57(1), 63(3), 63B(1), 67(1), 88(4)(b), 89(2), 92(1), 126(1), 131H(1), 207(1), 255(1), 280(1), 331(1), 345(2) (whether as a result of subsection (1) of that section or section 249(1)), 385(1) or 412B(4) or (8);

(b) a decision notice given in accordance with section 54(2), 57(3), 63(4), 63B(3), 67(4), 88(6)(b), 89(3), 92(4), 127(1), 131H(4), 208(1), 255(2), 280(2), 331(3), 345(3) (whether as a result of subsection (1) of that section or section 249(1)), 386(1) or 412B(5) or (9).

393 THIRD PARTY RIGHTS

(1) If any of the reasons contained in a warning notice to which this section applies relates to a matter which—
(a) identifies a person ("the third party") other than the person to whom the notice is given, and

(b) in the opinion of the Authority, is prejudicial to the third party,
a copy of the notice must be given to the third party.

(2) Subsection (1) does not require a copy to be given to the third party if the Authority—
(a) has given him a separate warning notice in relation to the same matter; or
(b) gives him such a notice at the same time as it gives the warning notice which identifies him.

(3) The notice copied to a third party under subsection (1) must specify a reasonable period (which may not be less than 28 days) within which he may make representations to the Authority.

(4) If any of the reasons contained in a decision notice to which this section applies relates to a matter which—
(a) identifies a person ("the third party") other than the person to whom the decision notice is given, and
(b) in the opinion of the Authority, is prejudicial to the third party,
a copy of the notice must be given to the third party.

(5) If the decision notice was preceded by a warning notice, a copy of the decision notice must (unless it has been given under subsection (4)) be given to each person to whom the warning notice was copied.

(6) Subsection (4) does not require a copy to be given to the third party if the Authority—
(a) has given him a separate decision notice in relation to the same matter; or
(b) gives him such a notice at the same time as it gives the decision notice which identifies him.

(7) Neither subsection (1) nor subsection (4) requires a copy of a notice to be given to a third party if the Authority considers it impracticable to do so.

(8) Subsections (9) to (11) apply if the person to whom a decision notice is given has a right to refer the matter to the Tribunal.

(9) A person to whom a copy of the notice is given under this section may refer to the Tribunal—
(a) the decision in question, so far as it is based on a reason of the kind mentioned in subsection (4); or
(b) any opinion expressed by the Authority in relation to him.

(10) The copy must be accompanied by an indication of the third party's right to make a reference under subsection (9) and of the procedure on such a reference.

(11) A person who alleges that a copy of the notice should have been given to him, but was not, may refer to the Tribunal the alleged failure and—
(a) the decision in question, so far as it is based on a reason of the kind mentioned in subsection (4); or
(b) any opinion expressed by the Authority in relation to him.

(12) Section 394 applies to a third party as it applies to the person to whom the notice to which this section applies was given, in so far as the material which the Authority must disclose under that section relates to the matter which identifies the third party.

(13) A copy of a notice given to a third party under this section must be accompanied by a description of the effect of section 394 as it applies to him.

(14) Any person to whom a warning notice or decision notice was copied under this section must be given a copy of a notice of discontinuance applicable to the proceedings to which the warning notice or decision notice related.

394 ACCESS TO AUTHORITY MATERIAL

(1) If the Authority gives a person ("A") a notice to which this section applies, it must—
(a) allow him access to the material on which it relied in taking the decision which gave rise to the obligation to give the notice;
(b) allow him access to any secondary material which, in the opinion of the Authority, might undermine that decision.

(2) But the Authority does not have to allow A access to material under subsection (1) if the material is excluded material or it—
(a) relates to a case involving a person other than A; and
(b) was taken into account by the Authority in A's case only for purposes of comparison with other cases.

(3) The Authority may refuse access A to particular material which it would otherwise have to allow him access to if, in its opinion, allowing him access to the material—
(a) would not be in the public interest; or
(b) would not be fair, having regard to—
(i) the likely significance of the material to A in relation to the matter in respect of which he has been given a notice to which this section applies; and
(ii) the potential prejudice to the commercial interests of a person other than A which would be caused by the material's disclosure.

(4) If the Authority does not allow A access to material because it is excluded material consisting of a protected item, it must give A written notice of—
(a) the existence of the protected item; and
(b) the Authority's decision not to allow him access to it.

(5) If the Authority refuses under subsection (3) to allow A access to material, it must give him written notice of—
(a) the refusal; and
(b) the reasons for it.

(6) "Secondary material" means material, other than material falling within paragraph (a) of subsection (1) which—
(a) was considered by the Authority in reaching the decision mentioned in that paragraph; or
(b) was obtained by the Authority in connection with the matter to which the notice to which this section applies relates but which was not considered by it in reaching that decision.

(7) "Excluded material" means material which—
(a) is material the disclosure of which for the purposes of or in connection with any legal proceedings is prohibited by section 17 of the Regulation of Investigatory Powers Act 2000; or
(c) is a protected item (as defined in section 413).

The Authority's procedures

395 THE AUTHORITY'S PROCEDURES

(1) The Authority must determine the procedure that it proposes to follow in relation to the giving of—
(a) supervisory notices; and
(b) warning notices and decision notices.

(2) That procedure must be designed to secure, among other things, that the decision which gives rise to the obligation to give any such notice is taken by a person not directly involved in establishing the evidence on which that decision is based.

(3) But the procedure may permit a decision which gives rise to an obligation to give a supervisory notice to be taken by a person other than a person mentioned in subsection (2) if—
  (a) the Authority considers that, in the particular case, it is necessary in order to protect the interests of consumers; and
  (b) the person taking the decision is of a level of seniority laid down by the procedure.

(4) A level of seniority laid down by the procedure for the purposes of subsection (3)(b) must be appropriate to the importance of the decision.

(5) The Authority must issue a statement of the procedure.

(6) The statement must be published in the way appearing to the Authority to be best calculated to bring it to the attention of the public.

(7) The Authority may charge a reasonable fee for providing a person with a copy of the statement.

(8) The Authority must, without delay, give the Treasury a copy of any statement which it issues under this section.

(9) When giving a supervisory notice, or a warning notice or decision notice, the Authority must follow its stated procedure.

(10) If the Authority changes the procedure in a material way, it must publish a revised statement.

(11) The Authority's failure in a particular case to follow its procedure as set out in the latest published statement does not affect the validity of a notice given in that case.

(12) But subsection (11) does not prevent the Tribunal from taking into account any such failure in considering a matter referred to it.

(13) "Supervisory notice" means a notice given in accordance with section—
  (a) 53(4), (7) or (8)(b);
  (b) 78(2) or (5);
  (bza) 78A(2) or (8)(b);
  (ba) 96C;
  (bb) 87O(2) or (5);
  (bc) 191B(1);
  (c) 197(3), (6) or (7)(b);
  (d) 259(3), (8) or (9)(b);
  (e) 268(3), (7)(a) or (9)(a) (as a result of subsection (8)(b));
  (f) 282(3), (6) or (7)(b);
  (fa) 301J(1);
  (g) 321(2) or (5).

396 STATEMENTS UNDER SECTION 395: CONSULTATION

(1) Before issuing a statement of procedure under section 395, the Authority must publish a draft of the proposed statement in the way appearing to the Authority to be best calculated to bring it to the attention of the public.

(2) The draft must be accompanied by notice that representations about the proposal may be made to the Authority within a specified time.

(3) Before issuing the proposed statement of procedure, the Authority must have regard to any representations made to it in accordance with subsection (2).

(4) If the Authority issues the proposed statement of procedure it must publish an account, in general terms, of—
(a) the representations made to it in accordance with subsection (2); and
(b) its response to them.

(5) If the statement of procedure differs from the draft published under subsection (1) in a way which is, in the opinion of the Authority, significant, the Authority must (in addition to complying with subsection (4)) publish details of the difference.

(6) The Authority may charge a reasonable fee for providing a person with a copy of a draft published under subsection (1).

(7) This section also applies to a proposal to revise a statement of policy.

Part XXVII OFFENCES

Miscellaneous offences

397 MISLEADING STATEMENTS AND PRACTICES

(1) This subsection applies to a person who—
(a) makes a statement, promise or forecast which he knows to be misleading, false or deceptive in a material particular;
(b) dishonestly conceals any material facts whether in connection with a statement, promise or forecast made by him or otherwise; or
(c) recklessly makes (dishonestly or otherwise) a statement, promise or forecast which is misleading, false or deceptive in a material particular.

(2) A person to whom subsection (1) applies is guilty of an offence if he makes the statement, promise or forecast or conceals the facts for the purpose of inducing, or is reckless as to whether it may induce, another person (whether or not the person to whom the statement, promise or forecast is made)—
(a) to enter or offer to enter into, or to refrain from entering or offering to enter into, a relevant agreement; or
(b) to exercise, or refrain from exercising, any rights conferred by a relevant investment.

(3) Any person who does any act or engages in any course of conduct which creates a false or misleading impression as to the market in or the price or value of any relevant investments is guilty of an offence if he does so for the purpose of creating that impression and of thereby inducing another person to acquire, dispose of, subscribe for or underwrite those investments or to refrain from doing so or to exercise, or refrain from exercising, any rights conferred by those investments.

(4) In proceedings for an offence under subsection (2) brought against a person to whom subsection (1) applies as a result of paragraph (a) of that subsection, it is a defence for him to show that the statement, promise or forecast was made in conformity with—
(a) price stabilising rules;
(b) control of information rules; or
(c) the relevant provisions of Commission Regulation (EC) No 2273/2003 of 22 December 2003 implementing Directive 2003/6/EC of the European Parliament and of the Council as regards exemptions for buy-back programmes and stabilisation of financial instruments.

(5) In proceedings brought against any person for an offence under subsection (3) it is a defence for him to show—
 (a) that he reasonably believed that his act or conduct would not create an impression that was false or misleading as to the matters mentioned in that subsection;
 (b) that he acted or engaged in the conduct—
  (i) for the purpose of stabilising the price of investments; and
  (ii) in conformity with price stabilising rules;
 (c) that he acted or engaged in the conduct in conformity with control of information rules; or
 (d) that he acted or engaged in the conduct in conformity with the relevant provisions of Commission Regulation (EC) No 2273/2003 of 22 December 2003 implementing Directive 2003/6/EC of the European Parliament and of the Council as regards exemptions for buy-back programmes and stabilisation of financial instruments.

(6) Subsections (1) and (2) do not apply unless—
 (a) the statement, promise or forecast is made in or from, or the facts are concealed in or from, the United Kingdom or arrangements are made in or from the United Kingdom for the statement, promise or forecast to be made or the facts to be concealed;
 (b) the person on whom the inducement is intended to or may have effect is in the United Kingdom; or
 (c) the agreement is or would be entered into or the rights are or would be exercised in the United Kingdom.

(7) Subsection (3) does not apply unless—
 (a) the act is done, or the course of conduct is engaged in, in the United Kingdom; or
 (b) the false or misleading impression is created there.

(8) A person guilty of an offence under this section is liable—
 (a) on summary conviction, to imprisonment for a term not exceeding six months or a fine not exceeding the statutory maximum, or both;
 (b) on conviction on indictment, to imprisonment for a term not exceeding seven years or a fine, or both.

...

(13) "Investment" includes any asset, right or interest.

(14) "Specified" means specified in an order made by the Treasury.

Part XXIX INTERPRETATION

417 DEFINITIONS

(1) In this Act—

...

"the Authority" means the Financial Services Authority;

"body corporate" includes a body corporate constituted under the law of a country or territory outside the United Kingdom;

...

"director", in relation to a body corporate, includes—
 (a) a person occupying in relation to it the position of a director (by whatever name called); and

(b) a person in accordance with whose directions or instructions (not being advice given in a professional capacity) the directors of that body are accustomed to act;

...

"prescribed" (where not otherwise defined) means prescribed in regulations made by the Treasury;

...

"rule" means a rule made by the Authority under this Act;

...

SCHEDULE 10 COMPENSATION: EXEMPTIONS

Statements believed to be true

1(1) In this paragraph "statement" means—

(a) any untrue or misleading statement in listing particulars; or

(b) the omission from listing particulars of any matter required to be included by section 80 or 81.

(2) A person does not incur any liability under section 90(1) for loss caused by a statement if he satisfies the court that, at the time when the listing particulars were submitted to the competent authority, he reasonably believed (having made such enquiries, if any, as were reasonable) that—

(a) the statement was true and not misleading, or

(b) the matter whose omission caused the loss was properly omitted,

and that one or more of the conditions set out in sub-paragraph (3) are satisfied.

(3) The conditions are that—

(a) he continued in his belief until the time when the securities in question were acquired;

(b) they were acquired before it was reasonably practicable to bring a correction to the attention of persons likely to acquire them;

(c) before the securities were acquired, he had taken all such steps as it was reasonable for him to have taken to secure that a correction was brought to the attention of those persons;

(d) he continued in his belief until after the commencement of dealings in the securities following their admission to the official list and they were acquired after such a lapse of time that he ought in the circumstances to be reasonably excused.

Statements by experts

2(1) In this paragraph "statement" means a statement included in listing particulars which—

(a) purports to be made by, or on the authority of, another person as an expert; and

(b) is stated to be included in the listing particulars with that other person's consent.

(2) A person does not incur any liability under section 90(1) for loss in respect of any securities caused by a statement if he satisfies the court that, at the time when the listing particulars were submitted to the competent authority, he reasonably believed that the other person—

(a) was competent to make or authorise the statement, and

(b) had consented to its inclusion in the form and context in which it was included,

and that one or more of the conditions set out in sub-paragraph (3) are satisfied.

(3) The conditions are that—

(a) he continued in his belief until the time when the securities were acquired;

(b) they were acquired before it was reasonably practicable to bring the fact that the expert was not competent, or had not consented, to the attention of persons likely to acquire the securities in question;
(c) before the securities were acquired he had taken all such steps as it was reasonable for him to have taken to secure that that fact was brought to the attention of those persons;
(d) he continued in his belief until after the commencement of dealings in the securities following their admission to the official list and they were acquired after such a lapse of time that he ought in the circumstances to be reasonably excused.

Corrections of statements

3(1) In this paragraph "statement" has the same meaning as in paragraph 1.

(2) A person does not incur liability under section 90(1) for loss caused by a statement if he satisfies the court—
(a) that before the securities in question were acquired, a correction had been published in a manner calculated to bring it to the attention of persons likely to acquire the securities; or
(b) that he took all such steps as it was reasonable for him to take to secure such publication and reasonably believed that it had taken place before the securities were acquired.

(3) Nothing in this paragraph is to be taken as affecting paragraph 1.

Corrections of statements by experts

4(1) In this paragraph "statement" has the same meaning as in paragraph 2.

(2) A person does not incur liability under section 90(1) for loss caused by a statement if he satisfies the court—
(a) that before the securities in question were acquired, the fact that the expert was not competent or had not consented had been published in a manner calculated to bring it to the attention of persons likely to acquire the securities; or
(b) that he took all such steps as it was reasonable for him to take to secure such publication and reasonably believed that it had taken place before the securities were acquired.

(3) Nothing in this paragraph is to be taken as affecting paragraph 2.

Official statements

5. A person does not incur any liability under section 90(1) for loss resulting from—
(a) a statement made by an official person which is included in the listing particulars, or
(b) a statement contained in a public official document which is included in the listing particulars,
if he satisfies the court that the statement is accurately and fairly reproduced.

False or misleading information known about

6. A person does not incur any liability under section 90(1) or (4) if he satisfies the court that the person suffering the loss acquired the securities in question with knowledge—
(a) that the statement was false or misleading,
(b) of the omitted matter, or
(c) of the change or new matter,
as the case may be.

Belief that supplementary listing particulars not called for

7. A person does not incur any liability under section 90(4) if he satisfies the court that he reasonably believed that the change or new matter in question was not such as to call for supplementary listing particulars.

Meaning of "expert"

8. "Expert" includes any engineer, valuer, accountant or other person whose profession, qualifications or experience give authority to a statement made by him.

SCHEDULE 10A LIABILITY OF ISSUERS IN CONNECTION WITH PUBLISHED INFORMATION

Part 1 SCOPE OF THIS SCHEDULE

SECURITIES TO WHICH THIS SCHEDULE APPLIES

1(1) This Schedule applies to securities that are, with the consent of the issuer, admitted to trading on a securities market, where—
(a) the market is situated or operating in the United Kingdom, or
(b) the United Kingdom is the issuer's home State.

(2) For the purposes of this Schedule—
(a) an issuer of securities is not taken to have consented to the securities being admitted to trading on a securities market by reason only of having consented to their admission to trading on another market as a result of which they are admitted to trading on the first-mentioned market;
(b) an issuer who has accepted responsibility (to any extent) for any document prepared for the purposes of the admission of the securities to trading on a securities market (such as a prospectus or listing particulars) is taken to have consented to their admission to trading on that market.

(3) For the purposes of this Schedule the United Kingdom is the home State of an issuer—
(a) in the case of securities in relation to which the transparency obligations directive(**a**) applies, if the United Kingdom is the home Member State for the purposes of that directive (see Article 2.1 of the directive);
(b) in any other case, if the issuer has its registered office (or, if it does not have a registered office, its head office) in the United Kingdom.

PUBLISHED INFORMATION TO WHICH THIS SCHEDULE APPLIES

4(1) This Schedule applies to information published by the issuer of securities to which this Schedule applies—
(a) by recognised means, or
(b) by other means where the availability of the information has been announced by the issuer by recognised means.

(2) It is immaterial whether the information is required to be published (by recognised means or otherwise).

(3) The following are "recognised means"—
(a) a recognised information service;
(b) other means required or authorised to be used to communicate information to the market in question, or to the public, when a recognised information service is unavailable.

(4) A "recognised information service" means—
(a) in relation to a securities market situated or operating in the EEA, a service used for the dissemination of information in accordance with Article 21 of the transparency obligations directive;

(b) in relation to a securities market situated or operating outside the EEA, a service used for the dissemination of information corresponding to that required to be disclosed under that directive; or
(c) in relation to any securities market, any other service used by issuers of securities for the dissemination of information required to be disclosed by the rules of the market.

Part 2 LIABILITY IN CONNECTION WITH PUBLISHED INFORMATION

LIABILITY OF ISSUER FOR MISLEADING STATEMENT OR DISHONEST OMISSION

3(1) An issuer of securities to which this Schedule applies is liable to pay compensation to a person who—
(a) acquires, continues to hold or disposes of the securities in reliance on published information to which this Schedule applies, and
(b) suffers loss in respect of the securities as a result of—
(i) any untrue or misleading statement in that published information, or
(ii) the omission from that published information of any matter required to be included in it.

(2) The issuer is liable in respect of an untrue or misleading statement only if a person discharging managerial responsibilities within the issuer knew the statement to be untrue or misleading or was reckless as to whether it was untrue or misleading.

(3) The issuer is liable in respect of the omission of any matter required to be included in published information only if a person discharging managerial responsibilities within the issuer knew the omission to be a dishonest concealment of a material fact.

(4) A loss is not regarded as suffered as a result of the statement or omission unless the person suffering it acquired, continued to hold or disposed of the relevant securities—
(a) in reliance on the information in question, and
(b) at a time when, and in circumstances in which, it was reasonable for him to rely on it.

4 An issuer of securities to which this Schedule applies is not liable under paragraph 3 to pay compensation to a person for loss suffered as a result of an untrue or misleading statement in, or omission from, published information to which this Schedule applies if—
(a) the published information is contained in listing particulars or a prospectus (or supplementary listing particulars or a supplementary prospectus), and
(b) the issuer is liable under section 90 (compensation for statements in listing particulars or prospectus) to pay compensation to the person in respect of the statement or omission.

LIABILITY OF ISSUER FOR DISHONEST DELAY IN PUBLISHING INFORMATION

5(1) An issuer of securities to which this Schedule applies is liable to pay compensation to a person who—
(a) acquires, continues to hold or disposes of the securities, and
(b) suffers loss in respect of the securities as a result of delay by the issuer in publishing information to which this Schedule applies.

(2) The issuer is liable only if a person discharging managerial responsibilities within the issuer acted dishonestly in delaying the publication of the information.

MEANING OF DISHONESTY

6 For the purposes of paragraphs 3(3) and 5(2) a person's conduct is regarded as dishonest if (and only if)—
(a) it is regarded as dishonest by persons who regularly trade on the securities market in question, and
(b) the person was aware (or must be taken to have been aware) that it was so regarded.

EXCLUSION OF CERTAIN OTHER LIABILITIES

7(1) The issuer is not subject—
(a) to any liability other than that provided for by paragraph 3 in respect of loss suffered as a result of reliance by any person on—
(i) an untrue or misleading statement in published information to which this Schedule applies, or
(ii) the omission from any such published information of any matter required to be included in it;
(b) to any liability other than that provided for by paragraph 5 in respect of loss suffered as a result of delay in the publication of information to which this Schedule applies.

(2) A person other than the issuer is not subject to any liability, other than to the issuer, in respect of any such loss.

(3) This paragraph does not affect—
(a) civil liability—
(i) under section 90 (compensation for statements in listing particulars or prospectus),
(ii) under rules made by virtue of section 954 of the Companies Act 2006 (compensation),
(iii) for breach of contract,
(iv) under the Misrepresentation Act 1967, or
(v) arising from a person's having assumed responsibility, to a particular person for a particular purpose, for the accuracy or completeness of the information concerned;
(b) liability to a civil penalty; or
(c) criminal liability.

(4) This paragraph does not affect the powers conferred by sections 382 and 384 (powers of the court to make a restitution order and of the Authority to require restitution).

(5) References in this paragraph to liability, in relation to a person, include a reference to another person being entitled as against that person to be granted any civil remedy or to rescind or repudiate an agreement.

Part 3 SUPPLEMENTARY PROVISIONS

INTERPRETATION

8(1) In this Schedule—
(a) "securities" means transferable securities within the meaning of Article 4.1.18 of the markets in financial instruments directive(**a**), other than money-market instruments as defined in Article 4.1.19 of that directive that have a maturity of less than 12 months (and includes instruments outside the EEA);
(b) "securities market" means—

(i) a regulated market as defined in Article 4.1.14 of the markets in financial instruments directive,
(ii) a multilateral trading facility as defined in Article 4.1.15 of the markets in financial instruments directive, or
(iii) a market or facility of a corresponding description outside the EEA.

(2) References in this Schedule to the issuer of securities are—
(a) in relation to a depositary receipt, derivative instrument or other financial instrument representing securities where the issuer of the securities represented has consented to the admission of the instrument to trading as mentioned in paragraph 1(1), to the issuer of the securities represented;
(b) in any other case, to the person who issued the securities.

(3) References in this Schedule to the acquisition or disposal of securities include—
(a) acquisition or disposal of any interest in securities, or
(b) contracting to acquire or dispose of securities or of any interest in securities, except where what is acquired or disposed of (or contracted to be acquired or disposed of) is a depositary receipt, derivative instrument or other financial instrument representing securities.

(4) References to continuing to hold securities have a corresponding meaning.

(5) For the purposes of this Schedule the following are persons "discharging managerial responsibilities" within an issuer—
(a) any director of the issuer (or person occupying the position of director, by whatever name called);
(b) in the case of an issuer whose affairs are managed by its members, any member of the issuer;
(c) in the case of an issuer that has no persons within paragraph (a) or (b), any senior executive of the issuer having responsibilities in relation to the information in question or its publication.

(6) The following definitions (which apply generally for the purposes of Part 6 of this Act) do not apply for the purposes of this Schedule:
(a) section 102A(1), (2) and (6) (meaning of "securities" and "issuer");
(b) section 102C (meaning of "home State" in relation to transferable securities).

SCHEDULE 15 INFORMATION AND INVESTIGATIONS: CONNECTED PERSONS

Part I RULES FOR SPECIFIC BODIES

Corporate bodies

1 If the authorised person ("BC") is a body corporate, a person who is or has been—
(a) an officer or manager of BC or of a parent undertaking of BC;
(b) an employee of BC;
(c) an agent of BC or of a parent undertaking of BC.

Partnerships

2 If the authorised person ("PP") is a partnership, a person who is or has been a member, manager, employee or agent of PP.

Unincorporated associations

3 If the authorised person ("UA") is an unincorporated association of persons which is neither a partnership nor an unincorporated friendly society, a person who is or has been an officer, manager, employee or agent of UA.

Friendly societies

4(1) If the authorised person ("FS") is a friendly society, a person who is or has been an officer, manager or employee of FS.

(2) In relation to FS, "officer" and "manager" have the same meaning as in section 119(1) of the Friendly Societies Act 1992.

Building societies

5(1) If the authorised person ("BS") is a building society, a person who is or has been an officer or employee of BS.

(2) In relation to BS, "officer" has the same meaning as it has in section 119(1) of the Building Societies Act 1986.

Individuals

6 If the authorised person ("IP") is an individual, a person who is or has been an employee or agent of IP.

Application to sections 171 and 172

7 For the purposes of sections 171 and 172, if the person under investigation is not an authorised person the references in this Part of this Schedule to an authorised person are to be taken to be references to the person under investigation.

Part II ADDITIONAL RULES

8 A person who is, or at the relevant time was, the partner, manager, employee, agent, appointed representative, banker, auditor, actuary or solicitor of—

(a) the person under investigation ("A");
(b) a parent undertaking of A;
(c) a subsidiary undertaking of A;
(d) a subsidiary undertaking of a parent undertaking of A; or
(e) a parent undertaking of a subsidiary undertaking of A.

As amended by the Regulation of Investigatory Powers Act 2000, Schedule 4, para 11; The Limted Liability Partnerships Regulations 2001 (SI 2001/1090), Schedule 5, para 21; Criminal Justice Act 2003, Schedule 26, para 54(2); The Financial Services and Markets Act 2000 (Market Abuse) Regulations 2005 (SI 2005/381), reg 7, Schedules 1–2; The Prospectus Regulations 2005 (SI 2005/1433), Schedule 1; Companies Act 2006, ss 1265, 1267–1271, Schedule 15, Part 1; The Financial Services and Markets Act 2000 (Markets in Financial Instruments) Regulations 2007 (SI 2007/126), Schedule 5, paras 6–11, 13–16; The Regulatory Reform (Financial Services and Markets Act 2000) Order 2007 (SI 2007/1973), arts 5–9; The Financial Services and Markets Act 2000 (Market Abuse) Regulations 2008 (SI 2008/1439), reg 3; The Definition of Financial Instrument Order 2008 (SI 2008/3053), art 3; The Financial Services and Markets Act 2000 (Controllers) Regulations 2009 (SI 2009/534), reg 6; The Financial Services and Markets Act 2000 (Market Abuse) Regulations 2009 (SI 2009/3128), reg 2; Financial Services Act 2010, ss 8–10, 13, 18(2)–(3), Schedule 2, paras 15–20, 28–29; The Transfer of Tribunal Functions Order 2010 (SI 2010/22), Schedule 2, para 47; The Financial Services and Markets Act 2000 (Liability of Issuers) Regulations 2010 (SI 2010/1192), reg 2(2)–(3), Sch; The Treaty of Lisbon (Changes in Terminology) Order 2011 (SI 2011/1043), arts 3, 6.

Limited Liability Partnerships Act 2000

Introductory

1 LIMITED LIABILITY PARTNERSHIPS

(1) There shall be a new form of legal entity to be known as a limited liability partnership.

(2) A limited liability partnership is a body corporate (with legal personality separate from that of its members) which is formed by being incorporated under this Act; and—
  (a) in the following provisions of this Act (except in the phrase "oversea limited liability partnership"), and
  (b) in any other enactment (except where provision is made to the contrary or the context otherwise requires), references to a limited liability partnership are to such a body corporate.

(3) A limited liability partnership has unlimited capacity.

(4) The members of a limited liability partnership have such liability to contribute to its assets in the event of its being wound up as is provided for by virtue of this Act.

(5) Accordingly, except as far as otherwise provided by this Act or any other enactment, the law relating to partnerships does not apply to a limited liability partnership.

(6) The Schedule (which makes provision about the names and registered offices of limited liability partnerships) has effect.

Incorporation

2 INCORPORATION DOCUMENT ETC.

(1) For a limited liability partnership to be incorporated—
  (a) two or more persons associated for carrying on a lawful business with a view to profit must have subscribed their names to an incorporation document,
  (b) the incorporation document or a copy of it must have been delivered to the registrar, and
  (c) there must have been so delivered a statement, made by either a solicitor engaged in the formation of the limited liability partnership or anyone who subscribed his name to the incorporation document, that the requirement imposed by paragraph (a) has been complied with.

(2) The incorporation document must—
  (b) state the name of the limited liability partnership,
  (c) state whether the registered office of the limited liability partnership is to be situated in England and Wales, in Wales, in Scotland or in Northern Ireland,
  (d) state the address of that registered office,
  (e) give the required particulars of each of the persons who are to be members of the limited liability partnership on incorporation, and

(f) either specify which of those persons are to be designated members or state that every person who from time to time is a member of the limited liability partnership is a designated member.

(2ZA) The required particulars mentioned in subsection (2)(e) are the particulars required to be stated in the LLP's register of members and register of members' residential addresses.

(3) If a person makes a false statement under subsection (1)(c) which he—
(a) knows to be false, or
(b) does not believe to be true,
he commits an offence.

(4) A person guilty of an offence under subsection (3) is liable—
(a) on summary conviction, to imprisonment for a period not exceeding six months or a fine not exceeding the statutory maximum, or to both, or
(b) on conviction on indictment, to imprisonment for a period not exceeding two years or a fine, or to both.

3 INCORPORATION BY REGISTRATION

(1) The registrar, if satisfied that the requirements of section 2 are complied with, shall—
(a) register the documents delivered under that section, and
(b) give a certificate that the limited liability partnership is incorporated.

(1A) The certificate must state—
(a) the name and registered number of the limited liability partnership,
(b) the date of its incorporation, and
(c) whether the limited liability partnership's registered office is situated in England and Wales (or in Wales), in Scotland or in Northern Ireland.

(2) The registrar may accept the statement delivered under paragraph (c) of subsection (1) of section 2 as sufficient evidence that the requirement imposed by paragraph (a) of that subsection has been complied with.

(3) The certificate shall either be signed by the registrar or be authenticated by his official seal.

(4) The certificate is conclusive evidence that the requirements of section 2 are complied with and that the limited liability partnership is incorporated by the name specified in the incorporation document.

Membership

4 MEMBERS

(1) On the incorporation of a limited liability partnership its members are the persons who subscribed their names to the incorporation document (other than any who have died or been dissolved).

(2) Any other person may become a member of a limited liability partnership by and in accordance with an agreement with the existing members.

(3) A person may cease to be a member of a limited liability partnership (as well as by death or dissolution) in accordance with an agreement with the other members or, in the absence of agreement with the other members as to cessation of membership, by giving reasonable notice to the other members.

(4) A member of a limited liability partnership shall not be regarded for any purpose as employed by the limited liability partnership unless, if he and the other members were partners in a partnership, he would be regarded for that purpose as employed by the partnership.

4A MINIMUM MEMBERSHIP FOR CARRYING ON BUSINESS

(1) This section applies where a limited liability partnership carries on business without having at least two members, and does so for more than 6 months.

(2) A person who, for the whole or any part of the period that it so carries on business after those 6 months—
   (a) is a member of the limited liability partnership, and
   (b) knows that it is carrying on business with only one member,
   is liable (jointly and severally with the limited liability partnership) for the payment of the limited liability partnership's debts contracted during the period or, as the case may be, that part of it.

5 RELATIONSHIP OF MEMBERS ETC.

(1) Except as far as otherwise provided by this Act or any other enactment, the mutual rights and duties of the members of a limited liability partnership, and the mutual rights and duties of a limited liability partnership and its members, shall be governed—
   (a) by agreement between the members, or between the limited liability partnership and its members, or
   (b) in the absence of agreement as to any matter, by any provision made in relation to that matter by regulations under section 15(c).

(2) An agreement made before the incorporation of a limited liability partnership between the persons who subscribe their names to the incorporation document may impose obligations on the limited liability partnership (to take effect at any time after its incorporation).

6 MEMBERS AS AGENTS

(1) Every member of a limited liability partnership is the agent of the limited liability partnership.

(2) But a limited liability partnership is not bound by anything done by a member in dealing with a person if—
   (a) the member in fact has no authority to act for the limited liability partnership by doing that thing, and
   (b) the person knows that he has no authority or does not know or believe him to be a member of the limited liability partnership.

(3) Where a person has ceased to be a member of a limited liability partnership, the former member is to be regarded (in relation to any person dealing with the limited liability partnership) as still being a member of the limited liability partnership unless—
   (a) the person has notice that the former member has ceased to be a member of the limited liability partnership, or
   (b) notice that the former member has ceased to be a member of the limited liability partnership has been delivered to the registrar.

(4) Where a member of a limited liability partnership is liable to any person (other than another member of the limited liability partnership) as a result of a wrongful act or

omission of his in the course of the business of the limited liability partnership or with its authority, the limited liability partnership is liable to the same extent as the member.

7 EX-MEMBERS

(1) This section applies where a member of a limited liability partnership has either ceased to be a member or—
  (a) has died,
  (b) has become bankrupt or had his estate sequestrated or has been wound up,
  (c) has granted a trust deed for the benefit of his creditors, or
  (d) has assigned the whole or any part of his share in the limited liability partnership (absolutely or by way of charge or security).

(2) In such an event the former member or—
  (a) his personal representative,
  (b) his trustee in bankruptcy or permanent or interim trustee (within the meaning of the [1985 c. 66.] Bankruptcy (Scotland) Act 1985) or liquidator,
  (c) his trustee under the trust deed for the benefit of his creditors, or
  (d) his assignee,

may not interfere in the management or administration of any business or affairs of the limited liability partnership.

(3) But subsection (2) does not affect any right to receive an amount from the limited liability partnership in that event.

8 DESIGNATED MEMBERS

(1) If the incorporation document specifies who are to be designated members—
  (a) they are designated members on incorporation, and
  (b) any member may become a designated member by and in accordance with an agreement with the other members, and a member may cease to be a designated member in accordance with an agreement with the other members.

(2) But if there would otherwise be no designated members, or only one, every member is a designated member.

(3) If the incorporation document states that every person who from time to time is a member of the limited liability partnership is a designated member, every member is a designated member.

(4) A limited liability partnership may at any time deliver to the registrar—
  (a) notice that specified members are to be designated members, or
  (b) notice that every person who from time to time is a member of the limited liability partnership is a designated member,

and, once it is delivered, subsection (1) (apart from paragraph (a)) and subsection (2), or subsection (3), shall have effect as if that were stated in the incorporation document.

(6) A person ceases to be a designated member if he ceases to be a member.

9 REGISTRATION OF MEMBERSHIP CHANGES

(1) A limited liability partnership must ensure that—

(a) where a person becomes or ceases to be a member or designated member, notice is delivered to the registrar within fourteen days, and
(b) where there is any change in the particulars contained in its register of members or its register of members' residential addresses, notice is delivered to the registrar within 14 days.

(2) Where all the members from time to time of a limited liability partnership are designated members, subsection (1)(a) does not require notice that a person has become or ceased to be a designated member as well as a member.

(3) A notice delivered under subsection (1) that relates to a person becoming a member or designated member must contain—
(a) a statement that the member or designated member consents to acting in that capacity, and
(b) in the case of a person becoming a member, a statement of the particulars of the new member that are required to be included in the limited liability partnership's register of members and its register of residential addresses.

(3ZA) Where—
(a) a limited liability partnership gives notice of a change of a member's service address as stated in its register of members, and
(b) the notice is not accompanied by notice of any resulting change in the particulars contained in its register of members' residential addresses,
the notice must be accompanied by a statement that no such change is required.

(4) If a limited liability partnership fails to comply with this section, the partnership and every designated member commits an offence.

(5) But it is a defence for a designated member charged with an offence under subsection (4) to prove that he took all reasonable steps for securing that this section was complied with.

(6) A person guilty of an offence under subsection (4) is liable on summary conviction to a fine not exceeding level 5 on the standard scale.

Supplementary

18 INTERPRETATION

In this Act—

"business" includes every trade, profession and occupation,

"designated member" shall be construed in accordance with section 8,

...

"incorporation document" shall be construed in accordance with section 2,

"limited liability partnership" has the meaning given by section 1(2),

"member" shall be construed in accordance with section 4,

"modifications" includes additions and omissions,

"name", in relation to a member of a limited liability partnership, means—
(a) if an individual, his forename and surname (or, in the case of a peer or other person usually known by a title, his title instead of or in addition to either or both his forename and surname), and

(b) if a corporation or Scottish firm, its corporate or firm name,

...

"the registrar" means—

(a) if the registered office of the limited liability partnership is, or is to be, in England and Wales (or Wales), the registrar of companies for England and Wales,

(b) if the registered office of the limited liability partnership is, or is to be, in Scotland, the registrar of companies for Scotland, and

(c) if the registered office of the limited liability partnership is, or is to be, in Northern Ireland, the registrar of companies for Northern Ireland;

...

19 COMMENCEMENT, EXTENT AND SHORT TITLE

(4) This Act extends to the whole of the United Kingdom.

SCHEDULE NAMES AND REGISTERED OFFICES

Part I NAMES

Name to indicate status

2(1) The name of a limited liability partnership must end with—

(a) the expression "limited liability partnership", or

(b) the abbreviation "llp" or "LLP".

(2) But if the incorporation document for a limited liability partnership states that the registered office is to be situated in Wales, its name must end with—

(a) one of the expressions "limited liability partnership" and "partneriaeth atebolrwydd cyfyngedig", or

(b) one of the abbreviations "llp", "LLP", "pac" and "PAC".

Improper use of "limited liability partnership" etc.

7(1) If any person carries on a business under a name or title which includes as the last words—

(a) the expression "limited liability partnership" or "partneriaeth atebolrwydd cyfyngedig", or

(b) any contraction or imitation of either of those expressions, that person, unless a limited liability partnership or oversea limited liability partnership, commits an offence.

(2) A person guilty of an offence under sub-paragraph (1) is liable on summary conviction to a fine not exceeding level 3 on the standard scale.

As amended by The Limited Liability Partnerships (Particulars of Usual Residential Address) (Confidentiality Orders) Regulations 2002 (SI 2002/915), Schedule 2, paras 1, 3; Companies (Audit, Investigations and Community Enterprise) Act 2004, Schedule 6, para 10; Companies Act 2006, Schedule 16; The Limited Liability Partnerships (Application of Companies Act 2006) Regulations 2009 (SI 2009/1804), Sch 3.

Council Regulation (EC) No 2157/2001 of 8 October 2001 on the Statute for a European company (SE)

Title I GENERAL PROVISIONS

Article 1

1. A company may be set up within the territory of the Community in the form of a European public limited-liability company (Societas Europaea or SE) on the conditions and in the manner laid down in this Regulation.

2. The capital of an SE shall be divided into shares. No shareholder shall be liable for more than the amount he has subscribed.

3. An SE shall have legal personality.

4. Employee involvement in an SE shall be governed by the provisions of Directive 2001/86/EC.

Article 2

1. Public limited-liability companies such as referred to in Annex I, formed under the law of a Member State, with registered offices and head offices within the Community may form an SE by means of a merger provided that at least two of them are governed by the law of different Member States.

2. Public and private limited-liability companies such as referred to in Annex II, formed under the law of a Member State, with registered offices and head offices within the Community may promote the formation of a holding SE provided that each of at least two of them:
   (a) is governed by the law of a different Member State, or
   (b) has for at least two years had a subsidiary company governed by the law of another Member State or a branch situated in another Member State.

3. Companies and firms within the meaning of the second paragraph of Article 48 of the Treaty and other legal bodies governed by public or private law, formed under the law of a Member State, with registered offices and head offices within the Community may form a subsidiary SE by subscribing for its shares, provided that each of at least two of them:

(a) is governed by the law of a different Member State, or
(b) has for at least two years had a subsidiary company governed by the law of another Member State or a branch situated in another Member State.

4. A public limited-liability company, formed under the law of a Member State, which has its registered office and head office within the Community may be transformed into an SE if for at least two years it has had a subsidiary company governed by the law of another Member State.

5. A Member State may provide that a company the head office of which is not in the Community may participate in the formation of an SE provided that company is formed under the law of a Member State, has its registered office in that Member State and has a real and continuous link with a Member State's economy.

Article 3

1. For the purposes of Article 2(1), (2) and (3), an SE shall be regarded as a public limited-liability company governed by the law of the Member State in which it has its registered office.

2. An SE may itself set up one or more subsidiaries in the form of SEs. The provisions of the law of the Member State in which a subsidiary SE has its registered office that require a public limited-liability company to have more than one shareholder shall not apply in the case of the subsidiary SE. The provisions of national law implementing the twelfth Council Company Law Directive (89/667/EEC) of 21 December 1989 on single-member private limited-liability companies (5) shall apply to SEs mutatis mutandis.

Article 4

1. The capital of an SE shall be expressed in euro.

2. The subscribed capital shall not be less than EUR 120000.

3. The laws of a Member State requiring a greater subscribed capital for companies carrying on certain types of activity shall apply to SEs with registered offices in that Member State.

Article 5

Subject to Article 4(1) and (2), the capital of an SE, its maintenance and changes thereto, together with its shares, bonds and other similar securities shall be governed by the provisions which would apply to a public limited-liability company with a registered office in the Member State in which the SE is registered.

Article 6

For the purposes of this Regulation, "the statutes of the SE" shall mean both the instrument of incorporation and, where they are the subject of a separate document, the statutes of the SE.

Article 7

The registered office of an SE shall be located within the Community, in the same Member State as its head office. A Member State may in addition impose on SEs registered in its territory the obligation of locating their head office and their registered office in the same place.

Article 8

1. The registered office of an SE may be transferred to another Member State in accordance with paragraphs 2 to 13. Such a transfer shall not result in the winding up of the SE or in the creation of a new legal person.

2. The management or administrative organ shall draw up a transfer proposal and publicise it in accordance with Article 13, without prejudice to any additional forms of publication provided for by the Member State of the registered office. That proposal shall state the current name, registered office and number of the SE and shall cover:
   (a) the proposed registered office of the SE;
   (b) the proposed statutes of the SE including, where appropriate, its new name;
   (c) any implication the transfer may have on employees' involvement;
   (d) the proposed transfer timetable;
   (e) any rights provided for the protection of shareholders and/or creditors.

3. The management or administrative organ shall draw up a report explaining and justifying the legal and economic aspects of the transfer and explaining the implications of the transfer for shareholders, creditors and employees.

4. An SE's shareholders and creditors shall be entitled, at least one month before the general meeting called upon to decide on the transfer, to examine at the SE's registered office the transfer proposal and the report drawn up pursuant to paragraph 3 and, on request, to obtain copies of those documents free of charge.

5. A Member State may, in the case of SEs registered within its territory, adopt provisions designed to ensure appropriate protection for minority shareholders who oppose a transfer.

6. No decision to transfer may be taken for two months after publication of the proposal. Such a decision shall be taken as laid down in Article 59.

7. Before the competent authority issues the certificate mentioned in paragraph 8, the SE shall satisfy it that, in respect of any liabilities arising prior to the publication of the transfer proposal, the interests of creditors and holders of other rights in respect of the SE (including those of public bodies) have been adequately protected in accordance with requirements laid down by the Member State where the SE has its registered office prior to the transfer.

   A Member State may extend the application of the first subparagraph to liabilities that arise (or may arise) prior to the transfer.

   The first and second subparagraphs shall be without prejudice to the application to SEs of the national legislation of Member States concerning the satisfaction or securing of payments to public bodies.

8. In the Member State in which an SE has its registered office the court, notary or other competent authority shall issue a certificate attesting to the completion of the acts and formalities to be accomplished before the transfer.

9. The new registration may not be effected until the certificate referred to in paragraph 8 has been submitted, and evidence produced that the formalities required for registration in the country of the new registered office have been completed.

10. The transfer of an SE's registered office and the consequent amendment of its statutes shall take effect on the date on which the SE is registered, in accordance with Article 12, in the register for its new registered office.

11. When the SE's new registration has been effected, the registry for its new registration shall notify the registry for its old registration. Deletion of the old registration shall be effected on receipt of that notification, but not before.

12. The new registration and the deletion of the old registration shall be publicised in the Member States concerned in accordance with Article 13.

13. On publication of an SE's new registration, the new registered office may be relied on as against third parties. However, as long as the deletion of the SE's registration from the register for its previous registered office has not been publicised, third parties may continue to rely on the previous registered office unless the SE proves that such third parties were aware of the new registered office.

14. The laws of a Member State may provide that, as regards SEs registered in that Member State, the transfer of a registered office which would result in a change of the law applicable shall not take effect if any of that Member State's competent authorities opposes it within the two-month period referred to in paragraph 6. Such opposition may be based only on grounds of public interest.

    Where an SE is supervised by a national financial supervisory authority according to Community directives the right to oppose the change of registered office applies to this authority as well.

    Review by a judicial authority shall be possible.

15. An SE may not transfer its registered office if proceedings for winding up, liquidation, insolvency or suspension of payments or other similar proceedings have been brought against it.

16. An SE which has transferred its registered office to another Member State shall be considered, in respect of any cause of action arising prior to the transfer as determined in paragraph 10, as having its registered office in the Member States where the SE was registered prior to the transfer, even if the SE is sued after the transfer.

Article 9

1. An SE shall be governed:
   (a) by this Regulation,
   (b) where expressly authorised by this Regulation, by the provisions of its statutes or
   (c) in the case of matters not regulated by this Regulation or, where matters are partly regulated by it, of those aspects not covered by it, by:
      (i) the provisions of laws adopted by Member States in implementation of Community measures relating specifically to SEs;
      (ii) the provisions of Member States' laws which would apply to a public limited-liability company formed in accordance with the law of the Member State in which the SE has its registered office;
      (iii) the provisions of its statutes, in the same way as for a public limited-liability company formed in accordance with the law of the Member State in which the SE has its registered office.

2. The provisions of laws adopted by Member States specifically for the SE must be in accordance with Directives applicable to public limited-liability companies referred to in Annex I.

3. If the nature of the business carried out by an SE is regulated by specific provisions of national laws, those laws shall apply in full to the SE.

Article 10

Subject to this Regulation, an SE shall be treated in every Member State as if it were a public limited-liability company formed in accordance with the law of the Member State in which it has its registered office.

Article 11

1. The name of an SE shall be preceded or followed by the abbreviation SE.

2. Only SEs may include the abbreviation SE in their name.

3. Nevertheless, companies, firms and other legal entities registered in a Member State before the date of entry into force of this Regulation in the names of which the abbreviation SE appears shall not be required to alter their names.

Article 12

1. Every SE shall be registered in the Member State in which it has its registered office in a register designated by the law of that Member State in accordance with Article 3 of the first Council Directive (68/151/EEC) of 9 March 1968 on coordination of safeguards which, for the protection of the interests of members and others, are required by Member States of companies within the meaning of the second paragraph of Article 58 of the Treaty, with a view to making such safeguards equivalent throughout the Community(6).

2. An SE may not be registered unless an agreement on arrangements for employee involvement pursuant to Article 4 of Directive 2001/86/EC has been concluded, or a decision pursuant to Article 3(6) of the Directive has been taken, or the period for negotiations pursuant to Article 5 of the Directive has expired without an agreement having been concluded.

3. In order for an SE to be registered in a Member State which has made use of the option referred to in Article 7(3) of Directive 2001/86/EC, either an agreement pursuant to Article 4 of the Directive must have been concluded on the arrangements for employee involvement, including participation, or none of the participating companies must have been governed by participation rules prior to the registration of the SE.

4. The statutes of the SE must not conflict at any time with the arrangements for employee involvement which have been so determined. Where new such arrangements determined pursuant to the Directive conflict with the existing statutes, the statutes shall to the extent necessary be amended.

In this case, a Member State may provide that the management organ or the administrative organ of the SE shall be entitled to proceed to amend the statutes without any further decision from the general shareholders meeting.

Article 13

Publication of the documents and particulars concerning an SE which must be publicised under this Regulation shall be effected in the manner laid down in the laws of the Member State in which the SE has its registered office in accordance with Directive 68/151/EEC.

Article 14

1. Notice of an SE's registration and of the deletion of such a registration shall be published for information purposes in the Official Journal of the European Communities after publication in accordance with Article 13. That notice shall state the name, number, date and place of registration of the SE, the date and place of publication and the title of publication, the registered office of the SE and its sector of activity.

2. Where the registered office of an SE is transferred in accordance with Article 8, notice shall be published giving the information provided for in paragraph 1, together with that relating to the new registration.

3. The particulars referred to in paragraph 1 shall be forwarded to the Office for Official Publications of the European Communities within one month of the publication referred to in Article 13.

Title II FORMATION

Section 1 GENERAL

Article 15

1. Subject to this Regulation, the formation of an SE shall be governed by the law applicable to public limited-liability companies in the Member State in which the SE establishes its registered office.

2. The registration of an SE shall be publicised in accordance with Article 13.

Article 16

1. An SE shall acquire legal personality on the date on which it is registered in the register referred to in Article 12.

2. If acts have been performed in an SE's name before its registration in accordance with Article 12 and the SE does not assume the obligations arising out of such acts after its registration, the natural persons, companies, firms or other legal entities which performed those acts shall be jointly and severally liable therefor, without limit, in the absence of agreement to the contrary.

Section 2 FORMATION BY MERGER

Article 17

1. An SE may be formed by means of a merger in accordance with Article 2(1).

2. Such a merger may be carried out in accordance with:
   (a) the procedure for merger by acquisition laid down in Article 3(1) of the third Council Directive (78/855/EEC) of 9 October 1978 based on Article 54(3)(g) of the Treaty concerning mergers of public limited-liability companies(7) or
   (b) the procedure for merger by the formation of a new company laid down in Article 4(1) of the said Directive.

   In the case of a merger by acquisition, the acquiring company shall take the form of an SE when the merger takes place. In the case of a merger by the formation of a new company, the SE shall be the newly formed company.

Article 18

For matters not covered by this section or, where a matter is partly covered by it, for aspects not covered by it, each company involved in the formation of an SE by merger shall be governed by the provisions of the law of the Member State to which it is subject that apply to mergers of public limited-liability companies in accordance with Directive 78/855/EEC.

Article 19

The laws of a Member State may provide that a company governed by the law of that Member State may not take part in the formation of an SE by merger if any of that Member State's competent authorities opposes it before the issue of the certificate referred to in Article 25(2).

Such opposition may be based only on grounds of public interest. Review by a judicial authority shall be possible.

Article 20

1. The management or administrative organs of merging companies shall draw up draft terms of merger. The draft terms of merger shall include the following particulars:
   (a) the name and registered office of each of the merging companies together with those proposed for the SE;

(b) the share-exchange ratio and the amount of any compensation;
(c) the terms for the allotment of shares in the SE;
(d) the date from which the holding of shares in the SE will entitle the holders to share in profits and any special conditions affecting that entitlement;
(e) the date from which the transactions of the merging companies will be treated for accounting purposes as being those of the SE;
(f) the rights conferred by the SE on the holders of shares to which special rights are attached and on the holders of securities other than shares, or the measures proposed concerning them;
(g) any special advantage granted to the experts who examine the draft terms of merger or to members of the administrative, management, supervisory or controlling organs of the merging companies;
(h) the statutes of the SE;
(i) information on the procedures by which arrangements for employee involvement are determined pursuant to Directive 2001/86/EC.

2. The merging companies may include further items in the draft terms of merger.

Article 21

For each of the merging companies and subject to the additional requirements imposed by the Member State to which the company concerned is subject, the following particulars shall be published in the national gazette of that Member State:

(a) the type, name and registered office of every merging company;

(b) the register in which the documents referred to in Article 3(2) of Directive 68/151/EEC are filed in respect of each merging company, and the number of the entry in that register;

(c) an indication of the arrangements made in accordance with Article 24 for the exercise of the rights of the creditors of the company in question and the address at which complete information on those arrangements may be obtained free of charge;

(d) an indication of the arrangements made in accordance with Article 24 for the exercise of the rights of minority shareholders of the company in question and the address at which complete information on those arrangements may be obtained free of charge;

(e) the name and registered office proposed for the SE.

Article 22

As an alternative to experts operating on behalf of each of the merging companies, one or more independent experts as defined in Article 10 of Directive 78/855/EEC, appointed for those purposes at the joint request of the companies by a judicial or administrative authority in the Member State of one of the merging companies or of the proposed SE, may examine the draft terms of merger and draw up a single report to all the shareholders.

The experts shall have the right to request from each of the merging companies any information they consider necessary to enable them to complete their function.

Article 23

1. The general meeting of each of the merging companies shall approve the draft terms of merger.

2. Employee involvement in the SE shall be decided pursuant to Directive 2001/86/EC. The general meetings of each of the merging companies may reserve the right to make registration of the SE conditional upon its express ratification of the arrangements so decided.

Article 24

1. The law of the Member State governing each merging company shall apply as in the case of a merger of public limited-liability companies, taking into account the cross-border nature of the merger, with regard to the protection of the interests of:
   (a) creditors of the merging companies;
   (b) holders of bonds of the merging companies;
   (c) holders of securities, other than shares, which carry special rights in the merging companies.

2. A Member State may, in the case of the merging companies governed by its law, adopt provisions designed to ensure appropriate protection for minority shareholders who have opposed the merger.

Article 25

1. The legality of a merger shall be scrutinised, as regards the part of the procedure concerning each merging company, in accordance with the law on mergers of public limited-liability companies of the Member State to which the merging company is subject.

2. In each Member State concerned the court, notary or other competent authority shall issue a certificate conclusively attesting to the completion of the pre-merger acts and formalities.

3. If the law of a Member State to which a merging company is subject provides for a procedure to scrutinise and amend the share-exchange ratio, or a procedure to compensate minority shareholders, without preventing the registration of the merger, such procedures shall only apply if the other merging companies situated in Member States which do not provide for such procedure explicitly accept, when approving the draft terms of the merger in accordance with Article 23(1), the possibility for the shareholders of that merging company to have recourse to such procedure. In such cases, the court, notary or other competent authorities may issue the certificate referred to in paragraph 2 even if such a procedure has been commenced. The certificate must, however, indicate that the procedure is pending. The decision in the procedure shall be binding on the acquiring company and all its shareholders.

Article 26

1. The legality of a merger shall be scrutinised, as regards the part of the procedure concerning the completion of the merger and the formation of the SE, by the court, notary or other authority competent in the Member State of the proposed registered office of the SE to scrutinise that aspect of the legality of mergers of public limited-liability companies.

2. To that end each merging company shall submit to the competent authority the certificate referred to in Article 25(2) within six months of its issue together with a copy of the draft terms of merger approved by that company.

3. The authority referred to in paragraph 1 shall in particular ensure that the merging companies have approved draft terms of merger in the same terms and that arrangements for employee involvement have been determined pursuant to Directive 2001/86/EC.

4. That authority shall also satisfy itself that the SE has been formed in accordance with the requirements of the law of the Member State in which it has its registered office in accordance with Article 15.

Article 27

1. A merger and the simultaneous formation of an SE shall take effect on the date on which the SE is registered in accordance with Article 12.

2. The SE may not be registered until the formalities provided for in Articles 25 and 26 have been completed.

Article 28

For each of the merging companies the completion of the merger shall be publicised as laid down by the law of each Member State in accordance with Article 3 of Directive 68/151/EEC.

Article 29

1. A merger carried out as laid down in Article 17(2)(a) shall have the following consequences ipso jure and simultaneously:
   (a) all the assets and liabilities of each company being acquired are transferred to the acquiring company;
   (b) the shareholders of the company being acquired become shareholders of the acquiring company;
   (c) the company being acquired ceases to exist;
   (d) the acquiring company adopts the form of an SE.

2. A merger carried out as laid down in Article 17(2)(b) shall have the following consequences ipso jure and simultaneously:
   (a) all the assets and liabilities of the merging companies are transferred to the SE;
   (b) the shareholders of the merging companies become shareholders of the SE;
   (c) the merging companies cease to exist.

3. Where, in the case of a merger of public limited-liability companies, the law of a Member State requires the completion of any special formalities before the transfer of certain assets, rights and obligations by the merging companies becomes effective against third parties, those formalities shall apply and shall be carried out either by the merging companies or by the SE following its registration.

4. The rights and obligations of the participating companies on terms and conditions of employment arising from national law, practice and individual employment contracts or employment relationships and existing at the date of the registration shall, by reason of such registration be transferred to the SE upon its registration.

Article 30

A merger as provided for in Article 2(1) may not be declared null and void once the SE has been registered.

The absence of scrutiny of the legality of the merger pursuant to Articles 25 and 26 may be included among the grounds for the winding-up of the SE.

Article 31

1. Where a merger within the meaning of Article 17(2)(a) is carried out by a company which holds all the shares and other securities conferring the right to vote at general meetings of another company, neither Article 20(1)(b), (c) and (d), Article 29(1)(b) nor Article 22 shall apply. National law governing each merging company and mergers of public limited-liability companies in accordance with Article 24 of Directive 78/855/EEC shall nevertheless apply.

2. Where a merger by acquisition is carried out by a company which holds 90% or more but not all of the shares and other securities conferring the right to vote at general meetings of another company, reports by the management or administrative body, reports by an independent expert or experts and the documents necessary for scrutiny shall be required only to the extent that the national law governing either the acquiring company or the company being acquired so requires.

Member States may, however, provide that this paragraph may apply where a company holds shares conferring 90% or more but not all of the voting rights.

Section 3 FORMATION OF A HOLDING SE

Article 32

1. A holding SE may be formed in accordance with Article 2(2). A company promoting the formation of a holding SE in accordance with Article 2(2) shall continue to exist.

2. The management or administrative organs of the companies which promote such an operation shall draw up, in the same terms, draft terms for the formation of the holding SE. The draft terms shall include a report explaining and justifying the legal and economic aspects of the formation and indicating the implications for the shareholders and for the employees of the adoption of the form of a holding SE. The draft terms shall also set out the particulars provided for in Article 20(1)(a), (b), (c), (f), (g), (h) and (i) and shall fix the minimum proportion of the shares in each of the companies promoting the operation which the shareholders must contribute to the formation of the holding SE. That proportion shall be shares conferring more than 50% of the permanent voting rights.

3. For each of the companies promoting the operation, the draft terms for the formation of the holding SE shall be publicised in the manner laid down in each Member State's national law in accordance with Article 3 of Directive 68/151/EEC at least one month before the date of the general meeting called to decide thereon.

4. One or more experts independent of the companies promoting the operation, appointed or approved by a judicial or administrative authority in the Member State to which each company is subject in accordance with national provisions adopted in implementation of Directive 78/855/EEC, shall examine the draft terms of formation drawn up in accordance with paragraph 2 and draw up a written report for the shareholders of each company. By agreement between the companies promoting the operation, a single written report may be drawn up for the shareholders of all the companies by one or more independent experts, appointed or approved by a judicial or administrative authority in the Member State to which one of the companies promoting the operation or the proposed SE is subject in accordance with national provisions adopted in implementation of Directive 78/855/EEC.

5. The report shall indicate any particular difficulties of valuation and state whether the proposed share-exchange ratio is fair and reasonable, indicating the methods used to arrive at it and whether such methods are adequate in the case in question.

6. The general meeting of each company promoting the operation shall approve the draft terms of formation of the holding SE.

   Employee involvement in the holding SE shall be decided pursuant to Directive 2001/86/EC. The general meetings of each company promoting the operation may reserve the right to make registration of the holding SE conditional upon its express ratification of the arrangements so decided.

7. These provisions shall apply mutatis mutandis to private limited-liability companies.

Article 33

1. The shareholders of the companies promoting such an operation shall have a period of three months in which to inform the promoting companies whether they intend to contribute their shares to the formation of the holding SE. That period shall begin on the

date upon which the terms for the formation of the holding SE have been finally determined in accordance with Article 32.

2. The holding SE shall be formed only if, within the period referred to in paragraph 1, the shareholders of the companies promoting the operation have assigned the minimum proportion of shares in each company in accordance with the draft terms of formation and if all the other conditions are fulfilled.

3. If the conditions for the formation of the holding SE are all fulfilled in accordance with paragraph 2, that fact shall, in respect of each of the promoting companies, be publicised in the manner laid down in the national law governing each of those companies adopted in implementation of Article 3 of Directive 68/151/EEC. Shareholders of the companies promoting the operation who have not indicated whether they intend to make their shares available to the promoting companies for the purpose of forming the holding SE within the period referred to in paragraph 1 shall have a further month in which to do so.

4. Shareholders who have contributed their securities to the formation of the SE shall receive shares in the holding SE.

5. The holding SE may not be registered until it is shown that the formalities referred to in Article 32 have been completed and that the conditions referred to in paragraph 2 have been fulfilled.

Article 34

A Member State may, in the case of companies promoting such an operation, adopt provisions designed to ensure protection for minority shareholders who oppose the operation, creditors and employees.

Section 4 FORMATION OF A SUBSIDIARY SE

Article 35

An SE may be formed in accordance with Article 2(3).

Article 36

Companies, firms and other legal entities participating in such an operation shall be subject to the provisions governing their participation in the formation of a subsidiary in the form of a public limited-liability company under national law.

Section 5 CONVERSION OF AN EXISTING PUBLIC LIMITED-LIABILITY COMPANY INTO AN SE

Article 37

1. An SE may be formed in accordance with Article 2(4).

2. Without prejudice to Article 12 the conversion of a public limited-liability company into an SE shall not result in the winding up of the company or in the creation of a new legal person.

3. The registered office may not be transferred from one Member State to another pursuant to Article 8 at the same time as the conversion is effected.

4. The management or administrative organ of the company in question shall draw up draft terms of conversion and a report explaining and justifying the legal and economic aspects of the conversion and indicating the implications for the shareholders and for the employees of the adoption of the form of an SE.

5. The draft terms of conversion shall be publicised in the manner laid down in each Member State's law in accordance with Article 3 of Directive 68/151/EEC at least one month before the general meeting called upon to decide thereon.

6. Before the general meeting referred to in paragraph 7 one or more independent experts appointed or approved, in accordance with the national provisions adopted in implementation of Article 10 of Directive 78/855/EEC, by a judicial or administrative authority in the Member State to which the company being converted into an SE is subject shall certify in compliance with Directive 77/91/EEC(8) mutatis mutandis that the company has net assets at least equivalent to its capital plus those reserves which must not be distributed under the law or the Statutes.

7. The general meeting of the company in question shall approve the draft terms of conversion together with the statutes of the SE. The decision of the general meeting shall be passed as laid down in the provisions of national law adopted in implementation of Article 7 of Directive 78/855/EEC.

8. Member States may condition a conversion to a favourable vote of a qualified majority or unanimity in the organ of the company to be converted within which employee participation is organised.

9. The rights and obligations of the company to be converted on terms and conditions of employment arising from national law, practice and individual employment contracts or employment relationships and existing at the date of the registration shall, by reason of such registration be transferred to the SE.

Title III STRUCTURE OF THE SE

Article 38

Under the conditions laid down by this Regulation an SE shall comprise:

(a) a general meeting of shareholders and

(b) either a supervisory organ and a management organ (two-tier system) or an administrative organ (one-tier system) depending on the form adopted in the statutes.

Section 1 TWO-TIER SYSTEM

Article 39

1. The management organ shall be responsible for managing the SE. A Member State may provide that a managing director or managing directors shall be responsible for the current management under the same conditions as for public limited-liability companies that have registered offices within that Member State's territory.

2. The member or members of the management organ shall be appointed and removed by the supervisory organ.

   A Member State may, however, require or permit the statutes to provide that the member or members of the management organ shall be appointed and removed by the general meeting under the same conditions as for public limited-liability companies that have registered offices within its territory.

3. No person may at the same time be a member of both the management organ and the supervisory organ of the same SE. The supervisory organ may, however, nominate one of its members to act as a member of the management organ in the event of a vacancy. During such a period the functions of the person concerned as a member of the supervisory organ shall be suspended. A Member State may impose a time limit on such a period.

4. The number of members of the management organ or the rules for determining it shall be laid down in the SE's statutes. A Member State may, however, fix a minimum and/or a maximum number.

5. Where no provision is made for a two-tier system in relation to public limited-liability companies with registered offices within its territory, a Member State may adopt the appropriate measures in relation to SEs.

Article 40

1. The supervisory organ shall supervise the work of the management organ. It may not itself exercise the power to manage the SE.

2. The members of the supervisory organ shall be appointed by the general meeting. The members of the first supervisory organ may, however, be appointed by the statutes. This shall apply without prejudice to Article 47(4) or to any employee participation arrangements determined pursuant to Directive 2001/86/EC.

3. The number of members of the supervisory organ or the rules for determining it shall be laid down in the statutes. A Member State may, however, stipulate the number of members of the supervisory organ for SEs registered within its territory or a minimum and/or a maximum number.

Article 41

1. The management organ shall report to the supervisory organ at least once every three months on the progress and foreseeable development of the SE's business.

2. In addition to the regular information referred to in paragraph 1, the management organ shall promptly pass the supervisory organ any information on events likely to have an appreciable effect on the SE.

3. The supervisory organ may require the management organ to provide information of any kind which it needs to exercise supervision in accordance with Article 40(1). A Member State may provide that each member of the supervisory organ also be entitled to this facility.

4. The supervisory organ may undertake or arrange for any investigations necessary for the performance of its duties.

5. Each member of the supervisory organ shall be entitled to examine all information submitted to it.

Article 42

The supervisory organ shall elect a chairman from among its members. If half of the members are appointed by employees, only a member appointed by the general meeting of shareholders may be elected chairman.

Section 2 THE ONE-TIER SYSTEM

Article 43

1. The administrative organ shall manage the SE. A Member State may provide that a managing director or managing directors shall be responsible for the day-to-day management under the same conditions as for public limited-liability companies that have registered offices within that Member State's territory.

2. The number of members of the administrative organ or the rules for determining it shall be laid down in the SE's statutes. A Member State may, however, set a minimum and, where necessary, a maximum number of members.

The administrative organ shall, however, consist of at least three members where employee participation is regulated in accordance with Directive 2001/86/EC.

3. The member or members of the administrative organ shall be appointed by the general meeting. The members of the first administrative organ may, however, be appointed by the statutes. This shall apply without prejudice to Article 47(4) or to any employee participation arrangements determined pursuant to Directive 2001/86/EC.

4. Where no provision is made for a one-tier system in relation to public limited-liability companies with registered offices within its territory, a Member State may adopt the appropriate measures in relation to SEs.

Article 44

1. The administrative organ shall meet at least once every three months at intervals laid down by the statutes to discuss the progress and foreseeable development of the SE's business.

2. Each member of the administrative organ shall be entitled to examine all information submitted to it.

Article 45

The administrative organ shall elect a chairman from among its members. If half of the members are appointed by employees, only a member appointed by the general meeting of shareholders may be elected chairman.

Section 3 RULES COMMON TO THE ONE-TIER AND TWO-TIER SYSTEMS

Article 46

1. Members of company organs shall be appointed for a period laid down in the statutes not exceeding six years.

2. Subject to any restrictions laid down in the statutes, members may be reappointed once or more than once for the period determined in accordance with paragraph 1.

Article 47

1. An SE's statutes may permit a company or other legal entity to be a member of one of its organs, provided that the law applicable to public limited-liability companies in the Member State in which the SE's registered office is situated does not provide otherwise.

   That company or other legal entity shall designate a natural person to exercise its functions on the organ in question.

2. No person may be a member of any SE organ or a representative of a member within the meaning of paragraph 1 who:
   (a) is disqualified, under the law of the Member State in which the SE's registered office is situated, from serving on the corresponding organ of a public limited-liability company governed by the law of that Member State, or
   (b) is disqualified from serving on the corresponding organ of a public limited-liability company governed by the law of a Member State owing to a judicial or administrative decision delivered in a Member State.

3. An SE's statutes may, in accordance with the law applicable to public limited-liability companies in the Member State in which the SE's registered office is situated, lay down special conditions of eligibility for members representing the shareholders.

4. This Regulation shall not affect national law permitting a minority of shareholders or other persons or authorities to appoint some of the members of a company organ.

Article 48

1. An SE's statutes shall list the categories of transactions which require authorisation of the management organ by the supervisory organ in the two-tier system or an express decision by the administrative organ in the one-tier system. A Member State may, however, provide that in the two-tier system the supervisory organ may itself make certain categories of transactions subject to authorisation.

2. A Member State may determine the categories of transactions which must at least be indicated in the statutes of SEs registered within its territory.

Article 49

The members of an SE's organs shall be under a duty, even after they have ceased to hold office, not to divulge any information which they have concerning the SE the disclosure of which might be prejudicial to the company's interests, except where such disclosure is required or permitted under national law provisions applicable to public limited-liability companies or is in the public interest.

Article 50

1. Unless otherwise provided by this Regulation or the statutes, the internal rules relating to quorums and decision-taking in SE organs shall be as follows:
   (a) quorum: at least half of the members must be present or represented;
   (b) decision-taking: a majority of the members present or represented.

2. Where there is no relevant provision in the statutes, the chairman of each organ shall have a casting vote in the event of a tie. There shall be no provision to the contrary in the statutes, however, where half of the supervisory organ consists of employees' representatives.

3. Where employee participation is provided for in accordance with Directive 2001/86/EC, a Member State may provide that the supervisory organ's quorum and decision-making shall, by way of derogation from the provisions referred to in paragraphs 1 and 2, be subject to the rules applicable, under the same conditions, to public limited-liability companies governed by the law of the Member State concerned.

Article 51

Members of an SE's management, supervisory and administrative organs shall be liable, in accordance with the provisions applicable to public limited-liability companies in the Member State in which the SE's registered office is situated, for loss or damage sustained by the SE following any breach on their part of the legal, statutory or other obligations inherent in their duties.

Section 4 GENERAL MEETING

Article 52

The general meeting shall decide on matters for which it is given sole responsibility by:

(a) this Regulation or

(b) the legislation of the Member State in which the SE's registered office is situated adopted in implementation of Directive 2001/86/EC.

Furthermore, the general meeting shall decide on matters for which responsibility is given to the general meeting of a public limited-liability company governed by the law of the Member State in which the SE's registered office is situated, either by the law of that Member State or by the SE's statutes in accordance with that law.

Article 53

Without prejudice to the rules laid down in this section, the organisation and conduct of general meetings together with voting procedures shall be governed by the law applicable to public limited-liability companies in the Member State in which the SE's registered office is situated.

Article 54

1. An SE shall hold a general meeting at least once each calendar year, within six months of the end of its financial year, unless the law of the Member State in which the SE's registered office is situated applicable to public limited-liability companies carrying on the same type of activity as the SE provides for more frequent meetings. A Member State may, however, provide that the first general meeting may be held at any time in the 18 months following an SE's incorporation.
2. General meetings may be convened at any time by the management organ, the administrative organ, the supervisory organ or any other organ or competent authority in accordance with the national law applicable to public limited-liability companies in the Member State in which the SE's registered office is situated.

Article 55

1. One or more shareholders who together hold at least 10% of an SE's subscribed capital may request the SE to convene a general meeting and draw up the agenda therefor; the SE's statutes or national legislation may provide for a smaller proportion under the same conditions as those applicable to public limited-liability companies.
2. The request that a general meeting be convened shall state the items to be put on the agenda.
3. If, following a request made under paragraph 1, a general meeting is not held in due time and, in any event, within two months, the competent judicial or administrative authority within the jurisdiction of which the SE's registered office is situated may order that a general meeting be convened within a given period or authorise either the shareholders who have requested it or their representatives to convene a general meeting. This shall be without prejudice to any national provisions which allow the shareholders themselves to convene general meetings.

Article 56

One or more shareholders who together hold at least 10% of an SE's subscribed capital may request that one or more additional items be put on the agenda of any general meeting. The procedures and time limits applicable to such requests shall be laid down by the national law of the Member State in which the SE's registered office is situated or, failing that, by the SE's statutes. The above proportion may be reduced by the statutes or by the law of the Member State in which the SE's registered office is situated under the same conditions as are applicable to public limited-liability companies.

Article 57

Save where this Regulation or, failing that, the law applicable to public limited-liability companies in the Member State in which an SE's registered office is situated requires a larger majority, the general meeting's decisions shall be taken by a majority of the votes validly cast.

Article 58

The votes cast shall not include votes attaching to shares in respect of which the shareholder has not taken part in the vote or has abstained or has returned a blank or spoilt ballot paper.

Article 59

1. Amendment of an SE's statutes shall require a decision by the general meeting taken by a majority which may not be less than two thirds of the votes cast, unless the law applicable to public limited-liability companies in the Member State in which an SE's registered office is situated requires or permits a larger majority.
2. A Member State may, however, provide that where at least half of an SE's subscribed capital is represented, a simple majority of the votes referred to in paragraph 1 shall suffice.
3. Amendments to an SE's statutes shall be publicised in accordance with Article 13.

Article 60

1. Where an SE has two or more classes of shares, every decision by the general meeting shall be subject to a separate vote by each class of shareholders whose class rights are affected thereby.
2. Where a decision by the general meeting requires the majority of votes specified in Article 59(1) or (2), that majority shall also be required for the separate vote by each class of shareholders whose class rights are affected by the decision.

Title IV ANNUAL ACCOUNTS AND CONSOLIDATED ACCOUNTS

Article 61

Subject to Article 62 an SE shall be governed by the rules applicable to public limited-liability companies under the law of the Member State in which its registered office is situated as regards the preparation of its annual and, where appropriate, consolidated accounts including the accompanying annual report and the auditing and publication of those accounts.

Article 62

1. An SE which is a credit or financial institution shall be governed by the rules laid down in the national law of the Member State in which its registered office is situated in implementation of Directive 2000/12/EC of the European Parliament and of the Council of 20 March 2000 relating to the taking up and pursuit of the business of credit institutions(9) as regards the preparation of its annual and, where appropriate, consolidated accounts, including the accompanying annual report and the auditing and publication of those accounts.
2. An SE which is an insurance undertaking shall be governed by the rules laid down in the national law of the Member State in which its registered office is situated in implementation of Council Directive 91/674/EEC of 19 December 1991 on the annual accounts and consolidated accounts of insurance undertakings(10) as regards the preparation of its annual and, where appropriate, consolidated accounts including the accompanying annual report and the auditing and publication of those accounts.

Title V WINDING UP, LIQUIDATION, INSOLVENCY AND CESSATION OF PAYMENTS

Article 63

As regards winding up, liquidation, insolvency, cessation of payments and similar procedures, an SE shall be governed by the legal provisions which would apply to a public limited-liability company formed in accordance with the law of the Member State in which its registered office is situated, including provisions relating to decision-making by the general meeting.

Article 64

1. When an SE no longer complies with the requirement laid down in Article 7, the Member State in which the SE's registered office is situated shall take appropriate measures to oblige the SE to regularise its position within a specified period either:
   (a) by re-establishing its head office in the Member State in which its registered office is situated or
   (b) by transferring the registered office by means of the procedure laid down in Article 8.
2. The Member State in which the SE's registered office is situated shall put in place the measures necessary to ensure that an SE which fails to regularise its position in accordance with paragraph 1 is liquidated.
3. The Member State in which the SE's registered office is situated shall set up a judicial remedy with regard to any established infringement of Article 7. That remedy shall have a suspensory effect on the procedures laid down in paragraphs 1 and 2.
4. Where it is established on the initiative of either the authorities or any interested party that an SE has its head office within the territory of a Member State in breach of Article 7, the authorities of that Member State shall immediately inform the Member State in which the SE's registered office is situated.

Article 65

Without prejudice to provisions of national law requiring additional publication, the initiation and termination of winding up, liquidation, insolvency or cessation of payment procedures and any decision to continue operating shall be publicised in accordance with Article 13.

Article 66

1. An SE may be converted into a public limited-liability company governed by the law of the Member State in which its registered office is situated. No decision on conversion may be taken before two years have elapsed since its registration or before the first two sets of annual accounts have been approved.
2. The conversion of an SE into a public limited-liability company shall not result in the winding up of the company or in the creation of a new legal person.
3. The management or administrative organ of the SE shall draw up draft terms of conversion and a report explaining and justifying the legal and economic aspects of the conversion and indicating the implications of the adoption of the public limited-liability company for the shareholders and for the employees.
4. The draft terms of conversion shall be publicised in the manner laid down in each Member State's law in accordance with Article 3 of Directive 68/151/EEC at least one month before the general meeting called to decide thereon.
5. Before the general meeting referred to in paragraph 6, one or more independent experts appointed or approved, in accordance with the national provisions adopted in implementation of Article 10 of Directive 78/855/EEC, by a judicial or administrative authority in the Member State to which the SE being converted into a public limited-liability company is subject shall certify that the company has assets at least equivalent to its capital.
6. The general meeting of the SE shall approve the draft terms of conversion together with the statutes of the public limited-liability company. The decision of the general meeting shall be passed as laid down in the provisions of national law adopted in implementation of Article 7 of Directive 78/855/EEC.

Title VI ADDITIONAL AND TRANSITIONAL PROVISIONS

Article 67

1. If and so long as the third phase of economic and monetary union (EMU) does not apply to it each Member State may make SEs with registered offices within its territory subject to the same provisions as apply to public limited-liability companies covered by its legislation as regards the expression of their capital. An SE may, in any case, express its capital in euro as well. In that event the national currency/euro conversion rate shall be that for the last day of the month preceding that of the formation of the SE.

2. If and so long as the third phase of EMU does not apply to the Member State in which an SE has its registered office, the SE may, however, prepare and publish its annual and, where appropriate, consolidated accounts in euro. The Member State may require that the SE's annual and, where appropriate, consolidated accounts be prepared and published in the national currency under the same conditions as those laid down for public limited-liability companies governed by the law of that Member State. This shall not prejudge the additional possibility for an SE of publishing its annual and, where appropriate, consolidated accounts in euro in accordance with Council Directive 90/604/EEC of 8 November 1990 amending Directive 78/60/EEC on annual accounts and Directive 83/349/EEC on consolidated accounts as concerns the exemptions for small and medium-sized companies and the publication of accounts in ecu.

Title VII FINAL PROVISIONS

Article 68

1. The Member States shall make such provision as is appropriate to ensure the effective application of this Regulation.

2. Each Member State shall designate the competent authorities within the meaning of Articles 8, 25, 26, 54, 55 and 64. It shall inform the Commission and the other Member States accordingly.

Article 69

Five years at the latest after the entry into force of this Regulation, the Commission shall forward to the Council and the European Parliament a report on the application of the Regulation and proposals for amendments, where appropriate. The report shall, in particular, analyse the appropriateness of:

(a) allowing the location of an SE's head office and registered office in different Member States;

(b) broadening the concept of merger in Article 17(2) in order to admit also other types of merger than those defined in Articles 3(1) and 4(1) of Directive 78/855/EEC;

(c) revising the jurisdiction clause in Article 8(16) in the light of any provision which may have been inserted in the 1968 Brussels Convention or in any text adopted by Member States or by the Council to replace such Convention;

(d) allowing provisions in the statutes of an SE adopted by a Member State in execution of authorisations given to the Member States by this Regulation or laws adopted to ensure the effective application of this Regulation in respect to the SE which deviate from or are complementary to these laws, even when such provisions would not be authorised in the statutes of a public limited-liability company having its registered office in the Member State.

Article 70
This Regulation shall enter into force on 8 October 2004.

This Regulation shall be binding in its entirety and directly applicable in all Member States.

ANNEX I PUBLIC LIMITED-LIABILITY COMPANIES REFERRED TO IN ARTICLE 2(1)

...

UNITED KINGDOM:

public companies limited by shares

public companies limited by guarantee having a share capital

ANNEX II PUBLIC AND PRIVATE LIMITED-LIABILITY COMPANIES REFERRED TO IN ARTICLE 2(2)

...

UNITED KINGDOM:

public companies limited by shares,

public companies limited by guarantee having a share capital,

private companies limited by shares,

private companies limited by guarantee having a share capital

The Insolvency Act 1986, Section 72A (Appointed Date) Order 2003 (SI 2003/2095)

APPOINTED DATE

2. The date appointed under section 72A(4)(a) of the Insolvency Act 1986 is 15th September 2003.

The Insolvency Act 1986 (Prescribed Part) Order 2003 (SI 2003/2097)

CITATION, COMMENCEMENT AND INTERPRETATION

1. ...

(2) In this order "the 1986 Act" means the Insolvency Act 1986.

MINIMUM VALUE OF THE COMPANY'S NET PROPERTY

2. For the purposes of section 176A(3)(a) of the 1986 Act the minimum value of the company's net property is £10,000.

CALCULATION OF PRESCRIBED PART

3(1) The prescribed part of the company's net property to be made available for the satisfaction of unsecured debts of the company pursuant to section 176A of the 1986 Act shall be calculated as follows—
- (a) where the company's net property does not exceed £10,000 in value, 50% of that property;
- (b) subject to paragraph (2), where the company's net property exceeds £10,000 in value the sum of—
  - (i) 50% of the first £10,000 in value; and
  - (ii) 20% of that part of the company's net property which exceeds £10,000 in value.

(2) The value of the prescribed part of the company's net property to be made available for the satisfaction of unsecured debts of the company pursuant to section 176A shall not exceed £600,000.

COMPANIES ACT 2006

Part 1 GENERAL INTRODUCTORY PROVISIONS

Companies and Companies Acts

1 COMPANIES

(1) In the Companies Acts, unless the context otherwise requires—

"company" means a company formed and registered under this Act, that is—
(a) a company so formed and registered after the commencement of this Part, or
(b) a company that immediately before the commencement of this Part—
  (i) was formed and registered under the Companies Act 1985 (c. 6) ... or
  (ii) was an existing company for the purposes of that Act ..., (which is to be treated on commencement as if formed and registered under this Act).

...

2 THE COMPANIES ACTS

(1) In this Act "the Companies Acts" means—
(a) the company law provisions of this Act,
...
(c) the provisions of the Companies Act 1985 (c. 6) ... that remain in force.

(2) The company law provisions of this Act are—
(a) the provisions of Parts 1 to 39 of this Act ...
...

Types of company

3 LIMITED AND UNLIMITED COMPANIES

(1) A company is a "limited company" if the liability of its members is limited by its constitution.

It may be limited by shares or limited by guarantee.

(2) If their liability is limited to the amount, if any, unpaid on the shares held by them, the company is "limited by shares".

(3) If their liability is limited to such amount as the members undertake to contribute to the assets of the company in the event of its being wound up, the company is "limited by guarantee".

(4) If there is no limit on the liability of its members, the company is an "unlimited company".

4 PRIVATE AND PUBLIC COMPANIES

(1) A "private company" is any company that is not a public company.

(2) A "public company" is a company limited by shares or limited by guarantee and having a share capital—
   (a) whose certificate of incorporation states that it is a public company, and
   (b) in relation to which the requirements of this Act, or the former Companies Acts, as to registration or re-registration as a public company have been complied with on or after the relevant date.

(3) For the purposes of subsection (2)(b) the relevant date is—
   (a) in relation to registration or re-registration in Great Britain, 22nd December 1980 ...

...

(4) For the two major differences between private and public companies, see Part 20.

5 COMPANIES LIMITED BY GUARANTEE AND HAVING SHARE CAPITAL

(1) A company cannot be formed as, or become, a company limited by guarantee with a share capital.

...

(3) Any provision in the constitution of a company limited by guarantee that purports to divide the company's undertaking into shares or interests is a provision for a share capital.

This applies whether or not the nominal value or number of the shares or interests is specified by the provision.

...

Part 2 COMPANY FORMATION

General

7 METHOD OF FORMING COMPANY

(1) A company is formed under this Act by one or more persons—
   (a) subscribing their names to a memorandum of association (see section 8), and
   (b) complying with the requirements of this Act as to registration (see sections 9 to 13).

(2) A company may not be so formed for an unlawful purpose.

8 MEMORANDUM OF ASSOCIATION

(1) A memorandum of association is a memorandum stating that the subscribers—
   (a) wish to form a company under this Act, and
   (b) agree to become members of the company and, in the case of a company that is to have a share capital, to take at least one share each.

(2) The memorandum must be in the prescribed form and must be authenticated by each subscriber.

Requirements for registration

9 REGISTRATION DOCUMENTS

(1) The memorandum of association must be delivered to the registrar together with an application for registration of the company, the documents required by this section and a statement of compliance.

(2) The application for registration must state—
(a) the company's proposed name,
(b) whether the company's registered office is to be situated in England and Wales (or in Wales), in Scotland or in Northern Ireland,
(c) whether the liability of the members of the company is to be limited, and if so whether it is to be limited by shares or by guarantee, and
(d) whether the company is to be a private or a public company.

(3) If the application is delivered by a person as agent for the subscribers to the memorandum of association, it must state his name and address.

(4) The application must contain—
(a) in the case of a company that is to have a share capital, a statement of capital and initial shareholdings (see section 10);
(b) in the case of a company that is to be limited by guarantee, a statement of guarantee (see section 11);
(c) a statement of the company's proposed officers (see section 12).

(5) The application must also contain—
(a) a statement of the intended address of the company's registered office; and
(b) a copy of any proposed articles of association (to the extent that these are not supplied by the default application of model articles: see section 20).

(6) The application must be delivered—
(a) to the registrar of companies for England and Wales, if the registered office of the company is to be situated in England and Wales (or in Wales);
(b) to the registrar of companies for Scotland, if the registered office of the company is to be situated in Scotland ...

...

10 STATEMENT OF CAPITAL AND INITIAL SHAREHOLDINGS

(1) The statement of capital and initial shareholdings required to be delivered in the case of a company that is to have a share capital must comply with this section.

(2) It must state—
(a) the total number of shares of the company to be taken on formation by the subscribers to the memorandum of association,
(b) the aggregate nominal value of those shares,
(c) for each class of shares—
(i) prescribed particulars of the rights attached to the shares,
(ii) the total number of shares of that class, and
(iii) the aggregate nominal value of shares of that class, and
(d) the amount to be paid up and the amount (if any) to be unpaid on each share (whether on account of the nominal value of the share or by way of premium).

(3) It must contain such information as may be prescribed for the purpose of identifying the subscribers to the memorandum of association.

(4) It must state, with respect to each subscriber to the memorandum—
   (a) the number, nominal value (of each share) and class of shares to be taken by him on formation, and
   (b) the amount to be paid up and the amount (if any) to be unpaid on each share (whether on account of the nominal value of the share or by way of premium).

(5) Where a subscriber to the memorandum is to take shares of more than one class, the information required under subsection (4)(a) is required for each class.

11 STATEMENT OF GUARANTEE

(1) The statement of guarantee required to be delivered in the case of a company that is to be limited by guarantee must comply with this section.

(2) It must contain such information as may be prescribed for the purpose of identifying the subscribers to the memorandum of association.

(3) It must state that each member undertakes that, if the company is wound up while he is a member, or within one year after he ceases to be a member, he will contribute to the assets of the company such amount as may be required for—
   (a) payment of the debts and liabilities of the company contracted before he ceases to be a member,
   (b) payment of the costs, charges and expenses of winding up, and
   (c) adjustment of the rights of the contributories among themselves, not exceeding a specified amount.

12 STATEMENT OF PROPOSED OFFICERS

(1) The statement of the company's proposed officers required to be delivered to the registrar must contain the required particulars of—
   (a) the person who is, or persons who are, to be the first director or directors of the company;
   (b) in the case of a company that is to be a private company, any person who is (or any persons who are) to be the first secretary (or joint secretaries) of the company;
   (c) in the case of a company that is to be a public company, the person who is (or the persons who are) to be the first secretary (or joint secretaries) of the company.

(2) The required particulars are the particulars that will be required to be stated—
   (a) in the case of a director, in the company's register of directors and register of directors' residential addresses (see sections 162 to 166);
   (b) in the case of a secretary, in the company's register of secretaries (see sections 277 to 279).

(3) The statement must also contain a consent by each of the persons named as a director, as secretary or as one of joint secretaries, to act in the relevant capacity.

If all the partners in a firm are to be joint secretaries, consent may be given by one partner on behalf of all of them.

13 STATEMENT OF COMPLIANCE

(1) The statement of compliance required to be delivered to the registrar is a statement that the requirements of this Act as to registration have been complied with.

(2) The registrar may accept the statement of compliance as sufficient evidence of compliance.

Registration and its effect

14 REGISTRATION

If the registrar is satisfied that the requirements of this Act as to registration are complied with, he shall register the documents delivered to him.

15 ISSUE OF CERTIFICATE OF INCORPORATION

(1) On the registration of a company, the registrar of companies shall give a certificate that the company is incorporated.

(2) The certificate must state—
(a) the name and registered number of the company,
(b) the date of its incorporation,
(c) whether it is a limited or unlimited company, and if it is limited whether it is limited by shares or limited by guarantee,
(d) whether it is a private or a public company, and
(e) whether the company's registered office is situated in England and Wales (or in Wales), in Scotland or in Northern Ireland.

(3) The certificate must be signed by the registrar or authenticated by the registrar's official seal.

(4) The certificate is conclusive evidence that the requirements of this Act as to registration have been complied with and that the company is duly registered under this Act.

16 EFFECT OF REGISTRATION

(1) The registration of a company has the following effects as from the date of incorporation.

(2) The subscribers to the memorandum, together with such other persons as may from time to time become members of the company, are a body corporate by the name stated in the certificate of incorporation.

(3) That body corporate is capable of exercising all the functions of an incorporated company.

(4) The status and registered office of the company are as stated in, or in connection with, the application for registration.

(5) In the case of a company having a share capital, the subscribers to the memorandum become holders of the shares specified in the statement of capital and initial shareholdings.

(6) The persons named in the statement of proposed officers—
(a) as director, or
(b) as secretary or joint secretary of the company,
are deemed to have been appointed to that office.

Part 3 A COMPANY'S CONSTITUTION

Chapter 1 INTRODUCTORY

17 A COMPANY'S CONSTITUTION

Unless the context otherwise requires, references in the Companies Acts to a company's constitution include—

(a) the company's articles, and

(b) any resolutions and agreements to which Chapter 3 applies (see section 29).

Chapter 2 ARTICLES OF ASSOCIATION

General

18 ARTICLES OF ASSOCIATION

(1) A company must have articles of association prescribing regulations for the company.

(2) Unless it is a company to which model articles apply by virtue of section 20 (default application of model articles in case of limited company), it must register articles of association.

(3) Articles of association registered by a company must—
(a) be contained in a single document, and
(b) be divided into paragraphs numbered consecutively.

(4) References in the Companies Acts to a company's "articles" are to its articles of association.

19 POWER OF SECRETARY OF STATE TO PRESCRIBE MODEL ARTICLES

(1) The Secretary of State may by regulations prescribe model articles of association for companies.

(2) Different model articles may be prescribed for different descriptions of company.

(3) A company may adopt all or any of the provisions of model articles.

(4) Any amendment of model articles by regulations under this section does not affect a company registered before the amendment takes effect.

"Amendment" here includes addition, alteration or repeal.

(5) Regulations under this section are subject to negative resolution procedure.

20 DEFAULT APPLICATION OF MODEL ARTICLES

(1) On the formation of a limited company—
(a) if articles are not registered, or
(b) if articles are registered, in so far as they do not exclude or modify the relevant model articles,
the relevant model articles (so far as applicable) form part of the company's articles in the same manner and to the same extent as if articles in the form of those articles had been duly registered.

(2) The "relevant model articles" means the model articles prescribed for a company of that description as in force at the date on which the company is registered.

Alteration of articles

21 AMENDMENT OF ARTICLES

(1) A company may amend its articles by special resolution.

...

22 ENTRENCHED PROVISIONS OF THE ARTICLES

(1) A company's articles may contain provision ("provision for entrenchment") to the effect that specified provisions of the articles may be amended or repealed only if conditions are met, or procedures are complied with, that are more restrictive than those applicable in the case of a special resolution.

(2) Provision for entrenchment may only be made—
(a) in the company's articles on formation, or
(b) by an amendment of the company's articles agreed to by all the members of the company.

(3) Provision for entrenchment does not prevent amendment of the company's articles—
(a) by agreement of all the members of the company, or
(b) by order of a court or other authority having power to alter the company's articles.

(4) Nothing in this section affects any power of a court or other authority to alter a company's articles.

23 NOTICE TO REGISTRAR OF EXISTENCE OF RESTRICTION ON AMENDMENT OF ARTICLES

(1) Where a company's articles—
(a) on formation contain provision for entrenchment,
(b) are amended so as to include such provision, or
(c) are altered by order of a court or other authority so as to restrict or exclude the power of the company to amend its articles,
the company must give notice of that fact to the registrar.

(2) Where a company's articles—
(a) are amended so as to remove provision for entrenchment, or
(b) are altered by order of a court or other authority—
(i) so as to remove such provision, or
(ii) so as to remove any other restriction on, or any exclusion of, the power of the company to amend its articles,
the company must give notice of that fact to the registrar.

24 STATEMENT OF COMPLIANCE WHERE AMENDMENT OF ARTICLES RESTRICTED

(1) This section applies where a company's articles are subject—
(a) to provision for entrenchment, or
(b) to an order of a court or other authority restricting or excluding the company's power to amend the articles.

(2) If the company—
(a) amends its articles, and
(b) is required to send to the registrar a document making or evidencing the amendment,
the company must deliver with that document a statement of compliance.

(3) The statement of compliance required is a statement certifying that the amendment has been made in accordance with the company's articles and, where relevant, any applicable order of a court or other authority.

(4) The registrar may rely on the statement of compliance as sufficient evidence of the matters stated in it.

25 EFFECT OF ALTERATION OF ARTICLES ON COMPANY'S MEMBERS

(1) A member of a company is not bound by an alteration to its articles after the date on which he became a member, if and so far as the alteration—
   (a) requires him to take or subscribe for more shares than the number held by him at the date on which the alteration is made, or
   (b) in any way increases his liability as at that date to contribute to the company's share capital or otherwise to pay money to the company.

(2) Subsection (1) does not apply in a case where the member agrees in writing, either before or after the alteration is made, to be bound by the alteration.

26 REGISTRAR TO BE SENT COPY OF AMENDED ARTICLES

(1) Where a company amends its articles it must send to the registrar a copy of the articles as amended not later than 15 days after the amendment takes effect.

(2) This section does not require a company to set out in its articles any provisions of model articles that—
   (a) are applied by the articles, or
   (b) apply by virtue of section 20 (default application of model articles).

(3) If a company fails to comply with this section an offence is committed by—
   (a) the company, and
   (b) every officer of the company who is in default.

(4) A person guilty of an offence under this section is liable on summary conviction to a fine not exceeding level 3 on the standard scale and, for continued contravention, a daily default fine not exceeding one-tenth of level 3 on the standard scale.

27 REGISTRAR'S NOTICE TO COMPLY IN CASE OF FAILURE WITH RESPECT TO AMENDED ARTICLES

(1) If it appears to the registrar that a company has failed to comply with any enactment requiring it—
   (a) to send to the registrar a document making or evidencing an alteration in the company's articles, or
   (b) to send to the registrar a copy of the company's articles as amended,
   the registrar may give notice to the company requiring it to comply.

(2) The notice must—
   (a) state the date on which it is issued, and
   (b) require the company to comply within 28 days from that date.

(3) If the company complies with the notice within the specified time, no criminal proceedings may be brought in respect of the failure to comply with the enactment mentioned in subsection (1).

(4) If the company does not comply with the notice within the specified time, it is liable to a civil penalty of £200.

   This is in addition to any liability to criminal proceedings in respect of the failure mentioned in subsection (1).

(5) The penalty may be recovered by the registrar and is to be paid into the Consolidated Fund.

Supplementary

28 EXISTING COMPANIES: PROVISIONS OF MEMORANDUM TREATED AS PROVISIONS OF ARTICLES

(1) Provisions that immediately before the commencement of this Part were contained in a company's memorandum but are not provisions of the kind mentioned in section 8 (provisions of new-style memorandum) are to be treated after the commencement of this Part as provisions of the company's articles.

(2) This applies not only to substantive provisions but also to provision for entrenchment (as defined in section 22).

(3) The provisions of this Part about provision for entrenchment apply to such provision as they apply to provision made on the company's formation, except that the duty under section 23(1)(a) to give notice to the registrar does not apply.

Chapter 3 RESOLUTIONS AND AGREEMENTS AFFECTING A COMPANY'S CONSTITUTION

29 RESOLUTIONS AND AGREEMENTS AFFECTING A COMPANY'S CONSTITUTION

(1) This Chapter applies to—
- (a) any special resolution;
- (b) any resolution or agreement agreed to by all the members of a company that, if not so agreed to, would not have been effective for its purpose unless passed as a special resolution;
- (c) any resolution or agreement agreed to by all the members of a class of shareholders that, if not so agreed to, would not have been effective for its purpose unless passed by some particular majority or otherwise in some particular manner;
- (d) any resolution or agreement that effectively binds all members of a class of shareholders though not agreed to by all those members;
- (e) any other resolution or agreement to which this Chapter applies by virtue of any enactment.

(2) References in subsection (1) to a member of a company, or of a class of members of a company, do not include the company itself where it is such a member by virtue only of its holding shares as treasury shares.

30 COPIES OF RESOLUTIONS OR AGREEMENTS TO BE FORWARDED TO REGISTRAR

(1) A copy of every resolution or agreement to which this Chapter applies, or (in the case of a resolution or agreement that is not in writing) a written memorandum setting out its terms, must be forwarded to the registrar within 15 days after it is passed or made.

(2) If a company fails to comply with this section, an offence is committed by—
- (a) the company, and
- (b) every officer of it who is in default.

(3) A person guilty of an offence under this section is liable on summary conviction to a fine not exceeding level 3 on the standard scale and, for continued contravention, a daily default fine not exceeding one-tenth of level 3 on the standard scale.

(4) For the purposes of this section, a liquidator of the company is treated as an officer of it.

Chapter 4 MISCELLANEOUS AND SUPPLEMENTARY PROVISIONS

Statement of company's objects

31 STATEMENT OF COMPANY'S OBJECTS

(1) Unless a company's articles specifically restrict the objects of the company, its objects are unrestricted.

(2) Where a company amends its articles so as to add, remove or alter a statement of the company's objects—
  (a) it must give notice to the registrar,
  (b) on receipt of the notice, the registrar shall register it, and
  (c) the amendment is not effective until entry of that notice on the register.

(3) Any such amendment does not affect any rights or obligations of the company or render defective any legal proceedings by or against it.

...

Other provisions with respect to a company's constitution

32 CONSTITUTIONAL DOCUMENTS TO BE PROVIDED TO MEMBERS

(1) A company must, on request by any member, send to him the following documents—
  (a) an up-to-date copy of the company's articles;
  (b) a copy of any resolution or agreement relating to the company to which Chapter 3 applies (resolutions and agreements affecting a company's constitution) and that is for the time being in force;
  (c) a copy of any document required to be sent to the registrar under—
    (i) section 34(2) (notice where company's constitution altered by enactment), or
    (ii) section 35(2)(a) (notice where order of court or other authority alters company's constitution);
  (d) a copy of any court order under section 899 (order sanctioning compromise or arrangement) or section 900 (order facilitating reconstruction or amalgamation);
  (e) a copy of any court order under section 996 (protection of members against unfair prejudice: powers of the court) that alters the company's constitution;
  (f) a copy of the company's current certificate of incorporation, and of any past certificates of incorporation;
  (g) in the case of a company with a share capital, a current statement of capital;
  (h) in the case of a company limited by guarantee, a copy of the statement of guarantee.

(2) The statement of capital required by subsection (1)(g) is a statement of—
  (a) the total number of shares of the company,
  (b) the aggregate nominal value of those shares,
  (c) for each class of shares—
    (i) prescribed particulars of the rights attached to the shares,
    (ii) the total number of shares of that class, and
    (iii) the aggregate nominal value of shares of that class, and
  (d) the amount paid up and the amount (if any) unpaid on each share (whether on account of the nominal value of the share or by way of premium).

(3) If a company makes default in complying with this section, an offence is committed by every officer of the company who is in default.

(4) A person guilty of an offence under this section is liable on summary conviction to a fine not exceeding level 3 on the standard scale.

33 EFFECT OF COMPANY'S CONSTITUTION

(1) The provisions of a company's constitution bind the company and its members to the same extent as if there were covenants on the part of the company and of each member to observe those provisions.

(2) Money payable by a member to the company under its constitution is a debt due from him to the company.

In England and Wales and Northern Ireland it is of the nature of an ordinary contract debt.

34 NOTICE TO REGISTRAR WHERE COMPANY'S CONSTITUTION ALTERED BY ENACTMENT

(1) This section applies where a company's constitution is altered by an enactment, other than an enactment amending the general law.

(2) The company must give notice of the alteration to the registrar, specifying the enactment, not later than 15 days after the enactment comes into force. In the case of a special enactment the notice must be accompanied by a copy of the enactment.

(3) If the enactment amends—
(a) the company's articles, or
(b) a resolution or agreement to which Chapter 3 applies (resolutions and agreements affecting a company's constitution),

the notice must be accompanied by a copy of the company's articles, or the resolution or agreement in question, as amended.

(4) A "special enactment" means an enactment that is not a public general enactment, and includes—
(a) an Act for confirming a provisional order,
(b) any provision of a public general Act in relation to the passing of which any of the standing orders of the House of Lords or the House of Commons relating to Private Business applied, or
(c) any enactment to the extent that it is incorporated in or applied for the purposes of a special enactment.

(5) If a company fails to comply with this section an offence is committed by—
(a) the company, and
(b) every officer of the company who is in default.

(6) A person guilty of an offence under this section is liable on summary conviction to a fine not exceeding level 3 on the standard scale and, for continued contravention, a daily default fine not exceeding one-tenth of level 3 on the standard scale.

35 NOTICE TO REGISTRAR WHERE COMPANY'S CONSTITUTION ALTERED BY ORDER

(1) Where a company's constitution is altered by an order of a court or other authority, the company must give notice to the registrar of the alteration not later than 15 days after the alteration takes effect.

(2) The notice must be accompanied by—
(a) a copy of the order, and
(b) if the order amends—
(i) the company's articles, or
(ii) a resolution or agreement to which Chapter 3 applies (resolutions and agreements affecting the company's constitution),
a copy of the company's articles, or the resolution or agreement in question, as amended.

(3) If a company fails to comply with this section an offence is committed by—
(a) the company, and
(b) every officer of the company who is in default.

(4) A person guilty of an offence under this section is liable on summary conviction to a fine not exceeding level 3 on the standard scale and, for continued contravention, a daily default fine not exceeding one-tenth of level 3 on the standard scale.

(5) This section does not apply where provision is made by another enactment for the delivery to the registrar of a copy of the order in question.

36 DOCUMENTS TO BE INCORPORATED IN OR ACCOMPANY COPIES OF ARTICLES ISSUED BY COMPANY

(1) Every copy of a company's articles issued by the company must be accompanied by—
(a) a copy of any resolution or agreement relating to the company to which Chapter 3 applies (resolutions and agreements affecting a company's constitution),
(b) where the company has been required to give notice to the registrar under section 34(2) (notice where company's constitution altered by enactment), a statement that the enactment in question alters the effect of the company's constitution,
(c) where the company's constitution is altered by a special enactment (see section 34(4)), a copy of the enactment, and
(d) a copy of any order required to be sent to the registrar under section 35(2)(a) (order of court or other authority altering company's constitution).

(2) This does not require the articles to be accompanied by a copy of a document or by a statement if—
(a) the effect of the resolution, agreement, enactment or order (as the case may be) on the company's constitution has been incorporated into the articles by amendment, or
(b) the resolution, agreement, enactment or order (as the case may be) is not for the time being in force.

(3) If the company fails to comply with this section, an offence is committed by every officer of the company who is in default.

(4) A person guilty of an offence under this section is liable on summary conviction to a fine not exceeding level 3 on the standard scale for each occasion on which copies are issued, or, as the case may be, requested.

(5) For the purposes of this section, a liquidator of the company is treated as an officer of it.

Supplementary provisions

37 RIGHT TO PARTICIPATE IN PROFITS OTHERWISE THAN AS MEMBER VOID

In the case of a company limited by guarantee and not having a share capital any provision in the company's articles, or in any resolution of the company, purporting to give a person a right to participate in the divisible profits of the company otherwise than as a member is void.

38 APPLICATION TO SINGLE MEMBER COMPANIES OF ENACTMENTS AND RULES OF LAW

Any enactment or rule of law applicable to companies formed by two or more persons or having two or more members applies with any necessary modification in relation to a company formed by one person or having only one person as a member.

Part 4 A COMPANY'S CAPACITY AND RELATED MATTERS

Capacity of company and power of directors to bind it

39 A COMPANY'S CAPACITY

(1) The validity of an act done by a company shall not be called into question on the ground of lack of capacity by reason of anything in the company's constitution.

...

40 POWER OF DIRECTORS TO BIND THE COMPANY

(1) In favour of a person dealing with a company in good faith, the power of the directors to bind the company, or authorise others to do so, is deemed to be free of any limitation under the company's constitution.

(2) For this purpose—
- (a) a person "deals with" a company if he is a party to any transaction or other act to which the company is a party,
- (b) a person dealing with a company—
  - (i) is not bound to enquire as to any limitation on the powers of the directors to bind the company or authorise others to do so,
  - (ii) is presumed to have acted in good faith unless the contrary is proved, and
  - (iii) is not to be regarded as acting in bad faith by reason only of his knowing that an act is beyond the powers of the directors under the company's constitution.

(3) The references above to limitations on the directors' powers under the company's constitution include limitations deriving—
- (a) from a resolution of the company or of any class of shareholders, or
- (b) from any agreement between the members of the company or of any class of shareholders.

(4) This section does not affect any right of a member of the company to bring proceedings to restrain the doing of an action that is beyond the powers of the directors.

But no such proceedings lie in respect of an act to be done in fulfilment of a legal obligation arising from a previous act of the company.

(5) This section does not affect any liability incurred by the directors, or any other person, by reason of the directors' exceeding their powers.

(6) This section has effect subject to—

section 41 (transactions with directors or their associates) ...

41 CONSTITUTIONAL LIMITATIONS: TRANSACTIONS INVOLVING DIRECTORS OR THEIR ASSOCIATES

(1) This section applies to a transaction if or to the extent that its validity depends on section 40 (power of directors deemed to be free of limitations under company's constitution in favour of person dealing with company in good faith).

Nothing in this section shall be read as excluding the operation of any other enactment or rule of law by virtue of which the transaction may be called in question or any liability to the company may arise.

(2) Where—
(a) a company enters into such a transaction, and
(b) the parties to the transaction include—
(i) a director of the company or of its holding company, or
(ii) a person connected with any such director,
the transaction is voidable at the instance of the company.

(3) Whether or not it is avoided, any such party to the transaction as is mentioned in subsection (2)(b)(i) or (ii), and any director of the company who authorised the transaction, is liable—
(a) to account to the company for any gain he has made directly or indirectly by the transaction, and
(b) to indemnify the company for any loss or damage resulting from the transaction.

(4) The transaction ceases to be voidable if—
(a) restitution of any money or other asset which was the subject matter of the transaction is no longer possible, or
(b) the company is indemnified for any loss or damage resulting from the transaction, or
(c) rights acquired bona fide for value and without actual notice of the directors' exceeding their powers by a person who is not party to the transaction would be affected by the avoidance, or
(d) the transaction is affirmed by the company.

(5) A person other than a director of the company is not liable under subsection (3) if he shows that at the time the transaction was entered into he did not know that the directors were exceeding their powers.

(6) Nothing in the preceding provisions of this section affects the rights of any party to the transaction not within subsection (2)(b)(i) or (ii).

But the court may, on the application of the company or any such party, make an order affirming, severing or setting aside the transaction on such terms as appear to the court to be just.

(7) In this section—
(a) "transaction" includes any act; and
(b) the reference to a person connected with a director has the same meaning as in Part 10 (company directors).

43 COMPANY CONTRACTS

(1) Under the law of England and Wales or Northern Ireland a contract may be made—
(a) by a company, by writing under its common seal, or
(b) on behalf of a company, by a person acting under its authority, express or implied.

(2) Any formalities required by law in the case of a contract made by an individual also apply, unless a contrary intention appears, to a contract made by or on behalf of a company.

44 EXECUTION OF DOCUMENTS

(1) Under the law of England and Wales or Northern Ireland a document is executed by a company—
(a) by the affixing of its common seal, or
(b) by signature in accordance with the following provisions.

(2) A document is validly executed by a company if it is signed on behalf of the company—
(a) by two authorised signatories, or
(b) by a director of the company in the presence of a witness who attests the signature.

(3) The following are "authorised signatories" for the purposes of subsection (2)—
(a) every director of the company, and
(b) in the case of a private company with a secretary or a public company, the secretary (or any joint secretary) of the company.

(4) A document signed in accordance with subsection (2) and expressed, in whatever words, to be executed by the company has the same effect as if executed under the common seal of the company.

(5) In favour of a purchaser a document is deemed to have been duly executed by a company if it purports to be signed in accordance with subsection (2).

A "purchaser" means a purchaser in good faith for valuable consideration and includes a lessee, mortgagee or other person who for valuable consideration acquires an interest in property.

(6) Where a document is to be signed by a person on behalf of more than one company, it is not duly signed by that person for the purposes of this section unless he signs it separately in each capacity.

(7) References in this section to a document being (or purporting to be) signed by a director or secretary are to be read, in a case where that office is held by a firm, as references to its being (or purporting to be) signed by an individual authorised by the firm to sign on its behalf.

(8) This section applies to a document that is (or purports to be) executed by a company in the name of or on behalf of another person whether or not that person is also a company.

45 COMMON SEAL

(1) A company may have a common seal, but need not have one.

(2) A company which has a common seal shall have its name engraved in legible characters on the seal.

(3) If a company fails to comply with subsection (2) an offence is committed by—
(a) the company, and
(b) every officer of the company who is in default.

(4) An officer of a company, or a person acting on behalf of a company, commits an offence if he uses, or authorises the use of, a seal purporting to be a seal of the company on which its name is not engraved as required by subsection (2).

(5) A person guilty of an offence under this section is liable on summary conviction to a fine not exceeding level 3 on the standard scale.

(6) This section does not form part of the law of Scotland.

47 EXECUTION OF DEEDS OR OTHER DOCUMENTS BY ATTORNEY

(1) Under the law of England and Wales or Northern Ireland a company may, by instrument executed as a deed, empower a person, either generally or in respect of specified matters, as its attorney to execute deeds or other documents on its behalf.

(2) A deed or other document so executed, whether in the United Kingdom or elsewhere, has effect as if executed by the company.

Formalities of doing business under the law of Scotland

48 EXECUTION OF DOCUMENTS BY COMPANIES

(1) The following provisions form part of the law of Scotland only.

(2) Notwithstanding the provisions of any enactment, a company need not have a company seal.

(3) For the purposes of any enactment—
  (a) providing for a document to be executed by a company by affixing its common seal, or
  (b) referring (in whatever terms) to a document so executed,

a document signed or subscribed by or on behalf of the company in accordance with the provisions of the Requirements of Writing (Scotland) Act 1995 (c. 7) has effect as if so executed.

Other matters

49 OFFICIAL SEAL FOR USE ABROAD

(1) A company that has a common seal may have an official seal for use outside the United Kingdom.

(2) The official seal must be a facsimile of the company's common seal, with the addition on its face of the place or places where it is to be used.

(3) The official seal when duly affixed to a document has the same effect as the company's common seal.

This subsection does not extend to Scotland.

(4) A company having an official seal for use outside the United Kingdom may—
  (a) by writing under its common seal, or
  (b) as respects Scotland, by writing subscribed in accordance with the Requirements of Writing (Scotland) Act 1995, authorise any person appointed for the purpose to affix the official seal to any deed or other document to which the company is party.

(5) As between the company and a person dealing with such an agent, the agent's authority continues—
  (a) during the period mentioned in the instrument conferring the authority, or
  (b) if no period is mentioned, until notice of the revocation or termination of the agent's authority has been given to the person dealing with him.

(6) The person affixing the official seal must certify in writing on the deed or other document to which the seal is affixed the date on which, and place at which, it is affixed.

50 OFFICIAL SEAL FOR SHARE CERTIFICATES ETC.

(1) A company that has a common seal may have an official seal for use—
 (a) for sealing securities issued by the company, or
 (b) for sealing documents creating or evidencing securities so issued.

(2) The official seal—
 (a) must be a facsimile of the company's common seal, with the addition on its face of the word "Securities", and
 (b) when duly affixed to the document has the same effect as the company's common seal.

51 PRE-INCORPORATION CONTRACTS, DEEDS AND OBLIGATIONS

(1) A contract that purports to be made by or on behalf of a company at a time when the company has not been formed has effect, subject to any agreement to the contrary, as one made with the person purporting to act for the company or as agent for it, and he is personally liable on the contract accordingly.

(2) Subsection (1) applies—
 (a) to the making of a deed under the law of England and Wales or Northern Ireland, and
 (b) to the undertaking of an obligation under the law of Scotland,
 as it applies to the making of a contract.

52 BILLS OF EXCHANGE AND PROMISSORY NOTES

A bill of exchange or promissory note is deemed to have been made, accepted or endorsed on behalf of a company if made, accepted or endorsed in the name of, or by or on behalf or on account of, the company by a person acting under its authority.

Part 5 A COMPANY'S NAME

Chapter 2 INDICATION OF COMPANY TYPE OR LEGAL FORM

Required indications for limited companies

58 PUBLIC LIMITED COMPANIES

(1) The name of a limited company that is a public company must end with "public limited company" or "p.l.c.".

(2) In the case of a Welsh company, its name may instead end with "cwmni cyfyngedig cyhoeddus" or "c.c.c".

59 PRIVATE LIMITED COMPANIES

(1) The name of a private limited company must end with "limited" or "ltd.".

(2) In the case of a Welsh company, its name may instead end with "cyfyngedig" or "cyf.".

Part 6 A COMPANY'S REGISTERED OFFICE

General

86 A COMPANY'S REGISTERED OFFICE

A company must at all times have a registered office to which all communications and notices may be addressed.

Part 7 RE-REGISTRATION AS A MEANS OF ALTERING A COMPANY'S STATUS

Introductory

89 ALTERATION OF STATUS BY RE-REGISTRATION

A company may by re-registration under this Part alter its status—

(a) from a private company to a public company (see sections 90 to 96);

(b) from a public company to a private company (see sections 97 to 101);

...

Private company becoming public

90 RE-REGISTRATION OF PRIVATE COMPANY AS PUBLIC

(1) A private company (whether limited or unlimited) may be re-registered as a public company limited by shares if—
- (a) a special resolution that it should be so re-registered is passed,
- (b) the conditions specified below are met, and

an application for re-registration is delivered to the registrar ..., together with—
- (i) the other documents required by that section, and
- (ii) a statement of compliance.

(2) The conditions are—
- (a) that the company has a share capital;
- (b) that the requirements of section 91 are met as regards its share capital;
- (c) that the requirements of section 92 are met as regards its net assets; ... and
- (c) that the company has not previously been re-registered as unlimited.

(3) The company must make such changes—
- (a) in its name, and
- (b) in its articles,

as are necessary in connection with its becoming a public company.

(4) If the company is unlimited it must also make such changes in its articles as are necessary in connection with its becoming a company limited by shares.

91 REQUIREMENTS AS TO SHARE CAPITAL

(1) The following requirements must be met at the time the special resolution is passed that the company should be re-registered as a public company—
- (a) the nominal value of the company's allotted share capital must be not less than the authorised minimum;
- (b) each of the company's allotted shares must be paid up at least as to one-quarter of the nominal value of that share and the whole of any premium on it;
- (c) if any shares in the company or any premium on them have been fully or partly paid up by an undertaking given by any person that he or another should do work or perform services (whether for the company or any other person), the undertaking must have been performed or otherwise discharged;
- (d) if shares have been allotted as fully or partly paid up as to their nominal value or any premium on them otherwise than in cash, and the consideration for the allotment consists of or includes an undertaking to the company (other than one to which paragraph (c) applies), then either—
  - (i) the undertaking must have been performed or otherwise discharged, or

(ii) there must be a contract between the company and some person pursuant to which the undertaking is to be performed within five years from the time the special resolution is passed.

(2) For the purpose of determining whether the requirements in subsection (1)(b), (c) and (d) are met, the following may be disregarded—
(a) shares allotted—
(i) before 22nd June 1982 in the case of a company then registered in Great Britain, or
(ii) before 31st December 1984 in the case of a company then registered in Northern Ireland;
(b) shares allotted in pursuance of an employees' share scheme by reason of which the company would, but for this subsection, be precluded under subsection (1)(b) (but not otherwise) from being re-registered as a public company.

(3) No more than one-tenth of the nominal value of the company's allotted share capital is to be disregarded under subsection (2)(a).

For this purpose the allotted share capital is treated as not including shares disregarded under subsection (2)(b).

(4) Shares disregarded under subsection (2) are treated as not forming part of the allotted share capital for the purposes of subsection (1)(a).

(5) A company must not be re-registered as a public company if it appears to the registrar that—
(a) the company has resolved to reduce its share capital,
(b) the reduction—
(i) is made under section 626 (reduction in connection with redenomination of share capital),
(ii) is supported by a solvency statement in accordance with section 643, or
(iii) has been confirmed by an order of the court under section 648, and
(c) the effect of the reduction is, or will be, that the nominal value of the company's allotted share capital is below the authorised minimum.

92 REQUIREMENTS AS TO NET ASSETS

(1) A company applying to re-register as a public company must obtain—
(a) a balance sheet prepared as at a date not more than seven months before the date on which the application is delivered to the registrar,
(b) an unqualified report by the company's auditor on that balance sheet, and
(c) a written statement by the company's auditor that in his opinion at the balance sheet date the amount of the company's net assets was not less than the aggregate of its called-up share capital and undistributable reserves.

(2) Between the balance sheet date and the date on which the application for re-registration is delivered to the registrar, there must be no change in the company's financial position that results in the amount of its net assets becoming less than the aggregate of its called-up share capital and undistributable reserves.

(3) In subsection (1)(b) an "unqualified report" means—
(a) if the balance sheet was prepared for a financial year of the company, a report stating without material qualification the auditor's opinion that the balance sheet has been properly prepared in accordance with the requirements of this Act;
(b) if the balance sheet was not prepared for a financial year of the company, a report stating without material qualification the auditor's opinion that the balance sheet has

been properly prepared in accordance with the provisions of this Act which would have applied if it had been prepared for a financial year of the company.

(4) For the purposes of an auditor's report on a balance sheet that was not prepared for a financial year of the company, the provisions of this Act apply with such modifications as are necessary by reason of that fact.

(5) For the purposes of subsection (3) a qualification is material unless the auditor states in his report that the matter giving rise to the qualification is not material for the purpose of determining (by reference to the company's balance sheet) whether at the balance sheet date the amount of the company's net assets was not less than the aggregate of its called-up share capital and undistributable reserves.

(6) In this Part "net assets" and "undistributable reserves" have the same meaning as in section 831 (net asset restriction on distributions by public companies).

96 ISSUE OF CERTIFICATE OF INCORPORATION ON RE-REGISTRATION

(1) If on an application for re-registration as a public company the registrar is satisfied that the company is entitled to be so re-registered, the company shall be re-registered accordingly.

(2) The registrar must issue a certificate of incorporation altered to meet the circumstances of the case.

(5) The certificate is conclusive evidence that the requirements of this Act as to re-registration have been complied with.

Public company becoming private

97 RE-REGISTRATION OF PUBLIC COMPANY AS PRIVATE LIMITED COMPANY

(1) A public company may be re-registered as a private limited company if—
- (a) a special resolution that it should be so re-registered is passed,
- (b) the conditions specified below are met, and
- (c) an application for re-registration is delivered to the registrar in accordance with section 100, together with—
  - (i) the other documents required by that section, and
  - (ii) a statement of compliance.

(2) The conditions are that—
- (a) where no application under section 98 for cancellation of the resolution has been made—
  - (i) having regard to the number of members who consented to or voted in favour of the resolution, no such application may be made, or
  - (ii) the period within which such an application could be made has expired, or
- (b) where such an application has been made—
  - (i) the application has been withdrawn, or
  - (ii) an order has been made confirming the resolution and a copy of that order has been delivered to the registrar.

(3) The company must make such changes—
- (a) in its name, and

(b) in its articles,

as are necessary in connection with its becoming a private company limited by shares or, as the case may be, by guarantee.

98 APPLICATION TO COURT TO CANCEL RESOLUTION

(1) Where a special resolution by a public company to be re-registered as a private limited company has been passed, an application to the court for the cancellation of the resolution may be made—
- (a) by the holders of not less in the aggregate than 5% in nominal value of the company's issued share capital or any class of the company's issued share capital (disregarding any shares held by the company as treasury shares);
- (b) if the company is not limited by shares, by not less than 5% of its members; or
- (c) by not less than 50 of the company's members;

but not by a person who has consented to or voted in favour of the resolution.

(2) The application must be made within 28 days after the passing of the resolution and may be made on behalf of the persons entitled to make it by such one or more of their number as they may appoint for the purpose.

(3) On the hearing of the application the court shall make an order either cancelling or confirming the resolution.

(4) The court may—
- (a) make that order on such terms and conditions as it thinks fit,
- (b) if it thinks fit adjourn the proceedings in order that an arrangement may be made to the satisfaction of the court for the purchase of the interests of dissentient members, and
- (c) give such directions, and make such orders, as it thinks expedient for facilitating or carrying into effect any such arrangement.

(5) The court's order may, if the court thinks fit—
- (a) provide for the purchase by the company of the shares of any of its members and for the reduction accordingly of the company's capital; and
- (b) make such alteration in the company's articles as may be required in consequence of that provision.

(6) The court's order may, if the court thinks fit, require the company not to make any, or any specified, amendments to its articles without the leave of the court.

100 APPLICATION AND ACCOMPANYING DOCUMENTS

(1) An application for re-registration as a private limited company must contain a statement of the company's proposed name on re-registration.

(2) The application must be accompanied by—
- (a) a copy of the resolution that the company should re-register as a private limited company (unless a copy has already been forwarded to the registrar under Chapter 3 of Part 3); and
- (b) a copy of the company's articles as proposed to be amended.

(3) The statement of compliance required to be delivered together with the application is a statement that the requirements of this Part as to re-registration as a private limited company have been complied with.

(4) The registrar may accept the statement of compliance as sufficient evidence that the company is entitled to be re-registered as a private limited company.

101 ISSUE OF CERTIFICATE OF INCORPORATION ON RE-REGISTRATION

(1) If on an application for re-registration as a private limited company the registrar is satisfied that the company is entitled to be so re-registered, the company shall be re-registered accordingly.

(2) The registrar must issue a certificate of incorporation altered to meet the circumstances of the case.

(5) The certificate is conclusive evidence that the requirements of this Act as to re-registration have been complied with.

Part 8 A COMPANY'S MEMBERS

Chapter 1 THE MEMBERS OF A COMPANY

112 THE MEMBERS OF A COMPANY

(1) The subscribers of a company's memorandum are deemed to have agreed to become members of the company, and on its registration become members and must be entered as such in its register of members.

(2) Every other person who agrees to become a member of a company, and whose name is entered in its register of members, is a member of the company.

Chapter 4 PROHIBITION ON SUBSIDIARY BEING MEMBER OF ITS HOLDING COMPANY

General prohibition

136 PROHIBITION ON SUBSIDIARY BEING A MEMBER OF ITS HOLDING COMPANY

(1) Except as provided by this Chapter—
- (a) a body corporate cannot be a member of a company that is its holding company, and
- (b) any allotment or transfer of shares in a company to its subsidiary is void.

...

Part 9 EXERCISE OF MEMBERS' RIGHTS

Effect of provisions in company's articles

145 EFFECT OF PROVISIONS OF ARTICLES AS TO ENJOYMENT OR EXERCISE OF MEMBERS' RIGHTS

(1) This section applies where provision is made by a company's articles enabling a member to nominate another person or persons as entitled to enjoy or exercise all or any specified rights of the member in relation to the company.

(2) So far as is necessary to give effect to that provision, anything required or authorised by any provision of the Companies Acts to be done by or in relation to the member shall

instead be done, or (as the case may be) may instead be done, by or in relation to the nominated person (or each of them) as if he were a member of the company.

(3) This applies, in particular, to the rights conferred by—
(a) sections 291 and 293 (right to be sent proposed written resolution);
(b) section 292 (right to require circulation of written resolution);
(c) section 303 (right to require directors to call general meeting);
(d) section 310 (right to notice of general meetings);
(e) section 314 (right to require circulation of a statement);
(ea) section 319A (right to ask question at meeting of traded company);
(f) section 324 (right to appoint proxy to act at meeting);
(g) section 338 (right to require circulation of resolution for AGM of public company); and
(ga) section 338A (traded companies: members' power to include matters in business dealt with at AGM);
(h) section 423 (right to be sent a copy of annual accounts and reports).

(4) This section and any such provision as is mentioned in subsection (1)—
(a) do not confer rights enforceable against the company by anyone other than the member, and
(b) do not affect the requirements for an effective transfer or other disposition of the whole or part of a member's interest in the company.

Information rights

146 TRADED COMPANIES: NOMINATION OF PERSONS TO ENJOY INFORMATION RIGHTS

(1) This section applies to a company whose shares are admitted to trading on a regulated market.

(2) A member of such a company who holds shares on behalf of another person may nominate that person to enjoy information rights.

(3) "Information rights" means—
(a) the right to receive a copy of all communications that the company sends to its members generally or to any class of its members that includes the person making the nomination, and
(b) the rights conferred by—
(i) section 431 or 432 (right to require copies of accounts and reports), and
(ii) section 1145 (right to require hard copy version of document or information provided in another form).

(4) The reference in subsection (3)(a) to communications that a company sends to its members generally includes the company's annual accounts and reports.

For the application of section 426 (option to provide summary financial statement) in relation to a person nominated to enjoy information rights, see subsection (5) of that section.

(5) A company need not act on a nomination purporting to relate to certain information rights only.

147 INFORMATION RIGHTS: FORM IN WHICH COPIES TO BE PROVIDED

(1) This section applies as regards the form in which copies are to be provided to a person nominated under section 146 (nomination of person to enjoy information rights).

(2) If the person to be nominated wishes to receive hard copy communications, he must—
(a) request the person making the nomination to notify the company of that fact, and
(b) provide an address to which such copies may be sent.
This must be done before the nomination is made.

(3) If having received such a request the person making the nomination—
(a) notifies the company that the nominated person wishes to receive hard copy communications, and
(b) provides the company with that address,
the right of the nominated person is to receive hard copy communications accordingly.

(4) This is subject to the provisions of Parts 3 and 4 of Schedule 5 (communications by company) under which the company may take steps to enable it to communicate in electronic form or by means of a website.

(5) If no such notification is given (or no address is provided), the nominated person is taken to have agreed that documents or information may be sent or supplied to him by the company by means of a website.

(6) That agreement—
(a) may be revoked by the nominated person, and
(b) does not affect his right under section 1145 to require a hard copy version of a document or information provided in any other form.

148 TERMINATION OR SUSPENSION OF NOMINATION

(1) The following provisions have effect in relation to a nomination under section 146 (nomination of person to enjoy information rights).

(2) The nomination may be terminated at the request of the member or of the nominated person.

(3) The nomination ceases to have effect on the occurrence in relation to the member or the nominated person of any of the following—
(a) in the case of an individual, death or bankruptcy;
(b) in the case of a body corporate, dissolution or the making of an order for the winding up of the body otherwise than for the purposes of reconstruction.

(4) In subsection (3)—
(a) the reference to bankruptcy includes—
(i) the sequestration of a person's estate, and
(ii) a person's estate being the subject of a protected trust deed (within the meaning of the Bankruptcy (Scotland) Act 1985 (c. 66)); and
(b) the reference to the making of an order for winding up is to—
(i) the making of such an order under the Insolvency Act 1986 (c. 45) or the Insolvency (Northern Ireland) Order 1989 (S.I. 1989/2405 (N.I. 19)), or
(ii) any corresponding proceeding under the law of a country or territory outside the United Kingdom.

(5) The effect of any nominations made by a member is suspended at any time when there are more nominated persons than the member has shares in the company.

(6) Where—
(a) the member holds different classes of shares with different information rights, and
(b) there are more nominated persons than he has shares conferring a particular right,
the effect of any nominations made by him is suspended to the extent that they confer that right.

(7) Where the company—
(a) enquires of a nominated person whether he wishes to retain information rights, and
(b) does not receive a response within the period of 28 days beginning with the date on which the company's enquiry was sent,
the nomination ceases to have effect at the end of that period.

Such an enquiry is not to be made of a person more than once in any twelve-month period.

(8) The termination or suspension of a nomination means that the company is not required to act on it.

It does not prevent the company from continuing to do so, to such extent or for such period as it thinks fit.

149 INFORMATION AS TO POSSIBLE RIGHTS IN RELATION TO VOTING

(1) This section applies where a company sends a copy of a notice of a meeting to a person nominated under section 146 (nomination of person to enjoy information rights)

(2) The copy of the notice must be accompanied by a statement that—
(a) he may have a right under an agreement between him and the member by whom he was nominated to be appointed, or to have someone else appointed, as a proxy for the meeting, and
(b) if he has no such right or does not wish to exercise it, he may have a right under such an agreement to give instructions to the member as to the exercise of voting rights.

(3) Section 325 (notice of meeting to contain statement of member's rights in relation to appointment of proxy) does not apply to the copy, and the company must either—
(a) omit the notice required by that section, or
(b) include it but state that it does not apply to the nominated person.

150 INFORMATION RIGHTS: STATUS OF RIGHTS

(1) This section has effect as regards the rights conferred by a nomination under section 146 (nomination of person to enjoy information rights).

(2) Enjoyment by the nominated person of the rights conferred by the nomination is enforceable against the company by the member as if they were rights conferred by the company's articles.

(3) Any enactment, and any provision of the company's articles, having effect in relation to communications with members has a corresponding effect (subject to any necessary adaptations) in relation to communications with the nominated person.

(4) In particular—
(a) where under any enactment, or any provision of the company's articles, the members of a company entitled to receive a document or information are determined as at a date or time before it is sent or supplied, the company need not send or supply it to a nominated person—
(i) whose nomination was received by the company after that date or time, or
(ii) if that date or time falls in a period of suspension of his nomination; and
(b) where under any enactment, or any provision of the company's articles, the right of a member to receive a document or information depends on the company having a current address for him, the same applies to any person nominated by him.

(5) The rights conferred by the nomination—
 (a) are in addition to the rights of the member himself, and
 (b) do not affect any rights exercisable by virtue of any such provision as is mentioned in section 145 (provisions of company's articles as to enjoyment or exercise of members' rights).

(6) A failure to give effect to the rights conferred by the nomination does not affect the validity of anything done by or on behalf of the company.

(7) References in this section to the rights conferred by the nomination are to—
 (a) the rights referred to in section 146(3) (information rights), and
 (b) where applicable, the rights conferred by section 147(3) (right to hard copy communications) and section 149 (information as to possible voting rights).

151 INFORMATION RIGHTS: POWER TO AMEND

(1) The Secretary of State may by regulations amend the provisions of sections 146 to 150 (information rights) so as to—
 (a) extend or restrict the classes of companies to which section 146 applies,
 (b) make other provision as to the circumstances in which a nomination may be made under that section, or
 (c) extend or restrict the rights conferred by such a nomination.

(2) The regulations may make such consequential modifications of any other provisions of this Part, or of any other enactment, as appear to the Secretary of State to be necessary.

(3) Regulations under this section are subject to affirmative resolution procedure.

Exercise of rights where shares held on behalf of others

152 EXERCISE OF RIGHTS WHERE SHARES HELD ON BEHALF OF OTHERS: EXERCISE IN DIFFERENT WAYS

(1) Where a member holds shares in a company on behalf of more than one person—
 (a) rights attached to the shares, and
 (b) rights under any enactment exercisable by virtue of holding the shares,
need not all be exercised, and if exercised, need not all be exercised in the same way.

(2) A member who exercises such rights but does not exercise all his rights, must inform the company to what extent he is exercising the rights.

(3) A member who exercises such rights in different ways must inform the company of the ways in which he is exercising them and to what extent they are exercised in each way.

(4) If a member exercises such rights without informing the company—
 (a) that he is not exercising all his rights, or
 (b) that he is exercising his rights in different ways,
the company is entitled to assume that he is exercising all his rights and is exercising them in the same way.

153 EXERCISE OF RIGHTS WHERE SHARES HELD ON BEHALF OF OTHERS: MEMBERS' REQUESTS

(1) This section applies for the purposes of—
 (a) section 314 (power to require circulation of statement),

(b) section 338 (public companies: power to require circulation of resolution for AGM),
(ba) section 338A (traded companies: members' power to include matters in business dealt with at AGM),
(c) section 342 (power to require independent report on poll), and
(d) section 527 (power to require website publication of audit concerns).

(2) A company is required to act under any of those sections if it receives a request in relation to which the following conditions are met—
(a) it is made by at least 100 persons;
(b) it is authenticated by all the persons making it;
(c) in the case of any of those persons who is not a member of the company, it is accompanied by a statement—
(i) of the full name and address of a person ("the member") who is a member of the company and holds shares on behalf of that person,
(ii) that the member is holding those shares on behalf of that person in the course of a business,
(iii) of the number of shares in the company that the member holds on behalf of that person,
(iv) of the total amount paid up on those shares,
(v) that those shares are not held on behalf of anyone else or, if they are, that the other person or persons are not among the other persons making the request,
(vi) that some or all of those shares confer voting rights that are relevant for the purposes of making a request under the section in question, and
(vii) that the person has the right to instruct the member how to exercise those rights;
(d) in the case of any of those persons who is a member of the company, it is accompanied by a statement—
(i) that he holds shares otherwise than on behalf of another person, or
(ii) that he holds shares on behalf of one or more other persons but those persons are not among the other persons making the request;
(e) it is accompanied by such evidence as the company may reasonably require of the matters mentioned in paragraph (c) and (d);
(f) the total amount of the sums paid up on—
(i) shares held as mentioned in paragraph (c), and
(ii) shares held as mentioned in paragraph (d),
divided by the number of persons making the request, is not less than £100;
(g) the request complies with any other requirements of the section in question as to contents, timing and otherwise.

Part 10 A COMPANY'S DIRECTORS

Chapter 1 APPOINTMENT AND REMOVAL OF DIRECTORS

Requirement to have directors

154 COMPANIES REQUIRED TO HAVE DIRECTORS

(1) A private company must have at least one director.

(2) A public company must have at least two directors.

155 COMPANIES REQUIRED TO HAVE AT LEAST ONE DIRECTOR WHO IS A NATURAL PERSON

(1) A company must have at least one director who is a natural person.

(2) This requirement is met if the office of director is held by a natural person as a corporation sole or otherwise by virtue of an office.

156 DIRECTION REQUIRING COMPANY TO MAKE APPOINTMENT

(1) If it appears to the Secretary of State that a company is in breach of—

section 154 (requirements as to number of directors), or
section 155 (requirement to have at least one director who is a natural person),
the Secretary of State may give the company a direction under this section.

(4) Where the company is in breach of section 154 or 155 it must comply with the direction by—
(a) making the necessary appointment or appointments, and
(b) giving notice of them under section 167,
before the end of the period specified in the direction.

(6) If a company fails to comply with a direction under this section, an offence is committed by—
(a) the company, and
(b) every officer of the company who is in default.
For this purpose a shadow director is treated as an officer of the company.

(7) A person guilty of an offence under this section is liable on summary conviction to a fine not exceeding level 5 on the standard scale and, for continued contravention, a daily default fine not exceeding one-tenth of level 5 on the standard scale.

Appointment

157 MINIMUM AGE FOR APPOINTMENT AS DIRECTOR

(1) A person may not be appointed a director of a company unless he has attained the age of 16 years.

(2) This does not affect the validity of an appointment that is not to take effect until the person appointed attains that age.

...

160 APPOINTMENT OF DIRECTORS OF PUBLIC COMPANY TO BE VOTED ON INDIVIDUALLY

(1) At a general meeting of a public company a motion for the appointment of two or more persons as directors of the company by a single resolution must not be made unless a resolution that it should be so made has first been agreed to by the meeting without any vote being given against it.

(2) A resolution moved in contravention of this section is void, whether or not its being so moved was objected to at the time.

But where a resolution so moved is passed, no provision for the automatic reappointment of retiring directors in default of another appointment applies.

(3) For the purposes of this section a motion for approving a person's appointment, or for nominating a person for appointment, is treated as a motion for his appointment.

(4) Nothing in this section applies to a resolution amending the company's articles.

161 VALIDITY OF ACTS OF DIRECTORS

(1) The acts of a person acting as a director are valid notwithstanding that it is afterwards discovered—
(a) that there was a defect in his appointment;
(b) that he was disqualified from holding office;
(c) that he had ceased to hold office;
(d) that he was not entitled to vote on the matter in question.

(2) This applies even if the resolution for his appointment is void under section 160 (appointment of directors of public company to be voted on individually).

Register of directors, etc.

162 REGISTER OF DIRECTORS

(1) Every company must keep a register of its directors.

(2) The register must contain the required particulars (see sections 163, 164 and 166) of each person who is a director of the company.

(3) The register must be kept available for inspection—
(a) at the company's registered office, or
(b) at a place specified in regulations under section 1136.

(4) The company must give notice to the registrar—
(a) of the place at which the register is kept available for inspection, and
(b) of any change in that place,
unless it has at all times been kept at the company's registered office.

(5) The register must be open to the inspection—
(a) of any member of the company without charge, and
(b) of any other person on payment of such fee as may be prescribed.

(6) If default is made in complying with subsection (1), (2) or (3) or if default is made for 14 days in complying with subsection (4), or if an inspection required under subsection (5) is refused, an offence is committed by—
(a) the company, and
(b) every officer of the company who is in default.
For this purpose a shadow director is treated as an officer of the company.

(7) A person guilty of an offence under this section is liable on summary conviction to a fine not exceeding level 5 on the standard scale and, for continued contravention, a daily default fine not exceeding one-tenth of level 5 on the standard scale.

(8) In the case of a refusal of inspection of the register, the court may by order compel an immediate inspection of it.

163 PARTICULARS OF DIRECTORS TO BE REGISTERED: INDIVIDUALS

(1) A company's register of directors must contain the following particulars in the case of an individual—
(a) name and any former name;
(b) a service address;
(c) the country or state (or part of the United Kingdom) in which he is usually resident;
(d) nationality;

(e) business occupation (if any);
(f) date of birth.

(5) A person's service address may be stated to be "The company's registered office".

165 REGISTER OF DIRECTORS' RESIDENTIAL ADDRESSES

(1) Every company must keep a register of directors' residential addresses.

(2) The register must state the usual residential address of each of the company's directors.

(3) If a director's usual residential address is the same as his service address (as stated in the company's register of directors), the register of directors' residential addresses need only contain an entry to that effect.

This does not apply if his service address is stated to be "The company's registered office".

(4) If default is made in complying with this section, an offence is committed by—
(a) the company, and
(b) every officer of the company who is in default.
For this purpose a shadow director is treated as an officer of the company.

(5) A person guilty of an offence under this section is liable on summary conviction to a fine not exceeding level 5 on the standard scale and, for continued contravention, a daily default fine not exceeding one-tenth of level 5 on the standard scale.

(6) This section applies only to directors who are individuals, not where the director is a body corporate or a firm that is a legal person under the law by which it is governed.

166 PARTICULARS OF DIRECTORS TO BE REGISTERED: POWER TO MAKE REGULATIONS

(1) The Secretary of State may make provision by regulations amending—

section 163 (particulars of directors to be registered: individuals),
section 164 (particulars of directors to be registered: corporate directors and firms), or
section 165 (register of directors' residential addresses),
so as to add to or remove items from the particulars required to be contained in a company's register of directors or register of directors' residential addresses.

(2) Regulations under this section are subject to affirmative resolution procedure.

167 DUTY TO NOTIFY REGISTRAR OF CHANGES

(1) A company must, within the period of 14 days from—
(a) a person becoming or ceasing to be a director, or
(c) the occurrence of any change in the particulars contained in its register of directors or its register of directors' residential addresses,
give notice to the registrar of the change and of the date on which it occurred.

...

Removal

168 RESOLUTION TO REMOVE DIRECTOR

(1) A company may by ordinary resolution at a meeting remove a director before the expiration of his period of office, notwithstanding anything in any agreement between it and him.

(2) Special notice is required of a resolution to remove a director under this section or to appoint somebody instead of a director so removed at the meeting at which he is removed.

(3) A vacancy created by the removal of a director under this section, if not filled at the meeting at which he is removed, may be filled as a casual vacancy.

(4) A person appointed director in place of a person removed under this section is treated, for the purpose of determining the time at which he or any other director is to retire, as if he had become director on the day on which the person in whose place he is appointed was last appointed a director.

(5) This section is not to be taken—
   (a) as depriving a person removed under it of compensation or damages payable to him in respect of the termination of his appointment as director or of any appointment terminating with that as director, or
   (b) as derogating from any power to remove a director that may exist apart from this section.

169 DIRECTOR'S RIGHT TO PROTEST AGAINST REMOVAL

(1) On receipt of notice of an intended resolution to remove a director under section 168, the company must forthwith send a copy of the notice to the director concerned.

(2) The director (whether or not a member of the company) is entitled to be heard on the resolution at the meeting.

(3) Where notice is given of an intended resolution to remove a director under that section, and the director concerned makes with respect to it representations in writing to the company (not exceeding a reasonable length) and requests their notification to members of the company, the company shall, unless the representations are received by it too late for it to do so—
   (a) in any notice of the resolution given to members of the company state the fact of the representations having been made; and
   (b) send a copy of the representations to every member of the company to whom notice of the meeting is sent (whether before or after receipt of the representations by the company).

(4) If a copy of the representations is not sent as required by subsection (3) because received too late or because of the company's default, the director may (without prejudice to his right to be heard orally) require that the representations shall be read out at the meeting.

(5) Copies of the representations need not be sent out and the representations need not be read out at the meeting if, on the application either of the company or of any other person who claims to be aggrieved, the court is satisfied that the rights conferred by this section are being abused.

(6) The court may order the company's costs (in Scotland, expenses) on an application under subsection (5) to be paid in whole or in part by the director, notwithstanding that he is not a party to the application.

Chapter 2 GENERAL DUTIES OF DIRECTORS

Introductory

170 SCOPE AND NATURE OF GENERAL DUTIES

(1) The general duties specified in sections 171 to 177 are owed by a director of a company to the company.

(2) A person who ceases to be a director continues to be subject—
   (a) to the duty in section 175 (duty to avoid conflicts of interest) as regards the exploitation of any property, information or opportunity of which he became aware at a time when he was a director, and
   (b) to the duty in section 176 (duty not to accept benefits from third parties) as regards things done or omitted by him before he ceased to be a director.

   To that extent those duties apply to a former director as to a director, subject to any necessary adaptations.

(3) The general duties are based on certain common law rules and equitable principles as they apply in relation to directors and have effect in place of those rules and principles as regards the duties owed to a company by a director.

(4) The general duties shall be interpreted and applied in the same way as common law rules or equitable principles, and regard shall be had to the corresponding common law rules and equitable principles in interpreting and applying the general duties.

(5) The general duties apply to shadow directors where, and to the extent that, the corresponding common law rules or equitable principles so apply.

The general duties

171 DUTY TO ACT WITHIN POWERS

A director of a company must—

(a) act in accordance with the company's constitution, and

(b) only exercise powers for the purposes for which they are conferred.

172 DUTY TO PROMOTE THE SUCCESS OF THE COMPANY

(1) A director of a company must act in the way he considers, in good faith, would be most likely to promote the success of the company for the benefit of its members as a whole, and in doing so have regard (amongst other matters) to—
   (a) the likely consequences of any decision in the long term,
   (b) the interests of the company's employees,
   (c) the need to foster the company's business relationships with suppliers, customers and others,
   (d) the impact of the company's operations on the community and the environment,
   (e) the desirability of the company maintaining a reputation for high standards of business conduct, and
   (f) the need to act fairly as between members of the company.

(2) Where or to the extent that the purposes of the company consist of or include purposes other than the benefit of its members, subsection (1) has effect as if the reference to promoting the success of the company for the benefit of its members were to achieving those purposes.

(3) The duty imposed by this section has effect subject to any enactment or rule of law requiring directors, in certain circumstances, to consider or act in the interests of creditors of the company.

173 DUTY TO EXERCISE INDEPENDENT JUDGMENT

(1) A director of a company must exercise independent judgment.

(2) This duty is not infringed by his acting—
(a) in accordance with an agreement duly entered into by the company that restricts the future exercise of discretion by its directors, or
(b) in a way authorised by the company's constitution.

174 DUTY TO EXERCISE REASONABLE CARE, SKILL AND DILIGENCE

(1) A director of a company must exercise reasonable care, skill and diligence.

(2) This means the care, skill and diligence that would be exercised by a reasonably diligent person with—
(a) the general knowledge, skill and experience that may reasonably be expected of a person carrying out the functions carried out by the director in relation to the company, and
(b) the general knowledge, skill and experience that the director has.

175 DUTY TO AVOID CONFLICTS OF INTEREST

(1) A director of a company must avoid a situation in which he has, or can have, a direct or indirect interest that conflicts, or possibly may conflict, with the interests of the company.

(2) This applies in particular to the exploitation of any property, information or opportunity (and it is immaterial whether the company could take advantage of the property, information or opportunity).

(3) This duty does not apply to a conflict of interest arising in relation to a transaction or arrangement with the company.

(4) This duty is not infringed—
(a) if the situation cannot reasonably be regarded as likely to give rise to a conflict of interest; or
(b) if the matter has been authorised by the directors.

(5) Authorisation may be given by the directors—
(a) where the company is a private company and nothing in the company's constitution invalidates such authorisation, by the matter being proposed to and authorised by the directors; or
(b) where the company is a public company and its constitution includes provision enabling the directors to authorise the matter, by the matter being proposed to and authorised by them in accordance with the constitution.

(6) The authorisation is effective only if—
(a) any requirement as to the quorum at the meeting at which the matter is considered is met without counting the director in question or any other interested director, and
(b) the matter was agreed to without their voting or would have been agreed to if their votes had not been counted.

(7) Any reference in this section to a conflict of interest includes a conflict of interest and duty and a conflict of duties.

176 DUTY NOT TO ACCEPT BENEFITS FROM THIRD PARTIES

(1) A director of a company must not accept a benefit from a third party conferred by reason of—
(a) his being a director, or
(b) his doing (or not doing) anything as director.

(2) A "third party" means a person other than the company, an associated body corporate or a person acting on behalf of the company or an associated body corporate.

(3) Benefits received by a director from a person by whom his services (as a director or otherwise) are provided to the company are not regarded as conferred by a third party.

(4) This duty is not infringed if the acceptance of the benefit cannot reasonably be regarded as likely to give rise to a conflict of interest.

(5) Any reference in this section to a conflict of interest includes a conflict of interest and duty and a conflict of duties.

177 DUTY TO DECLARE INTEREST IN PROPOSED TRANSACTION OR ARRANGEMENT

(1) If a director of a company is in any way, directly or indirectly, interested in a proposed transaction or arrangement with the company, he must declare the nature and extent of that interest to the other directors.

(2) The declaration may (but need not) be made—
- (a) at a meeting of the directors, or
- (b) by notice to the directors in accordance with—
  - (i) section 184 (notice in writing), or
  - (ii) section 185 (general notice).

(3) If a declaration of interest under this section proves to be, or becomes, inaccurate or incomplete, a further declaration must be made.

(4) Any declaration required by this section must be made before the company enters into the transaction or arrangement.

(5) This section does not require a declaration of an interest of which the director is not aware or where the director is not aware of the transaction or arrangement in question.

For this purpose a director is treated as being aware of matters of which he ought reasonably to be aware.

(6) A director need not declare an interest—
- (a) if it cannot reasonably be regarded as likely to give rise to a conflict of interest;
- (b) if, or to the extent that, the other directors are already aware of it (and for this purpose the other directors are treated as aware of anything of which they ought reasonably to be aware); or
- (c) if, or to the extent that, it concerns terms of his service contract that have been or are to be considered—
  - (i) by a meeting of the directors, or
  - (ii) by a committee of the directors appointed for the purpose under the company's constitution.

Supplementary provisions

178 CIVIL CONSEQUENCES OF BREACH OF GENERAL DUTIES

(1) The consequences of breach (or threatened breach) of sections 171 to 177 are the same as would apply if the corresponding common law rule or equitable principle applied.

(2) The duties in those sections (with the exception of section 174 (duty to exercise reasonable care, skill and diligence)) are, accordingly, enforceable in the same way as any other fiduciary duty owed to a company by its directors.

179 CASES WITHIN MORE THAN ONE OF THE GENERAL DUTIES

Except as otherwise provided, more than one of the general duties may apply in any given case.

180 CONSENT, APPROVAL OR AUTHORISATION BY MEMBERS

(1) In a case where—
(a) section 175 (duty to avoid conflicts of interest) is complied with by authorisation by the directors, or
(b) section 177 (duty to declare interest in proposed transaction or arrangement) is complied with,
the transaction or arrangement is not liable to be set aside by virtue of any common law rule or equitable principle requiring the consent or approval of the members of the company.

This is without prejudice to any enactment, or provision of the company's constitution, requiring such consent or approval.

(2) The application of the general duties is not affected by the fact that the case also falls within Chapter 4 (transactions requiring approval of members), except that where that Chapter applies and—
(a) approval is given under that Chapter, or
(b) the matter is one as to which it is provided that approval is not needed,
it is not necessary also to comply with section 175 (duty to avoid conflicts of interest) or section 176 (duty not to accept benefits from third parties).

(3) Compliance with the general duties does not remove the need for approval under any applicable provision of Chapter 4 (transactions requiring approval of members).

(4) The general duties—
(a) have effect subject to any rule of law enabling the company to give authority, specifically or generally, for anything to be done (or omitted) by the directors, or any of them, that would otherwise be a breach of duty, and
(b) where the company's articles contain provisions for dealing with conflicts of interest, are not infringed by anything done (or omitted) by the directors, or any of them, in accordance with those provisions.

(5) Otherwise, the general duties have effect (except as otherwise provided or the context otherwise requires) notwithstanding any enactment or rule of law.

Chapter 3 DECLARATION OF INTEREST IN EXISTING TRANSACTION OR ARRANGEMENT

182 DECLARATION OF INTEREST IN EXISTING TRANSACTION OR ARRANGEMENT

(1) Where a director of a company is in any way, directly or indirectly, interested in a transaction or arrangement that has been entered into by the company, he must declare the nature and extent of the interest to the other directors in accordance with this section.

This section does not apply if or to the extent that the interest has been declared under section 177 (duty to declare interest in proposed transaction or arrangement).

(2) The declaration must be made—
(a) at a meeting of the directors, or

(b) by notice in writing (see section 184), or
(c) by general notice (see section 185).

(3) If a declaration of interest under this section proves to be, or becomes, inaccurate or incomplete, a further declaration must be made.

(4) Any declaration required by this section must be made as soon as is reasonably practicable.

Failure to comply with this requirement does not affect the underlying duty to make the declaration.

(5) This section does not require a declaration of an interest of which the director is not aware or where the director is not aware of the transaction or arrangement in question.

For this purpose a director is treated as being aware of matters of which he ought reasonably to be aware.

(6) A director need not declare an interest under this section—
(a) if it cannot reasonably be regarded as likely to give rise to a conflict of interest;
(b) if, or to the extent that, the other directors are already aware of it (and for this purpose the other directors are treated as aware of anything of which they ought reasonably to be aware); or
(c) if, or to the extent that, it concerns terms of his service contract that have been or are to be considered—
(i) by a meeting of the directors, or
(ii) by a committee of the directors appointed for the purpose under the company's constitution.

183 OFFENCE OF FAILURE TO DECLARE INTEREST

(1) A director who fails to comply with the requirements of section 182 (declaration of interest in existing transaction or arrangement) commits an offence.

(2) A person guilty of an offence under this section is liable—
(a) on conviction on indictment, to a fine;
(b) on summary conviction, to a fine not exceeding the statutory maximum.

184 DECLARATION MADE BY NOTICE IN WRITING

(1) This section applies to a declaration of interest made by notice in writing.

(2) The director must send the notice to the other directors.

(3) The notice may be sent in hard copy form or, if the recipient has agreed to receive it in electronic form, in an agreed electronic form.

(4) The notice may be sent—
(a) by hand or by post, or
(b) if the recipient has agreed to receive it by electronic means, by agreed electronic means.

(5) Where a director declares an interest by notice in writing in accordance with this section—
(a) the making of the declaration is deemed to form part of the proceedings at the next meeting of the directors after the notice is given, and
(b) the provisions of section 248 (minutes of meetings of directors) apply as if the declaration had been made at that meeting.

185 GENERAL NOTICE TREATED AS SUFFICIENT DECLARATION

(1) General notice in accordance with this section is a sufficient declaration of interest in relation to the matters to which it relates.

(2) General notice is notice given to the directors of a company to the effect that the director—

(a) has an interest (as member, officer, employee or otherwise) in a specified body corporate or firm and is to be regarded as interested in any transaction or arrangement that may, after the date of the notice, be made with that body corporate or firm, or

(b) is connected with a specified person (other than a body corporate or firm) and is to be regarded as interested in any transaction or arrangement that may, after the date of the notice, be made with that person.

(3) The notice must state the nature and extent of the director's interest in the body corporate or firm or, as the case may be, the nature of his connection with the person.

(4) General notice is not effective unless—

(a) it is given at a meeting of the directors, or

(b) the director takes reasonable steps to secure that it is brought up and read at the next meeting of the directors after it is given.

186 DECLARATION OF INTEREST IN CASE OF COMPANY WITH SOLE DIRECTOR

(1) Where a declaration of interest under section 182 (duty to declare interest in existing transaction or arrangement) is required of a sole director of a company that is required to have more than one director—

(a) the declaration must be recorded in writing,

(b) the making of the declaration is deemed to form part of the proceedings at the next meeting of the directors after the notice is given, and

(c) the provisions of section 248 (minutes of meetings of directors) apply as if the declaration had been made at that meeting.

(2) Nothing in this section affects the operation of section 231 (contract with sole member who is also a director: terms to be set out in writing or recorded in minutes).

187 DECLARATION OF INTEREST IN EXISTING TRANSACTION BY SHADOW DIRECTOR

(1) The provisions of this Chapter relating to the duty under section 182 (duty to declare interest in existing transaction or arrangement) apply to a shadow director as to a director, but with the following adaptations.

(2) Subsection (2)(a) of that section (declaration at meeting of directors) does not apply.

(3) In section 185 (general notice treated as sufficient declaration), subsection (4) (notice to be given at or brought up and read at meeting of directors) does not apply.

(4) General notice by a shadow director is not effective unless given by notice in writing in accordance with section 184.

Chapter 4 TRANSACTION WITH DIRECTORS REQUIRING APPROVAL BY MEMBERS

Service contracts

188 DIRECTORS' LONG-TERM SERVICE CONTRACTS: REQUIREMENT OF MEMBERS' APPROVAL

(1) This section applies to provision under which the guaranteed term of a director's employment—
  (a) with the company of which he is a director, or
  (b) where he is the director of a holding company, within the group consisting of that company and its subsidiaries,
is, or may be, longer than two years.

(2) A company may not agree to such provision unless it has been approved—
  (a) by resolution of the members of the company, and
  (b) in the case of a director of a holding company, by resolution of the members of that company.

(3) The guaranteed term of a director's employment is—
  (a) the period (if any) during which the director's employment—
    (i) is to continue, or may be continued otherwise than at the instance of the company (whether under the original agreement or under a new agreement entered into in pursuance of it), and
    (ii) cannot be terminated by the company by notice, or can be so terminated only in specified circumstances, or
  (b) in the case of employment terminable by the company by notice, the period of notice required to be given,
or, in the case of employment having a period within paragraph (a) and a period within paragraph (b), the aggregate of those periods.

(4) If more than six months before the end of the guaranteed term of a director's employment the company enters into a further service contract (otherwise than in pursuance of a right conferred, by or under the original contract, on the other party to it), this section applies as if there were added to the guaranteed term of the new contract the unexpired period of the guaranteed term of the original contract.

(5) A resolution approving provision to which this section applies must not be passed unless a memorandum setting out the proposed contract incorporating the provision is made available to members—
  (a) in the case of a written resolution, by being sent or submitted to every eligible member at or before the time at which the proposed resolution is sent or submitted to him;
  (b) in the case of a resolution at a meeting, by being made available for inspection by members of the company both—
    (i) at the company's registered office for not less than 15 days ending with the date of the meeting, and
    (ii) at the meeting itself.

(6) No approval is required under this section on the part of the members of a body corporate that—
  (a) is not a UK-registered company, or
  (b) is a wholly-owned subsidiary of another body corporate.

(7) In this section "employment" means any employment under a director's service contract.

189 DIRECTORS' LONG-TERM SERVICE CONTRACTS: CIVIL CONSEQUENCES OF CONTRAVENTION

If a company agrees to provision in contravention of section 188 (directors' long-term service contracts: requirement of members' approval)—

(a) the provision is void, to the extent of the contravention, and

(b) the contract is deemed to contain a term entitling the company to terminate it at any time by the giving of reasonable notice.

Substantial property transactions

190 SUBSTANTIAL PROPERTY TRANSACTIONS: REQUIREMENT OF MEMBERS' APPROVAL

(1) A company may not enter into an arrangement under which—
  (a) a director of the company or of its holding company, or a person connected with such a director, acquires or is to acquire from the company (directly or indirectly) a substantial non-cash asset, or
  (b) the company acquires or is to acquire a substantial non-cash asset (directly or indirectly) from such a director or a person so connected, unless the arrangement has been approved by a resolution of the members of the company or is conditional on such approval being obtained.

For the meaning of "substantial non-cash asset" see section 191.

(2) If the director or connected person is a director of the company's holding company or a person connected with such a director, the arrangement must also have been approved by a resolution of the members of the holding company or be conditional on such approval being obtained.

(3) A company shall not be subject to any liability by reason of a failure to obtain approval required by this section.

(4) No approval is required under this section on the part of the members of a body corporate that—
  (a) is not a UK-registered company, or
  (b) is a wholly-owned subsidiary of another body corporate.

(5) For the purposes of this section—
  (a) an arrangement involving more than one non-cash asset, or
  (b) an arrangement that is one of a series involving non-cash assets,

shall be treated as if they involved a non-cash asset of a value equal to the aggregate value of all the non-cash assets involved in the arrangement or, as the case may be, the series.

(6) This section does not apply to a transaction so far as it relates—
  (a) to anything to which a director of a company is entitled under his service contract, or
  (b) to payment for loss of office as defined in section 215 (payments requiring members' approval).

191 MEANING OF "SUBSTANTIAL"

(1) This section explains what is meant in section 190 (requirement of approval for substantial property transactions) by a "substantial" non-cash asset.

(2) An asset is a substantial asset in relation to a company if its value—

(a) exceeds 10% of the company's asset value and is more than £5,000, or
(b) exceeds £100,000.

(3) For this purpose a company's "asset value" at any time is—
(a) the value of the company's net assets determined by reference to its most recent statutory accounts, or
(b) if no statutory accounts have been prepared, the amount of the company's called-up share capital.

(4) A company's "statutory accounts" means its annual accounts prepared in accordance with Part 15, and its "most recent" statutory accounts means those in relation to which the time for sending them out to members (see section 424) is most recent.

(5) Whether an asset is a substantial asset shall be determined as at the time the arrangement is entered into.

192 EXCEPTION FOR TRANSACTIONS WITH MEMBERS OR OTHER GROUP COMPANIES

Approval is not required under section 190 (requirement of members' approval for substantial property transactions)—

(a) for a transaction between a company and a person in his character as a member of that company, or

(b) for a transaction between—
(i) a holding company and its wholly-owned subsidiary, or
(ii) two wholly-owned subsidiaries of the same holding company.

193 EXCEPTION IN CASE OF COMPANY IN WINDING UP OR ADMINISTRATION

(1) This section applies to a company—
(a) that is being wound up (unless the winding up is a members' voluntary winding up), or
(b) that is in administration within the meaning of Schedule B1 to the Insolvency Act 1986 (c. 45) or the Insolvency (Northern Ireland) Order 1989 (S.I. 1989/2405 (N.I. 19)).

(2) Approval is not required under section 190 (requirement of members' approval for substantial property transactions)—
(a) on the part of the members of a company to which this section applies, or
(b) for an arrangement entered into by a company to which this section applies.

194 EXCEPTION FOR TRANSACTIONS ON RECOGNISED INVESTMENT EXCHANGE

(1) Approval is not required under section 190 (requirement of members' approval for substantial property transactions) for a transaction on a recognised investment exchange effected by a director, or a person connected with him, through the agency of a person who in relation to the transaction acts as an independent broker.

(2) For this purpose—
(a) "independent broker" means a person who, independently of the director or any person connected with him, selects the person with whom the transaction is to be effected; and

(b) "recognised investment exchange" has the same meaning as in Part 18 of the Financial Services and Markets Act 2000 (c. 8).

195 PROPERTY TRANSACTIONS: CIVIL CONSEQUENCES OF CONTRAVENTION

(1) This section applies where a company enters into an arrangement in contravention of section 190 (requirement of members' approval for substantial property transactions).

(2) The arrangement, and any transaction entered into in pursuance of the arrangement (whether by the company or any other person), is voidable at the instance of the company, unless—

(a) restitution of any money or other asset that was the subject matter of the arrangement or transaction is no longer possible,

(b) the company has been indemnified in pursuance of this section by any other persons for the loss or damage suffered by it, or

(c) rights acquired in good faith, for value and without actual notice of the contravention by a person who is not a party to the arrangement or transaction would be affected by the avoidance.

(3) Whether or not the arrangement or any such transaction has been avoided, each of the persons specified in subsection (4) is liable—

(a) to account to the company for any gain that he has made directly or indirectly by the arrangement or transaction, and

(b) (jointly and severally with any other person so liable under this section) to indemnify the company for any loss or damage resulting from the arrangement or transaction.

(4) The persons so liable are—

(a) any director of the company or of its holding company with whom the company entered into the arrangement in contravention of section 190,

(b) any person with whom the company entered into the arrangement in contravention of that section who is connected with a director of the company or of its holding company,

(c) the director of the company or of its holding company with whom any such person is connected, and

(d) any other director of the company who authorised the arrangement or any transaction entered into in pursuance of such an arrangement.

(5) Subsections (3) and (4) are subject to the following two subsections.

(6) In the case of an arrangement entered into by a company in contravention of section 190 with a person connected with a director of the company or of its holding company, that director is not liable by virtue of subsection (4)(c) if he shows that he took all reasonable steps to secure the company's compliance with that section.

(7) In any case—

(a) a person so connected is not liable by virtue of subsection (4)(b), and

(b) a director is not liable by virtue of subsection (4)(d),

if he shows that, at the time the arrangement was entered into, he did not know the relevant circumstances constituting the contravention.

(8) Nothing in this section shall be read as excluding the operation of any other enactment or rule of law by virtue of which the arrangement or transaction may be called in question or any liability to the company may arise.

196 PROPERTY TRANSACTIONS: EFFECT OF SUBSEQUENT AFFIRMATION

Where a transaction or arrangement is entered into by a company in contravention of section 190 (requirement of members' approval) but, within a reasonable period, it is affirmed—

(a) in the case of a contravention of subsection (1) of that section, by resolution of the members of the company, and

(b) in the case of a contravention of subsection (2) of that section, by resolution of the members of the holding company,

the transaction or arrangement may no longer be avoided under section 195.

Loans, quasi-loans and credit transactions

197 LOANS TO DIRECTORS: REQUIREMENT OF MEMBERS' APPROVAL

(1) A company may not—
 (a) make a loan to a director of the company or of its holding company, or
 (b) give a guarantee or provide security in connection with a loan made by any person to such a director,

unless the transaction has been approved by a resolution of the members of the company.

(2) If the director is a director of the company's holding company, the transaction must also have been approved by a resolution of the members of the holding company.

(3) A resolution approving a transaction to which this section applies must not be passed unless a memorandum setting out the matters mentioned in subsection (4) is made available to members—
 (a) in the case of a written resolution, by being sent or submitted to every eligible member at or before the time at which the proposed resolution is sent or submitted to him;
 (b) in the case of a resolution at a meeting, by being made available for inspection by members of the company both—
  (i) at the company's registered office for not less than 15 days ending with the date of the meeting, and
  (ii) at the meeting itself.

(4) The matters to be disclosed are—
 (a) the nature of the transaction,
 (b) the amount of the loan and the purpose for which it is required, and
 (c) the extent of the company's liability under any transaction connected with the loan.

(5) No approval is required under this section on the part of the members of a body corporate that—
 (a) is not a UK-registered company, or
 (b) is a wholly-owned subsidiary of another body corporate.

213 LOANS ETC.: CIVIL CONSEQUENCES OF CONTRAVENTION

(1) This section applies where a company enters into a transaction or arrangement in contravention of section 197 ... (requirement of members' approval for loans ...).

(2) The transaction or arrangement is voidable at the instance of the company, unless—
 (a) restitution of any money or other asset that was the subject matter of the transaction or arrangement is no longer possible,

(b) the company has been indemnified for any loss or damage resulting from the transaction or arrangement, or
(c) rights acquired in good faith, for value and without actual notice of the contravention by a person who is not a party to the transaction or arrangement would be affected by the avoidance.

(3) Whether or not the transaction or arrangement has been avoided, each of the persons specified in subsection (4) is liable—
(a) to account to the company for any gain that he has made directly or indirectly by the transaction or arrangement, and
(b) (jointly and severally with any other person so liable under this section) to indemnify the company for any loss or damage resulting from the transaction or arrangement.

(4) The persons so liable are—
(a) any director of the company or of its holding company with whom the company entered into the transaction or arrangement in contravention of section 197 ...,
... and
(d) any other director of the company who authorised the transaction or arrangement.

(7) In any case—
...
(b) a director is not liable by virtue of subsection (4)(d),
if he shows that, at the time the transaction or arrangement was entered into, he did not know the relevant circumstances constituting the contravention.

(8) Nothing in this section shall be read as excluding the operation of any other enactment or rule of law by virtue of which the transaction or arrangement may be called in question or any liability to the company may arise.

214 LOANS ETC.: EFFECT OF SUBSEQUENT AFFIRMATION

Where a transaction or arrangement is entered into by a company in contravention of section 197 ... (requirement of members' approval for loans ...) but, within a reasonable period, it is affirmed—

(a) in the case of a contravention of the requirement for a resolution of the members of the company, by a resolution of the members of the company, and
(b) in the case of a contravention of the requirement for a resolution of the members of the company's holding company, by a resolution of the members of the holding company,
the transaction or arrangement may no longer be avoided under section 213.

Payments for loss of office

215 PAYMENTS FOR LOSS OF OFFICE

(1) In this Chapter a "payment for loss of office" means a payment made to a director or past director of a company—
(a) by way of compensation for loss of office as director of the company,
(b) by way of compensation for loss, while director of the company or in connection with his ceasing to be a director of it, of—

(i) any other office or employment in connection with the management of the affairs of the company, or
(ii) any office (as director or otherwise) or employment in connection with the management of the affairs of any subsidiary undertaking of the company,

(c) as consideration for or in connection with his retirement from his office as director of the company, or

(d) as consideration for or in connection with his retirement, while director of the company or in connection with his ceasing to be a director of it, from—
(i) any other office or employment in connection with the management of the affairs of the company, or
(ii) any office (as director or otherwise) or employment in connection with the management of the affairs of any subsidiary undertaking of the company.

(2) The references to compensation and consideration include benefits otherwise than in cash and references in this Chapter to payment have a corresponding meaning.

(3) For the purposes of sections 217 to 221 (payments requiring members' approval)—
(a) payment to a person connected with a director, or
(b) payment to any person at the direction of, or for the benefit of, a director or a person connected with him,
is treated as payment to the director.

(4) References in those sections to payment by a person include payment by another person at the direction of, or on behalf of, the person referred to.

216 AMOUNTS TAKEN TO BE PAYMENTS FOR LOSS OF OFFICE

(1) This section applies where in connection with any such transfer as is mentioned in section 218 or 219 (payment in connection with transfer of undertaking, property or shares) a director of the company—
(a) is to cease to hold office, or
(b) is to cease to be the holder of—
(i) any other office or employment in connection with the management of the affairs of the company, or
(ii) any office (as director or otherwise) or employment in connection with the management of the affairs of any subsidiary undertaking of the company.

(2) If in connection with any such transfer—
(a) the price to be paid to the director for any shares in the company held by him is in excess of the price which could at the time have been obtained by other holders of like shares, or
(b) any valuable consideration is given to the director by a person other than the company,
the excess or, as the case may be, the money value of the consideration is taken for the purposes of those sections to have been a payment for loss of office.

217 PAYMENT BY COMPANY: REQUIREMENT OF MEMBERS' APPROVAL

(1) A company may not make a payment for loss of office to a director of the company unless the payment has been approved by a resolution of the members of the company.

(2) A company may not make a payment for loss of office to a director of its holding company unless the payment has been approved by a resolution of the members of each of those companies.

(3) A resolution approving a payment to which this section applies must not be passed unless a memorandum setting out particulars of the proposed payment (including its amount) is made available to the members of the company whose approval is sought—

(a) in the case of a written resolution, by being sent or submitted to every eligible member at or before the time at which the proposed resolution is sent or submitted to him;

(b) in the case of a resolution at a meeting, by being made available for inspection by the members both—

(i) at the company's registered office for not less than 15 days ending with the date of the meeting, and

(ii) at the meeting itself.

(4) No approval is required under this section on the part of the members of a body corporate that—

(a) is not a UK-registered company, or

(b) is a wholly-owned subsidiary of another body corporate.

222 PAYMENTS MADE WITHOUT APPROVAL: CIVIL CONSEQUENCES

(1) If a payment is made in contravention of section 217 (payment by company)—

(a) it is held by the recipient on trust for the company making the payment, and

(b) any director who authorised the payment is jointly and severally liable to indemnify the company that made the payment for any loss resulting from it.

...

Supplementary

223 TRANSACTIONS REQUIRING MEMBERS' APPROVAL: APPLICATION OF PROVISIONS TO SHADOW DIRECTORS

(1) For the purposes of—

(a) sections 188 and 189 (directors' service contracts),

(b) sections 190 to 196 (property transactions),

(c) [sections 197] (loans ...), and

(d) sections 215 to [217] (payments for loss of office),

a shadow director is treated as a director.

(2) Any reference in those provisions to loss of office as a director does not apply in relation to loss of a person's status as a shadow director.

224 APPROVAL BY WRITTEN RESOLUTION: ACCIDENTAL FAILURE TO SEND MEMORANDUM

(1) Where—

(a) approval under this Chapter is sought by written resolution, and

(b) a memorandum is required under this Chapter to be sent or submitted to every eligible member before the resolution is passed,

any accidental failure to send or submit the memorandum to one or more members shall be disregarded for the purpose of determining whether the requirement has been met.

(2) Subsection (1) has effect subject to any provision of the company's articles.

225 CASES WHERE APPROVAL IS REQUIRED UNDER MORE THAN ONE PROVISION

(1) Approval may be required under more than one provision of this Chapter.

(2) If so, the requirements of each applicable provision must be met.

(3) This does not require a separate resolution for the purposes of each provision.

Chapter 5 DIRECTORS' SERVICE CONTRACTS

227 DIRECTORS' SERVICE CONTRACTS

(1) For the purposes of this Part a director's "service contract", in relation to a company, means a contract under which—
  (a) a director of the company undertakes personally to perform services (as director or otherwise) for the company, or for a subsidiary of the company, or
  (b) services (as director or otherwise) that a director of the company undertakes personally to perform are made available by a third party to the company, or to a subsidiary of the company.

(2) The provisions of this Part relating to directors' service contracts apply to the terms of a person's appointment as a director of a company.

They are not restricted to contracts for the performance of services outside the scope of the ordinary duties of a director.

228 COPY OF CONTRACT OR MEMORANDUM OF TERMS TO BE AVAILABLE FOR INSPECTION

(1) A company must keep available for inspection—
  (a) a copy of every director's service contract with the company or with a subsidiary of the company, or
  (b) if the contract is not in writing, a written memorandum setting out the terms of the contract.

(2) All the copies and memoranda must be kept available for inspection at—
  (a) the company's registered office, or
  (b) a place specified in regulations under section 1136.

(3) The copies and memoranda must be retained by the company for at least one year from the date of termination or expiry of the contract and must be kept available for inspection during that time.

(4) The company must give notice to the registrar—
  (a) of the place at which the copies and memoranda are kept available for inspection, and
  (b) of any change in that place,
unless they have at all times been kept at the company's registered office.

(5) If default is made in complying with subsection (1), (2) or (3), or default is made for 14 days in complying with subsection (4), an offence is committed by every officer of the company who is in default.

(6) A person guilty of an offence under this section is liable on summary conviction to a fine not exceeding level 3 on the standard scale and, for continued contravention, a daily default fine not exceeding one-tenth of level 3 on the standard scale.

(7) The provisions of this section apply to a variation of a director's service contract as they apply to the original contract.

229 RIGHT OF MEMBER TO INSPECT AND REQUEST COPY

(1) Every copy or memorandum required to be kept under section 228 must be open to inspection by any member of the company without charge.

(2) Any member of the company is entitled, on request and on payment of such fee as may be prescribed, to be provided with a copy of any such copy or memorandum.

The copy must be provided within seven days after the request is received by the company.

(3) If an inspection required under subsection (1) is refused, or default is made in complying with subsection (2), an offence is committed by every officer of the company who is in default.

(4) A person guilty of an offence under this section is liable on summary conviction to a fine not exceeding level 3 on the standard scale and, for continued contravention, a daily default fine not exceeding one-tenth of level 3 on the standard scale.

(5) In the case of any such refusal or default the court may by order compel an immediate inspection or, as the case may be, direct that the copy required be sent to the person requiring it.

230 DIRECTORS' SERVICE CONTRACTS: APPLICATION OF PROVISIONS TO SHADOW DIRECTORS

A shadow director is treated as a director for the purposes of the provisions of this Chapter.

Chapter 6 CONTRACTS WITH SOLE MEMBERS WHO ARE DIRECTORS

231 CONTRACT WITH SOLE MEMBER WHO IS ALSO A DIRECTOR

(1) This section applies where—
- (a) a limited company having only one member enters into a contract with the sole member,
- (b) the sole member is also a director of the company, and
- (c) the contract is not entered into in the ordinary course of the company's business.

(2) The company must, unless the contract is in writing, ensure that the terms of the contract are either—
- (a) set out in a written memorandum, or
- (b) recorded in the minutes of the first meeting of the directors of the company following the making of the contract.

(3) If a company fails to comply with this section an offence is committed by every officer of the company who is in default.

(4) A person guilty of an offence under this section is liable on summary conviction to a fine not exceeding level 5 on the standard scale.

(5) For the purposes of this section a shadow director is treated as a director.

(6) Failure to comply with this section in relation to a contract does not affect the validity of the contract.

(7) Nothing in this section shall be read as excluding the operation of any other enactment or rule of law applying to contracts between a company and a director of the company.

Chapter 7 DIRECTORS' LIABILITIES

Provision protecting directors from liability

232 PROVISIONS PROTECTING DIRECTORS FROM LIABILITY

(1) Any provision that purports to exempt a director of a company (to any extent) from any liability that would otherwise attach to him in connection with any negligence, default, breach of duty or breach of trust in relation to the company is void.

(2) Any provision by which a company directly or indirectly provides an indemnity (to any extent) for a director of the company, or of an associated company, against any liability attaching to him in connection with any negligence, default, breach of duty or breach of trust in relation to the company of which he is a director is void, except as permitted by—
- (a) section 233 (provision of insurance), [or]
- (b) section 234 (qualifying third party indemnity provision) ...

(3) This section applies to any provision, whether contained in a company's articles or in any contract with the company or otherwise.

(4) Nothing in this section prevents a company's articles from making such provision as has previously been lawful for dealing with conflicts of interest.

233 PROVISION OF INSURANCE

Section 232(2) (voidness of provisions for indemnifying directors) does not prevent a company from purchasing and maintaining for a director of the company, or of an associated company, insurance against any such liability as is mentioned in that subsection.

234 QUALIFYING THIRD PARTY INDEMNITY PROVISION

(1) Section 232(2) (voidness of provisions for indemnifying directors) does not apply to qualifying third party indemnity provision.

(2) Third party indemnity provision means provision for indemnity against liability incurred by the director to a person other than the company or an associated company.

Such provision is qualifying third party indemnity provision if the following requirements are met.

(3) The provision must not provide any indemnity against—
- (a) any liability of the director to pay—
  - (i) a fine imposed in criminal proceedings, or
  - (ii) a sum payable to a regulatory authority by way of a penalty in respect of non-compliance with any requirement of a regulatory nature (however arising); or
- (b) any liability incurred by the director—
  - (i) in defending criminal proceedings in which he is convicted, or
  - (ii) in defending civil proceedings brought by the company, or an associated company, in which judgment is given against him, or
  - (iii) in connection with an application for relief (see subsection (6)) in which the court refuses to grant him relief.

(4) The references in subsection (3)(b) to a conviction, judgment or refusal of relief are to the final decision in the proceedings.

(5) For this purpose—
(a) a conviction, judgment or refusal of relief becomes final—
(i) if not appealed against, at the end of the period for bringing an appeal, or
(ii) if appealed against, at the time when the appeal (or any further appeal) is disposed of; and
(b) an appeal is disposed of—
(i) if it is determined and the period for bringing any further appeal has ended, or
(ii) if it is abandoned or otherwise ceases to have effect.

(6) The reference in subsection (3)(b)(iii) to an application for relief is to an application for relief under—

section 661(3) or (4) (power of court to grant relief in case of acquisition of shares by innocent nominee), or

section 1157 (general power of court to grant relief in case of honest and reasonable conduct).

236 QUALIFYING INDEMNITY PROVISION TO BE DISCLOSED IN DIRECTORS' REPORT

(1) This section requires disclosure in the directors' report of—
(a) qualifying third party indemnity provision …
…

Such provision is referred to in this section as "qualifying indemnity provision".

(2) If when a directors' report is approved any qualifying indemnity provision (whether made by the company or otherwise) is in force for the benefit of one or more directors of the company, the report must state that such provision is in force.

(3) If at any time during the financial year to which a directors' report relates any such provision was in force for the benefit of one or more persons who were then directors of the company, the report must state that such provision was in force.

(4) If when a directors' report is approved qualifying indemnity provision made by the company is in force for the benefit of one or more directors of an associated company, the report must state that such provision is in force.

(5) If at any time during the financial year to which a directors' report relates any such provision was in force for the benefit of one or more persons who were then directors of an associated company, the report must state that such provision was in force.

237 COPY OF QUALIFYING INDEMNITY PROVISION TO BE AVAILABLE FOR INSPECTION

(1) This section has effect where qualifying indemnity provision is made for a director of a company, and applies—
(a) to the company of which he is a director (whether the provision is made by that company or an associated company), and
(b) where the provision is made by an associated company, to that company.

(2) That company or, as the case may be, each of them must keep available for inspection—
(a) a copy of the qualifying indemnity provision, or

(b) if the provision is not in writing, a written memorandum setting out its terms.

(3) The copy or memorandum must be kept available for inspection at—
(a) the company's registered office, or
(b) a place specified in regulations under section 1136.

(4) The copy or memorandum must be retained by the company for at least one year from the date of termination or expiry of the provision and must be kept available for inspection during that time.

(5) The company must give notice to the registrar—
(a) of the place at which the copy or memorandum is kept available for inspection, and
(b) of any change in that place,
unless it has at all times been kept at the company's registered office.

(6) If default is made in complying with subsection (2), (3) or (4), or default is made for 14 days in complying with subsection (5), an offence is committed by every officer of the company who is in default.

(7) A person guilty of an offence under this section is liable on summary conviction to a fine not exceeding level 3 on the standard scale and, for continued contravention, a daily default fine not exceeding one-tenth of level 3 on the standard scale.

(8) The provisions of this section apply to a variation of a qualifying indemnity provision as they apply to the original provision.

(9) In this section "qualifying indemnity provision" means—
(a) qualifying third party indemnity provision ...

...

238 RIGHT OF MEMBER TO INSPECT AND REQUEST COPY

(1) Every copy or memorandum required to be kept by a company under section 237 must be open to inspection by any member of the company without charge.

(2) Any member of the company is entitled, on request and on payment of such fee as may be prescribed, to be provided with a copy of any such copy or memorandum.

The copy must be provided within seven days after the request is received by the company.

(3) If an inspection required under subsection (1) is refused, or default is made in complying with subsection (2), an offence is committed by every officer of the company who is in default.

(4) A person guilty of an offence under this section is liable on summary conviction to a fine not exceeding level 3 on the standard scale and, for continued contravention, a daily default fine not exceeding one-tenth of level 3 on the standard scale.

(5) In the case of any such refusal or default the court may by order compel an immediate inspection or, as the case may be, direct that the copy required be sent to the person requiring it.

Ratification of acts giving rise to liability

239 RATIFICATION OF ACTS OF DIRECTORS

(1) This section applies to the ratification by a company of conduct by a director amounting to negligence, default, breach of duty or breach of trust in relation to the company.

(2) The decision of the company to ratify such conduct must be made by resolution of the members of the company.

(3) Where the resolution is proposed as a written resolution neither the director (if a member of the company) nor any member connected with him is an eligible member.

(4) Where the resolution is proposed at a meeting, it is passed only if the necessary majority is obtained disregarding votes in favour of the resolution by the director (if a member of the company) and any member connected with him.

This does not prevent the director or any such member from attending, being counted towards the quorum and taking part in the proceedings at any meeting at which the decision is considered.

(5) For the purposes of this section—
(a) "conduct" includes acts and omissions;
(b) "director" includes a former director;
(c) a shadow director is treated as a director; and
(d) in section 252 (meaning of "connected person"), subsection (3) does not apply (exclusion of person who is himself a director).

(6) Nothing in this section affects—
(a) the validity of a decision taken by unanimous consent of the members of the company, or
(b) any power of the directors to agree not to sue, or to settle or release a claim made by them on behalf of the company.

(7) This section does not affect any other enactment or rule of law imposing additional requirements for valid ratification or any rule of law as to acts that are incapable of being ratified by the company.

Chapter 9 SUPPLEMENTARY PROVISIONS

Provision for employees on cessation or transfer of business

247 POWER TO MAKE PROVISION FOR EMPLOYEES ON CESSATION OR TRANSFER OF BUSINESS

(1) The powers of the directors of a company include (if they would not otherwise do so) power to make provision for the benefit of persons employed or formerly employed by the company, or any of its subsidiaries, in connection with the cessation or the transfer to any person of the whole or part of the undertaking of the company or that subsidiary.

(2) This power is exercisable notwithstanding the general duty imposed by section 172 (duty to promote the success of the company).

(4) The power may only be exercised if sanctioned—
(a) by a resolution of the company, or
(b) by a resolution of the directors,
in accordance with the following provisions.

(5) A resolution of the directors—
(a) must be authorised by the company's articles, and
(b) is not sufficient sanction for payments to or for the benefit of directors, former directors or shadow directors.

(6) Any other requirements of the company's articles as to the exercise of the power conferred by this section must be complied with.

(7) Any payment under this section must be made—
(a) before the commencement of any winding up of the company, and
(b) out of profits of the company that are available for dividend.

Records of meetings of directors

248 MINUTES OF DIRECTORS' MEETINGS

(1) Every company must cause minutes of all proceedings at meetings of its directors to be recorded.

(2) The records must be kept for at least ten years from the date of the meeting.

(3) If a company fails to comply with this section, an offence is committed by every officer of the company who is in default.

(4) A person guilty of an offence under this section is liable on summary conviction to a fine not exceeding level 3 on the standard scale and, for continued contravention, a daily default fine not exceeding one-tenth of level 3 on the standard scale.

249 MINUTES AS EVIDENCE

(1) Minutes recorded in accordance with section 248, if purporting to be authenticated by the chairman of the meeting or by the chairman of the next directors' meeting, are evidence (in Scotland, sufficient evidence) of the proceedings at the meeting.

(2) Where minutes have been made in accordance with that section of the proceedings of a meeting of directors, then, until the contrary is proved—
(a) the meeting is deemed duly held and convened,
(b) all proceedings at the meeting are deemed to have duly taken place, and
(c) all appointments at the meeting are deemed valid.

Meaning of "director" and "shadow director"

250 "DIRECTOR"

In the Companies Acts "director" includes any person occupying the position of director, by whatever name called.

251 "SHADOW DIRECTOR"

(1) In the Companies Acts "shadow director", in relation to a company, means a person in accordance with whose directions or instructions the directors of the company are accustomed to act.

(2) A person is not to be regarded as a shadow director by reason only that the directors act on advice given by him in a professional capacity.

(3) A body corporate is not to be regarded as a shadow director of any of its subsidiary companies for the purposes of—

Chapter 2 (general duties of directors),
Chapter 4 (transactions requiring members' approval), or
Chapter 6 (contract with sole member who is also a director),

by reason only that the directors of the subsidiary are accustomed to act in accordance with its directions or instructions.

Other definitions

252 PERSONS CONNECTED WITH A DIRECTOR

(1) This section defines what is meant by references in this Part to a person being "connected" with a director of a company (or a director being "connected" with a person).

(2) The following persons (and only those persons) are connected with a director of a company—
- (a) members of the director's family (see section 253);
- (b) a body corporate with which the director is connected (as defined in section 254);
- (c) a person acting in his capacity as trustee of a trust—
  - (i) the beneficiaries of which include the director or a person who by virtue of paragraph (a) or (b) is connected with him, or
  - (ii) the terms of which confer a power on the trustees that may be exercised for the benefit of the director or any such person,

  other than a trust for the purposes of an employees' share scheme or a pension scheme;
- (d) a person acting in his capacity as partner—
  - (i) of the director, or
  - (ii) of a person who, by virtue of paragraph (a), (b) or (c), is connected with that director;
- (e) a firm that is a legal person under the law by which it is governed and in which—
  - (i) the director is a partner,
  - (ii) a partner is a person who, by virtue of paragraph (a), (b) or (c) is connected with the director, or
  - (iii) a partner is a firm in which the director is a partner or in which there is a partner who, by virtue of paragraph (a), (b) or (c), is connected with the director.

(3) References in this Part to a person connected with a director of a company do not include a person who is himself a director of the company.

253 MEMBERS OF A DIRECTOR'S FAMILY

(1) This section defines what is meant by references in this Part to members of a director's family.

(2) For the purposes of this Part the members of a director's family are—
- (a) the director's spouse or civil partner;
- (b) any other person (whether of a different sex or the same sex) with whom the director lives as partner in an enduring family relationship;
- (c) the director's children or step-children;
- (d) any children or step-children of a person within paragraph (b) (and who are not children or step-children of the director) who live with the director and have not attained the age of 18;
- (e) the director's parents.

(3) Subsection (2)(b) does not apply if the other person is the director's grandparent or grandchild, sister, brother, aunt or uncle, or nephew or niece.

254 DIRECTOR "CONNECTED WITH" A BODY CORPORATE

(1) This section defines what is meant by references in this Part to a director being "connected with" a body corporate.

(2) A director is connected with a body corporate if, but only if, he and the persons connected with him together—
  (a) are interested in shares comprised in the equity share capital of that body corporate of a nominal value equal to at least 20% of that share capital, or
  (b) are entitled to exercise or control the exercise of more than 20% of the voting power at any general meeting of that body.

(3) The rules set out in Schedule 1 (references to interest in shares or debentures) apply for the purposes of this section.

(4) References in this section to voting power the exercise of which is controlled by a director include voting power whose exercise is controlled by a body corporate controlled by him.

(5) Shares in a company held as treasury shares, and any voting rights attached to such shares, are disregarded for the purposes of this section.

(6) For the avoidance of circularity in the application of section 252 (meaning of "connected person")—
  (a) a body corporate with which a director is connected is not treated for the purposes of this section as connected with him unless it is also connected with him by virtue of subsection (2)(c) or (d) of that section (connection as trustee or partner); and
  (b) a trustee of a trust the beneficiaries of which include (or may include) a body corporate with which a director is connected is not treated for the purposes of this section as connected with a director by reason only of that fact.

255 DIRECTOR "CONTROLLING" A BODY CORPORATE

(1) This section defines what is meant by references in this Part to a director "controlling" a body corporate.

(2) A director of a company is taken to control a body corporate if, but only if—
  (a) he or any person connected with him—
    (i) is interested in any part of the equity share capital of that body, or
    (ii) is entitled to exercise or control the exercise of any part of the voting power at any general meeting of that body, and
  (b) he, the persons connected with him and the other directors of that company, together—
    (i) are interested in more than 50% of that share capital, or
    (ii) are entitled to exercise or control the exercise of more than 50% of that voting power.

(3) The rules set out in Schedule 1 (references to interest in shares or debentures) apply for the purposes of this section.

(4) References in this section to voting power the exercise of which is controlled by a director include voting power whose exercise is controlled by a body corporate controlled by him.

(5) Shares in a company held as treasury shares, and any voting rights attached to such shares, are disregarded for the purposes of this section.

(6) For the avoidance of circularity in the application of section 252 (meaning of "connected person")—
  (a) a body corporate with which a director is connected is not treated for the purposes of this section as connected with him unless it is also connected with him by virtue of subsection (2)(c) or (d) of that section (connection as trustee or partner); and

(b) a trustee of a trust the beneficiaries of which include (or may include) a body corporate with which a director is connected is not treated for the purposes of this section as connected with a director by reason only of that fact.

256 ASSOCIATED BODIES CORPORATE

For the purposes of this Part—

(a) bodies corporate are associated if one is a subsidiary of the other or both are subsidiaries of the same body corporate, and

(b) companies are associated if one is a subsidiary of the other or both are subsidiaries of the same body corporate.

257 REFERENCES TO COMPANY'S CONSTITUTION

(1) References in this Part to a company's constitution include—
  (a) any resolution or other decision come to in accordance with the constitution, and
  (b) any decision by the members of the company, or a class of members, that is treated by virtue of any enactment or rule of law as equivalent to a decision by the company.

(2) This is in addition to the matters mentioned in section 17 (general provision as to matters contained in company's constitution).

General

258 POWER TO INCREASE FINANCIAL LIMITS

(1) The Secretary of State may by order substitute for any sum of money specified in this Part a larger sum specified in the order.

(2) An order under this section is subject to negative resolution procedure.

(3) An order does not have effect in relation to anything done or not done before it comes into force.

Accordingly, proceedings in respect of any liability incurred before that time may be continued or instituted as if the order had not been made.

259 TRANSACTIONS UNDER FOREIGN LAW

For the purposes of this Part it is immaterial whether the law that (apart from this Act) governs an arrangement or transaction is the law of the United Kingdom, or a part of it, or not.

Part 11 DERIVATIVE CLAIMS AND PROCEEDINGS BY MEMBERS

Chapter 1 DERIVATIVE CLAIMS IN ENGLAND AND WALES OR NORTHERN IRELAND

260 DERIVATIVE CLAIMS

(1) This Chapter applies to proceedings in England and Wales ... by a member of a company—
  (a) in respect of a cause of action vested in the company, and
  (b) seeking relief on behalf of the company.

This is referred to in this Chapter as a "derivative claim".

(2) A derivative claim may only be brought—
  (a) under this Chapter, or
  (b) in pursuance of an order of the court in proceedings under section 994 (proceedings for protection of members against unfair prejudice).

(3) A derivative claim under this Chapter may be brought only in respect of a cause of action arising from an actual or proposed act or omission involving negligence, default, breach of duty or breach of trust by a director of the company.

The cause of action may be against the director or another person (or both).

(4) It is immaterial whether the cause of action arose before or after the person seeking to bring or continue the derivative claim became a member of the company.

(5) For the purposes of this Chapter—
(a) "director" includes a former director;
(b) a shadow director is treated as a director; and
(c) references to a member of a company include a person who is not a member but to whom shares in the company have been transferred or transmitted by operation of law.

261 APPLICATION FOR PERMISSION TO CONTINUE DERIVATIVE CLAIM

(1) A member of a company who brings a derivative claim under this Chapter must apply to the court for permission ... to continue it.

(2) If it appears to the court that the application and the evidence filed by the applicant in support of it do not disclose a prima facie case for giving permission ..., the court—
(a) must dismiss the application, and
(b) may make any consequential order it considers appropriate.

(3) If the application is not dismissed under subsection (2), the court—
(a) may give directions as to the evidence to be provided by the company, and
(b) may adjourn the proceedings to enable the evidence to be obtained.

(4) On hearing the application, the court may—
(a) give permission ... to continue the claim on such terms as it thinks fit,
(b) refuse permission ... and dismiss the claim, or
(c) adjourn the proceedings on the application and give such directions as it thinks fit.

262 APPLICATION FOR PERMISSION TO CONTINUE CLAIM AS A DERIVATIVE CLAIM

(1) This section applies where—
(a) a company has brought a claim, and
(b) the cause of action on which the claim is based could be pursued as a derivative claim under this Chapter.

(2) A member of the company may apply to the court for permission ... to continue the claim as a derivative claim on the ground that—
(a) the manner in which the company commenced or continued the claim amounts to an abuse of the process of the court,
(b) the company has failed to prosecute the claim diligently, and
(c) it is appropriate for the member to continue the claim as a derivative claim.

(3) If it appears to the court that the application and the evidence filed by the applicant in support of it do not disclose a prima facie case for giving permission ..., the court—
(a) must dismiss the application, and
(b) may make any consequential order it considers appropriate.

(4) If the application is not dismissed under subsection (3), the court—
(a) may give directions as to the evidence to be provided by the company, and
(b) may adjourn the proceedings to enable the evidence to be obtained.

(5) On hearing the application, the court may—
(a) give permission ... to continue the claim as a derivative claim on such terms as it thinks fit,
(b) refuse permission ... and dismiss the application, or
(c) adjourn the proceedings on the application and give such directions as it thinks fit.

263 WHETHER PERMISSION TO BE GIVEN

(1) The following provisions have effect where a member of a company applies for permission ... under section 261 or 262.

(2) Permission ... must be refused if the court is satisfied—
(a) that a person acting in accordance with section 172 (duty to promote the success of the company) would not seek to continue the claim, or
(b) where the cause of action arises from an act or omission that is yet to occur, that the act or omission has been authorised by the company, or
(c) where the cause of action arises from an act or omission that has already occurred, that the act or omission—
(i) was authorised by the company before it occurred, or
(ii) has been ratified by the company since it occurred.

(3) In considering whether to give permission ... the court must take into account, in particular—
(a) whether the member is acting in good faith in seeking to continue the claim;
(b) the importance that a person acting in accordance with section 172 (duty to promote the success of the company) would attach to continuing it;
(c) where the cause of action results from an act or omission that is yet to occur, whether the act or omission could be, and in the circumstances would be likely to be—
(i) authorised by the company before it occurs, or
(ii) ratified by the company after it occurs;
(d) where the cause of action arises from an act or omission that has already occurred, whether the act or omission could be, and in the circumstances would be likely to be, ratified by the company;
(e) whether the company has decided not to pursue the claim;
(f) whether the act or omission in respect of which the claim is brought gives rise to a cause of action that the member could pursue in his own right rather than on behalf of the company.

(4) In considering whether to give permission ... the court shall have particular regard to any evidence before it as to the views of members of the company who have no personal interest, direct or indirect, in the matter.

(5) The Secretary of State may by regulations—
(a) amend subsection (2) so as to alter or add to the circumstances in which permission ... is to be refused;
(b) amend subsection (3) so as to alter or add to the matters that the court is required to take into account in considering whether to give permission... .

(6) Before making any such regulations the Secretary of State shall consult such persons as he considers appropriate.

(7) Regulations under this section are subject to affirmative resolution procedure.

264 APPLICATION FOR PERMISSION TO CONTINUE DERIVATIVE CLAIM BROUGHT BY ANOTHER MEMBER

(1) This section applies where a member of a company ("the claimant")—
  (a) has brought a derivative claim,
  (b) has continued as a derivative claim a claim brought by the company, or
  (c) has continued a derivative claim under this section.

(2) Another member of the company ("the applicant") may apply to the court for permission ... to continue the claim on the ground that—
  (a) the manner in which the proceedings have been commenced or continued by the claimant amounts to an abuse of the process of the court,
  (b) the claimant has failed to prosecute the claim diligently, and
  (c) it is appropriate for the applicant to continue the claim as a derivative claim.

(3) If it appears to the court that the application and the evidence filed by the applicant in support of it do not disclose a prima facie case for giving permission ..., the court—
  (a) must dismiss the application, and
  (b) may make any consequential order it considers appropriate.

(4) If the application is not dismissed under subsection (3), the court—
  (a) may give directions as to the evidence to be provided by the company, and
  (b) may adjourn the proceedings to enable the evidence to be obtained.

(5) On hearing the application, the court may—
  (a) give permission ... to continue the claim on such terms as it thinks fit,
  (b) refuse permission ... and dismiss the application, or
  (c) adjourn the proceedings on the application and give such directions as it thinks fit.

Chapter 2 DERIVATIVE PROCEEDINGS IN SCOTLAND

265 DERIVATIVE PROCEEDINGS

(1) In Scotland, a member of a company may raise proceedings in respect of an act or omission specified in subsection (3) in order to protect the interests of the company and obtain a remedy on its behalf.

(2) A member of a company may raise such proceedings only under subsection (1).

(3) The act or omission referred to in subsection (1) is any actual or proposed act or omission involving negligence, default, breach of duty or breach of trust by a director of the company.

(4) Proceedings may be raised under subsection (1) against (either or both)—
  (a) the director referred to in subsection (3), or
  (b) another person.

(5) It is immaterial whether the act or omission in respect of which the proceedings are to be raised or, in the case of continuing proceedings under section 267 or 269, are raised, arose before or after the person seeking to raise or continue them became a member of the company.

(6) This section does not affect—
  (a) any right of a member of a company to raise proceedings in respect of an act or omission specified in subsection (3) in order to protect his own interests and obtain a remedy on his own behalf, or

(b) the court's power to make an order under section 996(2)(c) or anything done under such an order.

(7) In this Chapter—
(a) proceedings raised under subsection (1) are referred to as "derivative proceedings",
(b) the act or omission in respect of which they are raised is referred to as the "cause of action",
(c) "director" includes a former director,
(d) references to a director include a shadow director, and
(e) references to a member of a company include a person who is not a member but to whom shares in the company have been transferred or transmitted by operation of law.

266 REQUIREMENT FOR LEAVE AND NOTICE

(1) Derivative proceedings may be raised by a member of a company only with the leave of the court.

(2) An application for leave must—
(a) specify the cause of action, and
(b) summarise the facts on which the derivative proceedings are to be based.

(3) If it appears to the court that the application and the evidence produced by the applicant in support of it do not disclose a prima facie case for granting it, the court—
(a) must refuse the application, and
(b) may make any consequential order it considers appropriate.

(4) If the application is not refused under subsection (3)—
(a) the applicant must serve the application on the company,
(b) the court—
(i) may make an order requiring evidence to be produced by the company, and
(ii) may adjourn the proceedings on the application to enable the evidence to be obtained, and
(c) the company is entitled to take part in the further proceedings on the application.

(5) On hearing the application, the court may—
(a) grant the application on such terms as it thinks fit,
(b) refuse the application, or
(c) adjourn the proceedings on the application and make such order as to further procedure as it thinks fit.

267 APPLICATION TO CONTINUE PROCEEDINGS AS DERIVATIVE PROCEEDINGS

(1) This section applies where—
(a) a company has raised proceedings, and
(b) the proceedings are in respect of an act or omission which could be the basis for derivative proceedings.

(2) A member of the company may apply to the court to be substituted for the company in the proceedings, and for the proceedings to continue in consequence as derivative proceedings, on the ground that—
(a) the manner in which the company commenced or continued the proceedings amounts to an abuse of the process of the court,

(b) the company has failed to prosecute the proceedings diligently, and
(c) it is appropriate for the member to be substituted for the company in the proceedings.

(3) If it appears to the court that the application and the evidence produced by the applicant in support of it do not disclose a prima facie case for granting it, the court—
(a) must refuse the application, and
(b) may make any consequential order it considers appropriate.

(4) If the application is not refused under subsection (3)—
(a) the applicant must serve the application on the company,
(b) the court—
(i) may make an order requiring evidence to be produced by the company, and
(ii) may adjourn the proceedings on the application to enable the evidence to be obtained, and
(c) the company is entitled to take part in the further proceedings on the application.

(5) On hearing the application, the court may—
(a) grant the application on such terms as it thinks fit,
(b) refuse the application, or
(c) adjourn the proceedings on the application and make such order as to further procedure as it thinks fit.

268 GRANTING OF LEAVE

(1) The court must refuse leave to raise derivative proceedings or an application under section 267 if satisfied—
(a) that a person acting in accordance with section 172 (duty to promote the success of the company) would not seek to raise or continue the proceedings (as the case may be), or
(b) where the cause of action is an act or omission that is yet to occur, that the act or omission has been authorised by the company, or
(c) where the cause of action is an act or omission that has already occurred, that the act or omission—
(i) was authorised by the company before it occurred, or
(ii) has been ratified by the company since it occurred.

(2) In considering whether to grant leave to raise derivative proceedings or an application under section 267, the court must take into account, in particular—
(a) whether the member is acting in good faith in seeking to raise or continue the proceedings (as the case may be),
(b) the importance that a person acting in accordance with section 172 (duty to promote the success of the company) would attach to raising or continuing them (as the case may be),
(c) where the cause of action is an act or omission that is yet to occur, whether the act or omission could be, and in the circumstances would be likely to be—
(i) authorised by the company before it occurs, or
(ii) ratified by the company after it occurs,
(d) where the cause of action is an act or omission that has already occurred, whether the act or omission could be, and in the circumstances would be likely to be, ratified by the company,
(e) whether the company has decided not to raise proceedings in respect of the same cause of action or to persist in the proceedings (as the case may be),
(f) whether the cause of action is one which the member could pursue in his own right rather than on behalf of the company.

(3) In considering whether to grant leave to raise derivative proceedings or an application under section 267, the court shall have particular regard to any evidence before it as to the views of members of the company who have no personal interest, direct or indirect, in the matter.

(4) The Secretary of State may by regulations—
(a) amend subsection (1) so as to alter or add to the circumstances in which leave or an application is to be refused,
(b) amend subsection (2) so as to alter or add to the matters that the court is required to take into account in considering whether to grant leave or an application.

(5) Before making any such regulations the Secretary of State shall consult such persons as he considers appropriate.

(6) Regulations under this section are subject to affirmative resolution procedure.

269 APPLICATION BY MEMBER TO BE SUBSTITUTED FOR MEMBER PURSUING DERIVATIVE PROCEEDINGS

(1) This section applies where a member of a company ("the claimant")—
(a) has raised derivative proceedings,
(b) has continued as derivative proceedings raised by the company, or
(c) has continued derivative proceedings under this section.

(2) Another member of the company ("the applicant") may apply to the court to be substituted for the claimant in the action on the ground that—
(a) the manner in which the proceedings have been commenced or continued by the claimant amounts to an abuse of the process of the court,
(b) the claimant has failed to prosecute the proceedings diligently, and
(c) it is appropriate for the applicant to be substituted for the claimant in the proceedings.

(3) If it appears to the court that the application and the evidence produced by the applicant in support of it do not disclose a prima facie case for granting it, the court—
(a) must refuse the application, and
(b) may make any consequential order it considers appropriate.

(4) If the application is not refused under subsection (3)—
(a) the applicant must serve the application on the company,
(b) the court—
(i) may make an order requiring evidence to be produced by the company, and
(ii) may adjourn the proceedings on the application to enable the evidence to be obtained, and
(c) the company is entitled to take part in the further proceedings on the application.

(5) On hearing the application, the court may—
(a) grant the application on such terms as it thinks fit,
(b) refuse the application, or
(c) adjourn the proceedings on the application and make such order as to further procedure as it thinks fit.

Part 12 COMPANY SECRETARIES

Private companies

270 PRIVATE COMPANY NOT REQUIRED TO HAVE SECRETARY

(1) A private company is not required to have a secretary.

Public companies

271 PUBLIC COMPANY REQUIRED TO HAVE SECRETARY

A public company must have a secretary.

273 QUALIFICATIONS OF SECRETARIES OF PUBLIC COMPANIES

(1) It is the duty of the directors of a public company to take all reasonable steps to secure that the secretary (or each joint secretary) of the company—
  (a) is a person who appears to them to have the requisite knowledge and experience to discharge the functions of secretary of the company, and
  (b) has one or more of the following qualifications.

(2) The qualifications are—
  (a) that he has held the office of secretary of a public company for at least three of the five years immediately preceding his appointment as secretary;
  (b) that he is a member of any of the bodies specified in subsection (3);
  (c) that he is a barrister, advocate or solicitor called or admitted in any part of the United Kingdom;
  (d) that he is a person who, by virtue of his holding or having held any other position or his being a member of any other body, appears to the directors to be capable of discharging the functions of secretary of the company.

(3) The bodies referred to in subsection (2)(b) are—
  (a) the Institute of Chartered Accountants in England and Wales;
  (b) the Institute of Chartered Accountants of Scotland;
  (c) the Association of Chartered Certified Accountants;
  (d) the Institute of Chartered Accountants in Ireland;
  (e) the Institute of Chartered Secretaries and Administrators;
  (f) the Chartered Institute of Management Accountants;
  (g) the Chartered Institute of Public Finance and Accountancy.

Part 13 RESOLUTIONS AND MEETINGS

Chapter 1 GENERAL PROVISIONS ABOUT RESOLUTIONS

281 RESOLUTIONS

(1) A resolution of the members (or of a class of members) of a private company must be passed—
  (a) as a written resolution in accordance with Chapter 2, or
  (b) at a meeting of the members (to which the provisions of Chapter 3 apply).

(2) A resolution of the members (or of a class of members) of a public company must be passed at a meeting of the members (to which the provisions of Chapter 3 and, where relevant, Chapter 4 apply).

(3) Where a provision of the Companies Acts—
  (a) requires a resolution of a company, or of the members (or a class of members) of a company, and
  (b) does not specify what kind of resolution is required,
what is required is an ordinary resolution unless the company's articles require a higher majority (or unanimity).

(4) Nothing in this Part affects any enactment or rule of law as to—

(a) things done otherwise than by passing a resolution,
(b) circumstances in which a resolution is or is not treated as having been passed, or
(c) cases in which a person is precluded from alleging that a resolution has not been duly passed.

282 ORDINARY RESOLUTIONS

(1) An ordinary resolution of the members (or of a class of members) of a company means a resolution that is passed by a simple majority.

(2) A written resolution is passed by a simple majority if it is passed by members representing a simple majority of the total voting rights of eligible members (see Chapter 2).

(3) A resolution passed at a meeting on a show of hands is passed by a simple majority if it is passed by a simple majority of the votes cast by those entitled to vote.

(4) A resolution passed on a poll taken at a meeting is passed by a simple majority if it is passed by members representing a simple majority of the total voting rights of members who (being entitled to do so) vote in person, by proxy or in advance (see section 322A) on the resolution.

(5) Anything that may be done by ordinary resolution may also be done by special resolution.

283 SPECIAL RESOLUTIONS

(1) A special resolution of the members (or of a class of members) of a company means a resolution passed by a majority of not less than 75%.

(2) A written resolution is passed by a majority of not less than 75% if it is passed by members representing not less than 75% of the total voting rights of eligible members (see Chapter 2).

(3) Where a resolution of a private company is passed as a written resolution—
(a) the resolution is not a special resolution unless it stated that it was proposed as a special resolution, and
(b) if the resolution so stated, it may only be passed as a special resolution.

(4) A resolution passed at a meeting on a show of hands is passed by a majority of not less than 75% if it is passed by not less than 75% of the votes cast by those entitled to vote.

(5) A resolution passed on a poll taken at a meeting is passed by a majority of not less than 75% if it is passed by members representing not less than 75% of the total voting rights of the members who (being entitled to do so) vote in person, by proxy or in advance (see section 322A) on the resolution.

(6) Where a resolution is passed at a meeting—
(a) the resolution is not a special resolution unless the notice of the meeting included the text of the resolution and specified the intention to propose the resolution as a special resolution, and
(b) if the notice of the meeting so specified, the resolution may only be passed as a special resolution.

284 VOTES: GENERAL RULES

(1) On a vote on a written resolution—
(a) in the case of a company having a share capital, every member has one vote in respect of each share or each £10 of stock held by him, and
(b) in any other case, every member has one vote.

(2) On a vote on a resolution on a show of hands at a meeting, each member present in person has one vote.

(3) On a vote on a resolution on a poll taken at a meeting—
(a) in the case of a company having a share capital, every member has one vote in respect of each share or each £10 of stock held by him, and
(b) in any other case, every member has one vote.

(4) The provisions of this section have effect subject to any provision of the company's articles.

(5) Nothing in this section is to be read as restricting the effect of—

section 152 (exercise of rights by nominees),
section 285 (voting by proxy),
section 322 (exercise of voting rights on poll),
section 322A (voting on a poll: votes cast in advance), or
section 323 (representation of corporations at meetings).

285 VOTING BY PROXY

(1) On a vote on a resolution on a show of hands at a meeting, every proxy present who has been duly appointed by one or more members entitled to vote on the resolution has one vote.

This is subject to subsection (2).

(2) On a vote on a resolution on a show of hands at a meeting, a proxy has one vote for and one vote against the resolution if—
(a) the proxy has been duly appointed by more than one member entitled to vote on the resolution, and
(b) the proxy has been instructed by one or more of those members to vote for the resolution and by one or more other of those members to vote against it.

(3) On a poll taken at a meeting of a company all or any of the voting rights of a member may be exercised by one or more duly appointed proxies.

(4) Where a member appoints more than one proxy, subsection (3) does not authorize the exercise by the proxies taken together of more extensive voting rights than could be exercised by the member in person.

(5) Subsections (1) and (2) have effect subject to any provision of the company's articles.

285A VOTING RIGHTS ON POLL OR WRITTEN RESOLUTION

In relation to a resolution required or authorised by an enactment, if a private company's articles provide that a member has a different number of votes in relation to a resolution when it is passed as a written resolution and when it is passed on a poll taken at a meeting—

(a) the provision about how many votes a member has in relation to the resolution passed on a poll is void, and

(b) a member has the same number of votes in relation to the resolution when it is passed on a poll as the member has when it is passed as a written resolution.

286 VOTES OF JOINT HOLDERS OF SHARES

(1) In the case of joint holders of shares of a company, only the vote of the senior holder who votes (and any proxies duly authorised by him) may be counted by the company.

(2) For the purposes of this section, the senior holder of a share is determined by the order in which the names of the joint holders appear in the register of members.

(3) Subsections (1) and (2) have effect subject to any provision of the company's articles.

287 SAVING FOR PROVISIONS OF ARTICLES AS TO DETERMINATION OF ENTITLEMENT TO VOTE

Nothing in this Chapter affects—

(a) any provision of a company's articles—
  (i) requiring an objection to a person's entitlement to vote on a resolution to be made in accordance with the articles, and
  (ii) for the determination of any such objection to be final and conclusive, or

(b) the grounds on which such a determination may be questioned in legal proceedings.

Chapter 2 WRITTEN RESOLUTIONS

General provisions about written resolutions

288 WRITTEN RESOLUTIONS OF PRIVATE COMPANIES

(1) In the Companies Acts a "written resolution" means a resolution of a private company proposed and passed in accordance with this Chapter.

(2) The following may not be passed as a written resolution—
  (a) a resolution under section 168 removing a director before the expiration of his period of office;
  (b) a resolution under section 510 removing an auditor before the expiration of his term of office.

(3) A resolution may be proposed as a written resolution—
  (a) by the directors of a private company (see section 291), or
  (b) by the members of a private company (see sections 292 to 295).

(4) References in enactments passed or made before this Chapter comes into force to—
  (a) a resolution of a company in general meeting, or
  (b) a resolution of a meeting of a class of members of the company,
  have effect as if they included references to a written resolution of the members, or of a class of members, of a private company (as appropriate).

(5) A written resolution of a private company has effect as if passed (as the case may be)—
  (a) by the company in general meeting, or
  (b) by a meeting of a class of members of the company,
  and references in enactments passed or made before this section comes into force to a meeting at which a resolution is passed or to members voting in favour of a resolution shall be construed accordingly.

289 ELIGIBLE MEMBERS

(1) In relation to a resolution proposed as a written resolution of a private company, the eligible members are the members who would have been entitled to vote on the resolution on the circulation date of the resolution (see section 290).

(2) If the persons entitled to vote on a written resolution change during the course of the day that is the circulation date of the resolution, the eligible members are the persons entitled to vote on the resolution at the time that the first copy of the resolution is sent or submitted to a member for his agreement.

Circulation of written resolutions

290 CIRCULATION DATE

References in this Part to the circulation date of a written resolution are to the date on which copies of it are sent or submitted to members in accordance with this Chapter (or if copies are sent or submitted to members on different days, to the first of those days).

291 CIRCULATION OF WRITTEN RESOLUTIONS PROPOSED BY DIRECTORS

(1) This section applies to a resolution proposed as a written resolution by the directors of the company.

(2) The company must send or submit a copy of the resolution to every eligible member.

(3) The company must do so—
 (a) by sending copies at the same time (so far as reasonably practicable) to all eligible members in hard copy form, in electronic form or by means of a website, or
 (b) if it is possible to do so without undue delay, by submitting the same copy to each eligible member in turn (or different copies to each of a number of eligible members in turn),

or by sending copies to some members in accordance with paragraph (a) and submitting a copy or copies to other members in accordance with paragraph (b).

(4) The copy of the resolution must be accompanied by a statement informing the member—
 (a) how to signify agreement to the resolution (see section 296), and
 (b) as to the date by which the resolution must be passed if it is not to lapse (see section 297).

(5) In the event of default in complying with this section, an offence is committed by every officer of the company who is in default.

(6) A person guilty of an offence under this section is liable—
 (a) on conviction on indictment, to a fine;
 (b) on summary conviction, to a fine not exceeding the statutory maximum.

(7) The validity of the resolution, if passed, is not affected by a failure to comply with this section.

292 MEMBERS' POWER TO REQUIRE CIRCULATION OF WRITTEN RESOLUTION

(1) The members of a private company may require the company to circulate a resolution that may properly be moved and is proposed to be moved as a written resolution.

(2) Any resolution may properly be moved as a written resolution unless—
 (a) it would, if passed, be ineffective (whether by reason of inconsistency with any enactment or the company's constitution or otherwise),
 (b) it is defamatory of any person, or
 (c) it is frivolous or vexatious.

(3) Where the members require a company to circulate a resolution they may require the company to circulate with it a statement of not more than 1,000 words on the subject matter of the resolution.

(4) A company is required to circulate the resolution and any accompanying statement once it has received requests that it do so from members representing not less than the requisite percentage of the total voting rights of all members entitled to vote on the resolution.

(5) The "requisite percentage" is 5% or such lower percentage as is specified for this purpose in the company's articles.

(6) A request—
(a) may be in hard copy form or in electronic form,
(b) must identify the resolution and any accompanying statement, and
(c) must be authenticated by the person or persons making it.

293 CIRCULATION OF WRITTEN RESOLUTION PROPOSED BY MEMBERS

(1) A company that is required under section 292 to circulate a resolution must send or submit to every eligible member—
(a) a copy of the resolution, and
(b) a copy of any accompanying statement.
This is subject to section 294(2) (deposit or tender of sum in respect of expenses of circulation) and section 295 (application not to circulate members' statement).

(2) The company must do so—
(a) by sending copies at the same time (so far as reasonably practicable) to all eligible members in hard copy form, in electronic form or by means of a website, or
(b) if it is possible to do so without undue delay, by submitting the same copy to each eligible member in turn (or different copies to each of a number of eligible members in turn),
or by sending copies to some members in accordance with paragraph (a) and submitting a copy or copies to other members in accordance with paragraph (b).

(3) The company must send or submit the copies (or, if copies are sent or submitted to members on different days, the first of those copies) not more than 21 days after it becomes subject to the requirement under section 292 to circulate the resolution.

(4) The copy of the resolution must be accompanied by guidance as to—
(a) how to signify agreement to the resolution (see section 296), and
(b) the date by which the resolution must be passed if it is not to lapse (see section 297).

(5) In the event of default in complying with this section, an offence is committed by every officer of the company who is in default.

(6) A person guilty of an offence under this section is liable—
(a) on conviction on indictment, to a fine;
(b) on summary conviction, to a fine not exceeding the statutory maximum.

(7) The validity of the resolution, if passed, is not affected by a failure to comply with this section.

294 EXPENSES OF CIRCULATION

(1) The expenses of the company in complying with section 293 must be paid by the members who requested the circulation of the resolution unless the company resolves otherwise.

(2) Unless the company has previously so resolved, it is not bound to comply with that section unless there is deposited with or tendered to it a sum reasonably sufficient to meet its expenses in doing so.

295 APPLICATION NOT TO CIRCULATE MEMBERS' STATEMENT

(1) A company is not required to circulate a members' statement under section 293 if, on an application by the company or another person who claims to be aggrieved, the court is satisfied that the rights conferred by section 292 and that section are being abused.

(2) The court may order the members who requested the circulation of the statement to pay the whole or part of the company's costs (in Scotland, expenses) on such an application, even if they are not parties to the application.

Agreeing to written resolutions

296 PROCEDURE FOR SIGNIFYING AGREEMENT TO WRITTEN RESOLUTION

(1) A member signifies his agreement to a proposed written resolution when the company receives from him (or from someone acting on his behalf) an authenticated document—
  (a) identifying the resolution to which it relates, and
  (b) indicating his agreement to the resolution.

(2) The document must be sent to the company in hard copy form or in electronic form.

(3) A member's agreement to a written resolution, once signified, may not be revoked.

(4) A written resolution is passed when the required majority of eligible members have signified their agreement to it.

297 PERIOD FOR AGREEING TO WRITTEN RESOLUTION

(1) A proposed written resolution lapses if it is not passed before the end of—
  (a) the period specified for this purpose in the company's articles, or
  (b) if none is specified, the period of 28 days beginning with the circulation date.

(2) The agreement of a member to a written resolution is ineffective if signified after the expiry of that period.

Supplementary

298 SENDING DOCUMENTS RELATING TO WRITTEN RESOLUTIONS BY ELECTRONIC MEANS

(1) Where a company has given an electronic address in any document containing or accompanying a proposed written resolution, it is deemed to have agreed that any document or information relating to that resolution may be sent by electronic means to that address (subject to any conditions or limitations specified in the document).

(2) In this section "electronic address" means any address or number used for the purposes of sending or receiving documents or information by electronic means.

299 PUBLICATION OF WRITTEN RESOLUTION ON WEBSITE

(1) This section applies where a company sends—

(a) a written resolution, or
(b) a statement relating to a written resolution,
to a person by means of a website.

(2) The resolution or statement is not validly sent for the purposes of this Chapter unless the resolution is available on the website throughout the period beginning with the circulation date and ending on the date on which the resolution lapses under section 297.

300 RELATIONSHIP BETWEEN THIS CHAPTER AND PROVISIONS OF COMPANY'S ARTICLES

A provision of the articles of a private company is void in so far as it would have the effect that a resolution that is required by or otherwise provided for in an enactment could not be proposed and passed as a written resolution.

Chapter 3 RESOLUTIONS AT MEETINGS

General provisions about resolutions at meetings

301 RESOLUTIONS AT GENERAL MEETINGS

A resolution of the members of a company is validly passed at a general meeting if—

(a) notice of the meeting and of the resolution is given, and

(b) the meeting is held and conducted,

in accordance with the provisions of this Chapter (and, where relevant, Chapter 4) and the company's articles.

Calling meetings

302 DIRECTORS' POWER TO CALL GENERAL MEETINGS

The directors of a company may call a general meeting of the company.

303 MEMBERS' POWER TO REQUIRE DIRECTORS TO CALL GENERAL MEETING

(1) The members of a company may require the directors to call a general meeting of the company.

(2) The directors are required to call a general meeting once the company has received requests to do so from—
(a) members representing at least 5% of such of the paid-up capital of the company as carries the right of voting at general meetings of the company (excluding any paid-up capital held as treasury shares); or
(b) in the case of a company not having a share capital, members who represent at least 5% of the total voting rights of all the members having a right to vote at general meetings.

(4) A request—
(a) must state the general nature of the business to be dealt with at the meeting, and
(b) may include the text of a resolution that may properly be moved and is intended to be moved at the meeting.

(5) A resolution may properly be moved at a meeting unless—
(a) it would, if passed, be ineffective (whether by reason of inconsistency with any enactment or the company's constitution or otherwise),
(b) it is defamatory of any person, or
(c) it is frivolous or vexatious.

(6) A request—
(a) may be in hard copy form or in electronic form, and
(b) must be authenticated by the person or persons making it.

304 DIRECTORS' DUTY TO CALL MEETINGS REQUIRED BY MEMBERS

(1) Directors required under section 303 to call a general meeting of the company must call a meeting—
(a) within 21 days from the date on which they become subject to the requirement, and
(b) to be held on a date not more than 28 days after the date of the notice convening the meeting.

(2) If the requests received by the company identify a resolution intended to be moved at the meeting, the notice of the meeting must include notice of the resolution.

(3) The business that may be dealt with at the meeting includes a resolution of which notice is given in accordance with this section.

(4) If the resolution is to be proposed as a special resolution, the directors are treated as not having duly called the meeting if they do not give the required notice of the resolution in accordance with section 283.

305 POWER OF MEMBERS TO CALL MEETING AT COMPANY'S EXPENSE

(1) If the directors—
(a) are required under section 303 to call a meeting, and
(b) do not do so in accordance with section 304,
the members who requested the meeting, or any of them representing more than one half of the total voting rights of all of them, may themselves call a general meeting.

(2) Where the requests received by the company included the text of a resolution intended to be moved at the meeting, the notice of the meeting must include notice of the resolution.

(3) The meeting must be called for a date not more than three months after the date on which the directors become subject to the requirement to call a meeting.

(4) The meeting must be called in the same manner, as nearly as possible, as that in which meetings are required to be called by directors of the company.

(5) The business which may be dealt with at the meeting includes a resolution of which notice is given in accordance with this section.

(6) Any reasonable expenses incurred by the members requesting the meeting by reason of the failure of the directors duly to call a meeting must be reimbursed by the company.

(7) Any sum so reimbursed shall be retained by the company out of any sums due or to become due from the company by way of fees or other remuneration in respect of the services of such of the directors as were in default.

306 POWER OF COURT TO ORDER MEETING

(1) This section applies if for any reason it is impracticable—
  (a) to call a meeting of a company in any manner in which meetings of that company may be called, or
  (b) to conduct the meeting in the manner prescribed by the company's articles or this Act.

(2) The court may, either of its own motion or on the application—
  (a) of a director of the company, or
  (b) of a member of the company who would be entitled to vote at the meeting,
order a meeting to be called, held and conducted in any manner the court thinks fit.

(3) Where such an order is made, the court may give such ancillary or consequential directions as it thinks expedient.

(4) Such directions may include a direction that one member of the company present at the meeting be deemed to constitute a quorum.

(5) A meeting called, held and conducted in accordance with an order under this section is deemed for all purposes to be a meeting of the company duly called, held and conducted.

Notice of meetings

307 NOTICE REQUIRED OF GENERAL MEETING

(A1) This section applies to—
  (a) a general meeting of a company that is not a traded company; and
  (b) a general meeting of a traded company that is an opted-in company (as defined by section 971(1)), where—
    (i) the meeting is held to decide whether to take any action that might result in the frustration of a takeover bid for the company; or
    (ii) the meeting is held by virtue of section 969 (power of offeror to require general meeting to be held).

(A2) For corresponding provision in relation to general meetings of traded companies (other than meetings within subsection (A1)(b)), see section 307A.

(1) A general meeting of a private company (other than an adjourned meeting) must be called by notice of at least 14 days.

(2) A general meeting of a public company (other than an adjourned meeting) must be called by notice of—
  (a) in the case of an annual general meeting, at least 21 days, and
  (b) in any other case, at least 14 days.

(3) The company's articles may require a longer period of notice than that specified in subsection (1) or (2).

(4) A general meeting may be called by shorter notice than that otherwise required if shorter notice is agreed by the members.

(5) The shorter notice must be agreed to by a majority in number of the members having a right to attend and vote at the meeting, being a majority who—
  (a) together hold not less than the requisite percentage in nominal value of the shares giving a right to attend and vote at the meeting (excluding any shares in the company held as treasury shares), or
  (b) in the case of a company not having a share capital, together represent not less than the requisite percentage of the total voting rights at that meeting of all the members.

(6) The requisite percentage is—
(a) in the case of a private company, 90% or such higher percentage (not exceeding 95%) as may be specified in the company's articles;
(b) in the case of a public company, 95%.

(7) Subsections (5) and (6) do not apply to an annual general meeting of a public company (see instead section 337(2)).

307A NOTICE REQUIRED OF GENERAL MEETING: CERTAIN MEETINGS OF TRADED COMPANIES

(1) A general meeting of a traded company must be called by notice of—
(a) in a case where conditions A to C (set out below) are met, at least 14 days;
(b) in any other case, at least 21 days.

(2) Condition A is that the general meeting is not an annual general meeting.

(3) Condition B is that the company offers the facility for members to vote by electronic means accessible to all members who hold shares that carry rights to vote at general meetings.

This condition is met if there is a facility, offered by the company and accessible to all such members, to appoint a proxy by means of a website.

(4) Condition C is that a special resolution reducing the period of notice to not less than 14 days has been passed—
(a) at the immediately preceding annual general meeting, or
(b) at a general meeting held since that annual general meeting.

(5) In the case of a company which has not yet held an annual general meeting, condition C is that a special resolution reducing the period of notice to not less than 14 days has been passed at a general meeting.

(6) The company's articles may require a longer period of notice than that specified in subsection (1).

(7) Where a general meeting is adjourned, the adjourned meeting may be called by shorter notice than required by subsection (1).

But in the case of an adjournment for lack of a quorum this subsection applies only if—
(a) no business is to be dealt with at the adjourned meeting the general nature of which was not stated in the notice of the original meeting, and
(b) the adjourned meeting is to be held at least 10 days after the original meeting.

(8) Nothing in this section applies in relation to a general meeting of a kind mentioned in section 307(A1)(b) (certain meetings regarding takeover of opted-in company).

308 MANNER IN WHICH NOTICE TO BE GIVEN

Notice of a general meeting of a company must be given—

(a) in hard copy form,

(b) in electronic form, or

(c) by means of a website (see section 309),

or partly by one such means and partly by another.

309 PUBLICATION OF NOTICE OF MEETING ON WEBSITE

(1) Notice of a meeting is not validly given by a company by means of a website unless it is given in accordance with this section.

(2) When the company notifies a member of the presence of the notice on the website the notification must—
(a) state that it concerns a notice of a company meeting,
(b) specify the place, date and time of the meeting, and
(c) in the case of a public company, state whether the meeting will be an annual general meeting.

(3) The notice must be available on the website throughout the period beginning with the date of that notification and ending with the conclusion of the meeting.

310 PERSONS ENTITLED TO RECEIVE NOTICE OF MEETINGS

(1) Notice of a general meeting of a company must be sent to—
(a) every member of the company, and
(b) every director.

(2) In subsection (1), the reference to members includes any person who is entitled to a share in consequence of the death or bankruptcy of a member, if the company has been notified of their entitlement.

(3) In subsection (2), the reference to the bankruptcy of a member includes—
(a) the sequestration of the estate of a member;
(b) a member's estate being the subject of a protected trust deed (within the meaning of the Bankruptcy (Scotland) Act 1985 (c. 66)).

(4) This section has effect subject to—
(a) any enactment, and
(b) any provision of the company's articles.

311 CONTENTS OF NOTICES OF MEETINGS

(1) Notice of a general meeting of a company must state—
(a) the time and date of the meeting, and
(b) the place of the meeting.

(2) Notice of a general meeting of a company must state the general nature of the business to be dealt with at the meeting.

In relation to a company other than a traded company, this subsection has effect subject to any provision of the company's articles.

(3) Notice of a general meeting of a traded company must also include—
(a) a statement giving the address of the website on which the information required by section 311A (traded companies: publication of information in advance of general meeting) is published;
(b) a statement—
(i) that the right to vote at the meeting is determined by reference to the register of members, and
(ii) of the time when that right will be determined in accordance with section 360B(2) (traded companies: share dealings before general meetings);

(c) a statement of the procedures with which members must comply in order to be able to attend and vote at the meeting (including the date by which they must comply);
(d) a statement giving details of any forms to be used for the appointment of a proxy;
(e) where the company offers the facility for members to vote in advance (see section 322A) or by electronic means (see section 360A), a statement of the procedure for doing so (including the date by which it must be done, and details of any forms to be used); and
(f) a statement of the right of members to ask questions in accordance with section 319A (traded companies: questions at meetings).

311A TRADED COMPANIES: PUBLICATION OF INFORMATION IN ADVANCE OF GENERAL MEETING

(1) A traded company must ensure that the following information relating to a general meeting of the company is made available on a website—
(a) the matters set out in the notice of the meeting;
(b) the total numbers of—
(i) shares in the company, and
(ii) shares of each class,
in respect of which members are entitled to exercise voting rights at the meeting;
(c) the totals of the voting rights that members are entitled to exercise at the meeting in respect of the shares of each class;
(d) members' statements, members' resolutions and members' matters of business received by the company after the first date on which notice of the meeting is given.

(2) The information must be made available on a website that—
(a) is maintained by or on behalf of the company, and
(b) identifies the company.

(3) Access to the information on the website, and the ability to obtain a hard copy of the information from the website, must not be conditional on payment of a fee or otherwise restricted.

(4) The information—
(a) must be made available—
(i) in the case of information required by subsection (1)(a) to (c), on or before the first date on which notice of the meeting is given, and
(ii) in the case of information required by subsection (1)(d), as soon as reasonably practicable, and
(b) must be kept available throughout the period of two years beginning with the date on which it is first made available on a website in accordance with this section.

(5) A failure to make information available throughout the period specified in subsection (4)(b) is disregarded if—
(a) the information is made available on the website for part of that period, and
(b) the failure is wholly attributable to circumstances that it would not be reasonable to have expected the company to prevent or avoid.

(6) The amounts mentioned in subsection (1)(b) and (c) must be ascertained at the latest practicable time before the first date on which notice of the meeting is given.

(7) Failure to comply with this section does not affect the validity of the meeting or of anything done at the meeting.

(8) If this section is not complied with as respects any meeting, an offence is committed by every officer of the company who is in default.

(9) A person guilty of an offence under this section is liable on summary conviction to a fine not exceeding level 3 on the standard scale.

312 RESOLUTION REQUIRING SPECIAL NOTICE

(1) Where by any provision of the Companies Acts special notice is required of a resolution, the resolution is not effective unless notice of the intention to move it has been given to the company at least 28 days before the meeting at which it is moved.

(2) The company must, where practicable, give its members notice of any such resolution in the same manner and at the same time as it gives notice of the meeting.

(3) Where that is not practicable, the company must give its members notice at least 14 days before the meeting—
(a) by advertisement in a newspaper having an appropriate circulation, or
(b) in any other manner allowed by the company's articles.

(4) If, after notice of the intention to move such a resolution has been given to the company, a meeting is called for a date 28 days or less after the notice has been given, the notice is deemed to have been properly given, though not given within the time required.

313 ACCIDENTAL FAILURE TO GIVE NOTICE OF RESOLUTION OR MEETING

(1) Where a company gives notice of—
(a) a general meeting, or
(b) a resolution intended to be moved at a general meeting,
any accidental failure to give notice to one or more persons shall be disregarded for the purpose of determining whether notice of the meeting or resolution (as the case may be) is duly given.

(2) Except in relation to notice given under—
(a) section 304 (notice of meetings required by members),
(b) section 305 (notice of meetings called by members), or
(c) section 339 (notice of resolutions at AGMs proposed by members),
subsection (1) has effect subject to any provision of the company's articles.

Members' statements

314 MEMBERS' POWER TO REQUIRE CIRCULATION OF STATEMENTS

(1) The members of a company may require the company to circulate, to members of the company entitled to receive notice of a general meeting, a statement of not more than 1,000 words with respect to—
(a) a matter referred to in a proposed resolution to be dealt with at that meeting, or
(b) other business to be dealt with at that meeting.

(2) A company is required to circulate a statement once it has received requests to do so from—

(a) members representing at least 5% of the total voting rights of all the members who have a relevant right to vote (excluding any voting rights attached to any shares in the company held as treasury shares), or
(b) at least 100 members who have a relevant right to vote and hold shares in the company on which there has been paid up an average sum, per member, of at least £100.

See also section 153 (exercise of rights where shares held on behalf of others).

(3) In subsection (2), a "relevant right to vote" means—
(a) in relation to a statement with respect to a matter referred to in a proposed resolution, a right to vote on that resolution at the meeting to which the requests relate, and
(b) in relation to any other statement, a right to vote at the meeting to which the requests relate.

(4) A request—
(a) may be in hard copy form or in electronic form,
(b) must identify the statement to be circulated,
(c) must be authenticated by the person or persons making it, and
(d) must be received by the company at least one week before the meeting to which it relates.

315 COMPANY'S DUTY TO CIRCULATE MEMBERS' STATEMENT

(1) A company that is required under section 314, to circulate a statement must send a copy of it to each member of the company entitled to receive notice of the meeting—
(a) in the same manner as the notice of the meeting, and
(b) at the same time as, or as soon as reasonably practicable after, it gives notice of the meeting.

(2) Subsection (1) has effect subject to section 316(2) (deposit or tender of sum in respect of expenses of circulation) and section 317 (application not to circulate members' statement).

(3) In the event of default in complying with this section, an offence is committed by every officer of the company who is in default.

(4) A person guilty of an offence under this section is liable—
(a) on conviction on indictment, to a fine;
(b) on summary conviction, to a fine not exceeding the statutory maximum.

316 EXPENSES OF CIRCULATING MEMBERS' STATEMENT

(1) The expenses of the company in complying with section 315 need not be paid by the members who requested the circulation of the statement if—
(a) the meeting to which the requests relate is an annual general meeting of a public company, and
(b) requests sufficient to require the company to circulate the statement are received before the end of the financial year preceding the meeting.

(2) Otherwise—
(a) the expenses of the company in complying with that section must be paid by the members who requested the circulation of the statement unless the company resolves otherwise, and
(b) unless the company has previously so resolved, it is not bound to comply with that section unless there is deposited with or tendered to it, not later than one week before the meeting, a sum reasonably sufficient to meet its expenses in doing so.

317 APPLICATION NOT TO CIRCULATE MEMBERS' STATEMENT

(1) A company is not required to circulate a members' statement under section 315 if, on an application by the company or another person who claims to be aggrieved, the court is satisfied that the rights conferred by section 314 and that section are being abused.

(2) The court may order the members who requested the circulation of the statement to pay the whole or part of the company's costs (in Scotland, expenses) on such an application, even if they are not parties to the application.

Procedure at meetings

318 QUORUM AT MEETINGS

(1) In the case of a company limited by shares or guarantee and having only one member, one qualifying person present at a meeting is a quorum.

(2) In any other case, subject to the provisions of the company's articles, two qualifying persons present at a meeting are a quorum, unless—
- (a) each is a qualifying person only because he is authorised under section 323 to act as the representative of a corporation in relation to the meeting, and they are representatives of the same corporation; or
- (b) each is a qualifying person only because he is appointed as proxy of a member in relation to the meeting, and they are proxies of the same member.

(3) For the purposes of this section a "qualifying person" means—
- (a) an individual who is a member of the company,
- (b) a person authorised under section 323 (representation of corporations at meetings) to act as the representative of a corporation in relation to the meeting, or
- (c) a person appointed as proxy of a member in relation to the meeting.

319 CHAIRMAN OF MEETING

(1) A member may be elected to be the chairman of a general meeting by a resolution of the company passed at the meeting.

(2) Subsection (1) is subject to any provision of the company's articles that states who may or may not be chairman.

319A TRADED COMPANIES: QUESTIONS AT MEETINGS

(1) At a general meeting of a traded company, the company must cause to be answered any question relating to the business being dealt with at the meeting put by a member attending the meeting.

(2) No such answer need be given—
- (a) if to do so would—
  - (i) interfere unduly with the preparation for the meeting, or
  - (ii) involve the disclosure of confidential information;
- (b) if the answer has already been given on a website in the form of an answer to a question; or
- (c) if it is undesirable in the interests of the company or the good order of the meeting that the question be answered.

320 DECLARATION BY CHAIRMAN ON A SHOW OF HANDS

(1) On a vote on a resolution at a meeting on a show of hands, a declaration by the chairman that the resolution—
(a) has or has not been passed, or
(b) passed with a particular majority,
is conclusive evidence of that fact without proof of the number or proportion of the votes recorded in favour of or against the resolution.

(2) An entry in respect of such a declaration in minutes of the meeting recorded in accordance with section 355 is also conclusive evidence of that fact without such proof.

(3) This section does not have effect if a poll is demanded in respect of the resolution (and the demand is not subsequently withdrawn).

321 RIGHT TO DEMAND A POLL

(1) A provision of a company's articles is void in so far as it would have the effect of excluding the right to demand a poll at a general meeting on any question other than—
(a) the election of the chairman of the meeting, or
(b) the adjournment of the meeting.

(2) A provision of a company's articles is void in so far as it would have the effect of making ineffective a demand for a poll on any such question which is made—
(a) by not less than 5 members having the right to vote on the resolution; or
(b) by a member or members representing not less than 10% of the total voting rights of all the members having the right to vote on the resolution (excluding any voting rights attached to any shares in the company held as treasury shares); or
(c) by a member or members holding shares in the company conferring a right to vote on the resolution, being shares on which an aggregate sum has been paid up equal to not less than 10% of the total sum paid up on all the shares conferring that right (excluding shares in the company conferring a right to vote on the resolution which are held as treasury shares).

322 VOTING ON A POLL

On a poll taken at a general meeting of a company, a member entitled to more than one vote need not, if he votes, use all his votes or cast all the votes he uses in the same way.

322A VOTING ON A POLL: VOTES CAST IN ADVANCE

(1) A company's articles may contain provision to the effect that on a vote on a resolution on a poll taken at a meeting, the votes may include votes cast in advance.

(2) In the case of a traded company any such provision in relation to voting at a general meeting may be made subject only to such requirements and restrictions as are—
(a) necessary to ensure the identification of the person voting, and
(b) proportionate to the achievement of that objective.
Nothing in this subsection affects any power of a company to require reasonable evidence of the entitlement of any person who is not a member to vote.

(3) Any provision of a company's articles is void in so far as it would have the effect of requiring any document casting a vote in advance to be received by the company or another person earlier than the following time—

(a) in the case of a poll taken more than 48 hours after it was demanded, 24 hours before the time appointed for the taking of the poll;
(b) in the case of any other poll, 48 hours before the time for holding the meeting or adjourned meeting.

(4) In calculating the periods mentioned in subsection (3), no account is to be taken of any part of a day that is not a working day.

323 REPRESENTATION OF CORPORATIONS AT MEETINGS

(1) If a corporation (whether or not a company within the meaning of this Act) is a member of a company, it may by resolution of its directors or other governing body authorise a person or persons to act as its representative or representatives at any meeting of the company.

(2) A person authorised by a corporation is entitled to exercise (on behalf of the corporation) the same powers as the corporation could exercise if it were an individual member of the company.

Where a corporation authorises more than one person, this subsection is subject to subsections (3) and (4).

(3) On a vote on a resolution on a show of hands at a meeting of the company, each authorised person has the same voting rights as the corporation would be entitled to.

(4) Where subsection (3) does not apply and more than one authorised person purport to exercise a power under subsection (2) in respect of the same shares—
(a) if they purport to exercise the power in the same way as each other, the power is treated as exercised in that way;
(b) if they do not purport to exercise the power in the same way as each other, the power is treated as not exercised.

Proxies

324 RIGHTS TO APPOINT PROXIES

(1) A member of a company is entitled to appoint another person as his proxy to exercise all or any of his rights to attend and to speak and vote at a meeting of the company.

(2) In the case of a company having a share capital, a member may appoint more than one proxy in relation to a meeting, provided that each proxy is appointed to exercise the rights attached to a different share or shares held by him, or (as the case may be) to a different £10, or multiple of £10, of stock held by him.

324A OBLIGATION OF PROXY TO VOTE IN ACCORDANCE WITH INSTRUCTIONS

A proxy must vote in accordance with any instructions given by the member by whom the proxy is appointed.

325 NOTICE OF MEETING TO CONTAIN STATEMENT OF RIGHTS

(1) In every notice calling a meeting of a company there must appear, with reasonable prominence, a statement informing the member of—
(a) his rights under section 324, and
(b) any more extensive rights conferred by the company's articles to appoint more than one proxy.

(2) Failure to comply with this section does not affect the validity of the meeting or of anything done at the meeting.

(3) If this section is not complied with as respects any meeting, an offence is committed by every officer of the company who is in default.

(4) A person guilty of an offence under this section is liable on summary conviction to a fine not exceeding level 3 on the standard scale.

326 COMPANY-SPONSORED INVITATIONS TO APPOINT PROXIES

(1) If for the purposes of a meeting there are issued at the company's expense invitations to members to appoint as proxy a specified person or a number of specified persons, the invitations must be issued to all members entitled to vote at the meeting.

(2) Subsection (1) is not contravened if—
   (a) there is issued to a member at his request a form of appointment naming the proxy or a list of persons willing to act as proxy, and
   (b) the form or list is available on request to all members entitled to vote at the meeting.

(3) If subsection (1) is contravened as respects a meeting, an offence is committed by every officer of the company who is in default.

(4) A person guilty of an offence under this section is liable on summary conviction to a fine not exceeding level 3 on the standard scale.

327 NOTICE REQUIRED OF APPOINTMENT OF PROXY ETC.

(A1) In the case of a traded company —
   (a) the appointment of a person as proxy for a member must be notified to the company in writing;
   (b) where such an appointment is made, the company may require reasonable evidence of—
      (i) the identity of the member and of the proxy,
      (ii) the member's instructions (if any) as to how the proxy is to vote, and
      (iii) where the proxy is appointed by a person acting on behalf of the member, authority of that person to make the appointment;
   but may not require to be provided with anything else relating to the appointment.

(1) The following provisions apply in the case of traded companies and other companies as regards—
   (a) the appointment of a proxy, and
   (b) any document necessary to show the validity of, or otherwise relating to, the appointment of a proxy.

(2) Any provision of the company's articles is void in so far as it would have the effect of requiring any such appointment or document to be received by the company or another person earlier than the following time—
   (a) in the case of a meeting or adjourned meeting, 48 hours before the time for holding the meeting or adjourned meeting;
   (b) in the case of a poll taken more than 48 hours after it was demanded, 24 hours before the time appointed for the taking of the poll;
   (c) in the case of a poll taken not more than 48 hours after it was demanded, the time at which it was demanded.

(3) In calculating the periods mentioned in subsection (2) no account shall be taken of any part of a day that is not a working day.

328 CHAIRING MEETINGS

(1) A proxy may be elected to be the chairman of a general meeting by a resolution of the company passed at the meeting.

(2) Subsection (1) is subject to any provision of the company's articles that states who may or who may not be chairman.

329 RIGHT OF PROXY TO DEMAND A POLL

(1) The appointment of a proxy to vote on a matter at a meeting of a company authorises the proxy to demand, or join in demanding, a poll on that matter.

(2) In applying the provisions of section 321(2) (requirements for effective demand), a demand by a proxy counts—
(a) for thc purposes of paragraph (a), as a demand by the member;
(b) for the purposes of paragraph (b), as a demand by a member representing the voting rights that the proxy is authorised to exercise;
(c) for the purposes of paragraph (c), as a demand by a member holding the shares to which those rights are attached.

330 NOTICE REQUIRED OF TERMINATION OF PROXY'S AUTHORITY

(A1) In the case of a traded company the termination of the authority of a person to act as proxy must be notified to the company in writing.

(1) The following provisions apply in the case of traded companies and other companies as regards notice that the authority of a person to act as proxy is terminated ("notice of termination").

(2) The termination of the authority of a person to act as proxy does not affect—
(a) whether he counts in deciding whether there is a quorum at a meeting,
(b) the validity of anything he does as chairman of a meeting, or
(c) the validity of a poll demanded by him at a meeting,
unless the company receives notice of the termination before the commencement of the meeting.

(3) The termination of the authority of a person to act as proxy does not affect the validity of a vote given by that person unless the company receives notice of the termination—
(a) before the commencement of the meeting or adjourned meeting at which the vote is given, or
(b) in the case of a poll taken more than 48 hours after it is demanded, before the time appointed for taking the poll.

(4) If the company's articles require or permit members to give notice of termination to a person other than the company, the references above to the company receiving notice have effect as if they were or (as the case may be) included a reference to that person.

(5) Subsections (2) and (3) have effect subject to any provision of the company's articles which has the effect of requiring notice of termination to be received by the company or another person at a time earlier than that specified in those subsections.

This is subject to subsection (6).

(6) Any provision of the company's articles is void in so far as it would have the effect of requiring notice of termination to be received by the company or another person earlier than the following time—

(a) in the case of a meeting or adjourned meeting, 48 hours before the time for holding the meeting or adjourned meeting;
(b) in the case of a poll taken more than 48 hours after it was demanded, 24 hours before the time appointed for the taking of the poll;
(c) in the case of a poll taken not more than 48 hours after it was demanded, the time at which it was demanded.

(7) In calculating the periods mentioned in subsections (3)(b) and (6) no account shall be taken of any part of a day that is not a working day.

331 SAVING FOR MORE EXTENSIVE RIGHTS CONFERRED BY ARTICLES

Nothing in sections 324 to 330 (proxies) prevents a company's articles from conferring more extensive rights on members or proxies than are conferred by those sections.

Adjourned meetings

332 RESOLUTION PASSED AT ADJOURNED MEETING

Where a resolution is passed at an adjourned meeting of a company, the resolution is for all purposes to be treated as having been passed on the date on which it was in fact passed, and is not to be deemed passed on any earlier date.

Electronic communications

333 SENDING DOCUMENTS RELATING TO MEETINGS ETC. IN ELECTRONIC FORM

(1) Where a company has given an electronic address in a notice calling a meeting, it is deemed to have agreed that any document or information relating to proceedings at the meeting may be sent by electronic means to that address (subject to any conditions or limitations specified in the notice).

(2) Where a company has given an electronic address—
(a) in an instrument of proxy sent out by the company in relation to the meeting, or
(b) in an invitation to appoint a proxy issued by the company in relation to the meeting,
it is deemed to have agreed that any document or information relating to proxies for that meeting may be sent by electronic means to that address (subject to any conditions or limitations specified in the notice).

(3) In subsection (2), documents relating to proxies include—
(a) the appointment of a proxy in relation to a meeting,
(b) any document necessary to show the validity of, or otherwise relating to, the appointment of a proxy, and
(c) notice of the termination of the authority of a proxy.

(4) In this section "electronic address" means any address or number used for the purposes of sending or receiving documents or information by electronic means.

333A TRADED COMPANY: DUTY TO PROVIDE ELECTRONIC ADDRESS FOR RECEIPT OF PROXIES ETC.

(1) A traded company must provide an electronic address for the receipt of any document or information relating to proxies for a general meeting.

(2) The company must provide the address either—
(a) by giving it when sending out an instrument of proxy for the purposes of the meeting or issuing an invitation to appoint a proxy for those purposes; or
(b) by ensuring that it is made available, throughout the period beginning with the first date on which notice of the meeting is given and ending with the conclusion of the meeting, on the website on which the information required by section 311A(1) is made available.

(3) The company is deemed to have agreed that any document or information relating to proxies for the meeting may be sent by electronic means to the address provided (subject to any limitations specified by the company when providing the address).

(4) In this section—
(a) documents relating to proxies include—
(i) the appointment of a proxy for a meeting,
(ii) any document necessary to show the validity of, or otherwise relating to, the appointment of a proxy, and
(iii) notice of the termination of the authority of a proxy;
(b) "electronic address" has the meaning given by section 333(4).

Application to class meetings

334 APPLICATION TO CLASS MEETINGS

(1) The provisions of this Chapter apply (with necessary modifications) in relation to a meeting of holders of a class of shares as they apply in relation to a general meeting.

This is subject to subsections (2) to (3).

(2) The following provisions of this Chapter do not apply in relation to a meeting of holders of a class of shares—
(a) sections 303 to 305 (members' power to require directors to call general meeting),
(b) section 306 (power of court to order meeting), and
(c) sections 311(3), 311A, 319A, 327(A1), 330(A1) and 333A (additional requirements relating to traded companies).

(2A) Section 307(1) to (6) apply in relation to a meeting of holders of a class of shares in a traded company as they apply in relation to a meeting of holders of a class of shares in a company other than a traded company (and, accordingly, section 307A does not apply in relation to such a meeting).

(3) The following provisions (in addition to those mentioned in subsection (2)) do not apply in relation to a meeting in connection with the variation of rights attached to a class of shares (a "variation of class rights meeting")—
(a) section 318 (quorum), and
(b) section 321 (right to demand a poll).

(4) The quorum for a variation of class rights meeting is—
(a) for a meeting other than an adjourned meeting, two persons present holding at least one-third in nominal value of the issued shares of the class in question (excluding any shares of that class held as treasury shares);
(b) for an adjourned meeting, one person present holding shares of the class in question.

(5) For the purposes of subsection (4), where a person is present by proxy or proxies, he is treated as holding only the shares in respect of which those proxies are authorised to exercise voting rights.

(6) At a variation of class rights meeting, any holder of shares of the class in question present may demand a poll.

(7) For the purposes of this section—
(a) any amendment of a provision contained in a company's articles for the variation of the rights attached to a class of shares, or the insertion of any such provision into the articles, is itself to be treated as a variation of those rights, and
(b) references to the variation of rights attached to a class of shares include references to their abrogation.

Chapter 5 PUBLIC COMPANIES AND TRADED COMPANIES: ADDITIONAL REQUIREMENTS FOR AGMS

336 PUBLIC COMPANIES AND TRADED COMPANIES: ANNUAL GENERAL MEETING

(1) Every public company must hold a general meeting as its annual general meeting in each period of 6 months beginning with the day following its accounting reference date (in addition to any other meetings held during that period).

(1A) Every private company that is a traded company must hold a general meeting as its annual general meeting in each period of 9 months beginning with the day following its accounting reference date (in addition to any other meetings held during that period).

(2) A company that fails to comply with subsection (1) or (1A) as a result of giving notice under section 392 (alteration of accounting reference date)—
(a) specifying a new accounting reference date, and
(b) stating that the current accounting reference period or the previous accounting reference period is to be shortened,
shall be treated as if it had complied with subsection (1) or (1A) if it holds a general meeting as its annual general meeting within 3 months of giving that notice.

(3) If a company fails to comply with subsection (1) or (1A), an offence is committed by every officer of the company who is in default.

(4) A person guilty of an offence under this section is liable—
(a) on conviction on indictment, to a fine;
(b) on summary conviction, to a fine not exceeding the statutory maximum.

337 PUBLIC COMPANIES AND TRADED COMPANIES: NOTICE OF AGM

(1) A notice calling an annual general meeting of a public company or a private company that is a traded company must state that the meeting is an annual general meeting.

(2) An annual general meeting of a public company that is not a traded company may be called by shorter notice than that required by section 307(2) or by the company's articles (as the case may be), if all the members entitled to attend and vote at the meeting agree to the shorter notice.

(3) Where a notice calling an annual general meeting of a traded company is given more than 6 weeks before the meeting, the notice must include—
(a) if the company is a public company, a statement of the right under section 338 to require the company to give notice of a resolution to be moved at the meeting, and

(b) whether or not the company is a public company, a statement of the right under section 338A to require the company to include a matter in the business to be dealt with at the meeting.

338 PUBLIC COMPANIES: MEMBERS' POWER TO REQUIRE CIRCULATION OF RESOLUTIONS FOR AGMS

(1) The members of a public company may require the company to give, to members of the company entitled to receive notice of the next annual general meeting, notice of a resolution which may properly be moved and is intended to be moved at that meeting.

(2) A resolution may properly be moved at an annual general meeting unless—
(a) it would, if passed, be ineffective (whether by reason of inconsistency with any enactment or the company's constitution or otherwise),
(b) it is defamatory of any person, or
(c) it is frivolous or vexatious.

(3) A company is required to give notice of a resolution once it has received requests that it do so from—
(a) members representing at least 5% of the total voting rights of all the members who have a right to vote on the resolution at the annual general meeting to which the requests relate (excluding any voting rights attached to any shares in the company held as treasury shares), or
(b) at least 100 members who have a right to vote on the resolution at the annual general meeting to which the requests relate and hold shares in the company on which there has been paid up an average sum, per member, of at least £100.
See also section 153 (exercise of rights where shares held on behalf of others).

(4) A request—
(a) may be in hard copy form or in electronic form,
(b) must identify the resolution of which notice is to be given,
(c) must be authenticated by the person or persons making it, and
(d) must be received by the company not later than—
(i) 6 weeks before the annual general meeting to which the requests relate, or
(ii) if later, the time at which notice is given of that meeting.

338A TRADED COMPANIES: MEMBERS' POWER TO INCLUDE OTHER MATTERS IN BUSINESS DEALT WITH AT AGM

(1) The members of a traded company may request the company to include in the business to be dealt with at an annual general meeting any matter (other than a proposed resolution) which may properly be included in the business.

(2) A matter may properly be included in the business at an annual general meeting unless—
(a) it is defamatory of any person, or
(b) it is frivolous or vexatious.

(3) A company is required to include such a matter once it has received requests that it do so from—
(a) members representing at least 5% of the total voting rights of all the members who have a right to vote at the meeting, or
(b) at least 100 members who have a right to vote at the meeting and hold shares in the company on which there has been paid up an average sum, per member, of at least £100.
See also section 153 (exercise of rights where shares held on behalf of others).

(4) A request—
  (a) may be in hard copy form or in electronic form,
  (b) must identify the matter to be included in the business,
  (c) must be accompanied by a statement setting out the grounds for the request, and
  (d) must be authenticated by the person or persons making it.

(5) A request must be received by the company not later than—
  (a) 6 weeks before the meeting, or
  (b) if later, the time at which notice is given of the meeting.

339 PUBLIC COMPANIES: COMPANY'S DUTY TO CIRCULATE MEMBERS' RESOLUTIONS FOR AGMS

(1) A company that is required under section 338 to give notice of a resolution must send a copy of it to each member of the company entitled to receive notice of the annual general meeting—
  (a) in the same manner as notice of the meeting, and
  (b) at the same time as, or as soon as reasonably practicable after, it gives notice of the meeting.

(2) Subsection (1) has effect subject to section 340(2) (deposit or tender of sum in respect of expenses of circulation).

(3) The business which may be dealt with at an annual general meeting includes a resolution of which notice is given in accordance with this section.

(4) In the event of default in complying with this section, an offence is committed by every officer of the company who is in default.

(5) A person guilty of an offence under this section is liable—
  (a) on conviction on indictment, to a fine;
  (b) on summary conviction, to a fine not exceeding the statutory maximum.

340 PUBLIC COMPANIES: EXPENSES OF CIRCULATING MEMBERS' RESOLUTIONS FOR AGM

(1) The expenses of the company in complying with section 339 need not be paid by the members who requested the circulation of the resolution if requests sufficient to require the company to circulate it are received before the end of the financial year preceding the meeting.

(2) Otherwise—
  (a) the expenses of the company in complying with that section must be paid by the members who requested the circulation of the resolution unless the company resolves otherwise, and
  (b) unless the company has previously so resolved, it is not bound to comply with that section unless there is deposited with or tendered to it, not later than—
    (i) six weeks before the annual general meeting to which the requests relate, or
    (ii) if later, the time at which notice is given of that meeting,
  a sum reasonably sufficient to meet its expenses in complying with that section.

340A TRADED COMPANIES: DUTY TO CIRCULATE MEMBERS' MATTERS FOR AGM

(1) A company that is required under section 338A to include any matter in the business to be dealt with at an annual general meeting must—

(a) give notice of it to each member of the company entitled to receive notice of the annual general meeting—
(i) in the same manner as notice of the meeting, and
(ii) at the same time as, or as soon as reasonably practicable after, it gives notice of the meeting, and
(b) publish it on the same website as that on which the company published the information required by section 311A.

(2) Subsection (1) has effect subject to section 340B(2) (deposit or tender of sum in respect of expenses of circulation).

(3) In the event of default in complying with this section, an offence is committed by every officer of the company who is in default.

(4) A person guilty of an offence under this section is liable—
(a) on conviction on indictment, to a fine;
(b) on summary conviction, to a fine not exceeding the statutory maximum.

340B TRADED COMPANIES: EXPENSES OF CIRCULATING MEMBERS' MATTERS TO BE DEALT WITH AT AGM

(1) The expenses of the company in complying with section 340A need not be paid by the members who requested the inclusion of the matter in the business to be dealt with at the annual general meeting if requests sufficient to require the company to include the matter are received before the end of the financial year preceding the meeting.

(2) Otherwise—
(a) the expenses of the company in complying with that section must be paid by the members who requested the inclusion of the matter unless the company resolves otherwise, and
(b) unless the company has previously so resolved, it is not bound to comply with that section unless there is deposited with or tendered to it, not later than—
(i) six weeks before the annual general meeting to which the requests relate, or
(ii) if later, the time at which notice is given of that meeting,
a sum reasonably sufficient to meet its expenses in complying with that section.

Chapter 5 ADDITIONAL REQUIREMENTS FOR QUOTED COMPANIES

Website publication of poll results

341 RESULTS OF POLL TO BE MADE AVAILABLE ON WEBSITE

(1) Where a poll is taken at a general meeting of a quoted company that is not a traded company, the company must ensure that the following information is made available on a website—
(a) the date of the meeting,
(b) the text of the resolution or, as the case may be, a description of the subject matter of the poll,
(c) the number of votes cast in favour, and
(d) the number of votes cast against.

(1A) Where a poll is taken at a general meeting of a traded company, the company must ensure that the following information is made available on a website—
(a) the date of the meeting,
(b) the text of the resolution or, as the case may be, a description of the subject matter of the poll,

(c) the number of votes validly cast,
(d) the proportion of the company's issued share capital (determined at the time at which the right to vote is determined under section 360B(2)) represented by those votes,
(e) the number of votes cast in favour,
(f) the number of votes cast against, and
(g) the number of abstentions (if counted).

(1B) A traded company must comply with subsection (1A) by—
(a) the end of 16 days beginning with the day of the meeting, or
(b) if later, the end of the first working day after the day on which the result of the poll is declared.

(2) The provisions of section 353 (requirements as to website availability) apply.

(3) In the event of default in complying with this section (or with the requirements of section 353 as it applies for the purposes of this section), an offence is committed by every officer of the company who is in default.

(4) A person guilty of an offence under subsection (3) is liable on summary conviction to a fine not exceeding level 3 on the standard scale.

(5) Failure to comply with this section (or the requirements of section 353) does not affect the validity of—
(a) the poll, or
(b) the resolution or other business (if passed or agreed to) to which the poll relates.

(6) This section only applies to polls taken after this section comes into force.

Chapter 6 RECORDS OF RESOLUTIONS AND MEETINGS

355 RECORDS OF RESOLUTIONS AND MEETINGS ETC.

(1) Every company must keep records comprising—
(a) copies of all resolutions of members passed otherwise than at general meetings,
(b) minutes of all proceedings of general meetings, and
(c) details provided to the company in accordance with section 357 (decisions of sole member).

(2) The records must be kept for at least ten years from the date of the resolution, meeting or decision (as appropriate).

(3) If a company fails to comply with this section, an offence is committed by every officer of the company who is in default.

(4) A person guilty of an offence under this section is liable on summary conviction to a fine not exceeding level 3 on the standard scale and, for continued contravention, a daily default fine not exceeding one-tenth of level 3 on the standard scale.

356 RECORDS AS EVIDENCE OF RESOLUTIONS ETC.

(1) This section applies to the records kept in accordance with section 355.

(2) The record of a resolution passed otherwise than at a general meeting, if purporting to be signed by a director of the company or by the company secretary, is evidence (in Scotland, sufficient evidence) of the passing of the resolution.

(3) Where there is a record of a written resolution of a private company, the requirements of this Act with respect to the passing of the resolution are deemed to be complied with unless the contrary is proved.

(4) The minutes of proceedings of a general meeting, if purporting to be signed by the chairman of that meeting or by the chairman of the next general meeting, are evidence (in Scotland, sufficient evidence) of the proceedings at the meeting.

(5) Where there is a record of proceedings of a general meeting of a company, then, until the contrary is proved—
(a) the meeting is deemed duly held and convened,
(b) all proceedings at the meeting are deemed to have duly taken place, and
(c) all appointments at the meeting are deemed valid.

357 RECORDS OF DECISIONS BY SOLE MEMBER

(1) This section applies to a company limited by shares or by guarantee that has only one member.

(2) Where the member takes any decision that—
(a) may be taken by the company in general meeting, and
(b) has effect as if agreed by the company in general meeting,
he must (unless that decision is taken by way of a written resolution) provide the company with details of that decision.

(3) If a person fails to comply with this section he commits an offence.

(4) A person guilty of an offence under this section is liable on summary conviction to a fine not exceeding level 2 on the standard scale.

(5) Failure to comply with this section does not affect the validity of any decision referred to in subsection (2).

358 INSPECTION OF RECORDS OF RESOLUTIONS AND MEETINGS

(1) The records referred to in section 355 (records of resolutions etc.) relating to the previous ten years must be kept available for inspection—
(a) at the company's registered office, or
(b) at a place specified in regulations under section 1136.

(2) The company must give notice to the registrar—
(a) of the place at which the records are kept available for inspection, and
(b) of any change in that place,
unless they have at all times been kept at the company's registered office.

(3) The records must be open to the inspection of any member of the company without charge.

(4) Any member may require a copy of any of the records on payment of such fee as may be prescribed.

(5) If default is made for 14 days in complying with subsection (2) or an inspection required under subsection (3) is refused, or a copy requested under subsection (4) is not sent, an offence is committed by every officer of the company who is in default.

(6) A person guilty of an offence under this section is liable on summary conviction to a fine not exceeding level 3 on the standard scale and, for continued contravention, a daily default fine not exceeding one-tenth of level 3 on the standard scale.

(7) In a case in which an inspection required under subsection (3) is refused or a copy requested under subsection (4) is not sent, the court may by order compel an immediate inspection of the records or direct that the copies required be sent to the persons who requested them.

359 RECORDS OF RESOLUTIONS AND MEETINGS OF CLASS OF MEMBERS

The provisions of this Chapter apply (with necessary modifications) in relation to resolutions and meetings of—

(a) holders of a class of shares, and

(b) in the case of a company without a share capital, a class of members, as they apply in relation to resolutions of members generally and to general meetings.

Chapter 7 SUPPLEMENTARY PROVISIONS

360 COMPUTATION OF PERIODS OF NOTICE ETC.: CLEAR DAY RULE

(1) This section applies for the purposes of the following provisions of this Part—

section 307(1) and (2) (notice required of general meeting),

section 307A(1), (4), (5) and (7)(b) (notice required of general meeting of traded company),

section 312(1) and (3) (resolution requiring special notice),

section 314(4)(d) (request to circulate members' statement),

section 316(2)(b) (expenses of circulating statement to be deposited or tendered before meeting),

section 337(3) (contents of notice of AGM of traded company),

section 338(4)(d)(i) (request to circulate member's resolution at AGM of public company),

section 338A(5) (request to include matter in the business to be dealt with at AGM of traded company),

section 340(2)(b)(i) (expenses of circulating statement to be deposited or tendered before meeting), and

section 340B(2)(b) (traded companies: duty to circulate members' matters for AGM).

(2) Any reference in those provisions to a period of notice, or to a period before a meeting by which a request must be received or sum deposited or tendered, is to a period of the specified length excluding—
(a) the day of the meeting, and
(b) the day on which the notice is given, the request received or the sum deposited or tendered.

360A ELECTRONIC MEETINGS AND VOTING

(1) Nothing in this Part is to be taken to preclude the holding and conducting of a meeting in such a way that persons who are not present together at the same place may by electronic means attend and speak and vote at it.

(2) In the case of a traded company the use of electronic means for the purpose of enabling members to participate in a general meeting may be made subject only to such requirements and restrictions as are—

(a) necessary to ensure the identification of those taking part and the security of the electronic communication, and
(b) proportionate to the achievement of those objectives.

(3) Nothing in subsection (2) affects any power of a company to require reasonable evidence of the entitlement of any person who is not a member to participate in the meeting.

360B TRADED COMPANIES: REQUIREMENTS FOR PARTICIPATING IN AND VOTING AT GENERAL MEETINGS

(1) Any provision of a traded company's articles is void in so far as it would have the effect of—
(a) imposing a restriction on a right of a member to participate in and vote at a general meeting of the company unless the member's shares have (after having been acquired by the member and before the meeting) been deposited with, or transferred to, or registered in the name of another person, or
(b) imposing a restriction on the right of a member to transfer shares in the company during the period of 48 hours before the time for the holding of a general meeting of the company if that right would not otherwise be subject to that restriction.

(2) A traded company must determine the right to vote at a general meeting of the company by reference to the register of members as at a time (determined by the company) that is not more than 48 hours before the time for the holding of the meeting.

(3) In calculating the period mentioned in subsection (1)(b) or (2), no account is to be taken of any part of a day that is not a working day.

(4) Nothing in this section affects—
(a) the operation of—
(i) Part 22 of this Act (information about interests in a company's shares),
(ii) Part 15 of the Companies Act 1985(a) (orders imposing restrictions on shares), or
(iii) any provision in a company's articles relating to the application of any provision of either of those Parts; or
(b) the validity of articles prescribed, or to the same effect as articles prescribed, under section 19 of this Act (power of Secretary of State to prescribe model articles).

360C MEANING OF "TRADED COMPANY"

In this Part, "traded company" means a company any shares of which—
(a) carry rights to vote at general meetings, and
(b) are admitted to trading on a regulated market in an EEA State by or with the consent of the company.

361 MEANING OF "QUOTED COMPANY"

In this Part "quoted company" has the same meaning as in Part 15 of this Act.

Part 14 CONTROL OF POLITICAL DONATIONS AND EXPENDITURE

Introductory

362 INTRODUCTORY

This Part has effect for controlling—

(a) political donations made by companies to political parties, to other political organisations and to independent election candidates, and

(b) political expenditure incurred by companies.

Donations and expenditure to which this Part applies

363 POLITICAL PARTIES, ORGANISATIONS ETC., TO WHICH THIS PART APPLIES

(1) This Part applies to a political party if—
- (a) it is registered under Part 2 of the Political Parties, Elections and Referendums Act 2000 (c. 41), or
- (b) it carries on, or proposes to carry on, activities for the purposes of or in connection with the participation of the party in any election or elections to public office held in a member State other than the United Kingdom.

(2) This Part applies to an organisation (a "political organisation") if it carries on, or proposes to carry on, activities that are capable of being reasonably regarded as intended—
- (a) to affect public support for a political party to which, or an independent election candidate to whom, this Part applies, or
- (b) to influence voters in relation to any national or regional referendum held under the law of the United Kingdom or another member State.

(3) This Part applies to an independent election candidate at any election to public office held in the United Kingdom or another member State.

(4) Any reference in the following provisions of this Part to a political party, political organisation or independent election candidate, or to political expenditure, is to a party, organisation, independent candidate or expenditure to which this Part applies.

364 MEANING OF "POLITICAL DONATION"

(1) The following provisions have effect for the purposes of this Part as regards the meaning of "political donation".

(2) In relation to a political party or other political organisation—
- (a) "political donation" means anything that in accordance with sections 50 to 52 of the Political Parties, Elections and Referendums Act 2000—
  - (i) constitutes a donation for the purposes of Chapter 1 of Part 4 of that Act (control of donations to registered parties), or
  - (ii) would constitute such a donation reading references in those sections to a registered party as references to any political party or other political organisation,

  and
- (b) section 53 of that Act applies, in the same way, for the purpose of determining the value of a donation.

(3) In relation to an independent election candidate—
- (a) "political donation" means anything that, in accordance with sections 50 to 52 of that Act, would constitute a donation for the purposes of Chapter 1 of Part 4 of that Act (control of donations to registered parties) reading references in those sections to a registered party as references to the independent election candidate,

  and
- (b) section 53 of that Act applies, in the same way, for the purpose of determining the value of a donation.

(4) For the purposes of this section, sections 50 and 53 of the Political Parties, Elections and Referendums Act 2000 (c. 41) (definition of "donation" and value of donations) shall be treated as if the amendments to those sections made by the Electoral Administration Act 2006 (which remove from the definition of "donation" loans made otherwise than on commercial terms) had not been made.

365 MEANING OF "POLITICAL EXPENDITURE"

(1) In this Part "political expenditure", in relation to a company, means expenditure incurred by the company on—
- (a) the preparation, publication or dissemination of advertising or other promotional or publicity material—
  - (i) of whatever nature, and
  - (ii) however published or otherwise disseminated,

  that, at the time of publication or dissemination, is capable of being reasonably regarded as intended to affect public support for a political party or other political organisation, or an independent election candidate, or
- (b) activities on the part of the company that are capable of being reasonably regarded as intended—
  - (i) to affect public support for a political party or other political organisation, or an independent election candidate, or
  - (ii) to influence voters in relation to any national or regional referendum held under the law of a member State.

(2) For the purposes of this Part a political donation does not count as political expenditure.

Authorisation required for donations or expenditure

366 AUTHORISATION REQUIRED FOR DONATIONS OR EXPENDITURE

(1) A company must not—
- (a) make a political donation to a political party or other political organisation, or to an independent election candidate, or
- (b) incur any political expenditure,

unless the donation or expenditure is authorised in accordance with the following provisions.

(2) The donation or expenditure must be authorised—
- (a) in the case of a company that is not a subsidiary of another company, by a resolution of the members of the company;
- (b) in the case of a company that is a subsidiary of another company by—
  - (i) a resolution of the members of the company, and
  - (ii) a resolution of the members of any relevant holding company.

(3) No resolution is required on the part of a company that is a wholly-owned subsidiary of a UK-registered company.

(4) For the purposes of subsection (2)(b)(ii) a "relevant holding company" means a company that, at the time the donation was made or the expenditure was incurred—
- (a) was a holding company of the company by which the donation was made or the expenditure was incurred,
- (b) was a UK-registered company, and
- (c) was not a subsidiary of another UK-registered company.

(5) The resolution or resolutions required by this section—
(a) must comply with section 367 (form of authorising resolution), and
(b) must be passed before the donation is made or the expenditure incurred.

(6) Nothing in this section enables a company to be authorised to do anything that it could not lawfully do apart from this section.

367 FORM OF AUTHORISING RESOLUTION

(1) A resolution conferring authorisation for the purposes of this Part may relate to—
(a) the company passing the resolution,
(b) one or more subsidiaries of that company, or
(c) the company passing the resolution and one or more subsidiaries of that company.

(2) A resolution may be expressed to relate to all companies that are subsidiaries of the company passing the resolution—
(a) at the time the resolution is passed, or
(b) at any time during the period for which the resolution has effect, without identifying them individually.

(3) The resolution may authorise donations or expenditure under one or more of the following heads—
(a) donations to political parties or independent election candidates;
(b) donations to political organisations other than political parties;
(c) political expenditure.

(4) The resolution must specify a head or heads—
(a) in the case of a resolution under subsection (2), for all of the companies to which it relates taken together;
(b) in the case of any other resolution, for each company to which it relates.

(5) The resolution must be expressed in general terms conforming with subsection (3) and must not purport to authorise particular donations or expenditure.

(6) For each of the specified heads the resolution must authorise donations or, as the case may be, expenditure up to a specified amount in the period for which the resolution has effect (see section 368).

(7) The resolution must specify such amounts—
(a) in the case of a resolution under subsection (2), for all of the companies to which it relates taken together;
(b) in the case of any other resolution, for each company to which it relates.

368 PERIOD FOR WHICH RESOLUTION HAS EFFECT

(1) A resolution conferring authorisation for the purposes of this Part has effect for a period of four years beginning with the date on which it is passed unless the directors determine, or the articles require, that it is to have effect for a shorter period beginning with that date.

(2) The power of the directors to make a determination under this section is subject to any provision of the articles that operates to prevent them from doing so.

Remedies in case of unauthorised donations or expenditure

369 LIABILITY OF DIRECTORS IN CASE OF UNAUTHORISED DONATION OR EXPENDITURE

(1) This section applies where a company has made a political donation or incurred political expenditure without the authorisation required by this Part.

(2) The directors in default are jointly and severally liable—
(a) to make good to the company the amount of the unauthorised donation or expenditure, with interest, and
(b) to compensate the company for any loss or damage sustained by it as a result of the unauthorised donation or expenditure having been made.

(3) The directors in default are—
(a) those who, at the time the unauthorised donation was made or the unauthorised expenditure was incurred, were directors of the company by which the donation was made or the expenditure was incurred, and
(b) where—
(i) that company was a subsidiary of a relevant holding company, and
(ii) the directors of the relevant holding company failed to take all reasonable steps to prevent the donation being made or the expenditure being incurred,
the directors of the relevant holding company.

(4) For the purposes of subsection (3)(b) a "relevant holding company" means a company that, at the time the donation was made or the expenditure was incurred—
(a) was a holding company of the company by which the donation was made or the expenditure was incurred,
(b) was a UK-registered company, and
(c) was not a subsidiary of another UK-registered company.

(5) The interest referred to in subsection (2)(a) is interest on the amount of the unauthorised donation or expenditure, so far as not made good to the company—
(a) in respect of the period beginning with the date when the donation was made or the expenditure was incurred, and
(b) at such rate as the Secretary of State may prescribe by regulations. Section 379(2) (construction of references to date when donation made or expenditure incurred) does not apply for the purposes of this subsection.

(6) Where only part of a donation or expenditure was unauthorised, this section applies only to so much of it as was unauthorised.

370 ENFORCEMENT OF DIRECTORS' LIABILITIES BY SHAREHOLDER ACTION

(1) Any liability of a director under section 369 is enforceable—
(a) in the case of a liability of a director of a company to that company, by proceedings brought under this section in the name of the company by an authorised group of its members;
(b) in the case of a liability of a director of a holding company to a subsidiary, by proceedings brought under this section in the name of the subsidiary by—
(i) an authorised group of members of the subsidiary, or
(ii) an authorised group of members of the holding company.

(2) This is in addition to the right of the company to which the liability is owed to bring proceedings itself to enforce the liability.

(3) An "authorised group" of members of a company means—
  (a) the holders of not less than 5% in nominal value of the company's issued share capital,
  (b) if the company is not limited by shares, not less than 5% of its members, or
  (c) not less than 50 of the company's members.

(4) The right to bring proceedings under this section is subject to the provisions of section 371.

(5) Nothing in this section affects any right of a member of a company to bring or continue proceedings under Part 11 (derivative claims or proceedings).

371 ENFORCEMENT OF DIRECTORS' LIABILITIES BY SHAREHOLDER ACTION: SUPPLEMENTARY

(1) A group of members may not bring proceedings under section 370 in the name of a company unless—
  (a) the group has given written notice to the company stating—
    (i) the cause of action and a summary of the facts on which the proceedings are to be based,
    (ii) the names and addresses of the members comprising the group, and
    (iii) the grounds on which it is alleged that those members constitute an authorised group; and
  (b) not less than 28 days have elapsed between the date of the giving of the notice to the company and the bringing of the proceedings.

(2) Where such a notice is given to a company, any director of the company may apply to the court within the period of 28 days beginning with the date of the giving of the notice for an order directing that the proposed proceedings shall not be brought, on one or more of the following grounds—
  (a) that the unauthorised amount has been made good to the company;
  (b) that proceedings to enforce the liability have been brought, and are being pursued with due diligence, by the company;
  (c) that the members proposing to bring proceedings under this section do not constitute an authorised group.

(3) Where an application is made on the ground mentioned in subsection (2)(b), the court may as an alternative to directing that the proposed proceedings under section 370 are not to be brought, direct—
  (a) that such proceedings may be brought on such terms and conditions as the court thinks fit, and
  (b) that the proceedings brought by the company—
    (i) shall be discontinued, or
    (ii) may be continued on such terms and conditions as the court thinks fit.

(4) The members by whom proceedings are brought under section 370 owe to the company in whose name they are brought the same duties in relation to the proceedings as would be owed by the company's directors if the proceedings were being brought by the company.

But proceedings to enforce any such duty may be brought by the company only with the permission of the court.

(5) Proceedings brought under section 370 may not be discontinued or settled by the group except with the permission of the court, which may be given on such terms as the court thinks fit.

372 COSTS OF SHAREHOLDER ACTION

(1) This section applies in relation to proceedings brought under section 370 in the name of a company ("the company") by an authorised group ("the group").

(2) The group may apply to the court for an order directing the company to indemnify the group in respect of costs incurred or to be incurred by the group in connection with the proceedings.

The court may make such an order on such terms as it thinks fit.

(3) The group is not entitled to be paid any such costs out of the assets of the company except by virtue of such an order.

(4) If no such order has been made with respect to the proceedings, then—
(a) if the company is awarded costs in connection with the proceedings, or it is agreed that costs incurred by the company in connection with the proceedings should be paid by any defendant, the costs shall be paid to the group; and
(b) if any defendant is awarded costs in connection with the proceedings, or it is agreed that any defendant should be paid costs incurred by him in connection with the proceedings, the costs shall be paid by the group.

(5) In the application of this section to Scotland for "costs" read "expenses" and for "defendant" read "defender".

373 INFORMATION FOR PURPOSES OF SHAREHOLDER ACTION

(1) Where proceedings have been brought under section 370 in the name of a company by an authorised group, the group is entitled to require the company to provide it with all information relating to the subject matter of the proceedings that is in the company's possession or under its control or which is reasonably obtainable by it.

(2) If the company, having been required by the group to do so, refuses to provide the group with all or any of that information, the court may, on an application made by the group, make an order directing—
(a) the company, and
(b) any of its officers or employees specified in the application,
to provide the group with the information in question in such form and by such means as the court may direct.

Exemptions

374 TRADE UNIONS

(1) A donation to a trade union, other than a contribution to the union's political fund, is not a political donation for the purposes of this Part.

(2) A trade union is not a political organisation for the purposes of section 365 (meaning of "political expenditure").

(3) In this section—

"trade union" has the meaning given by section 1 of Trade Union and Labour Relations (Consolidation) Act 1992 (c. 52) or Article 3 of the Industrial Relations (Northern Ireland) Order 1992 (S.I. 1992/807 (N.I. 5));

"political fund" means the fund from which payments by a trade union in the furtherance of political objects are required to be made by virtue of section 82(1)(a) of that Act or Article 57(2)(a) of that Order.

375 SUBSCRIPTION FOR MEMBERSHIP OF TRADE ASSOCIATION

(1) A subscription paid to a trade association for membership of the association is not a political donation for the purposes of this Part.

(2) For this purpose—

"trade association" means an organisation formed for the purpose of furthering the trade interests of its members, or of persons represented by its members, and

"subscription" does not include a payment to the association to the extent that it is made for the purpose of financing any particular activity of the association.

376 ALL-PARTY PARLIAMENTARY GROUPS

(1) An all-party parliamentary group is not a political organisation for the purposes of this Part.

(2) An "all-party parliamentary group" means an all-party group composed of members of one or both of the Houses of Parliament (or of such members and other persons).

377 POLITICAL EXPENDITURE EXEMPTED BY ORDER

(1) Authorisation under this Part is not needed for political expenditure that is exempt by virtue of an order of the Secretary of State under this section.

(2) An order may confer an exemption in relation to—
   (a) companies of any description or category specified in the order, or
   (b) expenditure of any description or category so specified (whether framed by reference to goods, services or other matters in respect of which such expenditure is incurred or otherwise),

or both.

(3) If or to the extent that expenditure is exempt from the requirement of authorisation under this Part by virtue of an order under this section, it shall be disregarded in determining what donations are authorised by any resolution of the company passed for the purposes of this Part.

(4) An order under this section is subject to affirmative resolution procedure.

378 DONATIONS NOT AMOUNTING TO MORE THAN £5,000 IN ANY TWELVE MONTH PERIOD

(1) Authorisation under this Part is not needed for a donation except to the extent that the total amount of—
   (a) that donation, and
   (b) other relevant donations made in the period of 12 months ending with the date on which that donation is made,

exceeds £5,000.

(2) In this section—

"donation" means a donation to a political party or other political organisation or to an independent election candidate; and

"other relevant donations" means—
   (a) in relation to a donation made by a company that is not a subsidiary, any other donations made by that company or by any of its subsidiaries;

(b) in relation to a donation made by a company that is a subsidiary, any other donations made by that company, by any holding company of that company or by any other subsidiary of any such holding company.

(3) If or to the extent that a donation is exempt by virtue of this section from the requirement of authorisation under this Part, it shall be disregarded in determining what donations are authorised by any resolution passed for the purposes of this Part.

Supplementary provisions

379 MINOR DEFINITIONS

(1) In this Part—

"director" includes shadow director; and

"organisation" includes any body corporate or unincorporated association and any combination of persons.

(2) Except as otherwise provided, any reference in this Part to the time at which a donation is made or expenditure is incurred is, in a case where the donation is made or expenditure incurred in pursuance of a contract, any earlier time at which that contract is entered into by the company.

Part 15 ACCOUNTS AND REPORTS

Chapter 1 INTRODUCTION

General

380 SCHEME OF THIS PART

(1) The requirements of this Part as to accounts and reports apply in relation to each financial year of a company.

(2) In certain respects different provisions apply to different kinds of company.

(3) The main distinctions for this purpose are—
(a) between companies subject to the small companies regime (see section 381) and companies that are not subject to that regime; and
(b) between quoted companies (see section 385) and companies that are not quoted.

Companies subject to the small companies regime

381 COMPANIES SUBJECT TO THE SMALL COMPANIES REGIME

The small companies regime applies to a company for a financial year in relation to which the company—

(a) qualifies as small (see sections 382 and 383), and

(b) is not excluded from the regime (see section 384).

382 COMPANIES QUALIFYING AS SMALL: GENERAL

(1) A company qualifies as small in relation to its first financial year if the qualifying conditions are met in that year.

(2) A company qualifies as small in relation to a subsequent financial year—
(a) if the qualifying conditions are met in that year and the preceding financial year;
(b) if the qualifying conditions are met in that year and the company qualified as small in relation to the preceding financial year;
(c) if the qualifying conditions were met in the preceding financial year and the company qualified as small in relation to that year.

(3) The qualifying conditions are met by a company in a year in which it satisfies two or more of the following requirements—

1. Turnover	Not more than £6.5 million
2. Balance sheet total	Not more than £3.26 million
3. Number of employees	Not more than 50

(4) For a period that is a company's financial year but not in fact a year the maximum figures for turnover must be proportionately adjusted.

(5) The balance sheet total means the aggregate of the amounts shown as assets in the company's balance sheet.

(6) The number of employees means the average number of persons employed by the company in the year, determined as follows—
(a) find for each month in the financial year the number of persons employed under contracts of service by the company in that month (whether throughout the month or not),
(b) add together the monthly totals, and
(c) divide by the number of months in the financial year.

(7) This section is subject to section 383 (companies qualifying as small: parent companies).

383 COMPANIES QUALIFYING AS SMALL: PARENT COMPANIES

(1) A parent company qualifies as a small company in relation to a financial year only if the group headed by it qualifies as a small group.

(2) A group qualifies as small in relation to the parent company's first financial year if the qualifying conditions are met in that year.

(3) A group qualifies as small in relation to a subsequent financial year of the parent company—
(a) if the qualifying conditions are met in that year and the preceding financial year;
(b) if the qualifying conditions are met in that year and the group qualified as small in relation to the preceding financial year;
(c) if the qualifying conditions were met in the preceding financial year and the group qualified as small in relation to that year.

(4) The qualifying conditions are met by a group in a year in which it satisfies two or more of the following requirements—

1. Aggregate turnover	Not more than £6.5 million net (or £7.8 million gross)
2. Aggregate balance sheet total	Not more than £3.26 million net (or £3.9 million gross)
3. Aggregate number of employees	Not more than 50

(5) The aggregate figures are ascertained by aggregating the relevant figures determined in accordance with section 382 for each member of the group.

(7) The figures for each subsidiary undertaking shall be those included in its individual accounts for the relevant financial year, that is—
(a) if its financial year ends with that of the parent company, that financial year, and
(b) if not, its financial year ending last before the end of the financial year of the parent company.

If those figures cannot be obtained without disproportionate expense or undue delay, the latest available figures shall be taken.

384 COMPANIES EXCLUDED FROM THE SMALL COMPANIES REGIME

(1) The small companies regime does not apply to a company that is, or was at any time within the financial year to which the accounts relate—
(a) a public company ... or
(c) a member of an ineligible group.

(2) A group is ineligible if any of its members is—
(a) a public company [or]
(b) a body corporate (other than a company) whose shares are admitted to trading on a regulated market in an EEA State...

...

(3) A company is a small company for the purposes of subsection (2) if it qualified as small in relation to its last financial year ending on or before the end of the financial year to which the accounts relate.

Quoted and unquoted companies

385 QUOTED AND UNQUOTED COMPANIES

(1) For the purposes of this Part a company is a quoted company in relation to a financial year if it is a quoted company immediately before the end of the accounting reference period by reference to which that financial year was determined.

(2) A "quoted company" means a company whose equity share capital—
(a) has been included in the official list in accordance with the provisions of Part 6 of the Financial Services and Markets Act 2000 (c. 8), or
(b) is officially listed in an EEA State, or
(c) is admitted to dealing on either the New York Stock Exchange or the exchange known as Nasdaq.

In paragraph (a) "the official list" has the meaning given by section 103(1) of the Financial Services and Markets Act 2000.

(3) An "unquoted company" means a company that is not a quoted company.

(4) The Secretary of State may by regulations amend or replace the provisions of subsections (1) to (2) so as to limit or extend the application of some or all of the provisions of this Part that are expressed to apply to quoted companies.

(5) Regulations under this section extending the application of any such provision of this Part are subject to affirmative resolution procedure.

(6) Any other regulations under this section are subject to negative resolution procedure.

Chapter 2 ACCOUNTING RECORDS

386 DUTY TO KEEP ACCOUNTING RECORDS

(1) Every company must keep adequate accounting records.

(2) Adequate accounting records means records that are sufficient—
(a) to show and explain the company's transactions,
(b) to disclose with reasonable accuracy, at any time, the financial position of the company at that time, and
(c) to enable the directors to ensure that any accounts required to be prepared comply with the requirements of this Act (and, where applicable, of Article 4 of the IAS Regulation).

(3) Accounting records must, in particular, contain—
(a) entries from day to day of all sums of money received and expended by the company and the matters in respect of which the receipt and expenditure takes place, and
(b) a record of the assets and liabilities of the company.

(4) If the company's business involves dealing in goods, the accounting records must contain—
(a) statements of stock held by the company at the end of each financial year of the company,
(b) all statements of stocktakings from which any statement of stock as is mentioned in paragraph (a) has been or is to be prepared, and
(c) except in the case of goods sold by way of ordinary retail trade, statements of all goods sold and purchased, showing the goods and the buyers and sellers in sufficient detail to enable all these to be identified.

(5) A parent company that has a subsidiary undertaking in relation to which the above requirements do not apply must take reasonable steps to secure that the undertaking keeps such accounting records as to enable the directors of the parent company to ensure that any accounts required to be prepared under this Part comply with the requirements of this Act (and, where applicable, of Article 4 of the IAS Regulation).

387 DUTY TO KEEP ACCOUNTING RECORDS: OFFENCE

(1) If a company fails to comply with any provision of section 386 (duty to keep accounting records), an offence is committed by every officer of the company who is in default.

(2) It is a defence for a person charged with such an offence to show that he acted honestly and that in the circumstances in which the company's business was carried on the default was excusable.

(3) A person guilty of an offence under this section is liable—
(a) on conviction on indictment, to imprisonment for a term not exceeding two years or a fine (or both);
(b) on summary conviction—
(i) in England and Wales, to imprisonment for a term not exceeding twelve months or to a fine not exceeding the statutory maximum (or both);
(ii) in Scotland or Northern Ireland, to imprisonment for a term not exceeding six months, or to a fine not exceeding the statutory maximum (or both).

388 WHERE AND FOR HOW LONG RECORDS TO BE KEPT

(1) A company's accounting records—

(a) must be kept at its registered office or such other place as the directors think fit, and
(b) must at all times be open to inspection by the company's officers.

(4) Accounting records that a company is required by section 386 to keep must be preserved by it—
(a) in the case of a private company, for three years from the date on which they are made;
(b) in the case of a public company, for six years from the date on which they are made.

389 WHERE AND FOR HOW LONG RECORDS TO BE KEPT: OFFENCES

(1) If a company fails to comply with any provision of [subsection (1)] of section 388 (requirements as to keeping of accounting records), an offence is committed by every officer of the company who is in default.

(2) It is a defence for a person charged with such an offence to show that he acted honestly and that in the circumstances in which the company's business was carried on the default was excusable.

(3) An officer of a company commits an offence if he—
(a) fails to take all reasonable steps for securing compliance by the company with subsection (4) of that section (period for which records to be preserved), or
(b) intentionally causes any default by the company under that subsection.

(4) A person guilty of an offence under this section is liable—
(a) on conviction on indictment, to imprisonment for a term not exceeding two years or a fine (or both);
(b) on summary conviction—
(i) in England and Wales, to imprisonment for a term not exceeding twelve months or to a fine not exceeding the statutory maximum (or both);
(ii) in Scotland or Northern Ireland, to imprisonment for a term not exceeding six months, or to a fine not exceeding the statutory maximum (or both).

Chapter 4 ANNUAL ACCOUNTS

General

393 ACCOUNTS TO GIVE TRUE AND FAIR VIEW

(1) The directors of a company must not approve accounts for the purposes of this Chapter unless they are satisfied that they give a true and fair view of the assets, liabilities, financial position and profit or loss—
(a) in the case of the company's individual accounts, of the company;
(b) in the case of the company's group accounts, of the undertakings included in the consolidation as a whole, so far as concerns members of the company.

(2) The auditor of a company in carrying out his functions under this Act in relation to the company's annual accounts must have regard to the directors' duty under subsection (1).

Individual accounts

394 DUTY TO PREPARE INDIVIDUAL ACCOUNTS

The directors of every company must prepare accounts for the company for each of its financial years.

Those accounts are referred to as the company's "individual accounts".

395 INDIVIDUAL ACCOUNTS: APPLICABLE ACCOUNTING FRAMEWORK

(1) A company's individual accounts may be prepared—
  (a) in accordance with section 396 ("Companies Act individual accounts"), or
  (b) in accordance with international accounting standards ("IAS individual accounts").

...

396 COMPANIES ACT INDIVIDUAL ACCOUNTS

(1) Companies Act individual accounts must comprise—
  (a) a balance sheet as at the last day of the financial year, and
  (b) a profit and loss account.

(2) The accounts must—
  (a) in the case of the balance sheet, give a true and fair view of the state of affairs of the company as at the end of the financial year, and
  (b) in the case of the profit and loss account, give a true and fair view of the profit or loss of the company for the financial year.

(3) The accounts must comply with provision made by the Secretary of State by regulations as to—
  (a) the form and content of the balance sheet and profit and loss account, and
  (b) additional information to be provided by way of notes to the accounts.

(4) If compliance with the regulations, and any other provision made by or under this Act as to the matters to be included in a company's individual accounts or in notes to those accounts, would not be sufficient to give a true and fair view, the necessary additional information must be given in the accounts or in a note to them.

(5) If in special circumstances compliance with any of those provisions is inconsistent with the requirement to give a true and fair view, the directors must depart from that provision to the extent necessary to give a true and fair view.

Particulars of any such departure, the reasons for it and its effect must be given in a note to the accounts.

397 IAS INDIVIDUAL ACCOUNTS

Where the directors of a company prepare IAS individual accounts, they must state in the notes to the accounts that the accounts have been prepared in accordance with international accounting standards.

Group accounts: small companies

398 OPTION TO PREPARE GROUP ACCOUNTS

If at the end of a financial year a company subject to the small companies regime is a parent company the directors, as well as preparing individual accounts for the year, may prepare group accounts for the year.

Group accounts: other companies

399 DUTY TO PREPARE GROUP ACCOUNTS

(1) This section applies to companies that are not subject to the small companies regime.

(2) If at the end of a financial year the company is a parent company the directors, as well as preparing individual accounts for the year, must prepare group accounts for the year unless the company is exempt from that requirement.

404 COMPANIES ACT GROUP ACCOUNTS

(1) Companies Act group accounts must comprise—
(a) a consolidated balance sheet dealing with the state of affairs of the parent company and its subsidiary undertakings, and
(b) a consolidated profit and loss account dealing with the profit or loss of the parent company and its subsidiary undertakings.

(2) The accounts must give a true and fair view of the state of affairs as at the end of the financial year, and the profit or loss for the financial year, of the undertakings included in the consolidation as a whole, so far as concerns members of the company.

(3) The accounts must comply with provision made by the Secretary of State by regulations as to—
(a) the form and content of the consolidated balance sheet and consolidated profit and loss account, and
(b) additional information to be provided by way of notes to the accounts.

(4) If compliance with the regulations, and any other provision made by or under this Act as to the matters to be included in a company's group accounts or in notes to those accounts, would not be sufficient to give a true and fair view, the necessary additional information must be given in the accounts or in a note to them.

(5) If in special circumstances compliance with any of those provisions is inconsistent with the requirement to give a true and fair view, the directors must depart from that provision to the extent necessary to give a true and fair view.

Particulars of any such departure, the reasons for it and its effect must be given in a note to the accounts.

405 COMPANIES ACT GROUP ACCOUNTS: SUBSIDIARY UNDERTAKINGS INCLUDED IN THE CONSOLIDATION

(1) Where a parent company prepares Companies Act group accounts, all the subsidiary undertakings of the company must be included in the consolidation, subject to the following exceptions.

(2) A subsidiary undertaking may be excluded from consolidation if its inclusion is not material for the purpose of giving a true and fair view (but two or more undertakings may be excluded only if they are not material taken together).

(3) A subsidiary undertaking may be excluded from consolidation where—
(a) severe long-term restrictions substantially hinder the exercise of the rights of the parent company over the assets or management of that undertaking, or
(b) the information necessary for the preparation of group accounts cannot be obtained without disproportionate expense or undue delay, or

(c) the interest of the parent company is held exclusively with a view to subsequent resale.

(4) The reference in subsection (3)(a) to the rights of the parent company and the reference in subsection (3)(c) to the interest of the parent company are, respectively, to rights and interests held by or attributed to the company for the purposes of the definition of "parent undertaking" (see section 1162) in the absence of which it would not be the parent company.

406 IAS GROUP ACCOUNTS

Where the directors of a company prepare IAS group accounts, they must state in the notes to those accounts that the accounts have been prepared in accordance with international accounting standards.

407 CONSISTENCY OF FINANCIAL REPORTING WITHIN GROUP

(1) The directors of a parent company must secure that the individual accounts of—
(a) the parent company, and
(b) each of its subsidiary undertakings,
are all prepared using the same financial reporting framework, except to the extent that in their opinion there are good reasons for not doing so.

Information to be given in notes to the accounts

409 INFORMATION ABOUT RELATED UNDERTAKINGS

(1) The Secretary of State may make provision by regulations requiring information about related undertakings to be given in notes to a company's annual accounts.

411 INFORMATION ABOUT EMPLOYEE NUMBERS AND COSTS

(1) In the case of a company not subject to the small companies regime, the following information with respect to the employees of the company must be given in notes to the company's annual accounts—
(a) the average number of persons employed by the company in the financial year, and
(b) the average number of persons so employed within each category of persons employed by the company.

(2) The categories by reference to which the number required to be disclosed by subsection (1)(b) is to be determined must be such as the directors may select having regard to the manner in which the company's activities are organised.

(5) In respect of all persons employed by the company during the financial year who are taken into account in determining the relevant annual number for the purposes of subsection (1)(a) there must also be stated the aggregate amounts respectively of—
(a) wages and salaries paid or payable in respect of that year to those persons;
(b) social security costs incurred by the company on their behalf; and
(c) other pension costs so incurred.
This does not apply in so far as those amounts, or any of them, are stated elsewhere in the company's accounts.

(7) This section applies in relation to group accounts as if the undertakings included in the consolidation were a single company.

412 INFORMATION ABOUT DIRECTORS' BENEFITS: REMUNERATION

(1) The Secretary of State may make provision by regulations requiring information to be given in notes to a company's annual accounts about directors' remuneration.

(2) The matters about which information may be required include—
(a) gains made by directors on the exercise of share options;
(b) benefits received or receivable by directors under long-term incentive schemes;
(c) payments for loss of office (as defined in section 215);
(d) benefits receivable, and contributions for the purpose of providing benefits, in respect of past services of a person as director or in any other capacity while director;
(e) consideration paid to or receivable by third parties for making available the services of a person as director or in any other capacity while director.

(5) It is the duty of—
(a) any director of a company, and
(b) any person who is or has at any time in the preceding five years been a director of the company, to give notice to the company of such matters relating to himself as may be necessary for the purposes of regulations under this section.

(6) A person who makes default in complying with subsection (5) commits an offence and is liable on summary conviction to a fine not exceeding level 3 on the standard scale.

413 INFORMATION ABOUT DIRECTORS' BENEFITS: ADVANCES, CREDIT AND GUARANTEES

(1) In the case of a company that does not prepare group accounts, details of—
(a) advances and credits granted by the company to its directors, and
(b) guarantees of any kind entered into by the company on behalf of its directors,
must be shown in the notes to its individual accounts.

(2) In the case of a parent company that prepares group accounts, details of—
(a) advances and credits granted to the directors of the parent company, by that company or by any of its subsidiary undertakings, and
(b) guarantees of any kind entered into on behalf of the directors of the parent company, by that company or by any of its subsidiary undertakings,
must be shown in the notes to the group accounts.

Approval and signing of accounts

414 APPROVAL AND SIGNING OF ACCOUNTS

(1) A company's annual accounts must be approved by the board of directors and signed on behalf of the board by a director of the company.

(2) The signature must be on the company's balance sheet.

(3) If the accounts are prepared in accordance with the provisions applicable to companies subject to the small companies regime, the balance sheet must contain a statement to that effect in a prominent position above the signature.

(4) If annual accounts are approved that do not comply with the requirements of this Act (and, where applicable, of Article 4 of the IAS Regulation), every director of the company who—
(a) knew that they did not comply, or was reckless as to whether they complied, and

(b) failed to take reasonable steps to secure compliance with those requirements or, as the case may be, to prevent the accounts from being approved,

commits an offence.

(5) A person guilty of an offence under this section is liable—
(a) on conviction on indictment, to a fine;
(b) on summary conviction, to a fine not exceeding the statutory maximum.

Chapter 5 DIRECTORS' REPORT

Directors' report

415 DUTY TO PREPARE DIRECTORS' REPORT

(1) The directors of a company must prepare a directors' report for each financial year of the company.

(2) For a financial year in which—
(a) the company is a parent company, and
(b) the directors of the company prepare group accounts,

the directors' report must be a consolidated report (a "group directors' report") relating to the undertakings included in the consolidation.

(3) A group directors' report may, where appropriate, give greater emphasis to the matters that are significant to the undertakings included in the consolidation, taken as a whole.

(4) In the case of failure to comply with the requirement to prepare a directors' report, an offence is committed by every person who—
(a) was a director of the company immediately before the end of the period for filing accounts and reports for the financial year in question, and
(b) failed to take all reasonable steps for securing compliance with that requirement.

(5) A person guilty of an offence under this section is liable—
(a) on conviction on indictment, to a fine;
(b) on summary conviction, to a fine not exceeding the statutory maximum.

415A DIRECTORS' REPORT: SMALL COMPANIES EXEMPTION

(1) A company is entitled to small companies exemption in relation to the directors' report for a financial year if—
(a) it is entitled to prepare accounts for the year in accordance with the small companies regime, or
(b) it would be so entitled but for being or having been a member of an ineligible group.

(2) The exemption is relevant to—

section 416(3) (contents of report: statement of amount recommended by way of dividend), [and]

section 417 (contents of report: business review)...

...

416 CONTENTS OF DIRECTORS' REPORT: GENERAL

(1) The directors' report for a financial year must state—
(a) the names of the persons who, at any time during the financial year, were directors of the company, and
(b) the principal activities of the company in the course of the year.

(2) In relation to a group directors' report subsection (1)(b) has effect as if the reference to the company was to the undertakings included in the consolidation.

(3) Except in the case of a company entitled to the small companies exemption, the report must state the amount (if any) that the directors recommend should be paid by way of dividend.

(4) The Secretary of State may make provision by regulations as to other matters that must be disclosed in a directors' report.

Without prejudice to the generality of this power, the regulations may make any such provision as was formerly made by Schedule 7 to the Companies Act 1985.

417 CONTENTS OF DIRECTORS' REPORT: BUSINESS REVIEW

(1) Unless the company is entitled to the small companies exemption, the directors' report must contain a business review.

(2) The purpose of the business review is to inform members of the company and help them assess how the directors have performed their duty under section 172 (duty to promote the success of the company).

(3) The business review must contain—
(a) a fair review of the company's business, and
(b) a description of the principal risks and uncertainties facing the company.

(4) The review required is a balanced and comprehensive analysis of—
(a) the development and performance of the company's business during the financial year, and
(b) the position of the company's business at the end of that year,
consistent with the size and complexity of the business.

(5) In the case of a quoted company the business review must, to the extent necessary for an understanding of the development, performance or position of the company's business, include—
(a) the main trends and factors likely to affect the future development, performance and position of the company's business; and
(b) information about—
(i) environmental matters (including the impact of the company's business on the environment),
(ii) the company's employees, and
(iii) social and community issues,
including information about any policies of the company in relation to those matters and the effectiveness of those policies; and
(c) subject to subsection (11), information about persons with whom the company has contractual or other arrangements which are essential to the business of the company.
If the review does not contain information of each kind mentioned in paragraphs (b)(i), (ii) and (iii) and (c), it must state which of those kinds of information it does not contain.

(6) The review must, to the extent necessary for an understanding of the development, performance or position of the company's business, include—
(a) analysis using financial key performance indicators, and
(b) where appropriate, analysis using other key performance indicators, including information relating to environmental matters and employee matters.

"Key performance indicators" means factors by reference to which the development, performance or position of the company's business can be measured effectively.

...

(8) The review must, where appropriate, include references to, and additional explanations of, amounts included in the company's annual accounts.

(9) In relation to a group directors' report this section has effect as if the references to the company were references to the undertakings included in the consolidation.

(10) Nothing in this section requires the disclosure of information about impending developments or matters in the course of negotiation if the disclosure would, in the opinion of the directors, be seriously prejudicial to the interests of the company.

(11) Nothing in subsection (5)(c) requires the disclosure of information about a person if the disclosure would, in the opinion of the directors, be seriously prejudicial to that person and contrary to the public interest.

418 CONTENTS OF DIRECTORS' REPORT: STATEMENT AS TO DISCLOSURE TO AUDITORS

(1) This section applies to a company unless—
(a) it is exempt for the financial year in question from the requirements of Part 16 as to audit of accounts, and
(b) the directors take advantage of that exemption.

(2) The directors' report must contain a statement to the effect that, in the case of each of the persons who are directors at the time the report is approved—
(a) so far as the director is aware, there is no relevant audit information of which the company's auditor is unaware, and
(b) he has taken all the steps that he ought to have taken as a director in order to make himself aware of any relevant audit information and to establish that the company's auditor is aware of that information.

(3) "Relevant audit information" means information needed by the company's auditor in connection with preparing his report.

(4) A director is regarded as having taken all the steps that he ought to have taken as a director in order to do the things mentioned in subsection (2)(b) if he has—
(a) made such enquiries of his fellow directors and of the company's auditors for that purpose, and
(b) taken such other steps (if any) for that purpose,
as are required by his duty as a director of the company to exercise reasonable care, skill and diligence.

(5) Where a directors' report containing the statement required by this section is approved but the statement is false, every director of the company who—
(a) knew that the statement was false, or was reckless as to whether it was false, and
(b) failed to take reasonable steps to prevent the report from being approved,
commits an offence.

(6) A person guilty of an offence under subsection (5) is liable—
(a) on conviction on indictment, to imprisonment for a term not exceeding two years or a fine (or both);
(b) on summary conviction—

(i) in England and Wales, to imprisonment for a term not exceeding twelve months or to a fine not exceeding the statutory maximum (or both);
(ii) in Scotland or Northern Ireland, to imprisonment for a term not exceeding six months, or to a fine not exceeding the statutory maximum (or both).

419 APPROVAL AND SIGNING OF DIRECTORS' REPORT

(1) The directors' report must be approved by the board of directors and signed on behalf of the board by a director or the secretary of the company.

(2) If in preparing the report advantage is taken of the small companies exemption, it must contain a statement to that effect in a prominent position above the signature.

(3) If a directors' report is approved that does not comply with the requirements of this Act, every director of the company who—
(a) knew that it did not comply, or was reckless as to whether it complied, and
(b) failed to take reasonable steps to secure compliance with those requirements or, as the case may be, to prevent the report from being approved,
commits an offence.

(4) A person guilty of an offence under this section is liable—
(a) on conviction on indictment, to a fine;
(b) on summary conviction, to a fine not exceeding the statutory maximum.

419A APPROVAL AND SIGNING OF SEPARATE CORPORATE GOVERNANCE STATEMENT

Any separate corporate governance statement must be approved by the board of directors and signed on behalf of the board by a director or the secretary of the company.

Chapter 6 QUOTED COMPANIES: DIRECTORS' REMUNERATION REPORT

420 DUTY TO PREPARE DIRECTORS' REMUNERATION REPORT

(1) The directors of a quoted company must prepare a directors' remuneration report for each financial year of the company.

421 CONTENTS OF DIRECTORS' REMUNERATION REPORT

(1) The Secretary of State may make provision by regulations as to—
(a) the information that must be contained in a directors' remuneration report,
(b) how information is to be set out in the report, and
(c) what is to be the auditable part of the report.

(2) Without prejudice to the generality of this power, the regulations may make any such provision as was made, immediately before the commencement of this Part, by Schedule 7A to the Companies Act 1985 (c. 6).

(3) It is the duty of—
(a) any director of a company, and
(b) any person who is or has at any time in the preceding five years been a director of the company, to give notice to the company of such matters relating to himself as may be necessary for the purposes of regulations under this section.

422 APPROVAL AND SIGNING OF DIRECTORS' REMUNERATION REPORT

(1) The directors' remuneration report must be approved by the board of directors and signed on behalf of the board by a director or the secretary of the company.

Chapter 7 PUBLICATION OF ACCOUNTS AND REPORTS

Duty to circulate copies of accounts and reports

423 DUTY TO CIRCULATE COPIES OF ANNUAL ACCOUNTS AND REPORTS

(1) Every company must send a copy of its annual accounts and reports for each financial year to—
(a) every member of the company,
(b) every holder of the company's debentures, and
(c) every person who is entitled to receive notice of general meetings.

(6) This section has effect subject to section 426 (option to provide summary financial statement).

424 TIME ALLOWED FOR SENDING OUT COPIES OF ACCOUNTS AND REPORTS

(1) The time allowed for sending out copies of the company's annual accounts and reports is as follows.

(2) A private company must comply with section 423 not later than—
(a) the end of the period for filing accounts and reports, or
(b) if earlier, the date on which it actually delivers its accounts and reports to the registrar.

(3) A public company must comply with section 423 at least 21 days before the date of the relevant accounts meeting.

(4) If in the case of a public company copies are sent out later than is required by subsection (3), they shall, despite that, be deemed to have been duly sent if it is so agreed by all the members entitled to attend and vote at the relevant accounts meeting.

...

(6) In this section the "relevant accounts meeting" means the accounts meeting of the company at which the accounts and reports in question are to be laid.

Option to provide summary financial statement

426 OPTION TO PROVIDE SUMMARY FINANCIAL STATEMENT

(1) A company may—
(a) in such cases as may be specified by regulations made by the Secretary of State, and
(b) provided any conditions so specified are complied with,
provide a summary financial statement instead of copies of the accounts and reports required to be sent out in accordance with section 423.

(2) Copies of those accounts and reports must, however, be sent to any person entitled to be sent them in accordance with that section and who wishes to receive them.

(4) A summary financial statement must comply with the requirements of—

section 427 (form and contents of summary financial statement: unquoted companies), or

section 428 (form and contents of summary financial statement: quoted companies).

427 FORM AND CONTENTS OF SUMMARY FINANCIAL STATEMENT: UNQUOTED COMPANIES

(1) A summary financial statement by a company that is not a quoted company must—
- (a) be derived from the company's annual accounts, and
- (b) be prepared in accordance with this section and regulations made under it.

(2) The summary financial statement must be in such form, and contain such information, as the Secretary of State may specify by regulations.

The regulations may require the statement to include information derived from the directors' report.

428 FORM AND CONTENTS OF SUMMARY FINANCIAL STATEMENT: QUOTED COMPANIES

(1) A summary financial statement by a quoted company must—
- (a) be derived from the company's annual accounts and the directors' remuneration report, and
- (b) be prepared in accordance with this section and regulations made under it.

(2) The summary financial statement must be in such form, and contain such information, as the Secretary of State may specify by regulations.

The regulations may require the statement to include information derived from the directors' report.

Quoted companies: requirements as to website publication

430 QUOTED COMPANIES: ANNUAL ACCOUNTS AND REPORTS TO BE MADE AVAILABLE ON WEBSITE

(1) A quoted company must ensure that its annual accounts and reports—
- (a) are made available on a website, and
- (b) remain so available until the annual accounts and reports for the company's next financial year are made available in accordance with this section.

Right of member or debenture holder to demand copies of accounts and reports

431 RIGHT OF MEMBER OR DEBENTURE HOLDER TO COPIES OF ACCOUNTS AND REPORTS: UNQUOTED COMPANIES

(1) A member of, or holder of debentures of, an unquoted company is entitled to be provided, on demand and without charge, with a copy of—
- (a) the company's last annual accounts,
- (b) the last directors' report, and
- (c) the auditor's report on those accounts (including the statement on that report).

432 RIGHT OF MEMBER OR DEBENTURE HOLDER TO COPIES OF ACCOUNTS AND REPORTS: QUOTED COMPANIES

(1) A member of, or holder of debentures of, a quoted company is entitled to be provided, on demand and without charge, with a copy of—
- (a) the company's last annual accounts,
- (b) the last directors' remuneration report,
- (c) the last directors' report, and
- (d) the auditor's report on those accounts (including the report on the directors' remuneration report and on the directors' report).

434 REQUIREMENTS IN CONNECTION WITH PUBLICATION OF STATUTORY ACCOUNTS

(1) If a company publishes any of its statutory accounts, they must be accompanied by the auditor's report on those accounts (unless the company is exempt from audit and the directors have taken advantage of that exemption).

(2) A company that prepares statutory group accounts for a financial year must not publish its statutory individual accounts for that year without also publishing with them its statutory group accounts.

(6) This section does not apply in relation to the provision by a company of a summary financial statement (see section 426).

Chapter 8 PUBLIC COMPANIES: LAYING OF ACCOUNTS AND REPORTS BEFORE GENERAL MEETING

437 PUBLIC COMPANIES: LAYING OF ACCOUNTS AND REPORTS BEFORE GENERAL MEETING

(1) The directors of a public company must lay before the company in general meeting copies of its annual accounts and reports.

Chapter 9 QUOTED COMPANIES: MEMBERS' APPROVAL OF DIRECTORS' REMUNERATION REPORT

439 QUOTED COMPANIES: MEMBERS' APPROVAL OF DIRECTORS' REMUNERATION REPORT

(1) A quoted company must, prior to the accounts meeting, give to the members of the company entitled to be sent notice of the meeting notice of the intention to move at the meeting, as an ordinary resolution, a resolution approving the directors' remuneration report for the financial year.

(4) The existing directors must ensure that the resolution is put to the vote of the meeting.

(5) No entitlement of a person to remuneration is made conditional on the resolution being passed by reason only of the provision made by this section.

(6) In this section—

"the accounts meeting" means the general meeting of the company before which the company's annual accounts for the financial year are to be laid; and

"existing director" means a person who is a director of the company immediately before that meeting.

Chapter 10 FILING OF ACCOUNTS AND REPORTS

Duty to file accounts and reports

442 PERIOD ALLOWED FOR FILING ACCOUNTS

(1) This section specifies the period allowed for the directors of a company to comply with their obligation … to deliver accounts and reports for a financial year to the registrar.

This is referred to in the Companies Acts as the "period for filing" those accounts and reports.

(2) The period is—
(a) for a private company, nine months after the end of the relevant accounting reference period, and
(b) for a public company, six months after the end of that period.
…

Chapter 11 REVISION OF DEFECTIVE ACCOUNTS AND REPORTS

Voluntary revision

454 VOLUNTARY REVISION OF ACCOUNTS ETC.

(1) If it appears to the directors of a company that—
(a) the company's annual accounts,
(b) the directors' remuneration report or the directors' report, or
(c) a summary financial statement of the company,
did not comply with the requirements of this Act (or, where applicable, of Article 4 of the IAS Regulation), they may prepare revised accounts or a revised report or statement.

Secretary of State's notice

455 SECRETARY OF STATE'S NOTICE IN RESPECT OF ACCOUNTS OR REPORTS

(1) This section applies where—
(a) copies of a company's annual accounts or directors' report have been sent out under section 423, or
(b) a copy of a company's annual accounts or directors' report has been delivered to the registrar or (in the case of a public company) laid before the company in general meeting,
and it appears to the Secretary of State that there is, or may be, a question whether the accounts or report comply with the requirements of this Act (or, where applicable, of Article 4 of the IAS Regulation).

(2) The Secretary of State may give notice to the directors of the company indicating the respects in which it appears that such a question arises or may arise.

(3) The notice must specify a period of not less than one month for the directors to give an explanation of the accounts or report or prepare revised accounts or a revised report.

(4) If at the end of the specified period, or such longer period as the Secretary of State may allow, it appears to the Secretary of State that the directors have not—
(a) given a satisfactory explanation of the accounts or report, or

(b) revised the accounts or report so as to comply with the requirements of this Act (or, where applicable, of Article 4 of the IAS Regulation),

the Secretary of State may apply to the court.

(5) The provisions of this section apply equally to revised annual accounts and revised directors' reports, in which case they have effect as if the references to revised accounts or reports were references to further revised accounts or reports.

Application to court

456 APPLICATION TO COURT IN RESPECT OF DEFECTIVE ACCOUNTS OR REPORTS

(1) An application may be made to the court—

(a) by the Secretary of State, after having complied with section 455, or

(b) by a person authorised by the Secretary of State for the purposes of this section,

for a declaration (in Scotland, a declarator) that the annual accounts of a company do not comply, or a directors' report does not comply, with the requirements of this Act (or, where applicable, of Article 4 of the IAS Regulation) and for an order requiring the directors of the company to prepare revised accounts or a revised report.

Chapter 12 SUPPLEMENTARY PROVISIONS

Liability for false or misleading statements in reports

463 LIABILITY FOR FALSE OR MISLEADING STATEMENTS IN REPORTS

(1) The reports to which this section applies are—

(a) the directors' report,

(b) the directors' remuneration report, and

(c) a summary financial statement so far as it is derived from either of those reports.

(2) A director of a company is liable to compensate the company for any loss suffered by it as a result of—

(a) any untrue or misleading statement in a report to which this section applies, or

(b) the omission from a report to which this section applies of anything required to be included in it.

(3) He is so liable only if—

(a) he knew the statement to be untrue or misleading or was reckless as to whether it was untrue or misleading, or

(b) he knew the omission to be dishonest concealment of a material fact.

(4) No person shall be subject to any liability to a person other than the company resulting from reliance, by that person or another, on information in a report to which this section applies.

(5) The reference in subsection (4) to a person being subject to a liability includes a reference to another person being entitled as against him to be granted any civil remedy or to rescind or repudiate an agreement.

(6) This section does not affect—

(a) liability for a civil penalty, or

(b) liability for a criminal offence.

Companies qualifying as medium-sized

465 COMPANIES QUALIFYING AS MEDIUM-SIZED: GENERAL

(1) A company qualifies as medium-sized in relation to its first financial year if the qualifying conditions are met in that year.

(2) A company qualifies as medium-sized in relation to a subsequent financial year—
(a) if the qualifying conditions are met in that year and the preceding financial year;
(b) if the qualifying conditions are met in that year and the company qualified as medium-sized in relation to the preceding financial year;
(c) if the qualifying conditions were met in the preceding financial year and the company qualified as medium-sized in relation to that year.

(3) The qualifying conditions are met by a company in a year in which it satisfies two or more of the following requirements—

1. Turnover	Not more than £25.9 million
2. Balance sheet total	Not more than £12.9 million
3. Number of employees	Not more than 250

(4) For a period that is a company's financial year but not in fact a year the maximum figures for turnover must be proportionately adjusted.

(5) The balance sheet total means the aggregate of the amounts shown as assets in the company's balance sheet.

(6) The number of employees means the average number of persons employed by the company in the year, determined as follows—
(a) find for each month in the financial year the number of persons employed under contracts of service by the company in that month (whether throughout the month or not),
(b) add together the monthly totals, and
(c) divide by the number of months in the financial year.

(7) This section is subject to section 466 (companies qualifying as medium-sized: parent companies).

466 COMPANIES QUALIFYING AS MEDIUM-SIZED: PARENT COMPANIES

(1) A parent company qualifies as a medium-sized company in relation to a financial year only if the group headed by it qualifies as a medium-sized group.

(2) A group qualifies as medium-sized in relation to the parent company's first financial year if the qualifying conditions are met in that year.

(3) A group qualifies as medium-sized in relation to a subsequent financial year of the parent company—
(a) if the qualifying conditions are met in that year and the preceding financial year;
(b) if the qualifying conditions are met in that year and the group qualified as medium-sized in relation to the preceding financial year;
(c) if the qualifying conditions were met in the preceding financial year and the group qualified as medium-sized in relation to that year.

(4) The qualifying conditions are met by a group in a year in which it satisfies two or more of the following requirements—

1. Aggregate turnover	Not more than £25.9 million net (or £31.1 million gross)
2. Aggregate balance sheet total	Not more than £12.9 million net (or £15.5 million gross)
3. Aggregate number of employees	Not more than 250

(5) The aggregate figures are ascertained by aggregating the relevant figures determined in accordance with section 465 for each member of the group.

(7) The figures for each subsidiary undertaking shall be those included in its individual accounts for the relevant financial year, that is—
(a) if its financial year ends with that of the parent company, that financial year, and
(b) if not, its financial year ending last before the end of the financial year of the parent company.
If those figures cannot be obtained without disproportionate expense or undue delay, the latest available figures shall be taken.

467 COMPANIES EXCLUDED FROM BEING TREATED AS MEDIUM-SIZED

(1) A company is not entitled to take advantage of any of the provisions of this Part relating to companies qualifying as medium-sized if it was at any time within the financial year in question—
(a) a public company,
..., or
(c) a member of an ineligible group.

(2) A group is ineligible if any of its members is—
(a) a public company,
(b) a body corporate (other than a company) whose shares are admitted to trading on a regulated market...
...

(3) A company is a small company for the purposes of subsection (2) if it qualified as small in relation to its last financial year ending on or before the end of the financial year in question.

Other supplementary provisions

469 PREPARATION AND FILING OF ACCOUNTS IN EUROS

(1) The amounts set out in the annual accounts of a company may also be shown in the same accounts translated into euros.

471 MEANING OF "ANNUAL ACCOUNTS" AND RELATED EXPRESSIONS

(1) In this Part a company's "annual accounts", in relation to a financial year, means—
(a) the company's individual accounts for that year (see section 394), and
(b) any group accounts prepared by the company for that year (see sections 398 and 399).
...

(2) In the case of an unquoted company, its "annual accounts and reports" for a financial year are—
(a) its annual accounts,

(b) the directors' report, and
(c) the auditor's report on those accounts and the directors' report (unless the company is exempt from audit).

(3) In the case of a quoted company, its "annual accounts and reports" for a financial year are—
(a) its annual accounts,
(b) the directors' remuneration report,
(c) the directors' report, and
(d) the auditor's report on those accounts, on the auditable part of the directors' remuneration report and on the directors' report.

472 NOTES TO THE ACCOUNTS

(1) Information required by this Part to be given in notes to a company's annual accounts may be contained in the accounts or in a separate document annexed to the accounts.

(2) References in this Part to a company's annual accounts, or to a balance sheet or profit and loss account, include notes to the accounts giving information which is required by any provision of this Act or international accounting standards, and required or allowed by any such provision to be given in a note to company accounts.

472A MEANING OF "CORPORATE GOVERNANCE STATEMENT" ETC.

(1) In this Part "corporate governance statement" means the statement required by rules 7.2.1 to 7.2.11 in the Disclosure Rules and Transparency Rules sourcebook issued by the Financial Services Authority.

(2) Those rules were inserted by Annex C of the Disclosure Rules and Transparency Rules Sourcebook (Corporate Governance Rules) Instrument 2008 made by the Authority on 26th June 2008 (FSA 2008/32).

(3) A "separate" corporate governance statement means one that is not included in the directors' report.

474 MINOR DEFINITIONS

(1) In this Part—

...

"group" means a parent undertaking and its subsidiary undertakings;

"IAS Regulation" means EC Regulation No. 1606/2002 of the European Parliament and of the Council of 19 July 2002 on the application of international accounting standards;

...

"international accounting standards" means the international accounting standards, within the meaning of the IAS Regulation, adopted from time to time by the European Commission in accordance with that Regulation;

...

Part 16 AUDIT

Chapter 1 REQUIREMENT FOR AUDITED ACCOUNTS

Requirement for audited accounts

475 REQUIREMENT FOR AUDITED ACCOUNTS

(1) A company's annual accounts for a financial year must be audited in accordance with this Part unless the company—
  (a) is exempt from audit under—
  section 477 (small companies)...
  ...

(2) A company is not entitled to any such exemption unless its balance sheet contains a statement by the directors to that effect.

476 RIGHT OF MEMBERS TO REQUIRE AUDIT

(1) The members of a company that would otherwise be entitled to exemption from audit under any of the provisions mentioned in section 475(1)(a) may by notice under this section require it to obtain an audit of its accounts for a financial year.

(2) The notice must be given by—
  (a) members representing not less in total than 10% in nominal value of the company's issued share capital, or any class of it...
  ...

(3) The notice may not be given before the financial year to which it relates and must be given not later than one month before the end of that year.

Exemption from audit: small companies

477 SMALL COMPANIES: CONDITIONS FOR EXEMPTION FROM AUDIT

(1) A company that meets the following conditions in respect of a financial year is exempt from the requirements of this Act relating to the audit of accounts for that year.

(2) The conditions are—
  (a) that the company qualifies as a small company in relation to that year,
  (b) that its turnover in that year is not more than £6.5 million, and
  (c) that its balance sheet total for that year is not more than £3.26 million.

(4) For the purposes of this section—
  (a) whether a company qualifies as a small company shall be determined in accordance with section 382(1) to (6), and
  (b) "balance sheet total" has the same meaning as in that section.

(5) This section has effect subject to—
section 475(2) ... (requirements as to statements to be contained in balance sheet),
section 476 (right of members to require audit),
section 478 (companies excluded from small companies exemption), and
section 479 (availability of small companies exemption in case of group company).

478 COMPANIES EXCLUDED FROM SMALL COMPANIES EXEMPTION

A company is not entitled to the exemption conferred by section 477 (small companies) if it was at any time within the financial year in question—

(a) a public company...

...

479 AVAILABILITY OF SMALL COMPANIES EXEMPTION IN CASE OF GROUP COMPANY

(1) A company is not entitled to the exemption conferred by section 477 (small companies) in respect of a financial year during any part of which it was a group company unless—
   (a) the conditions specified in subsection (2) below are met, or
   (b) subsection (3) applies.

(2) The conditions are—
   (a) that the group—
      (i) qualifies as a small group in relation to that financial year, and
      (ii) was not at any time in that year an ineligible group;
   (b) that the group's aggregate turnover in that year is not more than £6.5 million net (or £7.8 million gross);
   (c) that the group's aggregate balance sheet total for that year is not more than £3.26 million net (or £3.9 million gross).

...

(4) In this section—
   (a) "group company" means a company that is a parent company or a subsidiary undertaking, and
   (b) "the group", in relation to a group company, means that company together with all its associated undertakings.

   For this purpose undertakings are associated if one is a subsidiary undertaking of the other or both are subsidiary undertakings of a third undertaking.

(5) For the purposes of this section—
   (a) whether a group qualifies as small shall be determined in accordance with section 383 (companies qualifying as small: parent companies);
   (b) "ineligible group" has the meaning given by section 384(2) and (3);
   (c) a group's aggregate turnover and aggregate balance sheet total shall be determined as for the purposes of section 383;
   (d) "net" and "gross" have the same meaning as in that section;
   (e) a company may meet any relevant requirement on the basis of either the gross or the net figure.

(6) The provisions mentioned in subsection (5) apply for the purposes of this section as if all the bodies corporate in the group were companies.

Chapter 2 APPOINTMENT OF AUDITORS

Private companies

485 APPOINTMENT OF AUDITORS OF PRIVATE COMPANY: GENERAL

(1) An auditor or auditors of a private company must be appointed for each financial year of the company, unless the directors reasonably resolve otherwise on the ground that audited accounts are unlikely to be required.

(2) For each financial year for which an auditor or auditors is or are to be appointed (other than the company's first financial year), the appointment must be made before the end of the period of 28 days beginning with—
(a) the end of the time allowed for sending out copies of the company's annual accounts and reports for the previous financial year (see section 424), or
(b) if earlier, the day on which copies of the company's annual accounts and reports for the previous financial year are sent out under section 423.
This is the "period for appointing auditors".

(3) The directors may appoint an auditor or auditors of the company—
(a) at any time before the company's first period for appointing auditors...
...

(4) The members may appoint an auditor or auditors by ordinary resolution—
(a) during a period for appointing auditors,
(b) if the company should have appointed an auditor or auditors during a period for appointing auditors but failed to do so, or
(c) where the directors had power to appoint under subsection (3) but have failed to make an appointment.

(5) An auditor or auditors of a private company may only be appointed—
(a) in accordance with this section, or
(b) in accordance with section 486 (default power of Secretary of State).
This is without prejudice to any deemed re-appointment under section 487.

486 APPOINTMENT OF AUDITORS OF PRIVATE COMPANY: DEFAULT POWER OF SECRETARY OF STATE

(1) If a private company fails to appoint an auditor or auditors in accordance with section 485, the Secretary of State may appoint one or more persons to fill the vacancy.

487 TERM OF OFFICE OF AUDITORS OF PRIVATE COMPANY

(1) An auditor or auditors of a private company hold office in accordance with the terms of their appointment, subject to the requirements that—
(a) they do not take office until any previous auditor or auditors cease to hold office, and
(b) they cease to hold office at the end of the next period for appointing auditors unless re-appointed.

(2) Where no auditor has been appointed by the end of the next period for appointing auditors, any auditor in office immediately before that time is deemed to be re-appointed at that time, unless—
(a) he was appointed by the directors, or
(b) the company's articles require actual re-appointment, or
(c) the deemed re-appointment is prevented by the members under section 488, or
(d) the members have resolved that he should not be re-appointed, or
(e) the directors have resolved that no auditor or auditors should be appointed for the financial year in question.

(3) This is without prejudice to the provisions of this Part as to removal and resignation of auditors.

488 PREVENTION BY MEMBERS OF DEEMED RE-APPOINTMENT OF AUDITOR

(1) An auditor of a private company is not deemed to be re-appointed under section 487(2) if the company has received notices under this section from members representing at least the requisite percentage of the total voting rights of all members who would be entitled to vote on a resolution that the auditor should not be re-appointed.

(2) The "requisite percentage" is 5%, or such lower percentage as is specified for this purpose in the company's articles.

Public companies

489 APPOINTMENT OF AUDITORS OF PUBLIC COMPANY: GENERAL

(1) An auditor or auditors of a public company must be appointed for each financial year of the company, unless the directors reasonably resolve otherwise on the ground that audited accounts are unlikely to be required.

(2) For each financial year for which an auditor or auditors is or are to be appointed (other than the company's first financial year), the appointment must be made before the end of the accounts meeting of the company at which the company's annual accounts and reports for the previous financial year are laid.

(3) The directors may appoint an auditor or auditors of the company—
 (a) at any time before the company's first accounts meeting...
 ...

(4) The members may appoint an auditor or auditors by ordinary resolution—
 (a) at an accounts meeting;
 (b) if the company should have appointed an auditor or auditors at an accounts meeting but failed to do so;
 (c) where the directors had power to appoint under subsection (3) but have failed to make an appointment.

(5) An auditor or auditors of a public company may only be appointed—
 (a) in accordance with this section, or
 (b) in accordance with section 490 (default power of Secretary of State).

490 APPOINTMENT OF AUDITORS OF PUBLIC COMPANY: DEFAULT POWER OF SECRETARY OF STATE

(1) If a public company fails to appoint an auditor or auditors in accordance with section 489, the Secretary of State may appoint one or more persons to fill the vacancy.

491 TERM OF OFFICE OF AUDITORS OF PUBLIC COMPANY

(1) The auditor or auditors of a public company hold office in accordance with the terms of their appointment, subject to the requirements that—
 (a) they do not take office until the previous auditor or auditors have ceased to hold office, and
 (b) they cease to hold office at the conclusion of the accounts meeting next following their appointment, unless re-appointed.

(2) This is without prejudice to the provisions of this Part as to removal and resignation of auditors.

General provisions

492 FIXING OF AUDITOR'S REMUNERATION

(1) The remuneration of an auditor appointed by the members of a company must be fixed by the members by ordinary resolution or in such manner as the members may by ordinary resolution determine.

(2) The remuneration of an auditor appointed by the directors of a company must be fixed by the directors.

(3) The remuneration of an auditor appointed by the Secretary of State must be fixed by the Secretary of State.

(4) For the purposes of this section "remuneration" includes sums paid in respect of expenses.

(5) This section applies in relation to benefits in kind as to payments of money.

493 DISCLOSURE OF TERMS OF AUDIT APPOINTMENT

(1) The Secretary of State may make provision by regulations for securing the disclosure of the terms on which a company's auditor is appointed, remunerated or performs his duties.

Nothing in the following provisions of this section affects the generality of this power.

494 DISCLOSURE OF SERVICES PROVIDED BY AUDITOR OR ASSOCIATES AND RELATED REMUNERATION

(1) The Secretary of State may make provision by regulations for securing the disclosure of—
- (a) the nature of any services provided for a company by the company's auditor (whether in his capacity as auditor or otherwise) or by his associates;
- (b) the amount of any remuneration received or receivable by a company's auditor, or his associates, in respect of any such services.

Nothing in the following provisions of this section affects the generality of this power.

(2) The regulations may provide—
- (a) for disclosure of the nature of any services provided to be made by reference to any class or description of services specified in the regulations (or any combination of services, however described);
- (b) for the disclosure of amounts of remuneration received or receivable in respect of services of any class or description specified in the regulations (or any combination of services, however described);
- (c) for the disclosure of separate amounts so received or receivable by the company's auditor or any of his associates, or of aggregate amounts so received or receivable by all or any of those persons.

Chapter 3 FUNCTIONS OF AUDITOR

Auditor's report

495 AUDITOR'S REPORT ON COMPANY'S ANNUAL ACCOUNTS

(1) A company's auditor must make a report to the company's members on all annual accounts of the company of which copies are, during his tenure of office—

(a) in the case of a private company, to be sent out to members under section 423;
(b) in the case of a public company, to be laid before the company in general meeting under section 437.

(2) The auditor's report must include—
(a) an introduction identifying the annual accounts that are the subject of the audit and the financial reporting framework that has been applied in their preparation, and
(b) a description of the scope of the audit identifying the auditing standards in accordance with which the audit was conducted.

(3) The report must state clearly whether, in the auditor's opinion, the annual accounts—
(a) give a true and fair view—
(i) in the case of an individual balance sheet, of the state of affairs of the company as at the end of the financial year,
(ii) in the case of an individual profit and loss account, of the profit or loss of the company for the financial year,
(iii) in the case of group accounts, of the state of affairs as at the end of the financial year and of the profit or loss for the financial year of the undertakings included in the consolidation as a whole, so far as concerns members of the company;
(b) have been properly prepared in accordance with the relevant financial reporting framework; and
(c) have been prepared in accordance with the requirements of this Act (and, where applicable, Article 4 of the IAS Regulation).

Expressions used in this subsection that are defined for the purposes of Part 15 (see section 474) have the same meaning as in that Part.

(4) The auditor's report—
(a) must be either unqualified or qualified, and
(b) must include a reference to any matters to which the auditor wishes to draw attention by way of emphasis without qualifying the report.

496 AUDITOR'S REPORT ON DIRECTORS' REPORT

The auditor must state in his report on the company's annual accounts whether in his opinion the information given in the directors' report for the financial year for which the accounts are prepared is consistent with those accounts.

497 AUDITOR'S REPORT ON AUDITABLE PART OF DIRECTORS' REMUNERATION REPORT

(1) If the company is a quoted company, the auditor, in his report on the company's annual accounts for the financial year, must—
(a) report to the company's members on the auditable part of the directors' remuneration report, and
(b) state whether in his opinion that part of the directors' remuneration report has been properly prepared in accordance with this Act.

(2) For the purposes of this Part, "the auditable part" of a directors' remuneration report is the part identified as such by regulations under section 421.

497A AUDITOR'S REPORT ON SEPARATE CORPORATE GOVERNANCE STATEMENT

(1) Where the company prepares a separate corporate governance statement in respect of a financial year the auditor must state in his report on the company's annual accounts for that year whether in his opinion the information given in the statement in compliance with rules 7.2.5 and 7.2.6 in the Disclosure Rules and Transparency Rules sourcebook issued by the Financial Services Authority (information about internal control and risk management systems in relation to financial reporting processes and about share capital structures) is consistent with those accounts.

(2) The rules referred to above were inserted by Annex C of the Disclosure Rules and Transparency Rules Sourcebook (Corporate Governance Rules) Instrument 2008 made by the Authority on 26th June 2008 (FSA 2008/32).

Duties and rights of auditors

498 DUTIES OF AUDITOR

(1) A company's auditor, in preparing his report, must carry out such investigations as will enable him to form an opinion as to—
- (a) whether adequate accounting records have been kept by the company and returns adequate for their audit have been received from branches not visited by him, and
- (b) whether the company's individual accounts are in agreement with the accounting records and returns, and
- (c) in the case of a quoted company, whether the auditable part of the company's directors' remuneration report is in agreement with the accounting records and returns.

(2) If the auditor is of the opinion—
- (a) that adequate accounting records have not been kept, or that returns adequate for their audit have not been received from branches not visited by him, or
- (b) that the company's individual accounts are not in agreement with the accounting records and returns, or
- (c) in the case of a quoted company, that the auditable part of its directors' remuneration report is not in agreement with the accounting records and returns,

the auditor shall state that fact in his report.

(3) If the auditor fails to obtain all the information and explanations which, to the best of his knowledge and belief, are necessary for the purposes of his audit, he shall state that fact in his report.

(4) If—
- (a) the requirements of regulations under section 412 (disclosure of directors' benefits: remuneration, pensions and compensation for loss of office) are not complied with in the annual accounts, or
- (b) in the case of a quoted company, the requirements of regulations under section 421 as to information forming the auditable part of the directors' remuneration report are not complied with in that report,

the auditor must include in his report, so far as he is reasonably able to do so, a statement giving the required particulars.

(5) If the directors of the company—
- (a) have prepared accounts in accordance with the small companies regime, or
- (b) have taken advantage of small companies exemption in preparing the directors' report,

and in the auditor's opinion they were not entitled to do so, the auditor shall state that fact in his report

498A AUDITOR'S DUTIES IN RELATION TO SEPARATE CORPORATE GOVERNANCE STATEMENT

Where the company is required to prepare a corporate governance statement in respect of a financial year and no such statement is included in the directors' report—

(a) the company's auditor, in preparing his report on the company's annual accounts for that year, must ascertain whether a corporate governance statement has been prepared, and

(b) if it appears to the auditor that no such statement has been prepared, he must state that fact in his report.

499 AUDITOR'S GENERAL RIGHT TO INFORMATION

(1) An auditor of a company—
   (a) has a right of access at all times to the company's books, accounts and vouchers (in whatever form they are held), and
   (b) may require any of the following persons to provide him with such information or explanations as he thinks necessary for the performance of his duties as auditor.

(2) Those persons are—
   (a) any officer or employee of the company;
   (b) any person holding or accountable for any of the company's books, accounts or vouchers;
   (c) any subsidiary undertaking of the company which is a body corporate incorporated in the United Kingdom;
   (d) any officer, employee or auditor of any such subsidiary undertaking or any person holding or accountable for any books, accounts or vouchers of any such subsidiary undertaking;
   (e) any person who fell within any of paragraphs (a) to (d) at a time to which the information or explanations required by the auditor relates or relate.

(3) A statement made by a person in response to a requirement under this section may not be used in evidence against him in criminal proceedings except proceedings for an offence under section 501.

(4) Nothing in this section compels a person to disclose information in respect of which a claim to legal professional privilege (in Scotland, to confidentiality of communications) could be maintained in legal proceedings.

500 AUDITOR'S RIGHT TO INFORMATION FROM OVERSEAS SUBSIDIARIES

(1) Where a parent company has a subsidiary undertaking that is not a body corporate incorporated in the United Kingdom, the auditor of the parent company may require it to obtain from any of the following persons such information or explanations as he may reasonably require for the purposes of his duties as auditor.

(2) Those persons are—
   (a) the undertaking;
   (b) any officer, employee or auditor of the undertaking;

(c) any person holding or accountable for any of the undertaking's books, accounts or vouchers;
(d) any person who fell within paragraph (b) or (c) at a time to which the information or explanations relates or relate.

(3) If so required, the parent company must take all such steps as are reasonably open to it to obtain the information or explanations from the person concerned.

(4) A statement made by a person in response to a requirement under this section may not be used in evidence against him in criminal proceedings except proceedings for an offence under section 501.

(5) Nothing in this section compels a person to disclose information in respect of which a claim to legal professional privilege (in Scotland, to confidentiality of communications) could be maintained in legal proceedings.

501 AUDITOR'S RIGHTS TO INFORMATION: OFFENCES

(1) A person commits an offence who knowingly or recklessly makes to an auditor of a company a statement (oral or written) that—
(a) conveys or purports to convey any information or explanations which the auditor requires, or is entitled to require, under section 499, and
(b) is misleading, false or deceptive in a material particular.

(2) A person guilty of an offence under subsection (1) is liable—
(a) on conviction on indictment, to imprisonment for a term not exceeding two years or a fine (or both);
(b) on summary conviction—
(i) in England and Wales, to imprisonment for a term not exceeding twelve months or to a fine not exceeding the statutory maximum (or both);
(ii) in Scotland or Northern Ireland, to imprisonment for a term not exceeding six months or to a fine not exceeding the statutory maximum (or both).

(3) A person who fails to comply with a requirement under section 499 without delay commits an offence unless it was not reasonably practicable for him to provide the required information or explanations.

(4) If a parent company fails to comply with section 500, an offence is committed by—
(a) the company, and
(b) every officer of the company who is in default.

(5) A person guilty of an offence under subsection (3) or (4) is liable on summary conviction to a fine not exceeding level 3 on the standard scale.

(6) Nothing in this section affects any right of an auditor to apply for an injunction (in Scotland, an interdict or an order for specific performance) to enforce any of his rights under section 499 or 500.

502 AUDITOR'S RIGHTS IN RELATION TO RESOLUTIONS AND MEETINGS

(1) In relation to a written resolution proposed to be agreed to by a private company, the company's auditor is entitled to receive all such communications relating to the resolution as, by virtue of any provision of Chapter 2 of Part 13 of this Act, are required to be supplied to a member of the company.

(2) A company's auditor is entitled—
(a) to receive all notices of, and other communications relating to, any general meeting which a member of the company is entitled to receive,
(b) to attend any general meeting of the company, and
(c) to be heard at any general meeting which he attends on any part of the business of the meeting which concerns him as auditor.

(3) Where the auditor is a firm, the right to attend or be heard at a meeting is exercisable by an individual authorised by the firm in writing to act as its representative at the meeting.

Offences in connection with auditor's report

507 OFFENCES IN CONNECTION WITH AUDITOR'S REPORT

(1) A person to whom this section applies commits an offence if he knowingly or recklessly causes a report under section 495 (auditor's report on company's annual accounts) to include any matter that is misleading, false or deceptive in a material particular.

(2) A person to whom this section applies commits an offence if he knowingly or recklessly causes such a report to omit a statement required by—
(a) section 498(2)(b) (statement that company's accounts do not agree with accounting records and returns),
(b) section 498(3) (statement that necessary information and explanations not obtained), or
(c) section 498(5) (statement that directors wrongly took advantage of exemption from obligation to prepare group accounts).

(3) This section applies to—
(a) where the auditor is an individual, that individual and any employee or agent of his who is eligible for appointment as auditor of the company;
(b) where the auditor is a firm, any director, member, employee or agent of the firm who is eligible for appointment as auditor of the company.

(4) A person guilty of an offence under this section is liable—
(a) on conviction on indictment, to a fine;
(b) on summary conviction, to a fine not exceeding the statutory maximum.

Chapter 4 REMOVAL, RESIGNATION, ETC. OF AUDITORS

Removal of auditor

510 RESOLUTION REMOVING AUDITOR FROM OFFICE

(1) The members of a company may remove an auditor from office at any time.

(2) This power is exercisable only—
(a) by ordinary resolution at a meeting, and
(b) in accordance with section 511 (special notice of resolution to remove auditor).

(3) Nothing in this section is to be taken as depriving the person removed of compensation or damages payable to him in respect of the termination—
(a) of his appointment as auditor, or
(b) of any appointment terminating with that as auditor.

(4) An auditor may not be removed from office before the expiration of his term of office except by resolution under this section.

511 SPECIAL NOTICE REQUIRED FOR RESOLUTION REMOVING AUDITOR FROM OFFICE

(1) Special notice is required for a resolution at a general meeting of a company removing an auditor from office.

(2) On receipt of notice of such an intended resolution the company must immediately send a copy of it to the auditor proposed to be removed.

(3) The auditor proposed to be removed may make with respect to the intended resolution representations in writing to the company (not exceeding a reasonable length) and request their notification to members of the company.

(4) The company must (unless the representations are received by it too late for it to do so)—
   (a) in any notice of the resolution given to members of the company, state the fact of the representations having been made, and
   (b) send a copy of the representations to every member of the company to whom notice of the meeting is or has been sent.

(5) If a copy of any such representations is not sent out as required because received too late or because of the company's default, the auditor may (without prejudice to his right to be heard orally) require that the representations be read out at the meeting.

(6) Copies of the representations need not be sent out and the representations need not be read at the meeting if, on the application either of the company or of any other person claiming to be aggrieved, the court is satisfied that the auditor is using the provisions of this section to secure needless publicity for defamatory matter.

The court may order the company's costs (in Scotland, expenses) on the application to be paid in whole or in part by the auditor, notwithstanding that he is not a party to the application.

512 NOTICE TO REGISTRAR OF RESOLUTION REMOVING AUDITOR FROM OFFICE

(1) Where a resolution is passed under section 510 (resolution removing auditor from office), the company must give notice of that fact to the registrar within 14 days.

513 RIGHTS OF AUDITOR WHO HAS BEEN REMOVED FROM OFFICE

(1) An auditor who has been removed by resolution under section 510 has, notwithstanding his removal, the rights conferred by section 502(2) in relation to any general meeting of the company—
   (a) at which his term of office would otherwise have expired, or
   (b) at which it is proposed to fill the vacancy caused by his removal.

(2) In such a case the references in that section to matters concerning the auditor as auditor shall be construed as references to matters concerning him as a former auditor.

Resignation of auditor

516 RESIGNATION OF AUDITOR

(1) An auditor of a company may resign his office by depositing a notice in writing to that effect at the company's registered office.

(2) The notice is not effective unless it is accompanied by the statement required by section 519.

(3) An effective notice of resignation operates to bring the auditor's term of office to an end as of the date on which the notice is deposited or on such later date as may be specified in it.

517 NOTICE TO REGISTRAR OF RESIGNATION OF AUDITOR

(1) Where an auditor resigns the company must within 14 days of the deposit of a notice of resignation send a copy of the notice to the registrar of companies.

518 RIGHTS OF RESIGNING AUDITOR

(1) This section applies where an auditor's notice of resignation is accompanied by a statement of the circumstances connected with his resignation (see section 519).

(2) He may deposit with the notice a signed requisition calling on the directors of the company forthwith duly to convene a general meeting of the company for the purpose of receiving and considering such explanation of the circumstances connected with his resignation as he may wish to place before the meeting.

(10) An auditor who has resigned has, notwithstanding his resignation, the rights conferred by section 502(2) in relation to any such general meeting of the company as is mentioned in subsection (3)(a) or (b) above.

In such a case the references in that section to matters concerning the auditor as auditor shall be construed as references to matters concerning him as a former auditor.

Statement by auditor on ceasing to hold office

519 STATEMENT BY AUDITOR TO BE DEPOSITED WITH COMPANY

(1) Where an auditor of an unquoted company ceases for any reason to hold office, he must deposit at the company's registered office a statement of the circumstances connected with his ceasing to hold office, unless he considers that there are no circumstances in connection with his ceasing to hold office that need to be brought to the attention of members or creditors of the company.

(2) If he considers that there are no circumstances in connection with his ceasing to hold office that need to be brought to the attention of members or creditors of the company, he must deposit at the company's registered office a statement to that effect.

(3) Where an auditor of a quoted company ceases for any reason to hold office, he must deposit at the company's registered office a statement of the circumstances connected with his ceasing to hold office.

Chapter 6 AUDITORS' LIABILITY

Voidness of provisions protecting auditors from liability

532 VOIDNESS OF PROVISIONS PROTECTING AUDITORS FROM LIABILITY

(1) This section applies to any provision—
   (a) for exempting an auditor of a company (to any extent) from any liability that would otherwise attach to him in connection with any negligence, default, breach of duty or

breach of trust in relation to the company occurring in the course of the audit of accounts, or

(b) by which a company directly or indirectly provides an indemnity (to any extent) for an auditor of the company, or of an associated company, against any liability attaching to him in connection with any negligence, default, breach of duty or breach of trust in relation to the company of which he is auditor occurring in the course of the audit of accounts.

(2) Any such provision is void, except as permitted by—
(a) section 533 (indemnity for costs of successfully defending proceedings), or
(b) sections 534 to 536 (liability limitation agreements).

(3) This section applies to any provision, whether contained in a company's articles or in any contract with the company or otherwise.

(4) For the purposes of this section companies are associated if one is a subsidiary of the other or both are subsidiaries of the same body corporate.

Indemnity for costs of defending proceedings

533 INDEMNITY FOR COSTS OF SUCCESSFULLY DEFENDING PROCEEDINGS

Section 532 (general voidness of provisions protecting auditors from liability) does not prevent a company from indemnifying an auditor against any liability incurred by him—

(a) in defending proceedings (whether civil or criminal) in which judgment is given in his favour or he is acquitted, or

(b) in connection with an application under section 1157 (power of court to grant relief in case of honest and reasonable conduct) in which relief is granted to him by the court.

Liability limitation agreements

534 LIABILITY LIMITATION AGREEMENTS

(1) A "liability limitation agreement" is an agreement that purports to limit the amount of a liability owed to a company by its auditor in respect of any negligence, default, breach of duty or breach of trust, occurring in the course of the audit of accounts, of which the auditor may be guilty in relation to the company.

(2) Section 532 (general voidness of provisions protecting auditors from liability) does not affect the validity of a liability limitation agreement that—
(a) complies with section 535 (terms of liability limitation agreement) and of any regulations under that section, and
(b) is authorised by the members of the company (see section 536).

(3) Such an agreement—
(a) is effective to the extent provided by section 537, and
(b) is not subject—
(i) in England and Wales or Northern Ireland, to section 2(2) or 3(2)(a) of the Unfair Contract Terms Act 1977 (c. 50);
(ii) in Scotland, to section 16(1)(b) or 17(1)(a) of that Act.

535 TERMS OF LIABILITY LIMITATION AGREEMENT

(1) A liability limitation agreement—
(a) must not apply in respect of acts or omissions occurring in the course of the audit of accounts for more than one financial year, and
(b) must specify the financial year in relation to which it applies.

(2) The Secretary of State may by regulations—
(a) require liability limitation agreements to contain specified provisions or provisions of a specified description;
(b) prohibit liability limitation agreements from containing specified provisions or provisions of a specified description.
"Specified" here means specified in the regulations.

536 AUTHORISATION OF AGREEMENT BY MEMBERS OF THE COMPANY

(1) A liability limitation agreement is authorised by the members of the company if it has been authorised under this section and that authorisation has not been withdrawn.

(2) A liability limitation agreement between a private company and its auditor may be authorised—
(a) by the company passing a resolution, before it enters into the agreement, waiving the need for approval,
(b) by the company passing a resolution, before it enters into the agreement, approving the agreement's principal terms, or
(c) by the company passing a resolution, after it enters into the agreement, approving the agreement.

(3) A liability limitation agreement between a public company and its auditor may be authorised—
(a) by the company passing a resolution in general meeting, before it enters into the agreement, approving the agreement's principal terms, or
(b) by the company passing a resolution in general meeting, after it enters into the agreement, approving the agreement.

(4) The "principal terms" of an agreement are terms specifying, or relevant to the determination of—
(a) the kind (or kinds) of acts or omissions covered,
(b) the financial year to which the agreement relates, or
(c) the limit to which the auditor's liability is subject.

(5) Authorisation under this section may be withdrawn by the company passing an ordinary resolution to that effect—
(a) at any time before the company enters into the agreement, or
(b) if the company has already entered into the agreement, before the beginning of the financial year to which the agreement relates.
Paragraph (b) has effect notwithstanding anything in the agreement.

537 EFFECT OF LIABILITY LIMITATION AGREEMENT

(1) A liability limitation agreement is not effective to limit the auditor's liability to less than such amount as is fair and reasonable in all the circumstances of the case having regard (in particular) to—

(a) the auditor's responsibilities under this Part,
(b) the nature and purpose of the auditor's contractual obligations to the company, and
(c) the professional standards expected of him.

(2) A liability limitation agreement that purports to limit the auditor's liability to less than the amount mentioned in subsection (1) shall have effect as if it limited his liability to that amount.

(3) In determining what is fair and reasonable in all the circumstances of the case no account is to be taken of—
(a) matters arising after the loss or damage in question has been incurred, or
(b) matters (whenever arising) affecting the possibility of recovering compensation from other persons liable in respect of the same loss or damage.

538 DISCLOSURE OF AGREEMENT BY COMPANY

(1) A company which has entered into a liability limitation agreement must make such disclosure in connection with the agreement as the Secretary of State may require by regulations.

(2) The regulations may provide, in particular, that any disclosure required by the regulations shall be made—
(a) in a note to the company's annual accounts (in the case of its individual accounts) or in such manner as is specified in the regulations (in the case of group accounts), or
(b) in the directors' report.

(3) Regulations under this section are subject to negative resolution procedure.

538A MEANING OF "CORPORATE GOVERNANCE STATEMENT" ETC.

(1) In this Part "corporate governance statement" means the statement required by rules 7.2.1 to 7.2.11 in the Disclosure Rules and Transparency Rules sourcebook issued by the Financial Services Authority.

(2) Those rules were inserted by Annex C of the Disclosure Rules and Transparency Rules Sourcebook (Corporate Governance Rules) Instrument 2008 made by the Authority on 26th June 2008 (FSA 2008/32).

(3) A "separate" corporate governance statement means one that is not included in the directors' report.

Part 17 A COMPANY'S SHARE CAPITAL

Chapter 1 SHARES AND SHARE CAPITAL OF A COMPANY

Shares

540 SHARES

(1) In the Companies Acts "share", in relation to a company, means share in the company's share capital.

541 NATURE OF SHARES

The shares or other interest of a member in a company are personal property (or, in Scotland, moveable property) and are not in the nature of real estate (or heritage).

542 NOMINAL VALUE OF SHARES

(1) Shares in a limited company having a share capital must each have a fixed nominal value.

544 TRANSFERABILITY OF SHARES

(1) The shares or other interest of any member in a company are transferable in accordance with the company's articles.

545 COMPANIES HAVING A SHARE CAPITAL

References in the Companies Acts to a company having a share capital are to a company that has power under its constitution to issue shares.

546 ISSUED AND ALLOTTED SHARE CAPITAL

(1) References in the Companies Acts—
- (a) to "issued share capital" are to shares of a company that have been issued;
- (b) to "allotted share capital" are to shares of a company that have been allotted.

(2) References in the Companies Acts to issued or allotted shares, or to issued or allotted share capital, include shares taken on the formation of the company by the subscribers to the company's memorandum.

Share capital

547 CALLED-UP SHARE CAPITAL

In the Companies Acts—

"called-up share capital", in relation to a company, means so much of its share capital as equals the aggregate amount of the calls made on its shares (whether or not those calls have been paid), together with—
- (a) any share capital paid up without being called, and
- (b) any share capital to be paid on a specified future date under the articles, the terms of allotment of the relevant shares or any other arrangements for payment of those shares; and

"uncalled share capital" is to be construed accordingly.

548 EQUITY SHARE CAPITAL

In the Companies Acts "equity share capital", in relation to a company, means its issued share capital excluding any part of that capital that, neither as respects dividends nor as respects capital, carries any right to participate beyond a specified amount in a distribution.

Chapter 2 ALLOTMENT OF SHARES: GENERAL PROVISIONS

Power of directors to allot shares

549 EXERCISE BY DIRECTORS OF POWER TO ALLOT SHARES ETC.

(1) The directors of a company must not exercise any power of the company—
- (a) to allot shares in the company, or
- (b) to grant rights to subscribe for, or to convert any security into, shares in the company,

except in accordance with section 550 (private company with single class of shares) or section 551 (authorisation by company).

(2) Subsection (1) does not apply—
(a) to the allotment of shares in pursuance of an employees' share scheme, or
(b) to the grant of a right to subscribe for, or to convert any security into, shares so allotted.

(3) Subsection (1) does not apply to the allotment of shares pursuant to a right to subscribe for, or to convert any security into, shares in the company.

(4) A director who knowingly contravenes, or permits or authorises a contravention of, this section commits an offence.

(5) A person guilty of an offence under this section is liable—
(a) on conviction on indictment, to a fine;
(b) on summary conviction, to a fine not exceeding the statutory maximum.

(6) Nothing in this section affects the validity of an allotment or other transaction.

550 POWER OF DIRECTORS TO ALLOT SHARES ETC.: PRIVATE COMPANY WITH ONLY ONE CLASS OF SHARES

Where a private company has only one class of shares, the directors may exercise any power of the company—

(a) to allot shares of that class, or

(b) to grant rights to subscribe for or to convert any security into such shares,

except to the extent that they are prohibited from doing so by the company's articles.

551 POWER OF DIRECTORS TO ALLOT SHARES ETC.: AUTHORISATION BY COMPANY

(1) The directors of a company may exercise a power of the company—
(a) to allot shares in the company, or
(b) to grant rights to subscribe for or to convert any security into shares in the company,
if they are authorised to do so by the company's articles or by resolution of the company.

(2) Authorisation may be given for a particular exercise of the power or for its exercise generally, and may be unconditional or subject to conditions.

(3) Authorisation must—
(a) state the maximum amount of shares that may be allotted under it, and
(b) specify the date on which it will expire, which must be not more than five years from—
(i) in the case of authorisation contained in the company's articles at the time of its original incorporation, the date of that incorporation;
(ii) in any other case, the date on which the resolution is passed by virtue of which the authorisation is given.

(4) Authorisation may—
(a) be renewed or further renewed by resolution of the company for a further period not exceeding five years, and
(b) be revoked or varied at any time by resolution of the company.

(5) A resolution renewing authorisation must—
(a) state (or restate) the maximum amount of shares that may be allotted under the authorisation or, as the case may be, the amount remaining to be allotted under it, and
(b) specify the date on which the renewed authorisation will expire.

(8) A resolution of a company to give, vary, revoke or renew authorisation under this section may be an ordinary resolution, even though it amends the company's articles.

(9) Chapter 3 of Part 3 (resolutions affecting a company's constitution) applies to a resolution under this section.

Registration of allotment

554 REGISTRATION OF ALLOTMENT

(1) A company must register an allotment of shares as soon as practicable and in any event within two months after the date of the allotment.

Supplementary provisions

558 WHEN SHARES ARE ALLOTTED

For the purposes of the Companies Acts shares in a company are taken to be allotted when a person acquires the unconditional right to be included in the company's register of members in respect of the shares.

559 PROVISIONS ABOUT ALLOTMENT NOT APPLICABLE TO SHARES TAKEN ON FORMATION

The provisions of this Chapter have no application in relation to the taking of shares by the subscribers to the memorandum on the formation of the company.

Chapter 3 ALLOTMENT OF EQUITY SECURITIES: EXISTING SHAREHOLDERS' RIGHT OF PRE-EMPTION

Introductory

560 MEANING OF "EQUITY SECURITIES" AND RELATED EXPRESSIONS

(1) In this Chapter—
"equity securities" means—
(a) ordinary shares in the company, or
(b) rights to subscribe for, or to convert securities into, ordinary shares in the company;

"ordinary shares" means shares other than shares that as respects dividends and capital carry a right to participate only up to a specified amount in a distribution.

(2) References in this Chapter to the allotment of equity securities—
(a) include the grant of a right to subscribe for, or to convert any securities into, ordinary shares in the company, and
(b) do not include the allotment of shares pursuant to such a right.

(3) References in this Chapter to the allotment of equity securities include the sale of ordinary shares in the company that immediately before the sale were held by the company as treasury shares.

Existing shareholders' right of pre-emption

561 EXISTING SHAREHOLDERS' RIGHT OF PRE-EMPTION

(1) A company must not allot equity securities to a person on any terms unless—
   (a) it has made an offer to each person who holds ordinary shares in the company to allot to him on the same or more favourable terms a proportion of those securities that is as nearly as practicable equal to the proportion in nominal value held by him of the ordinary share capital of the company, and
   (b) the period during which any such offer may be accepted has expired or the company has received notice of the acceptance or refusal of every offer so made.

562 COMMUNICATION OF PRE-EMPTION OFFERS TO SHAREHOLDERS

(1) This section has effect as to the manner in which offers required by section 561 are to be made to holders of a company's shares.

(2) The offer may be made in hard copy or electronic form.

(4) The offer must state a period during which it may be accepted and the offer shall not be withdrawn before the end of that period.

(5) The period must be a period of at least 14 days beginning—
   (a) in the case of an offer made in hard copy form, with the date on which the offer is sent or supplied;
   (b) in the case of an offer made in electronic form, with the date on which the offer is sent;

...

563 LIABILITY OF COMPANY AND OFFICERS IN CASE OF CONTRAVENTION

(1) This section applies where there is a contravention of—

section 561 (existing shareholders' right of pre-emption), or
section 562 (communication of pre-emption offers to shareholders).

(2) The company and every officer of it who knowingly authorised or permitted the contravention are jointly and severally liable to compensate any person to whom an offer should have been made in accordance with those provisions for any loss, damage, costs or expenses which the person has sustained or incurred by reason of the contravention.

Exceptions to right of pre-emption

564 EXCEPTION TO PRE-EMPTION RIGHT: BONUS SHARES

Section 561(1) (existing shareholders' right of pre-emption) does not apply in relation to the allotment of bonus shares.

565 EXCEPTION TO PRE-EMPTION RIGHT: ISSUE FOR NON-CASH CONSIDERATION

Section 561(1) (existing shareholders' right of pre-emption) does not apply to a particular allotment of equity securities if these are, or are to be, wholly or partly paid up otherwise than in cash.

566 EXCEPTIONS TO PRE-EMPTION RIGHT: EMPLOYEES' SHARE SCHEMES

Section 561 (existing shareholders' right of pre-emption) does not apply to the allotment of equity securities that would, apart from any renunciation or assignment of the right to their allotment, be held under or allotted or transferred pursuant to an employees' share scheme.

Exclusion of right of pre-emption

567 EXCLUSION OF REQUIREMENTS BY PRIVATE COMPANIES

(1) All or any of the requirements of—
 (a) section 561 (existing shareholders' right of pre-emption), or
 (b) section 562 (communication of pre-emption offers to shareholders)
 may be excluded by provision contained in the articles of a private company.

Disapplication of pre-emption rights

569 DISAPPLICATION OF PRE-EMPTION RIGHTS: PRIVATE COMPANY WITH ONLY ONE CLASS OF SHARES

(1) The directors of a private company that has only one class of shares may be given power by the articles, or by a special resolution of the company, to allot equity securities of that class as if section 561 (existing shareholders' right of pre-emption)—
 (a) did not apply to the allotment, or
 (b) applied to the allotment with such modifications as the directors may determine.

570 DISAPPLICATION OF PRE-EMPTION RIGHTS: DIRECTORS ACTING UNDER GENERAL AUTHORISATION

(1) Where the directors of a company are generally authorised for the purposes of section 551 (power of directors to allot shares etc.: authorisation by company), they may be given power by the articles, or by a special resolution of the company, to allot equity securities pursuant to that authorisation as if section 561 (existing shareholders' right of pre-emption)—
 (a) did not apply to the allotment, or
 (b) applied to the allotment with such modifications as the directors may determine.

571 DISAPPLICATION OF PRE-EMPTION RIGHTS BY SPECIAL RESOLUTION

(1) Where the directors of a company are authorised for the purposes of section 551 (power of directors to allot shares etc.: authorisation by company), whether generally or otherwise, the company may by special resolution resolve that section 561 (existing shareholders' right of pre-emption)—
 (a) does not apply to a specified allotment of equity securities to be made pursuant to that authorisation, or

(b) applies to such an allotment with such modifications as may be specified in the resolution.

573 DISAPPLICATION OF PRE-EMPTION RIGHTS: SALE OF TREASURY SHARES

(1) This section applies in relation to a sale of shares that is an allotment of equity securities by virtue of section 560(3) (sale of shares held by company as treasury shares).

(2) The directors of a company may be given power by the articles, or by a special resolution of the company, to allot equity securities as if section 561 (existing shareholders' right of pre-emption)—
(a) did not apply to the allotment, or
(b) applied to the allotment with such modifications as the directors may determine.

577 PROVISIONS ABOUT PRE-EMPTION NOT APPLICABLE TO SHARES TAKEN ON FORMATION

The provisions of this Chapter have no application in relation to the taking of shares by the subscribers to the memorandum on the formation of the company.

Chapter 4 PUBLIC COMPANIES: ALLOTMENT WHERE ISSUE NOT FULLY SUBSCRIBED

578 PUBLIC COMPANIES: ALLOTMENT WHERE ISSUE NOT FULLY SUBSCRIBED

(1) No allotment shall be made of shares of a public company offered for subscription unless—
(a) the issue is subscribed for in full, or
(b) the offer is made on terms that the shares subscribed for may be allotted—
(i) in any event, or
(ii) if specified conditions are met (and those conditions are met).

(2) If shares are prohibited from being allotted by subsection (1) and 40 days have elapsed after the first making of the offer, all money received from applicants for shares must be repaid to them forthwith, without interest.

(3) If any of the money is not repaid within 48 days after the first making of the offer, the directors of the company are jointly and severally liable to repay it, with interest at the rate for the time being specified under section 17 of the Judgments Act 1838 (c. 110) from the expiration of the 48th day.

A director is not so liable if he proves that the default in the repayment of the money was not due to any misconduct or negligence on his part.

(6) Any condition requiring or binding an applicant for shares to waive compliance with any requirement of this section is void.

579 PUBLIC COMPANIES: EFFECT OF IRREGULAR ALLOTMENT WHERE ISSUE NOT FULLY SUBSCRIBED

(1) An allotment made by a public company to an applicant in contravention of section 578 (public companies: allotment where issue not fully subscribed) is voidable at the instance of the applicant within one month after the date of the allotment, and not later.

Chapter 5 PAYMENT FOR SHARES

General rules

580 SHARES NOT TO BE ALLOTTED AT A DISCOUNT

(1) A company's shares must not be allotted at a discount.

(2) If shares are allotted in contravention of this section, the allottee is liable to pay the company an amount equal to the amount of the discount, with interest at the appropriate rate.

581 PROVISION FOR DIFFERENT AMOUNTS TO BE PAID ON SHARES

A company, if so authorised by its articles, may—

(a) make arrangements on the issue of shares for a difference between the shareholders in the amounts and times of payment of calls on their shares;

(b) accept from any member the whole or part of the amount remaining unpaid on any shares held by him, although no part of that amount has been called up;

(c) pay a dividend in proportion to the amount paid up on each share where a larger amount is paid up on some shares than on others.

582 GENERAL RULE AS TO MEANS OF PAYMENT

(1) Shares allotted by a company, and any premium on them, may be paid up in money or money's worth (including goodwill and know-how).

(2) This section does not prevent a company—
  (a) from allotting bonus shares to its members, or
  (b) from paying up, with sums available for the purpose, any amounts for the time being unpaid on any of its shares (whether on account of the nominal value of the shares or by way of premium).

(3) This section has effect subject to the following provisions of this Chapter (additional rules for public companies).

Additional rules for public companies

584 PUBLIC COMPANIES: SHARES TAKEN BY SUBSCRIBERS OF MEMORANDUM

Shares taken by a subscriber to the memorandum of a public company in pursuance of an undertaking of his in the memorandum, and any premium on the shares, must be paid up in cash.

585 PUBLIC COMPANIES: MUST NOT ACCEPT UNDERTAKING TO DO WORK OR PERFORM SERVICES

(1) A public company must not accept at any time, in payment up of its shares or any premium on them, an undertaking given by any person that he or another should do work or perform services for the company or any other person.

(2) If a public company accepts such an undertaking in payment up of its shares or any premium on them, the holder of the shares when they or the premium are treated as paid up (in whole or in part) by the undertaking is liable—
  (a) to pay the company in respect of those shares an amount equal to their nominal value, together with the whole of any premium or, if the case so requires, such proportion of that amount as is treated as paid up by the undertaking; and
  (b) to pay interest at the appropriate rate on the amount payable under paragraph (a).

586 PUBLIC COMPANIES: SHARES MUST BE AT LEAST ONE-QUARTER PAID UP

(1) A public company must not allot a share except as paid up at least as to one-quarter of its nominal value and the whole of any premium on it.

(2) This does not apply to shares allotted in pursuance of an employees' share scheme.

(3) If a company allots a share in contravention of this section—
  (a) the share is to be treated as if one-quarter of its nominal value, together with the whole of any premium on it, had been received, and
  (b) the allottee is liable to pay the company the minimum amount which should have been received in respect of the share under subsection (1) (less the value of any consideration actually applied in payment up, to any extent, of the share and any premium on it), with interest at the appropriate rate.

(4) Subsection (3) does not apply to the allotment of bonus shares, unless the allottee knew or ought to have known the shares were allotted in contravention of this section.

587 PUBLIC COMPANIES: PAYMENT BY LONG-TERM UNDERTAKING

(1) A public company must not allot shares as fully or partly paid up (as to their nominal value or any premium on them) otherwise than in cash if the consideration for the allotment is or includes an undertaking which is to be, or may be, performed more than five years after the date of the allotment.

(2) If a company allots shares in contravention of subsection (1), the allottee is liable to pay the company an amount equal to the aggregate of their nominal value and the whole of any premium (or, if the case so requires, so much of that aggregate as is treated as paid up by the undertaking), with interest at the appropriate rate.

Supplementary provisions

588 LIABILITY OF SUBSEQUENT HOLDERS OF SHARES

(1) If a person becomes a holder of shares in respect of which—
  (a) there has been a contravention of any provision of this Chapter, and
  (b) by virtue of that contravention another is liable to pay any amount under the provision contravened,

that person is also liable to pay that amount (jointly and severally with any other person so liable), subject as follows.

(2) A person otherwise liable under subsection (1) is exempted from that liability if either—

(a) he is a purchaser for value and, at the time of the purchase, he did not have actual notice of the contravention concerned, or
(b) he derived title to the shares (directly or indirectly) from a person who became a holder of them after the contravention and was not liable under subsection (1).

589 POWER OF COURT TO GRANT RELIEF

(1) This section applies in relation to liability under—

section 585(2) (liability of allottee in case of breach by public company of prohibition on accepting undertaking to do work or perform services),

section 587(2) … (liability of allottee in case of breach by public company of prohibition on payment by long-term undertaking), or

section 588 (liability of subsequent holders of shares),

as it applies in relation to a contravention of those sections.

(2) A person who—
(a) is subject to any such liability to a company in relation to payment in respect of shares in the company…

…

may apply to the court to be exempted in whole or in part from the liability.

(3) In the case of a liability within subsection (2)(a), the court may exempt the applicant from the liability only if and to the extent that it appears to the court just and equitable to do so…

590 PENALTY FOR CONTRAVENTION OF THIS CHAPTER

(1) If a company contravenes any of the provisions of this Chapter, an offence is committed by—
(a) the company, and
(b) every officer of the company who is in default.

(2) A person guilty of an offence under this section is liable—
(a) on conviction on indictment, to a fine;
(b) on summary conviction, to a fine not exceeding the statutory maximum.

591 ENFORCEABILITY OF UNDERTAKINGS TO DO WORK ETC.

(1) An undertaking given by any person, in or in connection with payment for shares in a company, to do work or perform services or to do any other thing, if it is enforceable by the company apart from this Chapter, is so enforceable notwithstanding that there has been a contravention in relation to it of a provision of this Chapter or Chapter 6.

(2) This is without prejudice to section 589 (power of court to grant relief etc. in respect of liabilities).

592 THE APPROPRIATE RATE OF INTEREST

(1) For the purposes of this Chapter the "appropriate rate" of interest is 5% per annum or such other rate as may be specified by order made by the Secretary of State.

(2) An order under this section is subject to negative resolution procedure.

Chapter 6 PUBLIC COMPANIES: INDEPENDENT VALUATION OF NON-CASH CONSIDERATION

Non-cash consideration for shares

593 PUBLIC COMPANY: VALUATION OF NON-CASH CONSIDERATION FOR SHARES

(1) A public company must not allot shares as fully or partly paid up (as to their nominal value or any premium on them) otherwise than in cash unless—
 (a) the consideration for the allotment has been independently valued in accordance with the provisions of this Chapter,
 (b) the valuer's report has been made to the company during the six months immediately preceding the allotment of the shares, and
 (c) a copy of the report has been sent to the proposed allottee.

(2) For this purpose the application of an amount standing to the credit of—
 (a) any of a company's reserve accounts, or
 (b) its profit and loss account,
in paying up (to any extent) shares allotted to members of the company, or premiums on shares so allotted, does not count as consideration for the allotment.

Accordingly, subsection (1) does not apply in that case.

(3) If a company allots shares in contravention of subsection (1) and either—
 (a) the allottee has not received the valuer's report required to be sent to him, or
 (b) there has been some other contravention of the requirements of this section or section 596 that the allottee knew or ought to have known amounted to a contravention,
the allottee is liable to pay the company an amount equal to the aggregate of the nominal value of the shares and the whole of any premium (or, if the case so requires, so much of that aggregate as is treated as paid up by the consideration), with interest at the appropriate rate.

(4) This section has effect subject to—

section 594 (exception to valuation requirement: arrangement with another company), and

section 595 (exception to valuation requirement: merger).

594 EXCEPTION TO VALUATION REQUIREMENT: ARRANGEMENT WITH ANOTHER COMPANY

(1) Section 593 (valuation of non-cash consideration) does not apply to the allotment of shares by a company ("company A") in connection with an arrangement to which this section applies.

(2) This section applies to an arrangement for the allotment of shares in company A on terms that the whole or part of the consideration for the shares allotted is to be provided by—
 (a) the transfer to that company, or
 (b) the cancellation,
of all or some of the shares, or of all or some of the shares of a particular class, in another company ("company B").

(3) It is immaterial whether the arrangement provides for the issue to company A of shares, or shares of any particular class, in company B.

(4) This section applies to an arrangement only if under the arrangement it is open to all the holders of the shares in company B (or, where the arrangement applies only to shares of a particular class, to all the holders of shares of that class) to take part in the arrangement.

(5) In determining whether that is the case, the following shall be disregarded—
(a) shares held by or by a nominee of company A;
(b) shares held by or by a nominee of a company which is—
(i) the holding company, or a subsidiary, of company A, or
(ii) a subsidiary of such a holding company;
(c) shares held as treasury shares by company B.

(6) In this section—
(a) "arrangement" means any agreement, scheme or arrangement (including an arrangement sanctioned in accordance with—
(i) Part 26 (arrangements and reconstructions), or
(ii) section 110 of the Insolvency Act 1986 (c. 45) or Article 96 of the Insolvency (Northern Ireland) Order 1989 (S.I. 1989/2405 (N.I. 19)) (liquidator in winding up accepting shares as consideration for sale of company property)), and
(b) "company", except in reference to company A, includes any body corporate.

595 EXCEPTION TO VALUATION REQUIREMENT: MERGER

(1) Section 593 (valuation of non-cash consideration) does not apply to the allotment of shares by a company in connection with a proposed merger with another company.

(2) A proposed merger is where one of the companies proposes to acquire all the assets and liabilities of the other in exchange for the issue of shares or other securities of that one to shareholders of the other, with or without any cash payment to shareholders.

(3) In this section "company", in reference to the other company, includes any body corporate.

596 NON-CASH CONSIDERATION FOR SHARES: REQUIREMENTS AS TO VALUATION AND REPORT

(1) The provisions of sections 1150 to 1153 (general provisions as to independent valuation and report) apply to the valuation and report required by section 593 (public company: valuation of non-cash consideration for shares).

(2) The valuer's report must state—
(a) the nominal value of the shares to be wholly or partly paid for by the consideration in question;
(b) the amount of any premium payable on the shares;
(c) the description of the consideration and, as respects so much of the consideration as he himself has valued, a description of that part of the consideration, the method used to value it and the date of the valuation;
(d) the extent to which the nominal value of the shares and any premium are to be treated as paid up—
(i) by the consideration;
(ii) in cash.

(3) The valuer's report must contain or be accompanied by a note by him—
(a) in the case of a valuation made by a person other than himself, that it appeared to himself reasonable to arrange for it to be so made or to accept a valuation so made,

(b) whoever made the valuation, that the method of valuation was reasonable in all the circumstances,
(c) that it appears to the valuer that there has been no material change in the value of the consideration in question since the valuation, and
(d) that, on the basis of the valuation, the value of the consideration, together with any cash by which the nominal value of the shares or any premium payable on them is to be paid up, is not less than so much of the aggregate of the nominal value and the whole of any such premium as is treated as paid up by the consideration and any such cash.

(4) Where the consideration to be valued is accepted partly in payment up of the nominal value of the shares and any premium and partly for some other consideration given by the company, section 593 and the preceding provisions of this section apply as if references to the consideration accepted by the company included the proportion of that consideration that is properly attributable to the payment up of that value and any premium.

(5) In such a case—
(a) the valuer must carry out, or arrange for, such other valuations as will enable him to determine that proportion, and
(b) his report must state what valuations have been made under this subsection and also the reason for, and method and date of, any such valuation and any other matters which may be relevant to that determination.

597 COPY OF REPORT TO BE DELIVERED TO REGISTRAR

(1) A company to which a report is made under section 593 as to the value of any consideration for which, or partly for which, it proposes to allot shares must deliver a copy of the report to the registrar for registration.

Transfer of non-cash asset in initial period

598 PUBLIC COMPANY: AGREEMENT FOR TRANSFER OF NON-CASH ASSET IN INITIAL PERIOD

(1) A public company formed as such must not enter into an agreement—
(a) with a person who is a subscriber to the company's memorandum,
(b) for the transfer by him to the company, or another, before the end of the company's initial period of one or more non-cash assets, and
(c) under which the consideration for the transfer to be given by the company is at the time of the agreement equal in value to one-tenth or more of the company's issued share capital,

unless the conditions referred to below have been complied with.

(2) The company's "initial period" means the period of two years beginning with the date of the company being issued with a certificate under section 761 (trading certificate).

(3) The conditions are those specified in—

section 599 (requirement of independent valuation), and

section 601 (requirement of approval by members).

(4) This section does not apply where—
(a) it is part of the company's ordinary business to acquire, or arrange for other persons to acquire, assets of a particular description, and
(b) the agreement is entered into by the company in the ordinary course of that business.

(5) This section does not apply to an agreement entered into by the company under the supervision of the court or of an officer authorised by the court for the purpose.

599 AGREEMENT FOR TRANSFER OF NON-CASH ASSET: REQUIREMENT OF INDEPENDENT VALUATION

(1) The following conditions must have been complied with—
- (a) the consideration to be received by the company, and any consideration other than cash to be given by the company, must have been independently valued in accordance with the provisions of this Chapter,
- (b) the valuer's report must have been made to the company during the six months immediately preceding the date of the agreement, and
- (c) a copy of the report must have been sent to the other party to the proposed agreement not later than the date on which copies have to be circulated to members under section 601(3).

(2) The reference in subsection (1)(a) to the consideration to be received by the company is to the asset to be transferred to it or, as the case may be, to the advantage to the company of the asset's transfer to another person.

(3) The reference in subsection (1)(c) to the other party to the proposed agreement is to the person referred to in section 598(1)(a).

If he has received a copy of the report under section 601 in his capacity as a member of the company, it is not necessary to send another copy under this section.

(4) This section does not affect any requirement to value any consideration for purposes of section 593 (valuation of non-cash consideration for shares).

600 AGREEMENT FOR TRANSFER OF NON-CASH ASSET: REQUIREMENTS AS TO VALUATION AND REPORT

(1) The provisions of sections 1150 to 1153 (general provisions as to independent valuation and report) apply to the valuation and report required by section 599 (public company: transfer of non-cash asset).

(2) The valuer's report must state—
- (a) the consideration to be received by the company, describing the asset in question (specifying the amount to be received in cash) and the consideration to be given by the company (specifying the amount to be given in cash), and
- (b) the method and date of valuation.

(3) The valuer's report must contain or be accompanied by a note by him—
- (a) in the case of a valuation made by a person other than himself, that it appeared to himself reasonable to arrange for it to be so made or to accept a valuation so made,
- (b) whoever made the valuation, that the method of valuation was reasonable in all the circumstances,
- (c) that it appears to the valuer that there has been no material change in the value of the consideration in question since the valuation, and
- (d) that, on the basis of the valuation, the value of the consideration to be received by the company is not less than the value of the consideration to be given by it.

(4) Any reference in section 599 or this section to consideration given for the transfer of an asset includes consideration given partly for its transfer.

(5) In such a case—
  (a) the value of any consideration partly so given is to be taken as the proportion of the consideration properly attributable to its transfer,
  (b) the valuer must carry out or arrange for such valuations of anything else as will enable him to determine that proportion, and
  (c) his report must state what valuations have been made for that purpose and also the reason for and method and date of any such valuation and any other matters which may be relevant to that determination.

601 AGREEMENT FOR TRANSFER OF NON-CASH ASSET: REQUIREMENT OF APPROVAL BY MEMBERS

(1) The following conditions must have been complied with—
  (a) the terms of the agreement must have been approved by an ordinary resolution of the company,
  (b) copies of the valuer's report must have been circulated to the members entitled to notice of the meeting at which the resolution is proposed, not later than the date on which notice of the meeting is given, and
  (c) a copy of the proposed resolution must have been sent to the other party to the proposed agreement.

(2) The reference in subsection (1)(c) to the other party to the proposed agreement is to the person referred to in section 598(1)(a).

602 COPY OF RESOLUTION TO BE DELIVERED TO REGISTRAR

(1) A company that has passed a resolution under section 601 with respect to the transfer of an asset must, within 15 days of doing so, deliver to the registrar a copy of the resolution together with the valuer's report required by that section.

603 ADAPTATION OF PROVISIONS IN RELATION TO COMPANY RE-REGISTERING AS PUBLIC

The provisions of sections 598 to 602 (public companies: transfer of non-cash assets) apply with the following adaptations in relation to a company re-registered as a public company—

(a) the reference in section 598(1)(a) to a person who is a subscriber to the company's memorandum shall be read as a reference to a person who is a member of the company on the date of re-registration;

(b) the reference in section 598(2) to the date of the company being issued with a certificate under section 761 (trading certificate) shall be read as a reference to the date of re-registration.

604 AGREEMENT FOR TRANSFER OF NON-CASH ASSET: EFFECT OF CONTRAVENTION

(1) This section applies where a public company enters into an agreement in contravention of section 598 and either—
  (a) the other party to the agreement has not received the valuer's report required to be sent to him, or

(b) there has been some other contravention of the requirements of this Chapter that the other party to the agreement knew or ought to have known amounted to a contravention.

(2) In those circumstances—
(a) the company is entitled to recover from that person any consideration given by it under the agreement, or an amount equal to the value of the consideration at the time of the agreement, and
(b) the agreement, so far as not carried out, is void.

(3) If the agreement is or includes an agreement for the allotment of shares in the company, then—
(a) whether or not the agreement also contravenes section 593 (valuation of non-cash consideration for shares), this section does not apply to it in so far as it is for the allotment of shares, and
(b) the allottee is liable to pay the company an amount equal to the aggregate of the nominal value of the shares and the whole of any premium (or, if the case so requires, so much of that aggregate as is treated as paid up by the consideration), with interest at the appropriate rate.

Supplementary provisions

605 LIABILITY OF SUBSEQUENT HOLDERS OF SHARES

(1) If a person becomes a holder of shares in respect of which—
(a) there has been a contravention of section 593 (public company: valuation of non-cash consideration for shares), and
(b) by virtue of that contravention another is liable to pay any amount under the provision contravened,
that person is also liable to pay that amount (jointly and severally with any other person so liable), unless he is exempted from liability under subsection (3) below.

(3) A person otherwise liable under subsection (1) ... is exempted from that liability if either—
(a) he is a purchaser for value and, at the time of the purchase, he did not have actual notice of the contravention concerned, or
(b) he derived title to the shares (directly or indirectly) from a person who became a holder of them after the contravention and was not liable under subsection (1)...

606 POWER OF COURT TO GRANT RELIEF

(1) A person who—
(a) is liable to a company under any provision of this Chapter in relation to payment in respect of any shares in the company, or
(b) is liable to a company by virtue of an undertaking given to it in, or in connection with, payment for any shares in the company,
may apply to the court to be exempted in whole or in part from the liability.

(2) In the case of a liability within subsection (1)(a), the court may exempt the applicant from the liability only if and to the extent that it appears to the court just and equitable to do so ...

607 PENALTY FOR CONTRAVENTION OF THIS CHAPTER

(1) This section applies where a company contravenes—

section 593 (public company allotting shares for non-cash consideration), or

section 598 (public company entering into agreement for transfer of non-cash asset).

(2) An offence is committed by—
(a) the company, and
(b) every officer of the company who is in default.

(3) A person guilty of an offence under this section is liable—
(a) on conviction on indictment, to a fine;
(b) on summary conviction, to a fine not exceeding the statutory maximum.

608 ENFORCEABILITY OF UNDERTAKINGS TO DO WORK ETC

(1) An undertaking given by any person, in or in connection with payment for shares in a company, to do work or perform services or to do any other thing, if it is enforceable by the company apart from this Chapter, is so enforceable notwithstanding that there has been a contravention in relation to it of a provision of this Chapter or Chapter 5.

(2) This is without prejudice to section 606 (power of court to grant relief etc in respect of liabilities).

609 THE APPROPRIATE RATE OF INTEREST

(1) For the purposes of this Chapter the "appropriate rate" of interest is 5% per annum or such other rate as may be specified by order made by the Secretary of State.

(2) An order under this section is subject to negative resolution procedure.

Chapter 7 SHARE PREMIUMS

The share premium account

610 APPLICATION OF SHARE PREMIUMS

(1) If a company issues shares at a premium, whether for cash or otherwise, a sum equal to the aggregate amount or value of the premiums on those shares must be transferred to an account called "the share premium account".

(2) Where, on issuing shares, a company has transferred a sum to the share premium account, it may use that sum to write off—
(a) the expenses of the issue of those shares;
(b) any commission paid on the issue of those shares.

(3) The company may use the share premium account to pay up new shares to be allotted to members as fully paid bonus shares.

(4) Subject to subsections (2) and (3), the provisions of the Companies Acts relating to the reduction of a company's share capital apply as if the share premium account were part of its paid up share capital.

...

Chapter 8 ALTERATION OF SHARE CAPITAL

How share capital may be altered

617 ALTERATION OF SHARE CAPITAL OF LIMITED COMPANY

(1) A limited company having a share capital may not alter its share capital except in the following ways.

(2) The company may—
(a) increase its share capital by allotting new shares in accordance with this Part, or
(b) reduce its share capital in accordance with Chapter 10.

(3) The company may—
(a) sub-divide or consolidate all or any of its share capital in accordance with section 618...
...

(5) Nothing in this section affects—
(a) the power of a company to purchase its own shares, or to redeem shares, in accordance with Part 18...
...

Sub-division or consolidation of shares

618 SUB-DIVISION OR CONSOLIDATION OF SHARES

(1) A limited company having a share capital may—
(a) sub-divide its shares, or any of them, into shares of a smaller nominal amount than its existing shares, or
(b) consolidate and divide all or any of its share capital into shares of a larger nominal amount than its existing shares.

(2) In any sub-division, consolidation or division of shares under this section, the proportion between the amount paid and the amount (if any) unpaid on each resulting share must be the same as it was in the case of the share from which that share is derived.

(3) A company may exercise a power conferred by this section only if its members have passed a resolution authorising it to do so.

619 NOTICE TO REGISTRAR OF SUB-DIVISION OR CONSOLIDATION

(1) If a company exercises the power conferred by section 618 (sub-division or consolidation of shares) it must within one month after doing so give notice to the registrar, specifying the shares affected.

Chapter 9 CLASSES OF SHARE AND CLASS RIGHTS

Introductory

629 CLASSES OF SHARES

(1) For the purposes of the Companies Acts shares are of one class if the rights attached to them are in all respects uniform.

(2) For this purpose the rights attached to shares are not regarded as different from those attached to other shares by reason only that they do not carry the same rights to dividends in the twelve months immediately following their allotment.

Variation of class rights

630 VARIATION OF CLASS RIGHTS: COMPANIES HAVING A SHARE CAPITAL

(1) This section is concerned with the variation of the rights attached to a class of shares in a company having a share capital.

(2) Rights attached to a class of a company's shares may only be varied—
 (a) in accordance with provision in the company's articles for the variation of those rights, or
 (b) where the company's articles contain no such provision, if the holders of shares of that class consent to the variation in accordance with this section.

(3) This is without prejudice to any other restrictions on the variation of the rights.

(4) The consent required for the purposes of this section on the part of the holders of a class of a company's shares is—
 (a) consent in writing from the holders of at least three-quarters in nominal value of the issued shares of that class (excluding any shares held as treasury shares), or
 (b) a special resolution passed at a separate general meeting of the holders of that class sanctioning the variation.

(5) Any amendment of a provision contained in a company's articles for the variation of the rights attached to a class of shares, or the insertion of any such provision into the articles, is itself to be treated as a variation of those rights.

(6) In this section, and (except where the context otherwise requires) in any provision in a company's articles for the variation of the rights attached to a class of shares, references to the variation of those rights include references to their abrogation.

632 VARIATION OF CLASS RIGHTS: SAVING FOR COURT'S POWERS UNDER OTHER PROVISIONS

Nothing in section 630 ... (variation of class rights) affects the power of the court under—

section 98 (application to cancel resolution for public company to be re-registered as private),

Part 26 (arrangements and reconstructions), or

Part 30 (protection of members against unfair prejudice).

633 RIGHT TO OBJECT TO VARIATION: COMPANIES HAVING A SHARE CAPITAL

(1) This section applies where the rights attached to any class of shares in a company are varied under section 630 (variation of class rights: companies having a share capital).

(2) The holders of not less in the aggregate than 15% of the issued shares of the class in question (being persons who did not consent to or vote in favour of the resolution for the variation) may apply to the court to have the variation cancelled. For this purpose any of the company's share capital held as treasury shares is disregarded.

(3) If such an application is made, the variation has no effect unless and until it is confirmed by the court.

(4) Application to the court—

(a) must be made within 21 days after the date on which the consent was given or the resolution was passed (as the case may be), and

(b) may be made on behalf of the shareholders entitled to make the application by such one or more of their number as they may appoint in writing for the purpose.

(5) The court, after hearing the applicant and any other persons who apply to the court to be heard and appear to the court to be interested in the application, may, if satisfied having regard to all the circumstances of the case that the variation would unfairly prejudice the shareholders of the class represented by the applicant, disallow the variation, and shall if not so satisfied confirm it.

The decision of the court on any such application is final.

(6) References in this section to the variation of the rights of holders of a class of shares include references to their abrogation.

635 COPY OF COURT ORDER TO BE FORWARDED TO THE REGISTRAR

(1) The company must within 15 days after the making of an order by the court on an application under section 633 … 634 (objection to variation of class rights) forward a copy of the order to the registrar.

636 NOTICE OF NAME OR OTHER DESIGNATION OF CLASS OF SHARES

(1) Where a company assigns a name or other designation, or a new name or other designation, to any class or description of its shares, it must within one month from doing so deliver to the registrar a notice giving particulars of the name or designation so assigned.

637 NOTICE OF PARTICULARS OF VARIATION OF RIGHTS ATTACHED TO SHARES

(1) Where the rights attached to any shares of a company are varied, the company must within one month from the date on which the variation is made deliver to the registrar a notice giving particulars of the variation.

638 NOTICE OF NEW CLASS OF MEMBERS

(1) If a company not having a share capital creates a new class of members, the company must within one month from the date on which the new class is created deliver to the registrar a notice containing particulars of the rights attached to that class.

Chapter 10 REDUCTION OF SHARE CAPITAL

Introductory

641 CIRCUMSTANCES IN WHICH A COMPANY MAY REDUCE ITS SHARE CAPITAL

(1) A limited company having a share capital may reduce its share capital—

(a) in the case of a private company limited by shares, by special resolution supported by a solvency statement (see sections 642 to 644);

(b) in any case, by special resolution confirmed by the court (see sections 645 to 651).

(2) A company may not reduce its capital under subsection (1)(a) if as a result of the reduction there would no longer be any member of the company holding shares other than redeemable shares.

(3) Subject to that, a company may reduce its share capital under this section in any way.

(4) In particular, a company may—
(a) extinguish or reduce the liability on any of its shares in respect of share capital not paid up, or
(b) either with or without extinguishing or reducing liability on any of its shares—
(i) cancel any paid-up share capital that is lost or unrepresented by available assets, or
(ii) repay any paid-up share capital in excess of the company's wants.

(5) A special resolution under this section may not provide for a reduction of share capital to take effect later than the date on which the resolution has effect in accordance with this Chapter.

(6) This Chapter (apart from subsection (5) above) has effect subject to any provision of the company's articles restricting or prohibiting the reduction of the company's share capital.

Private companies: reduction of capital supported by solvency statement

642 REDUCTION OF CAPITAL SUPPORTED BY SOLVENCY STATEMENT

(1) A resolution for reducing share capital of a private company limited by shares is supported by a solvency statement if—
(a) the directors of the company make a statement of the solvency of the company in accordance with section 643 (a "solvency statement") not more than 15 days before the date on which the resolution is passed, and
(b) the resolution and solvency statement are registered in accordance with section 644.

(2) Where the resolution is proposed as a written resolution, a copy of the solvency statement must be sent or submitted to every eligible member at or before the time at which the proposed resolution is sent or submitted to him.

(3) Where the resolution is proposed at a general meeting, a copy of the solvency statement must be made available for inspection by members of the company throughout that meeting.

(4) The validity of a resolution is not affected by a failure to comply with subsection (2) or (3).

643 SOLVENCY STATEMENT

(1) A solvency statement is a statement that each of the directors—
(a) has formed the opinion, as regards the company's situation at the date of the statement, that there is no ground on which the company could then be found to be unable to pay (or otherwise discharge) its debts; and
(b) has also formed the opinion—
(i) if it is intended to commence the winding up of the company within twelve months of that date, that the company will be able to pay (or otherwise discharge) its debts in full within twelve months of the commencement of the winding up; or

(ii) in any other case, that the company will be able to pay (or otherwise discharge) its debts as they fall due during the year immediately following that date.

(2) In forming those opinions, the directors must take into account all of the company's liabilities (including any contingent or prospective liabilities).

(3) The solvency statement must be in the prescribed form and must state—
(a) the date on which it is made, and
(b) the name of each director of the company.

(4) If the directors make a solvency statement without having reasonable grounds for the opinions expressed in it, and the statement is delivered to the registrar, an offence is committed by every director who is in default.

(5) A person guilty of an offence under subsection (4) is liable—
(a) on conviction on indictment, to imprisonment for a term not exceeding two years or a fine (or both);
(b) on summary conviction—
(i) in England and Wales, to imprisonment for a term not exceeding twelve months or to a fine not exceeding the statutory maximum (or both);
(ii) in Scotland or Northern Ireland, to imprisonment for a term not exceeding six months, or to a fine not exceeding the statutory maximum (or both).

644 REGISTRATION OF RESOLUTION AND SUPPORTING DOCUMENTS

(1) Within 15 days after the resolution for reducing share capital is passed the company must deliver to the registrar—
(a) a copy of the solvency statement, and
(b) a statement of capital.
This is in addition to the copy of the resolution itself that is required to be delivered to the registrar under Chapter 3 of Part 3.

Reduction of capital confirmed by the court

645 APPLICATION TO COURT FOR ORDER OF CONFIRMATION

(1) Where a company has passed a resolution for reducing share capital, it may apply to the court for an order confirming the reduction.

(2) If the proposed reduction of capital involves either—
(a) diminution of liability in respect of unpaid share capital, or
(b) the payment to a shareholder of any paid-up share capital,
section 646 (creditors entitled to object to reduction) applies unless the court directs otherwise.

(3) The court may, if having regard to any special circumstances of the case it thinks proper to do so, direct that section 646 is not to apply as regards any class or classes of creditors.

(4) The court may direct that section 646 is to apply in any other case.

646 CREDITORS ENTITLED TO OBJECT TO REDUCTION

(1) Where this section applies (see section 645(2) and (4)), every creditor of the company who—

(a) at the date fixed by the court is entitled to any debt or claim that, if that date were the commencement of the winding up of the company would be admissible in proof against the company, and
(b) can show that there is a real likelihood that the reduction would result in the company being unable to discharge his debt or claim when it fell due,

is entitled to object to the reduction of capital.

(2) The court shall settle a list of creditors entitled to object.

(3) For that purpose the court—
(a) shall ascertain, as far as possible without requiring an application from any creditor, the names of those creditors and the nature and amount of their debts or claims, and
(b) may publish notices fixing a day or days within which creditors not entered on the list are to claim to be so entered or are to be excluded from the right of objecting to the reduction of capital.

(4) If a creditor entered on the list whose debt or claim is not discharged or has not determined does not consent to the reduction, the court may, if it thinks fit, dispense with the consent of that creditor on the company securing payment of his debt or claim.

(5) For this purpose the debt or claim must be secured by appropriating (as the court may direct) the following amount—
(a) if the company admits the full amount of the debt or claim or, though not admitting it, is willing to provide for it, the full amount of the debt or claim;
(b) if the company does not admit, and is not willing to provide for, the full amount of the debt or claim, or if the amount is contingent or not ascertained, an amount fixed by the court after the like enquiry and adjudication as if the company were being wound up by the court.

647 OFFENCES IN CONNECTION WITH LIST OF CREDITORS

(1) If an officer of the company—
(a) intentionally or recklessly—
(i) conceals the name of a creditor entitled to object to the reduction of capital, or
(ii) misrepresents the nature or amount of the debt or claim of a creditor, or
(b) is knowingly concerned in any such concealment or misrepresentation,

he commits an offence.

(2) A person guilty of an offence under this section is liable—
(a) on conviction on indictment, to a fine;
(b) on summary conviction, to a fine not exceeding the statutory maximum.

648 COURT ORDER CONFIRMING REDUCTION

(1) The court may make an order confirming the reduction of capital on such terms and conditions as it thinks fit.

(2) The court must not confirm the reduction unless it is satisfied, with respect to every creditor of the company who is entitled to object to the reduction of capital that either—
(a) his consent to the reduction has been obtained, or
(b) his debt or claim has been discharged, or has determined or has been secured.

(3) Where the court confirms the reduction, it may order the company to publish (as the court directs) the reasons for reduction of capital, or such other information in regard to it as

the court thinks expedient with a view to giving proper information to the public, and (if the court thinks fit) the causes that led to the reduction.

(4) The court may, if for any special reason it thinks proper to do so, make an order directing that the company must, during such period (commencing on or at any time after the date of the order) as is specified in the order, add to its name as its last words the words "and reduced".

If such an order is made, those words are, until the end of the period specified in the order, deemed to be part of the company's name.

649 REGISTRATION OF ORDER AND STATEMENT OF CAPITAL

(1) The registrar, on production of an order of the court confirming the reduction of a company's share capital and the delivery of a copy of the order and of a statement of capital (approved by the court), shall register the order and statement.

This is subject to section 650 (public company reducing capital below authorised minimum).

650 PUBLIC COMPANY REDUCING CAPITAL BELOW AUTHORISED MINIMUM

(1) This section applies where the court makes an order confirming a reduction of a public company's capital that has the effect of bringing the nominal value of its allotted share capital below the authorised minimum.

(2) The registrar must not register the order unless either—
(a) the court so directs, or
(b) the company is first re-registered as a private company.

(3) Section 651 provides an expedited procedure for re-registration in these circumstances.

651 EXPEDITED PROCEDURE FOR RE-REGISTRATION AS A PRIVATE COMPANY

(1) The court may authorise the company to be re-registered as a private company without its having passed the special resolution required by section 97.

(2) If it does so, the court must specify in the order the changes to the company's name and articles to be made in connection with the re-registration.

(3) The company may then be re-registered as a private company if an application to that effect is delivered to the registrar together with—
(a) a copy of the court's order, and
(b) notice of the company's name, and a copy of the company's articles, as altered by the court's order.

(4) On receipt of such an application the registrar must issue a certificate of incorporation altered to meet the circumstances of the case.

(5) The certificate must state that it is issued on re-registration and the date on which it is issued.

(6) On the issue of the certificate—
(a) the company by virtue of the issue of the certificate becomes a private company, and
(b) the changes in the company's name and articles take effect.

(7) The certificate is conclusive evidence that the requirements of this Act as to re-registration have been complied with.

Effect of reduction of capital

652 LIABILITY OF MEMBERS FOLLOWING REDUCTION OF CAPITAL

(1) Where a company's share capital is reduced a member of the company (past or present) is not liable in respect of any share to any call or contribution exceeding in amount the difference (if any) between—
  (a) the nominal amount of the share as notified to the registrar in the statement of capital delivered under section 644 or 649, and
  (b) the amount paid on the share or the reduced amount (if any) which is deemed to have been paid on it, as the case may be.

(2) This is subject to section 653 (liability to creditor in case of omission from list).

(3) Nothing in this section affects the rights of the contributories among themselves.

653 LIABILITY TO CREDITOR IN CASE OF OMISSION FROM LIST OF CREDITORS

(1) This section applies where, in the case of a reduction of capital confirmed by the court—
  (a) a creditor entitled to object to the reduction of share capital is by reason of his ignorance—
    (i) of the proceedings for reduction of share capital, or
    (ii) of their nature and effect with respect to his debt or claim,
  is not entered on the list of creditors, and
  (b) after the reduction of capital the company is unable to pay the amount of his debt or claim.

(2) Every person who was a member of the company at the date on which the resolution for reducing capital took effect under section 649(3) is liable to contribute for the payment of the debt or claim an amount not exceeding that which he would have been liable to contribute if the company had commenced to be wound up on the day before that date.

(3) If the company is wound up, the court on the application of the creditor in question, and proof of ignorance as mentioned in subsection (1)(a), may if it thinks fit—
  (a) settle accordingly a list of persons liable to contribute under this section, and
  (b) make and enforce calls and orders on them as if they were ordinary contributories in a winding up.

(4) The reference in subsection (1)(b) to a company being unable to pay the amount of a debt or claim has the same meaning as in section 123 of the Insolvency Act 1986 (c. 45) or Article 103 of the Insolvency (Northern Ireland) Order 1989 (S.I. 1989/2405 (N.I. 19)).

Chapter 11 **MISCELLANEOUS AND SUPPLEMENTARY PROVISIONS**

654 TREATMENT OF RESERVE ARISING FROM REDUCTION OF CAPITAL

(1) A reserve arising from the reduction of a company's share capital is not distributable, subject to any provision made by order under this section.

(2) The Secretary of State may by order specify cases in which—

(a) the prohibition in subsection (1) does not apply, and
(b) the reserve is to be treated for the purposes of Part 23 (distributions) as a realised profit.

(3) An order under this section is subject to affirmative resolution procedure.

655 SHARES NO BAR TO DAMAGES AGAINST COMPANY

A person is not debarred from obtaining damages or other compensation from a company by reason only of his holding or having held shares in the company or any right to apply or subscribe for shares or to be included in the company's register of members in respect of shares.

656 PUBLIC COMPANIES: DUTY OF DIRECTORS TO CALL MEETING ON SERIOUS LOSS OF CAPITAL

(1) Where the net assets of a public company are half or less of its called-up share capital, the directors must call a general meeting of the company to consider whether any, and if so what, steps should be taken to deal with the situation.

(2) They must do so not later than 28 days from the earliest day on which that fact is known to a director of the company.

(3) The meeting must be convened for a date not later than 56 days from that day.

(4) If there is a failure to convene a meeting as required by this section, each of the directors of the company who—
(a) knowingly authorises or permits the failure, or
(b) after the period during which the meeting should have been convened, knowingly authorises or permits the failure to continue,
commits an offence.

(5) A person guilty of an offence under this section is liable—
(a) on conviction on indictment, to a fine;
(b) on summary conviction, to a fine not exceeding the statutory maximum.

(6) Nothing in this section authorises the consideration at a meeting convened in pursuance of subsection (1) of any matter that could not have been considered at that meeting apart from this section.

Part 18 ACQUISITION BY LIMITED COMPANY OF ITS OWN SHARES

Chapter 1 GENERAL PROVISIONS

Introductory

658 GENERAL RULE AGAINST LIMITED COMPANY ACQUIRING ITS OWN SHARES

(1) A limited company must not acquire its own shares, whether by purchase, subscription or otherwise, except in accordance with the provisions of this Part.

(2) If a company purports to act in contravention of this section—
(a) an offence is committed by—
(i) the company, and
(ii) every officer of the company who is in default, and
(b) the purported acquisition is void.

(3) A person guilty of an offence under this section is liable—
  (a) on conviction on indictment, to imprisonment for a term not exceeding two years or a fine (or both);
  (b) on summary conviction—
    (i) in England and Wales, to imprisonment for a term not exceeding twelve months or a fine not exceeding the statutory maximum (or both);
    (ii) in Scotland or Northern Ireland, to imprisonment for a term not exceeding six months or a fine not exceeding the statutory maximum (or both).

Chapter 2 FINANCIAL ASSISTANCE FOR PURCHASE OF OWN SHARES

Introductory

677 MEANING OF "FINANCIAL ASSISTANCE"

(1) In this Chapter "financial assistance" means—
  (a) financial assistance given by way of gift,
  (b) financial assistance given—
    (i) by way of guarantee, security or indemnity (other than an indemnity in respect of the indemnifier's own neglect or default), or
    (ii) by way of release or waiver,
  (c) financial assistance given—
    (i) by way of a loan or any other agreement under which any of the obligations of the person giving the assistance are to be fulfilled at a time when in accordance with the agreement any obligation of another party to the agreement remains unfulfilled, or
    (ii) by way of the novation of, or the assignment (in Scotland, assignation) of rights arising under, a loan or such other agreement, or
  (d) any other financial assistance given by a company where—
    (i) the net assets of the company are reduced to a material extent by the giving of the assistance, or
    (ii) the company has no net assets.

(2) "Net assets" here means the aggregate amount of the company's assets less the aggregate amount of its liabilities.

Circumstances in which financial assistance prohibited

678 ASSISTANCE FOR ACQUISITION OF SHARES IN PUBLIC COMPANY

(1) Where a person is acquiring or proposing to acquire shares in a public company, it is not lawful for that company, or a company that is a subsidiary of that company, to give financial assistance directly or indirectly for the purpose of the acquisition before or at the same time as the acquisition takes place.

(2) Subsection (1) does not prohibit a company from giving financial assistance for the acquisition of shares in it or its holding company if—
  (a) the company's principal purpose in giving the assistance is not to give it for the purpose of any such acquisition, or
  (b) the giving of the assistance for that purpose is only an incidental part of some larger purpose of the company,

and the assistance is given in good faith in the interests of the company.

(3) Where—
(a) a person has acquired shares in a company, and
(b) a liability has been incurred (by that or another person) for the purpose of the acquisition,
it is not lawful for that company, or a company that is a subsidiary of that company, to give financial assistance directly or indirectly for the purpose of reducing or discharging the liability if, at the time the assistance is given, the company in which the shares were acquired is a public company.

(4) Subsection (3) does not prohibit a company from giving financial assistance if—
(a) the company's principal purpose in giving the assistance is not to reduce or discharge any liability incurred by a person for the purpose of the acquisition of shares in the company or its holding company, or
(b) the reduction or discharge of any such liability is only an incidental part of some larger purpose of the company,
and the assistance is given in good faith in the interests of the company.

(5) This section has effect subject to sections 681 and 682 (unconditional and conditional exceptions to prohibition).

680 PROHIBITED FINANCIAL ASSISTANCE AN OFFENCE

(1) If a company contravenes section 678(1) or (3) … (prohibited financial assistance) an offence is committed by—
(a) the company, and
(b) every officer of the company who is in default.

(2) A person guilty of an offence under this section is liable—
(a) on conviction on indictment, to imprisonment for a term not exceeding two years or a fine (or both);
(b) on summary conviction—
(i) in England and Wales, to imprisonment for a term not exceeding twelve months or to a fine not exceeding the statutory maximum (or both);
(ii) in Scotland or Northern Ireland, to imprisonment for a term not exceeding six months, or to a fine not exceeding the statutory maximum (or both).

Exceptions from prohibition

681 UNCONDITIONAL EXCEPTIONS

(1) Neither section 678 nor section 679 prohibits a transaction to which this section applies.

(2) Those transactions are—
(a) a distribution of the company's assets by way of—
(i) dividend lawfully made, or
(ii) distribution in the course of a company's winding up;
(b) an allotment of bonus shares;
(c) a reduction of capital under Chapter 10 of Part 17;
(d) a redemption of shares under Chapter 3 or a purchase of shares under Chapter 4 of this Part;
(e) anything done in pursuance of an order of the court under Part 26 (order sanctioning compromise or arrangement with members or creditors);

(f) anything done under an arrangement made in pursuance of section 110 of the Insolvency Act 1986 (c. 45) or Article 96 of the Insolvency (Northern Ireland) Order 1989 (S.I. 1989/2405 (N.I. 19)) (liquidator in winding up accepting shares as consideration for sale of company's property);

(g) anything done under an arrangement made between a company and its creditors that is binding on the creditors by virtue of Part 1 of the Insolvency Act 1986 or Part 2 of the Insolvency (Northern Ireland) Order 1989 (S.I. 1989/2405 (N.I. 19)).

682 CONDITIONAL EXCEPTIONS

(1) [Section 678 does not prohibit] a transaction to which this section applies—
(a) if the company giving the assistance is a private company, or
(b) if the company giving the assistance is a public company and—
(i) the company has net assets that are not reduced by the giving of the assistance, or
(ii) to the extent that those assets are so reduced, the assistance is provided out of distributable profits.

(2) The transactions to which this section applies are—
(a) where the lending of money is part of the ordinary business of the company, the lending of money in the ordinary course of the company's business;
(b) the provision by the company, in good faith in the interests of the company or its holding company, of financial assistance for the purposes of an employees' share scheme;
(c) the provision of financial assistance by the company for the purposes of or in connection with anything done by the company (or another company in the same group) for the purpose of enabling or facilitating transactions in shares in the first-mentioned company or its holding company between, and involving the acquisition of beneficial ownership of those shares by—
(i) bona fide employees or former employees of that company (or another company in the same group), or
(ii) spouses or civil partners, widows, widowers or surviving civil partners, or minor children or step-children of any such employees or former employees;
(d) the making by the company of loans to persons (other than directors) employed in good faith by the company with a view to enabling those persons to acquire fully paid shares in the company or its holding company to be held by them by way of beneficial ownership.

(3) The references in this section to "net assets" are to the amount by which the aggregate of the company's assets exceeds the aggregate of its liabilities.

(5) For the purposes of subsection (2)(c) a company is in the same group as another company if it is a holding company or subsidiary of that company or a subsidiary of a holding company of that company.

Supplementary

683 DEFINITIONS FOR THIS CHAPTER

(1) In this Chapter—

"distributable profits", in relation to the giving of any financial assistance—
(a) means those profits out of which the company could lawfully make a distribution equal in value to that assistance, and

...

"distribution" has the same meaning as in Part 23 (distributions) (see section 829).

Chapter 3 REDEEMABLE SHARES

684 POWER OF LIMITED COMPANY TO ISSUE REDEEMABLE SHARES

(1) A limited company having a share capital may issue shares that are to be redeemed or are liable to be redeemed at the option of the company or the shareholder ("redeemable shares"), subject to the following provisions.

(2) The articles of a private limited company may exclude or restrict the issue of redeemable shares.

(3) A public limited company may only issue redeemable shares if it is authorised to do so by its articles.

(4) No redeemable shares may be issued at a time when there are no issued shares of the company that are not redeemable.

685 TERMS AND MANNER OF REDEMPTION

(1) The directors of a limited company may determine the terms, conditions and manner of redemption of shares if they are authorised to do so—
(a) by the company's articles, or
(b) by a resolution of the company.

(2) A resolution under subsection (1)(b) may be an ordinary resolution, even though it amends the company's articles.

(3) Where the directors are authorised under subsection (1) to determine the terms, conditions and manner of redemption of shares—
(a) they must do so before the shares are allotted, and
(b) any obligation of the company to state in a statement of capital the rights attached to the shares extends to the terms, conditions and manner of redemption.

(4) Where the directors are not so authorised, the terms, conditions and manner of redemption of any redeemable shares must be stated in the company's articles.

686 PAYMENT FOR REDEEMABLE SHARES

(1) Redeemable shares in a limited company may not be redeemed unless they are fully paid.

(2) The terms of redemption of shares in a limited company may provide that the amount payable on redemption may, by agreement between the company and the holder of the shares, be paid on a date later than the redemption date.

(3) Unless redeemed in accordance with a provision authorised by subsection (2), the shares must be paid for on redemption.

687 FINANCING OF REDEMPTION

(1) A private limited company may redeem redeemable shares out of capital in accordance with Chapter 5.

(2) Subject to that, redeemable shares in a limited company may only be redeemed out of—
(a) distributable profits of the company, or
(b) the proceeds of a fresh issue of shares made for the purposes of the redemption.

(3) Any premium payable on redemption of shares in a limited company must be paid out of distributable profits of the company, subject to the following provision.

(4) If the redeemable shares were issued at a premium, any premium payable on their redemption may be paid out of the proceeds of a fresh issue of shares made for the purposes of the redemption, up to an amount equal to—
   (a) the aggregate of the premiums received by the company on the issue of the shares redeemed, or
   (b) the current amount of the company's share premium account (including any sum transferred to that account in respect of premiums on the new shares),
   whichever is the less.

(5) The amount of the company's share premium account is reduced by a sum corresponding (or by sums in the aggregate corresponding) to the amount of any payment made under subsection (4).

(6) This section is subject to section 735(4) (terms of redemption enforceable in a winding up).

688 REDEEMED SHARES TREATED AS CANCELLED

Where shares in a limited company are redeemed—

(a) the shares are treated as cancelled, and

(b) the amount of the company's issued share capital is diminished accordingly by the nominal value of the shares redeemed.

689 NOTICE TO REGISTRAR OF REDEMPTION

(1) If a limited company redeems any redeemable shares it must within one month after doing so give notice to the registrar, specifying the shares redeemed.

Chapter 4 PURCHASE OF OWN SHARES

General provisions

690 POWER OF LIMITED COMPANY TO PURCHASE OWN SHARES

(1) A limited company having a share capital may purchase its own shares (including any redeemable shares), subject to—
   (a) the following provisions of this Chapter, and
   (b) any restriction or prohibition in the company's articles.

(2) A limited company may not purchase its own shares if as a result of the purchase there would no longer be any issued shares of the company other than redeemable shares or shares held as treasury shares.

691 PAYMENT FOR PURCHASE OF OWN SHARES

(1) A limited company may not purchase its own shares unless they are fully paid.

(2) Where a limited company purchases its own shares, the shares must be paid for on purchase.

692 FINANCING OF PURCHASE OF OWN SHARES

(1) A private limited company may purchase its own shares out of capital in accordance with Chapter 5.

(2) Subject to that—
(a) a limited company may only purchase its own shares out of—
(i) distributable profits of the company, or
(ii) the proceeds of a fresh issue of shares made for the purpose of financing the purchase, and
(b) any premium payable on the purchase by a limited company of its own shares must be paid out of distributable profits of the company, subject to subsection (3).

(3) If the shares to be purchased were issued at a premium, any premium payable on their purchase by the company may be paid out of the proceeds of a fresh issue of shares made for the purpose of financing the purchase, up to an amount equal to—
(a) the aggregate of the premiums received by the company on the issue of the shares purchased, or
(b) the current amount of the company's share premium account (including any sum transferred to that account in respect of premiums on the new shares),
whichever is the less.

(4) The amount of the company's share premium account is reduced by a sum corresponding (or by sums in the aggregate corresponding) to the amount of any payment made under subsection (3).

(5) This section has effect subject to section 735(4) (terms of purchase enforceable in a winding up).

Authority for purchase of own shares

693 AUTHORITY FOR PURCHASE OF OWN SHARES

(1) A limited company may only purchase its own shares—
(a) by an off-market purchase, in pursuance of a contract approved in advance in accordance with section 694;
(b) by a market purchase, authorised in accordance with section 701.

(2) A purchase is "off-market" if the shares either—
(a) are purchased otherwise than on a recognised investment exchange, or
(b) are purchased on a recognised investment exchange but are not subject to a marketing arrangement on the exchange.

(3) For this purpose a company's shares are subject to a marketing arrangement on a recognised investment exchange if—
(a) they are listed under Part 6 of the Financial Services and Markets Act 2000 (c. 8), or
(b) the company has been afforded facilities for dealings in the shares to take place on the exchange—
(i) without prior permission for individual transactions from the authority governing that investment exchange, and
(ii) without limit as to the time during which those facilities are to be available.

(4) A purchase is a "market purchase" if it is made on a recognised investment exchange and is not an off-market purchase by virtue of subsection (2)(b).

(5) In this section "recognised investment exchange" means a recognised investment exchange (within the meaning of Part 18 of the Financial Services and Markets Act 2000) other than an overseas exchange (within the meaning of that Part).

Authority for off-market purchase

694 AUTHORITY FOR OFF-MARKET PURCHASE

(1) A company may only make an off-market purchase of its own shares in pursuance of a contract approved prior to the purchase in accordance with this section.

(2) Either—
- (a) the terms of the contract must be authorised by a special resolution of the company before the contract is entered into, or
- (b) the contract must provide that no shares may be purchased in pursuance of the contract until its terms have been authorised by a special resolution of the company.

(3) The contract may be a contract, entered into by the company and relating to shares in the company, that does not amount to a contract to purchase the shares but under which the company may (subject to any conditions) become entitled or obliged to purchase the shares.

(4) The authority conferred by a resolution under this section may be varied, revoked or from time to time renewed by a special resolution of the company.

(5) In the case of a public company a resolution conferring, varying or renewing authority must specify a date on which the authority is to expire, which must not be later than five years after the date on which the resolution is passed.

(6) A resolution conferring, varying, revoking or renewing authority under this section is subject to—

section 695 (exercise of voting rights), and

section 696 (disclosure of details of contract).

695 RESOLUTION AUTHORISING OFF-MARKET PURCHASE: EXERCISE OF VOTING RIGHTS

(1) This section applies to a resolution to confer, vary, revoke or renew authority for the purposes of section 694 (authority for off-market purchase of own shares).

(2) Where the resolution is proposed as a written resolution, a member who holds shares to which the resolution relates is not an eligible member.

(3) Where the resolution is proposed at a meeting of the company, it is not effective if—
- (a) any member of the company holding shares to which the resolution relates exercises the voting rights carried by any of those shares in voting on the resolution, and
- (b) the resolution would not have been passed if he had not done so.

(4) For this purpose—
- (a) a member who holds shares to which the resolution relates is regarded as exercising the voting rights carried by those shares not only if he votes in respect of them on a poll on the question whether the resolution shall be passed, but also if he votes on the resolution otherwise than on a poll;
- (b) any member of the company may demand a poll on that question;
- (c) a vote and a demand for a poll by a person as proxy for a member are the same respectively as a vote and a demand by the member.

696 RESOLUTION AUTHORISING OFF-MARKET PURCHASE: DISCLOSURE OF DETAILS OF CONTRACT

(1) This section applies in relation to a resolution to confer, vary, revoke or renew authority for the purposes of section 694 (authority for off-market purchase of own shares).

(2) A copy of the contract (if it is in writing) or a memorandum setting out its terms (if it is not) must be made available to members—
- (a) in the case of a written resolution, by being sent or submitted to every eligible member at or before the time at which the proposed resolution is sent or submitted to him;
- (b) in the case of a resolution at a meeting, by being made available for inspection by members of the company both—
  - (i) at the company's registered office for not less than 15 days ending with the date of the meeting, and
  - (ii) at the meeting itself.

(5) The resolution is not validly passed if the requirements of this section are not complied with

Authority for market purchase

701 AUTHORITY FOR MARKET PURCHASE

(1) A company may only make a market purchase of its own shares if the purchase has first been authorised by a resolution of the company.

(2) That authority—
- (a) may be general or limited to the purchase of shares of a particular class or description, and
- (b) may be unconditional or subject to conditions.

(3) The authority must—
- (a) specify the maximum number of shares authorised to be acquired, and
- (b) determine both the maximum and minimum prices that may be paid for the shares.

(4) The authority may be varied, revoked or from time to time renewed by a resolution of the company.

(5) A resolution conferring, varying or renewing authority must specify a date on which it is to expire, which must not be later than five years after the date on which the resolution is passed.

(8) Chapter 3 of Part 3 (resolutions affecting a company's constitution) applies to a resolution under this section.

Supplementary provisions

702 COPY OF CONTRACT OR MEMORANDUM TO BE AVAILABLE FOR INSPECTION

(1) This section applies where a company has entered into—
- (a) a contract approved under section 694 (authorisation of contract for off-market purchase), or
- (b) a contract for a purchase authorised under section 701 (authorisation of market purchase).

(2) The company must keep available for inspection—

(a) a copy of the contract, or
(b) if the contract is not in writing, a written memorandum setting out its terms.

704 NO ASSIGNMENT OF COMPANY'S RIGHT TO PURCHASE OWN SHARES

The rights of a company under a contract authorised under—

(a) section 694 (authority for off-market purchase), or

(b) section 701 (authority for market purchase)

are not capable of being assigned.

706 TREATMENT OF SHARES PURCHASED

Where a limited company makes a purchase of its own shares in accordance with this Chapter, then—

(a) if section 724 (treasury shares) applies, the shares may be held and dealt with in accordance with Chapter 6;

(b) if that section does not apply—
(i) the shares are treated as cancelled, and
(ii) the amount of the company's issued share capital is diminished accordingly by the nominal value of the shares cancelled.

Chapter 5 REDEMPTION OR PURCHASE BY PRIVATE COMPANY OUT OF CAPITAL

Introductory

709 POWER OF PRIVATE LIMITED COMPANY TO REDEEM OR PURCHASE OWN SHARES OUT OF CAPITAL

(1) A private limited company may in accordance with this Chapter, but subject to any restriction or prohibition in the company's articles, make a payment in respect of the redemption or purchase of its own shares otherwise than out of distributable profits or the proceeds of a fresh issue of shares.

(2) References below in this Chapter to payment out of capital are to any payment so made, whether or not it would be regarded apart from this section as a payment out of capital.

The permissible capital payment

710 THE PERMISSIBLE CAPITAL PAYMENT

(1) The payment that may, in accordance with this Chapter, be made by a company out of capital in respect of the redemption or purchase of its own shares is such amount as, after applying for that purpose—
(a) any available profits of the company, and
(b) the proceeds of any fresh issue of shares made for the purposes of the redemption or purchase,
is required to meet the price of redemption or purchase.

(2) That is referred to below in this Chapter as "the permissible capital payment" for the shares.

711 AVAILABLE PROFITS

(1) For the purposes of this Chapter the available profits of the company, in relation to the redemption or purchase of any shares, are the profits of the company that are available for distribution (within the meaning of Part 23).

(2) But the question whether a company has any profits so available, and the amount of any such profits, shall be determined in accordance with section 712 instead of in accordance with sections 836 to 842 in that Part.

712 DETERMINATION OF AVAILABLE PROFITS

(1) The available profits of the company are determined as follows.

(2) First, determine the profits of the company by reference to the following items as stated in the relevant accounts—
- (a) profits, losses, assets and liabilities,
- (b) provisions of the following kinds—
  - (i) where the relevant accounts are Companies Act accounts, provisions of a kind specified for the purposes of this subsection by regulations under section 396;
  - (ii) where the relevant accounts are IAS accounts, provisions of any kind;
- (c) share capital and reserves (including undistributable reserves).

(3) Second, reduce the amount so determined by the amount of—
- (a) any distribution lawfully made by the company, and
- (b) any other relevant payment lawfully made by the company out of distributable profits,

after the date of the relevant accounts and before the end of the relevant period.

(4) For this purpose "other relevant payment lawfully made" includes—
- (a) financial assistance lawfully given out of distributable profits in accordance with Chapter 2, [and]
- (b) payments lawfully made out of distributable profits in respect of the purchase by the company of any shares in the company...

...

(5) The resulting figure is the amount of available profits.

(6) For the purposes of this section "the relevant accounts" are any accounts that—
- (a) are prepared as at a date within the relevant period, and
- (b) are such as to enable a reasonable judgment to be made as to the amounts of the items mentioned in subsection (2).

(7) In this section "the relevant period" means the period of three months ending with the date on which the directors' statement is made in accordance with section 714.

Requirements for payment out of capital

713 REQUIREMENTS FOR PAYMENT OUT OF CAPITAL

(1) A payment out of capital by a private company for the redemption or purchase of its own shares is not lawful unless the requirements of the following sections are met—

section 714 (directors' statement and auditor's report);

section 716 (approval by special resolution);

section 719 (public notice of proposed payment);

section 720 (directors' statement and auditor's report to be available for inspection).

(2) This is subject to any order of the court under section 721 (power of court to extend period for compliance on application by persons objecting to payment).

714 DIRECTORS' STATEMENT AND AUDITOR'S REPORT

(1) The company's directors must make a statement in accordance with this section.

(2) The statement must specify the amount of the permissible capital payment for the shares in question.

(3) It must state that, having made full inquiry into the affairs and prospects of the company, the directors have formed the opinion—
- (a) as regards its initial situation immediately following the date on which the payment out of capital is proposed to be made, that there will be no grounds on which the company could then be found unable to pay its debts, and
- (b) as regards its prospects for the year immediately following that date, that having regard to—
  - (i) their intentions with respect to the management of the company's business during that year, and
  - (ii) the amount and character of the financial resources that will in their view be available to the company during that year,

the company will be able to continue to carry on business as a going concern (and will accordingly be able to pay its debts as they fall due) throughout that year.

(4) In forming their opinion for the purposes of subsection (3)(a), the directors must take into account all of the company's liabilities (including any contingent or prospective liabilities).

(5) The directors' statement must be in the prescribed form and must contain such information with respect to the nature of the company's business as may be prescribed.

(6) It must in addition have annexed to it a report addressed to the directors by the company's auditor stating that—
- (a) he has inquired into the company's state of affairs,
- (b) the amount specified in the statement as the permissible capital payment for the shares in question is in his view properly determined in accordance with sections 710 to 712, and
- (c) he is not aware of anything to indicate that the opinion expressed by the directors in their statement as to any of the matters mentioned in subsection (3) above is unreasonable in all the circumstances.

715 DIRECTORS' STATEMENT: OFFENCE IF NO REASONABLE GROUNDS FOR OPINION

(1) If the directors make a statement under section 714 without having reasonable grounds for the opinion expressed in it, an offence is committed by every director who is in default.

(2) A person guilty of an offence under this section is liable—
- (a) on conviction on indictment, to imprisonment for a term not exceeding two years or a fine (or both);
- (b) on summary conviction—

(i) in England and Wales, to imprisonment for a term not exceeding twelve months or a fine not exceeding the statutory maximum (or both);
(ii) in Scotland or Northern Ireland, to imprisonment for a term not exceeding six months or a fine not exceeding the statutory maximum (or both).

716 PAYMENT TO BE APPROVED BY SPECIAL RESOLUTION

(1) The payment out of capital must be approved by a special resolution of the company.

(2) The resolution must be passed on, or within the week immediately following, the date on which the directors make the statement required by section 714.

(3) A resolution under this section is subject to—

section 717 (exercise of voting rights), and

section 718 (disclosure of directors' statement and auditors' report).

717 RESOLUTION AUTHORISING PAYMENT: EXERCISE OF VOTING RIGHTS

(1) This section applies to a resolution under section 716 (authority for payment out of capital for redemption or purchase of own shares).

(2) Where the resolution is proposed as a written resolution, a member who holds shares to which the resolution relates is not an eligible member.

(3) Where the resolution is proposed at a meeting of the company, it is not effective if—
(a) any member of the company holding shares to which the resolution relates exercises the voting rights carried by any of those shares in voting on the resolution, and
(b) the resolution would not have been passed if he had not done so.

(4) For this purpose—
(a) a member who holds shares to which the resolution relates is regarded as exercising the voting rights carried by those shares not only if he votes in respect of them on a poll on the question whether the resolution shall be passed, but also if he votes on the resolution otherwise than on a poll;
(b) any member of the company may demand a poll on that question;
(c) a vote and a demand for a poll by a person as proxy for a member are the same respectively as a vote and a demand by the member.

718 RESOLUTION AUTHORISING PAYMENT: DISCLOSURE OF DIRECTORS' STATEMENT AND AUDITOR'S REPORT

(1) This section applies to a resolution under section 716 (resolution authorising payment out of capital for redemption or purchase of own shares).

(2) A copy of the directors' statement and auditor's report under section 714 must be made available to members—
(a) in the case of a written resolution, by being sent or submitted to every eligible member at or before the time at which the proposed resolution is sent or submitted to him;
(b) in the case of a resolution at a meeting, by being made available for inspection by members of the company at the meeting.

(3) The resolution is ineffective if this requirement is not complied with.

719 PUBLIC NOTICE OF PROPOSED PAYMENT

(1) Within the week immediately following the date of the resolution under section 716 the company must cause to be published in the Gazette a notice—
- (a) stating that the company has approved a payment out of capital for the purpose of acquiring its own shares by redemption or purchase or both (as the case may be),
- (b) specifying—
  - (i) the amount of the permissible capital payment for the shares in question, and
  - (ii) the date of the resolution,
- (c) stating where the directors' statement and auditor's report required by section 714 are available for inspection, and
- (d) stating that any creditor of the company may at any time within the five weeks immediately following the date of the resolution apply to the court under section 721 for an order preventing the payment.

(2) Within the week immediately following the date of the resolution the company must also either—
- (a) cause a notice to the same effect as that required by subsection (1) to be published in an appropriate national newspaper, or
- (b) give notice in writing to that effect to each of its creditors.

(3) "An appropriate national newspaper" means a newspaper circulating throughout the part of the United Kingdom in which the company is registered.

(4) Not later than the day on which the company—
- (a) first publishes the notice required by subsection (1), or
- (b) if earlier, first publishes or gives the notice required by subsection (2),

the company must deliver to the registrar a copy of the directors' statement and auditor's report required by section 714.

720 DIRECTORS' STATEMENT AND AUDITOR'S REPORT TO BE AVAILABLE FOR INSPECTION

(1) The directors' statement and auditor's report must be kept available for inspection throughout the period—
- (a) beginning with the day on which the company—
  - (i) first publishes the notice required by section 719(1), or
  - (ii) if earlier, first publishes or gives the notice required by section 719(2), and
- (b) ending five weeks after the date of the resolution for payment out of capital.

(2) They must be kept available for inspection—
- (a) at the company's registered office, or
- (b) at a place specified in regulations under section 1136.

(3) The company must give notice to the registrar—
- (a) of the place at which the statement and report are kept available for inspection, and
- (b) of any change in that place,

unless they have at all times been kept at the company's registered office.

(4) They must be open to the inspection of any member or creditor of the company without charge.

(5) If default is made for 14 days in complying with subsection (3), or an inspection under subsection (4) is refused, an offence is committed by—
- (a) the company, and
- (b) every officer of the company who is in default.

(6) A person guilty of an offence under this section is liable on summary conviction to a fine not exceeding level 3 on the standard scale and, for continued contravention, a daily default fine not exceeding one-tenth of level 3 on the standard scale.

(7) In the case of a refusal of an inspection required by subsection (4), the court may by order compel an immediate inspection.

Objection to payment by members or creditors

721 APPLICATION TO COURT TO CANCEL RESOLUTION

(1) Where a private company passes a special resolution approving a payment out of capital for the redemption or purchase of any of its shares—
(a) any member of the company (other than one who consented to or voted in favour of the resolution), and
(b) any creditor of the company,
may apply to the court for the cancellation of the resolution.

(2) The application—
(a) must be made within five weeks after the passing of the resolution, and
(b) may be made on behalf of the persons entitled to make it by such one or more of their number as they may appoint in writing for the purpose.

(3) On an application under this section the court may if it thinks fit—
(a) adjourn the proceedings in order that an arrangement may be made to the satisfaction of the court—
(i) for the purchase of the interests of dissentient members, or
(ii) for the protection of dissentient creditors, and
(b) give such directions and make such orders as it thinks expedient for facilitating or carrying into effect any such arrangement.

(4) Subject to that, the court must make an order either cancelling or confirming the resolution, and may do so on such terms and conditions as it thinks fit.

(5) If the court confirms the resolution, it may by order alter or extend any date or period of time specified—
(a) in the resolution, or
(b) in any provision of this Chapter applying to the redemption or purchase to which the resolution relates.

(6) The court's order may, if the court thinks fit—
(a) provide for the purchase by the company of the shares of any of its members and for the reduction accordingly of the company's capital, and
(b) make any alteration in the company's articles that may be required in consequence of that provision.

(7) The court's order may, if the court thinks fit, require the company not to make any, or any specified, amendments of its articles without the leave of the court.

722 NOTICE TO REGISTRAR OF COURT APPLICATION OR ORDER

(1) On making an application under section 721 (application to court to cancel resolution) the applicants, or the person making the application on their behalf, must immediately give notice to the registrar.

This is without prejudice to any provision of rules of court as to service of notice of the application.

(2) On being served with notice of any such application, the company must immediately give notice to the registrar.

(3) Within 15 days of the making of the court's order on the application, or such longer period as the court may at any time direct, the company must deliver to the registrar a copy of the order.

(4) If a company fails to comply with subsection (2) or (3) an offence is committed by—
(a) the company, and
(b) every officer of the company who is in default.

(5) A person guilty of an offence under this section is liable on summary conviction to a fine not exceeding level 3 on the standard scale and, for continued contravention, a daily default fine not exceeding one-tenth of level 3 on the standard scale.

Supplementary provisions

723 WHEN PAYMENT OUT OF CAPITAL TO BE MADE

(1) The payment out of capital must be made—
(a) no earlier than five weeks after the date on which the resolution under section 716 is passed, and
(b) no more than seven weeks after that date.

(2) This is subject to any exercise of the court's powers under section 721(5) (power to alter or extend time where resolution confirmed after objection).

Chapter 6 TREASURY SHARES

724 TREASURY SHARES

(1) This section applies where—
(a) a limited company makes a purchase of its own shares in accordance with Chapter 4,
(b) the purchase is made out of distributable profits, and
(c) the shares are qualifying shares.

(2) For this purpose "qualifying shares" means shares that—
(a) are included in the official list in accordance with the provisions of Part 6 of the Financial Services and Markets Act 2000 (c. 8),
(b) are traded on the market known as the Alternative Investment Market established under the rules of London Stock Exchange plc,
(c) are officially listed in an EEA State, or
(d) are traded on a regulated market.
In paragraph (a) "the official list" has the meaning given in section 103(1) of the Financial Services and Markets Act 2000.

(3) Where this section applies the company may—
(a) hold the shares (or any of them), or
(b) deal with any of them, at any time, in accordance with section 727 or 729.

(4) Where shares are held by the company, the company must be entered in its register of members as the member holding the shares.

(5) In the Companies Acts references to a company holding shares as treasury shares are to the company holding shares that—
   (a) were (or are treated as having been) purchased by it in circumstances in which this section applies, and
   (b) have been held by the company continuously since they were so purchased (or treated as purchased).

726 TREASURY SHARES: EXERCISE OF RIGHTS

(1) This section applies where shares are held by a company as treasury shares.

(2) The company must not exercise any right in respect of the treasury shares, and any purported exercise of such a right is void.

This applies, in particular, to any right to attend or vote at meetings.

(3) No dividend may be paid, and no other distribution (whether in cash or otherwise) of the company's assets (including any distribution of assets to members on a winding up) may be made to the company, in respect of the treasury shares.

(4) Nothing in this section prevents—
   (a) an allotment of shares as fully paid bonus shares in respect of the treasury shares, or
   (b) the payment of any amount payable on the redemption of the treasury shares (if they are redeemable shares).

(5) Shares allotted as fully paid bonus shares in respect of the treasury shares are treated as if purchased by the company, at the time they were allotted, in circumstances in which section 724(1) (treasury shares) applied.

727 TREASURY SHARES: DISPOSAL

(1) Where shares are held as treasury shares, the company may at any time—
   (a) sell the shares (or any of them) for a cash consideration, or
   (b) transfer the shares (or any of them) for the purposes of or pursuant to an employees' share scheme.

728 TREASURY SHARES: NOTICE OF DISPOSAL

(1) Where shares held by a company as treasury shares—
   (a) are sold, or
   (b) are transferred for the purposes of an employees' share scheme,

the company must deliver a return to the registrar not later than 28 days after the shares are disposed of.

(2) The return must state with respect to shares of each class disposed of—
   (a) the number and nominal value of the shares, and
   (b) the date on which they were disposed of.

729 TREASURY SHARES: CANCELLATION

(1) Where shares are held as treasury shares, the company may at any time cancel the shares (or any of them).

(2) If shares held as treasury shares cease to be qualifying shares, the company must forthwith cancel the shares.

(3) For this purpose shares are not to be regarded as ceasing to be qualifying shares by virtue only of—
   (a) the suspension of their listing in accordance with the applicable rules in the EEA State in which the shares are officially listed, or
   (b) the suspension of their trading in accordance with—
      (i) in the case of shares traded on the market known as the Alternative Investment Market, the rules of London Stock Exchange plc, and
      (ii) in any other case, the rules of the regulated market on which they are traded.

(4) If company cancels shares held as treasury shares, the amount of the company's share capital is reduced accordingly by the nominal amount of the shares cancelled.

(5) The directors may take any steps required to enable the company to cancel its shares under this section without complying with the provisions of Chapter 10 of Part 17 (reduction of share capital).

730 TREASURY SHARES: NOTICE OF CANCELLATION

(1) Where shares held by a company as treasury shares are cancelled, the company must deliver a return to the registrar not later than 28 days after the shares are cancelled.

This does not apply to shares that are cancelled forthwith on their acquisition by the company (see section 708).

(2) The return must state with respect to shares of each class cancelled—
   (a) the number and nominal value of the shares, and
   (b) the date on which they were cancelled.

731 TREASURY SHARES: TREATMENT OF PROCEEDS OF SALE

(1) Where shares held as treasury shares are sold, the proceeds of sale must be dealt with in accordance with this section.

(2) If the proceeds of sale are equal to or less than the purchase price paid by the company for the shares, the proceeds are treated for the purposes of Part 23 (distributions) as a realised profit of the company.

(3) If the proceeds of sale exceed the purchase price paid by the company—
   (a) an amount equal to the purchase price paid is treated as a realised profit of the company for the purposes of that Part, and
   (b) the excess must be transferred to the company's share premium account.

(4) For the purposes of this section—
   (a) the purchase price paid by the company must be determined by the application of a weighted average price method, and
   (b) if the shares were allotted to the company as fully paid bonus shares, the purchase price paid for them is treated as nil.

732 TREASURY SHARES: OFFENCES

(1) If a company contravenes any of the provisions of this Chapter (except section 730 (notice of cancellation)), an offence is committed by—
   (a) the company, and
   (b) every officer of the company who is in default.

(2) A person guilty of an offence under this section is liable—
(a) on conviction on indictment, to a fine;
(b) on summary conviction to a fine not exceeding the statutory maximum.

Chapter 7 SUPPLEMENTARY PROVISIONS

733 THE CAPITAL REDEMPTION RESERVE

(1) In the following circumstances a company must transfer amounts to a reserve, called the "capital redemption reserve".

(2) Where under this Part shares of a limited company are redeemed or purchased wholly out of the company's profits, the amount by which the company's issued share capital is diminished in accordance with—
(a) section 688(b) (on the cancellation of shares redeemed), or
(b) section 706(b)(ii) (on the cancellation of shares purchased), must be transferred to the capital redemption reserve.

(3) If—
(a) the shares are redeemed or purchased wholly or partly out of the proceeds of a fresh issue, and
(b) the aggregate amount of the proceeds is less than the aggregate nominal value of the shares redeemed or purchased,
the amount of the difference must be transferred to the capital redemption reserve.

This does not apply in the case of a private company if, in addition to the proceeds of the fresh issue, the company applies a payment out of capital under Chapter 5 in making the redemption or purchase.

(4) The amount by which a company's share capital is diminished in accordance with section 729(4) (on the cancellation of shares held as treasury shares) must be transferred to the capital redemption reserve.

(5) The company may use the capital redemption reserve to pay up new shares to be allotted to members as fully paid bonus shares.

(6) Subject to that, the provisions of the Companies Acts relating to the reduction of a company's share capital apply as if the capital redemption reserve were part of its paid up share capital.

734 ACCOUNTING CONSEQUENCES OF PAYMENT OUT OF CAPITAL

(1) This section applies where a payment out of capital is made in accordance with Chapter 5 (redemption or purchase of own shares by private company out of capital).

(2) If the permissible capital payment is less than the nominal amount of the shares redeemed or purchased, the amount of the difference must be transferred to the company's capital redemption reserve.

(3) If the permissible capital payment is greater than the nominal amount of the shares redeemed or purchased—
(a) the amount of any capital redemption reserve, share premium account or fully paid share capital of the company, and
(b) any amount representing unrealised profits of the company for the time being standing to the credit of any revaluation reserve maintained by the company,

may be reduced by a sum not exceeding (or by sums not in total exceeding) the amount by which the permissible capital payment exceeds the nominal amount of the shares.

(4) Where the proceeds of a fresh issue are applied by the company in making a redemption or purchase of its own shares in addition to a payment out of capital under this Chapter, the references in subsections (2) and (3) to the permissible capital payment are to be read as referring to the aggregate of that payment and those proceeds.

735 EFFECT OF COMPANY'S FAILURE TO REDEEM OR PURCHASE

(1) This section applies where a company—
- (a) issues shares on terms that they are or are liable to be redeemed, or
- (b) agrees to purchase any of its shares.

(2) The company is not liable in damages in respect of any failure on its part to redeem or purchase any of the shares.

This is without prejudice to any right of the holder of the shares other than his right to sue the company for damages in respect of its failure.

(3) The court shall not grant an order for specific performance of the terms of redemption or purchase if the company shows that it is unable to meet the costs of redeeming or purchasing the shares in question out of distributable profits.

(4) If the company is wound up and at the commencement of the winding up any of the shares have not been redeemed or purchased, the terms of redemption or purchase may be enforced against the company.

When shares are redeemed or purchased under this subsection, they are treated as cancelled.

(5) Subsection (4) does not apply if—
- (a) the terms provided for the redemption or purchase to take place at a date later than that of the commencement of the winding up, or
- (b) during the period—
  - (i) beginning with the date on which the redemption or purchase was to have taken place, and
  - (ii) ending with the commencement of the winding up,

the company could not at any time have lawfully made a distribution equal in value to the price at which the shares were to have been redeemed or purchased.

(6) There shall be paid in priority to any amount that the company is liable under subsection (4) to pay in respect of any shares—
- (a) all other debts and liabilities of the company (other than any due to members in their character as such), and
- (b) if other shares carry rights (whether as to capital or as to income) that are preferred to the rights as to capital attaching to the first-mentioned shares, any amount due in satisfaction of those preferred rights.

Subject to that, any such amount shall be paid in priority to any amounts due to members in satisfaction of their rights (whether as to capital or income) as members.

736 MEANING OF "DISTRIBUTABLE PROFITS"

In this Part (except in Chapter 2 (financial assistance): see section 683) "distributable profits", in relation to the making of any payment by a company, means profits out of which the company could lawfully make a distribution (within the meaning given by section 830) equal in value to the payment.

Part 19 DEBENTURES

General provisions

738 MEANING OF "DEBENTURE"

In the Companies Acts "debenture" includes debenture stock, bonds and any other securities of a company, whether or not constituting a charge on the assets of the company.

Part 20 PRIVATE AND PUBLIC COMPANIES

Chapter 1 PROHIBITION OF PUBLIC OFFERS BY PRIVATE COMPANIES

755 PROHIBITION OF PUBLIC OFFERS BY PRIVATE COMPANY

(1) A private company limited by shares or limited by guarantee and having a share capital must not—
 (a) offer to the public any securities of the company, or
 (b) allot or agree to allot any securities of the company with a view to their being offered to the public.

(2) Unless the contrary is proved, an allotment or agreement to allot securities is presumed to be made with a view to their being offered to the public if an offer of the securities (or any of them) to the public is made—
 (a) within six months after the allotment or agreement to allot, or
 (b) before the receipt by the company of the whole of the consideration to be received by it in respect of the securities.

(3) A company does not contravene this section if—
 (a) it acts in good faith in pursuance of arrangements under which it is to re-register as a public company before the securities are allotted, or
 (b) as part of the terms of the offer it undertakes to re-register as a public company within a specified period, and that undertaking is complied with.

(4) The specified period for the purposes of subsection (3)(b) must be a period ending not later than six months after the day on which the offer is made (or, in the case of an offer made on different days, first made).

(5) In this Chapter "securities" means shares or debentures.

756 MEANING OF "OFFER TO THE PUBLIC"

(1) This section explains what is meant in this Chapter by an offer of securities to the public.

(2) An offer to the public includes an offer to any section of the public, however selected.

(3) An offer is not regarded as an offer to the public if it can properly be regarded, in all the circumstances, as—
 (a) not being calculated to result, directly or indirectly, in securities of the company becoming available to persons other than those receiving the offer, or
 (b) otherwise being a private concern of the person receiving it and the person making it.

(4) An offer is to be regarded (unless the contrary is proved) as being a private concern of the person receiving it and the person making it if—
(a) it is made to a person already connected with the company and, where it is made on terms allowing that person to renounce his rights, the rights may only be renounced in favour of another person already connected with the company; or
(b) it is an offer to subscribe for securities to be held under an employees' share scheme and, where it is made on terms allowing that person to renounce his rights, the rights may only be renounced in favour of—
(i) another person entitled to hold securities under the scheme, or
(ii) a person already connected with the company.

(5) For the purposes of this section "person already connected with the company" means—
(a) an existing member or employee of the company,
(b) a member of the family of a person who is or was a member or employee of the company,
(c) the widow or widower, or surviving civil partner, of a person who was a member or employee of the company,
(d) an existing debenture holder of the company, or
(e) a trustee (acting in his capacity as such) of a trust of which the principal beneficiary is a person within any of paragraphs (a) to (d).

(6) For the purposes of subsection (5)(b) the members of a person's family are the person's spouse or civil partner and children (including step-children) and their descendants.

757 ENFORCEMENT OF PROHIBITION: ORDER RESTRAINING PROPOSED CONTRAVENTION

(1) If it appears to the court—
(a) on an application under this section, or
(b) in proceedings under Part 30 (protection of members against unfair prejudice),
that a company is proposing to act in contravention of section 755 (prohibition of public offers by private companies), the court shall make an order under this section.

(2) An order under this section is an order restraining the company from contravening that section.

(3) An application for an order under this section may be made by—
(a) a member or creditor of the company, or
(b) the Secretary of State.

758 ENFORCEMENT OF PROHIBITION: ORDERS AVAILABLE TO THE COURT AFTER CONTRAVENTION

(1) This section applies if it appears to the court—
(a) on an application under this section, or
(b) in proceedings under Part 30 (protection of members against unfair prejudice),
that a company has acted in contravention of section 755 (prohibition of public offers by private companies).

(2) The court must make an order requiring the company to re-register as a public company unless it appears to the court—
(a) that the company does not meet the requirements for re-registration as a public company, and
(b) that it is impractical or undesirable to require it to take steps to do so.

(3) If it does not make an order for re-registration, the court may make either or both of the following—

(a) a remedial order (see section 759), or
(b) an order for the compulsory winding up of the company.

(4) An application under this section may be made by—
(a) a member of the company who—
(i) was a member at the time the offer was made (or, if the offer was made over a period, at any time during that period), or
(ii) became a member as a result of the offer,
(b) a creditor of the company who was a creditor at the time the offer was made (or, if the offer was made over a period, at any time during that period), or
(c) the Secretary of State.

759 ENFORCEMENT OF PROHIBITION: REMEDIAL ORDER

(1) A "remedial order" is an order for the purpose of putting a person affected by anything done in contravention of section 755 (prohibition of public offers by private company) in the position he would have been in if it had not been done.

(2) The following provisions are without prejudice to the generality of the power to make such an order.

(3) Where a private company has—
(a) allotted securities pursuant to an offer to the public, or
(b) allotted or agreed to allot securities with a view to their being offered to the public,
a remedial order may require any person knowingly concerned in the contravention of section 755 to offer to purchase any of those securities at such price and on such other terms as the court thinks fit.

(4) A remedial order may be made—
(a) against any person knowingly concerned in the contravention, whether or not an officer of the company;
(b) notwithstanding anything in the company's constitution (which includes, for this purpose, the terms on which any securities of the company are allotted or held);
(c) whether or not the holder of the securities subject to the order is the person to whom the company allotted or agreed to allot them.

(5) Where a remedial order is made against the company itself, the court may provide for the reduction of the company's capital accordingly.

760 VALIDITY OF ALLOTMENT ETC. NOT AFFECTED

Nothing in this Chapter affects the validity of any allotment or sale of securities or of any agreement to allot or sell securities.

Chapter 2 MINIMUM SHARE CAPITAL REQUIREMENTS FOR PUBLIC COMPANIES

761 PUBLIC COMPANY: REQUIREMENT AS TO MINIMUM SHARE CAPITAL

(1) A company that is a public company (otherwise than by virtue of re-registration as a public company) must not do business or exercise any borrowing powers unless the registrar has issued it with a certificate under this section (a "trading certificate").

(2) The registrar shall issue a trading certificate if, on an application made in accordance with section 762, he is satisfied that the nominal value of the company's allotted share capital is not less than the authorised minimum.

(3) For this purpose a share allotted in pursuance of an employees' share scheme shall not be taken into account unless paid up as to—
(a) at least one-quarter of the nominal value of the share, and
(b) the whole of any premium on the share.

(4) A trading certificate has effect from the date on which it is issued and is conclusive evidence that the company is entitled to do business and exercise any borrowing powers.

763 THE AUTHORISED MINIMUM

(1) "The authorised minimum", in relation to the nominal value of a public company's allotted share capital is—
(a) £50,000, or
(b) the prescribed euro equivalent.

(2) The Secretary of State may by order prescribe the amount in euros that is for the time being to be treated as equivalent to the sterling amount of the authorised minimum.

767 CONSEQUENCES OF DOING BUSINESS ETC WITHOUT A TRADING CERTIFICATE

(1) If a company does business or exercises any borrowing powers in contravention of section 761, an offence is committed by—
(a) the company, and
(b) every officer of the company who is in default.

(2) A person guilty of an offence under subsection (1) is liable—
(a) on conviction on indictment, to a fine;
(b) on summary conviction, to a fine not exceeding the statutory maximum.

(3) A contravention of section 761 does not affect the validity of a transaction entered into by the company, but if a company—
(a) enters into a transaction in contravention of that section, and
(b) fails to comply with its obligations in connection with the transaction within 21 days from being called on to do so,
the directors of the company are jointly and severally liable to indemnify any other party to the transaction in respect of any loss or damage suffered by him by reason of the company's failure to comply with its obligations.

(4) The directors who are so liable are those who were directors at the time the company entered into the transaction.

Part 21 CERTIFICATION AND TRANSFER OF SECURITIES

Chapter 1 CERTIFICATION AND TRANSFER OF SECURITIES: GENERAL

Share certificates

768 SHARE CERTIFICATE TO BE EVIDENCE OF TITLE

(1) In the case of a company registered in England and Wales or Northern Ireland, a certificate under the common seal of the company specifying any shares held by a member is prima facie evidence of his title to the shares.

(2) In the case of a company registered in Scotland—
(a) a certificate under the common seal of the company specifying any shares held by a member, or
(b) a certificate specifying any shares held by a member and subscribed by the company in accordance with the Requirements of Writing (Scotland) Act 1995 (c. 7),
is sufficient evidence, unless the contrary is shown, of his title to the shares.

Issue of certificates etc. on allotment

769 DUTY OF COMPANY AS TO ISSUE OF CERTIFICATES ETC ON ALLOTMENT

(1) A company must, within two months after the allotment of any of its shares, debentures or debenture stock, complete and have ready for delivery—
(a) the certificates of the shares allotted,
(b) the debentures allotted, or
(c) the certificates of the debenture stock allotted.

(2) Subsection (1) does not apply—
(a) if the conditions of issue of the shares, debentures or debenture stock provide otherwise,
(b) in the case of allotment to a financial institution (see section 778), or
(c) in the case of an allotment of shares if, following the allotment, the company has issued a share warrant in respect of the shares (see section 779).

(3) If default is made in complying with subsection (1) an offence is committed by every officer of the company who is in default.

(4) A person guilty of an offence under subsection (3) is liable on summary conviction to a fine not exceeding level 3 on the standard scale and, for continued contravention, a daily default fine not exceeding one-tenth of level 3 on the standard scale.

Transfer of securities

770 REGISTRATION OF TRANSFER

(1) A company may not register a transfer of shares in or debentures of the company unless—
(a) a proper instrument of transfer has been delivered to it, or
(b) the transfer—
(i) is an exempt transfer within the Stock Transfer Act 1982 (c. 41), or
(ii) is in accordance with regulations under Chapter 2 of this Part.

(2) Subsection (1) does not affect any power of the company to register as shareholder or debenture holder a person to whom the right to any shares in or debentures of the company has been transmitted by operation of law.

771 PROCEDURE ON TRANSFER BEING LODGED

(1) When a transfer of shares in or debentures of a company has been lodged with the company, the company must either—
(a) register the transfer, or
(b) give the transferee notice of refusal to register the transfer, together with its reasons for the refusal,

as soon as practicable and in any event within two months after the date on which the transfer is lodged with it.

(2) If the company refuses to register the transfer, it must provide the transferee with such further information about the reasons for the refusal as the transferee may reasonably request.

This does not include copies of minutes of meetings of directors.

(3) If a company fails to comply with this section, an offence is committed by—
(a) the company, and
(b) every officer of the company who is in default.

(4) A person guilty of an offence under this section is liable on summary conviction to a fine not exceeding level 3 on the standard scale and, for continued contravention, a daily default fine not exceeding one-tenth of level 3 on the standard scale.

(5) This section does not apply—
(a) in relation to a transfer of shares if the company has issued a share warrant in respect of the shares (see section 779);
(b) in relation to the transmission of shares or debentures by operation of law.

772 TRANSFER OF SHARES ON APPLICATION OF TRANSFEROR

On the application of the transferor of any share or interest in a company, the company shall enter in its register of members the name of the transferee in the same manner and subject to the same conditions as if the application for the entry were made by the transferee.

773 EXECUTION OF SHARE TRANSFER BY PERSONAL REPRESENTATIVE

An instrument of transfer of the share or other interest of a deceased member of a company—

(a) may be made by his personal representative although the personal representative is not himself a member of the company, and

(b) is as effective as if the personal representative had been such a member at the time of the execution of the instrument.

774 EVIDENCE OF GRANT OF PROBATE ETC.

The production to a company of any document that is by law sufficient evidence of the grant of—

(a) probate of the will of a deceased person,

(b) letters of administration of the estate of a deceased person, or

(c) confirmation as executor of a deceased person,

shall be accepted by the company as sufficient evidence of the grant.

775 CERTIFICATION OF INSTRUMENT OF TRANSFER

(1) The certification by a company of an instrument of transfer of any shares in, or debentures of, the company is to be taken as a representation by the company to any person acting on the faith of the certification that there have been produced to the

company such documents as on their face show a prima facie title to the shares or debentures in the transferor named in the instrument.

(2) The certification is not to be taken as a representation that the transferor has any title to the shares or debentures.

(3) Where a person acts on the faith of a false certification by a company made negligently, the company is under the same liability to him as if the certification had been made fraudulently.

(4) For the purposes of this section—
(a) an instrument of transfer is certificated if it bears the words "certificate lodged" (or words to the like effect);
(b) the certification of an instrument of transfer is made by a company if—
(i) the person issuing the instrument is a person authorised to issue certificated instruments of transfer on the company's behalf, and
(ii) the certification is signed by a person authorised to certificate transfers on the company's behalf or by an officer or employee either of the company or of a body corporate so authorised;
(c) a certification is treated as signed by a person if—
(i) it purports to be authenticated by his signature or initials (whether handwritten or not), and
(ii) it is not shown that the signature or initials was or were placed there neither by himself nor by a person authorised to use the signature or initials for the purpose of certificating transfers on the company's behalf.

Issue of certificates etc. on transfer

776 DUTY OF COMPANY AS TO ISSUE OF CERTIFICATES ETC. ON TRANSFER

(1) A company must, within two months after the date on which a transfer of any of its shares, debentures or debenture stock is lodged with the company, complete and have ready for delivery—
(a) the certificates of the shares transferred,
(b) the debentures transferred, or
(c) the certificates of the debenture stock transferred.

(2) For this purpose a "transfer" means—
(a) a transfer duly stamped and otherwise valid, or
(b) an exempt transfer within the Stock Transfer Act 1982 (c. 41),
but does not include a transfer that the company is for any reason entitled to refuse to register and does not register.

(3) Subsection (1) does not apply—
(a) if the conditions of issue of the shares, debentures or debenture stock provide otherwise,
(b) in the case of a transfer to a financial institution (see section 778), or
(c) in the case of a transfer of shares if, following the transfer, the company has issued a share warrant in respect of the shares (see section 779).

(4) Subsection (1) has effect subject to section 777 (cases where the Stock Transfer Act 1982 applies).

(5) If default is made in complying with subsection (1) an offence is committed by every officer of the company who is in default.

(6) A person guilty of an offence under this section is liable on summary conviction to a fine not exceeding level 3 on the standard scale and, for continued contravention, a daily default fine not exceeding one-tenth of level 3 on the standard scale.

Part 23 DISTRIBUTIONS

Chapter 1 RESTRICTIONS ON WHEN DISTRIBUTIONS MAY BE MADE

Introductory

829 MEANING OF "DISTRIBUTION"

(1) In this Part "distribution" means every description of distribution of a company's assets to its members, whether in cash or otherwise, subject to the following exceptions.

(2) The following are not distributions for the purposes of this Part—
- (a) an issue of shares as fully or partly paid bonus shares;
- (b) the reduction of share capital—
  - (i) by extinguishing or reducing the liability of any of the members on any of the company's shares in respect of share capital not paid up, or
  - (ii) by repaying paid-up share capital;
- (c) the redemption or purchase of any of the company's own shares out of capital (including the proceeds of any fresh issue of shares) or out of unrealised profits in accordance with Chapter 3, 4 or 5 of Part 18;
- (d) a distribution of assets to members of the company on its winding up.

General rules

830 DISTRIBUTIONS TO BE MADE ONLY OUT OF PROFITS AVAILABLE FOR THE PURPOSE

(1) A company may only make a distribution out of profits available for the purpose.

(2) A company's profits available for distribution are its accumulated, realised profits, so far as not previously utilised by distribution or capitalisation, less its accumulated, realised losses, so far as not previously written off in a reduction or reorganisation of capital duly made.

831 NET ASSET RESTRICTION ON DISTRIBUTIONS BY PUBLIC COMPANIES

(1) A public company may only make a distribution—
- (a) if the amount of its net assets is not less than the aggregate of its called-up share capital and undistributable reserves, and
- (b) if, and to the extent that, the distribution does not reduce the amount of those assets to less than that aggregate.

(2) For this purpose a company's "net assets" means the aggregate of the company's assets less the aggregate of its liabilities.

(3) "Liabilities" here includes—
- (a) where the relevant accounts are Companies Act accounts, provisions of a kind specified for the purposes of this subsection by regulations under section 396;
- (b) where the relevant accounts are IAS accounts, provisions of any kind.

(4) A company's undistributable reserves are—
(a) its share premium account;
(b) its capital redemption reserve;
(c) the amount by which its accumulated, unrealised profits (so far as not previously utilised by capitalisation) exceed its accumulated, unrealised losses (so far as not previously written off in a reduction or reorganisation of capital duly made);
(d) any other reserve that the company is prohibited from distributing—
(i) by any enactment (other than one contained in this Part), or
(ii) by its articles.

The reference in paragraph (c) to capitalisation does not include a transfer of profits of the company to its capital redemption reserve.

(5) A public company must not include any uncalled share capital as an asset in any accounts relevant for purposes of this section.

Chapter 3 SUPPLEMENTARY PROVISIONS

Consequences of unlawful distribution

847 CONSEQUENCES OF UNLAWFUL DISTRIBUTION

(1) This section applies where a distribution, or part of one, made by a company to one of its members is made in contravention of this Part.

(2) If at the time of the distribution the member knows or has reasonable grounds for believing that it is so made, he is liable—
(a) to repay it (or that part of it, as the case may be) to the company, or
(b) in the case of a distribution made otherwise than in cash, to pay the company a sum equal to the value of the distribution (or part) at that time.

(3) This is without prejudice to any obligation imposed apart from this section on a member of a company to repay a distribution unlawfully made to him.

(4) This section does not apply in relation to—
(a) financial assistance given by a company in contravention of section 678 or 679, or
(b) any payment made by a company in respect of the redemption or purchase by the company of shares in itself.

849 RESTRICTION ON APPLICATION OF UNREALISED PROFITS

A company must not apply an unrealised profit in paying up debentures or any amounts unpaid on its issued shares.

852 SAVING FOR OTHER RESTRICTIONS ON DISTRIBUTIONS

The provisions of this Part are without prejudice to any enactment, or any provision of a company's articles, restricting the sums out of which, or the cases in which, a distribution may be made.

853 MINOR DEFINITIONS

(1) The following provisions apply for the purposes of this Part.

(2) References to profit or losses of any description—

(a) are to profits or losses of that description made at any time, and
(b) except where the context otherwise requires, are to profits or losses of a revenue or capital character.

(3) "Capitalisation", in relation to a company's profits, means any of the following operations (whenever carried out)—
(a) applying the profits in wholly or partly paying up unissued shares in the company to be allotted to members of the company as fully or partly paid bonus shares, or
(b) transferring the profits to capital redemption reserve.

(4) References to "realised profits" and "realised losses", in relation to a company's accounts, are to such profits or losses of the company as fall to be treated as realised in accordance with principles generally accepted at the time when the accounts are prepared, with respect to the determination for accounting purposes of realised profits or losses.

(5) Subsection (4) is without prejudice to—
(a) the construction of any other expression (where appropriate) by reference to accepted accounting principles or practice, or
(b) any specific provision for the treatment of profits or losses of any description as realised.

(6) "Fixed assets" means assets of a company which are intended for use on a continuing basis in the company's activities.

Part 26 ARRANGEMENTS AND RECONSTRUCTIONS

Application of this Part

895 APPLICATION OF THIS PART

(1) The provisions of this Part apply where a compromise or arrangement is proposed between a company and—
(a) its creditors, or any class of them, or
(b) its members, or any class of them.

(2) In this Part—

"arrangement" includes a reorganisation of the company's share capital by the consolidation of shares of different classes or by the division of shares into shares of different classes, or by both of those methods; and

"company"—
(a) in section 900 (powers of court to facilitate reconstruction or amalgamation) means a company within the meaning of this Act, and
(b) elsewhere in this Part means any company liable to be wound up under the Insolvency Act 1986 (c. 45) or the Insolvency (Northern Ireland) Order 1989 (S.I. 1989/2405 (N.I. 19)).

Meeting of creditors or members

896 COURT ORDER FOR HOLDING OF MEETING

(1) The court may, on an application under this section, order a meeting of the creditors or class of creditors, or of the members of the company or class of members (as the case may be), to be summoned in such manner as the court directs.

(2) An application under this section may be made by—
(a) the company,
(b) any creditor or member of the company,
(c) if the company is being wound up, the liquidator, or
(d) if the company is in administration, the administrator.

(3) Section 323 (representation of corporations at meetings) applies to a meeting of creditors under this section as to a meeting of the company (references to a member of the company being read as references to a creditor).

897 STATEMENT TO BE CIRCULATED OR MADE AVAILABLE

(1) Where a meeting is summoned under section 896—
(a) every notice summoning the meeting that is sent to a creditor or member must be accompanied by a statement complying with this section, and
(b) every notice summoning the meeting that is given by advertisement must either—
(i) include such a statement, or
(ii) state where and how creditors or members entitled to attend the meeting may obtain copies of such a statement.

(2) The statement must—
(a) explain the effect of the compromise or arrangement, and
(b) in particular, state—
(i) any material interests of the directors of the company (whether as directors or as members or as creditors of the company or otherwise), and
(ii) the effect on those interests of the compromise or arrangement, in so far as it is different from the effect on the like interests of other persons.

(3) Where the compromise or arrangement affects the rights of debenture holders of the company, the statement must give the like explanation as respects the trustees of any deed for securing the issue of the debentures as it is required to give as respects the company's directors.

(4) Where a notice given by advertisement states that copies of an explanatory statement can be obtained by creditors or members entitled to attend the meeting, every such creditor or member is entitled, on making application in the manner indicated by the notice, to be provided by the company with a copy of the statement free of charge.

(5) If a company makes default in complying with any requirement of this section, an offence is committed by—
(a) the company, and
(b) every officer of the company who is in default.
This is subject to subsection (7) below.

(6) For this purpose the following are treated as officers of the company—
(a) a liquidator or administrator of the company, and
(b) a trustee of a deed for securing the issue of debentures of the company.

(7) A person is not guilty of an offence under this section if he shows that the default was due to the refusal of a director or trustee for debenture holders to supply the necessary particulars of his interests.

(8) A person guilty of an offence under this section is liable—
(a) on conviction on indictment, to a fine;
(b) on summary conviction, to a fine not exceeding the statutory maximum.

898 DUTY OF DIRECTORS AND TRUSTEES TO PROVIDE INFORMATION

(1) It is the duty of—
(a) any director of the company, and
(b) any trustee for its debenture holders,
to give notice to the company of such matters relating to himself as may be necessary for the purposes of section 897 (explanatory statement to be circulated or made available).

Court sanction for compromise or arrangement

899 COURT SANCTION FOR COMPROMISE OR ARRANGEMENT

(1) If a majority in number representing 75% in value of the creditors or class of creditors or members or class of members (as the case may be), present and voting either in person or by proxy at the meeting summoned under section 896, agree a compromise or arrangement, the court may, on an application under this section, sanction the compromise or arrangement.

(2) An application under this section may be made by—
(a) the company,
(b) any creditor or member of the company,
(c) if the company is being wound up, the liquidator, or
(d) if the company is in administration, the administrator.

(3) A compromise or agreement sanctioned by the court is binding on—
(a) all creditors or the class of creditors or on the members or class of members (as the case may be), and
(b) the company or, in the case of a company in the course of being wound up, the liquidator and contributories of the company.

(4) The court's order has no effect until a copy of it has been delivered to the registrar.

(5) Section 323 (representation of corporations at meetings) applies to a meeting of creditors under this section as to a meeting of the company (references to a member of the company being read as references to a creditor).

Reconstructions and amalgamations

900 POWERS OF COURT TO FACILITATE RECONSTRUCTION OR AMALGAMATION

(1) This section applies where application is made to the court under section 899 to sanction a compromise or arrangement and it is shown that—
(a) the compromise or arrangement is proposed for the purposes of, or in connection with, a scheme for the reconstruction of any company or companies, or the amalgamation of any two or more companies, and
(b) under the scheme the whole or any part of the undertaking or the property of any company concerned in the scheme ("a transferor company") is to be transferred to another company ("the transferee company").

(2) The court may, either by the order sanctioning the compromise or arrangement or by a subsequent order, make provision for all or any of the following matters—
(a) the transfer to the transferee company of the whole or any part of the undertaking and of the property or liabilities of any transferor company;

(b) the allotting or appropriation by the transferee company of any shares, debentures, policies or other like interests in that company which under the compromise or arrangement are to be allotted or appropriated by that company to or for any person;
(c) the continuation by or against the transferee company of any legal proceedings pending by or against any transferor company;
(d) the dissolution, without winding up, of any transferor company;
(e) the provision to be made for any persons who, within such time and in such manner as the court directs, dissent from the compromise or arrangement;
(f) such incidental, consequential and supplemental matters as are necessary to secure that the reconstruction or amalgamation is fully and effectively carried out.

(3) If an order under this section provides for the transfer of property or liabilities—
(a) the property is by virtue of the order transferred to, and vests in, the transferee company, and
(b) the liabilities are, by virtue of the order, transferred to and become liabilities of that company.

(4) The property (if the order so directs) vests freed from any charge that is by virtue of the compromise or arrangement to cease to have effect.

(5) In this section—

"property" includes property, rights and powers of every description; and

"liabilities" includes duties.

(6) Every company in relation to which an order is made under this section must cause a copy of the order to be delivered to the registrar within seven days after its making.

Obligations of company with respect to articles etc.

901 OBLIGATIONS OF COMPANY WITH RESPECT TO ARTICLES ETC.

(1) This section applies—
(a) to any order under section 899 (order sanctioning compromise or arrangement), and
(b) to any order under section 900 (order facilitating reconstruction or amalgamation) that alters the company's constitution.

(2) If the order amends—
(a) the company's articles, or
(b) any resolution or agreement to which Chapter 3 of Part 3 applies (resolution or agreement affecting a company's constitution),
the copy of the order delivered to the registrar by the company under section 899(4) or section 900(6) must be accompanied by a copy of the company's articles, or the resolution or agreement in question, as amended.

(3) Every copy of the company's articles issued by the company after the order is made must be accompanied by a copy of the order, unless the effect of the order has been incorporated into the articles by amendment.

Part 28 TAKEOVERS ETC.

Chapter 1 THE TAKEOVER PANEL

The Panel and its rules

942 THE PANEL

(1) The body known as the Panel on Takeovers and Mergers ("the Panel") is to have the functions conferred on it by or under this Chapter.

(2) The Panel may do anything that it considers necessary or expedient for the purposes of, or in connection with, its functions.

(3) The Panel may make arrangements for any of its functions to be discharged by—
(a) a committee or sub-committee of the Panel, or
(b) an officer or member of staff of the Panel, or a person acting as such.
This is subject to section 943(4) and (5).

943 RULES

(1) The Panel must make rules giving effect to Articles 3.1, 4.2, 5, 6.1 to 6.3, 7 to 9 and 13 of the Takeovers Directive.

(2) Rules made by the Panel may also make other provision—
(a) for or in connection with the regulation of—
(i) takeover bids,
(ii) merger transactions, and
(iii) transactions (not falling within sub-paragraph (i) or (ii)) that have or may have, directly or indirectly, an effect on the ownership or control of companies;
(b) for or in connection with the regulation of things done in consequence of, or otherwise in relation to, any such bid or transaction;
(c) about cases where—
(i) any such bid or transaction is, or has been, contemplated or apprehended, or
(ii) an announcement is made denying that any such bid or transaction is intended.

(3) The provision that may be made under subsection (2) includes, in particular, provision for a matter that is, or is similar to, a matter provided for by the Panel in the City Code on Takeovers and Mergers as it had effect immediately before the passing of this Act.

(4) In relation to rules made by virtue of section 957 (fees and charges), functions under this section may be discharged either by the Panel itself or by a committee of the Panel (but not otherwise).

(5) In relation to rules of any other description, the Panel must discharge its functions under this section by a committee of the Panel.

(6) Section 1 (meaning of "company") does not apply for the purposes of this section.

(7) In this section "takeover bid" includes a takeover bid within the meaning of the Takeovers Directive.

(8) In this Chapter "the Takeovers Directive" means Directive 2004/25/EC of the European Parliament and of the Council.

(9) A reference to rules in the following provisions of this Chapter is to rules under this section.

944 FURTHER PROVISIONS ABOUT RULES

(1) Rules may—
(a) make different provision for different purposes;
(b) make provision subject to exceptions or exemptions;
(c) contain incidental, supplemental, consequential or transitional provision;
(d) authorise the Panel to dispense with or modify the application of rules in particular cases and by reference to any circumstances.
Rules made by virtue of paragraph (d) must require the Panel to give reasons for acting as mentioned in that paragraph.

(2) Rules must be made by an instrument in writing.

(3) Immediately after an instrument containing rules is made, the text must be made available to the public, with or without payment, in whatever way the Panel thinks appropriate.

(4) A person is not to be taken to have contravened a rule if he shows that at the time of the alleged contravention the text of the rule had not been made available as required by subsection (3).

(5) The production of a printed copy of an instrument purporting to be made by the Panel on which is endorsed a certificate signed by an officer of the Panel authorised by it for that purpose and stating—
(a) that the instrument was made by the Panel,
(b) that the copy is a true copy of the instrument, and
(c) that on a specified date the text of the instrument was made available to the public as required by subsection (3),
is evidence (or in Scotland sufficient evidence) of the facts stated in the certificate.

(6) A certificate purporting to be signed as mentioned in subsection (5) is to be treated as having been properly signed unless the contrary is shown.

(7) A person who wishes in any legal proceedings to rely on an instrument by which rules are made may require the Panel to endorse a copy of the instrument with a certificate of the kind mentioned in subsection (5).

945 RULINGS

(1) The Panel may give rulings on the interpretation, application or effect of rules.

(2) To the extent and in the circumstances specified in rules, and subject to any review or appeal, a ruling has binding effect.

946 DIRECTIONS

Rules may contain provision conferring power on the Panel to give any direction that appears to the Panel to be necessary in order—

(a) to restrain a person from acting (or continuing to act) in breach of rules;

(b) to restrain a person from doing (or continuing to do) a particular thing, pending determination of whether that or any other conduct of his is or would be a breach of rules;

(c) otherwise to secure compliance with rules.

Information

947 POWER TO REQUIRE DOCUMENTS AND INFORMATION

(1) The Panel may by notice in writing require a person—
(a) to produce any documents that are specified or described in the notice;
(b) to provide, in the form and manner specified in the notice, such information as may be specified or described in the notice.

(2) A requirement under subsection (1) must be complied with—
(a) at a place specified in the notice, and
(b) before the end of such reasonable period as may be so specified.

(3) This section applies only to documents and information reasonably required in connection with the exercise by the Panel of its functions.

(4) The Panel may require—
(a) any document produced to be authenticated, or
(b) any information provided (whether in a document or otherwise) to be verified,
in such manner as it may reasonably require.

(5) The Panel may authorise a person to exercise any of its powers under this section.

(6) A person exercising a power by virtue of subsection (5) must, if required to do so, produce evidence of his authority to exercise the power.

(7) The production of a document in pursuance of this section does not affect any lien that a person has on the document.

(8) The Panel may take copies of or extracts from a document produced in pursuance of this section.

(9) A reference in this section to the production of a document includes a reference to the production of—
(a) a hard copy of information recorded otherwise than in hard copy form, or
(b) information in a form from which a hard copy can be readily obtained.

(10) A person is not required by this section to disclose documents or information in respect of which a claim to legal professional privilege (in Scotland, to confidentiality of communications) could be maintained in legal proceedings.

948 RESTRICTIONS ON DISCLOSURE

(1) This section applies to information (in whatever form)—
(a) relating to the private affairs of an individual, or
(b) relating to any particular business,
that is provided to the Panel in connection with the exercise of its functions.

(2) No such information may, during the lifetime of the individual or so long as the business continues to be carried on, be disclosed without the consent of that individual or (as the case may be) the person for the time being carrying on that business.

(3) Subsection (2) does not apply to any disclosure of information that—
(a) is made for the purpose of facilitating the carrying out by the Panel of any of its functions, [or]
(b) is made to a person specified in Part 1 of Schedule 2...
...

(6) Subsection (2) does not apply to—
(a) the disclosure by an authority within subsection (7) of information disclosed to it by the Panel in reliance on subsection (3);
(b) the disclosure of such information by anyone who has obtained it directly or indirectly from an authority within subsection (7).

(7) The authorities within this subsection are—
(a) the Financial Services Authority;
(b) an authority designated as a supervisory authority for the purposes of Article 4.1 of the Takeovers Directive;
(c) any other person or body that exercises functions of a public nature, under legislation in an EEA State other than the United Kingdom, that are similar to the Panel's functions or those of the Financial Services Authority.

(8) This section does not prohibit the disclosure of information if the information is or has been available to the public from any other source.

(9) Nothing in this section authorises the making of a disclosure in contravention of the Data Protection Act 1998 (c. 29).

949 OFFENCE OF DISCLOSURE IN CONTRAVENTION OF SECTION 948

(1) A person who discloses information in contravention of section 948 is guilty of an offence, unless—
(a) he did not know, and had no reason to suspect, that the information had been provided as mentioned in section 948(1), or
(b) he took all reasonable steps and exercised all due diligence to avoid the commission of the offence.

Co-operation

950 PANEL'S DUTY OF CO-OPERATION

(1) The Panel must take such steps as it considers appropriate to co-operate with—
(a) the Financial Services Authority;
(b) an authority designated as a supervisory authority for the purposes of Article 4.1 of the Takeovers Directive;
(c) any other person or body that exercises functions of a public nature, under legislation in any country or territory outside the United Kingdom, that appear to the Panel to be similar to its own functions or those of the Financial Services Authority.

(2) Co-operation may include the sharing of information that the Panel is not prevented from disclosing.

Hearings and appeals

951 HEARINGS AND APPEALS

(1) Rules must provide for a decision of the Panel to be subject to review by a committee of the Panel (the "Hearings Committee") at the instance of such persons affected by the decision as are specified in the rules.

(2) Rules may also confer other functions on the Hearings Committee.

(3) Rules must provide for there to be a right of appeal against a decision of the Hearings Committee to an independent tribunal (the "Takeover Appeal Board") in such circumstances and subject to such conditions as are specified in the rules.

(5) Rules must contain provision—

...

(b) preventing a person who is or has been a member of the committee mentioned in section 943(5) from being a member of the Hearings Committee or the Takeover Appeal Board...

...

Contravention of rules etc.

952 SANCTIONS

(1) Rules may contain provision conferring power on the Panel to impose sanctions on a person who has—
(a) acted in breach of rules, or
(b) failed to comply with a direction given by virtue of section 946.

(2) Subsection (3) applies where rules made by virtue of subsection (1) confer power on the Panel to impose a sanction of a kind not provided for by the City Code on Takeovers and Mergers as it had effect immediately before the passing of this Act.

(3) The Panel must prepare a statement (a "policy statement") of its policy with respect to—
(a) the imposition of the sanction in question, and
(b) where the sanction is in the nature of a financial penalty, the amount of the penalty that may be imposed.
An element of the policy must be that, in making a decision about any such matter, the Panel has regard to the factors mentioned in subsection (4).

(4) The factors are—
(a) the seriousness of the breach or failure in question in relation to the nature of the rule or direction contravened;
(b) the extent to which the breach or failure was deliberate or reckless;
(c) whether the person on whom the sanction is to be imposed is an individual.

(5) The Panel may at any time revise a policy statement.

(6) The Panel must prepare a draft of any proposed policy statement (or revised policy statement) and consult such persons about the draft as the Panel considers appropriate.

(7) The Panel must publish, in whatever way it considers appropriate, any policy statement (or revised policy statement) that it prepares.

(8) In exercising, or deciding whether to exercise, its power to impose a sanction within subsection (2) in the case of any particular breach or failure, the Panel must have regard to any relevant policy statement published and in force at the time when the breach or failure occurred.

953 FAILURE TO COMPLY WITH RULES ABOUT BID DOCUMENTATION

(1) This section applies where a takeover bid is made for a company that has securities carrying voting rights admitted to trading on a regulated market in the United Kingdom.

(2) Where an offer document published in respect of the bid does not comply with offer document rules, an offence is committed by—
(a) the person making the bid, and
(b) where the person making the bid is a body of persons, any director, officer or member of that body who caused the document to be published.

(3) A person commits an offence under subsection (2) only if—
(a) he knew that the offer document did not comply, or was reckless as to whether it complied, and
(b) he failed to take all reasonable steps to secure that it did comply.

(4) Where a response document published in respect of the bid does not comply with response document rules, an offence is committed by any director or other officer of the company referred to in subsection (1) who—
(a) knew that the response document did not comply, or was reckless as to whether it complied, and
(b) failed to take all reasonable steps to secure that it did comply.

(5) Where an offence is committed under subsection (2)(b) or (4) by a company or other body corporate ("the relevant body")—
(a) subsection (2)(b) has effect as if the reference to a director, officer or member of the person making the bid included a reference to a director, officer or member of the relevant body;
(b) subsection (4) has effect as if the reference to a director or other officer of the company referred to in subsection (1) included a reference to a director, officer or member of the relevant body.

(6) A person guilty of an offence under this section is liable—
(a) on conviction on indictment, to a fine;
(b) on summary conviction, to a fine not exceeding the statutory maximum.

(7) Nothing in this section affects any power of the Panel in relation to the enforcement of its rules.

(8) Section 1 (meaning of "company") does not apply for the purposes of this section.

(9) In this section—

"designated" means designated in rules;

"offer document" means a document required to be published by rules giving effect to Article 6.2 of the Takeovers Directive;

"offer document rules" means rules designated as rules that give effect to Article 6.3 of that Directive;

"response document" means a document required to be published by rules giving effect to Article 9.5 of that Directive;

"response document rules" means rules designated as rules that give effect to the first sentence of Article 9.5 of that Directive;

"securities" means shares or debentures;

"takeover bid" has the same meaning as in that Directive;

"voting rights" means rights to vote at general meetings of the company in question, including rights that arise only in certain circumstances.

954 COMPENSATION

(1) Rules may confer power on the Panel to order a person to pay such compensation as it thinks just and reasonable if he is in breach of a rule the effect of which is to require the payment of money.

(2) Rules made by virtue of this section may include provision for the payment of interest (including compound interest).

955 ENFORCEMENT BY THE COURT

(1) If, on the application of the Panel, the court is satisfied—
(a) that there is a reasonable likelihood that a person will contravene a rule-based requirement, or
(b) that a person has contravened a rule-based requirement or a disclosure requirement,
the court may make any order it thinks fit to secure compliance with the requirement.

(2) In subsection (1) "the court" means the High Court or, in Scotland, the Court of Session.

956 NO ACTION FOR BREACH OF STATUTORY DUTY ETC.

(1) Contravention of a rule-based requirement or a disclosure requirement does not give rise to any right of action for breach of statutory duty.

(2) Contravention of a rule-based requirement does not make any transaction void or unenforceable or (subject to any provision made by rules) affect the validity of any other thing.

Funding

957 FEES AND CHARGES

(1) Rules may provide for fees or charges to be payable to the Panel for the purpose of meeting any part of its expenses.

958 LEVY

(1) For the purpose of meeting any part of the expenses of the Panel, the Secretary of State may by regulations provide for a levy to be payable to the Panel—
(a) by specified persons or bodies, or persons or bodies of a specified description, or
(b) on transactions, of a specified description, in securities on specified markets.
In this subsection "specified" means specified in the regulations.

(2) The power to specify (or to specify descriptions of) persons or bodies must be exercised in such a way that the levy is payable only by persons or bodies that appear to the Secretary of State—
(a) to be capable of being directly affected by the exercise of any of the functions of the Panel, or
(b) otherwise to have a substantial interest in the exercise of any of those functions.

959 RECOVERY OF FEES, CHARGES OR LEVY

An amount payable by any person or body by virtue of section 957 or 958 is a debt due from that person or body to the Panel, and is recoverable accordingly.

Miscellaneous and supplementary

960 PANEL AS PARTY TO PROCEEDINGS

The Panel is capable (despite being an unincorporated body) of—

(a) bringing proceedings under this Chapter in its own name;

(b) bringing or defending any other proceedings in its own name.

961 EXEMPTION FROM LIABILITY IN DAMAGES

(1) Neither the Panel, nor any person within subsection (2), is to be liable in damages for anything done (or omitted to be done) in, or in connection with, the discharge or purported discharge of the Panel's functions.

(2) A person is within this subsection if—
(a) he is (or is acting as) a member, officer or member of staff of the Panel,
(b) he is a person authorised under section 947(5).

(3) Subsection (1) does not apply—
(a) if the act or omission is shown to have been in bad faith, or
(b) so as to prevent an award of damages in respect of the act or omission on the ground that it was unlawful as a result of section 6(1) of the Human Rights Act 1998 (c. 42) (acts of public authorities incompatible with Convention rights).

963 ANNUAL REPORTS

(1) After the end of each financial year the Panel must publish a report.

(2) The report must—
(a) set out how the Panel's functions were discharged in the year in question;
(b) include the Panel's accounts for that year;
(c) mention any matters the Panel considers to be of relevance to the discharge of its functions.

Chapter 2 IMPEDIMENTS TO TAKEOVERS

Opting in and opting out

966 OPTING IN AND OPTING OUT

(1) A company may by special resolution (an "opting-in resolution") opt in for the purposes of this Chapter if the following three conditions are met in relation to the company.

(2) The first condition is that the company has voting shares admitted to trading on a regulated market.

(3) The second condition is that—
(a) the company's articles of association—
(i) do not contain any such restrictions as are mentioned in Article 11 of the Takeovers Directive, or
(ii) if they do contain any such restrictions, provide for the restrictions not to apply at a time when, or in circumstances in which, they would be disapplied by that Article,
and

(b) those articles do not contain any other provision which would be incompatible with that Article.

(4) The third condition is that—
(a) no shares conferring special rights in the company are held by—
(i) a minister,
(ii) a nominee of, or any other person acting on behalf of, a minister, or
(iii) a company directly or indirectly controlled by a minister,
and
(b) no such rights are exercisable by or on behalf of a minister under any enactment.

(5) A company may revoke an opting-in resolution by a further special resolution (an "opting-out resolution").

(6) For the purposes of subsection (3), a reference in Article 11 of the Takeovers Directive to Article 7.1 or 9 of that Directive is to be read as referring to rules under section 943(1) giving effect to the relevant Article.

(7) In subsection (4) "minister" means—
(a) the holder of an office in Her Majesty's Government in the United Kingdom;
(b) the Scottish Ministers;
(c) a Minister within the meaning given by section 7(3) of the Northern Ireland Act 1998 (c. 47);
(d) the Welsh Ministers;
and for the purposes of that subsection "minister" also includes the Treasury, the Board of Trade and the Defence Council.

(8) The Secretary of State may by order subject to negative resolution procedure provide that subsection (4) applies in relation to a specified person or body that exercises functions of a public nature as it applies in relation to a minister.

"Specified" means specified in the order.

967 FURTHER PROVISION ABOUT OPTING-IN AND OPTING-OUT RESOLUTIONS

(1) An opting-in resolution or an opting-out resolution must specify the date from which it is to have effect (the "effective date").

(2) The effective date of an opting-in resolution may not be earlier than the date on which the resolution is passed.

(3) The second and third conditions in section 966 must be met at the time when an opting-in resolution is passed, but the first one does not need to be met until the effective date.

(4) An opting-in resolution passed before the time when voting shares of the company are admitted to trading on a regulated market complies with the requirement in subsection (1) if, instead of specifying a particular date, it provides for the resolution to have effect from that time.

(5) An opting-in resolution passed before the commencement of this section complies with the requirement in subsection (1) if, instead of specifying a particular date, it provides for the resolution to have effect from that commencement.

(6) The effective date of an opting-out resolution may not be earlier than the first anniversary of the date on which a copy of the opting-in resolution was forwarded to the registrar.

(7) Where a company has passed an opting-in resolution, any alteration of its articles of association that would prevent the second condition in section 966 from being met is of no effect until the effective date of an opting-out resolution passed by the company.

Consequences of opting in

968 EFFECT ON CONTRACTUAL RESTRICTIONS

(1) The following provisions have effect where a takeover bid is made for an opted-in company.

(2) An agreement to which this section applies is invalid in so far as it places any restriction—
   (a) on the transfer to the offeror, or at his direction to another person, of shares in the company during the offer period;
   (b) on the transfer to any person of shares in the company at a time during the offer period when the offeror holds shares amounting to not less than 75% in value of all the voting shares in the company;
   (c) on rights to vote at a general meeting of the company that decides whether to take any action which might result in the frustration of the bid;
   (d) on rights to vote at a general meeting of the company that—
      (i) is the first such meeting to be held after the end of the offer period, and
      (ii) is held at a time when the offeror holds shares amounting to not less than 75% in value of all the voting shares in the company.

(3) This section applies to an agreement—
   (a) entered into between a person holding shares in the company and another such person on or after 21st April 2004, or
   (b) entered into at any time between such a person and the company,
   and it applies to such an agreement even if the law applicable to the agreement (apart from this section) is not the law of a part of the United Kingdom.

(4) The reference in subsection (2)(c) to rights to vote at a general meeting of the company that decides whether to take any action which might result in the frustration of the bid includes a reference to rights to vote on a written resolution concerned with that question.

(5) For the purposes of subsection (2)(c), action which might result in the frustration of a bid is any action of that kind specified in rules under section 943(1) giving effect to Article 9 of the Takeovers Directive.

(6) If a person suffers loss as a result of any act or omission that would (but for this section) be a breach of an agreement to which this section applies, he is entitled to compensation, of such amount as the court considers just and equitable, from any person who would (but for this section) be liable to him for committing or inducing the breach.

(7) In subsection (6) "the court" means the High Court or, in Scotland, the Court of Session.

(8) A reference in this section to voting shares in the company does not include—
   (a) debentures, or
   (b) shares that, under the company's articles of association, do not normally carry rights to vote at its general meetings (for example, shares carrying rights to vote that, under those articles, arise only where specified pecuniary advantages are not provided).

969 POWER OF OFFEROR TO REQUIRE GENERAL MEETING TO BE CALLED

(1) Where a takeover bid is made for an opted-in company, the offeror may by making a request to the directors of the company require them to call a general meeting of the company if, at the date at which the request is made, he holds shares amounting to not less than 75% in value of all the voting shares in the company.

(2) The reference in subsection (1) to voting shares in the company does not include—
(a) debentures, or
(b) shares that, under the company's articles of association, do not normally carry rights to vote at its general meetings (for example, shares carrying rights to vote that, under those articles, arise only where specified pecuniary advantages are not provided).

(3) Sections 303 to 305 (members' power to require general meetings to be called) apply as they would do if subsection (1) above were substituted for subsections (1) to (3) of section 303, and with any other necessary modifications.

Supplementary

970 COMMUNICATION OF DECISIONS

(1) A company that has passed an opting-in resolution or an opting-out resolution must notify—
(a) the Panel, and
(b) where the company—
(i) has voting shares admitted to trading on a regulated market in an EEA State other than the United Kingdom, or
(ii) has requested such admission,
the authority designated by that state as the supervisory authority for the purposes of Article 4.1 of the Takeovers Directive.

(2) Notification must be given within 15 days after the resolution is passed and, if any admission or request such as is mentioned in subsection (1)(b) occurs at a later time, within 15 days after that time.

(3) If a company fails to comply with this section, an offence is committed by—
(a) the company, and
(b) every officer of it who is in default.

(4) A person guilty of an offence under this section is liable on summary conviction to a fine not exceeding level 3 on the standard scale and, for continued contravention, a daily default fine not exceeding one-tenth of level 3 on the standard scale.

971 INTERPRETATION OF THIS CHAPTER

(1) In this Chapter—

"offeror" and "takeover bid" have the same meaning as in the Takeovers Directive;

"offer period", in relation to a takeover bid, means the time allowed for acceptance of the bid by—
(a) rules under section 943(1) giving effect to Article 7.1 of the Takeovers Directive, or
(b) where the rules giving effect to that Article which apply to the bid are those of an EEA State other than the United Kingdom, those rules;

"opted-in company" means a company in relation to which—

(a) an opting-in resolution has effect, and
(b) the conditions in section 966(2) and (4) continue to be met;

"opting-in resolution" has the meaning given by section 966(1);

"opting-out resolution" has the meaning given by section 966(5);

"the Takeovers Directive" means Directive 2004/25/EC of the European Parliament and of the Council;

"voting rights" means rights to vote at general meetings of the company in question, including rights that arise only in certain circumstances;

"voting shares" means shares carrying voting rights.

(2) For the purposes of this Chapter—
(a) securities of a company are treated as shares in the company if they are convertible into or entitle the holder to subscribe for such shares;
(b) debentures issued by a company are treated as shares in the company if they carry voting rights.

Chapter 3 "SQUEEZE-OUT" AND "SELL-OUT"

Takeover offers

974 MEANING OF "TAKEOVER OFFER"

(1) For the purposes of this Chapter an offer to acquire shares in a company is a "takeover offer" if the following two conditions are satisfied in relation to the offer.

(2) The first condition is that it is an offer to acquire—
(a) all the shares in a company, or
(b) where there is more than one class of shares in a company, all the shares of one or more classes,
other than shares that at the date of the offer are already held by the offeror.

...

(3) The second condition is that the terms of the offer are the same—
(a) in relation to all the shares to which the offer relates, or
(b) where the shares to which the offer relates include shares of different classes, in relation to all the shares of each class.

...

"Squeeze-out"

979 RIGHT OF OFFEROR TO BUY OUT MINORITY SHAREHOLDER

(1) Subsection (2) applies in a case where a takeover offer does not relate to shares of different classes.

(2) If the offeror has, by virtue of acceptances of the offer, acquired or unconditionally contracted to acquire—
(a) not less than 90% in value of the shares to which the offer relates, and
(b) in a case where the shares to which the offer relates are voting shares, not less than 90% of the voting rights carried by those shares,

he may give notice to the holder of any shares to which the offer relates which the offeror has not acquired or unconditionally contracted to acquire that he desires to acquire those shares.

(3) Subsection (4) applies in a case where a takeover offer relates to shares of different classes.

(4) If the offeror has, by virtue of acceptances of the offer, acquired or unconditionally contracted to acquire—
(a) not less than 90% in value of the shares of any class to which the offer relates, and
(b) in a case where the shares of that class are voting shares, not less than 90% of the voting rights carried by those shares,
he may give notice to the holder of any shares of that class to which the offer relates which the offeror has not acquired or unconditionally contracted to acquire that he desires to acquire those shares.

980 FURTHER PROVISION ABOUT NOTICES GIVEN UNDER SECTION 979

(1) A notice under section 979 must be given in the prescribed manner.

(2) No notice may be given under section 979(2) or (4) after the end of—
(a) the period of three months beginning with the day after the last day on which the offer can be accepted, or
(b) the period of six months beginning with the date of the offer, where that period ends earlier and the offer is one to which subsection (3) below applies.

(3) This subsection applies to an offer if the time allowed for acceptance of the offer is not governed by rules under section 943(1) that give effect to Article 7 of the Takeovers Directive.

In this subsection "the Takeovers Directive" has the same meaning as in section 943.

(4) At the time when the offeror first gives a notice under section 979 in relation to an offer, he must send to the company—
(a) a copy of the notice, and
(b) a statutory declaration by him in the prescribed form, stating that the conditions for the giving of the notice are satisfied.

(5) Where the offeror is a company (whether or not a company within the meaning of this Act) the statutory declaration must be signed by a director.

(6) A person commits an offence if—
(a) he fails to send a copy of a notice or a statutory declaration as required by subsection (4), or
(b) he makes such a declaration for the purposes of that subsection knowing it to be false or without having reasonable grounds for believing it to be true.

(7) It is a defence for a person charged with an offence for failing to send a copy of a notice as required by subsection (4) to prove that he took reasonable steps for securing compliance with that subsection.

(8) A person guilty of an offence under this section is liable—
(a) on conviction on indictment, to imprisonment for a term not exceeding two years or a fine (or both);
(b) on summary conviction—

(i) in England and Wales, to imprisonment for a term not exceeding twelve months or to a fine not exceeding the statutory maximum (or both) and, for continued contravention, a daily default fine not exceeding one-fiftieth of the statutory maximum;

(ii) in Scotland or Northern Ireland, to imprisonment for a term not exceeding six months, or to a fine not exceeding the statutory maximum (or both) and, for continued contravention, a daily default fine not exceeding one-fiftieth of the statutory maximum.

981 EFFECT OF NOTICE UNDER SECTION 979

(1) Subject to section 986 (applications to the court), this section applies where the offeror gives a shareholder a notice under section 979.

(2) The offeror is entitled and bound to acquire the shares to which the notice relates on the terms of the offer.

(6) At the end of six weeks from the date of the notice the offeror must immediately—
(a) send a copy of the notice to the company, and
(b) pay or transfer to the company the consideration for the shares to which the notice relates.

Where the consideration consists of shares or securities to be allotted by the offeror, the reference in paragraph (b) to the transfer of the consideration is to be read as a reference to the allotment of the shares or securities to the company.

(7) If the shares to which the notice relates are registered, the copy of the notice sent to the company under subsection (6)(a) must be accompanied by an instrument of transfer executed on behalf of the holder of the shares by a person appointed by the offeror.

On receipt of that instrument the company must register the offeror as the holder of those shares.

(9) The company must hold any money or other consideration received by it under subsection (6)(b) on trust for the person who, before the offeror acquired them, was entitled to the shares in respect of which the money or other consideration was received.

. . .

"Sell-out"

983 RIGHT OF MINORITY SHAREHOLDER TO BE BOUGHT OUT BY OFFEROR

(1) Subsections (2) and (3) apply in a case where a takeover offer relates to all the shares in a company.

For this purpose a takeover offer relates to all the shares in a company if it is an offer to acquire all the shares in the company within the meaning of section 974.

(2) The holder of any voting shares to which the offer relates who has not accepted the offer may require the offeror to acquire those shares if, at any time before the end of the period within which the offer can be accepted—
(a) the offeror has by virtue of acceptances of the offer acquired or unconditionally contracted to acquire some (but not all) of the shares to which the offer relates, and

(b) those shares, with or without any other shares in the company which he has acquired or contracted to acquire (whether unconditionally or subject to conditions being met)—
   (i) amount to not less than 90% in value of all the voting shares in the company (or would do so but for section 990(1)), and
   (ii) carry not less than 90% of the voting rights in the company (or would do so but for section 990(1)).

(3) The holder of any non-voting shares to which the offer relates who has not accepted the offer may require the offeror to acquire those shares if, at any time before the end of the period within which the offer can be accepted—
(a) the offeror has by virtue of acceptances of the offer acquired or unconditionally contracted to acquire some (but not all) of the shares to which the offer relates, and
(b) those shares, with or without any other shares in the company which he has acquired or contracted to acquire (whether unconditionally or subject to conditions being met), amount to not less than 90% in value of all the shares in the company (or would do so but for section 990(1)).

(4) If a takeover offer relates to shares of one or more classes and at any time before the end of the period within which the offer can be accepted—
(a) the offeror has by virtue of acceptances of the offer acquired or unconditionally contracted to acquire some (but not all) of the shares of any class to which the offer relates, and
(b) those shares, with or without any other shares of that class which he has acquired or contracted to acquire (whether unconditionally or subject to conditions being met)—
   (i) amount to not less than 90% in value of all the shares of that class, and
   (ii) in a case where the shares of that class are voting shares, carry not less than 90% of the voting rights carried by the shares of that class,

the holder of any shares of that class to which the offer relates who has not accepted the offer may require the offeror to acquire those shares.

984 FURTHER PROVISION ABOUT RIGHTS CONFERRED BY SECTION 983

(1) Rights conferred on a shareholder by subsection (2), (3) or (4) of section 983 are exercisable by a written communication addressed to the offeror.

(2) Rights conferred on a shareholder by subsection (2), (3) or (4) of that section are not exercisable after the end of the period of three months from—
(a) the end of the period within which the offer can be accepted, or
(b) if later, the date of the notice that must be given under subsection (3) below.

(3) Within one month of the time specified in subsection (2), (3) or (4) (as the case may be) of that section, the offeror must give any shareholder who has not accepted the offer notice in the prescribed manner of—
(a) the rights that are exercisable by the shareholder under that subsection, and
(b) the period within which the rights are exercisable.

If the notice is given before the end of the period within which the offer can be accepted, it must state that the offer is still open for acceptance.

(4) Subsection (3) does not apply if the offeror has given the shareholder a notice in respect of the shares in question under section 979.

(5) An offeror who fails to comply with subsection (3) commits an offence. If the offeror is a company, every officer of that company who is in default or to whose neglect the failure is attributable also commits an offence.

(6) If an offeror other than a company is charged with an offence for failing to comply with subsection (3), it is a defence for him to prove that he took all reasonable steps for securing compliance with that subsection.

(7) A person guilty of an offence under this section is liable—
(a) on conviction on indictment, to a fine;
(b) on summary conviction, to a fine not exceeding the statutory maximum and, for continued contravention, a daily default fine not exceeding one-fiftieth of the statutory maximum.

985 EFFECT OF REQUIREMENT UNDER SECTION 983

(1) Subject to section 986, this section applies where a shareholder exercises his rights under section 983 in respect of any shares held by him.

(2) The offeror is entitled and bound to acquire those shares on the terms of the offer or on such other terms as may be agreed.

Supplementary

986 APPLICATIONS TO THE COURT

(1) Where a notice is given under section 979 to a shareholder the court may, on an application made by him, order—
(a) that the offeror is not entitled and bound to acquire the shares to which the notice relates, or
(b) that the terms on which the offeror is entitled and bound to acquire the shares shall be such as the court thinks fit.

(2) An application under subsection (1) must be made within six weeks from the date on which the notice referred to in that subsection was given.

If an application to the court under subsection (1) is pending at the end of that period, section 981(6) does not have effect until the application has been disposed of.

(3) Where a shareholder exercises his rights under section 983 in respect of any shares held by him, the court may, on an application made by him or the offeror, order that the terms on which the offeror is entitled and bound to acquire the shares shall be such as the court thinks fit.

(4) On an application under subsection (1) or (3)—
(a) the court may not require consideration of a higher value than that specified in the terms of the offer ("the offer value") to be given for the shares to which the application relates unless the holder of the shares shows that the offer value would be unfair;
(b) the court may not require consideration of a lower value than the offer value to be given for the shares.

(5) No order for costs or expenses may be made against a shareholder making an application under subsection (1) or (3) unless the court considers that—
(a) the application was unnecessary, improper or vexatious,
(b) there has been unreasonable delay in making the application, or

(c) there has been unreasonable conduct on the shareholder's part in conducting the proceedings on the application.

(6) A shareholder who has made an application under subsection (1) or (3) must give notice of the application to the offeror.

(7) An offeror who is given notice of an application under subsection (1) or (3) must give a copy of the notice to—
(a) any person (other than the applicant) to whom a notice has been given under section 979;
(b) any person who has exercised his rights under section 983.

(8) An offeror who makes an application under subsection (3) must give notice of the application to—
(a) any person to whom a notice has been given under section 979;
(b) any person who has exercised his rights under section 983.

(9) Where a takeover offer has not been accepted to the extent necessary for entitling the offeror to give notices under subsection (2) or (4) of section 979 the court may, on an application made by him, make an order authorising him to give notices under that subsection if it is satisfied that—
(a) the offeror has after reasonable enquiry been unable to trace one or more of the persons holding shares to which the offer relates,
(b) the requirements of that subsection would have been met if the person, or all the persons, mentioned in paragraph (a) above had accepted the offer, and
(c) the consideration offered is fair and reasonable.
This is subject to subsection (10).

(10) The court may not make an order under subsection (9) unless it considers that it is just and equitable to do so having regard, in particular, to the number of shareholders who have been traced but who have not accepted the offer.

Interpretation

989 CONVERTIBLE SECURITIES

(1) For the purposes of this Chapter securities of a company are treated as shares in the company if they are convertible into or entitle the holder to subscribe for such shares.

References to the holder of shares or a shareholder are to be read accordingly.

(2) Subsection (1) is not to be read as requiring any securities to be treated—
(a) as shares of the same class as those into which they are convertible or for which the holder is entitled to subscribe, or
(b) as shares of the same class as other securities by reason only that the shares into which they are convertible or for which the holder is entitled to subscribe are of the same class.

990 DEBENTURES CARRYING VOTING RIGHTS

(1) For the purposes of this Chapter debentures issued by a company to which subsection (2) applies are treated as shares in the company if they carry voting rights.

991 INTERPRETATION

(1) In this Chapter—

"the company" means the company whose shares are the subject of a takeover offer;

"date of the offer" means—
(a) where the offer is published, the date of publication;
(b) where the offer is not published, or where any notices of the offer are given before the date of publication, the date when notices of the offer (or the first such notices) are given;

...

"non-voting shares" means shares that are not voting shares;

"offeror" means (subject to section 987) the person making a takeover offer;

"voting rights" means rights to vote at general meetings of the company, including rights that arise only in certain circumstances;

"voting shares" means shares carrying voting rights.

Part 29 FRAUDULENT TRADING

993 OFFENCE OF FRAUDULENT TRADING

(1) If any business of a company is carried on with intent to defraud creditors of the company or creditors of any other person, or for any fraudulent purpose, every person who is knowingly a party to the carrying on of the business in that manner commits an offence.

(2) This applies whether or not the company has been, or is in the course of being, wound up.

(3) A person guilty of an offence under this section is liable—
(a) on conviction on indictment, to imprisonment for a term not exceeding ten years or a fine (or both);
(b) on summary conviction—
(i) in England and Wales, to imprisonment for a term not exceeding twelve months or a fine not exceeding the statutory maximum (or both);
(ii) in Scotland or Northern Ireland, to imprisonment for a term not exceeding six months or a fine not exceeding the statutory maximum (or both).

Part 30 PROTECTION OF MEMBERS AGAINST UNFAIR PREJUDICE

Main provisions

994 PETITION BY COMPANY MEMBER

(1) A member of a company may apply to the court by petition for an order under this Part on the ground—
(a) that the company's affairs are being or have been conducted in a manner that is unfairly prejudicial to the interests of members generally or of some part of its members (including at least himself), or
(b) that an actual or proposed act or omission of the company (including an act or omission on its behalf) is or would be so prejudicial.

(1A) For the purposes of subsection (1)(a), a removal of the company's auditor from office—
(a) on grounds of divergence of opinions on accounting treatments or audit procedures, or
(b) on any other improper grounds,

shall be treated as being unfairly prejudicial to the interests of some part of the company's members.

(2) The provisions of this Part apply to a person who is not a member of a company but to whom shares in the company have been transferred or transmitted by operation of law as they apply to a member of a company.

(3) In this section, and so far as applicable for the purposes of this section in the other provisions of this Part, "company" means—
  (a) a company within the meaning of this Act, or
  ...

995 PETITION BY SECRETARY OF STATE

(1) This section applies to a company in respect of which—
  (a) the Secretary of State has received a report under section 437 of the Companies Act 1985 (c. 6) (inspector's report);
  (b) the Secretary of State has exercised his powers under section 447 or 448 of that Act (powers to require documents and information or to enter and search premises);
  ...

(2) If it appears to the Secretary of State that in the case of such a company—
  (a) the company's affairs are being or have been conducted in a manner that is unfairly prejudicial to the interests of members generally or of some part of its members, or
  (b) an actual or proposed act or omission of the company (including an act or omission on its behalf) is or would be so prejudicial, he may apply to the court by petition for an order under this Part.

(3) The Secretary of State may do this in addition to, or instead of, presenting a petition for the winding up of the company.

(4) In this section, and so far as applicable for the purposes of this section in the other provisions of this Part, "company" means any body corporate that is liable to be wound up under the Insolvency Act 1986 (c. 45)...

996 POWERS OF THE COURT UNDER THIS PART

(1) If the court is satisfied that a petition under this Part is well founded, it may make such order as it thinks fit for giving relief in respect of the matters complained of.

(2) Without prejudice to the generality of subsection (1), the court's order may—
  (a) regulate the conduct of the company's affairs in the future;
  (b) require the company—
    (i) to refrain from doing or continuing an act complained of, or
    (ii) to do an act that the petitioner has complained it has omitted to do;
  (c) authorise civil proceedings to be brought in the name and on behalf of the company by such person or persons and on such terms as the court may direct;
  (d) require the company not to make any, or any specified, alterations in its articles without the leave of the court;
  (e) provide for the purchase of the shares of any members of the company by other members or by the company itself and, in the case of a purchase by the company itself, the reduction of the company's capital accordingly.

Supplementary provisions

998 COPY OF ORDER AFFECTING COMPANY'S CONSTITUTION TO BE DELIVERED TO REGISTRAR

(1) Where an order of the court under this Part—
(a) alters the company's constitution, or
(b) gives leave for the company to make any, or any specified, alterations to its constitution,
the company must deliver a copy of the order to the registrar.

999 SUPPLEMENTARY PROVISIONS WHERE COMPANY'S CONSTITUTION ALTERED

(1) This section applies where an order under this Part alters a company's constitution.

(3) Every copy of a company's articles issued by the company after the order is made must be accompanied by a copy of the order, unless the effect of the order has been incorporated into the articles by amendment.

Part 36 OFFENCES UNDER THE COMPANIES ACTS

Liability of officer in default

1121 LIABILITY OF OFFICER IN DEFAULT

(1) This section has effect for the purposes of any provision of the Companies Acts to the effect that, in the event of contravention of an enactment in relation to a company, an offence is committed by every officer of the company who is in default.

(2) For this purpose "officer" includes—
(a) any director, manager or secretary, and
(b) any person who is to be treated as an officer of the company for the purposes of the provision in question.

(3) An officer is "in default" for the purposes of the provision if he authorises or permits, participates in, or fails to take all reasonable steps to prevent, the contravention.

1122 LIABILITY OF COMPANY AS OFFICER IN DEFAULT

(1) Where a company is an officer of another company, it does not commit an offence as an officer in default unless one of its officers is in default.

(2) Where any such offence is committed by a company the officer in question also commits the offence and is liable to be proceeded against and punished accordingly.

(3) In this section "officer" and "in default" have the meanings given by section 1121.

Production and inspection of documents

1132 PRODUCTION AND INSPECTION OF DOCUMENTS WHERE OFFENCE SUSPECTED

(1) An application under this section may be made—

(a) in England and Wales, to a judge of the High Court by the Director of Public Prosecutions, the Secretary of State or a chief officer of police;
(b) in Scotland, to one of the Lords Commissioners of Justiciary by the Lord Advocate;
(c) in Northern Ireland, to the High Court by the Director of Public Prosecutions for Northern Ireland, the Department of Enterprise, Trade and Investment or a chief superintendent of the Police Service of Northern Ireland.

(2) If on an application under this section there is shown to be reasonable cause to believe—
(a) that any person has, while an officer of a company, committed an offence in connection with the management of the company's affairs, and
(b) that evidence of the commission of the offence is to be found in any documents in the possession or control of the company,
an order under this section may be made.

(3) The order may—
(a) authorise any person named in it to inspect the documents in question, or any of them, for the purpose of investigating and obtaining evidence of the offence, or
(b) require the secretary of the company, or such other officer of it as may be named in the order, to produce the documents (or any of them) to a person named in the order at a place so named.

(4) This section applies also in relation to documents in the possession or control of a person carrying on the business of banking, so far as they relate to the company's affairs, as it applies to documents in the possession or control of the company, except that no such order as is referred to in subsection (3)(b) may be made by virtue of this subsection.

(5) The decision under this section of a judge of the High Court, any of the Lords Commissioners of Justiciary or the High Court is not appealable.

(6) In this section "document" includes information recorded in any form.

Part 37 COMPANIES: SUPPLEMENTARY PROVISIONS

Requirements as to independent valuation

1149 APPLICATION OF VALUATION REQUIREMENTS

The provisions of sections 1150 to 1153 apply to the valuation and report required by—

section 93 (re-registration as public company: recent allotment of shares for non-cash consideration);

section 593 (allotment of shares of public company in consideration of non-cash asset);

section 599 (transfer of non-cash asset to public company).

1150 VALUATION BY QUALIFIED INDEPENDENT PERSON

(1) The valuation and report must be made by a person ("the valuer") who—
(a) is eligible for appointment as a statutory auditor (see section 1212), and
(b) meets the independence requirement in section 1151.

(2) However, where it appears to the valuer to be reasonable for the valuation of the consideration, or part of it, to be made by (or for him to accept a valuation made by) another person who—

(a) appears to him to have the requisite knowledge and experience to value the consideration or that part of it, and
(b) is not an officer or employee of—
(i) the company, or
(ii) any other body corporate that is that company's subsidiary or holding company or a subsidiary of that company's holding company,
or a partner of or employed by any such officer or employee,

he may arrange for or accept such a valuation, together with a report which will enable him to make his own report under this section.

(3) The references in subsection (2)(b) to an officer or employee do not include an auditor.

(4) Where the consideration or part of it is valued by a person other than the valuer himself, the latter's report must state that fact and shall also—
(a) state the former's name and what knowledge and experience he has to carry out the valuation, and
(b) describe so much of the consideration as was valued by the other person, and the method used to value it, and specify the date of that valuation.

1151 THE INDEPENDENCE REQUIREMENT

(1) A person meets the independence requirement for the purposes of section 1150 only if—
(a) he is not—
(i) an officer or employee of the company, or
(ii) a partner or employee of such a person, or a partnership of which such a person is a partner;
(b) he is not—
(i) an officer or employee of an associated undertaking of the company, or
(ii) a partner or employee of such a person, or a partnership of which such a person is a partner; and
(c) there does not exist between—
(i) the person or an associate of his, and
(ii) the company or an associated undertaking of the company,
a connection of any such description as may be specified by regulations made by the Secretary of State.

(2) An auditor of the company is not regarded as an officer or employee of the company for this purpose.

(3) In this section—

"associated undertaking" means—
(a) a parent undertaking or subsidiary undertaking of the company, or
(b) a subsidiary undertaking of a parent undertaking of the company; and
"associate" has the meaning given by section 1152.

(4) Regulations under this section are subject to negative resolution procedure.

1152 MEANING OF "ASSOCIATE"

(1) This section defines "associate" for the purposes of section 1151 (valuation: independence requirement).

(2) In relation to an individual, "associate" means—
(a) that individual's spouse or civil partner or minor child or step-child,

(b) any body corporate of which that individual is a director, and
(c) any employee or partner of that individual.

(3) In relation to a body corporate, "associate" means—
(a) any body corporate of which that body is a director,
(b) any body corporate in the same group as that body, and
(c) any employee or partner of that body or of any body corporate in the same group.

(4) In relation to a partnership that is a legal person under the law by which it is governed, "associate" means—
(a) any body corporate of which that partnership is a director,
(b) any employee of or partner in that partnership, and
(c) any person who is an associate of a partner in that partnership.

(5) In relation to a partnership that is not a legal person under the law by which it is governed, "associate" means any person who is an associate of any of the partners.

(6) In this section, in relation to a limited liability partnership, for "director" read "member".

1153 VALUER ENTITLED TO FULL DISCLOSURE

(1) A person carrying out a valuation or making a report with respect to any consideration proposed to be accepted or given by a company, is entitled to require from the officers of the company such information and explanation as he thinks necessary to enable him to—
(a) carry out the valuation or make the report, and
(b) provide any note required by section 596(3) or 600(3) (note required where valuation carried out by another person).

(2) A person who knowingly or recklessly makes a statement to which this subsection applies that is misleading, false or deceptive in a material particular commits an offence.

(3) Subsection (2) applies to a statement—
(a) made (whether orally or in writing) to a person carrying out a valuation or making a report, and
(b) conveying or purporting to convey any information or explanation which that person requires, or is entitled to require, under subsection (1).

(4) A person guilty of an offence under subsection (2) is liable—
(a) on conviction on indictment, to imprisonment for a term not exceeding two years or a fine (or both);
(b) on summary conviction—
(i) in England and Wales, to imprisonment for a term not exceeding twelve months or to a fine not exceeding the statutory maximum (or both);
(ii) in Scotland or Northern Ireland, to imprisonment for a term not exceeding six months, or to a fine not exceeding the statutory maximum (or both).

Courts and legal proceedings

1156 MEANING OF "THE COURT"

(1) Except as otherwise provided, in the Companies Acts "the court" means—
(a) in England and Wales, the High Court or ... a county court;
(b) in Scotland, the Court of Session or the sheriff court;
(c) in Northern Ireland, the High Court.

1157 POWER OF COURT TO GRANT RELIEF IN CERTAIN CASES

(1) If in proceedings for negligence, default, breach of duty or breach of trust against—
 (a) an officer of a company, or
 (b) a person employed by a company as auditor (whether he is or is not an officer of the company),

it appears to the court hearing the case that the officer or person is or may be liable but that he acted honestly and reasonably, and that having regard to all the circumstances of the case (including those connected with his appointment) he ought fairly to be excused, the court may relieve him, either wholly or in part, from his liability on such terms as it thinks fit.

(2) If any such officer or person has reason to apprehend that a claim will or might be made against him in respect of negligence, default, breach of duty or breach of trust—
 (a) he may apply to the court for relief, and
 (b) the court has the same power to relieve him as it would have had if it had been a court before which proceedings against him for negligence, default, breach of duty or breach of trust had been brought.

(3) Where a case to which subsection (1) applies is being tried by a judge with a jury, the judge, after hearing the evidence, may, if he is satisfied that the defendant (in Scotland, the defender) ought in pursuance of that subsection to be relieved either in whole or in part from the liability sought to be enforced against him, withdraw the case from the jury and forthwith direct judgment to be entered for the defendant (in Scotland, grant decree of absolvitor) on such terms as to costs (in Scotland, expenses) or otherwise as the judge may think proper.

Part 38 COMPANIES: INTERPRETATION

Meaning of "UK-registered company"

1158 MEANING OF "UK-REGISTERED COMPANY"

In the Companies Acts "UK-registered company" means a company registered under this Act. The expression does not include an overseas company that has registered particulars under section 1046.

Meaning of "subsidiary" and related expressions

1159 MEANING OF "SUBSIDIARY" ETC.

(1) A company is a "subsidiary" of another company, its "holding company", if that other company—
 (a) holds a majority of the voting rights in it, or
 (b) is a member of it and has the right to appoint or remove a majority of its board of directors, or
 (c) is a member of it and controls alone, pursuant to an agreement with other members, a majority of the voting rights in it,

or if it is a subsidiary of a company that is itself a subsidiary of that other company.

(2) A company is a "wholly-owned subsidiary" of another company if it has no members except that other and that other's wholly-owned subsidiaries or persons acting on behalf of that other or its wholly-owned subsidiaries.

(4) In this section … "company" includes any body corporate.

Meaning of "undertaking" and related expressions

1161 MEANING OF "UNDERTAKING" AND RELATED EXPRESSIONS

(1) In the Companies Acts "undertaking" means—
 (a) a body corporate or partnership, or
 (b) an unincorporated association carrying on a trade or business, with or without a view to profit.

(4) References in the Companies Acts to "fellow subsidiary undertakings" are to undertakings which are subsidiary undertakings of the same parent undertaking but are not parent undertakings or subsidiary undertakings of each other.

(5) In the Companies Acts "group undertaking", in relation to an undertaking, means an undertaking which is—
 (a) a parent undertaking or subsidiary undertaking of that undertaking, or
 (b) a subsidiary undertaking of any parent undertaking of that undertaking.

1162 PARENT AND SUBSIDIARY UNDERTAKINGS

(1) This section ... defines "parent undertaking" and "subsidiary undertaking" for the purposes of the Companies Acts.

(2) An undertaking is a parent undertaking in relation to another undertaking, a subsidiary undertaking, if—
 (a) it holds a majority of the voting rights in the undertaking, or
 (b) it is a member of the undertaking and has the right to appoint or remove a majority of its board of directors, or
 (c) it has the right to exercise a dominant influence over the undertaking—
  (i) by virtue of provisions contained in the undertaking's articles, or
  (ii) by virtue of a control contract, or
 (d) it is a member of the undertaking and controls alone, pursuant to an agreement with other shareholders or members, a majority of the voting rights in the undertaking.

(3) For the purposes of subsection (2) an undertaking shall be treated as a member of another undertaking—
 (a) if any of its subsidiary undertakings is a member of that undertaking, or
 (b) if any shares in that other undertaking are held by a person acting on behalf of the undertaking or any of its subsidiary undertakings.

(4) An undertaking is also a parent undertaking in relation to another undertaking, a subsidiary undertaking, if—
 (a) it has the power to exercise, or actually exercises, dominant influence or control over it, or
 (b) it and the subsidiary undertaking are managed on a unified basis.

(5) A parent undertaking shall be treated as the parent undertaking of undertakings in relation to which any of its subsidiary undertakings are, or are to be treated as, parent undertakings; and references to its subsidiary undertakings shall be construed accordingly.

(7) In this section ... references to shares, in relation to an undertaking, are to allotted shares.

Other definitions

1163 "NON-CASH ASSET"

(1) In the Companies Acts "non-cash asset" means any property or interest in property, other than cash.

For this purpose "cash" includes foreign currency.

(2) A reference to the transfer or acquisition of a non-cash asset includes—
(a) the creation or extinction of an estate or interest in, or a right over, any property, and
(b) the discharge of a liability of any person, other than a liability for a liquidated sum.

1171 THE FORMER COMPANIES ACTS

In the Companies Acts—

"the former Companies Acts" means—
(a) the Joint Stock Companies Acts, the Companies Act 1862 (c. 89), the Companies (Consolidation) Act 1908 (c. 69), the Companies Act 1929 (c. 23), the Companies Act (Northern Ireland) 1932 (c. 7 (N.I.)), the Companies Acts 1948 to 1983, the Companies Act (Northern Ireland) 1960 (c. 22 (N.I.)), the Companies (Northern Ireland) Order 1986 (S.I. 1986/1032 (N.I. 6)) and the Companies Consolidation (Consequential Provisions) (Northern Ireland) Order 1986 (S.I. 1986/1035 (N.I. 9)), and
(b) the provisions of the Companies Act 1985 (c. 6) and the Companies Consolidation (Consequential Provisions) Act 1985 (c. 9) that are no longer in force;

"the Joint Stock Companies Acts" means the Joint Stock Companies Act 1856 (c. 47), the Joint Stock Companies Acts 1856, 1857 (20 & 21 Vict. c. 14), the Joint Stock Banking Companies Act 1857 (c. 49), and the Act to enable Joint Stock Banking Companies to be formed on the principle of limited liability (1858 c. 91), but does not include the Joint Stock Companies Act 1844 (c. 110).

General

1172 REFERENCES TO REQUIREMENTS OF THIS ACT

References in the company law provisions of this Act to the requirements of this Act include the requirements of regulations and orders made under it.

1173 MINOR DEFINITIONS: GENERAL

(1) In the Companies Acts—

"body corporate" and "corporation" include a body incorporated outside the United Kingdom, but do not include—
(a) a corporation sole, or
(b) a partnership that, whether or not a legal person, is not regarded as a body corporate under the law by which it is governed;

. . .

"firm" means any entity, whether or not a legal person, that is not an individual and includes a body corporate, a corporation sole and a partnership or other unincorporated association;

"the Gazette" means—

(a) as respects companies registered in England and Wales, the London Gazette,
(b) as respects companies registered in Scotland, the Edinburgh Gazette, and
(c) as respects companies registered in Northern Ireland, the Belfast Gazette;

. . .

"officer", in relation to a body corporate, includes a director, manager or secretary;

"parent company" means a company that is a parent undertaking (see section 1162 . . .);

"regulated market" has the same meaning as in Directive 2004/39/EC of the European Parliament and of the Council on markets in financial instruments (see Article 4.1(14));

"working day", in relation to a company, means a day that is not a Saturday or Sunday, Christmas Day, Good Friday or any day that is a bank holiday under the Banking and Financial Dealings Act 1971 (c. 80) in the part of the United Kingdom where the company is registered.

(2) In relation to an EEA State that has not implemented Directive 2004/39/EC of the European Parliament and of the Council on markets in financial instruments, the following definition of "regulated market" has effect in place of that in subsection (1)—

"regulated market" has the same meaning as it has in Council Directive 93/22/EEC on investment services in the securities field.

SCHEDULE 2 SPECIFIED PERSONS, DESCRIPTIONS OF DISCLOSURES ETC. FOR THE PURPOSES OF SECTION 948

Part 1 SPECIFIED PERSONS

1. The Secretary of State.

2. The Department of Enterprise, Trade and Investment for Northern Ireland.

3. The Treasury.

3A. The Treasury of the Isle of Man.

4. The Bank of England.

5. The Financial Services Authority.

5A. The Financial Supervision Commission of the Isle of Man.

6. The Commissioners for Her Majesty's Revenue and Customs.

7. The Lord Advocate.

7A. The Attorney General of the Isle of Man.

8. The Director of Public Prosecutions.

9. The Director of Public Prosecutions for Northern Ireland.

10. A constable.

11. A procurator fiscal.

12. The Scottish Ministers.

12A. The members and officers of each of the Departments constituted by section 1(1) of the Government Departments Act 1987 (an Act of Tynwald: c 13).

"Member" has the same meaning as it has by virtue of section 7(1) of that Act.

As amended by The Government of Wales Act 2006 (Consequential Modifications and Transitional Provisions) Order 2007 (SI 2007/1388), art 142; The Statutory Auditors and Third Country Auditors Regulations (SI 2007/3494), reg 42; The Companies Act 2006 (Amendment) (Accounts and Reports) Regulations 2008 (SI 2008/393), regs 3–5, 6(1)–(5), (10), 11; The Companies Act 2006 (Consequential Amendments etc) Order 2008 (SI 2008/948), Schedule 1, paras 249–250; The Companies Act 2006 (Amendment of Schedule 2) Order 2009 (SI 2009/202), art 2, Schedule, para 1; The Companies Act 2006 (Accounts, Reports and Audit) Regulations 2009 (SI 2009/1581); The Companies (Shareholders' Rights) Regulations 2009 (SI 2009/1632); The Companies Act 2006 (Consequential Amendments, Transitional Provisions and Savings) Order 2009 (SI 2009/1941), Schedule 1, para 260; The Companies (Share Capital and Acquisition by Company of its Own Shares) Regulations 2009 (SI 2009/2022); The Companies Act 2006 (Allotment of Shares and Right of Pre-emption) (Amendment) Regulations 2009 (SI 2009/2561).

Fraud Act 2006

Fraud

1 FRAUD

(1) A person is guilty of fraud if he is in breach of any of the sections listed in subsection (2) (which provide for different ways of committing the offence).

(2) The sections are—
- (a) section 2 (fraud by false representation),
- (b) section 3 (fraud by failing to disclose information), and
- (c) section 4 (fraud by abuse of position).

(3) A person who is guilty of fraud is liable—
- (a) on summary conviction, to imprisonment for a term not exceeding 12 months or to a fine not exceeding the statutory maximum (or to both);
- (b) on conviction on indictment, to imprisonment for a term not exceeding 10 years or to a fine (or to both).

2 FRAUD BY FALSE REPRESENTATION

(1) A person is in breach of this section if he—
- (a) dishonestly makes a false representation, and
- (b) intends, by making the representation—
  - (i) to make a gain for himself or another, or
  - (ii) to cause loss to another or to expose another to a risk of loss.

(2) A representation is false if—
- (a) it is untrue or misleading, and
- (b) the person making it knows that it is, or might be, untrue or misleading.

(3) "Representation" means any representation as to fact or law, including a representation as to the state of mind of—
- (a) the person making the representation, or
- (b) any other person.

(4) A representation may be express or implied.

(5) For the purposes of this section a representation may be regarded as made if it (or anything implying it) is submitted in any form to any system or device designed to receive, convey or respond to communications (with or without human intervention).

3 FRAUD BY FAILING TO DISCLOSE INFORMATION

A person is in breach of this section if he—

(a) dishonestly fails to disclose to another person information which he is under a legal duty to disclose, and

(b) intends, by failing to disclose the information—
  (i) to make a gain for himself or another, or
  (ii) to cause loss to another or to expose another to a risk of loss.

4 FRAUD BY ABUSE OF POSITION

(1) A person is in breach of this section if he—
  (a) occupies a position in which he is expected to safeguard, or not to act against, the financial interests of another person,
  (b) dishonestly abuses that position, and
  (c) intends, by means of the abuse of that position—
    (i) to make a gain for himself or another, or
    (ii) to cause loss to another or to expose another to a risk of loss.

(2) A person may be regarded as having abused his position even though his conduct consisted of an omission rather than an act.

5 "GAIN" AND "LOSS"

(1) The references to gain and loss in sections 2 to 4 are to be read in accordance with this section.

(2) "Gain" and "loss"—
  (a) extend only to gain or loss in money or other property;
  (b) include any such gain or loss whether temporary or permanent;
and "property" means any property whether real or personal (including things in action and other intangible property).

(3) "Gain" includes a gain by keeping what one has, as well as a gain by getting what one does not have.

(4) "Loss" includes a loss by not getting what one might get, as well as a loss by parting with what one has.

9 PARTICIPATING IN FRAUDULENT BUSINESS CARRIED ON BY SOLE TRADER ETC.

(1) A person is guilty of an offence if he is knowingly a party to the carrying on of a business to which this section applies.

(2) This section applies to a business which is carried on—

(a) by a person who is outside the reach of section 993 of the Companies Act 2006 (offence of fraudulent trading), and
(b) with intent to defraud creditors of any person or for any other fraudulent purpose.

(3) The following are within the reach of that section—
(a) a company (as defined in section 1(1) of the Companies Act 2006);
(b) a person to whom that section applies (with or without adaptations or modifications) as if the person were a company;
(c) a person exempted from the application of that section.

(5) "Fraudulent purpose" has the same meaning as in that section.

(6) A person guilty of an offence under this section is liable—
(a) on summary conviction, to imprisonment for a term not exceeding 12 months or to a fine not exceeding the statutory maximum (or to both);
(b) on conviction on indictment, to imprisonment for a term not exceeding 10 years or to a fine (or to both).

Supplementary

12 LIABILITY OF COMPANY OFFICERS FOR OFFENCES BY COMPANY

(1) Subsection (2) applies if an offence under this Act is committed by a body corporate.

(2) If the offence is proved to have been committed with the consent or connivance of—
(a) a director, manager, secretary or other similar officer of the body corporate, or
(b) a person who was purporting to act in any such capacity,
he (as well as the body corporate) is guilty of the offence and liable to be proceeded against and punished accordingly.

(3) If the affairs of a body corporate are managed by its members, subsection (2) applies in relation to the acts and defaults of a member in connection with his functions of management as if he were a director of the body corporate.

As amended by The Companies Act 2006 (Commencement No. 3, Consequential Amendments, Transitional Provisions and Savings) Order 2007 (SI 2007/2194), Schedule 4, para 111; The Companies Act 2006 (Consequential Amendments, Transitional Provisions and Savings) Order 2009 (SI 2009/1941), Schedule 1, para 257.

Bankruptcy and Diligence etc. (Scotland) Act 2007

Part 2 FLOATING CHARGES

Registration and creation etc.

37 REGISTER OF FLOATING CHARGES

(1) The Keeper of the Registers of Scotland (in this Part, the "Keeper") must establish and maintain a register to be known as the Register of Floating Charges.

(2) The Keeper must accept an application for registration of—

(a) any document delivered to the Keeper in pursuance of section 38, 41, 42, 43 or 44 of this Act; and
(b) any notice delivered to the Keeper in pursuance of section 39 or 45(2) of this Act,
provided that the application is accompanied by such information as the Keeper may require for the purposes of the registration.

(5) The Keeper must—
(a) make the Register of Floating Charges available for public inspection at all reasonable times;
(b) provide facilities for members of the public to obtain copies of the documents in the Register; and
(c) supply an extract of a document in the Register, certified as a true copy of the original, to any person requesting it.

38 CREATION OF FLOATING CHARGES

(1) It continues to be competent, for the purpose of securing any obligation to which this subsection applies, for a company to grant in favour of the creditor in the obligation a charge (known as a "floating charge") over all or any part of the property which may from time to time be comprised in the company's property and undertaking.

(2) Subsection (1) above applies to any debt or other obligation incurred or to be incurred by, or binding upon, the company or any other person.

(3) From the coming into force of this section, a floating charge is (subject to subsection (3A) and section 39 of this Act) created only when a document—
(a) granting a floating charge; and
(b) subscribed by the company granting the charge,
is registered in the Register of Floating Charges.

(3A) If a floating charge is granted in favour of a central institution, it is created only when the document granting the floating charge is executed by the company granting the charge.

(4) References in this Part to a document which grants a floating charge are to a document by means of which a floating charge is granted.

39 ADVANCE NOTICE OF FLOATING CHARGES

(1) Where a company proposes to grant a floating charge, the company and the person in whose favour the charge is to be granted may apply to have joint notice of the proposed charge registered in the Register of Floating Charges.

(2) Subsection (3) below applies where—
(a) a notice under subsection (1) above is registered in the Register of Floating Charges; and
(b) within 21 days of the notice being so registered, a document—
(i) granting a floating charge conforming with the particulars contained in the notice; and
(ii) subscribed by the company granting the charge,
is registered in the Register of Floating Charges.

(3) Where this subsection applies, the floating charge so created is to be treated as having been created when the notice under subsection (1) above was so registered.

(4) This section does not apply where a company proposes to grant a floating charge in favour of a central institution.

40 RANKING OF FLOATING CHARGES

(1) Subject to subsections (4) and (5) below, a floating charge—
(a) created on or after the coming into force of this section; and
(b) which has attached to all or any part of the property of a company,
ranks as described in subsection (2) below.

(2) The floating charge referred to in subsection (1) above—
(a) ranks with—
(i) any other floating charge which has attached to that property or any part of it; or
(ii) any fixed security over that property or any part of it,
according to date of creation; and
(b) ranks equally with any floating charge or fixed security referred to in paragraph (a) above which was created on the same date as the floating charge referred to in subsection (1) above.

(3) For the purposes of subsection (2) above—
(a) the date of creation of a fixed security is the date on which the right to the security was constituted as a real right; and
(b) the date of creation of a floating charge subsisting before the coming into force of this section is the date on which the instrument creating the charge was executed by the company granting the charge.

(4) Where all or any part of the property of a company is subject to both—
(a) a floating charge; and
(b) a fixed security arising by operation of law,
the fixed security has priority over the floating charge.

(5) Where the holder of a floating charge over all or any part of the property of a company has received intimation in writing of the subsequent creation of—
(a) another floating charge over the same property or any part of it; or
(b) a fixed security over the same property or any part of it,
the priority of ranking of the first-mentioned charge is restricted to security for the matters referred to in subsection (6) below.

(6) Those matters are—
(a) the present debt incurred (whenever payable);
(b) any future debt which, under the contract to which the charge relates, the holder is required to allow the debtor to incur;
(c) any interest due or to become due on the debts referred to in paragraphs (a) and (b) above;
(d) any expenses or outlays which may be reasonably incurred by the holder; and
(e) in the case of a floating charge to secure a contingent liability (other than a liability arising under any further debts incurred from time to time), the maximum sum to which the contingent liability is capable of amounting, whether or not it is contractually limited.

(7) Subsections (1) to (6) above, and any provision made under section 41(1) of this Act, are subject to sections 175 and 176A (provision for preferential debts and share of assets) of the Insolvency Act 1986 (c. 45).

41 RANKING CLAUSES

(1) The document granting a floating charge over all or any part of the property of a company may make provision regulating the order in which the charge ranks with any

other floating charge or any fixed security (including a future floating charge or fixed security) over that property or any part of it.

(2) Provision under subsection (1) above—
(a) may displace in whole or part—
(i) subsections (1) and (2) of section 40 of this Act;
(ii) subsections (5) and (6) of that section;
(b) may not affect the operation of subsection (4) of that section (whether as against subsections (1) and (2) of that section or other provision under subsection (1) above).

(3) Accordingly, subsections (1), (2), (5) and (6) of that section have effect subject to any provision made under subsection (1) above.

(4) Provision under subsection (1) above is not valid unless it is made with the consent of the holder of any subsisting floating charge, or any subsisting fixed security, which would be adversely affected by the provision.

(5) A document of consent for the purpose of subsection (4) above may be registered in the Register of Floating Charges.

42 ASSIGNATION OF FLOATING CHARGES

(1) A floating charge may be assigned (and the rights under it vested in the assignee) by the registration in the Register of Floating Charges of a document of assignation subscribed by the holder of the charge.

(2) An assignation under subsection (1) above may be in whole or to such extent as may be specified in the document of assignation.

(3) This section is without prejudice to any other enactment, or any rule of law, by virtue of which a floating charge may be assigned.

(4) This section does not apply where a floating charge is assigned (whether in whole or to a specified extent) to or by a central institution.

43 ALTERATION OF FLOATING CHARGES

(1) A document of alteration may alter (whether by addition, deletion or substitution of text or otherwise) the terms of a document granting a floating charge.

(2) If (and in so far as) an alteration to the terms of a document granting a floating charge concerns—
(a) the ranking of the charge with any other floating charge or any fixed security; or
(b) the specification of—
(i) the property that is subject to the charge; or
(ii) the obligations that are secured by the charge,
the alteration is not valid unless subsection (3) below is satisfied.

(3) This subsection is satisfied if the alteration is made by a document of alteration which is—
(a) subscribed by—
(i) the company which granted the charge;
(ii) the holder of the charge; and
(iii) the holder of any other subsisting floating charge, or any subsisting fixed security, which would be adversely affected by the alteration; and
(b) registered in the Register of Floating Charges.

(4) Paragraph (a)(i) of subsection (3) above does not apply in respect of an alteration which—

(a) relates only to the ranking of the floating charge first-mentioned in that subsection with any other floating charge or any fixed security; and
(b) does not adversely affect the interests of the company which granted the charge.

(4A) Paragraph (b) of subsection (3) above does not apply in respect of an alteration if—
(a) the holder of the floating charge is a central institution, or
(b) the holder of the floating charge is not a central institution but the alteration is to be made in connection with a floating charge which is held (or which has been or is to be held) by a central institution.

(5) The granting, by the holder of a floating charge, of consent to the release from the scope of the charge of any particular property, or class of property, which is subject to the charge is to be treated as constituting an alteration—
(a) to the terms of the document granting the charge; and
(b) as to the specification of the property that is subject to the charge.

(6) For the purpose of subsection (5) above, property is not to be regarded as released from the scope of a floating charge by reason only of its ceasing to be the property of the company which granted the charge.

44 DISCHARGE OF FLOATING CHARGES

(1) A floating charge may be discharged by the registration in the Register of Floating Charges of a document of discharge subscribed by the holder of the charge.

(2) A discharge under subsection (1) above may be in whole or to such extent as may be specified in the document of discharge.

(3) This section is without prejudice to any other means by which a floating charge may be discharged or extinguished.

(4) This section does not apply where the floating charge to be discharged (whether in whole or to a specified extent) is or has been held by a central institution.

45 EFFECT OF FLOATING CHARGES ON WINDING UP

(1) Where a company goes into liquidation, a floating charge created over property of the company attaches to the property to which it relates.

(2) But, in a case mentioned in subsection (7)(a) below, there is no attachment under subsection (1) above until such time as a notice of attachment is registered in the Register of Floating Charges on the application of the holder of the charge.

(3) The attachment of a floating charge to property under subsection (1) above is subject to the rights of any person who—
(a) has effectually executed diligence on the property to which the charge relates or any part of it;
(b) holds over that property or any part of it a fixed security ranking in priority to the floating charge; or
(c) holds over that property or any part of it another floating charge so ranking.

(4) Interest accrues in respect of a floating charge which has attached to property until payment is made of any sum due under the charge.

(5) Part IV, except section 185, of the Insolvency Act 1986 has (subject to subsection (1) above) effect in relation to a floating charge as if the charge were a fixed security over the

property to which it has attached in respect of the principal of the debt or obligation to which it relates and any interest due or to become due on it.

(6) Subsections (1) to (5) above do not affect the operation of—

(a) sections 53(7) and 54(6) (attachment of floating charge on appointment of receiver) of the Insolvency Act 1986;

(b) sections 175 and 176A of that Act; or

...

(7) For the purposes of this section, reference to a company going into liquidation—

(a) in a case where a court of a member State has under the EC Regulation jurisdiction as respects the company which granted the relevant floating charge, means the opening of insolvency proceedings in that State;

(b) in any other case, is to be construed in accordance with section 247(2) and (3) of the Insolvency Act 1986 (c. 45).

(8) In subsection (7)(a) above—

"the EC Regulation" is the Regulation of the Council of the European Union published as Council Regulation (EC) No 1346/2000 on insolvency proceedings;

"court" is to be construed in accordance with Article 2(d) of that Regulation;

"insolvency proceedings" is to be construed in accordance with Article 2(a) of that Regulation;

"member State" means a member State of the European Union apart from the United Kingdom.

46 REPEALS, SAVINGS AND TRANSITIONAL ARRANGEMENTS

(2) Nothing in this Part (except sections 40 and 41 so far as they concern the ranking of floating charges subsisting immediately before the coming into force of this section) affects the validity or operation of floating charges subsisting before the coming into force of this section.

47 INTERPRETATION

In this Part—

"central institution" means—

(a) the Bank of England,

(b) the central bank of a country or territory outside the United Kingdom, or

(c) the European Central Bank;

"company" means an incorporated company (whether or not a company as defined in section 1(1) of the Companies Act 2006);

"fixed security", in relation to any property of a company, means any security (other than a floating charge or a charge having the character of a floating charge) which on the winding up of the company in Scotland would be treated as an effective security over that property including, in particular, a heritable security (within the meaning of section 9(8) of the Conveyancing and Feudal Reform (Scotland) Act 1970 (c. 35)).

As amended by The Banking Act 2009, s 253; The Companies Act 2006 (Consequential Amendments, Transitional Provisions and Savings) Order 2009 (SI 2009/1941), Schedule 1, para 267.

Corporate Manslaughter and Corporate Homicide Act 2007

Corporate manslaughter and corporate homicide

1 THE OFFENCE

(1) An organisation to which this section applies is guilty of an offence if the way in which its activities are managed or organised—
(a) causes a person's death, and
(b) amounts to a gross breach of a relevant duty of care owed by the organisation to the deceased.

(2) The organisations to which this section applies are—
(a) a corporation;
. . .
(d) a partnership, or a trade union or employers' association, that is an employer.

(3) An organisation is guilty of an offence under this section only if the way in which its activities are managed or organised by its senior management is a substantial element in the breach referred to in subsection (1).

(4) For the purposes of this Act—
(a) "relevant duty of care" has the meaning given by section 2 . . . ;
(b) a breach of a duty of care by an organisation is a "gross" breach if the conduct alleged to amount to a breach of that duty falls far below what can reasonably be expected of the organisation in the circumstances;
(c) "senior management", in relation to an organisation, means the persons who play significant roles in—
(i) the making of decisions about how the whole or a substantial part of its activities are to be managed or organised, or
(ii) the actual managing or organising of the whole or a substantial part of those activities.

(5) The offence under this section is called—
(a) corporate manslaughter, in so far as it is an offence under the law of England and Wales or Northern Ireland;
(b) corporate homicide, in so far as it is an offence under the law of Scotland.

(6) An organisation that is guilty of corporate manslaughter or corporate homicide is liable on conviction on indictment to a fine.

(7) The offence of corporate homicide is indictable only in the High Court of Justiciary.

Relevant duty of care

2 MEANING OF "RELEVANT DUTY OF CARE"

(1) A "relevant duty of care", in relation to an organisation, means any of the following duties owed by it under the law of negligence—
   (a) a duty owed to its employees or to other persons working for the organisation or performing services for it;
   (b) a duty owed as occupier of premises;
   (c) a duty owed in connection with—
      (i) the supply by the organisation of goods or services (whether for consideration or not),
      (ii) the carrying on by the organisation of any construction or maintenance operations,
      (iii) the carrying on by the organisation of any other activity on a commercial basis, or
      (iv) the use or keeping by the organisation of any plant, vehicle or other thing;

   . . .

. . .

(4) A reference in subsection (1) to a duty owed under the law of negligence includes a reference to a duty that would be owed under the law of negligence but for any statutory provision under which liability is imposed in place of liability under that law.

(5) For the purposes of this Act, whether a particular organisation owes a duty of care to a particular individual is a question of law.
The judge must make any findings of fact necessary to decide that question.

(6) For the purposes of this Act there is to be disregarded—
   (a) any rule of the common law that has the effect of preventing a duty of care from being owed by one person to another by reason of the fact that they are jointly engaged in unlawful conduct;
   (b) any such rule that has the effect of preventing a duty of care from being owed to a person by reason of his acceptance of a risk of harm.

(7) In this section—

"construction or maintenance operations" means operations of any of the following descriptions—
   (a) construction, installation, alteration, extension, improvement, repair, maintenance, decoration, cleaning, demolition or dismantling of—
      (i) any building or structure,
      (ii) anything else that forms, or is to form, part of the land, or
      (iii) any plant, vehicle or other thing;
   (b) operations that form an integral part of, or are preparatory to, or are for rendering complete, any operations within paragraph (a);

. . .

Gross breach

8 FACTORS FOR JURY

(1) This section applies where—
   (a) it is established that an organisation owed a relevant duty of care to a person, and
   (b) it falls to the jury to decide whether there was a gross breach of that duty.

(2) The jury must consider whether the evidence shows that the organisation failed to comply with any health and safety legislation that relates to the alleged breach, and if so—
(a) how serious that failure was;
(b) how much of a risk of death it posed.

(3) The jury may also—
(a) consider the extent to which the evidence shows that there were attitudes, policies, systems or accepted practices within the organisation that were likely to have encouraged any such failure as is mentioned in subsection (2), or to have produced tolerance of it;
(b) have regard to any health and safety guidance that relates to the alleged breach.

(4) This section does not prevent the jury from having regard to any other matters they consider relevant.

(5) In this section "health and safety guidance" means any code, guidance, manual or similar publication that is concerned with health and safety matters and is made or issued (under a statutory provision or otherwise) by an authority responsible for the enforcement of any health and safety legislation.

Remedial orders and publicity orders

9 POWER TO ORDER BREACH ETC TO BE REMEDIED

(1) A court before which an organisation is convicted of corporate manslaughter or corporate homicide may make an order (a "remedial order") requiring the organisation to take specified steps to remedy—
(a) the breach mentioned in section 1(1) ("the relevant breach");
(b) any matter that appears to the court to have resulted from the relevant breach and to have been a cause of the death;
(c) any deficiency, as regards health and safety matters, in the organisation's policies, systems or practices of which the relevant breach appears to the court to be an indication.

(2) A remedial order may be made only on an application by the prosecution specifying the terms of the proposed order.
Any such order must be on such terms (whether those proposed or others) as the court considers appropriate having regard to any representations made, and any evidence adduced, in relation to that matter by the prosecution or on behalf of the organisation.

(3) Before making an application for a remedial order the prosecution must consult such enforcement authority or authorities as it considers appropriate having regard to the nature of the relevant breach.

(4) A remedial order—
(a) must specify a period within which the steps referred to in subsection (1) are to be taken;
(b) may require the organisation to supply to an enforcement authority consulted under subsection (3), within a specified period, evidence that those steps have been taken.
A period specified under this subsection may be extended or further extended by order of the court on an application made before the end of that period or extended period.

(5) An organisation that fails to comply with a remedial order is guilty of an offence, and liable on conviction on indictment to a fine.

10 POWER TO ORDER CONVICTION ETC TO BE PUBLICISED

(1) A court before which an organisation is convicted of corporate manslaughter or corporate homicide may make an order (a "publicity order") requiring the organisation to publicise in a specified manner—
  (a) the fact that it has been convicted of the offence;
  (b) specified particulars of the offence;
  (c) the amount of any fine imposed;
  (d) the terms of any remedial order made.

(2) In deciding on the terms of a publicity order that it is proposing to make, the court must—
  (a) ascertain the views of such enforcement authority or authorities (if any) as it considers appropriate, and
  (b) have regard to any representations made by the prosecution or on behalf of the organisation.

(3) A publicity order—
  (a) must specify a period within which the requirements referred to in subsection (1) are to be complied with;
  (b) may require the organisation to supply to any enforcement authority whose views have been ascertained under subsection (2), within a specified period, evidence that those requirements have been complied with.

(4) An organisation that fails to comply with a publicity order is guilty of an offence, and liable on conviction on indictment to a fine.

Application to particular categories of organisation

...

14 APPLICATION TO PARTNERSHIPS

(1) For the purposes of this Act a partnership is to be treated as owing whatever duties of care it would owe if it were a body corporate.

(2) Proceedings for an offence under this Act alleged to have been committed by a partnership are to be brought in the name of the partnership (and not in that of any of its members).

(3) A fine imposed on a partnership on its conviction of an offence under this Act is to be paid out of the funds of the partnership.

(4) This section does not apply to a partnership that is a legal person under the law by which it is governed.

Miscellaneous

...

17 DPP'S CONSENT REQUIRED FOR PROCEEDINGS

Proceedings for an offence of corporate manslaughter—

(a) may not be instituted in England and Wales without the consent of the Director of Public Prosecutions;

(b) may not be instituted in Northern Ireland without the consent of the Director of Public Prosecutions for Northern Ireland.

18 NO INDIVIDUAL LIABILITY

(1) An individual cannot be guilty of aiding, abetting, counselling or procuring the commission of an offence of corporate manslaughter.

(1A) An individual cannot be guilty of an offence under Part 2 of the Serious Crime Act 2007 (encouraging or assisting crime) by reference to an offence of corporate manslaughter.

(2) An individual cannot be guilty of aiding, abetting, counselling or procuring, or being art and part in, the commission of an offence of corporate homicide.

19 CONVICTIONS UNDER THIS ACT AND UNDER HEALTH AND SAFETY LEGISLATION

(1) Where in the same proceedings there is—
   (a) a charge of corporate manslaughter or corporate homicide arising out of a particular set of circumstances, and
   (b) a charge against the same defendant of a health and safety offence arising out of some or all of those circumstances,

the jury may, if the interests of justice so require, be invited to return a verdict on each charge.

(2) An organisation that has been convicted of corporate manslaughter or corporate homicide arising out of a particular set of circumstances may, if the interests of justice so require, be charged with a health and safety offence arising out of some or all of those circumstances.

(3) In this section "health and safety offence" means an offence under any health and safety legislation.

20 ABOLITION OF LIABILITY OF CORPORATIONS FOR MANSLAUGHTER AT COMMON LAW

The common law offence of manslaughter by gross negligence is abolished in its application to corporations, and in any application it has to other organisations to which section 1 applies.

General and supplemental

25 INTERPRETATION

In this Act—

...

- "corporation" does not include a corporation sole but includes any body corporate wherever incorporated;
- "employee" means an individual who works under a contract of employment or apprenticeship (whether express or implied and, if express, whether oral or in writing), and related expressions are to be construed accordingly; ...
- "employers' association" has the meaning given by section 122 of the Trade Union and Labour Relations (Consolidation) Act 1992 (c. 52) or Article 4 of the Industrial Relations (Northern Ireland) Order 1992 (S.I. 1992/807 (N.I. 5));
- "enforcement authority" means an authority responsible for the enforcement of any health and safety legislation;
- "health and safety legislation" means any statutory provision dealing with health and safety matters, including in particular provision contained in the Health and Safety at

Work etc. Act 1974 (c. 37) or the Health and Safety at Work (Northern Ireland) Order 1978 (S.I. 1978/1039 (N.I. 9));

...

- "partnership" means—
  (a) a partnership within the Partnership Act 1890 (c. 39), or
  (b) a limited partnership registered under the Limited Partnerships Act 1907 (c. 24),
  or a firm or entity of a similar character formed under the law of a country or territory outside the United Kingdom;

...

- "premises" includes land, buildings and moveable structures;

...

- "publicity order" means an order under section 10(1);
- "remedial order" means an order under section 9(1);
- "statutory provision", except in section 15, means provision contained in, or in an instrument made under, any Act, any Act of the Scottish Parliament or any Northern Ireland legislation;
- "trade union" has the meaning given by section 1 of the Trade Union and Labour Relations (Consolidation) Act 1992 (c. 52) or Article 3 of the Industrial Relations (Northern Ireland) Order 1992 (S.I. 1992/807 (N.I. 5)).

...

As amended by the Serious Crime Act 2007, s 62.

The Companies (Disclosure of Auditor Remuneration and Liability Limitation Agreements) Regulations 2008 (SI 2008/489)

3 INTERPRETATION

(1) In these Regulations—

"the Act" means the Companies Act 2006;

"associated pension scheme" means, in relation to a company, a scheme for the provision of benefits for or in respect of directors or employees (or former directors or employees) of the company or any subsidiary of the company where—

(a) the benefits consist of or include any pension, lump sum, gratuity or other like benefit given or to be given on retirement or on death or in anticipation of retirement or, in connection with past service, after retirement or death; and

(b) either—

  (i) a majority of the trustees are appointed by, or by a person acting on behalf of, the company or a subsidiary of the company; or

  (ii) the company, or a subsidiary of the company, exercises a dominant influence over the appointment of the auditor (if any) of the scheme;

"parent" means a parent undertaking (as defined in section 1162 of the Act) which is a body corporate, and "parent company" is a parent which is a company;

"principal terms" has the meaning in section 536(4) of the Act;

"remuneration" includes payments in respect of expenses and benefits in kind;

"subsidiary" means a subsidiary undertaking (as defined in section 1162 of the Act) which is a body corporate, and "subsidiary company" is a subsidiary which is a company.

(2) For the purposes of these Regulations—
 (a) a company is small in relation to a financial year if the small companies regime as defined in section 381 of the Act applies to it for that year;
 (b) a company is medium-sized in relation to a financial year if—
  (i) it qualifies as medium-sized in relation to that year under section 465 of the Act; and
  (ii) it is not excluded from being medium-sized under section 467(1) of the Act;
 (c) references to an associate of a company are references to—
  (i) any subsidiary of that company, other than a subsidiary in respect of which severe long-term restrictions substantially hinder the exercise of the rights of the company over the assets or management of that subsidiary; and
  (ii) any scheme which is an associated pension scheme in relation to that company?...
 ...

Part 2 DISCLOSURE OF REMUNERATION

4 DISCLOSURE OF REMUNERATION: SMALL AND MEDIUM-SIZED COMPANIES

(1) A note to the annual accounts of a small or medium-sized company must disclose the amount of any remuneration receivable by the company's auditor for the auditing of those accounts.

(2) Where the remuneration includes benefits in kind, the nature and estimated money-value of those benefits must also be disclosed in a note.

(3) Where more than one person has been appointed as a company's auditor in respect of the period to which the accounts relate, separate disclosure is required in respect of the remuneration of each such person.

(4) For the purposes of section 1224 of the Act, the functions of the Secretary of State under Part 42 of the Act include (without prejudice to the generality of that section) consideration of the total remuneration receivable by the auditor of a medium-sized company for the supply by the auditor to the company of each of the following types of service where that remuneration is not disclosed in a note to the company's annual accounts—
 (a) assurance services other than the auditing of the company's accounts;
 (b) tax advisory services;
 (c) other services.

5 DISCLOSURE OF REMUNERATION: OTHER COMPANIES

(1) A note to the annual accounts of a company which is not a small or medium-sized company must disclose the amount of—
 (a) any remuneration receivable by the company's auditor for the auditing of those accounts; and

(b) subject to paragraph (6) and regulation 6(2), any remuneration receivable in respect of the period to which the accounts relate by—
  (i) the company's auditor; or
  (ii) any person who was, at any time during the period to which the accounts relate, an associate of the company's auditor,

for the supply of other services to the company or any associate of the company.

(2) Where the remuneration includes benefits in kind, the nature and estimated money-value of those benefits must also be disclosed in a note.

(3) Separate disclosure is required in respect of the auditing of the accounts in question and of each type of service specified in Schedule 2, but not in respect of each service falling within a type of service.

(4) Separate disclosure is required in respect of services supplied to the company and its subsidiaries on the one hand and to associated pension schemes on the other.

(5) Where more than one person has been appointed as a company's auditor in respect of the period to which the accounts relate, separate disclosure is required in respect of the remuneration of each such person and his associates.

(6) Disclosure is not required of remuneration receivable for the supply of services falling within paragraph 10 of Schedule 2 supplied by a distant associate of the company's auditor where the total remuneration receivable for all of those services supplied by that associate does not exceed either—
  (a) £10,000, or
  (b) 1% of the total audit remuneration received by the company's auditor in the most recent financial year of the auditor which ended no later than the end of the financial year of the company to which the accounts relate.

6 GROUP ACCOUNTS

(1) Group accounts must comply with regulation 5(1)(b) as if the undertakings included in the consolidation were a single company except where the group—
  (a) qualifies as small or medium-sized under section 383 or 466 of the Act; and
  (b) is not an ineligible group under section 384(2) or 467(2) of the Act.

(2) A note to the individual accounts of—
  (a) a parent company which is required to prepare and does prepare group accounts in accordance with the Act; and
  (b) a subsidiary company where its parent is required to prepare and does prepare group accounts in accordance with the Act and the company is included in the consolidation;

does not have to disclose the information required by regulation 5(1)(b) if the conditions in paragraph (3) are satisfied.

(3) Those conditions are that—
  (a) the group accounts are required to comply with paragraph (1); and
  (b) the individual accounts state that the group accounts are so required.

7 DUTY OF AUDITOR TO SUPPLY INFORMATION

The auditor of a company must supply the directors of the company with such information as is necessary to enable the disclosure required by regulation 5(1)(b) or 6(1) to be made.

Part 3 LIABILITY LIMITATION AGREEMENTS

8 DISCLOSURE OF LIABILITY LIMITATION AGREEMENTS

(1) A company which has entered into a liability limitation agreement must disclose—
(a) its principal terms; and
(b) the date of the resolution approving the agreement or the agreement's principal terms or, in the case of a private company, the date of the resolution waiving the need for such approval,
in a note to the company's annual accounts.

(2) The annual accounts in which the disclosure required by paragraph (1) must be made shall be those for the financial year to which the agreement relates unless the agreement was entered into too late for it to be reasonably practicable for the disclosure to be made in those accounts.

(3) If the agreement was entered into too late for it to be reasonably practicable for the disclosure required by paragraph (1) to be made in the accounts for the financial year to which the agreement relates, the disclosure shall be made in a note to the company's next following annual accounts.

SCHEDULE 2 TYPE OF SERVICE IN RESPECT OF WHICH DISCLOSURE IS TO BE MADE

1. The auditing of accounts of associates of the company pursuant to legislation (including that of countries and territories outside the United Kingdom).
2. Other services supplied pursuant to such legislation.
3. Other services relating to taxation.
4. Services relating to information technology.
5. Internal audit services.
6. Valuation and actuarial services.
7. Services relating to litigation.
8. Services relating to recruitment and remuneration.
9. Services relating to corporate finance transactions entered into or proposed to be entered into on behalf of the company or any of its associates.
10. All other services.

The Companies (Model Articles) Regulations 2008 (SI 2008/3229)

1 CITATION AND COMMENCEMENT

These Regulations may be cited as the Companies (Model Articles) Regulations 2008 and come into force on 1st October 2009.

2 MODEL ARTICLES FOR PRIVATE COMPANIES LIMITED BY SHARES

Schedule 1 to these Regulations prescribes the model articles of association for private companies limited by shares.

4 MODEL ARTICLES FOR PUBLIC COMPANIES

Schedule 3 to these Regulations prescribes the model articles of association for public companies.

SCHEDULE 1 MODEL ARTICLES FOR PRIVATE COMPANIES LIMITED BY SHARES

Part 1 INTERPRETATION AND LIMITATION OF LIABILITY

1 DEFINED TERMS

In the articles, unless the context requires otherwise—

"articles" means the company's articles of association;

...

"chairman" has the meaning given in article 12;

"chairman of the meeting" has the meaning given in article 39;

"Companies Acts" means the Companies Acts (as defined in section 2 of the Companies Act 2006), in so far as they apply to the company;

"director" means a director of the company, and includes any person occupying the position of director, by whatever name called;

...

"document" includes, unless otherwise specified, any document sent or supplied in electronic form;

"electronic form" has the meaning given in section 1168 of the Companies Act 2006;

"fully paid" in relation to a share, means that the nominal value and any premium to be paid to the company in respect of that share have been paid to the company;

"hard copy form" has the meaning given in section 1168 of the Companies Act 2006;

"holder" in relation to shares means the person whose name is entered in the register of members as the holder of the shares;

"instrument" means a document in hard copy form;

"ordinary resolution" has the meaning given in section 282 of the Companies Act 2006;

"paid" means paid or credited as paid;

"participate", in relation to a directors' meeting, has the meaning given in article 10;

"proxy notice" has the meaning given in article 45;

"shareholder" means a person who is the holder of a share;

"shares" means shares in the company;

"special resolution" has the meaning given in section 283 of the Companies Act 2006;

"subsidiary" has the meaning given in section 1159 of the Companies Act 2006;

"transmittee" means a person entitled to a share by reason of the death or bankruptcy of a shareholder or otherwise by operation of law; and

"writing" means the representation or reproduction of words, symbols or other information in a visible form by any method or combination of methods, whether sent or supplied in electronic form or otherwise.

Unless the context otherwise requires, other words or expressions contained in these articles bear the same meaning as in the Companies Act 2006 as in force on the date when these articles become binding on the company.

2 LIABILITY OF MEMBERS

The liability of the members is limited to the amount, if any, unpaid on the shares held by them.

Part 2 DIRECTORS

DIRECTORS' POWERS AND RESPONSIBILITIES

3 DIRECTORS' GENERAL AUTHORITY

Subject to the articles, the directors are responsible for the management of the company's business, for which purpose they may exercise all the powers of the company.

4 SHAREHOLDERS' RESERVE POWER

(1) The shareholders may, by special resolution, direct the directors to take, or refrain from taking, specified action.

(2) No such special resolution invalidates anything which the directors have done before the passing of the resolution.

5 DIRECTORS MAY DELEGATE

(1) Subject to the articles, the directors may delegate any of the powers which are conferred on them under the articles—
(a) to such person or committee;
(b) by such means (including by power of attorney);
(c) to such an extent;
(d) in relation to such matters or territories; and
(e) on such terms and conditions;
as they think fit.

(2) If the directors so specify, any such delegation may authorise further delegation of the directors' powers by any person to whom they are delegated.

(3) The directors may revoke any delegation in whole or part, or alter its terms and conditions.

6 COMMITTEES

(1) Committees to which the directors delegate any of their powers must follow procedures which are based as far as they are applicable on those provisions of the articles which govern the taking of decisions by directors.

(2) The directors may make rules of procedure for all or any committees, which prevail over rules derived from the articles if they are not consistent with them.

DECISION-MAKING BY DIRECTORS

7 DIRECTORS TO TAKE DECISIONS COLLECTIVELY

(1) The general rule about decision-making by directors is that any decision of the directors must be either a majority decision at a meeting or a decision taken in accordance with article 8.

(2) If—
(a) the company only has one director, and
(b) no provision of the articles requires it to have more than one director,
the general rule does not apply, and the director may take decisions without regard to any of the provisions of the articles relating to directors' decision-making.

8 UNANIMOUS DECISIONS

(1) A decision of the directors is taken in accordance with this article when all eligible directors indicate to each other by any means that they share a common view on a matter.

(2) Such a decision may take the form of a resolution in writing, copies of which have been signed by each eligible director or to which each eligible director has otherwise indicated agreement in writing.

(3) References in this article to eligible directors are to directors who would have been entitled to vote on the matter had it been proposed as a resolution at a directors' meeting.

(4) A decision may not be taken in accordance with this article if the eligible directors would not have formed a quorum at such a meeting.

9 CALLING A DIRECTORS' MEETING

(1) Any director may call a directors' meeting by giving notice of the meeting to the directors or by authorising the company secretary (if any) to give such notice.

(2) Notice of any directors' meeting must indicate—
(a) its proposed date and time;
(b) where it is to take place; and
(c) if it is anticipated that directors participating in the meeting will not be in the same place, how it is proposed that they should communicate with each other during the meeting.

(3) Notice of a directors' meeting must be given to each director, but need not be in writing.

(4) Notice of a directors' meeting need not be given to directors who waive their entitlement to notice of that meeting, by giving notice to that effect to the company not more than 7 days after the date on which the meeting is held. Where such notice is given after the meeting has been held, that does not affect the validity of the meeting, or of any business conducted at it.

10 PARTICIPATION IN DIRECTORS' MEETINGS

(1) Subject to the articles, directors participate in a directors' meeting, or part of a directors' meeting, when—
(a) the meeting has been called and takes place in accordance with the articles, and
(b) they can each communicate to the others any information or opinions they have on any particular item of the business of the meeting.

(2) In determining whether directors are participating in a directors' meeting, it is irrelevant where any director is or how they communicate with each other.

(3) If all the directors participating in a meeting are not in the same place, they may decide that the meeting is to be treated as taking place wherever any of them is.

11 QUORUM FOR DIRECTORS' MEETINGS

(1) At a directors' meeting, unless a quorum is participating, no proposal is to be voted on, except a proposal to call another meeting.

(2) The quorum for directors' meetings may be fixed from time to time by a decision of the directors, but it must never be less than two, and unless otherwise fixed it is two.

(3) If the total number of directors for the time being is less than the quorum required, the directors must not take any decision other than a decision—
(a) to appoint further directors, or
(b) to call a general meeting so as to enable the shareholders to appoint further directors.

12 CHAIRING OF DIRECTORS' MEETINGS

(1) The directors may appoint a director to chair their meetings.

(2) The person so appointed for the time being is known as the chairman.

(3) The directors may terminate the chairman's appointment at any time.

(4) If the chairman is not participating in a directors' meeting within ten minutes of the time at which it was to start, the participating directors must appoint one of themselves to chair it.

13 CASTING VOTE

(1) If the numbers of votes for and against a proposal are equal, the chairman or other director chairing the meeting has a casting vote.

(2) But this does not apply if, in accordance with the articles, the chairman or other director is not to be counted as participating in the decision-making process for quorum or voting purposes.

14 CONFLICTS OF INTEREST

(1) If a proposed decision of the directors is concerned with an actual or proposed transaction or arrangement with the company in which a director is interested, that director is not to be counted as participating in the decision-making process for quorum or voting purposes.

(2) But if paragraph (3) applies, a director who is interested in an actual or proposed transaction or arrangement with the company is to be counted as participating in the decision-making process for quorum and voting purposes.

(3) This paragraph applies when—
 (a) the company by ordinary resolution disapplies the provision of the articles which would otherwise prevent a director from being counted as participating in the decision-making process;
 (b) the director's interest cannot reasonably be regarded as likely to give rise to a conflict of interest; or
 (c) the director's conflict of interest arises from a permitted cause.

(4) For the purposes of this article, the following are permitted causes—
 (a) a guarantee given, or to be given, by or to a director in respect of an obligation incurred by or on behalf of the company or any of its subsidiaries;
 (b) subscription, or an agreement to subscribe, for shares or other securities of the company or any of its subsidiaries, or to underwrite, sub-underwrite, or guarantee subscription for any such shares or securities; and
 (c) arrangements pursuant to which benefits are made available to employees and directors or former employees and directors of the company or any of its subsidiaries which do not provide special benefits for directors or former directors.

(5) For the purposes of this article, references to proposed decisions and decision-making processes include any directors' meeting or part of a directors' meeting.

(6) Subject to paragraph (7), if a question arises at a meeting of directors or of a committee of directors as to the right of a director to participate in the meeting (or part of the meeting) for voting or quorum purposes, the question may, before the conclusion of the meeting, be referred to the chairman whose ruling in relation to any director other than the chairman is to be final and conclusive.

(7) If any question as to the right to participate in the meeting (or part of the meeting) should arise in respect of the chairman, the question is to be decided by a decision of the directors at that meeting, for which purpose the chairman is not to be counted as participating in the meeting (or that part of the meeting) for voting or quorum purposes.

15 RECORDS OF DECISIONS TO BE KEPT

The directors must ensure that the company keeps a record, in writing, for at least 10 years from the date of the decision recorded, of every unanimous or majority decision taken by the directors.

16 DIRECTORS' DISCRETION TO MAKE FURTHER RULES

Subject to the articles, the directors may make any rule which they think fit about how they take decisions, and about how such rules are to be recorded or communicated to directors.

APPOINTMENT OF DIRECTORS

17 METHODS OF APPOINTING DIRECTORS

(1) Any person who is willing to act as a director, and is permitted by law to do so, may be appointed to be a director—
 (a) by ordinary resolution, or
 (b) by a decision of the directors.

(2) In any case where, as a result of death, the company has no shareholders and no directors, the personal representatives of the last shareholder to have died have the right, by notice in writing, to appoint a person to be a director.

(3) For the purposes of paragraph (2), where 2 or more shareholders die in circumstances rendering it uncertain who was the last to die, a younger shareholder is deemed to have survived an older shareholder.

18 TERMINATION OF DIRECTOR'S APPOINTMENT

A person ceases to be a director as soon as—

(a) that person ceases to be a director by virtue of any provision of the Companies Act 2006 or is prohibited from being a director by law;

(b) a bankruptcy order is made against that person;

(c) a composition is made with that person's creditors generally in satisfaction of that person's debts;

(d) a registered medical practitioner who is treating that person gives a written opinion to the company stating that that person has become physically or mentally incapable of acting as a director and may remain so for more than three months;

(e) by reason of that person's mental health, a court makes an order which wholly or partly prevents that person from personally exercising any powers or rights which that person would otherwise have;

(f) notification is received by the company from the director that the director is resigning from office, and such resignation has taken effect in accordance with its terms.

19 DIRECTORS' REMUNERATION

(1) Directors may undertake any services for the company that the directors decide.

(2) Directors are entitled to such remuneration as the directors determine—
 (a) for their services to the company as directors, and
 (b) for any other service which they undertake for the company.

(3) Subject to the articles, a director's remuneration may—
 (a) take any form, and
 (b) include any arrangements in connection with the payment of a pension, allowance or gratuity, or any death, sickness or disability benefits, to or in respect of that director.

(4) Unless the directors decide otherwise, directors' remuneration accrues from day to day.

(5) Unless the directors decide otherwise, directors are not accountable to the company for any remuneration which they receive as directors or other officers or employees of the company's subsidiaries or of any other body corporate in which the company is interested.

20 DIRECTORS' EXPENSES

The company may pay any reasonable expenses which the directors properly incur in connection with their attendance at—

(a) meetings of directors or committees of directors,

(b) general meetings, or

(c) separate meetings of the holders of any class of shares or of debentures of the company,

or otherwise in connection with the exercise of their powers and the discharge of their responsibilities in relation to the company.

Part 3 SHARES AND DISTRIBUTIONS

SHARES

21 ALL SHARES TO BE FULLY PAID UP

(1) No share is to be issued for less than the aggregate of its nominal value and any premium to be paid to the company in consideration for its issue.

(2) This does not apply to shares taken on the formation of the company by the subscribers to the company's memorandum.

22 POWERS TO ISSUE DIFFERENT CLASSES OF SHARE

(1) Subject to the articles, but without prejudice to the rights attached to any existing share, the company may issue shares with such rights or restrictions as may be determined by ordinary resolution.

(2) The company may issue shares which are to be redeemed, or are liable to be redeemed at the option of the company or the holder, and the directors may determine the terms, conditions and manner of redemption of any such shares.

23 COMPANY NOT BOUND BY LESS THAN ABSOLUTE INTERESTS

Except as required by law, no person is to be recognised by the company as holding any share upon any trust, and except as otherwise required by law or the articles, the company is not in any way to be bound by or recognise any interest in a share other than the holder's absolute ownership of it and all the rights attaching to it.

24 SHARE CERTIFICATES

(1) The company must issue each shareholder, free of charge, with one or more certificates in respect of the shares which that shareholder holds.

(2) Every certificate must specify—
(a) in respect of how many shares, of what class, it is issued;
(b) the nominal value of those shares;

(c) that the shares are fully paid; and
(d) any distinguishing numbers assigned to them.

(3) No certificate may be issued in respect of shares of more than one class.

(4) If more than one person holds a share, only one certificate may be issued in respect of it.

(5) Certificates must—
(a) have affixed to them the company's common seal, or
(b) be otherwise executed in accordance with the Companies Acts.

26 SHARE TRANSFERS

(1) Shares may be transferred by means of an instrument of transfer in any usual form or any other form approved by the directors, which is executed by or on behalf of the transferor.

(2) No fee may be charged for registering any instrument of transfer or other document relating to or affecting the title to any share.

(3) The company may retain any instrument of transfer which is registered.

(4) The transferor remains the holder of a share until the transferee's name is entered in the register of members as holder of it.

(5) The directors may refuse to register the transfer of a share, and if they do so, the instrument of transfer must be returned to the transferee with the notice of refusal unless they suspect that the proposed transfer may be fraudulent.

27 TRANSMISSION OF SHARES

(1) If title to a share passes to a transmittee, the company may only recognise the transmittee as having any title to that share.

(2) A transmittee who produces such evidence of entitlement to shares as the directors may properly require—
(a) may, subject to the articles, choose either to become the holder of those shares or to have them transferred to another person, and
(b) subject to the articles, and pending any transfer of the shares to another person, has the same rights as the holder had.

(3) But transmittees do not have the right to attend or vote at a general meeting, or agree to a proposed written resolution, in respect of shares to which they are entitled, by reason of the holder's death or bankruptcy or otherwise, unless they become the holders of those shares.

DIVIDENDS AND OTHER DISTRIBUTIONS

30 PROCEDURE FOR DECLARING DIVIDENDS

(1) The company may by ordinary resolution declare dividends, and the directors may decide to pay interim dividends.

(2) A dividend must not be declared unless the directors have made a recommendation as to its amount. Such a dividend must not exceed the amount recommended by the directors.

(3) No dividend may be declared or paid unless it is in accordance with shareholders' respective rights.

(4) Unless the shareholders' resolution to declare or directors' decision to pay a dividend, or the terms on which shares are issued, specify otherwise, it must be paid by reference to

each shareholder's holding of shares on the date of the resolution or decision to declare or pay it.

(5) If the company's share capital is divided into different classes, no interim dividend may be paid on shares carrying deferred or non-preferred rights if, at the time of payment, any preferential dividend is in arrear.

(6) The directors may pay at intervals any dividend payable at a fixed rate if it appears to them that the profits available for distribution justify the payment.

(7) If the directors act in good faith, they do not incur any liability to the holders of shares conferring preferred rights for any loss they may suffer by the lawful payment of an interim dividend on shares with deferred or non-preferred rights.

32 NO INTEREST ON DISTRIBUTIONS

The company may not pay interest on any dividend or other sum payable in respect of a share unless otherwise provided by—

(a) the terms on which the share was issued, or

(b) the provisions of another agreement between the holder of that share and the company.

33 UNCLAIMED DISTRIBUTIONS

(1) All dividends or other sums which are—
(a) payable in respect of shares, and
(b) unclaimed after having been declared or become payable,
may be invested or otherwise made use of by the directors for the benefit of the company until claimed.

(2) The payment of any such dividend or other sum into a separate account does not make the company a trustee in respect of it.

(3) If—
(a) twelve years have passed from the date on which a dividend or other sum became due for payment, and
(b) the distribution recipient has not claimed it,
the distribution recipient is no longer entitled to that dividend or other sum and it ceases to remain owing by the company.

34 NON-CASH DISTRIBUTIONS

(1) Subject to the terms of issue of the share in question, the company may, by ordinary resolution on the recommendation of the directors, decide to pay all or part of a dividend or other distribution payable in respect of a share by transferring non-cash assets of equivalent value (including, without limitation, shares or other securities in any company).

Part 4 DECISION-MAKING BY SHAREHOLDERS

ORGANISATION OF GENERAL MEETINGS

37 ATTENDANCE AND SPEAKING AT GENERAL MEETINGS

(1) A person is able to exercise the right to speak at a general meeting when that person is in a position to communicate to all those attending the meeting, during the meeting, any information or opinions which that person has on the business of the meeting.

(2) A person is able to exercise the right to vote at a general meeting when—
(a) that person is able to vote, during the meeting, on resolutions put to the vote at the meeting, and
(b) that person's vote can be taken into account in determining whether or not such resolutions are passed at the same time as the votes of all the other persons attending the meeting.

(3) The directors may make whatever arrangements they consider appropriate to enable those attending a general meeting to exercise their rights to speak or vote at it.

(4) In determining attendance at a general meeting, it is immaterial whether any two or more members attending it are in the same place as each other.

(5) Two or more persons who are not in the same place as each other attend a general meeting if their circumstances are such that if they have (or were to have) rights to speak and vote at that meeting, they are (or would be) able to exercise them.

38 QUORUM FOR GENERAL MEETINGS

No business other than the appointment of the chairman of the meeting is to be transacted at a general meeting if the persons attending it do not constitute a quorum.

39 CHAIRING GENERAL MEETINGS

(1) If the directors have appointed a chairman, the chairman shall chair general meetings if present and willing to do so.

(2) If the directors have not appointed a chairman, or if the chairman is unwilling to chair the meeting or is not present within ten minutes of the time at which a meeting was due to start—
(a) the directors present, or
(b) (if no directors are present), the meeting,
must appoint a director or shareholder to chair the meeting, and the appointment of the chairman of the meeting must be the first business of the meeting.

(3) The person chairing a meeting in accordance with this article is referred to as "the chairman of the meeting".

40 ATTENDANCE AND SPEAKING BY DIRECTORS AND NON-SHAREHOLDERS

(1) Directors may attend and speak at general meetings, whether or not they are shareholders.

(2) The chairman of the meeting may permit other persons who are not—
(a) shareholders of the company, or
(b) otherwise entitled to exercise the rights of shareholders in relation to general meetings,
to attend and speak at a general meeting.

41 ADJOURNMENT

(1) If the persons attending a general meeting within half an hour of the time at which the meeting was due to start do not constitute a quorum, or if during a meeting a quorum ceases to be present, the chairman of the meeting must adjourn it.

(2) The chairman of the meeting may adjourn a general meeting at which a quorum is present if—
 (a) the meeting consents to an adjournment, or
 (b) it appears to the chairman of the meeting that an adjournment is necessary to protect the safety of any person attending the meeting or ensure that the business of the meeting is conducted in an orderly manner.

(3) The chairman of the meeting must adjourn a general meeting if directed to do so by the meeting.

(4) When adjourning a general meeting, the chairman of the meeting must—
 (a) either specify the time and place to which it is adjourned or state that it is to continue at a time and place to be fixed by the directors, and
 (b) have regard to any directions as to the time and place of any adjournment which have been given by the meeting.

(5) If the continuation of an adjourned meeting is to take place more than 14 days after it was adjourned, the company must give at least 7 clear days' notice of it (that is, excluding the day of the adjourned meeting and the day on which the notice is given)—
 (a) to the same persons to whom notice of the company's general meetings is required to be given, and
 (b) containing the same information which such notice is required to contain.

(6) No business may be transacted at an adjourned general meeting which could not properly have been transacted at the meeting if the adjournment had not taken place.

VOTING AT GENERAL MEETINGS

42 VOTING: GENERAL

A resolution put to the vote of a general meeting must be decided on a show of hands unless a poll is duly demanded in accordance with the articles.

43 ERRORS AND DISPUTES

(1) No objection may be raised to the qualification of any person voting at a general meeting except at the meeting or adjourned meeting at which the vote objected to is tendered, and every vote not disallowed at the meeting is valid.

(2) Any such objection must be referred to the chairman of the meeting, whose decision is final.

44 POLL VOTES

(1) A poll on a resolution may be demanded—
 (a) in advance of the general meeting where it is to be put to the vote, or
 (b) at a general meeting, either before a show of hands on that resolution or immediately after the result of a show of hands on that resolution is declared.

(2) A poll may be demanded by—
 (a) the chairman of the meeting;
 (b) the directors;
 (c) two or more persons having the right to vote on the resolution; or
 (d) a person or persons representing not less than one tenth of the total voting rights of all the shareholders having the right to vote on the resolution.

(3) A demand for a poll may be withdrawn if—
  (a) the poll has not yet been taken, and
  (b) the chairman of the meeting consents to the withdrawal.

(4) Polls must be taken immediately and in such manner as the chairman of the meeting directs.

45 CONTENT OF PROXY NOTICES

(1) Proxies may only validly be appointed by a notice in writing (a "proxy notice") which—
  (a) states the name and address of the shareholder appointing the proxy;
  (b) identifies the person appointed to be that shareholder's proxy and the general meeting in relation to which that person is appointed;
  (c) is signed by or on behalf of the shareholder appointing the proxy, or is authenticated in such manner as the directors may determine; and
  (d) is delivered to the company in accordance with the articles and any instructions contained in the notice of the general meeting to which they relate.

(2) The company may require proxy notices to be delivered in a particular form, and may specify different forms for different purposes.

(3) Proxy notices may specify how the proxy appointed under them is to vote (or that the proxy is to abstain from voting) on one or more resolutions.

(4) Unless a proxy notice indicates otherwise, it must be treated as—
  (a) allowing the person appointed under it as a proxy discretion as to how to vote on any ancillary or procedural resolutions put to the meeting, and
  (b) appointing that person as a proxy in relation to any adjournment of the general meeting to which it relates as well as the meeting itself.

46 DELIVERY OF PROXY NOTICES

(1) A person who is entitled to attend, speak or vote (either on a show of hands or on a poll) at a general meeting remains so entitled in respect of that meeting or any adjournment of it, even though a valid proxy notice has been delivered to the company by or on behalf of that person.

(2) An appointment under a proxy notice may be revoked by delivering to the company a notice in writing given by or on behalf of the person by whom or on whose behalf the proxy notice was given.

(3) A notice revoking a proxy appointment only takes effect if it is delivered before the start of the meeting or adjourned meeting to which it relates.

(4) If a proxy notice is not executed by the person appointing the proxy, it must be accompanied by written evidence of the authority of the person who executed it to execute it on the appointor's behalf.

47 AMENDMENTS TO RESOLUTIONS

(1) An ordinary resolution to be proposed at a general meeting may be amended by ordinary resolution if—
  (a) notice of the proposed amendment is given to the company in writing by a person entitled to vote at the general meeting at which it is to be proposed not less than 48 hours before the meeting is to take place (or such later time as the chairman of the meeting may determine), and

(b) the proposed amendment does not, in the reasonable opinion of the chairman of the meeting, materially alter the scope of the resolution.

(2) A special resolution to be proposed at a general meeting may be amended by ordinary resolution, if—
 (a) the chairman of the meeting proposes the amendment at the general meeting at which the resolution is to be proposed, and
 (b) the amendment does not go beyond what is necessary to correct a grammatical or other non-substantive error in the resolution.

(3) If the chairman of the meeting, acting in good faith, wrongly decides that an amendment to a resolution is out of order, the chairman's error does not invalidate the vote on that resolution.

Part 5 ADMINISTRATIVE ARRANGEMENTS

48 MEANS OF COMMUNICATION TO BE USED

(1) Subject to the articles, anything sent or supplied by or to the company under the articles may be sent or supplied in any way in which the Companies Act 2006 provides for documents or information which are authorised or required by any provision of that Act to be sent or supplied by or to the company.

(2) Subject to the articles, any notice or document to be sent or supplied to a director in connection with the taking of decisions by directors may also be sent or supplied by the means by which that director has asked to be sent or supplied with such notices or documents for the time being.

50 NO RIGHT TO INSPECT ACCOUNTS AND OTHER RECORDS

Except as provided by law or authorised by the directors or an ordinary resolution of the company, no person is entitled to inspect any of the company's accounting or other records or documents merely by virtue of being a shareholder.

51 PROVISION FOR EMPLOYEES ON CESSATION OF BUSINESS

The directors may decide to make provision for the benefit of persons employed or formerly employed by the company or any of its subsidiaries (other than a director or former director or shadow director) in connection with the cessation or transfer to any person of the whole or part of the undertaking of the company or that subsidiary.

DIRECTORS' INDEMNITY AND INSURANCE

52 INDEMNITY

(1) Subject to paragraph (2), a relevant director of the company or an associated company may be indemnified out of the company's assets against—
 (a) any liability incurred by that director in connection with any negligence, default, breach of duty or breach of trust in relation to the company or an associated company,

 ...

 (c) any other liability incurred by that director as an officer of the company or an associated company.

(2) This article does not authorise any indemnity which would be prohibited or rendered void by any provision of the Companies Acts or by any other provision of law.

(3) In this article—
(a) companies are associated if one is a subsidiary of the other or both are subsidiaries of the same body corporate, and
(b) a "relevant director" means any director or former director of the company or an associated company.

53 INSURANCE

(1) The directors may decide to purchase and maintain insurance, at the expense of the company, for the benefit of any relevant director in respect of any relevant loss.

(2) In this article—
(a) a "relevant director" means any director or former director of the company or an associated company,
(b) a "relevant loss" means any loss or liability which has been or may be incurred by a relevant director in connection with that director's duties or powers in relation to the company, any associated company or any pension fund or employees' share scheme of the company or associated company, and
(c) companies are associated if one is a subsidiary of the other or both are subsidiaries of the same body corporate.

SCHEDULE 3 MODEL ARTICLES FOR PUBLIC COMPANIES

Part 1 INTERPRETATION AND LIMITATION OF LIABILITY

1 DEFINED TERMS

In the articles, unless the context requires otherwise—

...

"articles" means the company's articles of association;

...

"call" has the meaning given in article 54;

"call notice" has the meaning given in article 54;

"certificate" means a paper certificate (other than a share warrant) evidencing a person's title to specified shares or other securities;

"certificated" in relation to a share, means that it is not an uncertificated share or a share in respect of which a share warrant has been issued and is current;

"chairman" has the meaning given in article 12;

"chairman of the meeting" has the meaning given in article 31;

"Companies Acts" means the Companies Acts (as defined in section 2 of the Companies Act 2006), in so far as they apply to the company;

...

"director" means a director of the company, and includes any person occupying the position of director, by whatever name called;

...

"document" includes, unless otherwise specified, any document sent or supplied in electronic form;

"electronic form" has the meaning given in section 1168 of the Companies Act 2006;

"fully paid" in relation to a share, means that the nominal value and any premium to be paid to the company in respect of that share have been paid to the company;

"hard copy form" has the meaning given in section 1168 of the Companies Act 2006;

"holder" in relation to shares means the person whose name is entered in the register of members as the holder of the shares, or, in the case of a share in respect of which a share warrant has been issued (and not cancelled), the person in possession of that warrant;

"instrument" means a document in hard copy form;

...

"member" has the meaning given in section 112 of the Companies Act 2006;

"ordinary resolution" has the meaning given in section 282 of the Companies Act 2006;

"paid" means paid or credited as paid;

"participate", in relation to a directors' meeting, has the meaning given in article 9;

"partly paid" in relation to a share means that part of that share's nominal value or any premium at which it was issued has not been paid to the company;

"proxy notice" has the meaning given in article 38;

"securities seal" has the meaning given in article 47;

"shares" means shares in the company;

"special resolution" has the meaning given in section 283 of the Companies Act 2006;

"subsidiary" has the meaning given in section 1159 of the Companies Act 2006;

"transmittee" means a person entitled to a share by reason of the death or bankruptcy of a shareholder or otherwise by operation of law;

"uncertificated" in relation to a share means that, by virtue of legislation (other than section 778 of the Companies Act 2006) permitting title to shares to be evidenced and transferred without a certificate, title to that share is evidenced and may be transferred without a certificate; and

"writing" means the representation or reproduction of words, symbols or other information in a visible form by any method or combination of methods, whether sent or supplied in electronic form or otherwise.

Unless the context otherwise requires, other words or expressions contained in these articles bear the same meaning as in the Companies Act 2006 as in force on the date when these articles become binding on the company.

2 LIABILITY OF MEMBERS

The liability of the members is limited to the amount, if any, unpaid on the shares held by them.

Part 2 DIRECTORS

DIRECTORS' POWERS AND RESPONSIBILITIES

3 DIRECTORS' GENERAL AUTHORITY

Subject to the articles, the directors are responsible for the management of the company's business, for which purpose they may exercise all the powers of the company.

4 MEMBERS' RESERVE POWER

(1) The members may, by special resolution, direct the directors to take, or refrain from taking, specified action.

(2) No such special resolution invalidates anything which the directors have done before the passing of the resolution.

5 DIRECTORS MAY DELEGATE

(1) Subject to the articles, the directors may delegate any of the powers which are conferred on them under the articles—
   (a) to such person or committee;
   (b) by such means (including by power of attorney);
   (c) to such an extent;
   (d) in relation to such matters or territories; and
   (e) on such terms and conditions;
   as they think fit.

(2) If the directors so specify, any such delegation may authorise further delegation of the directors' powers by any person to whom they are delegated.

(3) The directors may revoke any delegation in whole or part, or alter its terms and conditions.

6 COMMITTEES

(1) Committees to which the directors delegate any of their powers must follow procedures which are based as far as they are applicable on those provisions of the articles which govern the taking of decisions by directors.

(2) The directors may make rules of procedure for all or any committees, which prevail over rules derived from the articles if they are not consistent with them.

DECISION-MAKING BY DIRECTORS

7 DIRECTORS TO TAKE DECISIONS COLLECTIVELY

Decisions of the directors may be taken—

(a) at a directors' meeting, or

(b) in the form of a directors' written resolution.

8 CALLING A DIRECTORS' MEETING

(1) Any director may call a directors' meeting.

(2) The company secretary must call a directors' meeting if a director so requests.

(3) A directors' meeting is called by giving notice of the meeting to the directors.

(4) Notice of any directors' meeting must indicate—
(a) its proposed date and time;
(b) where it is to take place; and
(c) if it is anticipated that directors participating in the meeting will not be in the same place, how it is proposed that they should communicate with each other during the meeting.

(5) Notice of a directors' meeting must be given to each director, but need not be in writing.

(6) Notice of a directors' meeting need not be given to directors who waive their entitlement to notice of that meeting, by giving notice to that effect to the company not more than 7 days after the date on which the meeting is held. Where such notice is given after the meeting has been held, that does not affect the validity of the meeting, or of any business conducted at it.

9 PARTICIPATION IN DIRECTORS' MEETINGS

(1) Subject to the articles, directors participate in a directors' meeting, or part of a directors' meeting, when—
(a) the meeting has been called and takes place in accordance with the articles, and
(b) they can each communicate to the others any information or opinions they have on any particular item of the business of the meeting.

(2) In determining whether directors are participating in a directors' meeting, it is irrelevant where any director is or how they communicate with each other.

(3) If all the directors participating in a meeting are not in the same place, they may decide that the meeting is to be treated as taking place wherever any of them is.

10 QUORUM FOR DIRECTORS' MEETINGS

(1) At a directors' meeting, unless a quorum is participating, no proposal is to be voted on, except a proposal to call another meeting.

(2) The quorum for directors' meetings may be fixed from time to time by a decision of the directors, but it must never be less than two, and unless otherwise fixed it is two.

11 MEETINGS WHERE TOTAL NUMBER OF DIRECTORS LESS THAN QUORUM

(1) This article applies where the total number of directors for the time being is less than the quorum for directors' meetings.

(2) If there is only one director, that director may appoint sufficient directors to make up a quorum or call a general meeting to do so.

(3) If there is more than one director—
(a) a directors' meeting may take place, if it is called in accordance with the articles and at least two directors participate in it, with a view to appointing sufficient directors to make up a quorum or calling a general meeting to do so, and
(b) if a directors' meeting is called but only one director attends at the appointed date and time to participate in it, that director may appoint sufficient directors to make up a quorum or call a general meeting to do so.

12 CHAIRING DIRECTORS' MEETINGS

(1) The directors may appoint a director to chair their meetings.

(2) The person so appointed for the time being is known as the chairman.

(3) The directors may appoint other directors as deputy or assistant chairmen to chair directors' meetings in the chairman's absence.

(4) The directors may terminate the appointment of the chairman, deputy or assistant chairman at any time.

(5) If neither the chairman nor any director appointed generally to chair directors' meetings in the chairman's absence is participating in a meeting within ten minutes of the time at which it was to start, the participating directors must appoint one of themselves to chair it.

13 VOTING AT DIRECTORS' MEETINGS: GENERAL RULES

(1) Subject to the articles, a decision is taken at a directors' meeting by a majority of the votes of the participating directors.

(2) Subject to the articles, each director participating in a directors' meeting has one vote.

(3) Subject to the articles, if a director has an interest in an actual or proposed transaction or arrangement with the company—
(a) that director and that director's alternate may not vote on any proposal relating to it, but
(b) this does not preclude the alternate from voting in relation to that transaction or arrangement on behalf of another appointor who does not have such an interest.

14 CHAIRMAN'S CASTING VOTE AT DIRECTORS' MEETINGS

(1) If the numbers of votes for and against a proposal are equal, the chairman or other director chairing the meeting has a casting vote.

(2) But this does not apply if, in accordance with the articles, the chairman or other director is not to be counted as participating in the decision-making process for quorum or voting purposes.

15 ALTERNATES VOTING AT DIRECTORS' MEETINGS

A director who is also an alternate director has an additional vote on behalf of each appointor who is—

(a) not participating in a directors' meeting, and

(b) would have been entitled to vote if they were participating in it.

16 CONFLICTS OF INTEREST

(1) If a directors' meeting, or part of a directors' meeting, is concerned with an actual or proposed transaction or arrangement with the company in which a director is interested, that director is not to be counted as participating in that meeting, or part of a meeting, for quorum or voting purposes.

(2) But if paragraph (3) applies, a director who is interested in an actual or proposed transaction or arrangement with the company is to be counted as participating in a decision at a directors' meeting, or part of a directors' meeting, relating to it for quorum and voting purposes.

(3) This paragraph applies when—
(a) the company by ordinary resolution disapplies the provision of the articles which would otherwise prevent a director from being counted as participating in, or voting at, a directors' meeting;
(b) the director's interest cannot reasonably be regarded as likely to give rise to a conflict of interest; or
(c) the director's conflict of interest arises from a permitted cause.

(4) For the purposes of this article, the following are permitted causes—
(a) a guarantee given, or to be given, by or to a director in respect of an obligation incurred by or on behalf of the company or any of its subsidiaries;
(b) subscription, or an agreement to subscribe, for shares or other securities of the company or any of its subsidiaries, or to underwrite, sub-underwrite, or guarantee subscription for any such shares or securities; and
(c) arrangements pursuant to which benefits are made available to employees and directors or former employees and directors of the company or any of its subsidiaries which do not provide special benefits for directors or former directors.

(5) Subject to paragraph (6), if a question arises at a meeting of directors or of a committee of directors as to the right of a director to participate in the meeting (or part of the meeting) for voting or quorum purposes, the question may, before the conclusion of the meeting, be referred to the chairman whose ruling in relation to any director other than the chairman is to be final and conclusive.

(6) If any question as to the right to participate in the meeting (or part of the meeting) should arise in respect of the chairman, the question is to be decided by a decision of the directors at that meeting, for which purpose the chairman is not to be counted as participating in the meeting (or that part of the meeting) for voting or quorum purposes.

17 PROPOSING DIRECTORS' WRITTEN RESOLUTIONS

(1) Any director may propose a directors' written resolution.

(2) The company secretary must propose a directors' written resolution if a director so requests.

(3) A directors' written resolution is proposed by giving notice of the proposed resolution to the directors.

(4) Notice of a proposed directors' written resolution must indicate—
(a) the proposed resolution, and
(b) the time by which it is proposed that the directors should adopt it.

(5) Notice of a proposed directors' written resolution must be given in writing to each director.

(6) Any decision which a person giving notice of a proposed directors' written resolution takes regarding the process of adopting that resolution must be taken reasonably in good faith.

18 ADOPTION OF DIRECTORS' WRITTEN RESOLUTIONS

(1) A proposed directors' written resolution is adopted when all the directors who would have been entitled to vote on the resolution at a directors' meeting have signed one or more copies of it, provided that those directors would have formed a quorum at such a meeting.

(2) It is immaterial whether any director signs the resolution before or after the time by which the notice proposed that it should be adopted.

(3) Once a directors' written resolution has been adopted, it must be treated as if it had been a decision taken at a directors' meeting in accordance with the articles.

(4) The company secretary must ensure that the company keeps a record, in writing, of all directors' written resolutions for at least ten years from the date of their adoption.

19 DIRECTORS' DISCRETION TO MAKE FURTHER RULES

Subject to the articles, the directors may make any rule which they think fit about how they take decisions, and about how such rules are to be recorded or communicated to directors.

APPOINTMENT OF DIRECTORS

20 METHODS OF APPOINTING DIRECTORS

Any person who is willing to act as a director, and is permitted by law to do so, may be appointed to be a director—

(a) by ordinary resolution, or

(b) by a decision of the directors.

21 RETIREMENT OF DIRECTORS BY ROTATION

(1) At the first annual general meeting all the directors must retire from office.

(2) At every subsequent annual general meeting any directors—
 (a) who have been appointed by the directors since the last annual general meeting, or
 (b) who were not appointed or reappointed at one of the preceding two annual general meetings,

must retire from office and may offer themselves for reappointment by the members.

22 TERMINATION OF DIRECTOR'S APPOINTMENT

A person ceases to be a director as soon as—

(a) that person ceases to be a director by virtue of any provision of the Companies Act 2006 or is prohibited from being a director by law;

(b) a bankruptcy order is made against that person;

(c) a composition is made with that person's creditors generally in satisfaction of that person's debts;

(d) a registered medical practitioner who is treating that person gives a written opinion to the company stating that that person has become physically or mentally incapable of acting as a director and may remain so for more than three months;

(e) by reason of that person's mental health, a court makes an order which wholly or partly prevents that person from personally exercising any powers or rights which that person would otherwise have;

(f) notification is received by the company from the director that the director is resigning from office as director, and such resignation has taken effect in accordance with its terms.

23 DIRECTORS' REMUNERATION

(1) Directors may undertake any services for the company that the directors decide.

(2) Directors are entitled to such remuneration as the directors determine—
  (a) for their services to the company as directors, and
  (b) for any other service which they undertake for the company.

(3) Subject to the articles, a director's remuneration may—
  (a) take any form, and
  (b) include any arrangements in connection with the payment of a pension, allowance or gratuity, or any death, sickness or disability benefits, to or in respect of that director.

(4) Unless the directors decide otherwise, directors' remuneration accrues from day to day.

(5) Unless the directors decide otherwise, directors are not accountable to the company for any remuneration which they receive as directors or other officers or employees of the company's subsidiaries or of any other body corporate in which the company is interested.

24 DIRECTORS' EXPENSES

The company may pay any reasonable expenses which the directors properly incur in connection with their attendance at—

(a) meetings of directors or committees of directors,

(b) general meetings, or

(c) separate meetings of the holders of any class of shares or of debentures of the company,

or otherwise in connection with the exercise of their powers and the discharge of their responsibilities in relation to the company.

Part 3 DECISION-MAKING BY MEMBERS

ORGANISATION OF GENERAL MEETINGS

28 MEMBERS CAN CALL GENERAL MEETING IF NOT ENOUGH DIRECTORS

If—

(a) the company has fewer than two directors, and

(b) the director (if any) is unable or unwilling to appoint sufficient directors to make up a quorum or to call a general meeting to do so,

then two or more members may call a general meeting (or instruct the company secretary to do so) for the purpose of appointing one or more directors.

29 ATTENDANCE AND SPEAKING AT GENERAL MEETINGS

(1) A person is able to exercise the right to speak at a general meeting when that person is in a position to communicate to all those attending the meeting, during the meeting, any information or opinions which that person has on the business of the meeting.

(2) A person is able to exercise the right to vote at a general meeting when—
  (a) that person is able to vote, during the meeting, on resolutions put to the vote at the meeting, and

(b) that person's vote can be taken into account in determining whether or not such resolutions are passed at the same time as the votes of all the other persons attending the meeting.

(3) The directors may make whatever arrangements they consider appropriate to enable those attending a general meeting to exercise their rights to speak or vote at it.

(4) In determining attendance at a general meeting, it is immaterial whether any two or more members attending it are in the same place as each other.

(5) Two or more persons who are not in the same place as each other attend a general meeting if their circumstances are such that if they have (or were to have) rights to speak and vote at that meeting, they are (or would be) able to exercise them.

30 QUORUM FOR GENERAL MEETINGS

No business other than the appointment of the chairman of the meeting is to be transacted at a general meeting if the persons attending it do not constitute a quorum.

31 CHAIRING GENERAL MEETINGS

(1) If the directors have appointed a chairman, the chairman shall chair general meetings if present and willing to do so.

(2) If the directors have not appointed a chairman, or if the chairman is unwilling to chair the meeting or is not present within ten minutes of the time at which a meeting was due to start—
(a) the directors present, or
(b) (if no directors are present), the meeting,
must appoint a director or member to chair the meeting, and the appointment of the chairman of the meeting must be the first business of the meeting.

(3) The person chairing a meeting in accordance with this article is referred to as "the chairman of the meeting".

32 ATTENDANCE AND SPEAKING BY DIRECTORS AND NON-MEMBERS

(1) Directors may attend and speak at general meetings, whether or not they are members.

(2) The chairman of the meeting may permit other persons who are not—
(a) members of the company, or
(b) otherwise entitled to exercise the rights of members in relation to general meetings,
to attend and speak at a general meeting.

33 ADJOURNMENT

(1) If the persons attending a general meeting within half an hour of the time at which the meeting was due to start do not constitute a quorum, or if during a meeting a quorum ceases to be present, the chairman of the meeting must adjourn it.

(2) The chairman of the meeting may adjourn a general meeting at which a quorum is present if—
(a) the meeting consents to an adjournment, or
(b) it appears to the chairman of the meeting that an adjournment is necessary to protect the safety of any person attending the meeting or ensure that the business of the meeting is conducted in an orderly manner.

(3) The chairman of the meeting must adjourn a general meeting if directed to do so by the meeting.

(4) When adjourning a general meeting, the chairman of the meeting must—
  (a) either specify the time and place to which it is adjourned or state that it is to continue at a time and place to be fixed by the directors, and
  (b) have regard to any directions as to the time and place of any adjournment which have been given by the meeting.

(5) If the continuation of an adjourned meeting is to take place more than 14 days after it was adjourned, the company must give at least 7 clear days' notice of it (that is, excluding the day of the adjourned meeting and the day on which the notice is given)—
  (a) to the same persons to whom notice of the company's general meetings is required to be given, and
  (b) containing the same information which such notice is required to contain.

(6) No business may be transacted at an adjourned general meeting which could not properly have been transacted at the meeting if the adjournment had not taken place.

VOTING AT GENERAL MEETINGS

34 VOTING: GENERAL

A resolution put to the vote of a general meeting must be decided on a show of hands unless a poll is duly demanded in accordance with the articles.

35 ERRORS AND DISPUTES

(1) No objection may be raised to the qualification of any person voting at a general meeting except at the meeting or adjourned meeting at which the vote objected to is tendered, and every vote not disallowed at the meeting is valid.

(2) Any such objection must be referred to the chairman of the meeting whose decision is final.

36 DEMANDING A POLL

(1) A poll on a resolution may be demanded—
  (a) in advance of the general meeting where it is to be put to the vote, or
  (b) at a general meeting, either before a show of hands on that resolution or immediately after the result of a show of hands on that resolution is declared.

(2) A poll may be demanded by—
  (a) the chairman of the meeting;
  (b) the directors;
  (c) two or more persons having the right to vote on the resolution; or
  (d) a person or persons representing not less than one tenth of the total voting rights of all the members having the right to vote on the resolution.

(3) A demand for a poll may be withdrawn if—
  (a) the poll has not yet been taken, and
  (b) the chairman of the meeting consents to the withdrawal.

37 PROCEDURE ON A POLL

(1) Subject to the articles, polls at general meetings must be taken when, where and in such manner as the chairman of the meeting directs.

(2) The chairman of the meeting may appoint scrutineers (who need not be members) and decide how and when the result of the poll is to be declared.

(3) The result of a poll shall be the decision of the meeting in respect of the resolution on which the poll was demanded.

(4) A poll on—
(a) the election of the chairman of the meeting, or
(b) a question of adjournment,
must be taken immediately.

(5) Other polls must be taken within 30 days of their being demanded.

(6) A demand for a poll does not prevent a general meeting from continuing, except as regards the question on which the poll was demanded.

(7) No notice need be given of a poll not taken immediately if the time and place at which it is to be taken are announced at the meeting at which it is demanded.

(8) In any other case, at least 7 days' notice must be given specifying the time and place at which the poll is to be taken.

38 CONTENT OF PROXY NOTICES

(1) Proxies may only validly be appointed by a notice in writing (a "proxy notice") which—
(a) states the name and address of the member appointing the proxy;
(b) identifies the person appointed to be that member's proxy and the general meeting in relation to which that person is appointed;
(c) is signed by or on behalf of the member appointing the proxy, or is authenticated in such manner as the directors may determine; and
(d) is delivered to the company in accordance with the articles and any instructions contained in the notice of the general meeting to which they relate.

(2) The company may require proxy notices to be delivered in a particular form, and may specify different forms for different purposes.

(3) Proxy notices may specify how the proxy appointed under them is to vote (or that the proxy is to abstain from voting) on one or more resolutions.

(4) Unless a proxy notice indicates otherwise, it must be treated as—
(a) allowing the person appointed under it as a proxy discretion as to how to vote on any ancillary or procedural resolutions put to the meeting, and
(b) appointing that person as a proxy in relation to any adjournment of the general meeting to which it relates as well as the meeting itself.

39 DELIVERY OF PROXY NOTICES

(1) Any notice of a general meeting must specify the address or addresses ("proxy notification address") at which the company or its agents will receive proxy notices relating to that meeting, or any adjournment of it, delivered in hard copy or electronic form.

(2) A person who is entitled to attend, speak or vote (either on a show of hands or on a poll) at a general meeting remains so entitled in respect of that meeting or any adjournment of it, even though a valid proxy notice has been delivered to the company by or on behalf of that person.

(3) Subject to paragraphs (4) and (5), a proxy notice must be delivered to a proxy notification address not less than 48 hours before the general meeting or adjourned meeting to which it relates.

(4) In the case of a poll taken more than 48 hours after it is demanded, the notice must be delivered to a proxy notification address not less than 24 hours before the time appointed for the taking of the poll.

(5) In the case of a poll not taken during the meeting but taken not more than 48 hours after it was demanded, the proxy notice must be delivered—
  (a) in accordance with paragraph (3), or
  (b) at the meeting at which the poll was demanded to the chairman, secretary or any director.

(6) An appointment under a proxy notice may be revoked by delivering a notice in writing given by or on behalf of the person by whom or on whose behalf the proxy notice was given to a proxy notification address.

(7) A notice revoking a proxy appointment only takes effect if it is delivered before—
  (a) the start of the meeting or adjourned meeting to which it relates, or
  (b) (in the case of a poll not taken on the same day as the meeting or adjourned meeting) the time appointed for taking the poll to which it relates.

(8) If a proxy notice is not signed by the person appointing the proxy, it must be accompanied by written evidence of the authority of the person who executed it to execute it on the appointor's behalf.

40 AMENDMENTS TO RESOLUTIONS

(1) An ordinary resolution to be proposed at a general meeting may be amended by ordinary resolution if—
  (a) notice of the proposed amendment is given to the company secretary in writing by a person entitled to vote at the general meeting at which it is to be proposed not less than 48 hours before the meeting is to take place (or such later time as the chairman of the meeting may determine), and
  (b) the proposed amendment does not, in the reasonable opinion of the chairman of the meeting, materially alter the scope of the resolution.

(2) A special resolution to be proposed at a general meeting may be amended by ordinary resolution, if—
  (a) the chairman of the meeting proposes the amendment at the general meeting at which the resolution is to be proposed, and
  (b) the amendment does not go beyond what is necessary to correct a grammatical or other non-substantive error in the resolution.

(3) If the chairman of the meeting, acting in good faith, wrongly decides that an amendment to a resolution is out of order, the chairman's error does not invalidate the vote on that resolution.

RESTRICTIONS ON MEMBERS' RIGHTS

41 NO VOTING OF SHARES ON WHICH MONEY OWED TO COMPANY

No voting rights attached to a share may be exercised at any general meeting, at any adjournment of it, or on any poll called at or in relation to it, unless all amounts payable to the company in respect of that share have been paid.

APPLICATION OF RULES TO CLASS MEETINGS

42 CLASS MEETINGS

The provisions of the articles relating to general meetings apply, with any necessary modifications, to meetings of the holders of any class of shares.

Part 4 SHARES AND DISTRIBUTIONS

ISSUE OF SHARES

43 POWERS TO ISSUE DIFFERENT CLASSES OF SHARE

(1) Subject to the articles, but without prejudice to the rights attached to any existing share, the company may issue shares with such rights or restrictions as may be determined by ordinary resolution.

(2) The company may issue shares which are to be redeemed, or are liable to be redeemed at the option of the company or the holder, and the directors may determine the terms, conditions and manner of redemption of any such shares.

44 PAYMENT OF COMMISSIONS ON SUBSCRIPTION FOR SHARES

(1) The company may pay any person a commission in consideration for that person—
  (a) subscribing, or agreeing to subscribe, for shares, or
  (b) procuring, or agreeing to procure, subscriptions for shares.

(2) Any such commission may be paid—
  (a) in cash, or in fully paid or partly paid shares or other securities, or partly in one way and partly in the other, and
  (b) in respect of a conditional or an absolute subscription.

INTERESTS IN SHARES

45 COMPANY NOT BOUND BY LESS THAN ABSOLUTE INTERESTS

Except as required by law, no person is to be recognised by the company as holding any share upon any trust, and except as otherwise required by law or the articles, the company is not in any way to be bound by or recognise any interest in a share other than the holder's absolute ownership of it and all the rights attaching to it.

SHARE CERTIFICATES

46 CERTIFICATES TO BE ISSUED EXCEPT IN CERTAIN CASES

(1) The company must issue each member with one or more certificates in respect of the shares which that member holds.

(2) This article does not apply to—
  (a) uncertificated shares?...
  ...

(3) Except as otherwise specified in the articles, all certificates must be issued free of charge.

(4) No certificate may be issued in respect of shares of more than one class.

(5) If more than one person holds a share, only one certificate may be issued in respect of it.

47 CONTENTS AND EXECUTION OF SHARE CERTIFICATES

(1) Every certificate must specify—
- (a) in respect of how many shares, of what class, it is issued;
- (b) the nominal value of those shares;
- (c) the amount paid up on them; and
- (d) any distinguishing numbers assigned to them.

(2) Certificates must—
- (a) have affixed to them the company's common seal or an official seal which is a facsimile of the company's common seal with the addition on its face of the word "Securities" (a "securities seal"), or
- (b) be otherwise executed in accordance with the Companies Acts.

SHARES NOT HELD IN CERTIFICATED FORM

50 UNCERTIFICATED SHARES

(4) Any share or class of shares of the company may be issued or held on such terms, or in such a way, that—
- (a) title to it or them is not, or must not be, evidenced by a certificate, or
- (b) it or they may or must be transferred wholly or partly without a certificate.

(5) The directors have power to take such steps as they think fit in relation to—
- (a) the evidencing of and transfer of title to uncertificated shares (including in connection with the issue of such shares);
- (b) any records relating to the holding of uncertificated shares;
- (c) the conversion of certificated shares into uncertificated shares; or
- (d) the conversion of uncertificated shares into certificated shares.

PARTLY PAID SHARES

54 CALL NOTICES

(1) Subject to the articles and the terms on which shares are allotted, the directors may send a notice (a "call notice") to a member requiring the member to pay the company a specified sum of money (a "call") which is payable in respect of shares which that member holds at the date when the directors decide to send the call notice.

55 LIABILITY TO PAY CALLS

(1) Liability to pay a call is not extinguished or transferred by transferring the shares in respect of which it is required to be paid.

57 FAILURE TO COMPLY WITH CALL NOTICE: AUTOMATIC CONSEQUENCES

(1) If a person is liable to pay a call and fails to do so by the call payment date—
- (a) the directors may issue a notice of intended forfeiture to that person, and
- (b) until the call is paid, that person must pay the company interest on the call from the call payment date at the relevant rate.

58 NOTICE OF INTENDED FORFEITURE

A notice of intended forfeiture—

(a) may be sent in respect of any share in respect of which a call has not been paid as required by a call notice;

(b) must be sent to the holder of that share or to a person entitled to it by reason of the holder's death, bankruptcy or otherwise;

(c) must require payment of the call and any accrued interest by a date which is not less than 14 days after the date of the notice;

(d) must state how the payment is to be made; and

(e) must state that if the notice is not complied with, the shares in respect of which the call is payable will be liable to be forfeited.

59 DIRECTORS' POWER TO FORFEIT SHARES

If a notice of intended forfeiture is not complied with before the date by which payment of the call is required in the notice of intended forfeiture, the directors may decide that any share in respect of which it was given is forfeited, and the forfeiture is to include all dividends or other moneys payable in respect of the forfeited shares and not paid before the forfeiture.

60 EFFECT OF FORFEITURE

(1) Subject to the articles, the forfeiture of a share extinguishes—
  (a) all interests in that share, and all claims and demands against the company in respect of it, and
  (b) all other rights and liabilities incidental to the share as between the person whose share it was prior to the forfeiture and the company.

(2) Any share which is forfeited in accordance with the articles—
  (a) is deemed to have been forfeited when the directors decide that it is forfeited;
  (b) is deemed to be the property of the company; and
  (c) may be sold, re-allotted or otherwise disposed of as the directors think fit.

(3) If a person's shares have been forfeited—
  (a) the company must send that person notice that forfeiture has occurred and record it in the register of members;
  (b) that person ceases to be a member in respect of those shares;
  (c) that person must surrender the certificate for the shares forfeited to the company for cancellation;
  (d) that person remains liable to the company for all sums payable by that person under the articles at the date of forfeiture in respect of those shares, including any interest (whether accrued before or after the date of forfeiture); and
  (e) the directors may waive payment of such sums wholly or in part or enforce payment without any allowance for the value of the shares at the time of forfeiture or for any consideration received on their disposal.

(4) At any time before the company disposes of a forfeited share, the directors may decide to cancel the forfeiture on payment of all calls and interest due in respect of it and on such other terms as they think fit.

61 PROCEDURE FOLLOWING FORFEITURE

(1) If a forfeited share is to be disposed of by being transferred, the company may receive the consideration for the transfer and the directors may authorise any person to execute the instrument of transfer.

(4) If the company sells a forfeited share, the person who held it prior to its forfeiture is entitled to receive from the company the proceeds of such sale, net of any commission, and excluding any amount which—

(a) was, or would have become, payable, and

(b) had not, when that share was forfeited, been paid by that person in respect of that share,

but no interest is payable to such a person in respect of such proceeds and the company is not required to account for any money earned on them.

62 SURRENDER OF SHARES

(1) A member may surrender any share—

(a) in respect of which the directors may issue a notice of intended forfeiture;

(b) which the directors may forfeit; or

(c) which has been forfeited.

(2) The directors may accept the surrender of any such share.

(3) The effect of surrender on a share is the same as the effect of forfeiture on that share.

(4) A share which has been surrendered may be dealt with in the same way as a share which has been forfeited.

TRANSFER AND TRANSMISSION OF SHARES

63 TRANSFERS OF CERTIFICATED SHARES

(1) Certificated shares may be transferred by means of an instrument of transfer in any usual form or any other form approved by the directors, which is executed by or on behalf of—

(a) the transferor, and

(b) (if any of the shares is partly paid) the transferee.

(2) No fee may be charged for registering any instrument of transfer or other document relating to or affecting the title to any share.

(3) The company may retain any instrument of transfer which is registered.

(4) The transferor remains the holder of a certificated share until the transferee's name is entered in the register of members as holder of it.

(5) The directors may refuse to register the transfer of a certificated share if—

(a) the share is not fully paid;

(b) the transfer is not lodged at the company's registered office or such other place as the directors have appointed;

(c) the transfer is not accompanied by the certificate for the shares to which it relates, or such other evidence as the directors may reasonably require to show the transferor's right to make the transfer, or evidence of the right of someone other than the transferor to make the transfer on the transferor's behalf;

(d) the transfer is in respect of more than one class of share; or

(e) the transfer is in favour of more than four transferees.

(6) If the directors refuse to register the transfer of a share, the instrument of transfer must be returned to the transferee with the notice of refusal unless they suspect that the proposed transfer may be fraudulent.

64 TRANSFER OF UNCERTIFICATED SHARES

A transfer of an uncertificated share must not be registered if it is in favour of more than four transferees.

65 TRANSMISSION OF SHARES

(1) If title to a share passes to a transmittee, the company may only recognise the transmittee as having any title to that share.

(2) Nothing in these articles releases the estate of a deceased member from any liability in respect of a share solely or jointly held by that member.

66 TRANSMITTEES' RIGHTS

(1) A transmittee who produces such evidence of entitlement to shares as the directors may properly require—
   (a) may, subject to the articles, choose either to become the holder of those shares or to have them transferred to another person, and
   (b) subject to the articles, and pending any transfer of the shares to another person, has the same rights as the holder had.

(2) But transmittees do not have the right to attend or vote at a general meeting in respect of shares to which they are entitled, by reason of the holder's death or bankruptcy or otherwise, unless they become the holders of those shares.

DISTRIBUTIONS

70 PROCEDURE FOR DECLARING DIVIDENDS

(1) The company may by ordinary resolution declare dividends, and the directors may decide to pay interim dividends.

(2) A dividend must not be declared unless the directors have made a recommendation as to its amount. Such a dividend must not exceed the amount recommended by the directors.

(3) No dividend may be declared or paid unless it is in accordance with members' respective rights.

(4) Unless the members' resolution to declare or directors' decision to pay a dividend, or the terms on which shares are issued, specify otherwise, it must be paid by reference to each member's holding of shares on the date of the resolution or decision to declare or pay it.

(5) If the company's share capital is divided into different classes, no interim dividend may be paid on shares carrying deferred or non-preferred rights if, at the time of payment, any preferential dividend is in arrear.

(6) The directors may pay at intervals any dividend payable at a fixed rate if it appears to them that the profits available for distribution justify the payment.

(7) If the directors act in good faith, they do not incur any liability to the holders of shares conferring preferred rights for any loss they may suffer by the lawful payment of an interim dividend on shares with deferred or non-preferred rights.

71 CALCULATION OF DIVIDENDS

(1) Except as otherwise provided by the articles or the rights attached to shares, all dividends must be—

(a) declared and paid according to the amounts paid up on the shares on which the dividend is paid, and
(b) apportioned and paid proportionately to the amounts paid up on the shares during any portion or portions of the period in respect of which the dividend is paid.

(2) If any share is issued on terms providing that it ranks for dividend as from a particular date, that share ranks for dividend accordingly.

(3) For the purposes of calculating dividends, no account is to be taken of any amount which has been paid up on a share in advance of the due date for payment of that amount.

74 NO INTEREST ON DISTRIBUTIONS

The company may not pay interest on any dividend or other sum payable in respect of a share unless otherwise provided by—

(a) the terms on which the share was issued, or

(b) the provisions of another agreement between the holder of that share and the company.

75 UNCLAIMED DISTRIBUTIONS

(1) All dividends or other sums which are—
(a) payable in respect of shares, and
(b) unclaimed after having been declared or become payable,
may be invested or otherwise made use of by the directors for the benefit of the company until claimed.

(2) The payment of any such dividend or other sum into a separate account does not make the company a trustee in respect of it.

(3) If—
(a) twelve years have passed from the date on which a dividend or other sum became due for payment, and
(b) the distribution recipient has not claimed it,
the distribution recipient is no longer entitled to that dividend or other sum and it ceases to remain owing by the company.

76 NON-CASH DISTRIBUTIONS

(1) Subject to the terms of issue of the share in question, the company may, by ordinary resolution on the recommendation of the directors, decide to pay all or part of a dividend or other distribution payable in respect of a share by transferring non-cash assets of equivalent value (including, without limitation, shares or other securities in any company).

(2) If the shares in respect of which such a non-cash distribution is paid are uncertificated, any shares in the company which are issued as a non-cash distribution in respect of them must be uncertificated.

Part 5 MISCELLANEOUS PROVISIONS

COMMUNICATIONS

79 MEANS OF COMMUNICATION TO BE USED

(1) Subject to the articles, anything sent or supplied by or to the company under the articles may be sent or supplied in any way in which the Companies Act 2006 provides for

documents or information which are authorised or required by any provision of that Act to be sent or supplied by or to the company.

(2) Subject to the articles, any notice or document to be sent or supplied to a director in connection with the taking of decisions by directors may also be sent or supplied by the means by which that director has asked to be sent or supplied with such notices or documents for the time being.

ADMINISTRATIVE ARRANGEMENTS

83 NO RIGHT TO INSPECT ACCOUNTS AND OTHER RECORDS

Except as provided by law or authorised by the directors or an ordinary resolution of the company, no person is entitled to inspect any of the company's accounting or other records or documents merely by virtue of being a member.

84 PROVISION FOR EMPLOYEES ON CESSATION OF BUSINESS

The directors may decide to make provision for the benefit of persons employed or formerly employed by the company or any of its subsidiaries (other than a director or former director or shadow director) in connection with the cessation or transfer to any person of the whole or part of the undertaking of the company or that subsidiary.

DIRECTORS' INDEMNITY AND INSURANCE

85 INDEMNITY

(1) Subject to paragraph (2), a relevant director of the company or an associated company may be indemnified out of the company's assets against—
   (a) any liability incurred by that director in connection with any negligence, default, breach of duty or breach of trust in relation to the company or an associated company?...
   ...
   (c) any other liability incurred by that director as an officer of the company or an associated company.

(2) This article does not authorise any indemnity which would be prohibited or rendered void by any provision of the Companies Acts or by any other provision of law.

(3) In this article—
   (a) companies are associated if one is a subsidiary of the other or both are subsidiaries of the same body corporate, and
   (b) a "relevant director" means any director or former director of the company or an associated company.

86 INSURANCE

(1) The directors may decide to purchase and maintain insurance, at the expense of the company, for the benefit of any relevant director in respect of any relevant loss.

(2) In this article—
   (a) a "relevant director" means any director or former director of the company or an associated company,

(b) a "relevant loss" means any loss or liability which has been or may be incurred by a relevant director in connection with that director's duties or powers in relation to the company, any associated company or any pension fund or employees' share scheme of the company or associated company, and

(c) companies are associated if one is a subsidiary of the other or both are subsidiaries of the same body corporate.

EXPLANATORY NOTE

(This note is not part of the Regulations)
These Regulations, made under section 19 of the Companies Act 2006 (c.46), prescribe model forms of articles of association for—

(a) private companies limited by shares (regulation 2 and Schedule 1), ... and

(c) public companies (regulation 4 and Schedule 3).

These model articles will automatically form the articles of association for companies formed under the Companies Act 2006 which, on their formation, either do not register their own articles of association with the registrar of companies under that Act, or, if they do so, do not exclude the model articles in whole or in part (section 20 of the 2006 Act). Other companies are free to adopt the model articles in whole or in part.

...

These Regulations came into force on 1st October 2009.

The Takeover Code (The Takeover Panel, March 2009)

GENERAL PRINCIPLES

1. All holders of the securities of an offeree company of the same class must be afforded equivalent treatment; moreover, if a person acquires control of a company, the other holders of securities must be protected.

2. The holders of the securities of an offeree company must have sufficient time and information to enable them to reach a properly informed decision on the bid; where it advises the holders of securities, the board of the offeree company must give its views on the effects of implementation of the bid on employment, conditions of employment and the locations of the company's places of business.

3. The board of an offeree company must act in the interests of the company as a whole and must not deny the holders of securities the opportunity to decide on the merits of the bid.

4. False markets must not be created in the securities of the offeree company, of the offeror company or of any other company concerned by the bid in such a way that the rise or fall of the prices of the securities becomes artificial and the normal functioning of the markets is distorted.

5. An offeror must announce a bid only after ensuring that he/she can fulfil in full any cash consideration, if such is offered, and after taking all reasonable measures to secure the implementation of any other type of consideration.

6. An offeree company must not be hindered in the conduct of its affairs for longer than is reasonable by a bid for its securities.

RULE 1 THE APPROACH

(a) The offer must be put forward in the first instance to the board of the offeree company or to its advisers.

(b) If the offer, or an approach with a view to an offer being made, is not made by the ultimate offeror or potential offeror, the identity of that person must be disclosed at the outset.

(c) A board so approached is entitled to be satisfied that the offeror is, or will be, in a position to implement the offer in full.

RULE 2 SECRECY BEFORE ANNOUNCEMENTS; THE TIMING AND CONTENTS OF ANNOUNCEMENTS

2.1 SECRECY

The vital importance of absolute secrecy before an announcement must be emphasised. All persons privy to confidential information, and particularly price-sensitive information, concerning an offer or contemplated offer must treat that information as secret and may only pass it to another person if it is necessary to do so and if that person is made aware of the need for secrecy. All such persons must conduct themselves so as to minimise the chances of an accidental leak of information.

2.2 WHEN AN ANNOUNCEMENT IS REQUIRED

An announcement is required:—

(a) when a firm intention to make an offer (the making of which is not, or has ceased to be, subject to any pre-condition) is notified to the board of the offeree company from a serious source, irrespective of the attitude of the board to the offer;

(b) immediately upon an acquisition of any interest in shares which gives rise to an obligation to make an offer under Rule 9. The announcement that an obligation has been incurred should not be delayed while full information is being obtained; additional information can be the subject of a later supplementary announcement;

(c) when, following an approach to the offeree company, the offeree company is the subject of rumour and speculation or there is an untoward movement in its share price;

(d) when, before an approach has been made, the offeree company is the subject of rumour and speculation or there is an untoward movement in its share price and there are reasonable grounds for concluding that it is the potential offeror's actions (whether through inadequate security or otherwise) which have led to the situation;

(e) when negotiations or discussions relating to a possible offer are about to be extended to include more than a very restricted number of people (outside those who need to know in the parties concerned and their immediate advisers); or

(f) when a purchaser is being sought for an interest, or interests, in shares carrying in aggregate 30% or more of the voting rights of a company or when the board of a company is seeking one or more potential offerors, and:
   (i) the company is the subject of rumour and speculation or there is an untoward movement in its share price; or
   (ii) the number of potential purchasers or offerors approached is about to be increased to include more than a very restricted number of people.

RULE 3. INDEPENDENT ADVICE

3.1 BOARD OF THE OFFEREE COMPANY

The board of the offeree company must obtain competent independent advice on any offer and the substance of such advice must be made known to its shareholders.

RULE 4

4.1 PROHIBITED DEALINGS BY PERSONS OTHER THAN THE OFFEROR

(a) No dealings of any kind in securities of the offeree company by any person, not being the offeror, who is privy to confidential price-sensitive information concerning an offer or contemplated offer may take place between the time when there is reason to suppose that an approach or an offer is contemplated and the announcement of the approach or offer or of the termination of the discussions.

(b) No person who is privy to such information may make any recommendation to any other person as to dealing in the relevant securities.

(c) No such dealings may take place in securities of the offeror except where the proposed offer is not price-sensitive in relation to such securities.

4.2 RESTRICTION ON DEALINGS BY THE OFFEROR AND CONCERT PARTIES

(a) During an offer period, the offeror and persons acting in concert with it must not sell any securities in the offeree company except with the prior consent of the Panel and following 24 hours public notice that such sales might be made. The Panel will not give consent for sales where a mandatory offer under Rule 9 is being made. Sales below the value of the offer will not be permitted. After there has been an announcement that sales may be made, neither the offeror nor persons acting in concert with it may acquire an interest in any securities of the offeree company and only in exceptional circumstances will the Panel permit the offer to be revised. The Panel should be consulted whenever the offeror or a person acting in concert with it proposes to enter into or close out any type of transaction which may result in securities in the offeree company being sold during the offer period either by that party or by the counterparty to the transaction.

RULE 9

9.1 WHEN A MANDATORY OFFER IS REQUIRED AND WHO IS PRIMARILY RESPONSIBLE FOR MAKING IT

Except with the consent of the Panel, when:—

(a) any person acquires, whether by a series of transactions over a period of time or not, an interest in shares which (taken together with shares in which persons acting in concert with him are interested) carry 30% or more of the voting rights of a company; or

(b) any person, together with persons acting in concert with him, is interested in shares which in the aggregate carry not less than 30% of the voting rights of a company but does not hold shares carrying more than 50% of such voting rights and such person, or any person acting in concert with him, acquires an interest in any other shares which increases the percentage of shares carrying voting rights in which he is interested,

such person shall extend offers, on the basis set out in Rules 9.3… and 9.5, to the holders of any class of equity share capital whether voting or non-voting and also to the holders of any other class of transferable securities carrying voting rights. Offers for different classes of equity share capital must be comparable; the Panel should be consulted in advance in such cases.

An offer will not be required under this Rule where control of the offeree company is acquired as a result of a voluntary offer made in accordance with the Code to all the holders of voting equity share capital and other transferable securities carrying voting rights.

9.3 CONDITIONS AND CONSENTS

Except with the consent of the Panel…:

(a) offers made under this Rule must be conditional only upon the offeror having received acceptances in respect of shares which, together with shares acquired or agreed to be acquired before or during the offer, will result in the offeror and any person acting in concert with it holding shares carrying more than 50% of the voting rights.

…

9.5 CONSIDERATION TO BE OFFERED

(a) An offer made under Rule 9 must, in respect of each class of share capital involved, be in cash or be accompanied by a cash alternative at not less than the highest price paid by the offeror or any person acting in concert with it for any interest in shares of that class during the 12 months prior to the announcement of that offer. The Panel should be consulted where there is more than one class of share capital involved.

RULE 21. RESTRICTIONS ON FRUSTRATING ACTION

21.1 WHEN SHAREHOLDERS' CONSENT IS REQUIRED

During the course of an offer, or even before the date of the offer if the board of the offeree company has reason to believe that a bona fide offer might be imminent, the board must not, without the approval of the shareholders in general meeting:—

(a) take any action which may result in any offer or bona fide possible offer being frustrated or in shareholders being denied the opportunity to decide on its merits; or

(b) (i) issue any authorised but unissued shares or transfer or sell, or agree to transfer or sell, any shares out of treasury;
(ii) issue or grant options in respect of any unissued shares;
(iii) create or issue, or permit the creation or issue of, any securities carrying rights of conversion into or subscription for shares;
(iv) sell, dispose of or acquire, or agree to sell, dispose of or acquire, assets of a material amount; or
(v) enter into contracts otherwise than in the ordinary course of business.

The Panel must be consulted in advance if there is any doubt as to whether any proposed action may fall within this Rule.

The notice convening any relevant meeting of shareholders must include information about the offer or anticipated offer.

Where it is felt that:

(a) the proposed action is in pursuance of a contract entered into earlier or another pre-existing obligation; or

(b) a decision to take the proposed action had been taken before the beginning of the period referred to above which:
(i) has been partly or fully implemented before the beginning of that period; or
(ii) has not been partly or fully implemented before the beginning of that period but is in the ordinary course of business,
the Panel must be consulted and its consent to proceed without a shareholders' meeting obtained.

RULE 23. THE GENERAL OBLIGATION AS TO INFORMATION

Shareholders must be given sufficient information and advice to enable them to reach a properly informed decision as to the merits or demerits of an offer. Such information must be available to shareholders early enough to enable them to make a decision in good time. No relevant information should be withheld from them. The obligation of the offeror in these respects towards the shareholders of the offeree company is no less than an offeror's obligation towards its own shareholders.

RULE 24. OFFEROR DOCUMENTS

24.1 INTENTIONS REGARDING THE OFFEREE COMPANY, THE OFFEROR COMPANY AND THEIR EMPLOYEES

An offeror will be required to cover the following points in the offer document:—

(a) its intentions regarding the future business of the offeree company;

(b) its strategic plans for the offeree company, and their likely repercussions on employment and the locations of the offeree company's places of business;

(c) its intentions regarding any redeployment of the fixed assets of the offeree company;

(d) the long-term commercial justification for the proposed offer; and

(e) its intentions with regard to the continued employment of the employees and management of the offeree company and of its subsidiaries, including any material change in the conditions of employment.

Where the offeror is a company and insofar as it is affected by the offer, the offeror must also cover (a), (b) and (e) with regard to itself.

RULE 25. OFFEREE BOARD CIRCULARS

25.1 VIEWS OF THE BOARD ON THE OFFER, INCLUDING THE OFFEROR'S PLANS FOR THE COMPANY AND ITS EMPLOYEES

(a) The board of the offeree company must send its opinion on the offer (including any alternative offers) to the offeree company's shareholders and persons with information rights. It must, at the same time, make known to its shareholders the substance of the advice given to it by the independent advisers appointed pursuant to Rule 3.1.

(b) The opinion referred to in (a) above must include the views of the board of the offeree company on:

(i) the effects of implementation of the offer on all the company's interests, including, specifically, employment; and

(ii) the offeror's strategic plans for the offeree company and their likely repercussions on employment and the locations of the offeree company's places of business, as set out in the offer document pursuant to Rule 24.1,

and must state the board's reasons for forming its opinion.

(c) If any document published in connection with an offer includes a recommendation or an opinion of a financial adviser for or against acceptance of the offer, the document must, unless published by the financial adviser in question, include a statement that the financial adviser has given and not withdrawn its consent to the publication of the document with the inclusion of its recommendation or opinion in the form and context in which it is included.

RULE 30. PUBLISHING THE OFFER DOCUMENT AND THE OFFEREE BOARD CIRCULAR

30.1 THE OFFER DOCUMENT

(a) The offer document should normally be sent to shareholders of the offeree company and persons with information rights within 28 days of the announcement of a firm intention to make an offer.

(b) At the same time, both the offeror and the offeree company must make the offer document readily available to their employee representatives or, where there are no such representatives, to the employees themselves.

30.2 THE OFFEREE BOARD CIRCULAR

(a) The board of the offeree company must publish a circular containing its opinion, as required by Rule 25.1(a), as soon as practicable after publication of the offer document and normally within 14 days and must:

(i) send it to its shareholders and to persons with information rights; and
(ii) make it readily and promptly available to its employee representatives or, where there are no such representatives, the employees themselves.

...

(b) The board of the offeree company must append to the circular containing its opinion a separate opinion from the representatives of its employees on the effects of the offer on employment, provided such opinion is received in good time before publication of that circular.

RULE 31. TIMING OF THE OFFER

31.1 FIRST CLOSING DATE

An offer must initially be open for at least 21 days following the date on which the offer document is published.

31.4 OFFER TO REMAIN OPEN FOR 14 DAYS AFTER UNCONDITIONAL AS TO ACCEPTANCES

After an offer has become or is declared unconditional as to acceptances, the offer must remain open for acceptance for not less than 14 days after the date on which it would otherwise have expired...

RULE 35

35.1 DELAY OF 12 MONTHS

Except with the consent of the Panel, where an offer has been announced or made but has not become or been declared wholly unconditional and has been withdrawn or has lapsed ..., neither the offeror, nor any person who acted in concert with the offeror in the course of the original offer, nor any person who is subsequently acting in concert with any of them, may within 12 months from the date on which such offer is withdrawn or lapses either:

(a) announce an offer or possible offer for the offeree company (including a partial offer which could result in the offeror and persons acting in concert with it being interested in shares carrying 30% or more of the voting rights of the offeree company);

(b) acquire any interest in shares of the offeree company if the offeror or any such person would thereby become obliged under Rule 9 to make an offer;

(c) acquire any interest in, or procure an irrevocable commitment in respect of, shares of the offeree company if the shares in which such person, together with any persons acting in concert with him, would be interested and the shares in respect of which he, or they, had acquired irrevocable commitments would in aggregate carry 30% or more of the voting rights of the offeree company;

(d) make any statement which raises or confirms the possibility that an offer might be made for the offeree company; or

(e) take any steps in connection with a possible offer for the offeree company where knowledge of the possible offer might be extended outside those who need to know in the offeror and its immediate advisers.

35.3 DELAY OF 6 MONTHS BEFORE ACQUISITIONS ABOVE THE OFFER VALUE

Except with the consent of the Panel, if a person, together with any person acting in concert with him, holds shares carrying more than 50% of the voting rights of a company, neither that person nor any person acting in concert with him may, within 6 months of the closure of any previous offer made by him to the shareholders of that company which became or was declared wholly unconditional, make a second offer to any shareholder in that company, or acquire any interest in shares in that company, on more favourable terms than those made available under the previous offer...?. For this purpose the value of a securities exchange offer shall be calculated as at the date the offer closed. In addition, special deals with favourable conditions attached may not be entered into during this 6 months period...?.

APPENDIX 3 DIRECTORS' RESPONSIBILITIES AND CONFLICTS OF INTEREST GUIDANCE NOTE

1 DIRECTORS' RESPONSIBILITIES

While a board of directors may delegate the day-to-day conduct of an offer to individual directors or a committee of directors, the board as a whole must ensure that proper arrangements are in place to enable it to monitor that conduct in order that each director may fulfil his responsibilities under the Code. These arrangements should ensure that:

(a) the board is provided promptly with copies of all documents and announcements published by or on behalf of their company which bear on the offer; the board receives promptly details of all dealings in relevant securities made by their company or its associates and details of any agreements, understandings, guarantees, expenditure (including fees) or other obligations entered into or incurred by or on behalf of their company in the context of the offer which do not relate to routine administrative matters;

(b) those directors with day-to-day responsibility for the offer are in a position to justify to the board all their actions and proposed courses of action; and

(c) the opinions of advisers are available to the board where appropriate.

The above procedures should be followed, and board meetings held, as and when necessary throughout the offer in order to ensure that all directors are kept up-to-date with events and with actions taken.

Any director who has a question concerning the propriety of any action as far as the Code is concerned should ensure that the Panel is consulted.

The Panel expects directors to co-operate with it in connection with its enquiries; this will include the provision, promptly on request, of copies of minutes of board meetings and other information in their possession, or in the possession of an offeror or the offeree company as appropriate, which may be relevant to the enquiry.

The UK Corporate Governance Code (Financial Reporting Council, June 2010)

GOVERNANCE AND THE CODE

1. The purpose of corporate governance is to facilitate effective, entrepreneurial and prudent management that can deliver the long-term success of the company.

2. The first version of the UK Code on Corporate Governance (the Code) was produced in 1992 by the Cadbury Committee. Its paragraph 2.5 is still the classic definition of the context of the Code:

   Corporate governance is the system by which companies are directed and controlled. Boards of directors are responsible for the governance of their companies. The shareholders' role in governance is to appoint the directors and the auditors and to satisfy themselves that an appropriate governance structure is in place. The responsibilities of the board include setting the company's strategic aims, providing the leadership to put them into effect, supervising the management of the business and reporting to shareholders on their stewardship. The board's actions are subject to laws, regulations and the shareholders in general meeting.

3. Corporate governance is therefore about what the board of a company does and how it sets the values of the company, and is to be distinguished from the day to day operational management of the company by full-time executives.

4. The Code is a guide to a number of key components of effective board practice. It is based on the underlying principles of all good governance: accountability, transparency, probity and focus on the sustainable success of an entity over the longer term.

5. The Code has been enduring, but it is not immutable. Its fitness for purpose in a permanently changing economic and social business environment requires its evaluation at appropriate intervals. The reviews preceding this one were in 2005 and 2007. The Preface, which should be regarded as an integral part of the Code, introduces the changes made in the current review.

6. The new Code applies to accounting periods beginning on or after 29 June 2010 and, as a result of the new Listing Regime introduced in April 2010, applies to all companies with a Premium Listing of equity shares regardless of whether they are incorporated in the UK or elsewhere.

PREFACE

1. The financial crisis which came to a head in 2008–09 triggered widespread reappraisal, locally and internationally, of the governance systems which might have alleviated it. In the UK, Sir David Walker was asked to review the governance of banks and other financial institutions, and the FRC decided to bring forward the Code review scheduled for 2010 so that corporate governance in other listed companies could be assessed at the same time.

2. Two principal conclusions were drawn by the FRC from its review. First, that much more attention needed to be paid to following the spirit of the Code as well as its letter. Secondly, that the impact of shareholders in monitoring the Code could and should be enhanced by better interaction between the boards of listed companies and their shareholders. To this end, the FRC has assumed responsibility for a stewardship code that will provide guidance on good practice for investors.

3. Nearly two decades of constructive usage have enhanced the prestige of the Code. Indeed, it seems that there is almost a belief that complying with the Code in itself constitutes good governance. The Code, however, is of necessity limited to being a guide only in general terms to principles, structure and processes. It cannot guarantee effective board behaviour because the range of situations in which it is applicable is much too great for it to attempt to mandate behaviour more specifically than it does. Boards therefore have a lot of room within the framework of the Code to decide for themselves how they should act.

4. To follow the spirit of the Code to good effect, boards must think deeply, thoroughly and on a continuing basis, about their overall tasks and the implications of these for the roles of their individual members. Absolutely key in this endeavour are the leadership of the chairman of a board, the support given to and by the CEO, and the frankness and openness of mind with which issues are discussed and tackled by all directors.

5. The challenge should not be underrated. To run a corporate board successfully is extremely demanding. Constraints on time and knowledge combine with the need to maintain mutual respect and openness between a cast of strong, able and busy directors dealing with each other across the different demands of executive and non-executive roles. To achieve good governance requires continuing and high quality effort.

6. The Code's function should be to help boards discharge their duties in the best interests of their companies. The FRC in this review has focussed on changing the "tone" of the Code by making limited but significant changes to signal the importance of the general principles which should guide board behaviours. It is to be hoped that these changes will promote greater clarity and understanding with regard to the tasks of a board and that communication with shareholders will be more effective as a result.

7. Chairmen are encouraged to report personally in their annual statements how the principles relating to the role and effectiveness of the board (in Sections A and B of the new Code) have been applied. Not only will this give investors a clearer picture of the steps taken by boards to operate effectively but also, by providing fuller context, it may make investors more willing to accept explanations when a company chooses to explain rather than to comply with one or more provisions. Above all, the personal reporting on governance by chairmen as the leaders of boards might be a turning point in attacking the fungus of "boiler-plate" which is so often the preferred and easy option in sensitive areas but which is dead communication.

8. The new Code recommends that, in the interests of greater accountability, all directors of FTSE 350 companies should be subject to annual reelection. As with all other provisions

of the Code, companies are free to explain rather than comply if they believe that their existing arrangements ensure proper accountability and underpin board effectiveness, or that a transitional period is needed before they introduce annual re-election. The boards of smaller companies are also encouraged to consider their policy on director re-election.

COMPLY OR EXPLAIN

1. The "comply or explain" approach is the trademark of corporate governance in the UK. It has been in operation since the Code's beginnings and is the foundation of the Code's flexibility. It is strongly supported by both companies and shareholders and has been widely admired and imitated internationally.

2. The Code is not a rigid set of rules. It consists of principles (main and supporting) and provisions. The Listing Rules require companies to apply the Main Principles and report to shareholders on how they have done so. The principles are the core of the Code and the way in which they are applied should be the central question for a board as it determines how it is to operate according to the Code.

3. It is recognised that an alternative to following a provision may be justified in particular circumstances if good governance can be achieved by other means. A condition of doing so is that the reasons for it should be explained clearly and carefully to shareholders, who may wish to discuss the position with the company and whose voting intentions may be influenced as a result. In providing an explanation, the company should aim to illustrate how its actual practices are both consistent with the principle to which the particular provision relates and contribute to good governance.

4. In their responses to explanations, shareholders should pay due regard to companies' individual circumstances and bear in mind, in particular, the size and complexity of the company and the nature of the risks and challenges it faces. Whilst shareholders have every right to challenge companies' explanations if they are unconvincing, they should not be evaluated in a mechanistic way and departures from the Code should not be automatically treated as breaches. Shareholders should be careful to respond to the statements from companies in a manner that supports the "comply or explain" process and bearing in mind the purpose of good corporate governance. They should put their views to the company and both parties should be prepared to discuss the position.

5. Smaller listed companies, in particular those new to listing, may judge that some of the provisions are disproportionate or less relevant in their case. Some of the provisions do not apply to companies below the FTSE 350. Such companies may nonetheless consider that it would be appropriate to adopt the approach in the Code and they are encouraged to do so. Externally managed investment companies typically have a different board structure which may affect the relevance of particular provisions; the Association of Investment Companies' Corporate Governance Code and Guide can assist them in meeting their obligations under the Code.

6. Satisfactory engagement between company boards and investors is crucial to the health of the UK's corporate governance regime. Companies and shareholders both have responsibility for ensuring that "comply or explain" remains an effective alternative to a rules-based system. There are practical and administrative obstacles to improved interaction between boards and shareholders. But certainly there is also scope for an increase in trust which could generate a virtuous upward spiral in attitudes to the Code and in its constructive use.

THE MAIN PRINCIPLES OF THE CODE

Section A: LEADERSHIP

Every company should be headed by an effective board which is collectively responsible for the long-term success of the company.

There should be a clear division of responsibilities at the head of the company between the running of the board and the executive responsibility for the running of the company's business. No one individual should have unfettered powers of decision.

The chairman is responsible for leadership of the board and ensuring its effectiveness on all aspects of its role.

As part of their role as members of a unitary board, non-executive directors should constructively challenge and help develop proposals on strategy.

Section B: EFFECTIVENESS

The board and its committees should have the appropriate balance of skills, experience, independence and knowledge of the company to enable them to discharge their respective duties and responsibilities effectively.

There should be a formal, rigorous and transparent procedure for the appointment of new directors to the board.

All directors should be able to allocate sufficient time to the company to discharge their responsibilities effectively.

All directors should receive induction on joining the board and should regularly update and refresh their skills and knowledge.

The board should be supplied in a timely manner with information in a form and of a quality appropriate to enable it to discharge its duties.

The board should undertake a formal and rigorous annual evaluation of its own performance and that of its committees and individual directors.

All directors should be submitted for re-election at regular intervals, subject to continued satisfactory performance.

Section C: ACCOUNTABILITY

The board should present a balanced and understandable assessment of the company's position and prospects.

The board is responsible for determining the nature and extent of the significant risks it is willing to take in achieving its strategic objectives. The board should maintain sound risk management and internal control systems.

The board should establish formal and transparent arrangements for considering how they should apply the corporate reporting and risk management and internal control principles and for maintaining an appropriate relationship with the company's auditor.

Section D: REMUNERATION

Levels of remuneration should be sufficient to attract, retain and motivate directors of the quality required to run the company successfully, but a company should avoid paying more than is necessary for this purpose. A significant proportion of executive directors' remuneration should be structured so as to link rewards to corporate and individual performance.

There should be a formal and transparent procedure for developing policy on executive remuneration and for fixing the remuneration packages of individual directors. No director should be involved in deciding his or her own remuneration.

Section E: RELATIONS WITH SHAREHOLDERS

There should be a dialogue with shareholders based on the mutual understanding of objectives. The board as a whole has responsibility for ensuring that a satisfactory dialogue with shareholders takes place.

The board should use the AGM to communicate with investors and to encourage their participation.

SECTION A: LEADERSHIP

A.1 The Role of the Board

MAIN PRINCIPLE

Every company should be headed by an effective board which is collectively responsible for the long-term success of the company.

SUPPORTING PRINCIPLES

The board's role is to provide entrepreneurial leadership of the company within a framework of prudent and effective controls which enables risk to be assessed and managed. The board should set the company's strategic aims, ensure that the necessary financial and human resources are in place for the company to meet its objectives and review management performance. The board should set the company's values and standards and ensure that its obligations to its shareholders and others are understood and met.

All directors must act in what they consider to be the best interests of the company, consistent with their statutory duties.

CODE PROVISIONS

A.1.1 The board should meet sufficiently regularly to discharge its duties effectively. There should be a formal schedule of matters specifically reserved for its decision. The annual report should include a statement of how the board operates, including a high level statement of which types of decisions are to be taken by the board and which are to be delegated to management.

A.1.2 The annual report should identify the chairman, the deputy chairman (where there is one), the chief executive, the senior independent director and the chairmen and members of the board committees. It should also set out the number of meetings of the board and its committees and individual attendance by directors.

A.1.3 The company should arrange appropriate insurance cover in respect of legal action against its directors.

A.2 Division of Responsibilities

MAIN PRINCIPLE

There should be a clear division of responsibilities at the head of the company between the running of the board and the executive responsibility for the running of the company's business. No one individual should have unfettered powers of decision.

CODE PROVISION

A.2.1 The roles of chairman and chief executive should not be exercised by the same individual. The division of responsibilities between the chairman and chief executive should be clearly established, set out in writing and agreed by the board.

A.3 The Chairman

MAIN PRINCIPLE

The chairman is responsible for leadership of the board and ensuring its effectiveness on all aspects of its role.

SUPPORTING PRINCIPLES

The chairman is responsible for setting the board's agenda and ensuring that adequate time is available for discussion of all agenda items, in particular strategic issues. The chairman should also promote a culture of openness and debate by facilitating the effective contribution of non-executive directors in particular and ensuring constructive relations between executive and non-executive directors.

The chairman is responsible for ensuring that the directors receive accurate, timely and clear information. The chairman should ensure effective communication with shareholders.

CODE PROVISION

A.3.1 The chairman should on appointment meet the independence criteria set out in B.1.1 below. A chief executive should not go on to be chairman of the same company. If, exceptionally, a board decides that a chief executive should become chairman, the board should consult major shareholders in advance and should set out its reasons to shareholders at the time of the appointment and in the next annual report.

A.4 Non-executive Directors

MAIN PRINCIPLE

As part of their role as members of a unitary board, non-executive directors should constructively challenge and help develop proposals on strategy.

SUPPORTING PRINCIPLE

Non-executive directors should scrutinise the performance of management in meeting agreed goals and objectives and monitor the reporting of performance. They should satisfy themselves on the integrity of financial information and that financial controls and systems of risk management are robust and defensible. They are responsible for determining appropriate levels of remuneration of executive directors and have a prime role in appointing, and where necessary removing, executive directors, and in succession planning.

CODE PROVISIONS

A.4.1 The board should appoint one of the independent non-executive directors to be the senior independent director to provide a sounding board for the chairman and to serve as an intermediary for the other directors when necessary. The senior independent director should be available to shareholders if they have concerns which contact through the normal channels of chairman, chief executive or other executive directors has failed to resolve or for which such contact is inappropriate.

A.4.2 The chairman should hold meetings with the non-executive directors without the executives present. Led by the senior independent director, the non-executive directors should meet without the chairman present at least annually to appraise the chairman's performance and on such other occasions as are deemed appropriate.

A.4.3 Where directors have concerns which cannot be resolved about the running of the company or a proposed action, they should ensure that their concerns are recorded in the board minutes. On resignation, a nonexecutive director should provide a written statement to the chairman, for circulation to the board, if they have any such concerns.

SECTION B: EFFECTIVENESS

B.1 The Composition of the Board

MAIN PRINCIPLE

The board and its committees should have the appropriate balance of skills, experience, independence and knowledge of the company to enable them to discharge their respective duties and responsibilities effectively.

SUPPORTING PRINCIPLES

The board should be of sufficient size that the requirements of the business can be met and that changes to the board's composition and that of its committees can be managed without undue disruption, and should not be so large as to be unwieldy.

The board should include an appropriate balance of executive and non-executive directors (and, in particular, independent non-executive directors) such that no individual or small group of individuals can dominate the board's decision taking.

The value of ensuring that committee membership is refreshed and that undue reliance is not placed on particular individuals should be taken into account in deciding chairmanship and membership of committees.

No one other than the committee chairman and members is entitled to be present at a meeting of the nomination, audit or remuneration committee, but others may attend at the invitation of the committee.

CODE PROVISIONS

B.1.1 The board should identify in the annual report each non-executive director it considers to be independent. The board should determine whether the director is independent in character and judgment and whether there are relationships or circumstances which are likely to affect, or could appear to affect, the director's judgment. The board should state its reasons if it determines that a director is independent notwithstanding the existence of relationships or circumstances which may appear relevant to its determination, including if the director:

- has been an employee of the company or group within the last five years;
- has, or has had within the last three years, a material business relationship with the company either directly, or as a partner, shareholder, director or senior employee of a body that has such a relationship with the company;
- has received or receives additional remuneration from the company apart from a director's fee, participates in the company's share option or a performance-related pay scheme, or is a member of the company's pension scheme;
- has close family ties with any of the company's advisers, directors or senior employees;
- holds cross-directorships or has significant links with other directors through involvement in other companies or bodies;
- represents a significant shareholder; or
- has served on the board for more than nine years from the date of their first election.

B.1.2 Except for smaller companies, at least half the board, excluding the chairman, should comprise non-executive directors determined by the board to be independent. A smaller company should have at least two independent non-executive directors.

B.2 Appointments to the Board

MAIN PRINCIPLE

There should be a formal, rigorous and transparent procedure for the appointment of new directors to the board.

SUPPORTING PRINCIPLES

The search for board candidates should be conducted, and appointments made, on merit, against objective criteria and with due regard for the benefits of diversity on the board, incuding gender.

The board should satisfy itself that plans are in place for orderly succession for appointments to the board and to senior management, so as to maintain an appropriate balance of skills and experience within the company and on the board and to ensure progressive refreshing of the board.

CODE PROVISIONS

B.2.1 There should be a nomination committee which should lead the process for board appointments and make recommendations to the board. A majority of members of the nomination committee should be independent non-executive directors. The chairman or an independent non-executive director should chair the committee, but the chairman should not chair the nomination committee when it is dealing with the appointment of a successor to the chairmanship. The nomination committee should make available its terms of reference, explaining its role and the authority delegated to it by the board.

B.2.2 The nomination committee should evaluate the balance of skills, experience, independence and knowledge on the board and, in the light of this evaluation, prepare a description of the role and capabilities required for a particular appointment.

B.2.3 Non-executive directors should be appointed for specified terms subject to re-election and to statutory provisions relating to the removal of a director. Any term beyond six years for a non-executive director should be subject to particularly rigorous review, and should take into account the need for progressive refreshing of the board.

B.2.4 A separate section of the annual report should describe the work of the nomination committee, including the process it has used in relation to board appointments. An explanation should be given if neither an external search consultancy nor open advertising has been used in the appointment of a chairman or a non-executive director.

B.3 Commitment

MAIN PRINCIPLE

All directors should be able to allocate sufficient time to the company to discharge their responsibilities effectively.

CODE PROVISIONS

B.3.1 For the appointment of a chairman, the nomination committee should prepare a job specification, including an assessment of the time commitment expected, recognising the need for availability in the event of crises. A chairman's other significant commitments should be disclosed to the board before appointment and included in the annual report. Changes to such commitments should be reported to the board as they arise, and their impact explained in the next annual report.

B.3.2 The terms and conditions of appointment of non-executive directors should be made available for inspection. The letter of appointment should set out the expected time commitment. Non-executive directors should undertake that they will have sufficient time to meet what is expected of them. Their other significant commitments should be disclosed to the board before appointment, with a broad indication of the time involved and the board should be informed of subsequent changes.

B.3.3 The board should not agree to a full time executive director taking on more than one non-executive directorship in a FTSE 100 company nor the chairmanship of such a company.

B.4 Development

MAIN PRINCIPLE

All directors should receive induction on joining the board and should regularly update and refresh their skills and knowledge.

SUPPORTING PRINCIPLES

The chairman should ensure that the directors continually update their skills and the knowledge and familiarity with the company required to fulfil their role both on the board and on board committees. The company should provide the necessary resources for developing and updating its directors' knowledge and capabilities.

To function effectively, all directors need appropriate knowledge of the company and access to its operations and staff.

CODE PROVISIONS

B.4.1 The chairman should ensure that new directors receive a full, formal and tailored induction on joining the board. As part of this, directors should avail themselves of opportunities to meet major shareholders.

B.4.2 The chairman should regularly review and agree with each director their training and development needs.

B.5 Information and Support

MAIN PRINCIPLE

The board should be supplied in a timely manner with information in a form and of a quality appropriate to enable it to discharge its duties.

SUPPORTING PRINCIPLES

The chairman is responsible for ensuring that the directors receive accurate, timely and clear information. Management has an obligation to provide such information but directors should seek clarification or amplification where necessary.

Under the direction of the chairman, the company secretary's responsibilities include ensuring good information flows within the board and its committees and between senior management and nonexecutive directors, as well as facilitating induction and assisting with professional development as required.

The company secretary should be responsible for advising the board through the chairman on all governance matters.

CODE PROVISIONS

B.5.1 The board should ensure that directors, especially non-executive directors, have access to independent professional advice at the company's expense where they judge it necessary to discharge their responsibilities as directors. Committees should be provided with sufficient resources to undertake their duties.

B.5.2 All directors should have access to the advice and services of the company secretary, who is responsible to the board for ensuring that board procedures are complied with. Both the appointment and removal of the company secretary should be a matter for the board as a whole.

B.6 Evaluation

MAIN PRINCIPLE

The board should undertake a formal and rigorous annual evaluation of its own performance and that of its committees and individual directors.

SUPPORTING PRINCIPLES

The chairman should act on the results of the performance evaluation by recognising the strengths and addressing the weaknesses of the board and, where appropriate, proposing new members be appointed to the board or seeking the resignation of directors.

Individual evaluation should aim to show whether each director continues to contribute effectively and to demonstrate commitment to the role (including commitment of time for board and committee meetings and any other duties).

CODE PROVISIONS

B.6.1 The board should state in the annual report how performance evaluation of the board, its committees and its individual directors has been conducted.

B.6.2 Evaluation of the board of FTSE 350 companies should be externally facilitated at least every three years. A statement should be made available of whether an external facilitator has any other connection with the company.

B.6.3 The non-executive directors, led by the senior independent director, should be responsible for performance evaluation of the chairman, taking into account the views of executive directors.

B.7 Re-election

MAIN PRINCIPLE

All directors should be submitted for re-election at regular intervals, subject to continued satisfactory performance.

CODE PROVISIONS

B.7.1 All directors of FTSE 350 companies should be subject to annual election by shareholders. All other directors should be subject to election by shareholders at the first annual general meeting after their appointment, and to re-election thereafter at intervals of no more than three years. Non-executive directors who have served longer than nine years should be subject to annual re-election. The names of directors submitted for election or re-election should be accompanied by sufficient biographical details and any other relevant information to enable shareholders to take an informed decision on their election.

B.7.2 The board should set out to shareholders in the papers accompanying a resolution to elect a non-executive director why they believe an individual should be elected. The chairman should confirm to shareholders when proposing re-election that, following formal performance evaluation, the individual's performance continues to be effective and to demonstrate commitment to the role.

SECTION C: ACCOUNTABILITY

C.1 Financial and Business Reporting

MAIN PRINCIPLE

The board should present a balanced and understandable assessment of the company's position and prospects.

SUPPORTING PRINCIPLE

The board's responsibility to present a balanced and understandable assessment extends to interim and other price-sensitive public reports and reports to regulators as well as to information required to be presented by statutory requirements.

CODE PROVISIONS

C.1.1 The directors should explain in the annual report their responsibility for preparing the annual report and accounts, and there should be a statement by the auditor about their reporting responsibilities.

C.1.2 The directors should include in the annual report an explanation of the basis on which the company generates or preserves value over the longer term (the business model) and the strategy for delivering the objectives of the company.

C.1.3 The directors should report in annual and half-yearly financial statements that the business is a going concern, with supporting assumptions or qualifications as necessary.

C.2 Risk Management and Internal Control

MAIN PRINCIPLE

The board is responsible for determining the nature and extent of the significant risks it is willing to take in achieving its strategic objectives. The board should maintain sound risk management and internal control systems.

CODE PROVISION

C.2.1 The board should, at least annually, conduct a review of the effectiveness of the company's risk management and internal control systems and should report to shareholders that they have done so. The review should cover all material controls, including financial, operational and compliance controls.

C.3 Audit Committee and Auditors

MAIN PRINCIPLE

The board should establish formal and transparent arrangements for considering how they should apply the corporate reporting and risk management and internal control principles and for maintaining an appropriate relationship with the company's auditor.

CODE PROVISIONS

C.3.1 The board should establish an audit committee of at least three, or in the case of smaller companies two, independent non-executive directors. In smaller companies the company chairman may be a member of, but not chair, the committee in addition to the independent non-executive directors, provided he or she was considered independent on appointment as chairman. The board should satisfy itself that at least one member of the audit committee has recent and relevant financial experience.

C.3.2 The main role and responsibilities of the audit committee should be set out in written terms of reference and should include:

- to monitor the integrity of the financial statements of the company, and any formal announcements relating to the company's financial performance, reviewing significant financial reporting judgments contained in them;
- to review the company's internal financial controls and, unless expressly addressed by a separate board risk committee composed of independent directors, or by the board itself, to review the company's internal control and risk management systems;

- to monitor and review the effectiveness of the company's internal audit function;
- to make recommendations to the board, for it to put to the shareholders for their approval in general meeting, in relation to the appointment, re-appointment and removal of the external auditor and to approve the remuneration and terms of engagement of the external auditor;
- to review and monitor the external auditor's independence and objectivity and the effectiveness of the audit process, taking into consideration relevant UK professional and regulatory requirements;
- to develop and implement policy on the engagement of the external auditor to supply non-audit services, taking into account relevant ethical guidance regarding the provision of non-audit services by the external audit firm; and to report to the board, identifying any matters in respect of which it considers that action or improvement is needed and making recommendations as to the steps to be taken.

C.3.3 The terms of reference of the audit committee, including its role and the authority delegated to it by the board, should be made available. A separate section of the annual report should describe the work of the committee in discharging those responsibilities.

C.3.4 The audit committee should review arrangements by which staff of the company may, in confidence, raise concerns about possible improprieties in matters of financial reporting or other matters. The audit committee's objective should be to ensure that arrangements are in place for the proportionate and independent investigation of such matters and for appropriate follow-up action.

C.3.5 The audit committee should monitor and review the effectiveness of the internal audit activities. Where there is no internal audit function, the audit committee should consider annually whether there is a need for an internal audit function and make a recommendation to the board, and the reasons for the absence of such a function should be explained in the relevant section of the annual report.

C.3.6 The audit committee should have primary responsibility for making a recommendation on the appointment, reappointment and removal of the external auditors. If the board does not accept the audit committee's recommendation, it should include in the annual report, and in any papers recommending appointment or re-appointment, a statement from the audit committee explaining the recommendation and should set out reasons why the board has taken a different position.

C.3.7 The annual report should explain to shareholders how, if the auditor provides non-audit services, auditor objectivity and independence is safeguarded.

SECTION D: REMUNERATION

D.1 The Level and Components of Remuneration

MAIN PRINCIPLES

Levels of remuneration should be sufficient to attract, retain and motivate directors of the quality required to run the company successfully, but a company should avoid paying more than is necessary for this purpose. A significant proportion of executive directors' remuneration should be structured so as to link rewards to corporate and individual performance.

SUPPORTING PRINCIPLE

The performance-related elements of executive directors' remuneration should be stretching and designed to promote the long-term success of the company.

The remuneration committee should judge where to position their company relative to other companies. But they should use such comparisons with caution, in view of the risk of an upward ratchet of remuneration levels with no corresponding improvement in performance.

They should also be sensitive to pay and employment conditions elsewhere in the group, especially when determining annual salary increases.

CODE PROVISIONS

D.1.1 In designing schemes of performance-related remuneration for executive directors, the remuneration committee should follow the provisions in Schedule A to this Code.

D.1.2 Where a company releases an executive director to serve as a nonexecutive director elsewhere, the remuneration report should include a statement as to whether or not the director will retain such earnings and, if so, what the remuneration is.

D.1.3 Levels of remuneration for non-executive directors should reflect the time commitment and responsibilities of the role. Remuneration for non-executive directors should not include share options or other performance-related elements. If, exceptionally, options are granted, shareholder approval should be sought in advance and any shares acquired by exercise of the options should be held until at least one year after the non-executive director leaves the board. Holding of share options could be relevant to the determination of a non-executive director's independence (as set out in provision B.1.1).

D.1.4 The remuneration committee should carefully consider what compensation commitments (including pension contributions and all other elements) their directors' terms of appointment would entail in the event of early termination. The aim should be to avoid rewarding poor performance. They should take a robust line on reducing compensation to reflect departing directors' obligations to mitigate loss.

D.1.5 Notice or contract periods should be set at one year or less. If it is necessary to offer longer notice or contract periods to new directors recruited from outside, such periods should reduce to one year or less after the initial period.

D.2 Procedure

MAIN PRINCIPLE

There should be a formal and transparent procedure for developing policy on executive remuneration and for fixing the remuneration packages of individual directors. No director should be involved in deciding his or her own remuneration.

SUPPORTING PRINCIPLES

The remuneration committee should consult the chairman and/or chief executive about their proposals relating to the remuneration of other executive directors. The remuneration committee should also be responsible for appointing any consultants in respect of executive director remuneration. Where executive directors or senior management are involved in advising or supporting the remuneration committee, care should be taken to recognise and avoid conflicts of interest.

The chairman of the board should ensure that the company maintains contact as required with its principal shareholders about remuneration.

CODE PROVISIONS

D.2.1 The board should establish a remuneration committee of at least three, or in the case of smaller companies two, independent non-executive directors. In addition the company chairman may also be a member of, but not chair, the committee if he or she was considered independent on appointment as chairman. The remuneration committee should make available its terms of reference, explaining its role and the authority delegated to it by the board. Where remuneration consultants are appointed, a statement should be made available of whether they have any other connection with the company.

D.2.2 The remuneration committee should have delegated responsibility for setting remuneration for all executive directors and the chairman, including pension rights and any compensation payments. The committee should also recommend and monitor the level and structure of remuneration for senior management. The definition of 'senior management' for this purpose should be determined by the board but should normally include the first layer of management below board level.

D.2.3 The board itself or, where required by the Articles of Association, the shareholders should determine the remuneration of the non-executive directors within the limits set in the Articles of Association. Where permitted by the Articles, the board may however delegate this responsibility to a committee, which might include the chief executive.

D.2.4 Shareholders should be invited specifically to approve all new long-term incentive schemes (as defined in the Listing Rules) and significant changes to existing schemes, save in the circumstances permitted by the Listing Rules.

SECTION E: RELATIONS WITH SHAREHOLDERS

E.1 Dialogue with Shareholders

MAIN PRINCIPLE

There should be a dialogue with shareholders based on the mutual understanding of objectives. The board as a whole has responsibility for ensuring that a satisfactory dialogue with shareholders takes place.

SUPPORTING PRINCIPLES

Whilst recognising that most shareholder contact is with the chief executive and finance director, the chairman should ensure that all directors are made aware of their major shareholders' issues and concerns.

The board should keep in touch with shareholder opinion in whatever ways are most practical and efficient.

CODE PROVISIONS

E.1.1 The chairman should ensure that the views of shareholders are communicated to the board as a whole. The chairman should discuss governance and strategy with major shareholders. Non-executive directors should be offered the opportunity to attend meetings with major shareholders and should expect to attend them if requested by major shareholders. The senior independent director should attend sufficient meetings with a range of major shareholders to listen to their views in order to help develop a balanced understanding of the issues and concerns of major shareholders.

E.1.2 The board should state in the annual report the steps they have taken to ensure that the members of the board, and in particular the non-executive directors, develop an understanding of the views of major shareholders about their company, for example through direct face-to-face contact, analysts' or brokers' briefings and surveys of shareholder opinion.

E.2 Constructive Use of the AGM

MAIN PRINCIPLE

The board should use the AGM to communicate with investors and to encourage their participation.

CODE PROVISIONS

E.2.1 At any general meeting, the company should propose a separate resolution on each substantially separate issue, and should in particular propose a resolution at the AGM relating to the report and accounts. For each resolution, proxy appointment forms should provide shareholders with the option to direct their proxy to vote either for or against the resolution or to withhold their vote. The proxy form and any announcement of the results of a vote should make it clear that a 'vote withheld' is not a vote in law and will not be counted in the calculation of the proportion of the votes for and against the resolution.

E.2.2 The company should ensure that all valid proxy appointments received for general meetings are properly recorded and counted. For each resolution, after a vote has been taken, except where taken on a poll, the company should ensure that the following information is given at the meeting and made available as soon as reasonably practicable on a website which is maintained by or on behalf of the company:

- the number of shares in respect of which proxy appointments have been validly made;
- the number of votes for the resolution;
- the number of votes against the resolution; and
- the number of shares in respect of which the vote was directed to be withheld.

E.2.3 The chairman should arrange for the chairmen of the audit, remuneration and nomination committees to be available to answer questions at the AGM and for all directors to attend.

E.2.4 The company should arrange for the Notice of the AGM and related papers to be sent to shareholders at least 20 working days before the meeting.

SCHEDULE A THE DESIGN OF PERFORMANCE-RELATED REMUNERATION FOR EXECUTIVE DIRECTORS

The remuneration committee should consider whether the directors should be eligible for annual bonuses. If so, performance conditions should be relevant, stretching and designed to promote the long-term success of the company.

Upper limits should be set and disclosed. There may be a case for part payment in shares to be held for a significant period.

The remuneration committee should consider whether the directors should be eligible for benefits under long-term incentive schemes. Traditional share option schemes should be weighed against other kinds of long-term incentive scheme.

Executive share options should not be offered at a discount save as permitted by the relevant provisions of the Listing Rules.

In normal circumstances, shares granted or other forms of deferred remuneration should not vest, and options should not be exercisable, in less than three years. Directors should be encouraged to hold their shares for a further period after vesting or exercise, subject to the need to finance any costs of acquisition and associated tax liabilities.

Any new long-term incentive schemes which are proposed should be approved by shareholders and should preferably replace any existing schemes or, at least, form part of a well considered overall plan incorporating existing schemes.

The total potentially available rewards should not be excessive.

Payouts or grants under all incentive schemes, including new grants under existing share option schemes, should be subject to challenging performance criteria reflecting the company's objectives, including non-financial performance metrics where appropriate. Remuneration incentives should be compatible with risk policies and systems.

Grants under executive share option and other long-term incentive schemes should normally be phased rather than awarded in one large block.

Consideration should be given to the use of provisions that permit the company to reclaim variable components in exceptional circumstances of misstatement or misconduct.

In general, only basic salary should be pensionable. The remuneration committee should consider the pension consequences and associated costs to the company of basic salary increases and any other changes in pensionable remuneration, especially for directors close to retirement.

The UK Stewardship Code (Financial Reporting Council, July 2010)

PREFACE

The Stewardship Code aims to enhance the quality of engagement between institutional investors and companies to help improve long-term returns to shareholders and the efficient exercise of governance responsibilities.

Engagement includes pursuing purposeful dialogue on strategy, performance and the management of risk, as well as on issues that are the immediate subject of votes at general meetings.

The Code sets out good practice on engagement with investee companies to which the FRC believes institutional investors should aspire. It provides an opportunity to build a critical mass of UK and overseas investors committed to the high quality dialogue with companies needed to underpin good governance. By creating a sound basis of engagement it should create a much needed stronger link between governance and the investment process, and lend greater substance to the concept of "comply or explain" as applied by listed companies. The FRC therefore sees it as complementary to the UK Corporate Governance Code for listed companies, as revised in June 2010.

Institutional shareholders are free to choose whether or not to engage but their choice should be a considered one based on their investment approach. Their managers or agents are then responsible for ensuring that they comply with the terms of the mandate as agreed.

Disclosures made by institutions under the Code should assist companies to understand the approach and expectations of their major shareholders. They should also assist those issuing mandates to institutional fund managers to make a better informed choice, thereby improving the functioning of the market and facilitating the exercise of responsibility to end-investors.

As with the UK Corporate Governance Code, the Code should be applied on a "comply or explain" basis. In reporting terms this entails providing a statement on the institution's website that contains:

- a description of how the principles of the Code have been applied, and
- disclosure of the specific information listed under Principles 1, 5, 6 and 7; or
- an explanation of these elements of the Code have not been complied with.

It should be noted that compliance with the Code does not constitute an invitation to manage the affairs of investee companies or preclude a decision to sell a holding, where this is considered in the best interest of end-investors.

The Code is addressed in the first instance to firms who manage assets on behalf of institutional shareholders such as pension funds, insurance companies, investment trusts and other collective investment vehicles. The FRC expects those firms to disclose on their websites how they have applied the Code. Institutions that manage several types of fund need to make only one statement.

However the responsibility for monitoring company performance does not rest with fund managers alone. Pension fund trustees and other owners can do so either directly or indirectly through the mandates given to fund managers. Their actions can have a significant impact on the quality and quantity of engagement with UK companies. The FRC therefore strongly encourages all institutional investors to report if and how they have complied with the Code.

Principle 1 of the Code states that institutional investors that make use of proxy voting and other advisory services should disclose how they are used. The FRC encourages those service providers in turn to disclose how they carry out the wishes of their clients by applying the principles of the Code that are relevant to their activities.

The FRC recognises that not all parts of the Code will be relevant to all institutional investors, while smaller institutions may judge that some of its principles and guidance are disproportionate in their case. In these circumstances, they should take advantage of the "comply or explain" approach and set out why this is the case.

Specifically, the "explain" option means that overseas investors who follow other national or international standards that have similar objectives should not feel application of the Code duplicates or confuses their responsibilities. Disclosures made in respect of those standards can also be used to demonstrate the extent to which they have complied with the Code. In a similar spirit, UK institutions that apply the Code should use their best efforts to apply its principles to overseas holdings.

The FRC will retain on its website a list of those investors that have published a statement on their compliance or otherwise with the Code, and requests that they notify the FRC when they have done so. The FRC also considers that it would be good practice for each institution to name in its statement an individual who can be contacted for further information and by those interested in collective engagement.

The FRC will carry out regular monitoring of the take-up and application of the Code.

The FRC expects the content of the Code to evolve over time to reflect developments in good engagement practice, in the structure and operation of the market, and the broader regulatory framework, and it will need to give further consideration to issues raised in response to the consultation on this Code in the same light. A decision on the timing of the first review of the content of the Code will be taken in the second half of 2011.

Financial Reporting Council
July 2010

THE PRINCIPLES OF THE CODE

Institutional investors should:

- publicly disclose their policy on how they will discharge their stewardship responsibilities.
- have a robust policy on managing conflicts of interest in relation to stewardship and this policy should be publicly disclosed.
- monitor their investee companies.
- establish clear guidelines on when and how they will escalate their activities as a method of protecting and enhancing shareholder value.
- be willing to act collectively with other investors where appropriate.
- have a clear policy on voting and disclosure of voting activity.
- report periodically on their stewardship and voting activities.

Principle 1

Institutional investors should publicly disclose their policy on how they will discharge their stewardship responsibilities.

Guidance

The disclosure should include:

- how investee companies will be monitored. In order for monitoring to be effective an active dialogue may, where necessary, need to be entered into with the investee company's board;
- the strategy on intervention;
- internal arrangements, including how stewardship is integrated with the wider investment process;
- the policy on voting and the use made of, if any, proxy voting or other voting advisory service, including information on how they are used; and
- the policy on considering explanations made in relation to the UK Corporate Governance Code.

Principle 2

Institutional investors should have a robust policy on managing conflicts of interest in relation to stewardship and this policy should be publicly disclosed.

Guidance

An institutional investor's duty is to act in the interests of all clients and/or beneficiaries when considering matters such as engagement and voting.

Conflicts of interest will inevitably arise from time to time, which may include when voting on matters affecting a parent company or client.

Institutional investors should put in place and maintain a policy for managing conflicts of interest.

Principle 3

Institutional investors should monitor their investee companies.

Guidance

Investee companies should be monitored to determine when it is necessary to enter into an active dialogue with their boards. This monitoring should be regular, and the process clearly communicable and checked periodically for its effectiveness.

As part of this monitoring, institutional investors should:

- seek to satisfy themselves, to the extent possible, that the investee company's board and committee structures are effective, and that independent directors provide adequate oversight, including by meeting the chairman and, where appropriate, other board members;
- maintain a clear audit trail, for example, records of private meetings held with companies, of votes cast, and of reasons for voting against the investee company's management, for abstaining, or for voting with management in a contentious situation; and
- attend the General Meetings of companies in which they have a major holding, where appropriate and practicable.

Institutional investors should consider carefully explanations given for departure from the UK Corporate Governance Code and make reasoned judgements in each case. They should give a timely explanation to the company, in writing where appropriate, and be prepared to enter a dialogue if they do not accept the company's position.

Institutional investors should endeavour to identify problems at an early stage to minimise any loss of shareholder value. If they have concerns they should seek to ensure that the appropriate members of the investee company's board are made aware of them.

Institutional investors may not wish to be made insiders. They will expect investee companies and their advisers to ensure that information that could affect their ability to deal in the shares of the company concerned is not conveyed to them without their agreement.

Principle 4

Institutional investors should establish clear guidelines on when and how they will escalate their activities as a method of protecting and enhancing shareholder value.

Guidance

Institutional investors should set out the circumstances when they will actively intervene and regularly assess the outcomes of doing so. Intervention should be considered regardless of whether an active or passive investment policy is followed. In addition, being underweight is not, of itself, a reason for not intervening. Instances when institutional investors may want to intervene include when they have concerns about the company's strategy and performance, its governance or its approach to the risks arising from social and environmental matters.

Initial discussions should take place on a confidential basis. However, if boards do not respond constructively when institutional investors intervene, then institutional investors will consider whether to escalate their action, for example, by:

- holding additional meetings with management specifically to discuss concerns;
- expressing concerns through the company's advisers;
- meeting with the chairman, senior independent director, or with all independent directors;
- intervening jointly with other institutions on particular issues;
- making a public statement in advance of the AGM or an EGM;
- submitting resolutions at shareholders' meetings; and
- requisitioning an EGM, in some cases proposing to change board membership.

Principle 5

Institutional investors should be willing to act collectively with other investors where appropriate.

Guidance

At times collaboration with other investors may be the most effective manner in which to engage.

Collaborative engagement may be most appropriate at times of significant corporate or wider economic stress, or when the risks posed threaten the ability of the company to continue.

Institutional investors should disclose their policy on collective engagement.

When participating in collective engagement, institutional investors should have due regard to their policies on conflicts of interest and insider information.

Principle 6

Institutional investors should have a clear policy on voting and disclosure of voting activity.

Guidance

Institutional investors should seek to vote all shares held. They should not automatically support the board.

If they have been unable to reach a satisfactory outcome through active dialogue then they should register an abstention or vote against the resolution. In both instances, it is good practice to inform the company in advance of their intention and the reasons why.

Institutional investors should disclose publicly voting records and if they do not explain why.

Principle 7

Institutional investors should report periodically on their stewardship and voting activities.

Guidance

Those that act as agents should regularly report to their clients details of how they have discharged their responsibilities. Such reports will be likely to comprise qualitative as well as quantitative information. The particular information reported, including the format in which details of how votes have been cast are presented, should be a matter for agreement between agents and their principals.

Transparency is an important feature of effective stewardship. Institutional investors should not, however, be expected to make disclosures that might be counterproductive. Confidentiality in specific situations may well be crucial to achieving a positive outcome.

Those that act as principals, or represent the interests of the end-investor, should report at least annually to those to whom they are accountable on their policy and its execution.

Those that sign up to this Code should consider obtaining an independent audit opinion on their engagement and voting processes having regard to the standards in AAF 01/061 and SAS 702. The existence of such assurance certification should be publicly disclosed.

BRIBERY ACT 2010

General bribery offences

1 OFFENCES OF BRIBING ANOTHER PERSON

(1) A person ("P") is guilty of an offence if either of the following cases applies.

(2) Case 1 is where—
- (a) P offers, promises or gives a financial or other advantage to another person, and
- (b) P intends the advantage—
  - (i) to induce a person to perform improperly a relevant function or activity, or
  - (ii) to reward a person for the improper performance of such a function or activity.

(3) Case 2 is where—
(a) P offers, promises or gives a financial or other advantage to another person, and
(b) P knows or believes that the acceptance of the advantage would itself constitute the improper performance of a relevant function or activity.

(4) In case 1 it does not matter whether the person to whom the advantage is offered, promised or given is the same person as the person who is to perform, or has performed, the function or activity concerned.

(5) In cases 1 and 2 it does not matter whether the advantage is offered, promised or given by P directly or through a third party.

2 OFFENCES RELATING TO BEING BRIBED

(1) A person ("R") is guilty of an offence if any of the following cases applies.

(2) Case 3 is where R requests, agrees to receive or accepts a financial or other advantage intending that, in consequence, a relevant function or activity should be performed improperly (whether by R or another person).

(3) Case 4 is where—
(a) R requests, agrees to receive or accepts a financial or other advantage, and
(b) the request, agreement or acceptance itself constitutes the improper performance by R of a relevant function or activity.

(4) Case 5 is where R requests, agrees to receive or accepts a financial or other advantage as a reward for the improper performance (whether by R or another person) of a relevant function or activity.

(5) Case 6 is where, in anticipation of or in consequence of R requesting, agreeing to receive or accepting a financial or other advantage, a relevant function or activity is performed improperly—
(a) by R, or
(b) by another person at R's request or with R's assent or acquiescence.

(6) In cases 3 to 6 it does not matter—
(a) whether R requests, agrees to receive or accepts (or is to request, agree to receive or accept) the advantage directly or through a third party,
(b) whether the advantage is (or is to be) for the benefit of R or another person.

(7) In cases 4 to 6 it does not matter whether R knows or believes that the performance of the function or activity is improper.

(8) In case 6, where a person other than R is performing the function or activity, it also does not matter whether that person knows or believes that the performance of the function or activity is improper.

3 FUNCTION OR ACTIVITY TO WHICH BRIBE RELATES

(1) For the purposes of this Act a function or activity is a relevant function or activity if—
(a) it falls within subsection (2), and
(b) meets one or more of conditions A to C.

(2) The following functions and activities fall within this subsection—
(a) any function of a public nature,
(b) any activity connected with a business,

(c) any activity performed in the course of a person's employment,
(d) any activity performed by or on behalf of a body of persons (whether corporate or unincorporate).

(3) Condition A is that a person performing the function or activity is expected to perform it in good faith.

(4) Condition B is that a person performing the function or activity is expected to perform it impartially.

(5) Condition C is that a person performing the function or activity is in a position of trust by virtue of performing it.

(6) A function or activity is a relevant function or activity even if it—
(a) has no connection with the United Kingdom, and
(b) is performed in a country or territory outside the United Kingdom.

(7) In this section "business" includes trade or profession.

4 IMPROPER PERFORMANCE TO WHICH BRIBE RELATES

(1) For the purposes of this Act a relevant function or activity—
(a) is performed improperly if it is performed in breach of a relevant expectation, and
(b) is to be treated as being performed improperly if there is a failure to perform the function or activity and that failure is itself a breach of a relevant expectation.

(2) In subsection (1) "relevant expectation"—
(a) in relation to a function or activity which meets condition A or B, means the expectation mentioned in the condition concerned, and
(b) in relation to a function or activity which meets condition C, means any expectation as to the manner in which, or the reasons for which, the function or activity will be performed that arises from the position of trust mentioned in that condition.

(3) Anything that a person does (or omits to do) arising from or in connection with that person's past performance of a relevant function or activity is to be treated for the purposes of this Act as being done (or omitted) by that person in the performance of that function or activity.

5 EXPECTATION TEST

(1) For the purposes of sections 3 and 4, the test of what is expected is a test of what a reasonable person in the United Kingdom would expect in relation to the performance of the type of function or activity concerned.

(2) In deciding what such a person would expect in relation to the performance of a function or activity where the performance is not subject to the law of any part of the United Kingdom, any local custom or practice is to be disregarded unless it is permitted or required by the written law applicable to the country or territory concerned.

(3) In subsection (2) "written law" means law contained in—
(a) any written constitution, or provision made by or under legislation, applicable to the country or territory concerned, or
(b) any judicial decision which is so applicable and is evidenced in published written sources.

Bribery of foreign public officials

6 BRIBERY OF FOREIGN PUBLIC OFFICIALS

(1) A person ("P") who bribes a foreign public official ("F") is guilty of an offence if P's intention is to influence F in F's capacity as a foreign public official.

(2) P must also intend to obtain or retain—
(a) business, or
(b) an advantage in the conduct of business.

(3) P bribes F if, and only if—
(a) directly or through a third party, P offers, promises or gives any financial or other advantage—
(i) to F, or
(ii) to another person at F's request or with F's assent or acquiescence, and
(b) F is neither permitted nor required by the written law applicable to F to be influenced in F's capacity as a foreign public official by the offer, promise or gift.

(4) References in this section to influencing F in F's capacity as a foreign public official mean influencing F in the performance of F's functions as such an official, which includes—
(a) any omission to exercise those functions, and
(b) any use of F's position as such an official, even if not within F's authority.

(5) "Foreign public official" means an individual who—
(a) holds a legislative, administrative or judicial position of any kind, whether appointed or elected, of a country or territory outside the United Kingdom (or any subdivision of such a country or territory),
(b) exercises a public function—
(i) for or on behalf of a country or territory outside the United Kingdom (or any subdivision of such a country or territory), or
(ii) for any public agency or public enterprise of that country or territory (or subdivision), or
(c) is an official or agent of a public international organisation.

(6) "Public international organisation" means an organisation whose members are any of the following—
(a) countries or territories,
(b) governments of countries or territories,
(c) other public international organisations,
(d) a mixture of any of the above.

(7) For the purposes of subsection (3)(b), the written law applicable to F is—
(a) where the performance of the functions of F which P intends to influence would be subject to the law of any part of the United Kingdom, the law of that part of the United Kingdom,
(b) where paragraph (a) does not apply and F is an official or agent of a public international organisation, the applicable written rules of that organisation,
(c) where paragraphs (a) and (b) do not apply, the law of the country or territory in relation to which F is a foreign public official so far as that law is contained in—
(i) any written constitution, or provision made by or under legislation, applicable to the country or territory concerned, or
(ii) any judicial decision which is so applicable and is evidenced in published written sources.

(8) For the purposes of this section, a trade or profession is a business.

Failure of commercial organisations to prevent bribery

7 FAILURE OF COMMERCIAL ORGANISATIONS TO PREVENT BRIBERY

(1) A relevant commercial organisation ("C") is guilty of an offence under this section if a person ("A") associated with C bribes another person intending—
(a) to obtain or retain business for C, or
(b) to obtain or retain an advantage in the conduct of business for C.

(2) But it is a defence for C to prove that C had in place adequate procedures designed to prevent persons associated with C from undertaking such conduct.

(3) For the purposes of this section, A bribes another person if, and only if, A—
(a) is, or would be, guilty of an offence under section 1 or 6 (whether or not A has been prosecuted for such an offence), or
(b) would be guilty of such an offence if section 12(2)(c) and (4) were omitted.

(4) See section 8 for the meaning of a person associated with C and see section 9 for a duty on the Secretary of State to publish guidance.

(5) In this section—
- "partnership" means—
  (a) a partnership within the Partnership Act 1890, or
  (b) a limited partnership registered under the Limited Partnerships Act 1907, or a firm or entity of a similar character formed under the law of a country or territory outside the United Kingdom,
- "relevant commercial organisation" means—
  (a) a body which is incorporated under the law of any part of the United Kingdom and which carries on a business (whether there or elsewhere),
  (b) any other body corporate (wherever incorporated) which carries on a business, or part of a business, in any part of the United Kingdom,
  (c) a partnership which is formed under the law of any part of the United Kingdom and which carries on a business (whether there or elsewhere), or
  (d) any other partnership (wherever formed) which carries on a business, or part of a business, in any part of the United Kingdom, and, for the purposes of this section, a trade or profession is a business.

8 MEANING OF ASSOCIATED PERSON

(1) For the purposes of section 7, a person ("A") is associated with C if (disregarding any bribe under consideration) A is a person who performs services for or on behalf of C.

(2) The capacity in which A performs services for or on behalf of C does not matter.

(3) Accordingly A may (for example) be C's employee, agent or subsidiary.

(4) Whether or not A is a person who performs services for or on behalf of C is to be determined by reference to all the relevant circumstances and not merely by reference to the nature of the relationship between A and C.

(5) But if A is an employee of C, it is to be presumed unless the contrary is shown that A is a person who performs services for or on behalf of C.

9 GUIDANCE ABOUT COMMERCIAL ORGANISATIONS PREVENTING BRIBERY

(1) The Secretary of State must publish guidance about procedures that relevant commercial organisations can put in place to prevent persons associated with them from bribing as mentioned in section 7(1).

(2) The Secretary of State may, from time to time, publish revisions to guidance under this section or revised guidance.

(3) The Secretary of State must consult the Scottish Ministers before publishing anything under this section.

(4) Publication under this section is to be in such manner as the Secretary of State considers appropriate.

(5) Expressions used in this section have the same meaning as in section 7.

Prosecution and penalties

10 CONSENT TO PROSECUTION

(1) No proceedings for an offence under this Act may be instituted in England and Wales except by or with the consent of—
- (a) the Director of Public Prosecutions,
- (b) the Director of the Serious Fraud Office, or
- (c) the Director of Revenue and Customs Prosecutions.

...

(3) No proceedings for an offence under this Act may be instituted in England and Wales or Northern Ireland by a person—
- (a) who is acting—
  - (i) under the direction or instruction of the Director of Public Prosecutions, the Director of the Serious Fraud Office or the Director of Revenue and Customs Prosecutions, or
  - (ii) on behalf of such a Director, or
- (b) to whom such a function has been assigned by such a Director,

except with the consent of the Director concerned to the institution of the proceedings.

(4) The Director of Public Prosecutions, the Director of the Serious Fraud Office and the Director of Revenue and Customs Prosecutions must exercise personally any function under subsection (1), (2) or (3) of giving consent.

(5) The only exception is if—
- (a) the Director concerned is unavailable, and
- (b) there is another person who is designated in writing by the Director acting personally as the person who is authorised to exercise any such function when the Director is unavailable.

(6) In that case, the other person may exercise the function but must do so personally.

(7) Subsections (4) to (6) apply instead of any other provisions which would otherwise have enabled any function of the Director of Public Prosecutions, the Director of the Serious Fraud Office or the Director of Revenue and Customs Prosecutions under subsection (1), (2) or (3) of giving consent to be exercised by a person other than the Director concerned.

(8) No proceedings for an offence under this Act may be instituted in Northern Ireland by virtue of section 36 of the Justice (Northern Ireland) Act 2002 (delegation of the functions of the Director of Public Prosecutions for Northern Ireland to persons other than the Deputy Director) except with the consent of the Director of Public Prosecutions for Northern Ireland to the institution of the proceedings.

(9) The Director of Public Prosecutions for Northern Ireland must exercise personally any function under subsection (2) or (8) of giving consent unless the function is exercised personally by the Deputy Director of Public Prosecutions for Northern Ireland by virtue of section 30(4) or (7) of the Act of 2002 (powers of Deputy Director to exercise functions of Director).

(10) Subsection (9) applies instead of section 36 of the Act of 2002 in relation to the functions of the Director of Public Prosecutions for Northern Ireland and the Deputy Director of Public Prosecutions for Northern Ireland under, or (as the case may be) by virtue of, subsections (2) and (8) above of giving consent.

11 PENALTIES

(1) An individual guilty of an offence under section 1, 2 or 6 is liable—
(a) on summary conviction, to imprisonment for a term not exceeding 12 months, or to a fine not exceeding the statutory maximum, or to both,
(b) on conviction on indictment, to imprisonment for a term not exceeding 10 years, or to a fine, or to both.

(2) Any other person guilty of an offence under section 1, 2 or 6 is liable—
(a) on summary conviction, to a fine not exceeding the statutory maximum,
(b) on conviction on indictment, to a fine.

(3) A person guilty of an offence under section 7 is liable on conviction on indictment to a fine.

(4) The reference in subsection (1)(a) to 12 months is to be read—
(a) in its application to England and Wales in relation to an offence committed before the commencement of section 154(1) of the Criminal Justice Act 2003, and
(b) in its application to Northern Ireland,
as a reference to 6 months.

Other provisions about offences

12 OFFENCES UNDER THIS ACT: TERRITORIAL APPLICATION

(1) An offence is committed under section 1, 2 or 6 in England and Wales, Scotland or Northern Ireland if any act or omission which forms part of the offence takes place in that part of the United Kingdom.

(2) Subsection (3) applies if—
(a) no act or omission which forms part of an offence under section 1, 2 or 6 takes place in the United Kingdom,
(b) a person's acts or omissions done or made outside the United Kingdom would form part of such an offence if done or made in the United Kingdom, and
(c) that person has a close connection with the United Kingdom.

(3) In such a case—
(a) the acts or omissions form part of the offence referred to in subsection (2)(a), and
(b) proceedings for the offence may be taken at any place in the United Kingdom.

(4) For the purposes of subsection (2)(c) a person has a close connection with the United Kingdom if, and only if, the person was one of the following at the time the acts or omissions concerned were done or made—
(a) a British citizen,
(b) a British overseas territories citizen,
(c) a British National (Overseas),
(d) a British Overseas citizen,
(e) a person who under the British Nationality Act 1981 was a British subject,
(f) a British protected person within the meaning of that Act,
(g) an individual ordinarily resident in the United Kingdom,
(h) a body incorporated under the law of any part of the United Kingdom,
(i) a Scottish partnership.

(5) An offence is committed under section 7 irrespective of whether the acts or omissions which form part of the offence take place in the United Kingdom or elsewhere.

(6) Where no act or omission which forms part of an offence under section 7 takes place in the United Kingdom, proceedings for the offence may be taken at any place in the United Kingdom.

(7) Subsection (8) applies if, by virtue of this section, proceedings for an offence are to be taken in Scotland against a person.

(8) Such proceedings may be taken—
(a) in any sheriff court district in which the person is apprehended or in custody, or
(b) in such sheriff court district as the Lord Advocate may determine.

(9) In subsection (8) "sheriff court district" is to be read in accordance with section 307(1) of the Criminal Procedure (Scotland) Act 1995.

13 DEFENCE FOR CERTAIN BRIBERY OFFENCES ETC.

(1) It is a defence for a person charged with a relevant bribery offence to prove that the person's conduct was necessary for—
(a) the proper exercise of any function of an intelligence service, or
(b) the proper exercise of any function of the armed forces when engaged on active service.

(2) The head of each intelligence service must ensure that the service has in place arrangements designed to ensure that any conduct of a member of the service which would otherwise be a relevant bribery offence is necessary for a purpose falling within subsection (1)(a).

(3) The Defence Council must ensure that the armed forces have in place arrangements designed to ensure that any conduct of—
(a) a member of the armed forces who is engaged on active service, or
(b) a civilian subject to service discipline when working in support of any person falling within paragraph (a),

which would otherwise be a relevant bribery offence is necessary for a purpose falling within subsection (1)(b).

(4) The arrangements which are in place by virtue of subsection (2) or (3) must be arrangements which the Secretary of State considers to be satisfactory.

(5) For the purposes of this section, the circumstances in which a person's conduct is necessary for a purpose falling within subsection (1)(a) or (b) are to be treated as including any circumstances in which the person's conduct—

(a) would otherwise be an offence under section 2, and
(b) involves conduct by another person which, but for subsection (1)(a) or (b), would be an offence under section 1.

(6) In this section—

- "active service" means service in—
  (a) an action or operation against an enemy,
  (b) an operation outside the British Islands for the protection of life or property, or
  (c) the military occupation of a foreign country or territory,
- "armed forces" means Her Majesty's forces (within the meaning of the Armed Forces Act 2006),
- "civilian subject to service discipline" and "enemy" have the same meaning as in the Act of 2006,
- "GCHQ" has the meaning given by section 3(3) of the Intelligence Services Act 1994,
- "head" means—
  (a) in relation to the Security Service, the Director General of the Security Service,
  (b) in relation to the Secret Intelligence Service, the Chief of the Secret Intelligence Service, and
  (c) in relation to GCHQ, the Director of GCHQ,
- "intelligence service" means the Security Service, the Secret Intelligence Service or GCHQ,
- "relevant bribery offence" means—
  (a) an offence under section 1 which would not also be an offence under section 6,
  (b) an offence under section 2,
  (c) an offence committed by aiding, abetting, counselling or procuring the commission of an offence falling within paragraph (a) or (b),
  (d) an offence of attempting or conspiring to commit, or of inciting the commission of, an offence falling within paragraph (a) or (b), or
  (e) an offence under Part 2 of the Serious Crime Act 2007 (encouraging or assisting crime) in relation to an offence falling within paragraph (a) or (b).

14 OFFENCES UNDER SECTIONS 1, 2 AND 6 BY BODIES CORPORATE ETC.

(1) This section applies if an offence under section 1, 2 or 6 is committed by a body corporate or a Scottish partnership.

(2) If the offence is proved to have been committed with the consent or connivance of—
(a) a senior officer of the body corporate or Scottish partnership, or
(b) a person purporting to act in such a capacity,
the senior officer or person (as well as the body corporate or partnership) is guilty of the offence and liable to be proceeded against and punished accordingly.

(3) But subsection (2) does not apply, in the case of an offence which is committed under section 1, 2 or 6 by virtue of section 12(2) to (4), to a senior officer or person purporting to act in such a capacity unless the senior officer or person has a close connection with the United Kingdom (within the meaning given by section 12(4)).

(4) In this section—

- "director", in relation to a body corporate whose affairs are managed by its members, means a member of the body corporate,
- "senior officer" means—
  (a) in relation to a body corporate, a director, manager, secretary or other similar officer of the body corporate, and
  (b) in relation to a Scottish partnership, a partner in the partnership.

15 OFFENCES UNDER SECTION 7 BY PARTNERSHIPS

(1) Proceedings for an offence under section 7 alleged to have been committed by a partnership must be brought in the name of the partnership (and not in that of any of the partners).

(2) For the purposes of such proceedings—
  (a) rules of court relating to the service of documents have effect as if the partnership were a body corporate, and
  (b) the following provisions apply as they apply in relation to a body corporate—
    (i) section 33 of the Criminal Justice Act 1925 and Schedule 3 to the Magistrates' Courts Act 1980,
    (ii) section 18 of the Criminal Justice Act (Northern Ireland) 1945 (c. 15 (N.I.)) and Schedule 4 to the Magistrates' Courts (Northern Ireland) Order 1981 (S.I. 1981/1675 (N.I.26)),
    (iii) section 70 of the Criminal Procedure (Scotland) Act 1995.

(3) A fine imposed on the partnership on its conviction for an offence under section 7 is to be paid out of the partnership assets.

(4) In this section "partnership" has the same meaning as in section 7.

Supplementary and final provisions

16 APPLICATION TO CROWN

This Act applies to individuals in the public service of the Crown as it applies to other individuals.

17 CONSEQUENTIAL PROVISION

(1) The following common law offences are abolished—
  (a) the offences under the law of England and Wales and Northern Ireland of bribery and embracery,
  (b) the offences under the law of Scotland of bribery and accepting a bribe.

...

(4) The relevant national authority may by order make such supplementary, incidental or consequential provision as the relevant national authority considers appropriate for the purposes of this Act or in consequence of this Act.

(5) The power to make an order under this section—
  (a) is exercisable by statutory instrument,
  (b) includes power to make transitional, transitory or saving provision,
  (c) may, in particular, be exercised by amending, repealing, revoking or otherwise modifying any provision made by or under an enactment (including any Act passed in the same Session as this Act).

(6) Subject to subsection (7), a statutory instrument containing an order of the Secretary of State under this section may not be made unless a draft of the instrument has been laid before, and approved by a resolution of, each House of Parliament.

(7) A statutory instrument containing an order of the Secretary of State under this section which does not amend or repeal a provision of a public general Act or of devolved legislation is subject to annulment in pursuance of a resolution of either House of Parliament.

(8) Subject to subsection (9), a statutory instrument containing an order of the Scottish Ministers under this section may not be made unless a draft of the instrument has been laid before, and approved by a resolution of, the Scottish Parliament.

(9) A statutory instrument containing an order of the Scottish Ministers under this section which does not amend or repeal a provision of an Act of the Scottish Parliament or of a public general Act is subject to annulment in pursuance of a resolution of the Scottish Parliament.

(10) In this section—

- "devolved legislation" means an Act of the Scottish Parliament, a Measure of the National Assembly for Wales or an Act of the Northern Ireland Assembly,
- "enactment" includes an Act of the Scottish Parliament and Northern Ireland legislation,
- "relevant national authority" means—
  (a) in the case of provision which would be within the legislative competence of the Scottish Parliament if it were contained in an Act of that Parliament, the Scottish Ministers, and
  (b) in any other case, the Secretary of State.

18 EXTENT

(1) Subject as follows, this Act extends to England and Wales, Scotland and Northern Ireland.

...

19 COMMENCEMENT AND TRANSITIONAL PROVISION ETC.

(1) Subject to subsection (2), this Act comes into force on such day as the Secretary of State may by order made by statutory instrument appoint.

(2) Sections 16, 17(4) to (10) and 18, this section (other than subsections (5) to (7)) and section 20 come into force on the day on which this Act is passed.

(3) An order under subsection (1) may—
(a) appoint different days for different purposes,
(b) make such transitional, transitory or saving provision as the Secretary of State considers appropriate in connection with the coming into force of any provision of this Act.

(4) The Secretary of State must consult the Scottish Ministers before making an order under this section in connection with any provision of this Act which would be within the legislative competence of the Scottish Parliament if it were contained in an Act of that Parliament.

(5) This Act does not affect any liability, investigation, legal proceeding or penalty for or in respect of—
(a) a common law offence mentioned in subsection (1) of section 17 which is committed wholly or partly before the coming into force of that subsection in relation to such an offence, or
(b) an offence under the Public Bodies Corrupt Practices Act 1889 or the Prevention of Corruption Act 1906 committed wholly or partly before the coming into force of the repeal of the Act by Schedule 2 to this Act.

(6) For the purposes of subsection (5) an offence is partly committed before a particular time if any act or omission which forms part of the offence takes place before that time.

(7) Subsections (5) and (6) are without prejudice to section 16 of the Interpretation Act 1978 (general savings on repeal).

At the time of preparation of this book, the Bribery Act 2010 is due to come into force in full on 1 July 2011.

United Kingdom Listing Authority Listing Rules (LR)

CONTINUING OBLIGATIONS (LR 9)

LR 9.8 ANNUAL FINANCIAL REPORT

Additional information

LR 9.8.6

In the case of a listed company incorporated in the United Kingdom, the following additional items must be included in its annual financial report:

(5) a statement of how the listed company has applied the Main Principles set out in the UK Corporate Governance Code, in a manner that would enable shareholders to evaluate how the principles have been applied.

(6) a statement as to whether the listed company has:
- (a) complied throughout the accounting period with all relevant provisions set out in the UK Corporate Governance Code; or
- (b) not complied throughout the accounting period with all relevant provisions set out in the UK Corporate Governance Code and if so, setting out:
  - (i) those provisions, if any it has not complied with;

(ii) in the case of provisions whose requirements are of a continuing nature, the period within which, if any, it did not comply with some or all of those provisions; and
(iii) the company's reasons for non-compliance....

LR 9.8.7

An overseas company with a premium listing must include in its annual report and accounts the information in LR 9.8.6(5) ... [and] LR 9.8.6(6)...

SIGNIFICANT TRANSACTIONS: PREMIUM LISTING (LR 10)

LR 10.1 PRELIMINARY

Application

LR 10.1.1

This chapter applies to a company that has a premium listing.

Purpose

LR 10.1.2

The purpose of this chapter is to ensure that shareholders of companies with equity shares listed:

(1) are notified of certain transactions entered into by the listed company; and

(2) have the opportunity to vote on larger proposed transactions.

Meaning of "transaction"

LR 10.1.3

In this chapter (except where specifically provided to the contrary) a reference to a transaction by a listed company:

(1) (subject to paragraphs (3),(4) and (5)) includes all agreements (including amendments to agreements) entered into by the listed company or its subsidiary undertakings;

(2) includes the grant or acquisition of an option as if the option had been exercised except that, if exercise is solely at the listed company's or subsidiary undertaking's discretion, the transaction will be classified on exercise and only the consideration (if any) for the option will be classified on the grant or acquisition;

(3) excludes a transaction of a revenue nature in the ordinary course of business;

(4) excludes an issue of securities, or a transaction to raise finance, which does not involve the acquisition or disposal of any fixed asset of the listed company or of its subsidiary undertakings; and

(5) excludes any transaction between the listed company and its wholly-owned subsidiary undertaking or between its wholly-owned subsidiary undertakings.

LR 10.1.4

This chapter is intended to cover transactions that are outside the ordinary course of the listed company's business and may change a security holder's economic interest in the company's assets or liabilities (whether or not the change in the assets or liabilities is recognised on the company's balance sheet).

LR 10.1.5

In assessing whether a transaction is in the ordinary course of a company's business under this chapter, the FSA will have regard to the size and incidence of similar transactions which the company has entered into. The FSA may determine that a transaction is not in the ordinary course of business because of its size or incidence.

LR 10.2 CLASSIFYING TRANSACTIONS

Classifying transactions

LR 10.2.1

A transaction is classified by assessing its size relative to that of the listed company proposing to make it. The comparison of size is made by using the percentage ratios resulting from applying the class test calculations to a transaction. The class tests are set out in LR 10 Annex 1 G....

LR 10.2.2

Except as otherwise provided in this chapter, transactions are classified as follows:

(1) Class 3 transaction: a transaction where all percentage ratios are less than 5%;

(2) Class 2 transaction: a transaction where any percentage ratio is 5% or more but each is less than 25%; [and]

(3) Class 1 transaction: a transaction where any percentage ratio is 25% or more.

Aggregating transactions

LR 10.2.10

(1) Transactions completed during the 12 months before the date of the latest transaction must be aggregated with that transaction for the purposes of classification if:
   (a) they are entered into by the company with the same person or with persons connected with one another;
   (b) they involve the acquisition or disposal of securities or an interest in one particular company; or
   (c) together they lead to substantial involvement in a business activity which did not previously form a significant part of the company's principal activities.

...

(3) If under this rule aggregation of transactions results in a requirement for shareholder approval, then that approval is required only for the latest transaction.

LR 10.3 CLASS 3 REQUIREMENTS

Notification of acquisitions involving the issue of securities

LR 10.3.1

(1) If:
  (a) a listed company agrees the terms of a class 3 transaction that involves an acquisition; and
  (b) the consideration for the acquisition includes the issue of securities for which listing will be sought;

  the company must notify a [Regulated Information Service] as soon as possible after the terms of the acquisition are agreed.

(2) The notification must include:
  (a) the amount of the securities being issued;
  (b) details of the transaction, including the name of the other party to the transaction; and
  (c) either the value of the consideration, and how this is being satisfied, or the value of the gross assets acquired, whichever is the greater.

Notification of other class 3 transactions

LR 10.3.2

(1) If:
  (a) a listed company agrees the terms of a class 3 transaction of a type other than that referred to in LR 10.3.1 R; and
  (b) it releases any details to the public;

  it must also notify those details to a [Regulated Information Service] by no later than the release of details to the public referred to in paragraph (b).

(2) The notification must include:
  (a) details of the transaction, including the name of the other party to the transaction; and
  (b) either the value of the consideration, and how this is being satisfied, or the value of the gross assets acquired or disposed of.

LR 10.4 CLASS 2 REQUIREMENTS

Notification of class 2 transactions

LR 10.4.1

(1) A listed company must notify a [Regulated Information Service] as soon as possible after the terms of a class 2 transaction are agreed.

(2) The notification must include:
  (a) details of the transaction, including the name of the other party to the transaction;
  (b) a description of the business carried on by, or using, the net assets the subject of the transaction;
  (c) the consideration, and how it is being satisfied (including the terms of any arrangements for deferred consideration);
  (d) the value of the gross assets the subject of the transaction;
  (e) the profits attributable to the assets the subject of the transaction;

(f) the effect of the transaction on the listed company including any benefits which are expected to accrue to the company as a result of the transaction;
(g) details of any service contracts of proposed directors of the listed company;
(h) for a disposal, the application of the sale proceeds;
(i) for a disposal, if securities are to form part of the consideration received, a statement whether the securities are to be sold or retained; and
(j) details of key individuals important to the business or company the subject of the transaction.

LR 10.5 CLASS 1 REQUIREMENTS

Notification and shareholder approval

LR 10.5.1

A listed company must, in relation to a class 1 transaction:

(1) comply with the requirements of LR 10.4 (Class 2 requirements) for the transaction;

(2) send an explanatory circular to its shareholders and obtain their prior approval in a general meeting for the transaction; and

(3) ensure that any agreement effecting the transaction is conditional on that approval being obtained.

LR 10.8 MISCELLANEOUS

Class 1 disposals by companies in severe financial difficulty

LR 10.8.1

(1) A listed company in severe financial difficulty may find itself with no alternative but to dispose of a substantial part of its business within a short time frame to meet its ongoing working capital requirements or to reduce its liabilities. Due to time constraints it may not be able to prepare a circular and convene an extraordinary general meeting to obtain prior shareholder approval.

(2) The FSA may modify the requirements in LR 10.5 to prepare a circular and to obtain shareholder approval for such a disposal, if the company:
(a) can demonstrate that it is in severe financial difficulty; and
(b) satisfies the conditions in LR 10.8.2 G to LR 10.8.6 G.

(3) An application to modify LR 10.5 should be brought to the FSA's attention at the earliest available opportunity and at least five clear business days before the terms of the disposal are agreed.

LR 10.8.2

The listed company should demonstrate to the FSA that it could not reasonably have entered into negotiations earlier to enable shareholder approval to be sought.

LR 10.8.3

The following documents should be provided in writing to the FSA:

(1) confirmation from the listed company that:
(a) negotiation does not allow time for shareholder approval;

(b) all alternative methods of financing have been exhausted and the only option remaining is to dispose of a substantial part of their business;
(c) by taking the decision to dispose of part of the business to raise cash, the directors are acting in the best interests of the company and shareholders as a whole and that unless the disposal is completed receivers, administrators or liquidators are likely to be appointed; and
(d) if the disposal is to a related party, that the disposal by the company to the related party is the only available option in the current circumstances.

(2) confirmation from the company's sponsor that, in its opinion and on the basis of information available to it, the company is in severe financial difficulty and that it will not be in a position to meet its obligations as they fall due unless the disposal takes place according to the proposed timetable;

(3) confirmation from the persons providing finance stating that further finance or facilities will not be made available and that unless the disposal is effected immediately, current facilities will be withdrawn; and

(4) an announcement that complies with LR 10.8.4 G and LR 10.8.5 G.

LR 10.8.4

An announcement should be notified to a [Regulated Information Service] no later than the date the terms of the disposal are agreed and should contain:

(1) all relevant information required to be notified under LR 10.4.1 R;

(2) the name of the acquirer and the expected date of completion of the disposal;

(3) full disclosure about the continuing groups prospects for at least the current financial year;

(4) a statement that the directors believe that the disposal is in the best interests of the company and shareholders as a whole. The directors should also state that if the disposal is not completed the company will be unable to meet its financial commitments as they fall due and consequently will be unable to continue to trade resulting in the appointment of receivers, liquidators or administrators;

(5) a statement incorporating the details of all the confirmations provided to the FSA in LR 10.8.3 G;

(6) details of any financing arrangements (either current or future) if they are contingent upon the disposal being effected;

...

(8) a statement by the listed company that in its opinion the working capital available to the continuing group is sufficient for the groups present requirements, that is, for at least 12 months from the date of the announcement, or, if not, how it is proposed to provide the additional working capital thought by the company to be necessary.

LR 10.8.5

The announcement should contain any further information that the company and its sponsors consider necessary. This should incorporate historical price sensitive information, which has already been published in relation to the disposal....

LR 10.8.8

The directors should also consider whether the listed company's financial situation is such that they should request the suspension of its listing pending publication of an announcement and clarification of its financial position.

LR 10 ANNEX 1 THE CLASS TESTS

LR 10 ANNEX 1.1

Class tests

This Annex sets out the following class tests:

(1) the gross assets test;

(2) the profits test;

(3) the consideration test; and

(4) the gross capital test.

The Gross assets test

(1) The assets test is calculated by dividing the gross assets the subject of the transaction by the gross assets of the listed company.

...

The Profits test

(1) The profits test is calculated by dividing the profits attributable to the assets the subject of the transaction by the profits of the listed company.

...

The Consideration test

(1) The consideration test is calculated by taking the consideration for the transaction as a percentage of the aggregate market value of all the ordinary shares (excluding treasury shares) of the listed company.

...

The Gross Capital test

(1) The gross capital test is calculated by dividing the gross capital of the company or business being acquired by the gross capital of the listed company.

(2) The test in paragraph (1) is only to be applied for an acquisition of a company or business.

...

Related party transactions: Premium listing (LR 11)

LR 11.1 RELATED PARTY TRANSACTIONS

Application

LR 11.1.1

This chapter applies to a company that has a premium listing.

Purpose

LR 11.1.2

(1) This chapter sets out safeguards that apply to:
  (a) transactions and arrangements between a listed company and a related party; and
  (b) transactions and arrangements between a listed company and any other person that may benefit a related party.

(2) The safeguards are intended to prevent a related party from taking advantage of its position and also to prevent any perception that it may have done so.

Transaction

LR 11.1.3

A reference in this chapter:

(1) to a transaction or arrangement by a listed company includes a transaction or arrangement by its subsidiary undertaking; and

(2) to a transaction or arrangement is, unless the contrary intention appears, a reference to the entering into of the agreement for the transaction or the entering into of the arrangement.

Definition of "related party"

LR 11.1.4

In LR, a "related party" means:

(1) a person who is (or was within the 12 months before the date of the transaction or arrangement) a substantial shareholder; or

(2) a person who is (or was within the 12 months before the date of the transaction or arrangement) a director or shadow director of the listed company or of any other company which is (and, if he has ceased to be such, was while he was a director or shadow director of such other company) its subsidiary undertaking or parent undertaking or a fellow subsidiary undertaking of its parent undertaking; or

(4) a person exercising significant influence; or

(5) an associate of a related party referred to in paragraph (1), (2) or (4).

Definition of "related party transaction"

LR 11.1.5

In LR, a "related party transaction" means:

(1) a transaction (other than a transaction of a revenue nature in the ordinary course of business) between a listed company and a related party; or

(2) an arrangement pursuant to which a listed company and a related party each invests in, or provides finance to, another undertaking or asset; or

(3) any other similar transaction or arrangement (other than a transaction of a revenue nature in the ordinary course of business) between a listed company and any other person the purpose and effect of which is to benefit a related party.

LR 11.1.5A

In assessing whether a transaction is in the ordinary course of business under this chapter, the FSA will have regard to the size and incidence of the transaction and also whether the terms and conditions of the transaction are unusual.

Transactions to which this chapter does not apply

LR 11.1.6

LR 11.1.7 R to LR 11.1.10 R do not apply to a related party transaction if it is a transaction or arrangement:

(1) of a kind referred to in paragraph 1 of LR 11 Annex 1R R (a small transaction)); or

(2) of a kind referred to in paragraph 2 to 10 of LR 11 Annex 1R R and does not have any unusual features.

...

Requirements for related party transactions

LR 11.1.7

If a listed company enters into a related party transaction, the listed company must:

(1) make a notification in accordance with LR 10.4.1 R (Notification of class 2 transactions) that contains the details required by that rule and also:
  (a) the name of the related party; and
  (b) details of the nature and extent of the related party's interest in the transaction or arrangement;

...

(3) obtain the approval of its shareholders for the transaction or arrangement either:
  (a) before it is entered into; or
  (b) if the transaction or arrangement is expressed to be conditional on that approval, before it is completed; and

(4) ensure that the related party:
  (a) does not vote on the relevant resolution; and
  (b) takes all reasonable steps to ensure that the related party's associates do not vote on the relevant resolution.

Modified requirements for smaller related party transactions

LR 11.1.10

(1) This rule applies to a related party transaction if each of the percentage ratios is less than 5%, but one or more of the percentage ratios exceeds 0.25%.

(2) Where this rule applies, LR 11.1.7 R does not apply but instead the listed company must before entering into the transaction or arrangement (as the case may be):

(a) inform the FSA in writing of the details of the proposed transaction or arrangement;
(b) provide the FSA with written confirmation from an independent adviser acceptable to the FSA that the terms of the proposed transaction or arrangement with the related party are fair and reasonable as far as the shareholders of the listed company are concerned; and
(c) undertake in writing to the FSA to include details of the transaction or arrangement in the listed company's next published annual accounts, including, if relevant, the identity of the related party, the value of the consideration for the transaction or arrangement and all other relevant circumstances.

Aggregation of transactions in any 12 month period

LR 11.1.11

(1) If a listed company enters into transactions or arrangements with the same related party (and any of its associates) in any 12 month period and the transactions or arrangements have not been approved by shareholders the transactions or arrangements must be aggregated.

(2) If any percentage ratio is 5% or more for the aggregated transactions or arrangements, the listed company must comply with LR 11.1.7 R in respect of the latest transaction or arrangement.

LR 11 ANNEX 1R TRANSACTIONS TO WHICH RELATED PARTY TRANSACTION RULES DO NOT APPLY

LR 11 ANNEX 1.1

Small transaction

1 A transaction or arrangement where each of the applicable percentage ratios is equal to or less than 0.25%.

ISSUE OF NEW SECURITIES AND SALE OF TREASURY SHARES

Transaction agreed before person became a related party

1A A transaction the terms of which:
(1) were agreed at a time when no party to the transaction or person who was to receive the benefit of the transaction was a related party; and
(2) have not been amended, or required the exercise of discretion by the listed company under those terms, since the party or person become a related party.

2 A transaction that consists of:
(1) the take up by a related party of new securities or treasury shares under its entitlement in a pre-emptive offering;
(2) an issue of new securities made under the exercise of conversion or subscription rights attaching to a listed class of securities.

EMPLOYEES' SHARE SCHEMES AND LONG-TERM INCENTIVE SCHEMES

The:

(1) receipt of any asset (including cash or securities of the listed company or any of its subsidiary undertakings) by a director of the listed company, its parent undertaking or any of its subsidiary undertakings; or

(2) grant of an option or other right to a director of the listed company, its parent undertaking, or any of its subsidiary undertakings to acquire (whether or not for consideration) any asset (including cash or new or existing securities of the listed company or any of its subsidiary undertakings); or

(3) provision of a gift or loan to the trustees of an employee benefit trust to finance the provision of assets as referred to in (1) or (2);

in accordance with the terms of an employees' share scheme or a long-term incentive scheme.

4 CREDIT

A grant of credit (including the lending of money or the guaranteeing of a loan):

(1) to the related party on normal commercial terms;
(2) to a director for an amount and on terms no more favourable than those offered to employees of the group generally; or
(3) by the related party on normal commercial terms and on an unsecured basis.

5 DIRECTORS' INDEMNITIES AND LOANS

(1) A transaction that consists of:
 (a) granting an indemnity to a director of the listed company (or any of its subsidiary undertakings) if the terms of the indemnity are in accordance with those specifically permitted to be given to a director under the Companies Act 2006; [or]
 (b) maintaining a contract of insurance if the insurance is in accordance with that specifically permitted to be maintained for a director under that the Companies Act 2006 (whether for a director of the listed company or for a director of any of its subsidiary undertakings)....

(2) Paragraph (1) applies to a listed company that is not subject to the Companies Act 2006 if the terms of the indemnity or contract of insurance are in accordance with those that would be specifically permitted under that Act (if it applied).

6 UNDERWRITING

(1) The underwriting by a related party of all or part of an issue of securities by the listed company (or any of its subsidiary undertakings) if the consideration to be paid by the listed company (or any of its subsidiary undertakings) for the underwriting:
 (a) is no more than the usual commercial underwriting consideration; and
 (b) is the same as that to be paid to the other underwriters (if any).

(2) Paragraph (1) does not apply to the extent that a related party is underwriting securities which it is entitled to take up under an issue of securities.

8 JOINT INVESTMENT ARRANGEMENTS

(1) An arrangement where a listed company, or any of its subsidiary undertakings, and a related party each invests in, or provides finance to, another undertaking or asset if the following conditions are satisfied:
 (a) the amount invested, or provided, by the related party is not more than 25% of the amount invested, or provided, by the listed company or its subsidiary undertaking (as

the case may be) and the listed company has advised the FSA in writing that this condition has been met; and

(b) an independent adviser acceptable to the FSA has provided a written opinion to the FSA stating that the terms and circumstances of the investment or provision of finance by the listed company or its subsidiary undertakings (as the case may be) are no less favourable than those applying to the investment or provision of finance by the related party.

(2) The advice in paragraph (1)(a) and the opinion in paragraph (1)(b) must be provided before the investment is made or the finance is provided.

9 INSIGNIFICANT SUBSIDIARY UNDERTAKING

(1) A transaction or arrangement where each of the conditions in paragraphs (2) to (6) (as far as applicable) is satisfied.

(2) The party to the transaction or arrangement is only a related party because:

(a) it is (or was within the 12 months before the date of the transaction or arrangement) a substantial shareholder or its associate; or

(b) it is a person who is (or was within the 12 months before the date of the transaction or arrangement) a director or shadow director or his associate;

of a subsidiary undertaking or subsidiary undertakings of the listed company that has, or if there is more than one subsidiary undertaking that have in aggregate, contributed less than 10% of the profits of, and represented less than 10% of the assets of, the listed company for the relevant period.

(3) The subsidiary undertaking or each of the subsidiary undertakings (as the case may be) have been in the listed company's group for 1 year or more.

(4) In paragraph (2), "relevant period" means:

(a) if the subsidiary undertaking or each of the subsidiary undertakings (as the case may be) have been part of the listed company's group for more than 1 year but less than 3 years, each of the financial years before the date of the transaction or arrangement for which accounts have been published; and

(b) if the subsidiary undertaking or any of the subsidiary undertakings (as the case may be) have been part of the listed company's group for 3 years or more, each of the 3 financial years before the date of the transaction or arrangement for which accounts have been published.

(5) If the subsidiary undertaking or any of the subsidiary undertakings (as the case may be) are themselves party to the transaction or arrangement or if securities in the subsidiary undertaking or any of the subsidiary undertakings or their assets are the subject of the transaction or arrangement, then the ratio of consideration to market capitalisation of the listed company is less than 10%.

(6) In this rule, the figures to be used to calculate profits, assets and consideration to market capitalisation are the same as those used to classify profits, assets and consideration to market capitalisation in LR 10 Annex 1....

United Kingdom Listing Authority Disclosure Rules and Transparency Rules (DTR)

DTR 1B INTRODUCTION (CORPORATE GOVERNANCE)

Application: Audit committees

DTR 1B.1.2

Except as set out in DTR 1B.1.3 R, DTR 7.1 applies to an issuer:

(1) whose transferable securities are admitted to trading; and

(2) which is required to appoint a statutory auditor.

Exemptions

DTR 1B.1.3

DTR 7.1 does not apply to:

(1) any issuer which is a subsidiary undertaking of a parent undertaking where the parent undertaking is subject to DTR 7.1, or to requirements implementing Article 41 of the Audit Directive in any other EEA State;

...

Application: Corporate governance statements

DTR 1B.1.5

Except as set out in DTR 1B.1.6 R, DTR 7.2 applies to an issuer:

(1) whose transferable securities are admitted to trading; and

(2) which is a company within the meaning of section 1(1) of the Companies Act 2006.

Exemption

DTR 1B.1.6

The rules in DTR 7.2.2 R, 7.2.3 R and 7.2.7 R do not apply to an issuer which has not issued shares which are admitted to trading unless it has issued shares which are traded on [a Multilateral Trading Facility].

DTR 5 VOTE HOLDER AND ISSUER NOTIFICATION RULES

DTR 5.1 NOTIFICATION OF THE ACQUISITION OR DISPOSAL OF MAJOR SHAREHOLDINGS

DTR 5.1.1

In this chapter:

(1) references to an "issuer", in relation to shares admitted to trading on a regulated market, are to an issuer whose Home State is the United Kingdom;

(2) references to a "non-UK issuer" are to an issuer whose shares are admitted to trading on a regulated market and whose Home State is the United Kingdom other than:
- (a) a public company within the meaning of section 4(2) of the Companies Act 2006; and
- (b) a company which is otherwise incorporated in, and whose principal place of business is in, the UK;

(3) references to "shares" are to shares which are:
- (a) already issued and carry rights to vote which are exercisable in all circumstances at general meetings of the issuer including shares (such as preference shares) which, following the exercise of an option for their conversion, event of default or otherwise, have become fully enfranchised for voting purposes; and
- (b) admitted to trading on a regulated or prescribed market;

(4) an acquisition or disposal of shares is to be regarded as effective when the relevant transaction is executed unless the transaction provides for settlement to be subject to conditions which are beyond the control of the parties in which case the acquisition or disposal is to be regarded as effective on the settlement of the transaction;

(5) a stock-lending agreement which provides for the outright transfer of securities and which provides the lender with a right to call for re-delivery of the lent stock (or its equivalent) is not (as respects the lender) to be taken as involving a disposal of any *shares* which may be the subject of the stock loan; and

(6) for the purposes of calculating whether any percentage threshold is reached, exceeded or fallen below and in any resulting notification, the proportion of voting rights held shall if necessary be rounded down to the next whole number.

DTR 5.1.2

...[A] person must notify the issuer of the percentage of its voting rights he holds as shareholder ... if the percentage of those voting rights:

(1) reaches, exceeds or falls below 3%, 4%, 5%, 6%, 7%, 8%, 9%, 10% and each 1% threshold thereafter up to 100% (or in the case of a non-UK issuer on the basis of thresholds at 5%, 10%, 15%, 20%, 25%, 30%, 50% and 75%) as a result of an acquisition or disposal of shares ...; or

(2) reaches, exceeds or falls below an applicable threshold in (1) as a result of events changing the breakdown of voting rights and on the basis of information disclosed by the issuer in accordance with DTR 5.6.1 R and DTR 5.6.1A R;

and in the case of an issuer which is not incorporated in an EEA State a notification under (2) must be made on the basis of equivalent events and disclosed information.

DTR 5.6 DISCLOSURES BY ISSUERS

DTR 5.6.1

An issuer must, at the end of each calendar month during which an increase or decrease has occurred, disclose to the public:

(1) the total number of voting rights and capital in respect of each class of share which it issues; and

(2) the total number of voting rights attaching to shares of the issuer which are held by it in treasury.

DTR 5.6.1A

(1) Notwithstanding DTR 5.6.1 R, if a relevant increase or decrease in the total number of voting rights of the kind described in (2) occurs, an *issuer* must disclose to the public the information in DTR 5.6.1R (1) and (2) as soon as possible and in any event no later than the end of the business day following the day on which the increase or decrease occurs.

(2) For the purpose of (1), a relevant increase or decrease is any increase or decrease in the total number of voting rights produced when an issuer completes a transaction unless its effect on the total number of voting rights is immaterial when compared with the position before completion.

DTR 5.6.1B

In relation to the obligation in DTR 5.6.1A R, it is for an issuer to assess whether the effect on the total number of voting rights is immaterial. In the FSA's view an increase or decrease of 1% or more is likely to be material, both to the issuer and to the public.

DTR 5.6.2

The disclosure of the total number of voting rights should be in respect of each class of share which is admitted to trading on a regulated or prescribed market.

DTR 5.6.3

Responsibility for all information drawn up and made public in accordance with DTR 5.6.1 R and DTR 5.6.1A R lies with the issuer.

DTR 7 CORPORATE GOVERNANCE

DTR 7.1 AUDIT COMMITTEES

Audit committees and their functions

DTR 7.1.1

An issuer must have a body which is responsible for performing the functions set out in DTR 7.1.3 R. At least one member of that body must be independent and at least one member must have competence in accounting and/or auditing.

DTR 7.1.2

The requirements for independence and competence in accounting and/or auditing may be satisfied by the same member or by different members of the relevant body.

DTR 7.1.3

An issuer must ensure that, as a minimum, the relevant body must:

(1) monitor the financial reporting process;

(2) monitor the effectiveness of the issuer's internal control, internal audit where applicable, and risk management systems;

(3) monitor the statutory audit of the annual and consolidated accounts;

(4) review and monitor the independence of the statutory auditor, and in particular the provision of additional services to the issuer.

DTR 7.1.4

An issuer must base any proposal to appoint a statutory auditor on a recommendation made by the relevant body.

DTR 7.1.5

The issuer must make a statement available to the public disclosing which body carries out the functions required by DTR 7.1.3 R and how it is composed.

DTR 7.1.6

An issuer may include the statement required by DTR 7.1.5 R in any statement it is required to make under DTR 7.2 (Corporate governance statements).

DTR 7.1.7

In the FSA's view, compliance with provisions A.1.2, C.3.1, C.3.2 and C.3.3 of the UK Corporate Governance Code will result in compliance with DTR 7.1.1 R to DTR 7.1.5 R.

DTR 7.2 CORPORATE GOVERNANCE STATEMENTS

DTR 7.2.1

An issuer to which this section applies must include a corporate governance statement in its directors' report. That statement must be included as a specific section of the directors' report and must contain at least the information set out in DTR 7.2.2 R to DTR 7.2.7 R and, where applicable, DTR 7.2.10 R.

DTR 7.2.2

The corporate governance statement must contain a reference to:

(1) the corporate governance code to which the issuer is subject; and/or

(2) the corporate governance code which the issuer may have voluntarily decided to apply; and/or

(3) all relevant information about the corporate governance practices applied beyond the requirements under national law.

DTR 7.2.3

(1) An issuer which is complying with DTR 7.2.2R (1) or DTR 7.2.2R (2) must:
  (a) state in its directors' report where the relevant corporate governance code is publicly available; and
  (b) to the extent that it departs from that corporate governance code, explain which parts of the corporate governance code it departs from and the reasons for doing so.

(2) Where DTR 7.2.2R (3) applies, the issuer must make its corporate governance practices publicly available and state in its directors' report where they can be found.

(3) If an issuer has decided not to apply any provisions of a corporate governance code referred to under DTR 7.2.2R (1) and DTR 7.2.2R (2), it must explain its reasons for that decision.

DTR 7.2.4

A listed company which complies with LR 9.8.6R (6) (the comply or explain rule in relation to the UK Corporate Governance Code) will satisfy the requirements of DTR 7.2.2 R and DTR 7.2.3 R.

DTR 7.2.5

The corporate governance statement must contain a description of the main features of the issuer's internal control and risk management systems in relation to the financial reporting process.

...

DTR 7.2.7

The corporate governance statement must contain a description of the composition and operation of the issuer's administrative, management and supervisory bodies and their committees.

DTR 7.2.8

In the FSA's view, the information specified in provisions A.1.1, A.1.2, B.2.4, D.2.1 and C.3.3 of the UK Corporate Governance Code will satisfy the requirements of DTR 7.2.7 R.

DTR 7.2.9

An issuer may elect that, instead of including its corporate governance statement in its directors' report, the information required by DTR 7.2.1 R to DTR 7.2.7 R may be set out:

(1) in a separate report published together with and in the same manner as its annual report. In the event of a separate report, the corporate governance statement must contain either the information required by DTR 7.2.6 R or a reference to the directors' report where that information is made available; or

(2) by means of a reference in its directors' report to where such document is publicly available on the issuer's website.

DTR 7.2.10

Subject to DTR 7.2.11 R, an issuer which is required to prepare a group directors' report within the meaning of section 415(2) of the Companies Act 2006 must include in that report a description of the main features of the group's internal control and risk management systems in relation to the process for preparing consolidated accounts. In the event that the issuer presents its own annual report and its consolidated annual report as a single report, this information must be included in the corporate governance statement required by DTR 7.2.1 R.

DTR 7.2.11

An issuer that elects to include its corporate governance statement in a separate report as permitted by DTR 7.2.9R (1) must provide the information required by DTR 7.2.10 R in that report.

Thematic Index